REWRITING CHILDREN'S RIGHTS JUDGMENTS

This important edited collection is the culmination of research undertaken by the Children's Rights Judgments Project. This initiative involved academic experts revisiting existing case law, drawn from a range of legal sub-disciplines and jurisdictions, and redrafting the judgment from a children's rights perspective. The rewritten judgments shed light on the conceptual and practical challenges of securing children's rights within judicial decision-making and explore how developments in theory and practice can inform and (re-)invigorate the legal protection of children's rights. Collectively, the judgments point to five key factors that support a children's rights-based approach to judgment writing. These include: using children's rights law and principles; drawing on academic insights and evidence; endorsing child friendly procedures; adopting a children's rights focused narrative; and using child-friendly language.

Each judgment is accompanied by a commentary explaining the historical and legal context of the original case and the rationale underpinning the revised judgment including the particular children's rights perspective adopted; the extent to which it addresses the children's rights deficiencies evident in the original judgment; and the potential impact the alternative version might have had on law, policy or practice. Presented thematically, with contributions from leading scholars in the field, this innovative collection offers a truly new and unique perspective on children's rights.

Rewriting Children's Rights Judgments

From Academic Vision to New Practice

Edited by
Helen Stalford, Kathryn Hollingsworth
and Stephen Gilmore

·HART·
PUBLISHING
OXFORD AND PORTLAND, OREGON
2017

Hart Publishing

An imprint of Bloomsbury Publishing Plc

Hart Publishing Ltd
Kemp House
Chawley Park
Cumnor Hill
Oxford OX2 9PH
UK

Bloomsbury Publishing Plc
50 Bedford Square
London
WC1B 3DP
UK

www.hartpub.co.uk
www.bloomsbury.com

Published in North America (US and Canada) by
Hart Publishing
c/o International Specialized Book Services
920 NE 58th Avenue, Suite 300
Portland, OR 97213-3786
USA

www.isbs.com

HART PUBLISHING, the Hart/Stag logo, BLOOMSBURY and the
Diana logo are trademarks of Bloomsbury Publishing Plc

First published 2017

British Library Cataloguing-in-Publication Data
A catalogue record for this book is available from the British Library.

ISBN: HB: 978-1-78225-925-1
       ePDF: 978-1-78225-927-5
       ePub: 978-1-78225-926-8

Library of Congress Cataloging-in-Publication Data

Names: Stalford, Helen, editor. | Hollingsworth, Kathryn, editor. | Gilmore, Stephen, editor.

Title: Rewriting children's rights judgments : from academic vision to new practice /
Edited by Helen Stalford, Kathryn Hollingsworth and Stephen Gilmore.

Description: Portland, Oregon : Hart Publishing, 2017. | Includes bibliographical references and index.

Identifiers: LCCN 2017025634 (print) | LCCN 2017027013 (ebook) | ISBN 9781782259268 (Epub) |
ISBN 9781782259251 (hardback : alk. paper)

Subjects: LCSH: Children—Legal status, laws, etc.—Great Britain. | Children's rights—Great Britain—Cases.

Classification: LCC KD735 (ebook) | LCC KD735 .R49 2017 (print) | DDC 342.4108/772—dc23

LC record available at https://lccn.loc.gov/2017025634

Typeset by Compuscript Ltd, Shannon
Printed and bound in Great Britain by CPI Group (UK) Ltd, Croydon CR0 4YY

To find out more about our authors and books visit www.hartpublishing.co.uk. Here you will find extracts,
author information, details of forthcoming events and the option to sign up for our newsletters.

This collection is dedicated to the children in our lives, especially Hannah, Emma and Idris (KH), Libby and Tom (SG) and Mairéad, Bethan, Siôn, Mair and Martha (HS).

FOREWORD

Are children human? Of course they are: long gone, one hopes, are the days when it was acceptable to dehumanise a child by referring to him or her in legislation or in court judgments as 'it'. But in what ways are children human? Once infancy is ended, historically at the age of seven, are they just little adults, to be treated by the law in the same way as adults? That seems to have been the approach of the criminal law, as the trial of *John Hudson*, aged going on nine, at the Old Bailey on 10 December 1783[1] demonstrates. He was subject to the same criminal law, the same trial process and the same penalties as an adult would have been. The only concessions to youth were the conclusive presumption that children under seven were *doli incapax*—incapable of knowing right from wrong—and a rebuttable presumption that children under 14 were similarly incapable. A children's rights analysis would have made greater allowances for the developmental status of the individual child and for his vulnerability to exploitation by others.

But are children quite different human beings from adults? They clearly have developmental needs which someone must meet if they are to grow up into healthy functioning adults, fit to play a proper part in civil society. So it has long been recognised that they have a right to have those needs met, at least at a basic level, either by their parents, their families, their communities or the state. The Constitution of the Republic of South Africa so provides, but in the famous case of *Government of the Republic of South Africa v Grootboom*,[2] the Constitutional Court held that their right to shelter was a right to be provided with shelter by whomever was looking after them, in that case their parents. A children's rights analysis might have held that if their parents could not provide them with shelter, the state should provide it, not only for them, but also for their parents.

Or are children something else, *sui generis* human beings, having some of the rights peculiar to childhood and some of the rights which all human beings have? Peculiar to childhood is the right to have their best interests regarded as a primary consideration in all actions concerning them.[3] In our law, this is translated into a duty placed on some, but by no means all, public authorities to have regard to the need to safeguard and promote the welfare of children when exercising their functions.[4] It also means that their best interests must be a factor in deciding whether an interference with the fundamental human rights which they enjoy as ordinary human beings can be justified.[5] The scope of this is much wider than might be thought. In *Collins v Secretary of State for Communities and Local*

---

[1] *Proceedings of the Old Bailey, 1674-1913,* accessible at www.oldbaileyonline.org. See ch 26.
[2] [2000] ZACC 19, 2001 (1) SA 46 (CC). See ch 17.
[3] United Nations Convention on the Rights of the Child, 1989, Article 3(1).
[4] Children Act 2005, s 11; Borders, Citizenship and Immigration Act 2009, s 55.
[5] *ZH (Tanzania) v Secretary of State for the Home Department* [2011] UKSC 4, [2011] 2 AC 166.

Government,[6] for example, it was held to apply to the decision of a local planning authority to enforce the refusal of planning permission to a community of Travellers, including 39 children, encamped on land which they owned. A children's rights analysis would, unlike the actual decisions in the case, properly explore and assess the best interests of the children involved and then ask whether there were countervailing interests of sufficient strength to outweigh them. In *AAA v Associated Newspapers*,[7] a much-read daily newspaper published a salacious story about an allegation that a high-profile politician had fathered a child as a result of a brief extra-marital liaison. The child was named and a picture of her and her mother was published. This was an invasion of the child's right to privacy and she was awarded damages in respect of the publication of the photograph. But she was not awarded damages in respect of the publication of her name or an injunction to prevent repetition. A children's rights analysis would not have held that the child's right to privacy was reduced because of her mother's indiscretion in talking about it; the child was a separate person from her mother; nor was the public interest in knowing about the alleged philandering of the politician a good reason to publish the child's name, which was not in her best interests.

These cases illustrate that children do indeed have the same fundamental rights as other human beings and that interfering with them may be more difficult to justify. Perhaps the most striking illustration of this is the 'largely overlooked' case of *R (on the application of Castle) v Commissioner of Police for the Metropolis*.[8] Three teenagers took part peacefully in a large demonstration in London against the rise in university tuition fees. When it appeared that matters were getting out of hand, the police decided to 'kettle' several thousand of the demonstrators, including these three, in Whitehall. It was near freezing, there were no or totally inadequate toilet facilities and no food or water. They were not allowed to leave, in one case for six and a half hours and in the other two for seven and a half to eight hours. They felt that they would be unable to go on demonstrations in future, for fear of being 'kettled' again. This was, of course, an interference in their right to freedom of expression and freedom of association and peaceful assembly. The court held that the police were under a duty to have regard to the need to safeguard and promote the welfare of children when policing the protest but that it had not been breached. A children's rights analysis would have taken the best interests of these three children more seriously. It would have included their need to develop their personalities and experiences through safely engaging in community activities, including political activities. Children should not be deterred from engaging in political demonstrations, thus aiding their development as active participants in democracy, particularly as they do not have the right to vote. The police should have foreseen that there would be large numbers of children at this particular demonstration and made specific plans to safeguard their welfare.

I have picked out only a few examples from this rich and varied collection to show how valuable it is to re-think and to re-write decided cases to reflect a children's rights analysis far more effectively than the original judgments did. As with its predecessor, the feminist judgments project,[9] this project aims to write plausible judgments, adopting the usual

---

[6] [2013] EWCA Civ 1193, [2013] PTSR 1594. See ch 16.
[7] [2013] EWCA Civ 554. See ch 10.
[8] [2011] EWHC 2317 (Admin), [2012] 1 All ER 953. See ch 15.
[9] R Hunter, C McGlynn and E Rackley (eds), *Feminist Judgments: From Theory to Practice*, (Oxford, Hart Publishing, 2010).

conventions of judgment-writing in the common law world, and using the legal and factual materials available at the time. The aim is to show that it is possible to write judgments which properly respect the rights of children, even within those conventional constraints. The moral for any court is to think of the child as a real human being, with his or her own distinctive personality and rights, and not as an extension of the adults involved.

Brenda Hale
31 May 2017

ACKNOWLEDGEMENTS

Many individuals and organisations supported the two-year project, *Children's Rights Judgments*, that underpins this collection. We are very grateful for the funding received through the Arts and Humanities Research Council (AHRC) Research Networking Scheme which enabled us to hold four of the developmental workshops that shaped ideas for the rewritten judgments and commentaries. We also received financial and administrative support for two earlier workshops from the Newcastle Forum for Human Rights and Social Justice, Newcastle Law School, and the Research Development Fund of the School of Law and Social Justice, University of Liverpool. The other four workshops were held at De Montfort University, Cambridge University (Robinson College), King's College London and Cardiff University. We are incredibly grateful to our friends at those institutions— Trevor Buck, Brian Sloan and Julie Doughty—for their help and patience in hosting the events, and to the various support staff, particularly Rachel Barrett, who provided such excellent administration. Thank you also to Amir Shehu and Chloe Lee for note-taking and transcribing, and helping with the organisation of the workshops on the day, and to the various other students of the Liverpool Law School for their assistance at the final editing stage.

We are especially indebted to our advisory group, Rosemary Hunter, Sonia Harris-Short and Sir Mark Hedley for their enormous encouragement and advice at all stages of the project. Rosemary Hunter generously gave of her time and experience of the methodology of judgment re-writing and provided detailed and constructive feedback on early drafts of the judgments and on the introductory chapters to this collection. Sir Mark Hedley shared with us his immense knowledge and experience of the family courts, his insightful 'seven steps to a bomb proof judgment', and gentle, patient 'reality checking' of some re-written drafts. Sonia Harris-Short offered a unique combination of her academic and judicial insights into children's rights judging to provide us with excellent guidance and confidence to push the boundaries in bringing children's rights to bear on judgment-writing.

Many other colleagues, judges and practitioners willingly shared their expertise of judging, of judgment writing projects and of children's rights in different jurisdictions, including: Michael Freeman, Aoife Nolan, Nuno Ferreira, Trevor Buck, Kanstantsin Dzehtsiarou, Christine Schwöbel and Sir Mathew Thorpe. We owe a particular debt of gratitude to Baroness Hale, not only for inspiring so many of the approaches featured in this collection, but for chairing a workshop session, providing feedback on two of the re-written judgments, and writing the Foreword for this collection.

Numerous other participants at the final three workshops provided constructive, honest, and valuable feedback to the contributors on their rewritten judgments and commentaries. Our thanks, in particular, go to those colleagues who attended from academia (law and psychology), both branches of the legal profession (including some who had been involved in the original cases), children's rights organisations (including the Children's Rights

Alliance for England, Save the Children Wales, and Just for Kids Law), the Office of the Children's Commissioners of Wales and of England, and the judiciary. We would particularly like to mention those who were tasked with the role of discussant: Kate Aubrey-Johnson, Lucy Blake, Gillian Douglas, Caoilfhionn Gallagher, Jessie Hohmann, Thomas Horsley, Eleanor Drywood, Shauneen Lamb, Aisling McMahon, Solange Mouthaan, Dan Rosenberg, Smita Shah, Nigel Stone, and Jane Williams. Many others offered assistance behind the scenes, responding to requests for contextual information to inform the re-written judgments. Their efforts to reflect and comment so thoughtfully upon work-in-progress truly enhanced the quality of the contributions featured in this collection.

The project has benefited from significant artistic input too: Clare Brown designed our flyers and logo at the beginning of the project, and Huw Davies produced the unique artwork featured on the front cover and within this book. We are immensely grateful to both for their creative sensitivity. We are thankful also for the excellent support of Emily Braggins, Sinead Moloney, Helen Kitto and the editorial team at Hart Publishing in preparing this manuscript for final publication.

We end with a note of gratitude to the 53 contributors with whom we are immensely privileged to have worked over the last two years. Many came from near and far (including Australia, Israel, the USA, Ireland, the Netherlands and Belgium) to attend the workshops. All invested significant enthusiasm and an inspiring level of creativity into the project, and responded conscientiously to our editorial suggestions. We purposefully invited contributors from the full spectrum of the academic life cycle—from doctoral students to the most renowned children's rights scholars—with a view to harnessing existing and nurturing new collaborations across generational, disciplinary and jurisdictional boundaries. We hope that the friendships and links supported through this network will thrive for many years to come.

TABLE OF CONTENTS

NOTES ON CONTRIBUTORS

Amel Alghrani is Senior Lecturer in Law at Liverpool Law School, University of Liverpool

Ray Arthur is Professor in Law at Northumbria Law School, Northumbria University

Thomas Bennett is Lecturer in Law at Newcastle Law School, Newcastle University

Lydia Bracken is Lecturer in the School of Law, University of Limerick

Jo Bridgeman is Professor of Healthcare Law and Feminist Ethics at Sussex Law School, University of Sussex

Marielle Bruning is Professor of Children and the Law at the Department of Child Law, Leiden Law School, Leiden University

Trevor Buck is Emeritus Professor of Socio-Legal Studies at Leicester De Montfort Law School, De Montfort University

Emily Buss is Professor of Law at the University of Chicago Law School

Seamus Byrne is a graduate teaching assistant and doctoral candidate at Liverpool Law School, University of Liverpool

Eugenia Caracciolo di Torella is Associate Professor at the University of Leicester

Emma Cave is Professor of Healthcare Law at Durham Law School, Durham University

Stephen Cottle is a barrister at Garden Court Chambers and ranked in the Legal 500 2016 for his work in both Social Housing, and Civil Liberties and Human Rights

Aoife Daly is Senior Lecturer at Liverpool Law School, University of Liverpool

Fiona Donson is Lecturer in Law, Faculty of Law, University College Cork

Julie Doughty is Lecturer in Law at the Cardiff School of Law and Politics, Cardiff University

Jenny Driscoll is Senior Lecturer in Child Studies at Kings College London and previously practised at the Family Law bar

Sue Farran is Professor of Laws, Northumbria Law School, Northumbria University

Claire Fenton-Glynn is University Lecturer in Law and Fellow of Jesus College, Cambridge University

Lucinda Ferguson is Associate Professor of Family Law at the University of Oxford, and Tutorial Fellow in Law, Oriel College, Oxford

Nuno Ferreira is Professor of Law at the University of Sussex

Michael Freeman is Emeritus Professor of English Law at UCL Laws

Stephen Gilmore is Professor of Family Law at King's College London

Sonja Grover is Professor in the Faculty of Education at Lakehead University, Canada

Neville Harris is Professor of Law at the University of Manchester

Connie Healy is Lecturer in Law at the NUI Galway

Jonathan Herring is Professor of Law at Exeter College, University of Oxford

Simon Hoffman is Associate Professor in Law in the College of Law, Swansea University and previously practised as a barrister

Kathryn Hollingsworth is Professor of Law at Newcastle Law School, Newcastle University

Kirsty Hughes is University Lecturer in Law and Fellow of Clare College, Cambridge University

Urfan Khaliq is Professor of Law at Cardiff School of Law and Politics, Cardiff University

Abdullah Khoso is a PhD student at the Faculty of Arts and Social Sciences, University of Malaya, Malaysia

Ursula Kilkelly is Professor of Law and Director of the Child Law Clinic, School of Law, University College Cork

Ruth Lamont is Senior Lecturer in Family and Child Law at the School of Law, University of Manchester

Dave Lane was previously a social worker and Children's Guardian and is now a doctoral candidate at Liverpool Law School, Liverpool University

Ton Liefaard is Professor of Children's Rights and holds the UNICEF Chair in Children's Rights at the Department of Child Law, Leiden Law School, Leiden University

Laura Lundy is Professor of Education and Children's Rights in the School of Social Science, Education and Social Work at Queen's University Belfast

Maria Federica Moscati is an Italian Advocate and Lecturer in Family Law at the University of Sussex

Ellen Nissen is a PhD student at the Centre for Migration Law and the Institute for Sociology of Law of the Radboud University Nijmegen

Aoife Nolan is Professor of Law at the University of Nottingham

Emma Nottingham is Lecturer in Law at the University of Winchester

Conrad Nyamutata is Lecturer in Law at Leicester de Montfort Law School, De Montfort University

Charlotte O'Brien is Senior Lecturer at the School of Law, York University

Maria Papaioannou is a Lawyer and a Teaching Assistant at the Department of International and European Studies, Panteion University, Greece

Noam Peleg is Lecturer in Law at the University of New South Wales, Australia

Anashri Pillay is Associate Professor of Law at Durham Law School, Durham University

Rhona Schuz is Professor of Law and Co-Director of the Center for the Rights of the Child and the Family at Sha'arei Mishpat Law School, Israel

Brian Simpson is Professor of Law at the School of Law, University of New England, Australia

Brian Sloan is College Lecturer and Fellow in Law at Robinson College, Cambridge University

Rhona Smith is Professor of Law at Newcastle Law School, Newcastle University

Helen Stalford is Professor of Law at Liverpool Law School, University of Liverpool

Gamze Erdem Türkelli is a PhD candidate at the University of Antwerp Law Faculty

Wouter Vandenhole is the UNICEF Chair in Children's Rights at the University of Antwerp

Lara Walker is Lecturer in Law at the University of Sussex

Emma Walmsley is a graduate teaching assistant and doctoral candidate at Liverpool Law School, University of Liverpool

Jane Williams is Associate Professor at the School of Law, Swansea University and previously practised as a barrister

Barbara Bennett Woodhouse is the L Q C Lamar Professor of Law, Emory University School of Law

Part I

Children's Rights Judgments: From Academic Vision to New Practice

1

Introducing
Children's Rights Judgments

HELEN STALFORD, KATHRYN HOLLINGSWORTH AND STEPHEN GILMORE

Baroness Hale of Richmond's opinion in *R (Kehoe) v Secretary of State for Work and Pensions* opens with the following observation: 'This is another case which has been presented to us largely as a case about adults' rights when in reality it is a case about children's rights.'[1] What is it that enables a judge to shift his or her gaze like this, sharpening the focus of the issue(s) in a case through the lens of children's rights? This book is concerned to explore this question and the possibilities for judgment writing with greater awareness of children's rights. The collection is based on a two-and-a-half year project, *Children's Rights Judgments*, funded primarily by the Arts and Humanities Research Council, which took place between January 2015 and June 2017 and involved 56 academics and legal practitioners from across the world. Its principal aim was to revisit existing legal judgments relating to children and consider how they might have been drafted if adjudicated from a children's rights perspective. An innovative and highly effective legal methodology—that of judgment re-writing—is thus extended in this book to the topic of children's rights.

Over the last two decades, judgment re-writing has evolved into a distinct approach to critical legal scholarship by which academics step outside the comfort zone of conventional evaluative commentary and compose alternative versions of existing judgments, bound by the same constraints and legal principles that apply in real-life cases. Erika Rackley suggests three reasons—the academic, the educational and the political—why judgment re-writing is a valuable form of (alternative) academic writing.[2] It allows scholars to test the real-life relevance of theories[3] and acts as a valuable rhetorical and persuasive tool for a scholar;[4] it has pedagogical value, exposing students to the myth of judicial neutrality/impartiality and allows them to question the objectivity of the law and the power structures that uphold it;[5] and its political value lies in demonstrating so well the influence of a judge's

---

[1] *R (Kehoe) v Secretary of State for Work and Pensions* [2005] UKHL 48 at para 49.

[2] E Rackley, 'Why Feminist Legal Scholars Should Write Judgments: Reflections on the Feminist Judgments Project in England and Wales' (2012) 24 Canadian Journal of Women and the Law 389. See also R Hunter, C McGlynn and E Rackley (eds), *Feminist Judgments: From Theory to Practice* (Oxford, Hart Publishing, 2010).

[3] D Réaume, 'The Women's Court of Canada: The Virtues of Blending Theory and Practice' [unpublished] at 2, online: Feminist Judgments Project, www.kent.ac.uk/law/fjp/links.html, cited by Rackley, ibid at 397.

[4] Rackley, above n 2 at 400.

[5] Rackley, above n 2 at 403, '[feminist judgments] provide a practical demonstration not only of the extent to which the original decision is often just one way of deciding the case and writing the judgment but also of the importance of the personality and perspective of the judge.'

personality, values and experiences on how he or she reasons and decides cases, thus feeding into debates about judicial diversity.[6] Furthermore, it also has potential practical impact, with the possibility of informing and guiding judicial practice.[7]

Early published examples in North America saw legal scholars re-write versions of two landmark US constitutional judgments, *Brown v Board of Education* and *Roe v Wade*,[8] and Canadian feminist scholars and litigators re-wrote 'shadow' judgments of key Canadian Supreme Court decisions to demonstrate how substantive equality principles could be brought to bear on decision-making.[9] The latter inspired the *Feminist Judgments*[10] project which engaged 51 academics in re-drafting judgments and writing accompanying commentaries from a feminist perspective on a range of cases decided by the courts in England and Wales.

Since then, a number of other such projects have emerged,[11] each one with its own distinct scope and ambition. Some, for example, have placed decisions of the international and supra-national courts under the spotlight. The project *Diversity and European Human Rights* includes 18 partially re-written judgments of the European Court of Human Rights (ECtHR) to demonstrate how interpretations of the European Convention on Human Rights (ECHR) in relation to decisions affecting women, children, LGBT persons, ethnic and religious minorities, and persons with disabilities can better accommodate and respond to diversity.[12] Extending this ambition, the *Human Rights Integration* project, in a challenge to the persistent fragmentation of international human rights law, demonstrates through the rewriting of landmark decisions of supranational human rights monitoring bodies how different human rights principles and sources can be 'integrated' more symbiotically.[13] Our book is inspired by such earlier works and, in particular, responds to the call of the convenors of the UK *Feminist Judgments* project to develop in other contexts and other jurisdictions the methodology of judgment re-writing.[14]

---

[6] See inter alia, E Rackley, *Women, Judging and Judiciary: From Difference to Diversity* (London, Routledge, 2013); R Hunter, 'More than just a Different Face? Judicial Diversity and Decision-Making' (2015) *Current Legal Problems* 1; RJ Cahill O'Callaghan, 'The Influence of Personal Values on Legal Judgments' (2013) 40 *Journal of Law and Society* 596 and 'Reframing the Judicial Diversity Debate: Personal Values and Tacit Diversity' (2015) 35 *Legal Studies* 1; and TT Arvind and L Stirton, 'Legal Ideology, Legal Doctrine and the UK's Top Judges' [2016] *Public Law* 418.

[7] It is anticipated that, as with feminist rewriting projects, the outputs of this project may guide judicial practice in relation to children.

[8] J Balkin (ed), *What Brown v Board of Education Should have Said: The Nation's Top Legal Experts Rewrite America's Landmark Civil Rights Decisions* (New York, New York University Press, 2002); J Balkin (ed), *What Roe v Wade Should have Said: The Nation's Top Legal Experts Rewrite America's most Controversial Decision* (New York, New York University Press, 2005).

[9] 'The Women's Court of Canada' (2006) 18(1) Special Issue *Canadian Journal of Women and the Law.*

[10] Hunter, McGlynn and Rackley, above n 2.

[11] M Enright, J McCandless, and A O'Donoghue (eds), *Northern / Irish Feminist Judgments: Judges' Troubles and the Gendered Politics of Identity* (Oxford, Hart Publishing, 2017) and H Douglas, F Bartlett, T Luker and R Hunter (eds), *Australian Feminist Judgments: Righting and Rewriting Law* (Oxford, Hart Publishing, 2015) provide alternative jurisdiction-specific perspectives on feminist judgment writing. See also SW Smith et al (eds), *Ethical Judgments: Re-Writing Medical Law* (Oxford, Hart Publishing, 2017).

[12] E Brems (ed), *Diversity and European Human Rights; Rewriting Judgments of the ECHR* (Cambridge, Cambridge University Press, 2012).

[13] E Brems and E Desmet (eds), *Integrated Human Rights in Practice. Rewriting Human Rights Decisions* (Surrey, Edward Elgar, Forthcoming).

[14] Hunter, McGlynn and Rackley, above n 2.

Children's Rights Judgments is concerned to explore precisely how children's rights can be integrated into judicial reasoning. The project is distinctive and innovative in several ways. First, it is the only project so far to have focused exclusively on children and to attempt to bring children's rights theories, law, principles and methods to bear on the re-written versions. It is also more ambitious than other judgment-writing projects in terms of its jurisdictional scope and the number of cases included. The project engages with 28 judgments spanning seven domestic jurisdictions, with 14 from England and Wales, six from other jurisdictions (Australia, the Netherlands, the USA, South Africa, Canada and Pakistan), and eight judgments from the international courts, including the International Criminal Court (ICC), the European Court of Human Rights (ECtHR), the Court of Justice of the European Union (CJEU), and the European Committee on Economic and Social Rights (ECESR). In adopting this broad scope, *Children's Rights Judgments* has a strong international and comparative element: contributors have been able to explore the role of the judiciary in enabling states' authorities to discharge effectively their obligations under international human rights law, and particularly the United Nations Convention on the Rights of the Child (CRC). This enables the project to tease out and draw comparisons between how (universal) children's rights standards are interpreted and applied in different jurisdictions to reflect the variable contexts, cultures and value-systems within which they are located; and to offer the first systematic analysis of how children's rights are and could be adjudicated more effectively in the *supra-national courts*, specifically the ECtHR, the CJEU and the ICC. Finally, the collection seeks to compare and contrast how children's rights can be interpreted and applied across different substantive areas of law, thereby avoiding the common tendency to locate children's rights' discussions within a single legal context (particularly family law and medical decision-making).

Extending the rewriting judgment methodology to children's rights is important for two primary reasons that point to the legitimacy of a judicial approach that seeks to prioritise the rights of one group (children) over another (adults).[15] First, it is in the courts that children acquire a legal voice (individually, and as a group) that is denied them in other decision-making processes (private and civic).[16] Therefore, the role of the courts in protecting and securing children's rights, promoting children as *active* legal protagonists, carries greater significance than for other groups. Second, it focuses on children as *central* legal subjects. Children's dependence on adults (usually their parents) means that cases concerning children and their rights often emerge in the context of disputes between adults: typically between doctors and parents (medical decision-making); one parent and another (residence, contact, relocation or abduction); or the parent and the state (care and protection, adoption, immigration, criminal justice or education). The child is central to the dispute and yet arguments have often been framed in terms of the rights of adult others or in paternalistic terms. This project allows such cases to be re-imagined with the child as the primary rights-bearing subject rather than a passive object of concern.

---

[15] On the question of bias in the adoption of a feminist perspective, see R Hunter, 'An Account of Feminist Judging' in Hunter, McGlynn and Rackley, above n 2.

[16] A Nolan, 'The Child as "Democratic Citizen": Challenging the "Participation Gap"' [2010] *Public Law* 767; and J Tobin, 'Courts and the Construction of Childhood: A New Way of Thinking' in M Freeman (ed), *Law and Childhood Studies: Current Legal Issues* (Oxford, Oxford University Press, 2012).

I. Towards Collaboration

While some judges have embraced and foregrounded children's rights, particularly over the last five years or so,[17] with some even going as far as to draft their judgments in child friendly language,[18] such examples remain few and far between. Judgments at all levels and across all jurisdictions routinely pursue limited, often distinctly disempowering approaches to children's rights. Many judgments fail to engage with children's rights issues, confining their adjudication to a factual review of the available evidence rather than a more nuanced understanding of how that evidence might be interpreted in the light of established children's rights norms and research intelligence. This tendency is symptomatic of a persistent gulf between legal practice on the one hand and academic research relating to children and their rights on the other. And yet we are living in an era in which international and domestic guidance on the nature, scope and meaning of children's rights, in which intelligence on children's cognitive, emotional, social, political and psychological capacities, and in which opportunities for promoting interdisciplinary and inter-professional knowledge exchange and capacity-building are abundant and supremely accessible. The challenge lies in bringing those insights to bear on judicial decision-making.

Existing doctrinal research has critiqued the application and conceptualisation of children's rights in specific judgments and has analysed the impact of international rights standards on judicial decision-making.[19] Similarly, there is a long tradition of academics providing detailed, critical commentary of specific judgments in the form of case notes. But while judges may be accused of adjudicating on children's lives in an empirical and theoretical vacuum, many academic theoretical and conceptual expositions of children's rights remain detached from the real life situations in which these issues are negotiated, impervious to the complex economic and structural, practical and emotional constraints that impede judges (examined in chapter two). And whilst there is a growing body of work exploring how front-line practitioners understand and negotiate children's rights and interests in various clinical and legal contexts, particularly in medical decision-making, criminal justice, family justice, education and social work, practical engagement between children's rights scholars and judges and magistrates has been largely confined to critical assessments of isolated judgments or judicial processes. There has been no systematic attempt to demonstrate how these judgments would actually look were they decided through a children's rights lens. Few have attempted to demonstrate, on judges' own terms and observing judicial conventions, how judgments could have looked had

---

[17] See for example in the United Kingdom (the jurisdiction with which the editors are most familiar): *R (on the application of ZH (Tanzania) v Secretary of State for the Home Department* [2011] UKSC 4; *R (on the application of SG and others) v Secretary of State for Work and Pensions* [2015] UKSC 16; *Nzolameso v City of Westminster* [2015] UKSC 22; *Mathieson v Secretary of State for Work and Pensions* [2015] UKSC 47.

[18] *Lancashire County Council v M & Ors (Rev 1)* [2016] EWFC 9; *A (Letter to a Young Person)* [2017] EWFC 48.

[19] See inter alia T Liefaard and J Doek (eds), *Litigating the Rights of the Child: The UN Convention on the Rights of the Child in Domestic and International Jurisprudence* (Dordrecht, Springer, 2015); U Kilkelly 'The Best of Both Worlds for Children's Rights? Interpreting the European Convention on Human Rights in the Light of the UN Convention on the Rights of the Child' (2001) 23 *Human Rights Quarterly* 308; M Freeman 'Children's Rights as Human Rights: Reading the UNCRC' in J Qvortrup, W Corsaro and M Honig (eds), *The Palgrave Handbook of Childhood Studies* (London, Palgrave Macmillan, 2009) 377.

they been adjudicated in a way that is more faithful to what we understand to be a children's rights-based approach.[20]

This disjunction—between academic children's rights on the one hand and judicial expression on the other—not only perpetuates shortcomings in children's rights protection by the courts, but deprives academics and other children's rights advocates of a full appreciation of judges' profound and unique experience of transposing rights from abstract expressions into meaningful, fruitful and enduring commitments by all of those associated with the child. *Children's Rights Judgments* is therefore presented as a unique method of addressing this theory/practice gulf in children's rights and children's invisibility as legal and political citizens, by re-examining legal judgments in light of established and emerging theoretical, doctrinal and empirical research. It also provides a testing ground for exploring the relevance and potential influence of academic research on real life decisions confronting judges.[21]

The judgments and commentaries in this collection draw inspiration from a range of sources not commonly tapped by the judiciary, including children's rights theories, empirical research, participatory methods and international guidance, including the Council of Europe Guidelines on Child Friendly Justice and the General Comments of the UN Committee on the Rights of the Child. We also highlight and seek to emulate best practice across different jurisdictions and different levels of decision-making—drawing attention to existing judgments or elements of judgments that adopt (whether explicitly or more subtly) a children's rights-based approach.

We hope ultimately that the collection will be used not only as an example of how the method of judgment writing can be used to enable us better to understand and innovate in judicial decision-making, but as a practical training guide for judges and other legal practitioners who have a commitment to bringing children's rights to bear more fully on the adjudicatory process. We hope that this, in turn, will provide us with a more informed appreciation of the challenges and tensions confronting judges which may inhibit their potential to engage more fully in children's rights-based decision-making, and to expose opportunities for more creative and open correspondence with broader children's rights research, practice and theory/discourse.

II. The Organisation of the Book

Part I of the book, including this introductory chapter (which explains and outlines the content of the project), sets the scene for engagement with the contributors' work. Chapter two, 'Judging Children's Rights: Tendencies, Tensions, Constraints and Opportunities', explains the conceptual foundation for the project, highlighting the extensive international provisions endorsing children's rights, yet also the highly contested nature of children's rights and their struggle to gain traction in political discourse and legal practice. The chapter discusses the transformative role the judiciary can play in upholding and advancing

---

[20] Various interpretations of what constitutes a children's rights based approach are explored in chapter 3.
[21] Chapter 3 illustrates how this has been achieved across the various judgments.

children's rights. At the same time, it contextualises the challenges for judgment writers by illustrating some of the tendencies, tensions and constraints which may inhibit or distract judges when deciding cases involving children. These include the tendency to reinforce fixed conceptualisations of children and childhood, various forms of resistance to seeing children as rights-holders, the tendency to conflate best interests (in the sense of protected interests, or rights pertaining to the child) and welfare decision-making, and the marginalisation of children within legal processes, in particular, the tendency to pursue children's claims on adults' terms. The chapter explores other constraints which may affect a judge's propensity and freedom to adopt a substantive children's rights approach, such as: constitutional, political and institutional factors; clear statutory language, binding precedent or the inferior status of an international treaty in domestic law; their individual values, characteristics and experiences; and the multiple layers of constraint that limit the utility of research evidence by the courts in children's cases. Chapter two sets the scene for a discussion in chapter three of the primary characteristics of a children's rights judgment.

Chapter three, 'Towards Children's Rights Judgments', illustrates with reference to the re-written judgments in this collection how some of the issues that constrain and frustrate judicial attempts to advance the rights of children can be navigated in order to reason and decide in ways that are more consistent with children's rights. It identifies and explores five markers of a children's rights judgment: (i) the utilisation of formal legal tools including the CRC in domestic proceedings and the cross-pollination potential of children's rights sources to inform judicial decision-making in the supranational courts; (ii) the use of scholarship to inform key concepts and tensions (such as the child's best interests and child autonomy); (iii) the endorsement of child friendly procedures to maximise children's participation in legal processes; (iv) the centralisation of the child's voice and experience in the narrative of the judgment; and (v) the communication of the judgment in a child-friendly way.

The rest of the book consists of the re-written judgments, each preceded by a short commentary. The commentary provides essential background information about the original decision along with an explanation of why and how the re-written version represents a more children's rights-sensitive approach. The contributions are arranged in Parts II to VI of the book under the following broad subject headings: II, Children's Rights and Family Life; III, Children's Rights and Medical Decision-Making; IV, Children's Rights and Public Authorities; V, Children's Rights and Criminal Justice; and VI, Children's Rights and International Movement.

III. Overview of Contributions

A. Selection and Development of the Rewritten Judgments

The cases that feature in *Children's Rights Judgments* are the result of an open call, issued at the beginning of the project, to children's rights academics across the globe. The response was overwhelming and ranged from PhD students and early career scholars to internationally leading scholars in the field. Judgments were selected for rewriting either because of the way in which they were originally reasoned, because their original outcome is regarded as antithetical to children's rights, or because the judgment fails to respond adequately and in a manner that is relevant to modern social, economic, legal, cultural or technological developments that impact upon children's lives.

Many of the judgments selected for rewriting attracted significant critical attention when they were originally passed down (for instance, the surrogacy case of *Re X and Y*; the child immunisation case of *F v F*; the 'celebrity's lovechild' case of *AAA*; and the US death penalty case of *Roper v Simmons*). Two (*Begum*, the school uniform case; and the conjoined twins case of *Re A*) had already been rewritten from other conceptual and ideological perspectives as part of previous judgment-writing projects.[22] Other children's rights cases that readers might expect to see—judgments that pushed the boundaries but could have gone further— are not included here (for example *Gillick v West Norfolk and Wisbech AHA* and *V and T v United Kingdom*). This was in part a consequence of the open call (and thus reflecting contributors' choices) and in part our editorial desire to allow the precedential legacy of some of these cases to be examined (for example in *Re W*). Some of the rewritten versions arrive at an outcome different from the original based on a different reasoning or different sources of children's rights. Others arrive at the same outcome as the original but via different (sometimes subtle, sometimes radically different) reasoning. In all cases, children are treated as central legal subjects.

Whilst *Children's Rights Judgments* is keen to push boundaries and challenge entrenched conventions in judgment writing, it has been equally concerned to produce authentic alternatives that could pass muster as genuine originals. Thus, consistent with other judgment-writing projects, a number of constraints were imposed on the authors. First, each judgment had to adhere broadly to the format, style and tone of the court from which the case originally arose. Second, consistent with the judicial function, authors were confined to interpreting and applying the law as it stood at the time of the original and were prohibited from making radical changes to the law. This was a particular challenge for the *Hudson* child burglar case, our oldest judgment (a trial transcript) dating back to 1783! Similarly, the judgment-writers had to be cognisant of evidence and fact-based limitations depending on the level at which they were adjudicating. In all cases, for practical purposes, we imposed a 5000-word limit on all of the re-written judgments.[23] This has, in some cases, required authors to focus on particular aspects of the original for rewriting and to be judicious in their editing of the factual background and legal context.

That said, writers were given significant scope for creativity in producing a persuasive 'cover version' of the original. Some have invented a fictitious appeal to a higher court or a new dissenting judgment. Some have presented the facts of the case from a different perspective to highlight from the outset the focus on the child's voice, interests and rights. A few (*Valsamis*, *Grootboom*, and *Re T*) have developed an additional, child friendly version of the judgment with a view to conveying the decision to the child or children affected by the decision.

Early drafts of the judgments and commentaries were developed through a series of workshops organised throughout the UK during 2015–16 and involving feedback from

---

[22] See Hunter, McGlynn, and Rackley, above n 2.
[23] Except Hudson which necessarily has a shorter 'judgment' (in fact, a rewritten trial transcript) and a longer commentary.

leading judges, practitioners, academics (including from the field of psychology as well as law) and children's rights advocates, some of whom were involved in representing the parties and adjudicating on the original cases.[24] These enabled participants to explore what it means to adopt a children's rights-based approach to decision-making and to examine both the opportunities and constraints on the judiciary in protecting children's rights. It also enabled participants to receive training and feedback on the art and craft of judgment writing from leading academics and judges such as Professor Rosemary Hunter, Professor Sonia Harris-Short, Sir Mark Hedley and Baroness Hale of Richmond.

B. Themes

As captured by the quotation from Baroness Hale's opinion at the beginning of this chapter, a theme which emerges in many of the contributions is just how easily the interests of the child can become subsumed by, or lost in discussion of, adults' interests. Not surprisingly, the problem arises frequently in the contributions in Part II of the book, which broadly examines children's rights in the context of family life. Many of the judgments in this part focus on the forging of legal family connections between adults and children (for example in the context of surrogacy or adoption), yet they also illustrate how in such decision-making a greater focus might be placed on the separate interests of the children involved. This is often achieved by drawing, to a greater extent than the original judgment, on supranational authority, such as the ECHR and the CRC.

Jo Bridgeman's re-write of *Re X and Y (Foreign Surrogacy)* reaches the same conclusion as the original judgment in making a parental order in respect of twins who were born as a result of a foreign surrogacy arrangement. However, her judgment is also much more mindful of the need, in scrutinising the relevant legislation, to focus on the children's rights to respect for private and family life under Article 8 ECHR, interpreted in light of Articles 3, 7 and 8 CRC. Similarly, Eugenia Caracciolo di Torella's re-written judgment in *CD v ST*, addressing whether maternity leave should be available to the intended mother of a surrogacy arrangement, expands the reasoning of the CJEU to place centre stage the rights of the child to care and protection under Article 3 of the CRC and Article 24 of the Charter of Fundamental Rights. Claire Fenton-Glynn's imagined dissent in *Re C v XYZ County Council* examines the issue of whether there should be an investigation of the child's father's potential to care for the child in the context of proposed adoption outside the child's family. Concluding that the majority view, with its emphasis on avoiding delay, subverted the required focus on the welfare of the child, the re-written judgment places greater focus on the child's identity rights with reference to Articles 7 and 8 of the CRC. The dissent thus produces a judgment with the child at the centre, as opposed to the original which, as Brian Sloan in his commentary observes, could be described as 'glaringly mother-centred.' Similarly, in Lydia Bracken's re-write of the ECtHR judgment in *Gas and Dubois v France*,

---

[24] Direct involvement of children and young people in the project was considered but it was concluded that meaningful participation would require careful and considerable adaptations to the planned activities to equip young people with the necessary knowledge and understanding of the legal, theoretical and procedural issues under scrutiny.

which addressed the applicants' claim of discriminatory treatment arising from the inability of same-sex couples to adopt under French law, the judgment is re-shaped from the perspective of the child's best interests with reference to Article 3 of the CRC. As Ursula Kilkelly observes in her commentary, this highlights that 'it is not relevant to children whether their parents are same or opposite sex, married or not.' Kirsty Hughes' re-written judgment in *AAA v Associated News* addresses a claim for damages and an injunction to prevent disclosure of paternity in a newspaper and focuses much more strongly than the original judgment upon the child's substantive privacy right.

Some of the cases also illustrate that even when the child's separate interest is recognised, such as the right to be heard in proceedings, a children's rights focus may prove significant in upholding the substance of such rights in practice. This is evident in the final two judgments in Part II, which are concerned with the issue of hearing children in legal proceedings. In her re-write of *Re P–S (Children)* Jane Williams allows the appeal of a 15 year old boy, who was a party in care proceedings, holding that he be permitted to give evidence in the proceedings. She concludes that the effect of Articles 6 and 8 of the ECHR, and Articles 3 and 12 of the CRC, is that in practice he enjoys that right and any judicial discretion must be exercised so as to give effect to those fundamental human rights requirements. Similarly, Ton Liefaard and Marielle Bruning re-write a judgment of the Netherlands Supreme Court (*De Hoge Raad* 5 December 2014) in which the core legal issue was a minor's right to access all files relating to the case in connection with his right to be heard in proceedings. In what is described as an 'aspirational document', urging the Dutch Supreme Court to show more willingness to take into account international standards beyond the ECHR, the re-written judgment examines a range of international standards (including guidance from the UN Committee on the Rights of the Child) in order to centre on the core question of whether the child can effectively exercise his right to be heard and participate effectively without having direct access to files.

Many of the themes which emerge in Part II—children's connectedness yet also the need for transparency and consideration of the separate interests that children might plausibly claim—are also evident in Part III, which focuses on children's rights and medical decision-making. In Stephen Gilmore's alternative Court of Appeal judgment in *Re W (A Minor)(Consent to Medical Treatment)*, the issue turns to the child's autonomy interest in the context of an adolescent's refusal to consent to medical treatment where refusal would lead to irreparable harm or death. While agreeing with much of the original reasoning, the re-written judgment goes further, drawing on general principle in *Gillick v West Norfolk and Wisbech AHA*[25] and on academic commentary to reason that judicial consideration of the child's best interests must take full account of the child's autonomy interest, with the conclusion that the fully competent, mature adolescent's views ought to be respected as conducing to his or her welfare.

In *F v F* Emma Cave grapples with a parental dispute about administration of the MMR vaccine to two children aged 15 and 11 years. Cave's re-written judgment focuses more strongly than the original on the children's perspective, characterising the issue as whether compulsory vaccination *in opposition to their wishes* is in their best interests. Unlike the original judgment, which authorised the vaccination for both children, Cave differentiates

---

[25] *Gillick v West Norfolk and Wisbech AHA* [1986] 1 AC 112.

between the children, concluding in the case of the older child that compulsory vaccination is not in her best interests in light of her maturity and understanding, and the risk to her emotional well-being of overriding her refusal.

Michael Freeman imagines a set of House of Lords' opinions on appeal from the controversial Court of Appeal decision in *Re T (A Minor) (Wardship: Medical Treatment)*. The Court of Appeal refused to authorise a life-saving liver transplantation for a two-year-old boy in the face of the mother's objection, despite unanimous medical opinion that the operation could be carried out successfully. This is another case which strikingly illustrates how easy it may be to lose sight of the child's fundamental interests, even when applying the child's welfare as the paramount consideration. The fictive majority opinion in the Lords concludes that the Court of Appeal got the balancing exercise plainly wrong, conflating the interests of the child and the mother and placing undue emphasis on the parents' views, and insufficient weight on the strong presumption in favour of prolonging life. The leading judgment also endorses a general practice of, where appropriate, producing a child-friendly judgment. An additional concurring opinion by Lord Freeman (fictitiously recently appointed to the Appellate Committee of the House of Lords from academia), allows the airing of several more adventurous obiter comments from a children's rights perspective about the treatment of children. While *Re T* illustrates the importance of separating out individuals' interests, Amel Alghrani's re-written judgment of the Court of Appeal in *Re A (conjoined twins)* reminds us also of the importance (and in this case inevitability) of children's connectedness to others.

Part IV examines children's rights in their engagement with public authorities in a variety of contexts (for example, children's freedom of expression, their education and rights to a home). It illustrates how there is a need for careful consideration in particular contexts of how children are perceived, and of the content of the protection of children's best interests. *R (On the Application of Castle) v Commissioner of Police for the Metropolis*, for example, illustrates that despite the claims of individual children in other contexts for differential treatment according to their competences, in some circumstances there may need to be acknowledgement of the vulnerabilities of all children as a group. *Castle* was a claim for judicial review of a police force's decision to 'kettle' (confine to a particular area) protesters during the protest. In particular, it raised the question whether the police's decision-making complied with its duty under section 11 of the Children Act 2004 to make arrangements to safeguard and promote the welfare of children affected. Aoife Daly's re-written judgment highlights the police's failure to classify all under 18 year olds for the purpose of section 11, and also holds that welfare must be interpreted by reference to Article 3 of the CRC, viewed in light of the wider rights contained in the Convention, such as the right to engage in political activity implied by Articles 12 and 15.

The children's protest in *Castle* was against proposed increases in university fees and it is perhaps not surprising that many of the cases in which children's engagement with public law issues occur in the context of their education, their most likely place of engagement with the public sphere of life. In *Valsamis v Greece* a child, Victoria Valsamis, who failed to attend a compulsory National Day military parade because of her pacifist beliefs as a Jehovah's Witness, was punished with suspension for a day from school. Her parents alleged breach of Protocol 1, Article 2 (P1-2) of the ECHR (state's respect for the right of parents to ensure education and teaching in conformity with their own religious and philosophical beliefs), and of the child's rights under Article 9 (freedom of religion). Unlike the original majority judgment, which found no violations, Laura Lundy's re-write upholds the claims, relying directly on CRC Article 12 (respect for the child's views) and Article 5 (provision of parental guidance in accordance with the child's evolving capacities) in relation to the breach of the ECHR Article 9; and on the CRC Articles 3 (the child's best interests) and 29 (the aims of education) in relation to P1-2. Lundy's judgment goes even further in concluding that the child's own rights under P1-2 were also breached.

Similar issues were raised in *R (On the application of Begum) v Head teacher and Governors of Denbigh High School*, in which a Muslim schoolgirl, Shabina Begum, who wished to attend school wearing a jilbab in contravention of the school's uniform policy, sought judicial review of the school's policy. She claimed violations of Articles 9 and Article 2 of the First Protocol of the ECHR. Unlike the original opinions, Maria Moscati's imagined dissent, explicitly utilising the CRC, concludes that Begum's rights to manifest her religion or belief and to education were unjustifiably infringed. Moscati's judgment is also implicitly informed (though necessarily in a minimal way) by interviews with Shabina Begum and her counsel, Cherie Booth QC (reported in Nuno Ferreira's commentary), in order more thoroughly to contextualise in the judgment Begum's experience. The re-written judgment concentrates more concretely on the impact of the school's policy on Begum's rights and not on unfounded violations of other pupils' rights.

Neville Harris' imagined judgment on appeal from Elias J's judgment in *S v Special Educational Needs and Disability Tribunal (SENDIST) and Oxfordshire County Council* addresses the issue of whether a child's exceptional ability combined with her emotional, social and behavioural difficulties warranted a statutory assessment of her Special Educational Needs with the possibility of a confirmed placement at an independent residential school at the Local Education Authority's expense. While Harris upholds the lower court's conclusion that the child did not have special educational needs by virtue of a learning difficulty or disability by reason of high ability level, he quashes the decision and remits it for reconsideration by the SENDIST on the basis that there is a difference in treatment in enjoyment of the right of education based upon a status within Article 14 of the ECHR, which required justification. In his reasoning, Harris highlights Articles 28 and 29 of the CRC focusing on inclusive education with the objective of 'development of the child's personality, talents and mental and physical abilities to their fullest potential'. Harris also examines Article 12 of the CRC, urging that the child's views should, consistently with that provision, play a part in the SENDIST's determination.

Some of the decisions in Part IV touch on children's socio-economic rights, such as a right to housing provision. Simon Hoffman's re-write of *Collins v Secretary of State for Communities and Local Government* provides insight into the content of children's best interests in the context of planning decisions. *Collins* concerned an appeal by an extended family of Irish Travellers, including 39 children, against the refusal of planning permission to stay on their land. Hoffman is concerned to ensure that there is proper compliance with Articles 3 and 12 CRC where the child's right to respect for private and family life are at stake. He thus highlights the need to hear the views of the children in the planning process, and also to ensure that the best interests of the children are given considerable weight in decision-making. The issue of children's rights to adequate shelter and housing was also raised in the South African Constitutional Court's decision in *Government of the Republic of South Africa and Others v Grootboom*, which examined the constitutional right of everyone to have access to adequate housing and the constitutional right of children to shelter.[26] Unlike the original ruling, which concluded that there was no primary state obligation to provide shelter on demand to parents and their children if children are being cared for by their parents or families, Anashri Pillay's re-write, drawing on international children's rights sources, concludes that the Constitution must be interpreted as obligating state provision of shelter to children within their families.

The final case in Part IV, Sonja Grover's reimagined dissent in the Canadian Supreme Court in *Canadian Foundation for Children, Youth and the Law v Canada (Attorney General)*, examines whether section 43 of the Canadian Criminal Code infringes the Canadian Charter of Rights and Freedoms. Section 43 provides a defence justifying the reasonable use of force by way of correction in the context of an assault under the criminal code, which applies to schoolteachers, parents and persons standing in the place of parents. Grover argues that the provision infringes section 12 of the Charter, the right not to be subjected to cruel and unusual treatment or punishment, as an infringement of a human right of dignity which should apply equally to adults and children.

Part V of the book focuses on children's rights and criminal justice, a subject matter in which tensions between children's cognitive abilities and notions of responsibility for their actions play out, often upon a broader political canvas, and with reference to the constraints of perceptions of social acceptability. Barbara Bennett Woodhouse re-writes the United States Supreme Court decision in *Roper v Simmons*, which held that sentencing juvenile offenders to death violated the US Constitution's Eighth Amendment prohibition against cruel and unusual punishment. Woodhouse reaches the same outcome on different reasoning, claiming special treatment for children as a distinct class. Having regard to the nature of childhood, she grounds her decision instead in children's fundamental rights protecting their potential for development, which she bases on the Constitution's due process and equal protection principles.

A focus on the child's developmental interest also surfaces in Ray Arthur's re-examination of *R v JTB*. In that case the UK House of Lords held that section 34 of the Crime and Disorder Act 1998 abolished not only the *presumption* that a child over the minimum age of criminal responsibility (10 years) but under the age of discretion (14 years) is incapable of committing a criminal offence (ie, *doli incapax*), but also removed the notion of *doli incapax* completely as a defence. Arthur's re-written opinion illustrates how there can be choice in the narrative adopted in a judgment, rejecting that adopted by Lord Phillips in the original opinion, which portrayed a benevolent youth justice system and the difficulty of securing prosecution which section 34 sought to address. Unlike the original opinion, Arthur cites both common law decisions and Articles 40 and 3 of the CRC to interpret section 34 as retaining the defence. But as Kathryn Hollingsworth observes in her commentary, even this is a compromise adopted against the backdrop of an extremely low minimum age of criminal responsibility.

The final three judgments in Part V highlight how the realities of children's lives and protection of their rights must sometimes contend with the political setting and prevailing societal attitudes to children. Trevor Buck's alternative majority judgment in the International Criminal Court in the trial of Thomas Lubanga Dyilo for enlisting and conscripting

---

[26] Ss 26 and 28 of the Final Constitution of South Africa.

children under 15 years into the Force Patriotique pour la Libération du Congo and using them in hostilities (*Prosecutor v Thomas Lubanga Dyilo*) shines a light on the plight of child soldiers. In convicting the defendant, Buck develops more detailed arguments based on international child law provisions than the original judgment, including drawing on the child's right to be heard in Article 12 of the CRC in support of greater participation of children in the proceedings as victims of the offences.

In *Farooq Ahmed v Pakistan* Abdullah Khoso imagines the Supreme Court of Pakistan's examination of the decision of the Punjab High Court to strike off the statute book the Juvenile Justice System Ordinance 2000 (JJSO), despite the Court's lack of competence to strike down legislation. This Ordinance provides various protections for persons under 18 within the criminal justice system, such as to be tried separately from adults, and protection from the death penalty. The High Court held that the age of 18 is arbitrary and inappropriate in a country where a hot climate and the 'consumption of hot and spicy food all lead towards speedy physical growth and an accelerated maturity'. It was concerned that the JJSO was being abused by criminals who were using children to commit serious crimes on behalf of their family, knowing that they would not be subject to the death penalty. Khoso rejects the anti-human rights and anti-child rights approach of the High Court, which, as Urfan Khaliq's commentary highlights, may have been motivated by wider political considerations.

Sue Farran and Rhona Smith's contribution is very different from others in the collection, being a re-write of a trial transcript of an eighteenth century criminal trial of an eight year old boy, John Hudson (*December 1783, trial of John Hudson (t17831210-19) Burglary case*). Hudson was found guilty of stealing and sentenced to transportation. Farran and Smith reach a different result, assisted by the addition of fictitious defence counsel, William Garrow, to employ defence techniques (such as cross-questioning) which were in their infancy at that time. The case is a reminder that the treatment of children is often temporally and culturally contingent and that what may seem appropriate in one generation can be looked on with horror in another, and yet also how difficult it may be for the current generation to see its own horrors.

The final part of the book (Part VI) engages with children's rights and international movement. In the first case in this part, Brian Simpson examines the issue of procedural fairness to children in the context of proceedings for return of a child under the Hague Convention on the Civil Aspects of International Child Abduction. His re-write of the Australian High Court decision in *RCB as Litigation Guardian of EKV, CEV, CIV and LRV v The Honourable Justice Colin James Forrest of the Family Court of Australia & Ors* concludes (unlike the original judgment) that procedural fairness to the children warranted their separate representation to test the veracity and reliability of the conclusions of a court report which advised as to the children's best interests. Developing the same theme in a European context, the rewritten version of *Povse v Austria* highlights the rigidity of the CJEU and ECtHR in addressing the children's rights implications of parental child abduction. Specifically, the policy of automatic return of the child, supported by EU law (the Brussels IIa Regulation)[27] can sit at odds with children's expressed objections and right

---

[27] Reg 2201/2003 concerning jurisdiction and the recognition and enforcement of judgments in matrimonial matters and the matters of parental responsibility, [2003] OJ L338/1.

to respect for family life under Article 8 ECHR. As Ruth Lamont notes in her commentary, 'The protection of children's rights is restricted to an assessment of *where* rights may be considered, rather than interrogating *whether* the procedural legal framework itself is compliant with Article 8.' Whilst accepting the constitutional and legal limitations of the European courts, Lara Walker re-writes *Povse* to achieve a more children's rights sensitive interpretation of Article 8, concluding that forcing a child to leave her mother to live with her father after years of only limited contact with him does, indeed, constitute a disproportionate breach of her ECHR rights.

Staying with the European courts, Helen Stalford reimagines the CJEU's treatment of the residence, welfare and employment rights of the third country national parents of EU citizen children in Case C-34/09 *Gerardo Ruiz Zambrano v Office national de l'emploi (ONEm)*. In doing so, the children's (rather than the parents') rights are placed at the forefront of the court's reasoning and full use is made of the children's rights architecture to which the EU has access (but which it routinely fails to exploit). The status of migrant children is considered also by Maria Papaioannou who examines the ECtHR decision in *Antwi v Norway*, concerning a 10 year old Norwegian girl whose father was threatened with deportation to Ghana. In concluding that there was no violation of Article 8 of the ECHR in deporting the father, the ECHR applied its doctrine in immigration cases that the court would only in exceptional circumstances find such a violation in the case of a person who is aware that his or her immigration status is precarious. The Court was of the view that the family could enjoy family life in Ghana. By contrast the re-written judgment recognises the child as an independent rights holder rather than simply an extension of the parents, considering the detrimental impact of a move on the child's interests, and characterising the issue as whether a separation of the father and child would violate Article 8 ECHR.

Remaining with the migration theme, Wouter Vandenhole brings children's rights principles and approaches to bear on an often overlooked quasi-judicial monitoring body, the European Committee on Social Rights. *DCI v Belgium* concerns a collective complaint brought against the Belgian authorities in respect of their failure to provide adequate medical treatment and protection for child asylum seekers, many of whom had arrived unaccompanied. Whilst the original ruling finds Belgium to be in breach of its obligations under the European Social Charter, Wouter Vandenhole drafts a fictitious concurring decision to highlight the specific vulnerabilities of unaccompanied minors and to draw attention to the vacuous nature of children's rights in the absence of adequate material resourcing.

These rewritten judgments have therefore explored, in a multitude of ways and across a variety of legal contexts and jurisdictions, how a children's rights judgment can be better achieved even within temporal, doctrinal and jurisdictional constraints. Some may disagree with the approach to certain judgments; some may think the fictive judges have gone too far, and others not far enough. Ultimately, our hope is that this book will prompt more serious consideration of the possibilities and, indeed, importance of embedding children's rights more firmly in judicial decision-making.

2

Judging Children's Rights: Tendencies, Tensions, Constraints and Opportunities

HELEN STALFORD AND KATHRYN HOLLINGSWORTH*

I. Introduction

This chapter explains the conceptual foundation for this project. It discusses the importance of the judiciary in upholding and advancing children's rights by reference, in particular, to contemporary trends in human rights law and politics. The discussion then examines the factors that constrain the judicial role that may inhibit and even misguide judges when deciding cases involving children. We consider also how these same factors may present opportunities and indeed a growing impulse on the part of the judiciary to adopt a more explicit children's rights-based approach to their decision-making. In doing so, we set the scene for a fuller discussion in chapter three of the components of and methodological approaches to children's rights judgments. To begin our discussion, we explain our explicit use of the term 'children's rights' and then proceed to defend a children's rights-based approach as a legitimate perspective for judicial decision-making.

II. Why *Children's Rights* Judgments?

Our use of the term 'children's rights' in the context of judgment writing (as opposed to 'Judging Children' or 'Judging Children's Lives') is deliberate. At its most basic level the term 'children's rights' refers to the range of civil, political, social, economic and cultural rights that pertain to children and childhood. In the same way that the ability to lay claim to human rights is central to adults' humanity, security and dignity, children's rights define basic standards of protection, autonomy and respect that enable them to thrive in the present and develop to their fullest potential in the future. In that sense, children's rights provide the rhetorical and moral context for the assertion that children require specific

* We are very grateful to Stephen Gilmore, Rosemary Hunter and John Tobin for their comments on earlier drafts of this chapter.

attention and protection and signal a call to action that moves beyond sentimental reliance on compassion or benevolence[1] toward an expectation that children should be facilitated in exercising their basic entitlements.

International consensus around the basic principle that children have rights worthy of protection has never been more comprehensive and vivid than it is today. Children's rights are now firmly embedded within the lexicon of international human rights with almost all of the world's states having voluntarily adhered to the United Nations Convention on the Rights of the Child (CRC).[2] In that sense, the term 'children's rights' invokes clearly defined legal duties for which duty-bearers can be held to account. In contrast with other judgment-writing projects, *Children's Rights Judgments* benefits from the explicit normative and legal framework of the CRC, typically the first port of call when seeking to apply a child rights-based approach to decision-making.[3] The substantive provisions of the CRC, its four general principles,[4] other associated 'soft law'[5] and the accompanying guidance of the Committee on the Rights of the Child,[6] provide a comprehensive framework of rights that exclusively focuses on children as distinct from other (adult) rights-holders. These sources leave little scope for manipulation or obfuscation of children's rights, but rather are explicit in their requirements as to how children's rights should be distinguished and prioritised, not only in defining their substance, but in determining the processes that should be followed to give them effect. In particular, as the product of over a decade of inter-state negotiation, the CRC is widely regarded as reliable and robust; an expression of international accord that can guide judges in all manner of jurisdictions, at all levels of seniority, across all areas of law affecting children. Indeed, the Committee on the Rights of the Child explicitly calls on judicial bodies to consider the impact of their decisions on children,[7] an appeal that is echoed in other General Comments.[8]

The CRC is not the only reference point in determining the content and scope of children's rights, however. The CRC builds upon a diffuse set of pre-existing rights that find (albeit much more modest) legal expression in a range of much earlier human rights instruments, including the 1924 Declaration of the Rights of the Child, the European Convention on Human Rights and Fundamental Freedoms 1950 (ECHR), the 1959 Declaration on the Rights of the Child, the International Covenant on Civil and Political Rights 1966, the International Covenant on Economic, Social and Cultural Rights 1966, and a succession of

---

[1] M Freeman, 'The Value and Values of Children's Rights' in A Invernizzi and J Williams (eds), *The Human Rights of Children* (Surrey, Ashgate, 2011) 33.

[2] R Frost, 'The Justification of Human Rights and the Basic Right to Justification: A Reflexive Approach' (2010) 120 *Ethics* 711; J Tobin, 'Justifying Children's Rights' (2013) 21 *International Journal of Children's Rights* 395, 398.

[3] As Tobin notes, the use of the CRC in judicial decision-making 'provides a very strong indication of the extent to which the relevant international norms have been internalised and brought to life within the domestic legal system'. J Tobin, 'Judging the Judges: Are They Adopting the Rights Approach in Matters Involving Children?' (2009) 33 *Melbourne University Law Review* 579, 580.

[4] Namely, non-discrimination (Art 2), best interests as a primary consideration (Art 3), right to survival and development (Art 6), and the right to be heard (Art 12).

[5] Including subject specific rules such as the United Nations Minimum Rules for the Administration of Juvenile Justice (The Beijing Rules) 1985; and the Council of Europe *Guidelines on Child-Friendly Justice* (Council of Europe, 2010).

[6] Derived from its General Comments and the Concluding Observations on reports by state parties.

[7] CRC Committee, General Comment No 5: General Measures of Implementation of the Convention on the Rights of the Child, CRC/GC/2003/5 (2003).

[8] See, for example, CRC Committee, General Comment No 10: Children's Rights in Criminal Justice, CRC/C/GC/10 (2007) at para 13.

International Labour Organisation Conventions.[9] Children's rights are rooted in numerous post-CRC instruments too, including the African Charter on the Rights and Welfare of Children, various private international law instruments of the Hague Conference,[10] successive conventions of the Council of Europe,[11] the landmark 1999 ILO Convention on the Worst Forms of Child Labour (Number 182), the 2006 UN Convention on the Rights of Persons with Disabilities and even the constitutional texts of the European Union (EU).[12]

Notwithstanding the extensive international endorsement of children's rights, both the idea and application of children's rights remain highly contested and still struggle to gain traction in political discourse and legal practice. It remains very much the case that the extent to which children's rights are experienced and enforceable on the ground is unpredictable and variable according to the constitutional, political, social and economic context within which children are situated. It is for this reason that there has been a concerted effort in the last two decades or so to locate children's rights within a firm, 'intellectually compelling'[13] conceptual framework to stimulate a stronger sense of reasoned loyalty from those who are instrumental to giving effect to such rights.[14] As Tobin notes:

> [I]n the absence of a secure conceptual foundation, children's rights risk becoming invisible to, or rejected by, those for whom they are not self-evident … They also become vulnerable to conscious or unconscious manipulation by those who wish to use them as a rhetorical device by which to advance a subjective vision of what children's rights should mean … A right for which there is no recognised conceptual foundation quickly risks becoming an empty rhetorical vessel into which subjective preferences or political agendas may be poured.[15]

Thus, a range of theoretical frameworks has been developed to advance our thinking and test presumptions concerning the very essence of children's rights. This literature has confronted questions about whether it is even helpful to talk about children in terms of their 'rights'[16] or whether alternative discourses such as 'well-being',[17] capability,[18]

---

[9] See notably ILO Convention *Concerning Minimum Age for Admission to Employment*, 1973 (No 138). For a discussion of the various international children's rights instruments, see P Veerman, *The Rights of the Child and the Changing Image of Childhood* (Dordrect, Martinus Nijhoff, 1992); P Alston and J Tobin, *Laying the Foundations for Children's Rights* (Florence, UNICEF Innocenti Research Centre, 2005).

[10] See for instance The Hague Convention of 29 May 1993 on Protection of Children and Co-operation in Respect of Intercountry Adoption; The Hague Convention of 19 October 1996 on Jurisdiction, Applicable Law, Recognition, Enforcement and Co-operation in Respect of Parental Responsibility and Measures for the Protection of Children; and the Hague Convention of 23 November 2007 on the International Recovery of Child Support and Other Forms of Family Maintenance.

[11] See notably the European Convention on the Exercise of Children's Rights 1996, ETS No 160; the revised European Social Charter 1996, ETS No 163; the European Convention on Contact concerning Children 2003, ETS No 192; and the Council of Europe Convention on the Protection of Children against Sexual Exploitation and Sexual Abuse 2007, CETS No 201.

[12] Charter of Fundamental Rights of the European Union, Arts 12, 24 and 32 (OJ 2012/C 326/02); Art 3(3) Treaty on European Union; Arts 79(2)(d) and 83(1) of the Treaty on the Functioning of the European Union.

[13] A Sen, 'Elements of a Theory of Human Rights' (2004) 32 *Philosophy and Public Affairs* 315, 317.

[14] D Archard and C MacLeod, *The Moral and Political Status of Children* (Oxford, Oxford University Press, 2002) 15; and J Fortin, *Children's Rights and the Developing Law* (Cambridge, Cambridge University Press, 2009) 3.

[15] J Tobin, above n 2.

[16] M Guggenheim, *What's Wrong with Children's Rights* (Cambridge MA, Harvard University Press, 2005); O O'Neill, 'Children's Rights and Children's Lives' (1988) 98 *Ethics* 445; and H Brighouse, 'What Right (if any) Do Children Have?' in Archard and MacLeod, above n 14.

[17] EKM Tisdall, 'Children's Wellbeing and Children's Rights in Tension?' (2015) 23 *International Journal of Children's Rights* 769–89; J Eekelaar, 'Beyond the Welfare Principle' (2002) 14(3) *Child and Family Law Quarterly* 237.

[18] See, for example, A Sen, *Development as Freedom* (Oxford, Oxford University Press, 1999) and M Nussbaum, *Creating Capabilities: The Human Development Approach* (Cambridge MA, Belknap Harvard, 2011).

the ethic of care,[19] or 'dignity'[20] might be better deployed to reflect the reality of children's dependence on those around them and to avoid the more individualistic, self-serving and responsibility-averse connotations of human rights discourse. But whilst these alternative frameworks may reject a certain conceptualisation of rights, they are certainly not antithetical to children's rights.[21] In fact such values are integral to a children's rights-based approach. For instance, 'well-being' and dignity are leitmotifs running through the CRC,[22] whilst children's relationship with their family, and particularly their parents, is upheld as fundamental for their growth (preamble and Article 18(1)).

But of course the CRC is not just an instrument for proclaiming the virtues of family relationships and happy childhoods; it is as much about setting out how those virtues should be achieved and who should be responsible when those relationships go wrong. Theorisations of children's rights offer a critical framework for interpreting these dynamics. They support parents' role (enshrined in Article 18 CRC) as the primary guardian of their children's rights unless their interests are in direct conflict or they are otherwise unable to fulfil their duties;[23] they illustrate how paternalistic considerations around children's welfare might be accommodated and balanced against rights of autonomy and agency;[24] they provide a compelling argument in support of the agency of even very young children;[25] and they enable us to envisage a situation in which the rights of children can be reconciled with notions of accountability when children do wrong.[26] In fact, such is the apparent success of children's rights discourse that more recent work has explored how it can inspire and be integrated into broader human rights developments in favour of adults.[27]

Dovetailing with the development of persuasive conceptual arguments for children's rights, a substantial body of empirical, interdisciplinary research has emerged exploring how such concepts translate into practice. This provides a rich resource of intelligence concerning the effects—actual and envisioned—of laws, policies and practices on children's

---

[19]   T Cockburn, 'Children and the Feminist Ethic of Care' (2003) 10 *Childhood* 71; F Kelly, 'Conceptualising the Child through an "Ethic of Care": Lessons for Family Law' (2005) 1 *International Journal of Law in Context* 375; V Held, *The Ethics of Care: Personal, Political and Global* (Oxford, Oxford University Press, 2006); and J Herring, *Caring and the Law* (Oxford, Hart Publishing, 2013).

[20]   M Freeman, 'Why It Remains Important to Take Children's Rights Seriously' (2007) 15 *International Journal of Children's Rights* 5.

[21]   On the inter-relationship between rights and other approaches (including relationality, capabilities and caring), and how such approaches can be used to theorise rights, see (inter alia) M Nussbaum, 'Capabilities and Human Rights' (1997) 66 *Fordham Law Review* 273; R Dixon and M Nussbaum, 'Children's Rights and a Capabilities Approach: The Question of Special Priority' (2013) 97 *Cornell Law Review* 549; Herring, above n 19; J Herring, 'Forging a Relational Approach: Best Interests of Human Rights?' (2013) 13 *Medical Law International* 32.

[22]   In the preamble and in Arts 3(2), 3(3), 9(4), 17; 17(e) and 40(3)(b).

[23]   See for example, M Freeman, *The Rights and Wrongs of Children* (London, Frances Pinter, 1983) ch 2; Dixon and Nussbaum, above n 21.

[24]   Fortin, above n 14; Freeman, ibid. J Eekelaar, 'The Interests of the Child and the Child's Wishes: The Role of Dynamic Self-determinism' (1994) 8 *International Journal of Law, Policy and the Family* 42, 43; D Archard and M Skivenes, 'Balancing a Child's Best Interests and a Child's Views' (2009) 17 *International Journal of Children's Rights* 1.

[25]   P Alderson, *Young Children's Rights: Explaining Beliefs, Principles and Practice* (London, Jessica Kingsley, 2000).

[26]   Freeman, above n 23, ch 3; K Hollingsworth, 'Theorising Children's Rights in Youth Justice: The Significance of Autonomy and Foundational Rights' (2013) 76 *Modern Law Review* 1046.

[27]   E Brems, E Desmet and W Wandenhole (eds), *Children's Rights Law in the Global Human Rights Landscape* (Oxford, Routledge, 2017).

lived experiences of their rights in an array of contexts. The voluminous work on the sociology of childhood, child developmental psychology, medicine, neuroscience and child participation has further enriched our understanding of the psychological, social, environmental and procedural factors that affect the operation of children's rights in practice, including: how children confront the decision-making processes; the ways in which adults approach decisions on children's behalf; and the range of strategies and models that can be applied to enable children to participate more directly and meaningfully in decisions that affect their lives.[28] The letter of the law and sound intellectual arguments are not enough in themselves, however: they have to be accompanied by tailored approaches that illustrate how to bring our conceptual and empirical understanding of children's rights to bear on real life decision-making. Equally, we have to reach a position whereby those charged with interpreting and implementing the law internalise and commit themselves to the values espoused by children's rights. It is the central role of the judiciary in this process to which our discussion now turns.

III. The Importance of the Judiciary in Advancing Children's Rights

The visibility of human rights norms in judicial decision-making is acknowledged as a litmus test against which their effective implementation can be assessed.[29] It is a welcome development that the literature on the role of the judiciary in developing (rather than simply interpreting and applying) the law[30] has turned its attention in the last two decades or so to their role in advancing children's rights.[31] This work highlights the ultimate power of the judge to activate legal rights, particularly given children's limited ability to assert their rights through other democratic processes.[32] In essence, the courts step in where other adults (state authorities, parents, doctors) fail or disagree on how to give effect to children's rights, often in the context of highly sensitive, emotionally and ethically-charged circumstances.

---

[28] See inter alia, C Jenks, *Childhood* (London, Routledge, 1996); A James and A Prout (eds), *Constructing and Reconstructing Childhood: Contemporary Issues in the New Sociology of Childhood* (Oxford, Routledge, 1997); M Freeman, 'The Sociology of Childhood and Children's Rights' (1998) 6 *International Journal of Children's Rights* 433; B Mayall, 'The Sociology of Childhood in Relation to Children's Rights' (2000) 8 *International Journal of Children's Rights* 243; H Shier, 'Participation in Decision-making, in line with Art 12(1) of the UNCRC' (2001) 15 *Children and Society* 107–17; L Lundy, 'Voice is not Enough: Conceptualising Article 12 of the United Nations Convention on the Rights of the Child' (2007) 33 *British Educational Research Journal* 927 at 937.

[29] Tobin, above n 3, 580.

[30] S Fredman, *Human Rights Transformed: Positive Rights and Positive Duties* (Oxford, Oxford University Press, 2008) Pt II; JM Eekelaar, 'Judges and Citizens: Two Conceptions of Law' (2002) 22(3) *Oxford Journal of Legal Studies* 497.

[31] M Hedley, *The Modern Judge—Power, Responsibility and Society's Expectations* (Bristol, Lexis Nexis, 2016); A Nolan, *Children's Socio-Economic Rights, Democracy and the Courts* (Oxford, Hart Publishing, 2011); Tobin, above n 3; JM Eekelaar, 'The Role of the Best Interests Principle in Decisions Affecting Children and Decisions about Children' (2015) 23 *International Journal of Children's Rights* 3; A Daly, *Children, Autonomy and the Courts* (Oxford, Routledge, 2017 forthcoming); J Fortin, 'A Decade of the HRA and its Impact on Children's Rights' (2011) 41 *Family Law* 176–83.

[32] A Nolan, 'The Child as "Democratic Citizen": Challenging the "Participation Gap"' [2010] *Public Law* 767; and Nolan, ibid.

It is thus children's invisibility and vulnerability within the law and their lack of political voice that gives even greater legitimacy to the explicit judicial adoption of a children's rights perspective.[33] Judicial remedies are a key form of redress when rights are breached, whether it be at the hands of state authorities or at the hands of other private individuals. No matter how well-defined and child-sensitive the law, policy or legal process is, it is ultimately up to the judge to interpret and apply the relevant legal provisions in the light of the values, skills and evidence available to him or her. We add to this body of work by pointing to specific features of our current legal, political and social environment that present both opportunities and obstacles to the judiciary in advancing children's rights. In doing so, we draw heavily on examples from the legal and research framework of England and Wales with which we, as UK-based academics, are most familiar. Our aim, however, is to tease out how the multi-levelled nature of children's rights governance impacts upon the function and accessibility of the judiciary across all jurisdictions. We also draw attention to some potent, global political trends that highlight the importance of the judiciary in protecting human rights, including those of children.

A. The Multi-levelled Nature of Children's Rights Governance

The globalised, multi-layered regulatory environment in which we live has simultaneously nurtured strong legal connections and exposed variances between our legal systems. In a European context, notwithstanding its historical ambivalence towards children as independent rights-holders,[34] the ECHR operates as a beacon of human rights protection across the 47 states parties to the Council of Europe. Moreover, at the time of writing, 28 countries are members of the European Union which evidences a growing commitment to embedding children's rights provisions within the fabric of its law and policy. On an even wider scale, there are 196 State Parties to the CRC, 160 to the 2006 UN Convention on the Rights of Persons with Disabilities, 142 to the 1951 UN Refugee Convention, and 53 out of 54 African States are subject to the African Charter on the Rights and Welfare of Children. Add to this the patchwork of multilateral and bilateral treaties, such as those agreed under the Hague Conference on Private International Law which governs cross-national co-ordination on all manner of private and commercial matters to provide individuals (including children) with a higher degree of legal certainty in matters that straddle jurisdictional boundaries.[35] All of these international frameworks create obligations at the domestic level, often requiring legislative, policy and procedural amendment to

---

[33] And as Rosemary Hunter further articulates in countering arguments of bias in relation to feminist judging, where the 'case directly raises issues of equality and discrimination … then a decision that promotes substantive equality is likely to be 'consistent with the fundamental principles of the law' and as such is hardly objectionable'. R Hunter, 'An Account of Feminist Judging' in R Hunter, C McGlynn and E Rackley (eds), *Feminist Judgments: From Theory to Practice* (Oxford, Hart Publishing, 2010) 32. Judges also often have a discretionary space within which they will draw on their experiences and judicial perspective and which may, legitimately (again as Hunter points out in defence of a feminist approach) be one inclined towards a children's rights perspective. See the discussion below.

[34] See U Kilkelly, *The Child and the European Convention on Human Rights* (Aldershot, Ashgate, 1999); J Fortin, 'Accommodating Children's Rights in a Post Human Rights Act Era' (2006) 69 *Modern Law Review* 299.

[35] H van Loon, 'The Hague Conference on Private International Law' in PJ van Krieken and D McKay (eds), *The Hague: Legal Capital of the World* (The Hague, 2005) Ch 14, 518–26.

give them effect. Where effective implementation of these commitments is lacking, it falls to our judiciary to interpret domestic law and procedures in a way that enables individuals to lay claim to their human rights entitlement. The success and consistency with which judges achieve this depends, of course, on a range of factors, considered in more detail below. Suffice to say that the potential to protect children's rights is undoubtedly most robust when explicitly embedded within the constitutional framework of domestic jurisdictions insofar as they are more readily accessible and enforceable on the ground.[36] Below this level again, decentralised administrations can bring children's rights to bear on a localised level often to greater effect than measures implemented in the centralised context, particularly in fields such as health, education, social care, culture and recreation.[37] In jurisdictions (such as India, Pakistan, the UK, Canada and Australia) that adopt a dualist approach to international human rights treaties, it falls to the judiciary to bring the rights protected therein to bear on domestic cases in the absence of any implementing legislation.

A 'human rights-facing' judiciary demands much more outward and upward perspectives in their interpretation of individual entitlement, not only in terms of ensuring correspondence with international human rights obligations, but in taking opportunities to learn from other domestic jurisdictions. Remarking on the increasingly 'internationalised' nature of the judiciary in this respect, Elaine Mak notes:

> Legal systems and actors within these legal systems are increasingly interconnected. These interconnections have brought an increasing number of cases with international or foreign aspects to the courts. Moreover, systemic changes, such as the development of the European legal order and the increase of international legal instruments, have obliged highest courts to develop expertise concerning the application of legal sources elaborated outside of their national legal system. At the same time, meetings in transnational judicial networks and the availability of foreign legal sources, for example through internet databases, have made it easier and natural for judges to take an interest in developments outside of their national borders.[38]

The capacity of judges to adopt international perspectives of this nature is particularly important in cases involving children. Not only do international instruments establish a strong benchmark for how children should be treated in a range of substantive contexts at domestic level but, increasingly, children are implicated in legal proceedings of an international and cross-national nature. For instance, it is estimated that more than 31 million children live outside their country of birth, including 11 million child refugees and asylum-seekers. By the end of 2015, some 41 million people were displaced by violence and conflict within their own countries, of which approximately 17 million were children.

---

[36] Alston and Tobin, above n 9 at 21; J Tobin, 'Increasingly Seen and Heard: the Constitutional Recognition of Children's Rights' (2005) 21 *South African Journal on Human Rights* 86.

[37] 11 of the 16 German Lander constitutions, for instance, contain explicit protection for children's rights which is not derived from or replicated in the federal constitution. In Wales, the Rights of Children and Young Persons (Wales) Measure 2011 imposes a duty on Ministers to have due regard to the CRC when exercising any of their functions, thus establishing a devolved framework for children's rights accountability through legal (judicial review) and Parliamentary (National Assembly) mechanisms. No such mechanism exists in a centralised UK context. See further J Williams, 'Multi-level Governance and CRC Implementation' in A Invernizzi and J Williams (eds), *The Human Rights of Children* (Surrey, Ashgate, 2011) 241.

[38] E Mak, *Judicial Decision-Making in a Globalised World: A Comparative Analysis of the Changing Practices of Western Highest Courts* (Oxford, Hart Publishing, 2015) 1.

And between 2005 and 2015, the total number of all child migrants rose by 21 per cent.[39] An estimated 3000 children are abducted across borders by parents every year in the EU alone;[40] approximately 14 per cent of the 30,000 registered victims of trafficking in the EU are under 18,[41] increasing to 33 per cent globally.[42] On a more mundane level, children negotiate cross-border family, social, contractual and financial relationships on a daily basis via multiple media, with concomitant (often complex, multi-layered) legal and policy implications. It is almost unthinkable, therefore, that the judiciary, when confronted by such complex, multi-jurisdictional cases, should seek to adjudicate them without a stable grounding in the unifying principles underpinning children's rights.

The CRC has become a favoured judicial reference point in all manner of litigation concerning children, not only cases that straddle jurisdictional boundaries.[43] As Dohrn observes:

> Twenty-five years after its adoption, the values and standards of children's human rights, as developed by the CRC, its ambitious Committee and three Optional Protocols, have encircled the world, setting down roots in unlikely soil, rock and sand, and adapting to climates, faiths and cultures, and a vast range of legal traditions.[44]

The jurisprudence of the notoriously recalcitrant United States is a notable example of such unlikely soil, with Dohrn noting: 'Despite the US's formal isolation on the issue of ratification, the CRC and its associated protocols and case law have flourished beyond what their drafters anticipated'.[45] The landmark 2005 decision in *Roper v Simmons*,[46] which abolished the death penalty for juvenile offenders (see Woodhouse and Buss in this collection), highlights the value of the CRC (in this case Article 37 prohibiting the execution of children) in offering new perspectives on the characteristics and vulnerabilities of children who offend. Regional courts such as the Court of Justice of the EU (CJEU) are another unlikely terrain on which children's rights are starting to blossom,[47] aided significantly by the EU's explicit (albeit tentative) engagement with the CRC over the last decade or so, evidenced perhaps most notably in the EU Charter of Fundamental Rights and the 100 or so CJEU judgments

---

[39]   UNICEF, *Uprooted: The Growing Crisis for Refugee and Migrant Children* (September 2016). It is worth noting also that the current conflicts in the Middle East are causing not only mass displacement of refugees, but also a surge in numbers of children born outside of their parents' country of nationality, leading to a risk of statelessness for increasingly large numbers of children. L van Waas, 'Nationality Matters. Statelessness under International Law' (2009) 28(4) *Refugee Survey Quarterly* 236.

[40]   ECORYS Nederland BV, *Missing Children in the European Union: Mapping, Data Collection and Statistics*, (European Commission DG Justice, 2013).

[41]   Eurostat, *Trafficking in Human Beings* (2015).

[42]   United Nations Office on Drugs and Crime, *Global Report on Trafficking in Persons* (UN Vienna, 2014).

[43]   T Liefaard and J Doek (eds), *Litigating the Rights of the Child: The UN Convention on the Rights of the Child in Domestic and International Jurisprudence* (Dordrecht, Springer, 2015) 3; and esp see B Dohrn, 'The Surprising Role of the CRC in a Non-State Party' in Liefaard and Doek, ibid, ch 5, 71–87.

[44]   Dohrn, ibid, 75.

[45]   ibid.

[46]   *Roper v Simmons* 543 US 551 (2005).

[47]   The other main European regional court, the ECtHR, already boasts a stronger tradition of interpreting its seemingly age-neutral provisions to accommodate the specific interests of children. See further U Kilkelly, 'The CRC in Litigation under the ECHR' in Liefaard and Doek, above n 43; C Smyth, 'The Best Interests of the Child in the Expulsion and First-entry Jurisprudence of the European Court of Human Rights: How Principled is the Court's Use of the Principle?' (2015) 17 *European Journal of Migration and the Law* 70, 79.

that make at least indirect reference to the CRC.[48] This is particularly remarkable in a context not traditionally associated with advancing children's rights.[49]

The judiciary can, therefore, play a transformative role in embedding children's rights standards into supra-national, domestic and internal regional regimes through creative interpretation and increasingly liberal cross-jurisdictional referencing.[50] In doing so, judges go beyond merely interpreting and applying legislation; they resolve gaps and ambiguities that might exist in a system of legal norms, essentially imbuing what may be age-neutral laws with a more acute sensitivity of the specific needs, interests and vulnerabilities of children.[51] But of course effective implementation of children's rights is not just down to allusion to the CRC, nor can it rely solely on judicial sensitivity and interpretative ingenuity; there has to be a sturdy political commitment to embedding those rights in domestic legislation and to investing sufficient resources in the structures and processes that give effect to that law. We point to two contemporary political phenomena that pose added risks to children's rights and that, by implication, have particular implications for children's rights judging: the increasing dominance of neoliberal agendas; and the rise in populist politics.

B. The Role of the Judiciary in the Context of Neoliberalism

In recent decades, neoliberal economic policies have grown in prominence and influence across the globe. The key features of neoliberalism appear immediately antithetical to children's rights: neoliberalism favours privatisation, liberalised trade, the erosion of the welfare state and self-sufficiency; the ideal global, neoliberal subject is autonomous, self-reliant, responsible and able to personally negotiate risk and the marketplace without relying on state support. The protection of socio-economic rights has been a particular casualty of neoliberalism insofar as social rights require commitment by the state to redistributive justice. An increasingly important function of the judiciary, therefore, is to moderate what have been identified as some of the more sinister symptoms of this process. Maria Saffon argues that progressive judicial protection of social rights constitutes effective resistance to neoliberal policies and cites a number of examples in which the Constitutional Court of Colombia has upheld basic education, labour, housing and health rights through an explicitly rights-based approach.[52] The South Africa Constitutional Court has been similarly activist, as highlighted by the case of *Grootboom*, rewritten for this collection by Anashri Pillay.[53] A modest level of judicial activism to counteract the negative effects

---

[48] See in particular Arts 24 and 32 of the Charter. For a discussion of the meaning and scope of these provisions see R Lamont 'Art 24—the Rights of the Child' and H Stalford 'Article 32—Prohibition of Child Labour and Protection of Young People at Work', both featured in S Peers, T Hervey, J Kenner and A Ward (eds), *The EU Charter of Fundamental Rights—A Commentary* (Oxford, Hart Publishing, 2013).

[49] See further H Stalford, 'The CRC in Litigation under EU Law' in Liefaard and Doek, above n 43, 211. See also the decisions of *Zambrano* and *CD v ST* in this collection.

[50] Dohrn, above n 43, 85.

[51] Nolan, above n 31, at 138 citing D Kenney, *A Critique of Adjudication (fin de siècle)* (Harvard MA, Harvard University Press, 1997) 28.

[52] M Saffon, 'Can Constitutional Courts be Counter-Hegemonic Powers vis-à-vis Neoliberalism? The Case of the Colombian Constitutional Court' (2006–07) 5(2) *Seattle Journal for Social Justice* 533 at 534.

[53] J Sloth-Nielsen and H Kruuse, 'A Maturing Manifesto: The Constitutionalisation of Children's Rights in South African Jurisprudence 2007–2012' (2013) 4 *The International Journal of Children's Rights* 646; and A Skelton 'South Africa' in Liefaard and Doek, above n 43, ch 2.

of neoliberalism is also evident in Europe. For example, the acute contraction of legal aid in England and Wales is a product of neoliberal ideology with significant implications for children caught up in legal proceedings. Rosemary Hunter, commenting on the effects of such cuts in a family justice context, notes:

> The government's aim was not merely to restrict spending on legal aid as a short-term austerity measure, but to limit permanently the use of public resources (both legal aid and the courts) for what were seen, in the family law context, as essentially 'private' disputes.[54]

In doing so, the government's alleged, parallel motivation was to move towards

> a simpler justice system: one which is more responsive to public needs, which allows people to resolve their issues out of court without recourse to public funds, using simpler, more informal, remedies where they are appropriate, and which encourages more efficient resolution of contested cases where necessary.[55]

What has happened, in fact, is that the costs to the public purse have simply been passed on to the individual and the not-for-profit legal advice sector. The cuts may have resulted in a slight dip in contested cases but such cases are taking up *more* time and causing *more* aggression and distress in court, not less. Rather than prompting individuals to pursue less litigious alternatives to dispute resolution, these cuts have triggered an unprecedented and worrying trend in self-representation before the courts, creating longer delays than ever and significantly disempowering those without the skills or knowledge to represent themselves effectively.[56] Those without the possibility (notably children and the poor) or will to represent themselves are denied access to justice altogether.[57]

Legal aid has similarly been restricted in a criminal justice context so that prison legal aid is no longer available for claims relating to treatment or sentencing.[58] This applies equally to detained children as it does adults, despite their heightened vulnerability to and from poor treatment and the greater legal complexity relating to their imprisonment and release.[59] The same legislation has also increased tribunal fees for immigration appeals, disproportionately affecting children's access to justice.[60]

---

[54] R Hunter, 'Inducing Demand for Family Mediation—Before and After LASPO' Special Issue 29(2) *Journal of Social Welfare and Family Law* 189, 192.

[55] Ministry of Justice, *Proposals for the Reform of Legal Aid in England and Wales Consultation Paper CP12/10* (2010) 5.

[56] Legal Aid Agency, *Legal Aid Statistics in England and Wales—January to March 2016* (Ministry of Justice, 30 June 2016).

[57] Children are known to be particularly adversely affected by the cuts in legal aid: see further Office of the Children's Commissioner, *Legal Aid Changes since April 2013: Child Rights Impact Assessment*. (London, Office of the Children's Commissioner 2014) and House of Commons Justice Committee, *Impact of Changes to Civil Legal Aid under Part 1 of the Legal Aid, Sentencing and Punishment of Offenders Act 2012*, (2015) Eighth Report of Session 2014–15, 23–25. It has been estimated that approximately 68,000 children per year are affected by the cuts in legal aid in private family cases alone. The Family Court Unions Parliamentary Group, *The Impact of Legal Aid Cuts on Family Justice* (April 2014) 3.

[58] See K Hollingsworth, 'Assuming Responsibility for Incarcerated Children: A Rights Case for Care-based Homes' [2014] *Current Legal Problems* 99.

[59] Particularly in relation to the legal obligations regarding children's resettlement. See further Hollingsworth, ibid at 112–13.

[60] See J Collinson, 'Immigration Tribunal Fees as a Barrier to Access to Justice and Substantive Human Rights Protection for Children' [2017] *Public Law* 1, 10. This is because the legislation is premised on 'choice' (a litigant making a cost-benefit analysis of bringing the claim) and ignores the fact that children are not—by

The judiciary in England and Wales have stepped in to mitigate some of these effects for the benefit of children and adults alike, suggesting at one point that court funds could be made available to ensure adequate legal representation and support for vulnerable parties to a case in the absence of other funding.[61] The fact that these isolated examples of judicial activism were subsequently rejected as beyond the court's powers, however, highlights that the judiciary is only partially effective in resisting neoliberal policies;[62] a culture of judicial activism, the existence of sturdy judicial protective mechanisms *and* a broad and rights-enriched constitutional and political landscape are all instrumental in confronting the elements of neoliberalism that are hostile to individuals' access to and enjoyment of their rights.

C. Judicial Responses to the Rise of Populist Politics

The spectre of populist politics presents an additional challenge to (and perhaps even opportunity for) judicial activism. Populism has resurfaced in recent years in response to global unrest and the economic crisis, bringing with it new questions around the status of human rights and, indeed, the role of the judiciary in protecting those rights, with some profound implications for children. It is difficult to define populism because it refers more to a language and a logic rather than a particular ideology, but it is commonly described as a political philosophy supporting the rights and power of the people in their struggle against the privileged elite or 'establishment'.[63] Just as there is no common ideology that defines populism, there is no one constituency that comprises 'the people'; they can be blue-collar workers, shopkeepers or students burdened by debt; they can be the poor locked out of employment and welfare benefits, or the middle class struggling to secure social care or pension entitlement. Equally, there is no common identification of the 'elite' or 'establishment'. What defines populism, rather, is the conflict between these forces.[64] The difficulty with populism, however, is that children are rarely considered to be 'the people' or voice of populist politics given their democratic invisibility.

Whilst historically populism has been regarded as a feature of right wing politics, in more recent years, populism has been appropriated by left wing campaigns, particularly in southern European countries most acutely affected by the global recession such as Spain, Greece and Italy. For the left, the populist priority has been austerity; for the right, it has

---

law—economically active agents; increasing their reliance on their parents and thus undermining 'children's status as independent holders of human rights'. More generally, see F Meyler and S Woodhouse, 'Changing the Immigration Rules and Withdrawing the "Currency" of Legal Aid: The Impact of LASPO 2012 on Migrants and their Families' (2013) 35(1) *Journal Of Social Welfare And Family Law* 58.

[61] *Q v Q; Re B; Re C* [2014] EWFC 31, Munby P; See also HHJ Bellamy in *Re K and H (Children: Unrepresented Father: Cross examination of Child)* [2015] EWFC 1, *Re K and H (Children)* [2015] EWCA Civ 543.

[62] See *Re K (Children) (Private Law: Public Funding)* [2015] EWCA Civ 543; [2015] 1 WLR 3801 where it was held that a general power or duty (such as under s 1 of the Courts Act 2003) could not be used to circumvent the detailed statutory provisions for legal aid set out in the 2012 Act; to interpret such general provisions as giving the court the power to require the Lord Chancellor to provide public funding would amount to judicial legislation, not interpretation.

[63] M Kazin, *The Populist Persuasion: An American History* (London, Cornell University Press, 1995).

[64] C Muddle, 'The Problem with Populism' *The Guardian (Europe Opinion)* (17 February 2015).

been immigration and religious extremism. These agendas have stimulated a seismic shift in contemporary politics and something of a constitutional and human rights crisis in certain parts of the world, ranging from the rise of left wing, anti-austerity parties in southern Europe to EU withdrawal and potential repeal of the Human Rights Act 1998 in the UK, and the election of Donald Trump in the US. These trends have intense implications for human rights both as a tool for populist campaigns and as a symptom of the crises they seek to address. As Kate Nash notes:

> Human rights are used strategically for particular ends, they are implicated in issues of power, access to resources and in practical and ideal, more or less achievable, visions of how society should be governed … 'Human rights' figure in constructions of a crisis of democracy in which self-serving elites ignore the demands of the people. For both parties the reform and reconstruction of human rights is necessary to restore 'national sovereignty' … Coming from the Left and the Right, of course, each constructs the crisis in different ways.[65]

Nash goes on to argue that for the left, the enforcement of human rights standards is seen as a key anti-austerity mechanism. For those on the right, insofar as international and European human rights are presented as a threat to democracy, the solution lies in limiting and 'repatriating' such rights by allowing primarily nation-made law to dictate the personal and material scope of such entitlement in line with national priorities.

Similarly paradoxical is that whilst populism routinely obscures and even undermines children's active role in shaping political agendas, it can provide a platform for drawing attention to issues that acutely affect them. For instance, populist reactions (predominantly led by the left) to austerity measures that have been introduced in response to the global recession have exposed the disproportionately adverse effects of those measures for children, particularly across Europe. Unicef's cross-national evaluation of the impact of the recession on children reveals that the number of children entering into poverty during the recession is 2.6 million higher than the number that have been able to escape from it since 2008 (6.6 million, as against 4 million) and that around 76.5 million children live in poverty in the 41 most affluent countries.[66] This situation has been explicitly attributed to widespread cuts in public services and welfare budgets, especially those relevant to children and young people.[67] The same arguments are advanced by the populist right, however, but in support of restrictions on EU migrants' (including children's) access to and portability of welfare benefits (as illustrated by Charlotte O'Brien in her commentary on the rewritten version of *Zambrano*).[68] Consequently, populist politics polarises communities, dividing them into crude 'insider' and 'outsider' categories: children on the inside (typically nationals) are placed in hostile competition with children (usually of foreign nationality) on the outside for finite resources relating to education, health, housing and welfare benefits. The UK government's recent decision to prohibit access to unaccompanied migrant children

---

[65] K Nash, 'Politicising Human Rights in Europe: Challenges to Legal Constitutionalism from the Left and the Right' (2016) 20(8) *International Journal of Human Rights* 1295 and 1297.

[66] UNICEF Innocenti Report Card 12: *Children of the Recession—The Impact of the Economic Crisis on Child Well-being in Rich Countries* (Florence, UNICEF Innocenti, Sept 2015). For a more qualitative review, see S Ruxton, *How the Economic and Financial Crisis is Affecting Children & Young People in Europe* (Brussels, Eurochild, 2012).

[67] H Aldridge and T Macinnes, *Multiple Cuts for the Poorest Families* (Oxfam Research Reports, April 2014).

[68] See also C O'Brien, 'The Pillory, the Precipice and the Slippery Slope: The Profound Effects of the UK's Legal Reform Programme Targeting EU Migrants' (2015) (37(1) *Journal of Social Welfare and Family Law* 111.

from refugee camps in mainland Europe on the grounds of local authorities' alleged inability to cope is a case in point. The argument is presented as follows: allowing more people in, no matter how vulnerable, requires the diversion of valuable resources away from vulnerable others already living here. The fact that children in these situations have human rights with corresponding obligations barely features in such debates. Instead, the fickle narrative of 'compassion' has re-emerged to both support and counter regressive admission policies, resonant of a post-industrial protectionist—rather than a rights-based—agenda.[69]

Whilst specific child-related issues might well be used as a political tool, there is a power in knowing that the protection of children's rights is beyond politics and that the independence of the judiciary offers a secure and influential brake on the unauthorised actions of the executive or legislature.[70] The ability to refer disputes to the supra-national courts acts as a further layer of objective accountability. Returning to the example of the impact of the current refugee crisis; conditions for entry, reception and ongoing support of refugee and asylum seeking children are governed by a range of EU secondary legislation with a view to encouraging EU Member States to share and co-ordinate responsibility for settling them. These provisions, in turn, correspond with and reinforce Member States' international obligations under the ECHR, the 1951 Refugee Convention and the CRC.[71] Recourse to the Court of Justice of the EU and, indeed, the European Court of Human Rights, is possible in the event of Member States' (such as the UK's) failure to comply with the obligations set out in those instruments.[72] Similarly, in a criminal justice context, we need only look back to the 1990s when penal populism fuelled some antipathy towards children's rights protection in the UK. The high profile trial of Robert Thompson and Jon Venables, in particular, exemplifies the importance of the judiciary in safeguarding children's right to a fair trial and sentencing in the face of acute hostility and an increasingly punitive approach to youth crime on the part of the executive.[73]

---

[69] See Freeman, above n 23, ch 1. See in particular the speech of Home Secretary, Amber Rudd at the 2016 Conservative Party Conference in stating 'Our compassion does not stop at the border'; and equally Tasmina Ahmed-Sheikh of the Scottish National Party, who in questioning the Conservative government's decision to renege on its commitment to allowing children, stated 'If we have the compassion and humanity—and, indeed, the capacity, which we do—to take in more, why are we not doing so?' (HC Debs, 9 February 2017, Hansard).

[70] Note that at the time of writing the UK Home Secretary's decision to refuse further resettlement of unaccompanied children from mainland Europe is the subject of a pending High Court appeal.

[71] For a notable example of successful strategic litigation that brings children's human rights to bear on the interpretation of EU law and domestic immigration policy, see the Upper Immigration Tribunal judgment in *R (ZAT and others) v Secretary of State for The Home Department* (JR/15401/2015 and JR/15405/2015). This upheld the rights of children stranded in the Calais refugee camp to be united with family members living in the UK, in accordance with their right to respect for private and family life under Art 8 ECHR. For further critical analysis of the use of strategic litigation in an immigration context, see A-M Bucataru, 'Is Strategic Litigation a Way of Ensuring that the Rights of Unaccompanied Minors are Fully Considered in Law, Policy and Practice?' (2016, European Database of Asylum Law: available at www.asylumlawdatabase.eu/en/journal/strategic-litigation-way-ensuring-rights-unaccompanied-minors-are-fully-considered-law).

[72] See for instance Case C-540/03, *European Parliament v the Council*, in which the Court of Justice held that when the signatory Member States apply the EU Directive on Family Reunification (OJ L251/12), they must pay due regard to the individual's right to a family life under Art 8 of the European Convention on Human Rights, and the best interests of the child. (See paras 56–63); Subsequent decisions of the CJEU compel the authorities to interpret EU family reunification law in a manner that is consistent with children's rights—see Case C-648/11, *MA, BT and DA v Secretary of State of the Home Department*, 6 June 2013.

[73] *T v UK and V v UK* (2000) 30 EHRR 121. See further S Snacken and E Dumortier (eds), *Resisting Punitiveness in Europe?: Welfare, Human Rights and Democracy* (Oxford, Routledge, 2012).

Counteracting populist politics in the name of human rights exposes the judiciary to significant backlash, however. The Trump administration's attack on the judiciary in the United States offers a very current illustration of this, as does the criticism from some parts of the media of the judges in the UK tasked with adjudicating the procedure for triggering its negotiations towards EU withdrawal. In spite of a clear mandate to determine questions of law, these judges have faced fierce criticism that they are 'enemies of the people', undermining democracy, and intruding on issues of political judgment.[74] But populist politics can have the opposite effect too: the EU Court of Justice's decision to subject EU migrants who claim child benefits and child tax credits to more stringent residence and financial tests has been interpreted by some as a benign attempt by the judiciary to curb the anti-migrant sentiment threatening the future of the UK's relationship with Europe (it was surely no coincidence that the judgment was issued only a week before the Brexit referendum).[75]

IV. Judging Children's Rights: Common Tendencies

The discussion up to now has highlighted the importance of the judiciary in advancing children's rights in the face of contemporary political and constitutional barriers. Many judges navigate this role with notable skill and humanity to produce inspired decisions, sometimes in the context of highly complex, legally technical cases.[76] But it is also the case that children routinely are prey to poor judicial processes and decision-making tendencies, often with damaging consequences for the individual child in any particular case, and for children's rights more generally. This is supported by a vast body of more thematically focused academic studies, empirical and otherwise, relating to children's experiences of the court process in different legal sub-contexts and jurisdictions. It is also evidenced in the original judgments rewritten for this collection. We summarise these tendencies as follows: fixed judicial conceptualisations of children and childhood; a resistance to seeing children as rights-holders; the tendency to obscure best interests assessments; the tendency to sideline children in court proceedings; and the tendency to undermine children's autonomy. It is to these tendencies that our articulation of the components of a children's rights-based approach to judgment writing (detailed fully in chapter three) respond.

---

[74] J Slack, 'Enemies of the People: Fury over "out of touch" judges who have "declared war on democracy" by defying 17.4 m Brexit voters and who could trigger a constitutional crisis' *Daily Mail* (4 November 2016) available at http://www.dailymail.co.uk/news/article-3903436/Enemies-people-Fury-touch-judges-defied-17-4m-Brexit-voters-trigger-constitutional-crisis.html.

[75] Case C-308/14 *Commission v UK*. See further C O'Brien 'Don't think of the children! CJEU approves automatic exclusions from family benefits in Case C-308/14 Commission v UK' http://eulawanalysis.blogspot. co.uk/2016/06/dont-think-of-children-cjeu-approves.html; and S Reynolds 'Bad news for most vulnerable as court rules UK can restrict child benefit for EU migrants' *The Conversation* (19 June 2016).

[76] In the UK, see for example Lady Hale in *ZH (Tanzania) v Secretary of State for the Home Department* [2011] UKSC 4; [2011] 2 AC 166 or *R (on the application of SG) v Secretary of State for Work and Pensions* [2015] UKSC 16; [2015] 1 WLR 1449. For numerous other examples in different jurisdictions, see Liefaard and Doek, above n 43. See also Sir Mark Hedley's reflections on his experiences of confronting the many legal, evidential and moral dilemmas in his judicial career, presented with characteristic candour and humanity in *The Modern Judge*, above n 31.

A. The Tendency to Reinforce Fixed Conceptualisations of Children and Childhood

There is little question now—in law at least—that children are the bearers of rights rather than mere objects of concern.[77] The CRC has helped significantly in this regard. Yet even within the detailed UN children's rights framework there remain philosophical tensions (or, as Ferguson puts it, a 'theory gap')[78] around the capacities of children and the nature and scope of their rights that play out in the courtroom. We consider some of these tensions in more detail in later sections; suffice to say that particular constructions of children's capacities and childhood experiences emerge in different legal contexts, presumptions that are compounded to some degree by the CRC. For instance, the bright line marking the end of childhood (Article 1) does not necessarily reflect the nature and scope of children's roles, capacities, responsibilities and, indeed, vulnerabilities in different cultures and contexts. In the same vein, NGOs, academics and other advocates for children have contributed to propagating fixed norms of childhood across the globe in their efforts to develop and entrench the CRC in domestic regimes, efforts that are identified as having their precursors in the 'civilizing mission' of colonialism.[79] As Alan Prout observes:

> As the twentieth century has progressed ... highly selective, stereotypical perceptions of childhood—of the innocent child victim on the one hand and the young deviant on the other—have been exported from the industrial world to the South ... It has been the explicit goal of children's rights specialists to crystallize in international law a universal system of rights for the child based on these norms.[80]

Today children are still constructed as 'other' to the adult norm, usually in the sense of being vulnerable, dependent, uncivilised and lacking rationality. By contrast, adults are perceived as independent, civilised and rational—the 'ideal' rights-holder. Consequently, the boundary between the two life-stages (adulthood/childhood) is regarded as fixed (somewhat arbitrarily) by age or by the progressive acquisition of maturity in seemingly predictable developmental stages. Where children do not act in conformity with those prescribed stages, one of two approaches are usually taken: they are either no longer regarded as 'children' in need of special treatment (notably in the criminal law, as evidenced in the original judgment of *JTB*, rewritten by Ray Arthur for this collection); or, they must go beyond what is required for the adult 'norm' in order to acquire entitlement to self-determination (for example, where they wish to determine their own medical treatment or ongoing contact with parents in private family proceedings).

Such presumptions quickly morph into established 'truths' that can exert a significant influence on judicial decision-making. Take, for instance, the original ruling of the Dutch

---

[77] See HLA Hart, 'Definition and Theory in Jurisprudence' (1954) 70 *Law Quarterly Review* 37 for the case against, and for a rebuttal drawing on interest theory see N MacCormick, 'Children's Rights: A Test Case for Theories of Rights' (1976) 62 *Archiv für Rechts-und Sozialphilosphie* 305.

[78] L Ferguson, 'Not Merely Rights for Children but Children's Rights: The Theory Gap and the Assumption of the Importance of Children's Rights' (2013) 21 *International Journal of Children's Rights* 177.

[79] A Prout, *The Future of Childhood: Towards the Interdisciplinary Study of Children* (Abingdon, Routledge Falmer, 2005) 32; and J Boyden, 'Childhood and the Policy-makers: A Comparative Perspective on the Globalization of Childhood' in James and Prout, above n 28, at 184.

[80] ibid.

Supreme Court (*de Hoge Raad*), rewritten for this collection by Marielle Bruning and Ton Liefaard. In prescribing that 'competent' children only have a right to be heard in court proceedings if they are 12 years or older, Dutch law significantly limits younger children's ability to have a say in family-related decisions, no matter how competent they might be. Whilst judges have a discretion to allow younger children to be heard in such proceedings, we are told that permission is rarely granted, such that the judiciary perpetuates and promotes an entirely arbitrary age threshold as if it were a verified point of transition into higher maturity and resilience.

Of course, the CRC has the potential (and, indeed, is designed) to be interpreted much more liberally than this and should rightly be credited with tackling rather than driving some of the most injurious abuses of children's rights that are otherwise legitimised on cultural, social or public policy grounds. It is thus the judiciary's amenability to the principles and provisions contained in the CRC that is key to ensuring its legitimate application. The ruling in *Farooq Ahmed v Federation of Pakistan* concerning the potential repeal of juvenile justice laws designed to protect young offenders from the most severe of adult sanctions (re-written for this collection by Abdullah Khoso) offers a powerful illustration of this point. There the Lahore High Court consciously dispensed with the CRC in favour of religious and cultural norms to justify the reinstatement of these sanctions. The contention by the Lahore High Court in that case was that 'a rights-based approach is not appropriate to Pakistan', where the climate, diet and other factors stimulate the physical (and, by implication moral, educational and social) development of young people, necessitating a higher level of accountability for serious offences. In accepting this reasoning, the High Court merely replaces the 'imperialist ideal' associated with the CRC with a similarly stereotypical and dubious 'Orientalist' approach.[81] The judgment is also illustrative of another 'tendency' of the judiciary: a widespread resistance to seeing children as rights-holders.

B. Resistance to Seeing Children as Rights-holders

Children's rights are not just about formalised entitlement; it is a way of thinking. Notwithstanding efforts to mainstream children's rights, and specifically the CRC, into domestic constitutions and into interpretations of international human rights instruments such as the ECHR,[82] in some areas of law and in some courts there is a resistance to using the language and tools of children's *rights*.[83] In other words, the normative articulation of children's rights at various regulatory levels has yet to stimulate the necessary paradigm shift among many members of the judiciary to ensure their meaningful and consistent application.

Writing in 2006 in the context of England and Wales, Jane Fortin laments the disturbingly 'haphazard' approach to dealing with children's cases,[84] concluding that the domestic

---

[81] See further Urfan Khaliq's commentary of *Farooq*, this collection, who also contextualises the wider political forces at stake.

[82] See the work of Ursula Kilkelly, especially *The Child and the European Convention on Human Rights* (Aldershot, Dartmouth, 1999) and 'Protecting Children's Rights under the ECHR: The Role of Positive Obligations' (2010) 61 *Northern Ireland Legal Quarterly* 245–61. For examples of the case law see *V and T v United Kingdom* (1999) 30 EHRR 121 and *Neulinger and Shrunk v Switzerland* (2010) 28 BHRC 706.

[83] Fortin, above n 34 at 300.

[84] ibid.

courts are still 'only flirting with the idea that children are rights-holders' even after the domestic incorporation of the ECHR by the Human Rights Act 1998.[85] In the same vein, Tobin identifies judicial allegiance to children's rights-based decision-making along a continuum ranging from invisible through to 'incidental', 'selective', rhetorical' or 'superficial', most of which 'tend to overlook, marginalise or misuse the notion of children as rights-bearers.'[86] Rarely do judgments fall into Tobin's 'substantive' category: judgments that conceptualise the issues, determine the content of rights, and follow processes in a way that is consistent with children's rights.

This is not just a peculiarity of the judiciary though; in practice, counsel commonly fails to invoke children's rights principles and provisions even when there are opportunities to do so.[87] Judges and magistrates, for their part, therefore, are reluctant to reason their decisions explicitly on children's rights grounds unless they are advanced as such in the legal arguments put before them or manifested in domestic law. Even when there is a willingness to allude explicitly to children's rights, it is often with a view to legitimising decisions that reinforce adults' or the state's interests rather than children's rights. Scratch beneath the surface and we often find that it impacts only superficially on the reasoning and outcome.[88] Take for instance the House of Lords' majority reasoning in *Begum* (rewritten for the purposes of this collection by Maria Moscati). The Court failed to engage in any detailed way with Begum's claim that her freedom to manifest her religious beliefs (protected under Article 9 ECHR) and right to education (protected under Article 2 of Protocol 1 ECHR) had been breached by the refusal to allow her to attend school whilst wearing full religious dress (the jilbab). Instead, the focus was on the scope of the authorities' discretion to derogate from such rights and on the circumstances under which children might be reasonably presumed to have 'contracted out' of such rights.

C. The Tendency to Obscure Assessments of Best Interests

Linked to this point are inconsistencies in the way that the best interests principle, as enshrined in Article 3(1) CRC, is conceptualised and applied in judicial decision-making. The best interests principle is a cornerstone of decision-making in cases involving children; it responds to perceptions of children's inherent and enhanced vulnerability relative to adults and to a desire to ensure the best possible outcomes for them. Judges are generally very much at ease with grounding their decisions in a principle that is adaptable to endless contexts and that places the child's needs over and above those of others. Yet whilst best interests offers a neat shorthand for promoting the best outcome for children, its ubiquity in legal and judicial parlance belies the complex, speculative and often highly subjective nature of a process that seeks to determine definitively what is best for children. Indeed, the best interests principle remains profoundly contested in practice.

---

[85] ibid at 299.
[86] Tobin, above n 3, at 582.
[87] Although there are many notable exceptions to this: see for instance, Ian Wise QC or Caoilfhionn Gallagher QC who consistently integrate children's rights arguments, and the strong membership of the Association of Child Lawyers who share a commitment to securing children's access to justice (www.alc.org.uk/).
[88] Liefaard and Doek, above n 43.

There is an abundant academic commentary critiquing the variance and lack of transparency in best interests assessments, even in relation to factually and legally comparable
cases.[89] The theoretical insights developed through this literature reveal some common
misconceptions and tensions underpinning best interests which are not easily resolved in
practice. Some cases, for instance, involve children only indirectly; some cases require a balancing up of the seemingly competing interests of different children (consider, for instance,
the child offender and child victims in *JTB*); some legal contexts militate against an individualised assessment of best interests in favour of endorsing a generalised policy stance
that a particular course of action is, at least prima facie, in the best interests of all children
(see for instance the abduction framework exemplified by *Povse* and *RCB*, rewritten for
this collection by Lara Walker and Brian Simpson respectively); some cases may involve
children directly but their interests are inextricably intertwined with the interests of others
involved in their care (such as in *Antwi*, *Zambrano* or *Gas and Dubois*, rewritten for this
collection by Maria Papaioannou, Helen Stalford and Lydia Bracken respectively). In many
cases the best possible outcome may entail a decision that appears positively antithetical
to the child's best interests and, instead, amounts to the 'least worst' outcome that can be
achieved in the circumstances (see, for instance, the conjoined twins decision in *Re A* or
the chronically ill child in *Re T*, redrafted for this collection by Amel Alghrani and Michael
Freeman respectively).

Embedding a rights-based approach in judicial decision-making is impeded further by
the blurring of the definitional lines between best interests and 'welfare', at least in certain
legal contexts in England and Wales. The Children's Rights Alliance for England have noted
the courts' preference for the language of 'welfare' and 'well-being' when adjudicating, in
particular, on children's socio-economic rights such as health, social welfare, employment
and housing.[90] Welfare and best interests are also used interchangeably in family law, immigration proceedings and even criminal justice proceedings;[91] increasingly judges allude to
the best interests principle, as enshrined in Article 3(1) CRC, to interpret questions that are
(legally speaking) strictly concerned with 'welfare'; other times, Article 3(1) is dispensed
with altogether in favour of a 'rights-blind' assessment of welfare (we consider how to
frame best interests as a 'right' in chapter three).[92]

Judges in the UK jurisdictions appear particularly comfortable with 'welfare' perhaps
because it chimes with a traditional, paternalistic approach to protecting children. Welfare

---

[89]   For a comprehensive overview, see M Freeman, 'Article 3: The Best Interests of the Child' in A Alen, J Vande
Lanotte, E Verhellen, F Ang, E Berghmans, M Verheyde and B Abramson (eds), *Commentary on the United Nations
Convention on the Rights of the Child* (Brill, Nijhoff, 2007).

[90]   Children's Rights Alliance for England, *Children's Rights in the Courts: Using the Convention of the Rights of
the Child in Legal Proceedings Concerning Children* (CRAE, London, 2012).

[91]   Fortin (above n 34) suggests the courts are more comfortable with using the language of rights for children
in some contexts, such as criminal justice, but continue to rely on welfare in other contexts (such as family law).
However, even in criminal justice there is some evidence that a paternalistic adoption of welfare has been used to
restrict the child's rights. See K Hollingsworth, 'Judicial Approaches to Children's Rights in Youth Crime' (2007)
19 *Child and Family Law Quarterly* 42.

[92]   Lady Hale noted in *Nzolameso v Westminster City Council* [2015] UKSC 22, paras 28–29 the lack of clarity as
to whether all statutory welfare provisions (in this case, s 11 Children Act 1989) are to be interpreted in the light
of Art 3(1). This is discussed further in the commentary by Fiona Donson on *Castle*, this collection. Ferguson also
differentiates between judicial protection of the 'rights of children' (those arising as a result of another status, such
as the child's *human* rights), where there is greater judicial engagement and 'children's rights' (which depend on
the child's status *qua* child), where there is less clarity. See Ferguson, above n 78.

holds strong political and social currency too: there is nothing threatening about it; on the contrary, it appeals to our inherent sense of benevolence and charity in conveying an image of vulnerability and marginalisation and in reaffirming adults' authority, knowledge and skills to make things better. Perhaps unsurprisingly, it is the rhetoric of 'welfare' that frames much of the legal guidance on how to interpret key tenets of children's rights protection.[93] The principle of welfare paramountcy and its accompanying checklist that sits at the heart of children's public and private family proceedings in England and Wales is a case in point,[94] as is the wording of UK legislation governing the adjudication of children's immigration claims,[95] and the general statutory duty placed on a range of public authorities under the Children Act 2004.[96] These legislative references to 'welfare' typically mark the definitive starting point and the end point of judicial deliberations, often with little or no evidence of any specific consideration of what aspects of children's rights should be engaged to inform such deliberations. As Fortin notes: 'Those representing children seem more interested in presenting the courts with evidence which can be slotted into rather vague assertions about a child's welfare than with analysing what specific rights might protect him or her.'[97]

As a consequence, the implication is that by engaging in a rigorous welfare assessment, particularly if it is treated as of paramount importance compared to other considerations, the courts are automatically fulfilling their obligations pertaining to children's rights. But the conflation of these two concepts has obscured and even undermined the currency of best interests as a distinct 'right' and perpetuated, explicitly or implicitly, narrower paternalistic interpretations. In that sense, as Eekelaar notes:

> The very ease of the welfare test encourages a laziness and unwillingness to pay proper attention to all the interests [and rights][98] that are at stake in these decisions and, possibly also a tendency to abdicate responsibility for decision-making to welfare professionals.[99]

On a more technical level, the conflation of 'welfare' considerations with 'best interests' assessments compounds inconsistencies or clashes between the different interpretative standards applied to best interests in different legal contexts. A classic example relates to the paramountcy standard attached to welfare considerations under family law proceedings in England and Wales. This implies a higher threshold than that attached to the best interests principle which is articulated as 'a primary' (as opposed to '*the* primary') consideration under Article 3(1) CRC. Academics and judges[100] alike have pondered at length the implications of this shift in nomenclature, particularly where different standards appear to clash.[101]

---

[93] Note, however, that the Welsh and Scottish Governments have demonstrated a preference for rights over welfare vis-à-vis the obligations of ministers and, in Scotland, local authorities. See respectively Rights of Children and Young Persons (Wales) Measure 2011 and Children and Young Persons (Scotland) Act 2014, ss 1 and 2.

[94] Children Act 1989, ss 1(1) and (3).

[95] See Borders, Citizenship, and Immigration Act 2009, s 55.

[96] Children Act 2004, s 11 which requires a range of agencies to make arrangements to ensure their functions are discharged having regard to the need to protect and safeguard children's welfare.

[97] Fortin, above n 34 at 303.

[98] Our addition.

[99] Eekelaar, above n 17.

[100] See notably the seminal guidance issued by Lady Hale in *ZH (Tanzania) v SSHD* [2011] UKSC 4.

[101] See for instance family-related claims, otherwise dealt with under the Children Act 1989, pursued under Art 8 ECHR which is routinely informed by the 'lower' interpretative standard of Art 3(1) CRC. Eekelaar, above n 17; Daly, above n 31 at 2; Fortin, above n 34.

Some have cautioned that deference to the latter framework effectively downgrades the status of welfare, placing the interests and needs of a child on more of a fragile footing and, therefore, more easily undermined by other interests.[102] This is particularly true in cases with a strong public policy element, such as immigration or criminal justice, whereby the wider interests of society call for a broader reflection on the extent to which upholding the individual rights of that child might impact upon the collective financial and security interests of society, or, indeed, the individual justice interests of victims of crime. Consider, for instance, the original ruling of *Castle* (rewritten for this project by our fictive judge, Aoife Daly) concerning the confinement ('kettling') of children who were participating in a public demonstration. In linking the duty to protect the children's welfare under section 11 of the Children Act 2004 with the best interests standard under Article 3(1) CRC, the court should have been able to engage in a more enriched rights-based assessment of the proportionality of the measures. Instead, however, the court legitimises introducing other justificatory factors into the balance (the wider public interests of preventing a breach of the peace) and, ultimately, affording them greater weight.

We note a number of problems with this tendency, other than the fact that the balancing act is not always undertaken in a transparent and well-'balanced' way. First it posits the individual interests of children against the interests of others, including the wider community, as if they are mutually exclusive. In doing so, it can close off opportunities for exploring how both sets of interests might be achieved simultaneously to full effect. Second, it fails to acknowledge that upholding children's individual best interests *is* in the inherent interests of society insofar as it acknowledges and nurtures children as active contributors in the present and future to the communities in which they live. Persuasive arguments along these lines have been advanced in the context of immigration proceedings involving children, with Lord Kerr asserting in the UK Supreme Court decision of *HH* that 'although the child has a right to her family life and to all that goes with it, there is also a strong public interest in ensuring that children are properly brought up'.[103] With this in mind, Lord Kerr noted, the best interests of the child 'must always be at the forefront of any decision-maker's mind' and the primacy of the child's best interests is the starting point in *all* decisions affecting children against which other considerations should be weighed. It is not a secondary or supplementary consideration that can be easily trumped, save in the most persuasive circumstances.

A third problem with the tendency to apply different thresholds to best interests assessments is that, in reality, cases involving children are often much more variegated, straddling different legal sub-disciplines and, by implication, different best interests standards. Thus, children are commonly implicated in private or public family proceedings simultaneously with immigration proceedings; child protection and juvenile justice proceedings often go hand-in-hand, as do children's asylum claims and housing and welfare appeals. These complex hybrid cases highlight the importance of transcending technical distinctions between

---

[102] J Fortin, 'Are Children's Best Interests Really Best? *ZH (Tanzania) (FC) v Secretary of State for the Home Department*' (2011) 74 *Modern Law Review* 947; Daly, above n 31, ch 2. For a defence of the welfare principle, see J Herring, 'Farewell Welfare?' (2005) 27 *Journal of Social Welfare And Family Law* 159.

[103] *R (on the application of HH) v Deputy Prosecutor of the Italian Republic* [2012] UKSC 25 at para 33. See further H Stalford and S Woodhouse 'Family Migration: A UK Perspective' in J Eekelaar and R George (eds), *Routledge Handbook of Family Law and Policy* (Oxford, Routledge, 2015).

best interests or welfare thresholds in favour of a more holistic appraisal of the best possible outcome for the child, a process that can only be achieved if underpinned by an unshifting and transparent allegiance to children's rights principles.[104]

D. The Tendency to Side-line Children in the Legal Process

A related tendency we identify is the marginalisation of children within legal processes and, in particular, the tendency to pursue children's claims on adults' terms. This is perpetuated by a number of legal, procedural and practical obstacles. It is logistically difficult for children to bring a legal claim themselves, even when it directly concerns them. In some cases they are legally barred from doing so or they may require permission of the court to be party to proceedings. Legal proceedings before the international courts have little or no mechanism for involving children directly. On a more practical level, children typically have limited knowledge about their legal rights (and thus whether they have been infringed)[105] or about where to find appropriate legal representation, and they usually have limited resources to bring a claim on their own behalf. Consequently, challenges are usually pursued by adults on children's behalf[106] with little or no direct participation of children in proceedings.[107] Such obstacles distort the way in which children's interests are argued, adjudicated and, ultimately, protected.

As a consequence of these obstacles, a common tendency is to conflate children's rights and interests with those of their parents and to reason from the perspective of the parents as holders of rights (including rights over their children) rather than from the perspective of children as rights-holders in their own regard.[108] Consider, for instance, the original ruling in *Collins* (re-written for this collection by Simon Hoffman) concerning the refusal of planning permission to enable a traveller community to station caravans for residential occupation on land which they owned. The Court of Appeal, in upholding the refusal, failed to consider the specific impact that this would have on the distinct needs and vulnerabilities of the 39 children living on the site, preferring instead to conflate the interests of the children with those of the adults. Consider also the original judgment in *Re T* concerning a dispute about the medical treatment of a baby with a life-threatening liver condition. In supporting the parents' objection to a potentially life-saving transplant, the Court of Appeal failed to

---

[104] See Eekelaar, above n 17 for a discussion of how this might be achieved in practice. Ch 3 develops these ideas in more detail.

[105] See for example M Ruck, DP Keating, R Abramovitch and CJ Koegl, 'Adolescents' and Children's Knowledge About Rights: Some Evidence for How Young People View Rights in Their Own Lives' (1998) 21 *Journal of Adolescence* 275; C Goodwin-De Faria and V Marinos, 'Youth Understanding & Assertion of Legal Rights: Examining the Roles of Age and Power' (2012) 20 *International Journal of Children's Rights* 343; M Peterson-Badali, MD Ruck and J Bone, 'Rights Conceptions of Maltreated Children Living in State Care' (2008) 16 *International Journal of Children's Rights* 99–119. See also *R (on the Application of the Children's Rights Alliance for England) v Secretary of State for Justice* [2013] EWCA Civ 34 and *R (on the application of C) v the Secretary of State for Justice* [2008] EWCA Civ 882 where it emerged that children detained in secure training centres did not recognise that the restraint used against them was unlawful.

[106] J Fortin, 'Children's Rights—Flattering to Deceive' (2014) 26 *Child and Family Law Quarterly* 51, at 53–54.

[107] We examine this below in more detail.

[108] See for example *Re J (Specific Issue Order: Muslim Upbringing and Circumcision)* [1999] 2 FLR 678; *R (on the application of Williamson) v Secretary of State for Education and Employment* [2005] UKHL 15 [2005] AC 246, per Baroness Hale at [86], discussed by Fortin, above n 34 at 300–01.

disentangle the interests of the child from those of the parents and ultimately 'gave more weight to the parents' wishes over the medical opinion and the child's right to life.'[109]

This tendency to overlook the specific rights of the child is replicated in the supra-national courts too: the original CJEU case of *CD v ST*, for instance, (re-written for this collection by Eugenia Caracciolo di Torrella) concerned a claim that pregnancy-related entitlement provided by EU law should be extended to parents who have acquired children as a result of a surrogacy arrangement. This was rationalised entirely on the basis of the adults' claim for equality with no reference whatsoever to the potential effect that a refusal to extend entitlement would have on the child, and specifically its reinforcement of the children's differential (inferior) treatment on grounds of their parents' reproductive circumstances.[110]

E. The Tendency to Undermine Children's Autonomy

In the (relatively uncommon) instances in which children's perspectives and wishes are aired in legal proceedings, perhaps the most common shortcoming on the part of some members of the judiciary is to minimise children's active participation in decision-making, to pay mere lip service to their views and wishes or, worse still, to ignore them altogether. This is in spite of universal acceptance of the right of the child, who is capable of forming his or her own views, 'to express those views freely in all matters affecting the child, the views of the child being given due weight in accordance with the age and maturity of the child' (Article 12(1) CRC). This provision has been 'much revered and celebrated',[111] perhaps even reified for its radical re-conceptualisation of the adult–child decision-making relationship.[112] Its importance is matched only by the perceived extent of its abuse, such that an entire sub-discipline has emerged within children's rights and childhood studies dedicated to analysing the nature and scope of child participation. We know more about what children's right to participate (or 'to be heard', to use the phrasing of Article 12) in legal decision-making should mean, both conceptually and in practice, than virtually any other aspect of children's rights. There is also an overwhelming consensus, mined through empirical work involving children and young people, that children want to be given a say in decisions that affect their lives and that facilitating such participation reveals richer, unique insights and yields more enduring, fairer decisions. Yet in spite of this abundance of evidence, some members of the judiciary—and legal processes more broadly—still struggle to give children a meaningful stake in decision-making. As Daly notes:

> In liberal democracies individual freedom is upheld as the ultimate ideal, yet the right to be heard provides very little, if any, respect for children's legal autonomy, and too many excuses to override children's wishes, because it still leaves adults (usually judges) with all of the discretion, and therefore all of the power.[113]

---

[109] N Peleg commentary on the rewritten version of *Re T*, this collection.
[110] In the context of the ECtHR, Jacobsen's analysis shows that there remain cases 'involving children where their best interest is not considered independently of the parents' interest' and that a 'child-centred approach is not yet an indispensable component of ECtHR adjudication'. See AF Jacobsen, 'Children's Rights in the European Court of Human Rights—an Emerging Power Structure' (2016) 24 *International Journal of Children's Rights* 548.
[111] Daly, above n 31.
[112] ibid.
[113] ibid.

The wide scope and implications of this failure are confronted by many of the judgments that have been re-written for this collection across numerous legal contexts including education,[114] child protection,[115] private family proceedings[116] and medical proceedings.[117] The original versions of these decisions highlight the reality that children's right to have a say in decisions about their lives is readily overridden by paternalistic assessments as to what is 'best' for the child's welfare. The problem arises, Archard and Skivenes note,

> because the two commitments seem to pull in different directions: the promotion of a child's welfare is essentially paternalistic since it asks us to do what we, but not necessarily the child, think is best for the child; whereas listening to the child's own views asks us to consider doing what the child, but not necessarily we, thinks is best for the child.[118]

This difficulty is compounded by the tendency to categorise children's rights into mutually exclusive groupings comprised of 'protective obligations' (provisions that seek to protect children against harm, including the harms that might result from being involved in court processes) and 'autonomy rights' (provisions that promote children's agency to lay claim to their own rights on their own terms).[119] This, in turn, presents a seemingly stark choice between, on the one hand, highly paternalistic assessments based largely on what adults think will achieve the best outcomes for the child, and, on the other, a liberalised, seemingly riskier adultification of children.

An analysis of the case law reveals additional trends in judicial approaches when confronted by requests to hear and add weight to what children say. In the absence of a hard and fast age-threshold by which they acquire legal autonomy, a high threshold of understanding and capacity is required of children for them to qualify for autonomous decision-making—higher, in fact, than that expected of most adults.[120] Even when this threshold is reached, judges are extremely resistant to contravening the advice and opinions of adult professionals and their parents, particularly in matters of life and death.[121]

This apparent dichotomy between autonomy and best interests is manifested in the other direction in legal contexts where the child's competency for autonomous decision-making *is* recognised, or at least presumed, by the law. In the context of juvenile justice, for example, the courts are more comfortable with recognising the child's autonomy-based *rights* as shared in common with adults (such as the right to a fair trial), but are less willing to engage with best interests.[122] Returning to the original decision of *R v JTB* concerning children's criminal responsibility, the words 'welfare' and 'best interests' are entirely absent from the court's reasoning. In such contexts, autonomy is more explicitly acknowledged, but risks

---

[114] *Valsamis, Begum* and *SENDIST.*

[115] *P-S (Children).*

[116] *De Hoge Raad.*

[117] *F v F* [2013] EWHC 2683.

[118] Archard and Skivenes, above n 24.

[119] A Quennerstedt, 'Children, but not Really Humans? Critical Reflections on the Hampering Effect of the "3 p's"' (2010) 18 *International Journal of Children's Rights* 619.

[120] M Freeman, 'Rethinking Gillick' (2005) 13 *International Journal of Children's Rights* 201, 211.

[121] J Fortin 'Children's Rights: Are the Courts Now Taking Them More Seriously?' (2004) 15 *King's Law Journal* 253. For an illustration, see the original judgment in *Re W*, rewritten by Stephen Gilmore for this collection.

[122] Though there is an increasing willingness of some judges in England and Wales to do so: see for example, *R (on the application of HC) v Secretary of State for the Home Department* [2013] EWHC 982 (Admin).

being instrumentalised to justify holding defendants to account for their actions rather than enabling children to participate in decisions about what should happen to them.[123]

In identifying these tendencies of the judiciary, we note two important caveats. The first is that the shortcomings are not uniformly observable in *all* cases involving children: there is considerable variation between jurisdictions (we note our selective bias towards England and Wales as examples), legal contexts, courts and individual judges. That said, many of the highest profile cases that we have scrutinised come from the senior courts, but we suspect that these tendencies may be even more pervasive at first instance or in quasi-judicial fora such as education tribunals. The second, related caveat is that judges do not operate in a vacuum; their freedom to innovate and their ability and motivation to adopt a proactive, substantive approach to children's rights is constrained—and, at times facilitated—by a range of institutional, constitutional, procedural, practical and personal tensions and constraints.[124] It is to these that we now turn.

V. Judging Children's Rights: Common Tensions and Constraints

In some legal disputes, clear statutory language,[125] binding precedent,[126] and the 'inferior domestic legal status'[127] of international rights treaties—including the CRC—limit a judge's freedom to adopt a 'substantive' children's rights approach. As Lord Justice Laws recently stated (whilst adopting a restrictive approach to the application of the CRC in a decision widely regarded as antithetical to the rights of child defendants):

> [T]he exercise [of statutory interpretation] … imposes a discipline on the court—a discipline fulfilled by giving first consideration to the language of the provision and to its perceived objective

---

[123] Where a child's welfare *is* taken into account in criminal justice cases, there is evidence of a similar tendency as in other areas of law to use it to displace the child's autonomy-based rights. For example, in *R (on the application of JC & RT) v Central Criminal Court*, [2014] EWCA Civ 1777, a case concerning the protection of anonymity into adulthood following a childhood conviction, Laws LJ focused narrowly on protecting the child's immediate welfare, with no real examination of the child's *rights* under the CRC. See also Lord Bingham in *R (on the application of R) v Durham Constabulary*, [2005] UKHL 21 where a focus on the child's welfare displaced the need to obtain his consent to being issued with a final warning (the child version of a caution).

[124] Tobin identifies three principal obstacles: 'the continuing controversy surrounding the concept of children's rights; the relatively open-ended nature of many of the norms; and procedural impediments at the court level' in addition to the 'inferior legal status' of international human rights treaties in domestic law: above n 3 at 581. We expand on these in the section below.

[125] For example, the UK Parliament recently legislated to clarify that lifelong reporting restrictions are available in criminal courts only to child victims and witnesses, not child defendants (Youth Justice and Criminal Evidence Act 1999, s 45A), thus removing the possibility of a children's rights compatible judicial interpretation of previous (ambiguous) legislation (albeit that the courts had not, in fact, previously adopted a more child-friendly approach! See *JC*, above n 123).

[126] In particular, judges can be constrained by the antiquity of common law doctrines (as well as statutes) and the difficulty with which the past can 'speak to the present' (see S Sheldon, 'British Abortion Law: Speaking from the Past to the Present' (2016) 79 *Modern Law Review* 283; and in the context of children's rights see *R v JTB* [2009] (rewritten in this collection) where the House of Lords was unwilling to interpret the ancient concept of *doli incapax* in ways that would have given it contemporary relevance for the rights of child defendants. There are, however, examples of judges (re)interpreting doctrine to take account of children's rights, for example, *R v G* [2003] UKHL 50 (see J Williams, 'England and Wales' in Liefaard and Doek, above n 43, ch 4)).

[127] Tobin, above n 3 at 581.

purpose, informed in this case by contrasting rights which our constitution acknowledges, rights principally articulated by Articles 8 and 10 of the ECHR. These considerations must be the primary drivers of the court's decision.[128]

However, as he also acknowledged, 'the exercise of interpretation is seldom value free and is often creative' and, argues Tobin, the significance of the legislative, precedential and constitutional constraints is 'often overstated'.[129] In most cases, and especially in constitutional or senior appellate courts, human rights disputes,[130] and legal proceedings where the best interests of the child is the governing principle, there is considerable room for judicial discretion, the exercise of which involves the engagement of moral reasoning.[131] It is within this discretionary space—the edges of which are defined by law—that variations between judges emerge, reflecting differences in their 'judicial philosophy'.[132] Such judicial philosophy is shaped by a variety of factors, some of which clearly constrain the adoption of a children's rights approach,[133] whilst others form part of a more dynamic relationship; in one context a particular factor may operate as an inhibitor and in another context the same factor may facilitate what we would regard as a children's rights-based judgment.[134] We have broadly categorised these factors as structural (considerations relating to issues beyond the individual judge, such as their place in the constitutional order or procedural issues) and individual (those factors that relate to the judge him or herself, such as personal characteristics, experience and values).

A. Structural Tensions and Constraints

Institutional, constitutional and practical factors impact on how judges decide. To illustrate, we focus on the factors that have particular resonance for this rewriting project, either because of the relevance to the subject matter (children) or the jurisdictional reach (the inclusion of supranational courts).

i. Institutional Tensions: A Focus on the Supra-national Courts

A range of institutional factors influence and potentially constrain the judiciary including rules of the court, organisational culture, relationships with judicial colleagues

---

[128] *JC*, above n 123 at para [19].

[129] Tobin, above n 3 at 582.

[130] Where rights are vague and broadly defined and where judges enjoy a wide interpretative power (see for example, in the context of the UK, Human Rights Act 1998, s 3).

[131] Mnookin has similarly noted that judges are called on to make predictions about the future which imply value-laden assessments of the nature, scope and weight of the interests at stake. He calls these the 'prediction problem' (the difficulty of predicting the consequences of alternative policies/decisions) and the 'value problem' (the difficulty of selecting the criteria that should be used to evaluate the alternative consequences'). R Mnookin, *In the Interests of Children: Advocacy, Law Reform and Public Policy* (WH Freeman, New York, 1985) 16–17.

[132] '[t]hat is to say their view of the judicial role'. T Etherton, 'Liberty, the Archetype and Diversity: a Philosophy of Judging' [2010] *Public Law* 727 at 728.

[133] For example, if the voices of children are not heard during the legal process, the likelihood of a children's rights decision is reduced. See for example Lady Hale in *Re D (A Child)(Abduction: Foreign Custody Rights)* [2006] UKHL 51 at para [57], drawing a clear link between hearing the child and his or her moral status as a rights-holder.

[134] See below in the context of personal values or how the judge views the relationship between the courts and the legislature.

and counsel,[135] and the intended audience of the judgment.[136] These factors operate on a number of levels: on the proceedings (for example, whether and to what extent expert evidence can be submitted, how the child's views are represented, and the degree to which the child is able to participate); the substance of the decision (family courts might be more likely to reason from a welfarist position and criminal courts within a rights framework, for example);[137] and the way in which the judgment is written (its tone, length and structure).[138] One of the unique features of this rewriting project is the inclusion of courts operating at a supra-national level and thus it is these courts that are the focus of this section.

The distinct constitutional and institutional setting within which judges operate at the supra-national level is not always recognised in the general literature on the role of the judiciary in upholding children's rights.[139] The supra-national courts (in this collection, the CJEU, the ECtHR, the International Criminal Court (ICC) and the European Committee on Economic and Social Rights (ECESR)) have a rather different mandate and competencies compared to domestic courts. Whilst they too are called upon (increasingly) to adjudicate on children's rights matters, they do so with a rather different aim in mind, usually in a more limited advisory or appeal capacity, and significantly more distanced from the original facts and evidence underpinning the case. In the case of some courts, the legal dispute is often concerned with 'dry' jurisdictional issues, or questions of legal competency, often hiding or distorting the experiences of the child at the heart of the dispute. This is compounded by the tone, style and purpose of the supranational courts, which is markedly different from domestic courts, or at least those of common law jurisdictions. The narrative element of judicial opinion-writing that characterises domestic jurisdictions such as England and Wales,[140] where judges make careful (and sometimes selective) use of the facts in order to arrive at their desired legal destination/outcome, is largely absent. This is partly because the court is unable to revisit decided facts,[141] and partly because the legal traditions within which the courts operate (notably civil jurisdictions) dictate a rather more laconic style and content.

The CJEU, in particular, has been largely resistant to developing its reasoning around the children's rights-related provisions of the EU's own Charter of Fundamental Rights and relevant international children's rights law. This is true even of areas that fall squarely within EU competence and even where the case concerns EU secondary legislation that explicitly enshrines children's rights provisions (such as immigration and asylum law).[142] Similarly, the ECtHR has not always been as progressive or 'child friendly' as we might expect.[143]

---

[135] See for example A Paterson, *The Final Judgment: The Last Law Lords and the Supreme Court* (Oxford, Hart Publishing, 2013).

[136] See E Rackley, 'The Art and Craft of Writing Judgments: Notes on the Feminist Judgments Project' in Hunter, McGlynn and Rackley, above n 33.

[137] Fortin, above n 34.

[138] What Rackley calls the 'art and craft' of the judgment. See Rackley, above n 136. For a broad consideration of the impact of these factors on judgments, see Hunter, McGlynn and Rackley, above n 33.

[139] Although a notable exception is the collection by Liefaard and Doek, above n 43.

[140] See further ch 3, s IV.

[141] True also of some domestic courts.

[142] See H Stalford and E Drywood, 'Using the CRC to Inform EU Law and Policy-Making' in Invernizzi and Williams, above n 1.

[143] See Jacobsen, above n 110, 554.

As Jacobsen notes, 'it has taken a surprising amount of time for a child-centred perspective to gain ground and come into more frequent use by the court', such that children's rights continue to be marginalised in cases where the child's interests have to be balanced against competing parental interests.[144] In a similar vein, Ursula Kilkelly has noted the failure of the ECtHR to embrace the autonomy ethic underpinning Article 12 CRC to inform its judgments of ECHR rights with quite the same confidence as Article 3 CRC.[145] Certainly the culture of judicial reasoning at the European level does not lend itself particularly well to expansive children's rights reasoning; neither the ECtHR nor the Court of Justice were originally intended to operate as platforms for the promotion and protection of children's rights; only two of the 47 judges from the ECtHR (and none of the 28 CJEU judges) have any background in children's rights; only a handful of the current Court of Justice judges has any experience in human rights more broadly. But there is also an ideological reason underpinning the European courts' resistance to extended reflection on such cases: it is a deeply embedded principle that children's rights, like other aspects of human rights—and particularly those of a socio-economic nature—should be determined and regulated at the closest possible level to the child in light of the specific cultural, economic, political, legal and social context within which the child is situated. As such, the supra-national courts concede a considerable margin of appreciation to Member States in interpreting and applying European standards in a way that is sensitive to their distinct contextual factors. Indeed, the political legitimacy of these courts is dependent on maintaining a high level of respect for Member States' margin of appreciation.[146]

ii. Constitutional Tensions

The executive and legislative branches of government have primary (state) responsibility for implementing children's rights,[147] yet the courts have a central role in defining the scope of those obligations and providing remedies in the event of their breach (thus fulfilling a strong expressive function about our commitment to children's rights). How a judge views the proper role of the courts within the constitutional structure—their relationship with the other branches of government and their understanding of overarching constitutional principles such as the separation of powers and the rule of law—is thus central to how they resolve children's rights cases. The courts have to tread a fine line between giving effect to children's rights and respecting the role of the legislature and executive to set appropriate, realistic legal parameters and to allocate resources accordingly.

Children's rights cases can be emotive, highly controversial and can have polycentric ramifications, impacting on those beyond the immediate dispute, especially where the outcome requires the re-distribution of scarce resources or the setting aside of law or policy. In such cases in particular, judges are conscious of their susceptibility to criticism on the grounds of their (purported) lack of democratic legitimacy: that is, that an unelected judiciary should not overstep the bounds of their constitutional role by substituting their own decision for that of the elected and accountable branches of government.[148] The (not uncontroversial)

---

[144] ibid.

[145] Kilkelly, above n 47.

[146] See further Jacobsen, above n 110 at 558 and 566.

[147] Where parents are unable or unwilling to do so. See Nolan, above n 31.

[148] For a full account of this 'counter-majoritarian' argument in the context of children's socio-economic rights, see Nolan, above n 31 and see again the discussion on legal aid above, text at fns 56–57.

language of deference may be employed by judges in order to sidestep rights-based claims where they believe that the legislature or the executive, rather than the court, should determine the issue at hand.[149] In some cases this may result in a pro-children's rights outcome: for example when the UK House of Lords overturned an earlier High Court decision that sought to abolish the centuries old concept of *doli incapax* (a valuable buffer from criminal responsibility for younger children), which the Lords held was a doctrine of such importance and longevity that it could only be removed by Parliament.[150] But in other instances the courts appear *too* deferential. Nolan, for example, has argued in the context of children's socio-economic rights that the courts fail to recognise that the counter-majoritarian argument (that it is undemocratic for an unelected judge to override the will of the elected branches) has much less force when applied to children. Children are excluded from democratic processes and are not directly represented by the legislature or the government. They have little political power to advance their own interests outside of the courts, and thus it must fall to judges to protect them.[151] The legitimacy of the judges to do so, even when it appears to thwart governmental will, is strengthened where the executive and legislative branches persistently fail to respond to their children's rights obligations.[152] The impact of legal aid contractions on the enforcement of children's rights, noted earlier in this chapter, is a case in point.

In addition to a (sometimes misplaced) concern with their own legitimacy to decide complex children's rights claims, judges may also defer to other constitutional actors where they regard themselves as lacking the capacity to decide the issue before them. This arises most obviously in cases where the court lacks the expertise to assess disputed evidence or where the outcome will have wider implications—particularly economic ones—that cannot be considered within the narrow confines of a specific legal dispute.[153] However, Nolan argues that again such concerns are over-inflated and that the so-called incompetence of the courts is often 'greatly overestimated'. Moreover, as she goes on to note, the key question is not whether the courts are the *ideal* forum for such decision-making but rather 'where no one else fulfils this function, will the court do the job so badly that it is better to let the breakdown continue rather than suffer judicial intervention in a desperate last resort'.[154]

The 'practical question'[155] of a judge's capacity to adjudicate children's rights cases is affected by the adequacy, relevance and type of evidence provided to the court. For cases involving children there are two sources of information that have particular importance: the voice of the child and research evidence about children. Yet, as the next two sections reveal, there are procedural and evidential constraints around both which potentially restrict the judicial function.

---

[149] For an example of judicial deference at the expense of children's rights, see Healy's commentary in this collection where she refers to a CJEU decision of an Advocate General who stated that it is not 'for the Court to substitute itself for the legislature by engaging in constructive interpretation that would involve reading into Directives 2006/54 ... something that is simply not there'; this would 'encroach[] upon the legislative prerogative.'

[150] Though Parliament subsequently abolished it in any event. See *C (A Minor) v Director of Public Prosecutions* [1996] 1 AC 1 and s 34 Crime and Disorder Act 1998. On *doli incapax*, see Arthur's contribution to this collection.

[151] Nolan, above n 31. The two do not always conflict of course; policies can be both favourable to children's rights and to wider public policy (for example, keeping children out of the criminal justice system).

[152] See Mnookin, above n 131, ch 3.

[153] Particularly in the context of socio-economic rights, see Nolan, above n 31, ch 5.

[154] Nolan, above n 31 at 219.

[155] As Mnookin calls it: above n 131.

iii. Procedural Constraints: Hearing the Child's Voice

In chapter three we discuss in detail the key markers of a children's rights judgment which, as we note there, includes the use of narrative to centralise children's experiences, and reasoning that is located within concrete, lived, experiences rather than 'in abstract, categorical terms'.[156] The adoption of this children's rights method to judging depends upon understanding the experiences and lives of the children involved which in turn depends on hearing the child in compliance with Article 12 CRC. Yet throughout legal proceedings, the voices of children are excluded, silenced or distorted, hindering the ability of even the most willing judge to produce a 'children's rights judgment'.

The silencing and distortion of the litigant's voice (or that of others centrally affected by the decision) is not confined to children. The judgment is the end point of a long legal process during which lawyers decide what evidence to present and what facts to use to create a 'story' which will most likely secure the best outcome for their client.[157] The litigant's voice—adult or child—is inevitably filtered through their counsel, removing the individual's control over how she and her experiences are presented in court.[158] This is especially likely where contact with the lawyer prior to the proceedings is limited or where the lawyer is applying tried and tested strategies (which may favour silencing the child) with a view to simply winning the case for the child.[159] The judge's ability to hear and reflect in his or her judgment an individual's experiences (including an individual child) is therefore constrained by the version of the facts and the evidence presented. There are also other factors, touched upon earlier in this chapter, that compound the silencing of *children* in particular. In some legal contexts (for example disputes between parents) the child's interests will usually be presented to the court via a welfare report and the child will not ordinarily be a party to the proceedings or have separate representation. Though some jurisdictions may make special provision to allow children to instigate proceedings,[160] to be a party, or to have separate legal representation, it is quite exceptional in practice[161] and usually requires that the child pass maturity and best interests thresholds.[162] And, where a child is granted (for example, in private law) or entitled (as in public law) to separate legal representation, a litigation friend usually instructs the lawyer on the child's behalf unless the child is

---

[156] These are also the methods of feminist judging. See R Hunter, 'More than just a Different Face? Judicial Diversity and Decision-Making' (2015) 68(1) *Current Legal Problems*, 119.

[157] '[T]he goal of storytelling in law is to persuade an official decision maker that one's story is true, to win the case, and thus to invoke the coercive force of the state on one's behalf'. P Brooks and P Gewtiz, *Law's Stories: Narrative and Rhetoric in the Law* (New Haven, Yale University Press, 1996) 5.

[158] See Brooks and Gewtiz, ibid (especially the contributory chapter by C MacKinnon); D Watkins, 'Recovering the Lost Human Stories of Law: Finding Mrs Burns' (2013) 7 *Law and Humanities* 68 and 'The Shaping and Misshaping of Identity through Legal Practice and Process: (Re)discovering Mr Kernott' (2014) 8 *Law and Humanities* 192.

[159] For example in immigration or criminal justice proceedings. Although some barristers may have more interaction with their clients, in most cases the barrister will construct the 'story' for the court based on materials compiled by the solicitor and a detailed knowledge of how particular courts and judges operate.

[160] For example, in England and Wales children can apply for leave to apply for a s 8 order under the Children Act 1989 (by virtue of s 10).

[161] For example, in relation to applications under Children Act 1989, s 10, Fortin notes there are two significant hurdles: first the child must convince a solicitor she has sufficient maturity to instruct without a guardian; and second, leave of the court is required, and can only be obtained if the child has 'sufficient understanding'. See Fortin, above n 14 at 133 and ch 7.

[162] Either to convince a solicitor to represent her and/or to get leave of the court. See Fortin, above n 14 at ch 4.

deemed competent by the court to do so (and can convince a lawyer that s/he is capable of instructing her).[163] There are also temporal limits placed on certain types of proceedings involving children that limit possibilities for developing the trust, capacity and level of dialogue required for meaningful participation. All domestic courts dealing with international parental child abduction proceedings, for instance, are currently subject to a six-week time limit for resolving such cases (save for exceptional cases which make this impossible or unfair), from the point at which proceedings are issued to the point of the child's return to their country of habitual residence.[164]

There are therefore multiple ways throughout legal proceedings where the child's voice is unheard, filtered or distorted even before it gets to the point at which the judge's discretion comes into play. Whether these restrictions are motivated by pragmatic, protective or strategic factors there is considerable scope for enhancing—normalising even—children's participation within domestic and international justice systems. These include, but go beyond, the issue of the child's direct involvement in the legal proceedings and are examined further in chapter three.

iv. Evidential Tensions

Children's status as quasi-legal citizens—they have rights but not always the legal power to claim those rights or the competency to provide their own testimony—means that the empirical and expert evidence available to judges takes on special importance in children's cases. Judges may be called on to assess the risk that a child has suffered or will suffer harm; they may have to decide on the child's future based on an assessment of his or her best interests; they may also have to determine whether the child has sufficient competence to be afforded certain legal rights (and responsibilities). A tendency observed on the part of the judiciary is to 'use an intellectual framework informed by training or reading that may be out of date, too general or vague, or inappropriate when interpreting research.'[165] Hearing evidence, therefore, whether it be expert evidence about the particular child or general research evidence about children, is potentially highly informative. Such evidence allows assumptions[166] underpinning judicial decision-making about children to be challenged[167] and can inform judges about the 'real world' where their own life experience may be

---

[163]   See the original decision in *de Hoge Raad*. This is in contrast to the criminal justice system where children (in England and Wales at least) are presumed competent to instruct a lawyer, regardless.

[164]   The Hague Convention on the Civil Aspects of International Child Abduction 1980, Art 11; and Council Regulation (EC) No 2201/2003 of 27 November 2003 concerning jurisdiction and the recognition and enforcement of judgments in matrimonial matters and the matters of parental responsibility, OJ L 338, 23/12/2003 P. 0001— 0029, Art 11(3).

[165]   B Rodgers, L Trinder and T Williams, *Towards a Family Justice Observatory to Improve the Generation and Application of Research* (London, Nuffield, 2015) 6.

[166]   C Piper, 'Assumptions about Children's Best Interests' (2001) 22 *Journal of Social Welfare and Family Law* 261. See also M King and C Piper, *How the Law Thinks about Children* (Alderhot, Gower, 1990).

[167]   See for example Lady Hale, 'Should Judges be Socio-Legal Scholars' (SLSA Annual Conference, York, 4 April 2013) (available at www.supremecourt.uk/news/speeches.html#2013), who notes that research by Nigel Lowe and Rhona Shultz challenged the 'paradigm' child abduction cases underpinning the operation of the Hague Convention. See also, inter alia, C Smart, B Neale and A Wade, *The Changing Experience of Childhood: Families and Divorce* (Oxford, Polity, 2001) and in the criminal context the growing reliance on neuroscience evidence regarding children's maturation (see for example the US Supreme Court in *Roper v Simmons* above n 46).

temporally far removed from the experiences of children or otherwise relatively narrow (thus helping to counter the lack of diversity in the judiciary).[168]

However, the use of research evidence in court is extremely complicated and there are multiple layers of constraint that limit its use by the courts.[169] First, Rodgers, Trinder and Williams observe in the context of family cases that the use of research evidence is often ad hoc with 'few mechanisms for bringing it together in a way that meets the needs of the parties and the courts for understanding issues relevant to a particular case.'[170] Moreover, courts see only a snapshot of the relevant research, which can be narrow and misleading.[171] Second, judges lack the necessary expertise, skills, resources and time to access some of the most up-to-date evidence and to weigh and assess its reliability and validity (a critical limitation where the parties disagree about the evidence).[172] And third, 'judges ... are uncertain about the extent to which they can rely on research evidence, particularly where it has not been adduced to the courts by the parties to the case'[173] and thus not subject to interrogation.[174] For these reasons, Rodgers et al conclude that the value of research evidence in family cases is undermined such that it has had limited influence on practice.[175]

Where judges are predisposed to drawing on research evidence other factors can limit its utility: judges may elevate certain types of research over others (reflecting wider societal biases that rate 'scientific', quantitative data over social science or experiential/qualitative data); legal, resource and time constraints may inhibit detailed judicial reflection on empirical findings;[176] and even where there is compelling empirical evidence, its influence may be minimal if it clashes with strong political agendas. In the context of immigration and asylum, for instance, it is very difficult (but simultaneously imperative) for judges to bring even the most unequivocal, empirically-verified insights to bear on interpretations of otherwise very restrictive laws that, themselves, may be informed by a hostile political narrative.[177]

Thus, despite the strong imperative for research evidence to inform judicial decision-making there are structural, practical and attitudinal barriers that constrain how judges have, and potentially can, use such evidence to achieve a more consistent children's rights approach.

---

[168] See Lady Hale, ibid: 'I agree with Lord Neuberger that the life-blood of the common law is experience and common sense ... it is therefore dangerous for the common law to rely upon the experience and common sense of a comparatively narrow section of society. One counter to this is the study of law in its wider context.'

[169] See generally Rodgers et al, above n 165.

[170] ibid at 6.

[171] Lady Hale, above n 167.

[172] ibid.

[173] Rodgers et al, above n 165.

[174] Lady Hale, above n 167.

[175] Rodgers et al, above n 165.

[176] For example, child protection proceedings in England and Wales have to be completed within 26 weeks; and child abduction cases under both Hague and EU Brussels II have to be resolved within 6 weeks. Legal limits and the limits of legal aid constrain how much expert evidence can be submitted (at least in family cases as a result of the family justice review).

[177] See for instance the unequivocal, empirically-verified evidence and recommendations compiled by the Law Centre's Network in relation to children in the asylum system: *Put Yourself in Our Shoes: Considering Children's Best Interests in the Asylum System* (LC, November, 2016) and of the report of the EU sub-committee on Home Affairs, *Children in Crisis: Unaccompanied migrant children in the EU* (London, House of Lords, 2017).

B. Individual Factors

The political, institutional, constitutional, procedural and evidential constraints identified above can heavily circumscribe judicial adoption of a children's rights approach. But judges are only human and their judicial perspective is shaped not only by the external context but also by their personal characteristics, experiences, values, political and doctrinal perspective. One of the achievements of earlier rewriting judgment projects,[178] alongside empirical studies of judicial opinions,[179] has been to expose the supposed neutrality of the law, and to highlight the ways in which a judge's characteristics, life experiences, perspectives and values are brought to bear on her judicial role.[180] Thus, as Rackley convincingly argues, it matters who the judge is and, in the context of feminist judgment projects where the focus was on gender, it matters that there are women judges.[181] In cases involving children, it also matters who the judge is and what experiences he or she brings to the judicial function. However, the connection between a particular characteristic and a particular judicial perspective is harder to draw,[182] with two caveats. First, in some legal contexts, there is an *over*-representation of children with personal characteristics that are *under*-represented in the judiciary. For example, in the criminal courts, males from lower socio-economic groups and of black ethnicity are disproportionately over-represented among child defendants and yet distinctly underrepresented among the judiciary. A judge *might* be less likely to adopt a child rights perspective where his or her presumptions about childhood, and about 'normal' childhood behaviour (shaped by his own class, gender and ethnicity) differ from the life experiences of the child before him.[183] Second, a feminist judge may be more likely to adopt a children's rights perspective because the methodology of feminist judging (the use of narrative, placing legal issues in wider structural contexts, and reasoning from 'lived experiences rather than in abstract, categorical terms'[184]) reveals the 'unfair consequences of the "neutral" application of the law and makes visible the experiences and interest of less powerful groups' including children.[185] If there is at least *some* correlation between gender and the adoption of a feminist perspective[186] then we might also speculate that

---

[178]   See especially Hunter, McGlynn and Rackley, above n 33.

[179]   In the context of the UK House of Lords/Supreme Court, see for example C Hanretty, 'The Decisions and Ideal Points of British Law Lords' (2013) 43 *British Journal of Political Science* 703; RJ Cahill-O'Callaghan, 'The Influence of Personal Values on Legal Judgments' (2013) 40 *Journal of Law and Society* 596; RJ Cahill-O'Callaghan, 'Reframing the Judicial Diversity Debate: Personal Values and Tacit Diversity' (2015) 35 *Legal Studies* 1; and TT Arvind and L Stirton, 'Legal Ideology, Legal Doctrine and the UK's Top Judges' [2016] *Public Law* 418.

[180]   See especially Hunter, above n 33.

[181]   See E Rackley, 'Detailing Judicial Difference' (2009) *Feminist Legal Studies* 11 and *Women, Judging and the Judiciary* (Oxford, Routledge, 2013).

[182]   See Hunter, above n 156 and Rackley, ibid, for a thorough critique of the relationship between gender and judicial perspective (including the strength of underpinning theories to support the claim that it matters).

[183]   For example, see the decision of Laws J in *C (a minor) v DPP* [1994] 3 WLR 888.

[184]   Hunter, above n 156 at 13.

[185]   K Hollingsworth, 'Judging Children's Rights and the Benefit Cap: *R (SG and others)*' (2015) 27 *Child and Family Law Quarterly* 445. See further the discussion in ch 3.

[186]   Rackley notes that there is 'qualitative, if not quantitative, evidence in support of the assertion that women judges can make a difference' (Rackley, above n 181). One of the most commonly proffered reasons for this difference is that women may be more likely to reason from the perspective of an ethic of care which, though controversial, does appear to 'contain some grains of truth' suggests Hunter (Hunter, above n 156).

there is a correlation between a judge's gender and a propensity to adopt a children's rights perspective.[187]

One characteristic that undoubtedly *separates* judges from children, and which may therefore constrain their ability to adopt a child rights perspective (where that involves hearing and understanding their experiences) is age. That all judges have once been children might provide limited insight, but judges are temporally far removed from childhood and looking back through the lens of time can falsify perceptions (particularly where there have been considerable social, economic, political and technological developments). Indeed, if the fact of once being a child were significant and reliable then we would see *all* judges adopting a children's rights approach! Perhaps *having* children affects the adoption, or not, of a children's rights approach: might judges who have children of their own better recognise children's capacity for self-determination or might they incline towards paternalism? Might they better understand the life experience of the child or might they presume (perhaps unconsciously) that their own child's experience is universal? Without empirical evidence it is impossible to know, although we can proceed on a basic common sense presumption that simply being a parent is by no means coterminous with being in tune with children's rights, interests and desires.[188]

Two other individual factors may have a closer correlation to the adoption of a children's rights approach. First, professional experience: judges with limited experience in areas of law that *directly* concern children, for example commercial law, may be less inclined towards a children's rights approach than judges who have 'prior exposure to the values that underpin [a children's rights] model'.[189] This may in part explain the paucity of children's rights reasoning in senior appeal and international courts which are traditionally comprised of very few family law judges. As Rackley notes in the context of gender, evidence of the impact of judicial professional background on judging is likely to be qualitative not quantitative,[190] a starting point for which might be Lady Hale's contribution to a growing body of children's rights jurisprudence in the UK Supreme Court (given her professional background as a family law academic).[191]

However, even a background in family law does not guarantee the adoption of a children's rights approach,[192] particularly if the judge's experience is acquired within an institutional culture that is inclined towards paternalism rather than rights. It will also depend on the personal values of the judge, the final constraining/facilitating factor we highlight. Cahill-O'Callaghan's empirical analysis of UK Supreme Court decisions revealed that 'personal values serve as tacit influences on judicial decision-making',[193] especially in hard cases where the law 'runs out'.[194] As noted earlier, many cases involving children's rights—in the

---

[187] Though the number of male contributors to this collection, many of whom adopt an ostensibly feminist methodology to judgment writing, demonstrates that gender is an indicative (rather than definitive) factor.

[188] Carol Smart highlights the important distinction between 'caring for' and 'caring about' children. See further 'From Children's Shoes to Children's Voices' (2002) 40(3) *Family Court Review* 307.

[189] Tobin, above n 3 at 623.

[190] Rackley, above n 181.

[191] A judge's impact can be seen both in relation to his or her own decisions and the influence he or she has on his or her judicial colleagues. See Paterson, above n 135.

[192] See for example, Lord Hughes in *SG*, above n 76.

[193] See Cahill-O'Callaghan, above n 179.

[194] See Rackley, above n 181 at 131.

family courts, in human rights cases[195] and in appeals—confer a large discretionary space within which a judge exercises judgment in determining the 'right' outcome and where their personal values are influential on their reasoning and decision. In children's rights judgments, values such as 'universalism' (defined by Cahill-O'Callaghan as 'understanding, appreciation, tolerance and protection for the welfare of all people ... and includes values such as equality, protection of the vulnerable and social justice'[196]) or 'self-direction' (autonomy and freedom) are likely to feature; and judges who score highly against these values may be more likely to consistently adjudicate in a way compatible with children's rights.[197] But the significance of certain values will be context-specific: a children's rights outcome that requires pushing against constitutional orthodoxy or existing precedent is unlikely to be forthcoming from a judge who values 'tradition' and 'conformity'[198] even if he or she also values universalism.[199] The same is true of the potential impact of what Arvind and Stirton refer (in the context of the UK) to as a judge's 'doctrinal disposition'.[200] Their research suggests that the outcome of 'hard' cases that involve a public body are (statistically) significantly affected by judicial attitude to deference to the executive: some judges consistently fall at the 'red light'[201] end of the spectrum, and are more likely to find against the state body, whilst other judges are consistently more likely to adopt a 'green light' approach.[202] In public law cases brought *by* children (or their supporters) against a government body, it seems that a UK judge at the red light end of the spectrum may—in outcome if not in reasoning—be more likely to adopt a children's rights approach. It is interesting to note that of all the House of Lords and Supreme Court justices since 1985 to 2015, Lord Kerr and Lady Hale—the two justices who have consistently reasoned in a way compatible with children's rights—were the two least likely to defer to the executive.[203]

VI. Concluding Comments

The various tendencies, tensions and constraints identified in this chapter intersect in complex and sometimes unpredictable ways in cases involving children. Some factors are more impervious to change than others. However, one thing that can be influenced is judicial

---

[195] Where judges must define vague principles and attribute weight and balance competing factors on contentious issues.

[196] Cahill-O'Callaghan, above n 179 at 12.

[197] Lady Hale and Lord Kerr both score high on universalism.

[198] Which encompass 'adherence to legal traditions such as precedent and respect for Parliamentary authority', Cahill-O'Callaghan, above n 179.

[199] It is noteworthy that Lord Kerr, who controversially (in obiter dicta) stated in *SG* that Art 3 UNCRC is directly effective in the UK, scores *low* against these values. See Hollingsworth, above n 185.

[200] A similar individual disposition to either a deferential ('statesmen') or an 'activist' approach in the judges of the ECtHR has been observed by Bruinsma. See F Bruinsma, 'Judicial Identities in the European Court of Human Rights' in A van Hoek, O Jansen, T Hol, P Rijpkema and R Widdershoven (eds), *Multilevel Governance in Enforcement and Adjudication* (Antwerpen-Oxford, Intersentia, 2006) cited by Jacobsen, above n 110 at 553.

[201] On Harlow and Rawlings' 'red light, green light' theory of administrative law, see C Harlow and R Rawlings, *Law and Administration* (Cambridge, Cambridge University Press, 1977).

[202] See Arvind and Stirton, above n 179.

[203] In other jurisdictions, notably the USA, it is *political* disposition (liberal-conservative) rather than doctrinal disposition which has been identified as significant.

knowledge, skills and attitude. Much depends, suggests Tobin, on how much exposure a judge has previously had to the values that underpin a children's rights approach and the extent to which their 'moral reasoning is informed by an interest theory of rights consistent with the model under the CRC'.[204] He advocates—as do we—judicial training to ensure that the values and principles underpinning a children's rights approach form part of the 'interpretative theory' applied by a judge to the case.[205] As Tobin notes:

> The problem … is that glib calls for judges to actively promote children's rights too often fail to take account of a range of factors which might render such an approach difficult or even impossible. There is thus a strong onus on proponents of a more active judicial approach in this area to recognise the extent of these potential obstacles and to articulate a coherent vision of how these might be overcome in order to facilitate more effective and systematic judicial involvement. In order to be persuasive, any such vision would also need to reflect the empirical realities encountered by judges in their day-to-day approach to these issues.[206]

This collection, we hope, provides some useful building blocks to inform such training and to assist in removing such obstacles. The contributors have re-examined existing cases in order to explore how far, within the existing constraints, a judge can adopt a more robust children's rights approach and how the constraints identified might be turned into opportunities. The rewritten judgments add to the growing body of existing jurisprudence that collectively demonstrate some techniques (both obvious and more creative) that lend themselves to delivering 'children's rights' judgments. In the next chapter, we articulate and illustrate more fully the content and scope of those techniques.

---

[204] Tobin, above n 3 at 622.
[205] ibid.
[206] Tobin, above n 3 at 581.

3

Towards Children's Rights Judgments

KATHRYN HOLLINGSWORTH AND HELEN STALFORD[*]

I. Introduction

This chapter sets out what we see as the primary characteristics of a children's rights judgment. Drawing on the rewritten judgments in this collection, we suggest how some of the issues that constrain and frustrate judicial attempts to advance the rights of children—identified in chapter two—might be navigated in ways that are more consistent with children's rights. The features we identify are indicative not prescriptive: there is no one way of 'doing' a children's rights judgment and judicial room to manoeuvre will always (rightly) be constrained in some ways and reflective of its temporal, political, legal and jurisdictional location in others.[1]

Notwithstanding such variances, we suggest that the overarching aim of a children's rights judgment is to increase the visibility of children within the law by ensuring that their status as rights-holders is recognised, that their voices are heard and that their interests are identified and factored into judicial decision-making. This chapter identifies five ways in which these goals might be achieved, leading to judgments that better conform to a children's rights-based approach.[2] First, judges can explicitly adopt a child-rights approach by drawing on and utilising to maximum effect the formal legal tools which give effect to children's rights, including (but not confined to) the UN Convention on the Rights of the Child (CRC).[3]

[*] Many thanks to Stephen Gilmore and Rosemary Hunter for comments on an earlier version of this chapter. All errors remain our own.

[1] Reflecting Sommerlad's observation that: 'the law in practice is and always has been nuanced, complex and contingent, responsive to and expressive of popular narratives, and its extreme variability is accentuated and manifest in: its antiquity; the range of "repertoires of legal governance" it comprises; differences in specialism, locality and personnel; and its function as an arena of struggle'. H Sommerlad, 'The Ethics of Relational Jurisprudence' (2014) 17 *Legal Ethics* 281, 291.

[2] These overlap with, but are not identical to, Tobin's markers of a 'substantive children's rights approach' which he describes as one that: (a) conceptualises the issue on children's rights grounds rather than on a welfare/paternalistic basis; (b) adopts procedures that are 'child friendly' when resolving the issue—including securing participation; (c) articulates the content of rights such that it is grounded in the lived experiences of children; (d) balances competing interests in a way that is nuanced and fact-specific. J Tobin, 'Judging the Judges: Are they Adopting the Rights Approach in Matters Concerning Children' (2009) 33 *Melbourne University Law Review* 590, 603.

[3] It also involves maximising regional and domestic rights protection, including (in the context of England and Wales for example), the EU Charter of Fundamental Rights, the European Convention on Human Rights ((ECHR) and the Human Rights Act 1998 (HRA)), and the common law, as well as other relevant international treaties.

Second, a children's rights judgment can draw on scholarly insights to address theoretical tensions, conceptual challenges and prevailing presumptions which stymie the resolution of cases in ways which best protect children's rights.[4] Third, legal processes should maximise children's participation by endorsing and conforming with, where possible, child-friendly procedures.[5] Fourth, the narrative employed in the judgment—as an aspect of the 'art and craft'[6] of judgment writing—should seek to centralise the child's perspective and voice. Fifth, and finally, children should be acknowledged as one of the audiences for legal judgments through the use of child-appropriate language, structure and style, either in the primary judgment itself or in an additional 'child-friendly' version.

II. Utilising Formal Legal Tools: The CRC in Children's Rights Judgments

In the previous chapter we defended our explicit use of 'children's rights' to frame this project to illustrate the obligations incumbent on states and private actors to respond to and facilitate fulfilment of children's legal entitlements. Such entitlement is extensive and multi-layered and is catalogued most comprehensively and visibly in the CRC. As noted in chapter two, explicit reference within judgments to the CRC is a key indicator of judicial attempts to recognise children as rights-holders and to engage with the interpretation of those rights. But judicial employment of the CRC must act as more than a signifier; it needs to be used substantively[7] if it is to deliver the type of effective remedial action for breaches of children's rights that is absent—notwithstanding the recent introduction of an individual complaints procedure[8]—within its own internal structures.[9] Utilising the children's Convention is certainly not the only way for judges to confer formal rights recognition on children,[10] but unsurprisingly it is the CRC and its potential as a vehicle

---

[4] On theoretical and conceptual difficulties see, inter alia, L Ferguson, 'Not Merely Rights for Children but Children's Rights: The Theory Gap and the Assumption of the Importance of Children's Rights' (2013) 21 *International Journal of Children's Rights* 177; on presumptions see, inter alia, C Piper, 'Assumptions about Children's Best Interests' (2001) 22 *Journal of Social Welfare and Family Law* 261.

[5] See especially Council of Europe, *Guidelines on Child-Friendly Justice* (Council of Europe, 2010).

[6] E Rackley, 'The Art and Craft of Writing Judgments: Notes on the Feminist Judgment Project' in R Hunter, C McGlynn and E Rackley (eds), *Feminist Judgments: From Theory to Practice* (Oxford, Hart Publishing, 2010).

[7] To adopt Tobin's terminology (above, n 2, at 603).

[8] See *Optional Protocol to the Convention on the Rights of the Child on a Communications Procedure* (A/RES/66/138 of 19 December 2011, entered into force on 14 April 2014). To date it has been ratified by only 27 of the 196 state parties. For a critique see T Buck and M Wabwile, 'The Potential and Promise of Communications Procedures under the Third Protocol to the Convention on the Rights of the Child' (2013) 2 *International Human Rights Law Review* 205.

[9] The primary enforcement mechanism within the CRC is periodic reporting of state parties to the Committee on the Rights of the Child, but this does not provide the possibility of individual remedies. See Art 44 CRC and, inter alia, JE Doek, 'The CRC: Dynamics and Directions of Monitoring its Implementation' in A Invernizzi and J Williams (eds), *The Human Rights of Children: From Visions to Implementation* (Farnham, Ashgate, 2011).

[10] In the context of England and Wales for example, the ECHR (via the vehicle of the Human Rights Act 1998) is especially important: see J Fortin, 'Accommodating Children's Rights in a Post Human Rights Act Era' (2006) 69 *Modern Law Review* 299. On rights as recognition see, inter alia C Douzinas, 'Identity, Recognition, Rights or What Can Hegel Teach us about Human Rights? (2002) 29 *Journal of Law and Society* 379; and J Anderson and A Honneth, 'Autonomy, Vulnerability, Recognition and Justice' in J Christman and J Anderson (eds), *Autonomy and the Challenges to Liberalism: New Essays* (New York, Cambridge University Press, 2005).

for promoting and protecting children's rights that provides a focal point for a number of our rewritten judgments. We examine this here in the context of both the supranational and domestic courts.

A. The Cross-pollination Potential of Children's Rights Sources to Inform Judicial Decision-making in the Supranational Courts

Judges in the supranational courts face a particular challenge: they are adjudicating in jurisdictions that cannot be signatories to the CRC. Therefore, in order to make use of the CRC they must rely on the Vienna Convention on the Interpretation of Treaties,[11] their own establishing Treaty/ies (as with the International Criminal Court (ICC)),[12] or, in the case of the European Union (EU), applicable general principles.[13] The specificity of the CRC and its near universal ratification increase its potential influence on supranational courts,[14] and emphasising these points can help to provide legitimacy for a judge conscious of the delicate political context within which its court operates. Trevor Buck employs this tactic in his rewritten ICC decision in *Lubanga* to justify his extensive use of the CRC and its underpinning ethos, and to emphasise the agency of child soldiers and their participation within the ICC's procedures.[15] But, even the employment of this strong rights rhetoric did not allow Buck to escape the confines of the ICC's governing statutes; he was thus unable, despite his inclination, to increase the upper age of childhood to 18 in order to align with the CRC.[16]

The EU's Court of Justice (CJEU) is similarly precluded from interpreting international human rights provisions (including those incorporated into the EU's own Charter of Fundamental Rights) beyond the legitimate confines of EU competence;[17] nor can the European Court of Human Rights (ECtHR) 'stretch an existing European Convention right to meet the global standard if it means creating a new right'.[18] Both Courts must, therefore,

---

[11] Art 31(3)(c) Vienna Convention on the Law of Treaties establishes that in interpreting treaties, in addition to the context, courts should take account of 'any relevant rules of international law applicable in relations between parties'. See further S McInerney-Lankford, 'Fragmentation of International Law Redux: The Case of Strasbourg' (2012) 32 *Oxford Journal of Legal Studies* 609.

[12] Art 21(1)(b) of the Rome Treaty: 'The court shall apply ... where appropriate, applicable treaties and the principles and rules of international law ...'

[13] It is a long-standing general principle, acknowledged by the EU Court of Justice (see notably Case 26/69 *Stauder v City of Ulm* (1969) ECR 419) and formally enshrined in the EU Constitution (Treaty on European Union (Art 6(3)) that EU law should operate in conformity with fundamental rights, as enshrined in the international treaties and in the constitutional traditions of the EU Member States.

[14] See M Forowicz, *The Reception of International Law in the European Court of Human Rights* (London, Oxford University Press, 2010).

[15] See ch 24 at para 7.

[16] ibid, para 35 (where he also draws on the African Charter on the Rights and Welfare of the Child of 1999). This is one of the challenges arising from the 'fragmentation' of international law where different systems may 'overlap, place different emphasis on different aspects and, at worst, contradict each other'. See S Hespel, J Put and M Rom, 'Navigating the Maze. The Interrelation of International Legal Norms, with Illustrations from International Juvenile Justice Standards' (2012) 6 *Human Rights and International Legal Discourse* 329, 337.

[17] Charter of Fundamental Rights of the European Union, OJ C 326/391, 26.10.2012, Art 51.

[18] G Van Bueren, *Child Rights in Europe* (Strasbourg, Council of Europe Publishing, 2007) 19.

tread a fine (often challenging) line[19] between respecting Member States' jurisdiction to implement and interpret rights in a way that fits their own social, economic and political context whilst retaining their role in reinforcing and reminding Member States of their shared children's rights obligations. If the latter aim is to be achieved with any effect, it demands more positive engagement with children's rights perspectives and more liberal, thoughtful cross-fertilisation of international norms and guidance that are designed to achieve precisely this level of synergy. Lara Walker's alternative judgment in *Povse v Austria* eloquently reminds us, for instance, of the role of the ECtHR in ensuring Member States' implementation of their obligations to take account of the views of the child in cross-border child abduction proceedings.[20] In doing so, we are encouraged to recognise that such obligations exist by virtue not only of Article 12 CRC, but also Article 11(1)–(6) of the EU Brussels II Regulation. Similarly, the rewritten judgments of *Zambrano* and *CD v ST* highlight the potential of EU law and jurisprudence to act as an important channel of children's rights protection, especially since the introduction of the EU's own Charter of Fundamental Rights in 2000 (elements of which are inspired by the CRC[21] and which now carries the same legal force as the EU's treaties). The CRC and Charter have certainly inspired various rulings by the CJEU on the precise scope and application of EU law in favour of children.[22] The rewritten judgments try to go even further, however, by exploring how children's rights to family life and to be cared for by their parents, as enshrined in Articles 7 and 24 of the EU Charter of Fundamental Rights, Article 8 European Convention on Human Rights (ECHR) and Article 7 CRC, can be brought to bear much more explicitly on the CJEU's reasoning within the respectful and realistic confines of EU competence.

A similar approach is endorsed by Maria Papaioannou in her alternative vision of the ECtHR decision in *Antwi v Norway*. There she alludes to Article 3 CRC to aid her detailed consideration of the effects that a parent's deportation would have on the child's best interests in the context of her right to respect for private and family life (Article 8 ECHR). In a creative adjunct to this, her judgment also engages with the non-legally binding United Nations High Commissioner for Refugees (UNHCR) Guidelines on Determining the Best Interests of the Child 2008 to ascertain the relevant factors that may inform a best interests assessment in the context of immigration proceedings.[23] The alternative versions of *Gas and Dubois* and *Valsamis* support this approach too, sensitively incorporating the CRC into

---

[19] See the case of *Neulinger and Shuruk v Switzerland* (Application no 41615/07, 6 July 2010) where the ECtHR was criticised for overstepping its function by articulating how the best interests standard should be interpreted by Switzerland in the context of child abduction proceedings. See L Walker, 'The Impact of the Hague Abduction Convention on the Rights of the Family in the Case-law of the European Court of Human Rights and the UN Human Rights Committee: the Danger of Neulinger' (2010) 6 *Journal of Private International Law* 649.

[20] Ch 28, paras 16–17.

[21] Arts 24 and 32. See, inter alia, R Lamont, 'Article 24 of the Charter of Fundamental Rights of the European Union' in S Peers, T Hervey, J Kenner and A Ward (eds), *The EU Charter of Fundamental Rights: A Commentary* (Oxford, Hart Publishing, 2014).

[22] See for example *Carpenter v Secretary of State for the Home Department* (Case C-60/00) [2002] ECR 1-06279; *Baumbast and R v Secretary of State for the Home Department* (Case C-413/99 [2002] ECR I-7091; *Metock—Blaise Baheten Metock and Others v Minister for Justice, Equality and Law Reform* (Case C-127/08) [2008] ECR I-6241; *Dynamic Medien Vertriebs GmbH v Avides Media AG* (Case C-244/06) [2008] ECR I-505; *Zhu and Chen v Secretary of State for the Home Department* (Case C-200/02) [2004] ECR I-9923. For a full analysis of these judgments, see H Stalford and E Drywood, 'Using the CRC to Inform EU Law and Policy-Making' in Invernizzi and Williams (eds), above n 9.

[23] Ch 30, para 94.

interpretations of the ECHR. In doing so, our fictive judges are eager to avoid tokenistic cross-referencing in favour of more creative and explicit linkages between these various international sources and a clearer explanation of how they have informed their deliberations. Lundy, for instance, cross-refers to a range of provisions of the CRC (including Articles 5, 12 and 29(1) in addition to the more typical references to Article 3(1)) as well as to the UN Committee on the Rights of the Child's *General Comment No 1 on the Aims of Education*. In doing so, she achieves a much more nuanced, child-focused interpretation of Article 2 Protocol 1 ECHR to challenge the proportionality of Valsamis' temporary exclusion from school.

B. Bringing International Children's Rights Obligations to bear on Domestic Proceedings: Pushing the Boundaries

The domestic legal force of international children's rights, including the CRC, depends on the constitutional framework of individual nation states. We noted in chapter two that even in those jurisdictions that accommodate direct enforcement of such obligations, the judiciary has largely failed to be as proactive and creative in giving expression to those rights as advocates of children's rights would hope. The challenge of judicial engagement is even greater in jurisdictions where the CRC has weaker legal standing.

Nonetheless, even where the CRC is not domestically enforceable, judges can innovate within the law to make greater use of its provisions. For example, in England and Wales (the jurisdiction featured most in this collection), the CRC can inform judicial interpretations of ambiguous legislation,[24] common law principles (including principles of judicial review), domestically enforceable ECHR and EU rights, and private law remedies (to secure horizontal protection of rights). Many of our fictive judges have followed the example set by some of the Justices of the UK Supreme Court and the South African Constitutional Court in their unapologetic use of the CRC, particularly the best interests standard enshrined in Article 3;[25] some have sought to innovate even further. For example, Aoife Daly (rewriting *Castle v Commissioner of the Police for the Metropolis*) uses a progressive two-step approach to secure children's rights during public protests. First, she uses Article 3 CRC (best interests as a primary consideration) to interpret 'welfare' in section 11 of the 2004 Children Act, a provision described as 'giving effect to the spirit if not the wording' of Article 3 but which has not (yet) been specifically interpreted in line with it.[26] Daly 'steps into this space'[27] and in interpreting welfare using Article 3 she follows the UN Committee

[24] The 'presumption of conformity' (that courts presume that parliament intended to legislate in conformity with its international obligations) applies generally to ratified, unincorporated international treaties, including the CRC.
[25] See notably *SG v Secretary of State for Work and Pensions* [2015] UKSC 16 (per Lady Hale and Lord Kerr dissenting) (for analysis see K Hollingsworth, 'Judging Children's Rights and the Benefit Cap: *R (SG and others) v Secretary of State for Work and Pensions*' (2015) 27 *Child and Family Law Quarterly* 445); *Mathieson v Secretary of State for Work and Pensions* [2015] UKSC 47 (per Lord Wilson); *Nzolameso v City of Westminster* [2015] UKSC 22 (per Lady Hale); *ZH Tanzania v Secretary of State for the Home Department* [2011] UKSC 4 (per Lady Hale); and *Makhlouf v Secretary of State for the Home Department* [2016] UKSC 59 (per Lord Kerr and Lady Hale). See also the South African Constitutional Court ruling in *M v State* [2007] ZACC 18 (per Sachs J).
[26] Lady Hale seems keen for the point to be argued in an appropriate case. See *Nzolameso*, ibid, para 29.
[27] F Donson, Commentary on *Castle*, ch 15 of this collection.

on the Rights of the Child in arguing that giving primacy to the child's best interests must mean respecting other CRC rights, including those that protect civil liberty interests such as freedom of assembly. Second, she draws on the ECHR to interpret the CRC (rather than, as is more common, using the CRC to interpret ECHR rights), arguing that states have a positive obligation to develop children's rights as political citizens. Daly's interpretative innovation is important not only for the substantive outcome in the case, but also because her use of the CRC to interpret key statutory provisions embeds the Convention within the law of England and Wales *beyond* its use as an interpretative tool for children's ECHR rights (enforceable domestically as per the Human Rights Act 1998 (HRA)). This is all the more important should the HRA ever be repealed by a rights-sceptic parliament.[28] Kirsty Hughes' rewritten decision in *AAA* also gives prominence to Article 3 CRC in an action for damages and injunctive relief in the tort of misuse of private information. In the process, she extends the CRC's horizontal reach into private law proceedings in order to protect the child's privacy.

Judicial creativity can flourish even where the CRC is not available, as demonstrated by the rewritten judgments from earlier periods and from non-ratifying jurisdictions (or rather, jurisdiction singular!). The USA is notoriously unique as the only state not to have ratified the CRC such that the instrument cannot form the basis of either domestic or internationally enforceable obligations. However, in Barbara Bennett Woodhouse's re-imagined US Supreme Court decision in *Roper v Simmons* she notes, in relation to the juvenile death penalty, that '[i]nternational norms confirm our own Nation's commitment to minority as a legal and cultural institution conferring special protections on our Nation's youth'.[29] Although this was as far as she felt able to go in *explicitly* referring to international rights standards,[30] this underlying principle was at the heart of her innovative—if not radical—reading into the US Bill of Rights of a new, child-specific right that she calls the 'right to grow up'.[31] Similarly, in *John Hudson*, Sue Farran and Rhona Smith are able to envisage a child-friendly criminal justice system 200 years BC (Before Convention!) by maximising the procedural protections and alternative sentences available at the time, as well as imagining a defence lawyer and judge informed by enlightenment-based philosophical writings of the day.

And so, whilst many of the judgments that feature in this collection demonstrate the value of the CRC as an interpretative guide and as a principal means of recognising children's status as rights-holders, we also acknowledge that a 'substantive children's rights approach' can be achieved regardless of the CRC's legal status. Put simply, the CRC is not the be all and end all of a children's rights judgment. We acknowledge the value of a range

---

[28] As proposed by the Conservative party in their election manifestoes in 2010 and 2015. Plans to introduce a 'British Bill of Rights' have, however, been temporarily shelved in light of Brexit (see HC Debs, 24 Jan 2017, vol 620, col 153).

[29] The original decision also makes reference, inter alia, to the CRC and states that 'The opinion of the world community, while not controlling our outcome, does provide respected and significant confirmation for our own conclusions'. *Roper v Simmons* 543 US 551 (2005), 24.

[30] As Emily Buss's commentary in this collection states, Woodhouse's 'avoidance [of the CRC], even in a rewritten judgment that aims to depart, in ambitious ways, from the original, suggests the depth of the United States' resistance to international legal influence'. See ch 22.

[31] Thus adopting a substantive approach which, as Tobin notes, can be achieved where the judgment is underpinned by the principles and values of the CRC, regardless of explicit reference. He suggests the original decision in *Roper v Simmons* is also reflective of this approach. See Tobin, above n 2.

of other sources that feed our understanding of what constitutes a children's rights-based approach to decision-making, many of which are not reflected in the judgments featured in this collection. In a European context, for instance, more explicit reference could be made to the many Council of Europe Conventions to inform decisions relating to violence against children;[32] contact with parents;[33] or the scope and meaning of children's socio-economic rights to education, housing, welfare and employment.[34] For judges in EU Member States, the EU has established more than 80 instruments containing explicit provision for children which impose binding obligations on the Member States' authorities to ensure that their basic rights are upheld when applying EU law. In the absence of faithful and timely reflection of these international and European provisions within domestic law, it falls on the judiciary to interpret them in a way that achieves their spirit and objectives.

III. Utilising Academic Scholarship: Unpacking Theoretical Tensions, Conceptual Challenges and Prevailing Presumptions

In some jurisdictions, including England and Wales, judges may refer to academic scholarship to support their reasoning (particularly in the senior courts). Where they do, it tends—unsurprisingly—to be work of a doctrinal nature.[35] However, other types of children's rights scholarship—particularly that which is theoretically or empirically informed—does not appear to have permeated the work, or indeed the consciousness, of judges in the same way. This may, partly, be attributable to the judiciary's (and legal counsel's) lack of exposure to advancements in conceptual thinking as well as a concomitant failure of scholars to disseminate their findings beyond the confines of the academy. In this section we therefore explore how scholarly insights can more broadly inform the backdrop to judicial reasoning, and how it might be used to untangle some of the knotty theoretical, conceptual and empirical challenges that arise in cases concerning children.

Academic insights can be especially useful in children's rights cases for at least three reasons. First, scholarship can help to address the 'theory gap' that has hindered the legal realisation of children's rights.[36] As explained in chapter two, children pose a philosophical challenge to the traditional liberal conceptualisation of rights (one that is premised on protecting the freedoms of the independent, atomistic, rational agent rather than the interests of the (inter)dependent, inter-related, (sometimes) non-rational, child), and this can negatively affect the way in which some judges understand the nature, content and scope of children's rights. Fortin has argued that a 'clear understanding of rights theory can inform the courts' approach when articulating their decisions in terms of children's ... rights'[37] and

---

[32] Council of Europe Convention on the Protection of Children against Sexual Exploitation and Sexual Abuse (commonly referred to as the Lanzarote Convention).

[33] Council of Europe Convention on Contact concerning Children, ETS No 192.

[34] European Social Charter 1961 and Revised European Social Charter 1996.

[35] Some of our judges use scholarship in a similar way: see for example, Arthur's use of Dicey's work in the rewritten *JTB* in ch 23.

[36] See Ferguson, above n 4.

[37] Fortin was writing in the context of the child's ECHR rights. See Fortin, above n 10. On how judges 'fudge' theoretical difficulties, see Ferguson, above n 4.

so, in this section, we consider some of the ways this might happen. Second, and relatedly, academic work can be used to unpack key concepts that sometimes trouble judges, in particular best interests and autonomy. Finally, research (including that which is empirical) can challenge or support the presumptions about children and childhood upon which some judicial decision-making is premised.

However, as well as providing opportunities, there are also hurdles to the judicial use of scholarship. In a *technical* sense, as Rosemary Hunter observes, academic scholarship cannot form part of the *ratio* of a judgment.[38] Thus, where a judge draws on children's rights theory, for example, this must be implicit within the narrative and the reasoning; it cannot amount to explicit judicial theorising. As noted in chapter two, there are similar restrictions in relation to the use of empirical social science data: judges are not free to rely on evidence that has not been tested during the proceedings.[39] In an *affective* sense, the application of an abstract theory to a real life case or empirical evidence that challenges in uncomfortable ways our presumptions and constructions of childhood can be incredibly confronting in cases involving children. One might think it theoretically sound, for example, to respect the autonomous choices of a competent adolescent, but if that teenager's choice to refuse medical treatment results in the death of the *actual* child in front of you, that theoretical perspective might prove harder to swallow. As former High Court judge, Sir Mark Hedley, commented at one of our workshops, 'ultimately, the judge has to make a decision that is going to enable him or her to sleep at night'. Thus, scholarly insights may appear to bear little relevance to the sobering complexity of the issues with which judges are commonly confronted. But this is also illustrative of the two-way nature of judgment rewriting projects: if the consequences of applying a theory or empirical 'truth' are unpalatable or unworkable in 'real life' then this provides valuable feedback to the academic on the practical utility of their research.[40]

Whilst being mindful of these constraints, we examine three examples of key issues where academic scholarship offers added insights for our fictive judges: the justification of the special treatment of children as rights-holders within the law; how children's interests are understood, including unpacking 'best interest' and the reconciliation of clashing interests; and the meaning and scope of children's autonomy.

A. Using Scholarship to Justify Special Treatment of Children as Rights-holders

A particularly fertile area of children's rights scholarship has been that which provides justification for the special treatment of children within legal and rights frameworks, including where differential treatment from adults is required. As some of the original versions of cases examined in this collection exemplify (for example *Grootboom, Collins, SENDIST, JTB, Castle, Farooq Ahmed* and *AAA*), judges can be reluctant to recognise, or to coherently respond to, children's differential or special treatment. Such treatment can take different

---

[38] R Hunter, 'An Account of Feminist Judging' in Hunter, McGlynn and Rackley, above n 6 at 42–43.
[39] Ch 2, at 47.
[40] E Rackley, 'Why Feminist Legal Scholars Should Write Judgments: Reflections on the Feminist Judgments Project in England and Wales' (2012) 24(2) *Canadian Journal of Women and Law* 389.

forms. It could, for example, absolve children from legal responsibilities; it might prioritise their interests over others (including in the distribution of scarce resources); it may confer on them additional rights; or it might limit their equal enjoyment of (usually) autonomy rights. Academic scholarship can fill the 'theory gap'[41] by providing intellectual credence to the idea of *children's* rights: a term that presupposes children are sufficiently similar to adults to be rights-holders, but sufficiently dissimilar such that their rights have different— special—legal effect.[42] A judge who is informed of coherent and convincing reasons for children's differential treatment might then be more likely to better protect their rights.

The first 'go-to' justification for treating children differently as rights-holders is that many children are physically, emotionally and cognitively less developed than most adults. In some areas of law, empirical research that evidences such differences can be essential to underpin children's rights. This is seen, for example, in the current turn towards neuroscience to support assertions that children lack the necessary capacities to be held fully criminally responsible.[43] Had such evidence been more widely available in the UK in 2009, perhaps Ray Arthur's fictive judge would have drawn on it in *JTB*, just as Woodhouse does in *Roper*.[44]

Where judges accept such 'empirical' differences, this is usually accompanied by presumptions (sometimes true, sometimes not) that children are more vulnerable and less competent than adults. This can impact both *substantively* on judicial articulation of children's rights (*equal* enjoyment of rights may require different treatment in terms of the content of the rights and the corresponding obligations)[45] and *procedurally* (it can justify conferring on adults decision-making powers in relation to the exercise of the child's rights). In both cases, theoretical or empirical scholarship can be informative. For example, a judge might draw on John Eekelaar's work[46] and be directed towards reconciling the child's basic and developmental interests with the child's autonomy interests through the idea of the child's achievement of 'full capacity' for decision-making (see for example, Gilmore's rewritten judgment in *Re W*); or we might see judges embracing Freeman's liberal paternalism approach,[47] only prohibiting choices by the child where that might prevent him or her from reaching a rationally autonomous adulthood (see Cave's differential treatment of the older and younger sister in the rewritten judgment of *F v F*—refusal of inoculation). Alternatively, a judge who locates children's difference in the physical/emotional/developmental realm might gain insight from the capabilities approach, both to justify differential treatment and to inform the content and scope of children's rights.[48] Nussbaum

---

[41] Ferguson again, above n 4.

[42] Theoretical explorations of children's rights can also provide guidance on *how* those distinct duties should be fulfilled. This is considered in the sections that follow.

[43] See *Roper v Simmons*, above n 29. Similar arguments are likely to be made in courts in England and Wales in the very near future.

[44] In line with the original Supreme Court decision. However, for a critique see E Buss, 'What the Law Should (and Should Not) Learn from Child Development' (2009) 38 *Hofstra Law Review* 13.

[45] For example, there might be a lower threshold before 'treatment' becomes degrading and inhuman; or increased support may be required to ensure a child can participate effectively in her trial.

[46] J Eekelaar, 'The Emergence of Children's Rights' (1986) 6 *Oxford Journal of Legal Studies* 161.

[47] MDA Freeman, *The Rights and Wrongs of Children* (London, Frances Pinter, 1983).

[48] See R Dixon and M Nussbaum, 'Children's Rights and a Capabilities Approach: The Question of Special Priority' (2012) 97 *Cornell Law Review* 549; however, they go beyond children's physical, emotional and developmental vulnerabilities/differences to also justify differential treatment on the basis of children's 'unique vulnerability'. See the discussion below.

has argued, for example, that rights should be directed towards developing to a minimum threshold 10 central capabilities for every individual.[49] As she further notes in her work with Rosalind Dixon, these central capabilities are especially fragile during childhood:[50] if support is not provided during this period then a child may grow up unable to reach the minimum threshold of a core capability. This approach can provide justification for limiting the adult carer's 'freedom' to act in a way that is harmful to the acquisition of such capabilities. This is evidenced in 'clear' cases such as that considered by the fictive Lord Gilmore in *Re T* (giving his opinion alongside the more adventurous Lord Freeman!), where the child's capability to live a life of normal length provided the justification to restrict the mother's choice regarding her child's medical treatment; and in less obvious cases such as *AAA* where it is implicit in Kirsty Hughes' refusal to allow a mother's actions to constitute a waiver of her child's privacy, thus supporting the child's future ability to form affiliations and shape her self-identity.[51] Depriving children of a stable home environment, including basic shelter (as in *Grootboom*), is also likely to inhibit the long-term development of their emotional, affiliative and 'practical reason' capabilities (including those derived from education: see *Collins*). Similarly, some capabilities are especially fertile during childhood and investment then can be cost-effective in the longer-term, thus providing the implicit justification for prioritising children in the distribution of scarce resources (for example, investing in children's education as advocated in the rewritten judgment of *SENDIST*).

Theoretical scholarship is particularly valuable to underpin special treatment of children in cases where the two commonly presumed reasons for differential treatment—increased vulnerability and/or diminished capacities—'run out'; that is, where there is purportedly no discernible 'empirical' difference between adults and children.[52] This is particularly, but not exclusively,[53] at the threshold of childhood and adulthood: even neuro-scientific evidence is unable adequately to provide a bright line between adults and children. As Woodhouse

---

[49] Thus applying to children's rights the capability approach developed by Sen and Nussbaum (on which see inter alia, A Sen, *Development as Freedom* (Oxford, Oxford University Press, 1999); M Nussbaum, *Women and Human Development: The Capabilities Approach* (Cambridge, Cambridge University Press, 2000); and *Creating Capabilities: The Human Development Approach* (Cambridge MA, Belknap Harvard, 2011). The 10 central capabilities are (1) life; (2) bodily health (including health, food, shelter); (3) bodily integrity; (4) sense, imagination and thought ('to imagine, to think, to reason … cultivated by an adequate education … being able to use one's mind in ways protected by guarantees of freedom of expression … being able to search for the ultimate meaning of life in one's own way'); (5) emotions ('being able to have attachments to things … not having one's emotional development blighted by overwhelming fear and anxiety, or by traumatic events of abuse and neglect'); (6) practical reason ('being able to form a conception of the good and to engage in critical reflection about the planning of one's life'); (7) affiliation (A—to have compassion and empathy and capacity for justice and friendship and B—having the social bases of self-respect and non-humiliation; being able to be treated as dignified and equal); (8) other species; (9) play; (10) control over one's environment (A—political, including political participation and free speech and B—material, being able to hold and enjoy property; right to seek employment equal with others). See M Nussbaum, 'Capabilities and Human Rights' (1997) 66 *Fordham Law Review* 273.

[50] Dixon and Nussbaum, above n 48.

[51] Choosing when and how to disclose personal information to others is an essential element in forging intimate relationships (or affiliations); this is not possible if personal details have already been revealed in the public sphere.

[52] As Archard notes, physicality-derived justifications for age-based boundaries are arbitrary and unreliable: D Archard, *Children: Rights and Childhood* (London, Routledge, 2004) 85ff.

[53] Newer theorisations of children's rights, such as Dixon and Nussbaum's application of the capabilities approach, or those drawing on relational or caring approaches, emphasise the similarities rather than the differences between adults and children; thus necessitating an alternative way to differentiate between the two groups.

notes in the rewritten *Roper* opinion (inspired by Buss's scholarship): '[w]hile developmental science confirms our societal judgment that children are different, it does not and cannot tell us when children pass from childhood to adulthood as a matter of law'.[54] Two alternative justifications for *children's* rights emerge from the literature. First, that children are *uniquely* vulnerable: their unequal position in the social, political, economic and legal world is such that they are dependent on others to meet their needs and to represent their interests (including politically).[55] This explanation provides one justification for conferring primacy on children's best interests: doing so helps to 'equal' the playing fields in an adult-dominated world.[56] It also explains why children's participation in decision-making should be afforded such prominence (again, to compensate for lack of power elsewhere), a position adopted in many of the judgments in this collection. Furthermore, it supports the assumed responsibility of the state for a child's needs when those ordinarily responsible for meeting them (parents or carers) are unable or unwilling to do so. The 'unique vulnerability' justification implicitly underpins Pillay's rewritten judgment of *Grootboom*, where her fictional dissent recognises (contrary to the original South African Constitutional Court's judgment) children's specific constitutional right to shelter as a right distinct from the right to adequate housing, owed to everyone. As Nolan notes in her commentary, Pillay's reasoning is premised on children's 'special vulnerability as a social group'.[57]

The second justification, generically referred to here as the developmental approach, is closely related to the first two outlined above but it applies even if—as Emily Buss noted at the Cardiff workshop—children's actual *or* unique vulnerability is reduced or removed (that is, if (older) children were to be conferred with full legal, political and economic independence). This approach regards childhood as a time of development qua rights-holders and is underpinned by a concern, as argued by Buss, with children's *potential*. This informs Woodhouse's rewritten judgment of *Roper* which creates a right underpinned by children's 'unique capacity to change'. Childhood is a time when that potential is being developed and, on this view, the courts have an obligation to *recognise* (as in *Roper*) *and enhance* that development. This can support a number of approaches: the provision of socio-economic rights (especially education in order to develop the skills for autonomous decision-making, necessary for exercising one's rights); protecting children from the harms of too much responsibility (for example, in the criminal justice system, see *JTB*); supporting the child to develop her status as political rights-holder (as in the *Castle* or *Valsamis* judgments); or allowing children to make decisions for themselves in order to *develop* their capacity for autonomy (see, for example, the rewritten judgments in *F v F* and *Re W*).

Drawing implicitly on scholarship can thus provide the necessary justification for judges to treat children as a 'special' class of rights holder. This can create a stronger impetus to find ways to protect fully the rights of children as articulated in the CRC (or other international rights-standards), particularly where those rights are vulnerable to diminution in the face of competing interests or limited resources. The next question is *how* to do so. We have touched on this in this section, and in the next two sections we focus on two core

---

[54] At 5, drawing on Buss, above n 44.
[55] See Dixon and Nussbaum, above n 48; and A Nolan, *Children's Socio-Economic Rights, Democracy and the Courts* (Oxford, Hart Publishing, 2011).
[56] See below.
[57] Aoife Nolan's commentary on Pillay's rewritten decision, ch 17.

concepts within children's rights that are intimately linked to differential treatment: their best interests (used as a proxy for the child's autonomous decision-making and as the tool to prioritise their interests over those of others); and autonomy (often the location of the supposed difference from adults).

B. Using Scholarship to Understand Children's (Best) Interests

The virtues of the best interests principle have been persuasively argued: it serves to prioritise children's interests in an adult-dominated world; it offers a mechanism for addressing potential clashes between the interests of adults and those of the child; and it serves a utilitarian function insofar as protecting the interests of children impacts positively on society to which these same children will contribute as adults.[58] In short, where it is applicable it provides an essential legal tool—one that judges are generally at ease with using given its adaptability to endless contexts—to secure the differential treatment that the scholarship outlined above aims to justify theoretically.

However, as discussed in chapter two, the voluminous academic commentary exposes significant variance and opacity in its interpretation, even in relation to factually and legally comparable cases.[59] So, whilst best interests offers a neat shorthand for promoting the best outcome for children, its ubiquity in legal and judicial parlance obscures four problematic aspects of the principle that lead to it being profoundly contested in practice. First, how can best interests be reconciled with children's 'welfare'?; second, how can we understand the *content* of best interests given that what is 'best' for children is complex, speculative and often highly subjective?;[60] third, what is the proper weight to be attributed to the child's best interests given the wide variation in the types of cases in which it is used?; and finally, how can we reconcile best interests with children's autonomy? These first three issues are the focus of the discussion here, whilst the latter is addressed in the next section which engages in a broader exploration of children's autonomy.

We start from the premise—as do most of the contributors to this book—that best interests, despite its misleading taxonomy, is a *right* and is thus distinct from a paternalistic welfare approach. Its long and stable history within the lexicon of international human rights is testimony to its status as such. Article 3(1) CRC is the most commonly cited source of the best interests principle as a right, although it finds expression in earlier human rights texts,[61] and has been enshrined in all children's rights treaties enumerated

[58] H Stalford, 'The Broader Relevance of Features of Children's Rights Law: the "Best Interests of the Child" Principle' in E Brems, E Desmet and W Vandenhole (eds), *Children's Rights Law in the Global Human Rights Landscape* (Oxford, Routledge, 2017) 37.

[59] For a comprehensive overview, see M Freeman, 'Article 3: the Best Interests of the Child' in A Alen, J Vande Lanotte, E Verhellen, F Ang, E Berghmans, M Verheyde and B Abramson (eds), *Commentary on the United Nations Convention on the Rights of the Child* (Leiden, Brill Nijhoff, 2007) and J Eekelaar, 'The Role of the Best Interest Principle in Decisions Affecting Children and Decisions about Children' (2015) 23 *International Journal of Children's Rights* 3.

[60] As Robert Mnookin declared more than 40 years ago, determining what is in a child's best interests 'poses a question no less ultimate than the purposes and values of life itself'. R Mnookin, 'Child Custody Adjudication: Judicial Functions in the Face of Indeterminacy' (1975) 39 *Law and Contemporary Problems* 226, 260.

[61] See for example Principles 2 and 7 of the 1959 Declaration on the Rights of the Child and Art 5(b) and 16(d) of the 1979 Convention on the Elimination of All Forms of Discrimination Against Women.

ever since.[62] It occupies the elevated status of a 'general principle' of children's rights and, as such, informs the interpretation of all other substantive provisions contained within the CRC.[63] Framing best interests as a right implies obligations and accountability for its fulfilment on the part of adults, and it also expresses the notion that it (whatever 'it' is determined to be in the specific context) is an interest that the child plausibly claims rather than something imposed on the child by others (as is implied by welfare) or that can be waived by the actions of another. For example, in her re-write of *AAA* Hughes notes that parental waiver (in this case relating to the child's reasonable expectation of privacy) 'is contrary to the best interests approach, which was introduced to protect the welfare of the child regardless of the actions and wishes of parents.' She powerfully writes that:

> What is unconscionable is that the human right of one person can be waived by the actions of another. There is no basis for departing from that position simply because the claimant is a child. To suggest otherwise is to undermine the fact that the child has her own rights under international and domestic law.[64]

Children's rights theory can assist judges' understanding and assessment of best interests insofar as it goes well beyond a mere re-articulation of rights as framed in law, to achieve a more intellectually compelling explanation as to why a particular course of action supports children's best interests.[65] Whilst such a strategy cannot claim to resolve all of the challenges associated with determining best interests in practice, there is strong evidence that locating best interests within an intellectually and morally sound rights paradigm stimulates more comprehensive, procedurally robust assessments of best interests and assists in engaging the confidence and commitment of those who have to live with the decision thereafter. Therefore we advocate here—as do many of the fictive judges in this collection—a much broader conceptualisation of welfare in the context of judicial decision-making which is consistent with the best interests principle enshrined in Article 3 CRC and with the expansive scholarly commentary on it.

Regarding best interests (and by implication, welfare) as a right thus demands more than passing reference to the principle or a presumption that its component parts are understood; it necessitates transparent, rigorous, systematic, even forensic, deliberations of the various factors that have comprised that assessment.[66] An abundance of guidance has been

---

[62] See for example Arts 7(2), 23(2) and 23(2) and (4) of the 1996 UN Convention on the Rights of Persons with Disabilities; and Art 24(1) of the EU Charter of Fundamental Rights 2000.

[63] Note that best interests is explicitly referred to in Arts 9(1) and (3), 18(1), 20(1), 21, 37(c) and 40(2)(b)(iii) of the CRC.

[64] Ch 10, para 25.

[65] Tobin, above n 2. For example, by drawing on the Capabilities Approach.

[66] A distinction between 'rights-based' and 'non-rights-based' approaches to best interests is drawn in the UNHCR Guidelines on Determining the Best Interests of the Child 2008 (text at n 23 above, at para 3.6) and in General Comment No 6 of the United Nations Committee on the Rights of the Child (2005), on the Treatment of Unaccompanied and Separated Children Outside their Country of Origin (para 85). On the benefits of a rights-based approach over a conflated best interests approach, see Fortin: '[b]y articulating children's interests as rights and incorporating evidence traditionally associated with ideas about their best interests within such rights, the courts can develop a more structured and analytical approach to decision-making'. Fortin, above n 10, at 326. This links to the wider point made by commentators (including A Bainham, 'Can we Protect Children and Protect their Rights?' (2002) 32 *Family Law* 279) that rights-based assessments more clearly articulate the interests at stake than does a 'traditional' best interests/welfare assessment; though as Ferguson argues (above n 4), a clear articulation of interests is not *necessarily* excluded by best interests. The point we make here is that unpacking those interests must be holistic and rigorous.

developed by the judiciary,[67] the Committee on the Rights of the Child,[68] the legislature[69] and policy-makers at various levels[70] to articulate the factors that a best interests assessment comprises (whilst also acknowledging that relevant factors cannot be exhaustively prescribed given the significant variation in cases). What such guidance demonstrates is that the best interests principle is neither free standing nor amorphous: it is inextricably linked with and expressed in a range of other substantive rights (see, for example, Fenton-Glynn's articulation of the child's best interests as including her right to identity in *C v XYZ*; and Bridgeman's reading of 'welfare' and rights for the children born as a result of surrogacy in *Re X and Y*).[71] Indeed, arguing that best interests is a right (that is, detaching it from paternalism, coupling it to the child's plausible claims, and unpacking the component interests), must include a holistic articulation of the other rights of the child: it is in her best interests to protect her rights.[72]

The reasoning (and sometimes the decision) in most of the rewritten judgments concerning best interests hinges on the articulation of interests that were absent, obscured or minimised in the original cases. This is demonstrated (inter alia) in the rewritten *Castle* judgment where, as noted above, Daly interprets 'welfare' in the Children Act 2004 by reference to other CRC rights, thus allowing the identification of a right to develop as a political actor as an essential element of best interests. Similarly, in *Collins*, Hoffman sets out the specific factors to be considered in planning decisions vis-à-vis children's best interests. In *Defence for Children International (DCI) v Belgium* Vandenhole states that the European Social Charter should be interpreted in accordance with the child's best interests and reminds us of the guidance issued by the Committee on the Rights of the Child in its *General Comment No 5*: 'Every legislative, administrative and judicial body or institution is required to apply the best interests principle by systematically considering how children's rights and interests are or will be affected by their decisions and actions'.

As well as being holistic, rigorous and inclusive of the other rights of the child, the identification and assessment of (best) interests must also be informed by evidence. First, and foremost, judges should insist on information about the best interests of the *specific child* in relation to the *specific issue* that is the subject of the proceedings. Thus, in the rewritten judgment of *AAA*, Hughes notes that information on the best interests of *this* child had not

---

[67] See Lady Hale's guidance in the UK Supreme Court decision in *ZH (Tanzania)* above n 25 and the Australian Federal Court's reasoning on best interests in *Wan v Minister for Immigration and Multi-cultural Affairs* [2001] FCA 568, para 32.

[68] Committee on the Rights of the Child, General Comment No 14 on the Right of the Child to have his or her Best Interests taken as a Primary Consideration (art 3, para 1) CRC/C/GC/14.

[69] For example, see the checklist in s 1(3) Children Act 1989 (England and Wales).

[70] For example, see UNHRC Guidelines for Determining the Best Interests of the Child 2008; General Comments 17 and 19 of the Human Rights Committee in relation to the International Covenant on Civil and Political Rights 1966 (UN Human Rights Committee (HRC), *CCPR General Comment No 17: Article 24 (Rights of the Child)*, 7 April 1989 and UN Human Rights Committee (HRC), *CCPR General Comment No 19: Article 23 (The Family) Protection of the Family, the Right to Marriage and Equality of the Spouses*, 27 July 1990).

[71] A number of our judges specifically follow the now common judicial practice in many European jurisdictions (following the lead of the ECtHR), to use best interests, as articulated in Art 3 CRC, to bolster claims to children's *right* to respect for private and family life under Art 8 ECHR. See, for example, *ZH (Tanzania)*, *SG*, and *Nzolameso* above n 25, and R Taylor, 'Putting Children First? Children's Interests as a Primary Consideration in Public Law' (2016) 28 *Child and Family Law Quarterly* 45.

[72] J Fortin, *Children's Rights and the Developing Law* (Cambridge, Cambridge University Press, 2009).

been made available to the court; in *P-S* Jane Williams finds that the judge who has taken account of 'general evidence' of harm felt by children giving evidence in court was unlawful; and in *Re W* Gilmore rues the absence of a specific assessment of the child's competence to refuse the particular treatment ordered (which, had she been competent to refuse, would have been pertinent to the best interests assessment as to whether the treatment should be ordered). Second, and notwithstanding the caveats set out in chapter two, in certain circumstances judges should be informed by wider empirical evidence about children. This can prove invaluable in a number of contexts: where specific evidence about the child is either unavailable or unknown because it relates to her future best interests (see Fenton-Glynn's use of scholarship to inform the impact on children of not knowing their biological origins); where the judges' 'background' information about children's experiences and perspective are circumscribed (for example by a judge's lack of personal experience or—as for most—where s/he is temporally very far-removed from childhood); where presumptions about children, or the 'paradigm case' upon which the law is based, are inaccurate (again see *C v XYZ*; and also *Farooq Ahmed*);[73] or where robust, empirically verified insights are needed to counter the dominance of strong political and economic factors (for example, as we see in *Zambrano* in the immigration and asylum context).

One compelling research finding to which judges should have regard is the importance of hearing from, and genuinely taking account of, the views and wishes of the child in determining their own best interests. Since the 1970s, academics have sought to interpret children's rights in a much more nuanced way to reflect the incremental (and sometimes messy) process by which children acquire the skills and capacities to determine how their best interests might be fulfilled, with a concomitant reduction in their parents' and other adults' monopoly over knowing and determining what is best for them. This same body of work has highlighted the value of seeking children's input into assessments of their best interests because it informs the practical challenges they may face in implementing the court's decision and because it contributes to the emotional and social empowerment that comes with affirming children's role in shaping their own lives. The fact that the wishes and feelings of the child are instrumental to determining what is in their best interests is now firmly entrenched in law and policy in a range of contexts,[74] and the Committee on the Rights of the Child notes unequivocally the complementarity between the child's best interest right and the right to be heard in Article 12 CRC, with one establishing the 'objective and the other provid[ing] the methodology for reaching the goal …'[75] This is not necessarily the same as allowing the child full self-determination rights (see the next section) but it is a central aspect of framing best interests as a right that positions the child as an active contributor to (as opposed to a passive object of) decision-making. The rewritten judgment of *P-S* by Jane Williams is especially clear on this point, suggesting that the

---

[73] And see Lady Hale's example of child abduction cases, set out in ch 2.

[74] In public and private family law proceedings in England and Wales, in giving paramount consideration to the welfare of the child, judges are required to have due regard to their wishes and feelings. In medical decision-making, children under the age of 16 have a right to make autonomous decisions about their medical treatment provided they have sufficient capacity and understanding. Similarly, the judiciary have acknowledged that an important part of affording primacy to the best interests of the child in immigration proceedings is discovering the child's own view.

[75] See *General Comment No 14* above n 68, at para 43.

'general evidence' about the impact of children participating in proceedings regarding their best interests 'must nowadays … include evidence about ensuring respect for the rights of children in proceedings which affect them'; rights which go beyond the CRC to also include the Article 6 ECHR right to a fair trial, the protection from which '[n]o person, however young, is excluded …'[76] *Re W, Collins, Lubanga* and the decision of the Dutch *Hoge Raad* provide four other examples of such an approach within this collection.

Once the relevant interests have been identified, a judge must give them proper weight. Domestic and international frameworks provide some guidance by attributing either paramountcy or primacy to the child's best interests, which, as noted, is best understood as an umbrella term to encompass the other rights/interests of the child (rather than being simply a vehicle for paternalistic decision-making). The presumptive use of best interests as a 'trump' card has been criticised by some scholars for its (in)compatibility with the ECHR (since it removes the possibility of a more nuanced balance of the interests of all rights-holders).[77] Moreover, the adoption of the 'paramountcy' standard by the ECtHR[78] (followed by Bracken in her rewritten *Gas and Dubois* judgment) is not uncontroversial. But the CRC requirement that children's best interests be *a primary* consideration is sensitively worded to avoid any arbitrary disregard for others' interests; rather, it enables those interests to be factored into decision-makers, allowing them to override the interests of the child only in the most compelling of circumstances.[79] This approach helps to ensure that best interests assessments are properly insulated from the inappropriate influence of the agenda of others, whether that be public authorities (as in *Antwi, Zambrano, Canadian Foundation for Children, Youth and the Law* and *DCI v Belgium*), other children (*Re A (Children)(Conjoined Twins)*), or parents and other adults (*Povse v Austria*; and *Re T*) whilst remaining cognisant of the need to arrive at a decision that the child and those around him or her can live with and implement or support.

In other cases, an apparent conflict between the child's best interests and the interests or rights of another may, in fact, dissipate if viewed through a different theoretical lens. Relational theory, for example, acknowledges the importance of relations between adults and children and how those relations can either inhibit or facilitate the exercise of children's rights.[80] In that sense, relational theory resonates with numerous provisions contained within the CRC that emphasise the role of the parent/child relationship in upholding the best interests of the child. Consistent with the CRC, a relational perspective does not

---

[76] Williams, ch 8, para 23.

[77] See for example, S Choudhry and H Fenwick, 'Taking the Rights of Parents and Children Seriously: Confronting the Welfare Principle Under the Human Rights Act' (2005) 25 *Oxford Journal of Legal Studies* 453.

[78] For example see *Yousef v The Netherlands* [2003] 1 FLR 210.

[79] See further S Parker, 'The Best Interests of the Child—Principles and Problems' (1994) 8 *International Journal of Law and the Family* 26.

[80] On relational theory see, inter alia, J Nedelsky, 'Reconceiving Autonomy: Sources, Thoughts and Possibilities' (1989) 1 *Yale Journal of Law and Feminism* 7; J Nedelsky, *Law's Relations: A Relational Theory of Self, Autonomy and Law* (Oxford, Oxford University Press, 2011); M Minow and ML Shanley, 'Relational Rights and Responsibilities: Revisioning the Family in Liberal Political theory and Law' (1996) 11 *Hypatia* 4; H Lim and J Roche, 'Feminism and Children's Rights' in J Bridgman and D Monk (eds), *Feminist Perspectives on Child Law* (Cavendish, London, 2000); F Kelly, 'Conceptualising the Child Through an "Ethic of Care": Lessons for Family Law' (2005) 1 *International Journal of Law in Context* 375; J Herring, *Relational Autonomy and Family Law* (London, Springer, 2014).

For example, see the original judgment of *Re T (A Minor)(Wardship: Medical Treatment)* [1997] 1 FLR 502 where Lady Butler-Sloss describes the child's and mother's interests as one.

abandon children to their relationships with their parents/family, nor does it pretend that children are isolated individuals reliant on state protection. Rather it seeks to support children's best interests by striving to achieve an outcome that is most likely to nurture a positive relationship with their parents (or an outcome that will have the least detrimental impact on that relationship) and to support parents in meeting their duties to protect the child's rights. An unhappy parent, after all, generally implies an unhappy child and vice versa.[81]

For example, Bracken's rewritten ECtHR decision of *Gas and Dubois v France* adopts a relational approach to emphasise the indissociability of parent/child interests,[82] thus holding that the child's best interests are a paramount consideration in upholding the discrimination claim brought by her same-sex parents regarding existing adoption laws. The best interests principle is deployed to expose the potential impact of preventing the adoption on the child's family life, even though the child was not party to the proceedings. A relational approach is also implicit in the rewritten *Grootboom* decision where Pillay dismantles the 'leapfrog' argument that was used by the Supreme Court of South Africa to justify denying priority to adults who are parents—and thus their children—over non-parents in the allocation of shelter. A relational approach also moves away from understanding rights—including best interests—as protecting individuals from interference by other, atomistic, self-sufficient agents in a 'winner takes all' way, towards seeing the inter-dependency of rights-holders who have a mutual interest in securing each other's wellbeing. Alghrani adopts a similar approach in her rewriting of *Re A (Conjoined Twins)*. She avoids the problematic 'parasitic' language of the original judgment and embraces a more nuanced understanding of the twins' inter-dependency, recognising that the lives and interests of the sisters are entwined and that (in this case, literal) separation may not be the most rights-consistent approach. The foundation of this judgment is in the 'caring approach' advocated by scholars such as Virginia Held and Jonathan Herring, both of whom emphasise the importance of care *and* justice (thus avoiding concerns that individual interests will be consumed by the relationship) in a way that recognises the importance of caring relationships to our wellbeing; something that is especially true for children.[83]

Identifying children's interests and how they inform their rights, including best interest as a right, is a highly complicated and nuanced process and the adjudication of such complex, seemingly intractable circumstances may not be assuaged by even the most fluid collaboration between theory and practice. Nonetheless, for the more 'typical' cases concerning children there is significant scope to achieve more informed, reasoned and accountable decision-making by: recognising best interests as a right; articulating clearly that right—informed by the wider rights of children including their right to be heard; giving appropriate weight to the child's interests (underpinned by the justifications set out in the previous section); ensuring other agenda do not displace the child's best interests; and being open to alternative ways of conceptualising best interests for example using a relational approach.

---

[81] See further Stalford above n 58, 46.
[82] The phrase used by Lord Kerr to emphasise the inter-relatedness of the child and mother's rights in *SG* (above n 25).
[83] J Herring, *Caring and the Law* (Oxford, Hart Publishing, 2013); V Held, *The Ethics of Care: Personal, Political, Global* (Oxford, Oxford University Press, 2006).

C. Using Scholarship to Understand Children's Autonomy

Autonomy provides both a justificatory and descriptive basis for rights, and for a long time children's (often presumed) lack of capacity to exercise autonomy justified the denial of their status as independent rights-holders.[84] One of the key achievements of the children's rights movement has therefore been to secure a shift from paternalistic decision-making to giving effect to children's autonomy.[85] Yet progress towards children's legal autonomy—having the *de jure* authority to make one's own decisions—has been tentative at best, with judges over-extending their substituted decision-making or paying only lip-service to children's autonomy.[86]

There are two challenges that arise most frequently in relation to children's autonomy: the level and type of competence required,[87] and how to resolve conflict between a competent child's wishes and the conflicting view of her best interests as determined by adult others (parent, doctor, judge, for example). The latter issue is particularly difficult where the decision is likely to dramatically change the course of the child's life, or even end it altogether: as Fortin notes, 'it remains questionable [in such circumstances] whether ... the judiciary is entirely ready to allow children to martyr themselves.'[88] The case law suggests that a teenager's claim to have a decisive say in such cases will hinge on her ability to comprehend the implications of such a decision. In such cases, as Archard and Skivenes note, 'The courts must ... determine what it is to give sufficient weight to a child's opinions, or what it is for the child to be of "sufficient maturity", or what is "best" for any child'.[89] Both involve procedural adaptations as well as insights which the judge may simply not possess; both involve a high degree of speculation and perhaps even professional disagreement;[90] both are often based on (perhaps erroneous, perhaps correct) presumptions about the child based on the judge's own values, and on available evidence and societal norms more broadly. Archard and Skivenes point also to the need to distinguish estimations of the child's maturity with evaluations of the child's opinion, 'otherwise there is a danger of allowing a judgment of immaturity to be inferred simply from a disagreement with the prudence of the child's view'.[91]

Some of the rewritten judgments grapple with these challenging issues (see especially *Re W* and *F v F*). Whilst not always reaching a different outcome to the original case they

---

[84] See HLA Hart, 'Definition and Theory in Jurisprudence' (1954) 70 *Law Quarterly Review* 37; and for a rebuttal drawing on interest theory see N MacCormick, 'Children's Rights: A Test Case for Theories of Rights' (1976) 62 *Archiv für Rechts-und Sozialphilosphie* 305.

[85] As exemplified in those cases hailed as landmark children's rights judgments. See for example Lord Denning in *Hewer v Bryant* [1970] 1 QB 357, 369; *Krishnan v Sutton London Borough Council* [1970] Ch 181; and *Gillick v West Norfolk and Wisbech AHA* [1986] AC 112.

[86] For a fuller discussion of the limitations of the judiciary in giving full effect to children's autonomy, see A Daly, *Children, Autonomy and the Courts: Beyond the Right to be Heard* (London, Routledge, forthcoming 2017).

[87] That is, for the views to be authoritative ('the view that must be taken as defining the persons' interests for the purpose of decision-making ...') rather than consultative. See H Brighouse, 'How Should Children Be Heard?' (2003) *Arizona Law Review* 691, 692–93 (quoted by D Archard and M Skivenes, 'Balancing a Child's Best Interests and a Child's Views' (2009) 17 *International Journal of Children's Rights* 1).

[88] Fortin, above n 10, at 323.

[89] Archard and Skivenes, above n 87, at 4.

[90] ibid, at 8.

[91] ibid, at 10.

attempt a fuller and more nuanced engagement with children's capacity for autonomy and its relationship to the child's best interest (as determined by others). Stephen Gilmore draws on John Eekelaar's work[92] in his rewriting of *Re W*, a medical-treatment refusal case, and refuses to shy away from the consequences of conferring on the competent child decision-making power, even if that choice may result in her death. This he justifies on the basis that respecting the child's autonomy is consistent with her welfare:

> [T]he court's message should be clear that the adolescent who is adjudged to be fully competent to take decisions in this sphere ... should be accorded the same respect for his or her autonomy inter-est as English law accords to an adult who is regarded as so fully competent.[93]

But he draws a careful distinction between the level of competence required to refuse *all* treatment (a higher bar) and the competence required to withhold consent for a specific treatment.[94] Implicit in Gilmore's reasoning is that the capacity for autonomy is not uni-form; it is specific to the particular decision *and* to the child in question and requires a close, evidenced examination by the court (and ultimately it was the lack of evidence before him that led him to concur with the original decision to make an emergency order). This emerges too in *F v F* where Emma Cave orders different outcomes for two sisters, both of whom wish to refuse inoculation but for whom the impact of overriding those wishes on their autonomy interests (it is a greater infringement on the older child), and thus on their overall welfare, differs.[95]

Other rewritten judgments attempt to tease out the difference between the child's compe-tence to make a decision (whether she has the necessary skills and knowledge to do so) and its authenticity (whether the decision aligns with her deeper held, stable values and her self-identity).[96] Legal autonomy is usually dependent only on the former, and for good reason (to maximise whom we regard as rights-holders and to maximally respect their choices); and there is a strong argument that children should not be judged to a higher standard than adults in this regard.[97] However, the limited life experience and evolving self-identity of children may justify closer judicial scrutiny of whether (i) the child's values and identity are sufficiently developed; (ii) the child has the requisite skills to balance the decision in ques-tion against those values; and (iii) there is an alignment between them.[98] The application

---

[92] Eekelaar, above n 46.

[93] Gilmore, ch 11, para 19.

[94] Inspired by S Gilmore and J Herring, '"No" is the Hardest Word; Consent and Children's Autonomy' (2011) 23 *Child and Family Law Quarterly* 3.

[95] See Cave, ch 12, at para 37. Other factors, including the health risks, were also relevant and differed between the girls.

[96] This distinction can be conceptualised in different ways: for example, see below, n 98.

[97] Archard and Skivenes, above n 87, at 10: 'a child should not be judged against a standard of competence by which even most adults would fail'. They identify (from cases) the following as factors deemed relevant vis-à-vis children's competence but not adults: emotional instability, ignorance or poor understanding of the relevant issues; a lack of decision-making independence; over-reliance on the judgment of others. See also J Coggon, 'Varied and Principled Understandings of Autonomy in English Law: Justifiable Inconsistency or Blinkered Moral-ism?' (2007) 15 *Health Care Analysis* 235 who suggests that in serious decisions the law might also enquire into the authenticity (or in his words, 'best desire autonomy') rather than simple competence to make the decision ('current desire autonomy').

[98] Criteria (i) and (ii) are elements of a person's 'procedural' autonomy, and (iii) assesses whether the decision is substantively autonomous. Substantive autonomy can also be measured against an objective standard of what, as a society, we think people *should* value. These distinctions can be conceptualised in different ways: for example, see also Coggon's ideal desire autonomy; best desire autonomy; and current desire autonomy (discussed in Gilmore

of the three elements Archard and Skivenes suggest to determine a child's competence—the consistency with which an opinion is expressed; the reasons given by the child for holding that opinion; and the child's appreciation of the consequences should their views be decisive[99]—could help to inform the 'authenticity' of the child's views. The rewritten decisions in *Begum* (concerning a Muslim school girl's choice to wear the jilbab), *Valsamis* (a Jehovah's Witness girl's refusal to attend a National Day parade), *JTB* (children's criminal responsibility) and *Lubanga* (whether children can consent to enlistment in a militia) all recognise either explicitly or implicitly this dual element of children's internal capacity for autonomy (that is, the distinction between competency on the one hand and authenticity on the other) and its relevance to their legal autonomy. However, as Trevor Buck notes in his *Lubanga* rewrite, there are various difficulties 'associated with identifying the reality of children's voluntariness' and thus their autonomous choices, particularly where the child's views align closely with their family's and/or the societal or religious environment within which they have been raised (indeed, we might ask whether it is possible—or desirable—for any of us to be truly 'autonomous' in this sense).[100] The task confronting the court, therefore, might be to examine 'with care and on a case by case basis',[101] not only whether the child has capacity to make the decision, but also whether that decision is 'authentic'. We might think it preferable—or at least more honest—to deny the child *de jure* (legal) autonomy (or limit the weight given to her views in the legal assessment of her best interests) on this basis (that the decision lacks alignment with her deeper values, or those values are insufficiently formed), after explicit consideration, than misleadingly to assert that the child lacks the more basic competence we usually require to make a specific legal decision.[102] This more fully accords with the notion of 'evolving capacities' and, importantly—in terms of the recognition of children as rights-holders and the message the law conveys to the child and to others—it constitutes a more limited denial of the child's autonomy (even though she is not conferred with *de jure*—legal—autonomy).[103] It also provides a more coherent basis for differential treatment of adults (a lower threshold confined to competence assessment)[104] and children (a higher threshold, requiring the capacity to assess the 'authenticity' of the decision and/or requiring the decision is, in fact, substantively 'authentic' (in line with the child's settled, deeper, values)).[105]

---

and Herring, above n 94. Wide disagreement exists about which is a preferable approach to autonomy, including within law. See further, C MacKenzie and N Stoljar, *Relational Autonomy: Feminist Perspectives on Autonomy, Agency and the Social Self* (Oxford, Oxford University Press, 2000) Introduction.

[99] Although there is a deeper penetration into the child's capacity for autonomy, the focus remains primarily on the child's *procedural* autonomy—the way in which the opinion is held and defended (14). They therefore advocate a procedural approach to autonomy rather than a substantive approach (that is, the wisdom of the decision and whether it accords with the child's 'best interests').

[100] On which see the wide-ranging literature on relational autonomy, including MacKenzie and Stoljar, above n 98 and the references above, n 80.

[101] Buck, ch 24, para 47.

[102] See again the quote from Archard and Skivenes, above n 87.

[103] This is important in terms of the 'message' that the law gives to children, which, as discussed below, can also feed into how they develop as autonomous agents.

[104] Coggon's 'current desire autonomy'.

[105] Coggon's 'best desire authonomy'.

As well as differentiating the two distinct 'internal' aspects of autonomy[106] (competence and authenticity), theoretical scholarship on autonomy has also addressed the external requirements for autonomy. Mackenzie identifies these as comprising 'freedom' conditions (the 'social and political constraints that interfere with the exercise of self-determination and the political and personal liberties that enable it') and opportunity conditions ('the opportunities that need to be available to agents in social environments for them to have claims about what to value, to be and to do').[107] Legal rights often protect citizens, including children, in relation to both (broadly—though inaccurately[108]—dichotomised as traditional civil liberties (negative rights) on the one hand and economic and social rights (positive rights) on the other). Examples of how judges reinforce children's capacity for autonomy through the articulation and protection of these rights, and the inter-relationship between them, are evident, for example, in *Farooq Ahmed* (where Khoso points out the impact of malnutrition on children's mental capacities) and *Collins* (where the absence of a stable home is likely to impact on education, and—by implication—the capacity to develop autonomy competences).

One of the key difficulties for the courts is how to reconcile children's claims that they are as entitled to autonomy-protecting rights as adults and yet, at the same time, because of the child's age and maturity those autonomy rights should differ in content, scope or application. This dilemma—and the concomitant justification for, and application of, differential treatment—is considered above. In this section we instead draw attention to the temporal dimension of children's rights: children have rights in the here and now *and* they are developing towards the acquisition of 'full autonomy'[109] and full rights-status in adulthood.[110] Earlier children's rights scholarship, drawing on literature from the sociology of childhood, rightly emphasised the rights of the child in the present in order to counter the paternalistic focus on the child as future adult. But, as Freeman notes, 'it is equally important to understand that appreciating that [children] are "beings" does not preclude their being also "becomings"'.[111] Indeed, to neglect any consideration of how decisions now might impact upon a child's future life would be to engage in only a partial assessment of their rights and interests. A children's rights judgment is, therefore, also one that recognises children's special position as both 'beings' and 'becomings', and which fulfils the

---

[106] What MacKenzie identifies as autonomy as 'self-regulation'. C MacKenzie, 'Three Dimensions of Autonomy: A Relational Analysis' in A Veltman and M Piper, *Autonomy, Oppression and Gender* (Oxford, Oxford University Press, 2014).

[107] ibid. The emphasis on the social environment helps to counter the neoliberal appropriation of participation rights as demonstrative of 'choice'; those choices and opportunities have to be capable of being realised. See again the discussion in ch 2.

[108] See S Fredman, *Human Rights Transformed: Positive Rights and Positive Duties* (Oxford, Oxford University Press, 2008).

[109] A phrase used in K Hollingsworth, 'Theorising Children's Rights in Youth Justice: The Significance of Autonomy and Foundational Rights' (2013) 76 *Modern Law Review* 1046, to denote an understanding of autonomy that goes beyond the 'rational' agent in liberal theory to capture a relational and capabilities-based approach to autonomy.

[110] See for example, T Campbell, 'The Rights of the Minor: As Person, as Child, as Juvenile, as Future Adult' (1992) 6 *International Journal of Law and the Family* 1; Eekelaar, above n 46; M Freeman, 'The Human Rights of Children' (2010) *Current Legal Problems* 1.

[111] Freeman, ibid, 13.

law's role 'as protectors and supporters of [children's] ongoing development'.[112] Developing children's potential as rights-holders *may* require restricting the child's choices where she will permanently inhibit her future autonomy (or, in Feinberg's words, her 'right to an open future'[113]); an approach that may have underpinned Emma Cave's decision in relation to the younger child in *F v F* (but would be antithetical to Gilmore's approach in the case of a competent child).[114] But equally importantly, it demands that the courts recognise the obligation the *state* has to acknowledge and nurture children's autonomy.[115] This emerges most explicitly in Barbara Bennett Woodhouse's rewritten judgment of *Roper v Simmons* and her location within the US Constitution of a fundamental right to 'grow up', thereby rendering the juvenile death penalty unconstitutional.[116] It also features strongly in the emphasis Lundy's fictional judge places on education as a forum for autonomy-development; in Daly's focus in *Castle* on legal references to children's 'development' as a component of their welfare in order to argue that this extends to their development as political actors (and thus founding an obligation on the police to secure conditions to facilitate this development); and in *AAA*, where Kirsty Hughes refuses to allow the parent's actions to 'waive' her child's expectation of privacy because of the impact on the child's ability to create her own future.

In addition to facilitating a better understanding of the *concept* of autonomy,[117] theoretical developments can inform legal judgments by opening up possibilities of new *conceptualisations* of autonomy that are either empirically better suited to children and/or are normatively preferred. As noted above, traditional liberal approaches to rights can be exclusionary of children in how they conceptualise the ideal rights-holder (as atomistic and independent) *and* in how they conceptualise rights (as offering protection from interference by others) and relational theory has developed as a response to these perceived limitations. It provides a rich resource for those seeking a more child-appropriate understanding of rights.[118] The basic premise of relational theory—that we are inter-dependent and that our choices, values and experiences are shaped by the relationships (intimate, familial, community and societal) within which we are embedded—has a number of consequences for children's autonomy. First, it recognises that we may make choices (or have them made for us) that take account of, or even promote above our own, the interests of another; this does not necessarily render that choice or decision non-autonomous or contrary to our rights (for example, see the rewritten decision in *P-S*), provided that the judge engages in a close and particular examination of the relationship in question to ensure it is nourishing and not oppressive.[119]

---

[112] Buss, ch 22 of this collection, text at fn 12, and see further Buss, above n 44.

[113] J Feinberg, 'The Child's Right to an Open Future' in W Aitken and H La Follette (eds), *Whose Child?* (Totawa, Littlefield, Adams and Co, 1980).

[114] Thus reflecting the diversity in 'children's rights approaches'.

[115] For justifications for this see A Franklin Hall, 'On Becoming an Adult: Autonomy and the Moral Relevance of Life Stages' (2013) 63 *The Philosophical Quarterly* 223; Dixon and Nussbaum, above n 48; and Hollingsworth, above n 109.

[116] Discussed above, and inspired by Buss, above n 44.

[117] That is, whether it requires internal and external conditions, or whether the internal conditions include both competence and authenticity, whether it includes autonomy now and autonomy in the future and so on. See further, Mackenzie, above n 106.

[118] See again the references in n 80 above.

[119] For a real life attempt by the judiciary to reflect the reality and value of children's interdependence, see Lord Kerr dissenting in the UK Supreme Court case of *SG* (above n 25, at para 266 and at 265: 'Justification of a discriminatory measure must directly address the impact that it will have on the children ... because that impact is inextricably bound up with the women's capacity to fulfil their role as mothers'.

Second, a relational approach allows the judge to recognise that children may need adult support to make decisions, and that this does not necessarily render the decision non-autonomous. The judge is thus able to treat with less suspicion children's decisions that align with a family member (as in Cave's decision in *F v F*[120]) whilst at the same time recognising that some relationships, particularly those that are traditionally hierarchical, *can be* oppressive and limiting.[121] A relational approach also draws attention to the ways in which autonomy is vulnerable to oppressive social relations (for example gender or racial stereotypes or culture-based harmful practices),[122] and it encourages a close scrutiny of the decisions of children raised (for example) in religious communities (as in *Begum* and *Valsamis*) to ensure that there is still space for the child to question and reject that lifestyle (or, in Nedelsky's words, to engage in 'creative reimagining'[123]) if she so chooses.[124] The fact that a child is influenced by the relationships, norms and structures within which she experiences life is no reason to automatically deem her to be lacking autonomy. It is noteworthy that the CRC is cautious in this regard, protecting only the child's 'own views', implying, perhaps, that views influenced by others (or indeed *about* others) are not to be protected as a right.[125]

IV. Child-friendly Justice: Protecting the Child's Right to be Heard in Legal Proceedings

Judgment re-writing projects focus primarily on how different (for example feminist) perspectives impact on the discretionary space available to judges to reason and decide cases. Yet a children's rights judgment is not only concerned with the substance of the judicial opinion, but also with legal procedures and the extent to which they themselves comply with Article 12 CRC and secure the child's right to be heard.[126] This is our third marker of a children's rights judgment.

Ensuring that the child's voice is heard, including through the facilitation of her participation in the case, helps to mitigate the many ways in which the views and experiences

---

[120] Where Cave notes at para 28 that: 'The fact that L and M share the mother's view does not automatically render her influence "undue", just as it would not if they happened to share their father's view. L in particular has articulated reasoning quite separate to her mother's'.

[121] Nedelsky, above n 80.

[122] See Anderson and Honneth, above n 10. For a recognition of this in the judgments in this collection, see Gilmore's rewritten *re W* at para 14 where he acknowledges the potential impact of social relations on the child's 'independent judgment'.

[123] Nedelsky, above n 80.

[124] See CM Macleod, 'Conceptions of Parental Autonomy' (1997) 25(1) *Politics and Society* 117–40 on different ways of approaching the balance between parental freedom to pass on to their children their own conception of the 'good' (ie various religious, cultural, philosophical or moral commitments) and the child's freedom not to be constrained by parental choices (conservative, democratic and liberal). He concludes that the exercise of parental autonomy must not limit children's 'free and full access to the deliberative resources available in the pluralistic public culture' so that they are not closed to other alternatives.

[125] M Cordero Acre, 'Towards an Emancipatory Discourse of Children's Rights' (2012) 20 *International Journal of Children's Rights* 365.

[126] See also Committee on the Rights of the Child, *General Comment No 12: The Right to be Heard* (1 July 2009) CRC/C/GC/12.

of the child litigant are silenced or distorted throughout legal proceedings.[127] It has both intrinsic and instrumental value: it conveys to the child that her views are worth listening to, an aspect of the recognitional function of rights that reinforces the child's dignity, autonomy and status as rights-holder;[128] it provides a space for her to exercise and develop her capacity for autonomy;[129] it makes available to the judge the child's views and experiences, thus promoting better-informed and effective decision-making; and it legitimises the outcome of the proceedings, especially from the viewpoint of the child.[130]

The concept of 'child-friendly justice', comprehensively articulated in the Council of Europe's Guidelines,[131] captures these and the other norms and principles that should apply at different stages of legal proceedings.[132] Given the weaknesses in domestic legal frameworks and the non-binding nature of international standards,[133] compliance with principles of child-friendly justice usually relies on professional awareness and willingness to adopt them—particularly on the part of judges.[134] Thus, the extent to which Article 12 CRC is, in practice, a child's *right* during legal proceedings very much depends on whether 'those exercising discretion—judicially, professionally or administratively—act in a manner which is compatible with the holistic interpretation required by the Convention'.[135] There are a number of ways in which judges can facilitate the child's communication of her wishes during proceedings:[136] by ensuring the child is adequately supported (by a 'trustworthy and empathetic' adult,[137] and which may require the appointment of an intermediary[138]); by helping her to understand proceedings (through the use of simple and non-technical language); by facilitating the child's participation (considering, for example, the way in which oral evidence is given,[139] the length of the day, ensuring the child is not talked-over, the courtroom architecture, and dress[140]); by providing the child with access to relevant information that she can understand[141] (including practical information about how the case will

---

[127] See further, ch 2 and Tobin, above n 2.

[128] See Douzinas, and Anderson and Honneth, above n 10.

[129] Which should take account of what is appropriate for that child at that time in her life.

[130] See generally, Daly, above n 86, ch 4.

[131] Council of Europe, above n 5. These aim to provide a 'practical tool for member states in adapting their judicial and non-judicial systems to the specific rights, interests and needs of children'. European Union Agency for Fundamental Rights, *Child-friendly Justice: Perspectives and Experiences of Professionals on Children's Participation in Civil and Criminal Judicial Proceedings in 10 EU Member States* (2015) (which notes the EU's commitment to the guidelines).

[132] For example, the rule of law, non-discrimination and best interests of the child.

[133] The Council of Europe Guidelines consolidate standards found elsewhere, including the UN.

[134] The need to secure the child's participation in legal proceedings begins prior to the court proceedings (see Daly, above n 86) but our focus is on those aspects that are under judicial control.

[135] Jane Williams, rewritten judgment of *P-S (Children)* in this collection, at para 25. As noted in ch 2, most domestic law confers considerable discretion on professionals to determine whether and how children's wishes are communicated to the court.

[136] nb Art 12 UNCRC does not guarantee the child's *direct* participation, only his or her right to be heard.

[137] Daly, above n 86, ch 4 at 2.3.3.

[138] In England and Wales, judges have discretionary powers to order an intermediary for a child defendant, for example (though this requires the judge to recognise that one is needed).

[139] For example, the use of screens or CCTV.

[140] See further, Daly, above n 86.

[141] H Stalford and L Cairns, 'Achieving Child Friendly Justice using Child Friendly Methods: the Meaning and Scope of the Right to Information' in (2017 forthcoming) Aug/Sept Issue *Social Inclusion* (Special Issue on Promoting Children's Participation in Research, Policy and Practice).

proceed, as well as relevant case files[142]); by ensuring that the child's *wishes*, and not only her interests, are communicated to the court (through a competent and specially trained lawyer[143] and/or through direct communication with the judge in chambers[144]); and that, where necessary and available, the judge should ensure there are adequate resources to meet these duties.[145]

Our fictive judges were unable to retrospectively adapt the processes of their rewritten cases because they were tasked with writing a judgment on the basis of the same facts and evidence that was available to the original judge. Therefore it was not open to them to include evidence obtained directly from the affected child unless (as in *F v F*) the original judge had done so. Thus, Maria Moscati—who, along with Nuno Ferreira, interviewed for this project Shabina Begum (the young woman at the heart of their case) and heard from her a different version/interpretation of the facts—was unable directly to bring such evidence to bear on her rewritten House of Lords opinion. Ferreira's commentary does, however, highlight how a particular version of events relied upon by the original Court may have overplayed the influence of Shabina's brothers on her decision, and did not allow space for her to challenge the way in which her rights were presented as in conflict with those of her classmates. Similarly, although Kilkelly explores in her commentary on *Gas and Dubois* whether there was greater possibility to ensure the child's involvement in the proceedings of the European Court of Human Rights, it would not have been possible for Bracken to go so far as to make the child a party to the proceedings.

However, the substantive focus (either directly or indirectly) of a number of the rewritten judgments was children's participation in the legal processes, and thus the importance of the child's right to be heard within legal proceedings is a key theme in this collection. In some cases the doctrinal framework constrained the court from finding that the failure to have proper regard to the child's views constituted a breach of the law; but nonetheless important dicta are provided that—carefully read—represent a shift away from paying lip-service to children's views towards a fuller engagement with the participation principle. Neville Harris notes, for example, that the child's views should be '*enabled* … to *inform* the decision',[146] highlighting both the need to support the child (in this case in tribunal decision-making) and to ensure those views actually shape judicial decision-making and are not used simply to reinforce adult views or as a 'sop' to the child. In *Collins*, Simon Hoffman holds that the Secretary of State (in exercising quasi-judicial powers vis-à-vis upholding

---

[142] ibid. This is necessary in order to instruct a lawyer. In some circumstances, such as criminal justice, it is presumed children can instruct a lawyer, regardless of their capacity. In other contexts, as noted in ch 2, the child must convince a judge, and a lawyer, that they are competent to instruct *and* that it is in their best interest to do so.

[143] The extent to which the particular legal system requires lawyers to be specially trained or accredited is beyond judicial control (on the wide variation see Daly, above n 86), but they should be satisfied that they are getting accurate representation of the child's wishes.

[144] Children '[m]ore than anything … want to speak directly with those who take decisions about them'. U Kilkelly, *Listening to Children about Justice: Report of the Council of Europe's Consultation with Children on Child Friendly Justice* (Council of Europe, 2010) 39. In England and Wales, judges have considerable discretion to hold a 'judicial interview' with a child; but Daly notes that the case law suggests this is an exception not the rule (Daly, above n 86, ch 4 at 3.2.1). To be effective, judges need to be specially trained and should see the process not only as a way to 'demystify' proceedings for the child, but for the child's views to inform the decision-making process. See J Caldwell, 'Common Law Judges and Judicial Interviewing' (2011) 23 *Child and Family Law Quarterly* 41.

[145] On judicial discretion to mitigate (for example) cuts to legal aid in this regard, see Daly, above n 86 and ch 2 this collection.

[146] Rewritten decision of *S v SENDIST* (emphasis added).

a planning enforcement notice) acted unlawfully by failing to take adequate account of the children's best interests. This decision, Hoffman asserts, should be informed by the children's *own* views and not just the views of their adult carers, noting that the child's views and the views of their carers may not always coincide.[147] In three of the rewritten judgments—*RCB*, *P-S* and *de Hoge Raad*—the legal challenge centred on the child's participation within court proceedings. All of these judgments focus on the need closely to scrutinise judicial *discretion* to hear children: Bruning and Liefaard note that a discretionary power is not equivalent to a child's *right* to be heard and Williams opines that Article 12 compatibility is only secure *if* those exercising discretionary powers do so using a 'holistic interpretation' of the CRC. We also see emerging a strong emphasis on a commitment to securing *genuine* participation: Bruning and Liefaard hold that children should have access to relevant files to ensure that 'hearing the child' does not become a 'superficial exercise and a meaningless experience for the child';[148] and Simpson (*RCB*) cites evidence of children's capacity (rather than incapacity) to participate in proceedings and the need for children's legal representation in order to cross-examine and challenge the purported interests of the child provided to the court through adult conduits.[149]

The facilitation of children's participation in legal proceedings may be constrained by the relevant legal framework (as indicated in Simpson's pleas to the Australian legislature to liberalise the law in relation to child abduction cases).[150] The rewritten judgments demonstrate, however, that judges retain considerable discretion to ensure the child's wishes form part of the decision-making process and the exercise of this discretion in line with Article 12 is an essential pre-requisite to a children's rights judgment.

V. Telling a Different Story: The Use of Narrative in Children's Rights Judgments

Asserting rights through the legal process is an essential way in which marginalised or oppressed groups can demand that account be taken of their interests. In the preceding sections we have focused on how this can be achieved substantively in the legal reasoning and outcome, and procedurally through the child's participation in the legal processes. However, a children's rights approach is concerned not only with the substance or 'what' of the judgment: as Rackley argues in the context of feminist judging, it is also concerned with 'stylistic and rhetorical choices'; the 'how'.[151] Two aspects of the 'art and craft'[152] of a

---

[147] See also the rewritten decision in *Povse v Austria* where a strong emphasis was placed on the child's objection to being returned to her father. As Daly notes, generally the courts place greater weight on hearing directly from the child in Hague Convention cases as the child's objection is a ground to refuse return to the child's habitual country of residence. See Daly, above n 86.

[148] Rewritten judgment at para 26.

[149] In that case via a social report.

[150] Rewritten *RCB* judgment at para 25.

[151] Rackley, above n 6 at 45.

[152] ibid.

children's rights judgment are discussed in the two final parts of this chapter. In this part, we explore how narrative and language can be employed in a way consistent with a children's rights approach; adopting one of the key methods of the feminist judgments projects to explore how telling a different story can result in alternative reasoning and outcomes.[153] In the fifth and final part of the chapter, we suggest that an essential aspect of a children's rights judgment is that it is effectively communicated to children themselves; judgments should aim—where possible—to be 'child-friendly'.

All judgments are narrative; they tell a story through facts, structure and language[154] and it is through this storytelling method that judges seek to convince their audience that they have made the right decision. Given that cases concerning children can be amongst the most contentious, emotionally-charged, value-ridden and life-changing of cases to be dealt with by the courts, the imperative to persuade through narrative is strong. The narrative employed within cases concerning children—whether intentional on the part of the individual judge or not—also conveys messages about the cultural and social backdrop to children's rights, and the extent to which adult 'fears and fantasies' about childhood are reflected in and potentially magnified by the law (as we see, for example in *JTB*, *Castle* and *Roper*). For these reasons—for how it persuades and what it reveals—it is important to examine 'not simply how law is found but how it is made, not simply what judges command but how the commands are constructed and framed'.[155]

Narrative can be used in a number of ways to better give effect to children's rights. First, judges can use the facts (given that facts 'are not objective. They are what the judge thinks they are'[156]) to create a story that centralises the experiences of children, thus allowing them to move out of the margins of the law.[157] As Brooks and Gewirtz note, judgment-writing as storytelling:

> [H]as a distinctive power for 'oppositionists' and other outsider groups, particularly racial, and religious minorities and women. Telling stories (rather than simply making arguments), it is said, has a distinctive power to challenge and unsettle the legal status quo, because stories give uniquely vivid representation to particular voices, perspectives, and experiences of victimisation traditionally left out of legal scholarship and ignored when shaping legal rules.[158]

---

[153] Hunter, above n 38. See also Hollingsworth, above n 25, who argues that a feminist methodology of judging is also likely to constitute a children's rights methodology of judging.

[154] See for example, P Brooks and P Gewirtz, *Law's Stories: Narrative and Rhetoric in the Law* (New Haven, Yale University Press, 1996); K Lane Scheppele, 'Telling Stories' (1989) 87 *Michigan Law Review* 2073; D Watkins, 'Recovering the Lost Human Stories of Law: Finding Mrs Burns' (2013) 7 *Law and Humanities* 68 and 'The Shaping and Misshaping of Identity through Legal Practice and Process: (Re)discovering Mr Kernott' (2014) 8 *Law and Humanities* 192; and P Brooks, 'Narrative Transactions: Does the Law Need a Narratology' (2006) 18 *Yale Journal of Law and Humanities* 1.

[155] Brooks and Gewirtz, ibid, at 3.

[156] Watkins, 'The Shaping and Misshaping of Identity', above n 154 at 216, citing J Frank, *Courts on Trial: Myth and Reality in American Justice* (Princeton, Princeton University Press, 1950): 'The "facts", it must never be overlooked, are not objective. They are what the judge thinks they are. And what he thinks depends on what he hears and what he sees as the witnesses testify—which may not be, and often is not, what another judge would hear and see … [and] since the 'facts' are only what the judge thinks they are, the decision will vary with the judge's apprehension of the facts'.

[157] For an example of where this was *not* done see *Re B (Wardship: Sterilisation)* and J Montgomery's discussion in 'Rhetoric and Welfare' (1989) 9 *Oxford Journal of Legal Studies* 395, 399.

[158] Brooks and Gewirtz, above n 154 at 5.

Thus, where the narrative is 'grounded in and reflects the experience' of children[159] it can unmask legal principles and concepts as adult-centric (consider, for example, how we understand criminal responsibility in *JTB* or *Roper*); and it can also serve to remind us that the category of 'child' is itself not homogeneous.[160] Although children as a group are united by their unique vulnerability in law, they are individuals whose experiences, needs and capacities may be affected by their upbringing or by characteristics such as gender, class, race, (dis)ability or religion.[161] Such intersectionalities and differences can be obscured, however, where a judge constructs a particular image of 'child'—for example one based on a judicial 'ideal' of childhood as innocence, dependence, vulnerability or danger—which she misleadingly presents as universal. The employment of narrative can guard against this by 'encourage[ing] awareness of the particular human lives that are the subjects or objects of the law, even when that particularity is subordinated to the generalising impulse of legal regulation'.[162] The judge can therefore use facts in ways that provide a holistic and contextual account of the child's life; gives a more accurate telling of the *child's* story; better emphasises the impact of the decision on the child; and, therefore, helps to support the outcome towards which the judge is reasoning.[163] For example, in the rewritten decisions in *JTB* and *Roper*, both judges downplay the crime the child has been convicted of and instead Judges Arthur and Woodhouse emphasise the wider circumstances of the child's life, thus providing greater context: a technique intended to generate empathy for the child. This can make uncomfortable reading where the facts are retold in a way which, by taking account of broader structural or individual factors in favour of the child, may simultaneously appear to minimise the harm to the child's victim (particularly where that victim is another child, as in *JTB*). But, as Brooks—again—notes, storytelling is not morally neutral; 'it always seeks to induce a point of view'.[164]

A child-focused narrative can also protect against the danger identified by Watkins that judgments may 'extinguish[] the living personality that might otherwise remain associated with it'.[165] That is, that the real life person in whose name a case is taken can become a caricature; stripped of their identity through the appropriation of their name and their story (and consequently their 'self') by the law. This is especially acute where it is a child who is at the centre of a high profile or controversial decision (as, for example, in *Begum*), given that a child's self-identity is still in flux and may be negatively affected by a distorted, and very public, alternative image.

However, despite considerable judicial discretion to shape the narrative through their presentation of the facts,[166] the creation of an accurate child-focused 'story' nonetheless

---

[159] Tobin, above n 2, at 609.

[160] A criticism aimed by some commentators at the CRC: See for example the discussion in Cordero Acre, above n 125.

[161] Some children experience greater harm or discrimination because of characteristics which intersect with their age (for example, girls' enhanced vulnerability to sexual exploitation; or the intersection of race and gender for boys in criminal justice processes).

[162] Brooks and Gewirtz, above n 154 at 3.

[163] This may be explicit or—as in *SG*—implicit. See Hollingsworth, above n 25.

[164] P Brooks, 'The Law as Narrative and Rhetoric' in Brooks and Gewirtz, above n 154 at 17.

[165] Watkins, 'Recovering the Lost Stories of Law', above n 154, at 89.

[166] Contrast, for example, Lady Hale and Lord Reed's judgments in *SG*, see Hollingsworth, above n 25.

depends to some extent on the proceedings that go before it and the information the judge is able to get from, and about, the child. In the original decision in *Begum*, for example, the House of Lords may not have been privy to the version of the facts that Moscati and Ferreira heard from Shabina herself when they interviewed her for this project. Although, as noted above, it was not possible to include that interview data in the rewritten judgment, Ferreira's commentary attempts to rewrite Shabina's story—at least the version of her story that now, looking back, she tells—back into the case.

In addition to the careful deployment of facts, the language used by judges is also important for moving from the abstract to the particular, and emphasising the variety of childhood experiences. The contributors in this collection sought to achieve this in a number of ways. The first is simple: to give the child a name. Most powerfully, for Barbara Bennett Woodhouse in the rewritten *Roper* decision—where the child was already named in the original judgment—this meant referring to him by his forename (Christopher) rather than his surname (Simmons). This has a number of effects. First, it encourages the audience to humanise the young man convicted of a horrific, very violent crime. Second, it challenges the equality that is implied by the case title—*Roper v Simmons*—which suggests a legal dispute between two people with matching power. By refusing to use Simmons' surname and instead referring to him throughout as Christopher, Woodhouse highlights the power differential at play between the distant, omnipotent, state agent (embodied here by Roper, the superintendent of the Potsoi correctional centre, but representing more broadly the state and the criminal justice system) and this very real, quite damaged, young man, Christopher. The use of his forename also encourages us to see him as an embedded (in his family relationships—an important part of the story created about him), affective individual, who was vulnerable at the time of the offence; in contrast to the distancing effect created by the use of his surname. In short, using his first name humanises the teenager and allows the judge to draw on the concrete experiences of his life to highlight vulnerabilities and regrets which would seem less authentic and persuasive were his surname to be used.

Second, some contributors chose to confer a name on a child instead of an initial (as Gilmore does in *Re W* where 'J' becomes 'Jenny', a pseudonym). In many legal cases involving children, children are given only an initial in order to protect their identity. This is important for children's privacy, but it can also be de-personalising. Using a name instead, even a pseudonym, can serve to remind us that it is the life of a *real* child at stake. This is particularly useful when the proceedings are (in effect) test cases that focus on general legal principles or doctrines where it is especially easy for the court, and the wider audience, to forget the impact that the decision will have on actual children (see for example *JTB* which concerned the abolition of the common law defence of *doli incapax* and where Ray Arthur thus changed 'T' to 'Tim').

Thus, the narrative and employment of language within many of our judgments is directed at bringing alive the experiences of the child, helping to ensure that *other people's* (ie adults') narratives *about* children are disrupted, especially where those stories suit the needs of others rather than the children themselves. A children's rights judgment should therefore seek to understand and persuade from the child, not adult, perspective. In this way, the *crafting* of judgments—as well as the reasoning, outcomes and proceedings—can become a vehicle for the child's right to be heard and for recognising her as an active, rights-bearing agent.

VI. Speaking to Children: the Audience for a Children's Rights Judgment

All judgments are written with a potential audience in mind.[167] Judgment writing is thus a 'transactional'[168] process between judge and reader, where the judge attempts to persuade *that* specific audience of *this* particular outcome. The type of court and the nature of the litigation shape the audience that is uppermost in the judge's mind and this in turn affects the construction of the judgment. For example, a family court judge deciding a parental dispute over child arrangements following relationship breakdown may direct their judgment to the 'losing' parent (conscious that they need to accept the decision) or write it to be 'appeal proof' if the appeal court is their primary audience.[169] In contrast a senior court may write for lower courts (to provide good precedent), legal and other practitioners (to provide guidance),[170] the legislature (to secure the decision against amendment or to encourage legislative action[171]), the government (to ensure compliance not only with the decision but with the 'spirit' of it as well[172]), or the public (to get them on board with the social and political developments that may follow the decision).[173] And international courts will be mindful of the political implications of their decision, directing the judgment to the Member States not only as parties to the litigation but as political entities upon whose cooperation the existence of the legal system depends.[174]

For a *children's rights* judgment, judges must be cognisant of an additional audience: children themselves.[175] In some types of case—for example where an infant child is removed from her parents into care—a judge may carefully write the judgment knowing that, when the child is an adult, she is likely to have access to her files and to the decision, and she will read what was written about her and her family. In this scenario, the judge may write for the child as future adult. However, a children's rights judgment is also one that can be understood by children *during* childhood: a judgment written with children in mind—with language, a structure and a narrative that is accessible to and understood by them in a way similar to other child-friendly documents that (ideally) are available to children as they navigate the legal system.

A number of our judges have attempted to produce, at least partially, this type of judgment. Bridgeman, for example, has included a final paragraph specifically directed to the adopted child(ren) at the heart of the case; and Pillay, Freeman and Lundy have all included

---

[167]   Rackley, above n 6.

[168]   As Brooks and Gewirtz note, above n 154, at 3.

[169]   Both of these points were made during the project workshops by Sir Mark Hedley, retired High Court judge who sat on the project advisory board.

[170]   For example, doctors in refusal of treatment cases; or social workers in child protection cases.

[171]   See the rewritten decision in *RCB*.

[172]   See *R (HC) v Secretary of State for the Home Department* [2013] EWHC 982 (Admin).

[173]   For example, the US Supreme Court decision of *Brown v Board of Education* (the challenge to racial segregation in public schools).

[174]   See ch 2.

[175]   See Council of Europe, *Guidelines on Child Friendly Justice*, above n 5 at para 34 'Judgments and court rulings affecting children should be duly reasoned and explained to them in language that children can understand, particularly those decisions in which the child's views and opinions have not been followed'.

an abridged 'child-friendly' version of their judgment. The inclusion of a children's version of the judgment is—as far as we are aware—an innovation in judicial writing, and Pillay's employment of an overt storytelling approach (more pronounced than even the narrative in her primary judgment) serves to highlight the distance between 'normal' legal opinions and those written with children in mind.

Had word-count restrictions not constrained our judges they may well have gone even further in their 'child-friendly' versions and produced a full alternative. However, this would not be without its complications. Although the production of two versions of the same judgment is not unique in law—it happens in bilingual/multilingual jurisdictions such as Wales, Canada and the Council of Europe—it nonetheless requires a clear understanding of the legal status of each judgment, and which has primacy in the event of (unintended) contradiction between the two versions. That said, a child-friendly judgment is not, by its very nature, an attempt to replicate exactly the original decision (unlike a language translation); it will differ in significant and intended ways including the use of different words from the same language. But this raises its own problems. In common law jurisdictions, although we are used to disagreement on the *ratio* of a decision (particularly where the court does not produce a unanimous decision), it would be troubling if the source of such disagreement was an incompatibility between different versions of the *same* judicial opinion (particularly where it has precedential effect). It is highly unlikely therefore, that a child-friendly judgment that is additional to the original would carry the status of 'law'. This is clear from the *Grootboom* child-friendly judgment: it purposively lacks the detailed legal framework and analysis that Pillay's main judgment includes and, for that reason, no matter how much we may wish to develop 'child-friendly' versions of judgments it would be impossible to regard these as having the same status as the main judgment.

Abridged children's versions of judgments are especially valuable for younger children or those with lower capacities. For older, more competent children there are some types of case where the judge can write the *primary* judgment for them. Mr Justice Peter Jackson did just this in *Lancashire County Council v Mr A, Mr B, The Children* where he noted that 'This judgment is as short as possible so that the mother and the older children can follow it'.[176] In doing so, he deliberately used simple language and short sentences and paragraphs, and presumed no prior knowledge. Rather than diluting the reasoning or impact of the ruling, this approach positively enhanced it. Such clarity is of value to children but also to adults; it makes the law accessible to its citizens in compliance with basic rule of law principles. 'Child-friendly' judgments, therefore, are simply *good* judgments.

Yet child-friendly judgments do more than simply communicate effectively to affected children the outcome of the specific legal decision. By *speaking to* children, a children's rights judgment has a broader communicative value; it explicitly tells children—and adults—that the law recognises and treats them as rights-holders who are worthy of respect. Crucially, a judgment written *for* children achieves this even in cases where the substantive outcome of the decision overrides the child's wishes. In such a scenario, the court curtails the child's autonomy and it ostensibly communicates to her a message that she is not a full rights-holder; her version of the 'good life' is not one to be respected. But, the decision limits only

---

[176] *Lancashire County Council v Mr A, Mr B, The Children* [2016] EWFC 9.

one aspect of her autonomy—her self-determination. A 'child-friendly' judgment can none-theless develop (or at least try not to stymie) a child's capacity for another dimension of autonomy—her self-authorisation.[177] Self-authorisation captures the idea that autonomy includes regarding oneself as having equal moral worth to others and as being a legitimate source of reason; seeing one's life, choices, commitments and values as 'meaningful, worth-while and valuable'.[178] Anderson and Honneth call this (in the context of autonomy) 'self esteem'.[179] A judgment may, therefore, limit the child's self-determination but it can nonetheless help to develop or preserve autonomy as self-authorisation ('self esteem') where it explains to her, in ways she can understand and in ways that are theoretically sound,[180] why the decision was taken. This is of value for all litigants but it is especially important for children because *as a group*, in some circumstances, the law restricts their self-determination regardless of their capacity. This makes them uniquely vulnerable to suffering harm *also* to their self esteem; that they may stop regarding *themselves* as being of equal moral worth or as a legitimate source of reason. A child-friendly judgment thus helps to protect children's rights in this way too.

There are inevitably challenges with advocating and executing judgments that adopt a 'child-friendly' method of communication. Children are not a homogenous group; they have varying intellectual and emotional capabilities, and choices need to be made as to whether the rewritten judgment is pitched towards (say) a 15 year old or a 7 year old (or both). A judge will also have to be alive to ethical considerations including what to tell the child and when (especially in family law decisions, where the judge will be mindful of preserving that child's relationships with others). Nonetheless, there is instrumental and intrinsic value in judges writing versions of their judgments that can be regarded as 'child-friendly'. Once it is accepted that a judicial opinion does not simply pronounce the law but is also a storytelling device that (as Brooks and Gewirtz explain) reveals and shapes culture,[181] including the prevailing culture towards children and their rights, then it is necessary to think about the audience to whom the 'story' is being told[182] and to ensure that one of those audiences is children themselves.

VII. Concluding Comments

In this chapter we have attempted to identify and explore five markers of a children's rights judgment: (i) the utilisation to maximum effect of formal legal tools including the CRC; (ii) the use of scholarship to inform key concepts, tensions and presumptions; (iii) the endorse-ment of child-friendly procedures to maximise children's participation in legal processes;

---

[177] See MacKenzie, above n 106.
[178] ibid at 37.
[179] Anderson and Honneth, above n 10.
[180] For example, because she lacks the capacity for self-regulation or because it is seeking to develop her poten-tial. See the discussion earlier in this chapter on autonomy.
[181] Brooks and Gewirtz, above n 154 at 3.
[182] As Brooks and Gewirtz note, legal decision-making is 'transactional … not just a directive but an activity involving audiences as well as sovereign law givers', above n 154, at 3.

(iv) the centralisation of the child's voice and experience in the narrative of the judgment; and (v) the communication of the judgment in a child-friendly way. Each of these factors aims, to a greater or lesser extent, to increase the visibility of children within the law by ensuring their status as rights-holder is recognised, that their voices are heard, and their interests factored into judicial decision-making.

One of the underpinning claims of judgment-rewriting projects is that different judges, having heard the same facts and the same legal arguments, can nonetheless reason and (sometimes) conclude differently.[183] Indeed, Mark Hedley suggests that, ultimately, in the face of so many uncertainties, tensions and constraints, the modern judge can only strive for humility and confidence:

> Humility is essential once it is appreciated that the system is inherently fallible, and humility requires courage: the courage to acknowledge that, however hard we try and however conscientiously we apply ourselves, we are bound to get some cases wrong … The job can only be done with the human tools that we have.[184]

Embracing the components of a children's rights-based approach presented in this chapter certainly demands a degree of humility and courage: the humility to acknowledge that there may be a different and better way of adjudicating cases involving children; and the courage to depart from established conventions. Adding these components to the judicial toolbox, we argue, offers a sturdier foundation for judicial decision-making, thereby protecting children from the vagaries of individual, structural and constitutional factors that may otherwise produce wildly inconsistent, unpredictable and unfair outcomes for them. The judgments and commentaries presented in the remainder of this book illustrate how this can be achieved in practice.

---

[183] See again Hunter, McGlynn and Rackley, above n 6.
[184] M Hedley, *The Modern Judge: Power, Responsibility and Society's Expectations* (Bristol, Lexis Nexis, 2016) 28.

Part II

Children's Rights and Family Life

4

Commentary on
Re X and Y (Foreign Surrogacy)

EMMA WALMSLEY

I. Introduction

Re X and Y (Foreign Surrogacy),[1] a decision of Hedley J in the Family Division of the High Court, concerned a Parental Order which was made pursuant to section 30 of the Human Fertilisation and Embryology Act 1990 (HFEA 1990) in the context of an international surrogacy arrangement. In this case the arrangement resulted in the birth of twins to a married Ukrainian surrogate. The intended parents seeking the order were an English married couple, the surrogate having been implanted with embryos conceived with the intended father's sperm and eggs from an anonymous donor. The original and rewritten judgments expose major shortcomings with the laws regulating surrogacy in the UK, particularly for the rights of the child. This commentary compares the original and rewritten judgments to discover whether Bridgeman J's children's rights approach can resolve some of the difficulties caused by international surrogacy arrangements. The commentary also explores subsequent legislative amendments and case law and whether these changes have resulted in children's rights becoming more centralised in this context.

II. Background

Surrogacy is a rapidly developing and ethically controversial practice, which raises legal questions for children's rights, for example with reference to their nationality, identity and parentage. In the UK, the practice is currently regulated by the Surrogacy Arrangements Act 1985 (SA Act 1985), the Human Fertilisation and Embryology Act 2008[2] and the Human Fertilisation and Embryology (Parental Orders) Regulations 2010 no. 985. The HFEA 1990 was drafted following the publication of a White Paper: 'Human Fertilisation and

---

[1] *Re X and Y (Foreign Surrogacy)* [2008] EWHC 3030 (Fam), Hedley J, hereafter '*Re X and Y*'.

[2] S 54 HFEA 2008 amended s 30 HFEA 1990. The other parenthood provisions of the 1990 Act remain in force in relation to determining motherhood and fatherhood.

Embryology: A Framework for Legislation' in 1987.[3] The HFEA 1990 'introduced a more positive recognition of surrogacy' than the SA Act 1985:[4] intended parents were allowed to formalise their relationship with their children through the award of a Parental Order which provided an alternative to adoption for some intended parents. The effect of a Parental Order is to confer joint and equal legal parenthood and parental responsibility upon the intended parents whilst fully extinguishing the parental status of the surrogate.[5] This ensures 'each child's security and identity as lifelong members of the applicants' family.'[6] At the time of *Re X and Y*, the Parental Order Regulations 1994[7] were in force, which meant the child's welfare was the court's 'first consideration'. Following the 2010 Regulations, which imported section 1 of the Adoption and Children Act 2002 (ACA 2002) into section 54 Parental Order applications,

> welfare is no longer merely the court's first consideration but becomes its paramount consideration ... it will only be in the clearest case of the abuse of public policy that the court will be able to withhold an order if otherwise welfare considerations support its making.[8]

Re X and Y exposes how some of the provisions in sections 27–30 HFEA 1990 are incompatible with children's rights. When the twins were born, the Ukrainian surrogate was recognised by the law in England and Wales as the legal mother of the children.[9] Moreover, her husband was recognised as the children's legal father.[10] However, under Ukrainian law neither the surrogate nor her husband had legal responsibility for the twins once they had been born.[11] This meant the children were 'marooned stateless and parentless' with no right to remain in the Ukraine and no right to enter the UK.[12] The same issue has arisen in subsequent cases.[13] In the rewritten judgment Bridgeman J proposes 'an international response such as with the conventions on inter-country adoption and international child abduction.'[14] This commentator supports the solution proposed by Kirsty Horsey to pre-authorise Parental Orders before the child is born 'so that legal parenthood is conferred on intended parents at birth.'[15] In order to protect the child, a Parental Order reporter from CAFCASS could still visit the family after the child is born, as it currently does, to confirm that the award of a Parental Order is justified.[16]

In *Re X and Y,* the children were given permission to enter into the UK once the intended parents had satisfied the UK immigration authorities that the intended father was related

[3] Cm 259 (London, HMSO).
[4] K Horsey and S Sheldon, 'Still Hazy After All These Years?' (2012) 20 *Medical Law Review* 67–89, 70.
[5] *J v G* [2013] EWHC 1432 (Fam) [27].
[6] ibid.
[7] Parental Orders (Human Fertilisation and Embryology) Regs 1994 (SI No 2767) Sch 1(1)(a).
[8] *Re L (A Child) (Parental Order: Foreign Surrogacy)* [2010] EWHC 3146 (Fam) [5], [9]–[10] (Hedley J).
[9] S 27 (1) HFEA 1990.
[10] S 28 HFEA 1990 recognises the common law presumption of legitimacy whereby the child is treated as the legitimate child of the parties to a marriage.
[11] Above n 1 [8] (Hedley J).
[12] ibid [10] (Hedley J).
[13] *Re: IJ (A Child)* [2011] EWHC 921 (Fam); *AB V DE* [2013] EWHC 2413 (Fam).
[14] Rewritten judgment [10] (Bridgeman J).
[15] K Horsey, *Surrogacy in the UK: Myth Busting and Reform. Report of the Surrogacy UK Working Group on Surrogacy Law Reform* (November 2015), available at www.kent.ac.uk/law/research/projects/current/surrogacy/Surrogacy%20in%20the%20UK%20Report%20FINAL.pdf.
[16] It is acknowledged that this could leave the surrogate in a vulnerable position as she would need to consent to the Parental Order before the child is born.

to the twins.[17] The intended parents then sought to regularise their status as parents of the children by applying for a Parental Order. Although neither the original nor rewritten judgments mention this, an adoption order would have been inappropriate given the bio-logical connection between the twins and the intended father. The importance of awarding a Parental Order (compared to an adoption order) was stated in *Re X (A Child) (Surrogacy: Time limit)*:[18]

> A parental order presents the optimum legal and psychological solution for X and is preferable to an adoption order because it confirms the important legal, practical and psychological reality of X's identity; the commissioning father is his biological father and all parties intended from the outset that the commissioning parents should be his legal parents.[19]

As noted in the rewritten judgment, despite the importance of a Parental Order for the child's welfare, current law does not compel intended parents to apply for an order.[20] Con-sequently, where the intended parents do not apply for an order there will be no opportu-nity for a court to create a legal relationship between the child and the parents. Fortunately, in this case the intended parents did apply for an order and both judgments were able to award a Parental Order for each of the twins respectively, having found that the conditions in section 30 HFEA 1990 had been satisfied. A number of the conditions for the making of a Parental Order were uncontentious. As required by section 30(1) both applicants were law-fully married to each other and the husband's sperm was used. Section 30(2) provides for a non-extendable time limit for issuing the application, of six months from the date of the child's birth. This provision had been complied with in this case. Nevertheless, as Hedley J observed, 'this requirement may especially cause problems where immigration issues have led to delay.'[21] The applicants were also domiciled in England and Wales and the children had their home with them, as required by section 30(3). Both applicants were aged over 18 (as provided by section 30(4)) and the surrogate's consent was given 'not less than six weeks' after the birth (thus fulfilling section 30(6)). The legal issues in the case centred on the interpretation to be given to section 30(5) and (7).

III. A Comparison of the Original and Rewritten Judgment

The first condition that required closer analysis by Hedley J and Bridgeman J was section 30(5) HFEA 1990: 'The Court must be satisfied that both the father of the child … and the woman who carried the child have freely, and with full understanding of what is involved, agreed unconditionally to the making of the order.' Hedley J found that the Ukrainian sur-rogate had given the requisite consent. The intended parents argued that although the sur-rogate's husband had given consent, it was not required as a matter of law because section 28(2) should not be applied extra-territorially.[22] Hedley J did not accept this and found

[17] Above n 1 [10] (Hedley J).
[18] *Re X (A Child) (Surrogacy: Time limit)* [2014] EWHC 3135 (Fam).
[19] ibid [7].
[20] Rewritten judgment [33] (Bridgeman J).
[21] Above n 1 [12] (Hedley J).
[22] ibid [14] (Hedley J).

that Parliament cannot be taken to have had any different intention in relation to husbands of foreign domicile.[23] By contrast, the rewritten judgment criticises the provision which allows the surrogate's husband to 'withhold consent and prevent a parental order being granted … whilst the laws of his own country relieve him of any responsibility for the children.'[24] Bridgeman J laments that this is yet 'another way in which the current law fails to protect the rights of children who are born in such circumstances.'[25] The rewritten judgment explains that there is nothing to suggest Parliament has even considered whether the law should apply extra-territorially, thereby implying that the issue needs to be examined.

The second requirement that needed closer examination was section 30(7) HFEA 1990: 'The court must be satisfied that no money or other benefit (other than for expenses reasonably incurred) has been given or received by the husband or wife … unless authorised by the court.' Hedley J and Bridgeman J agreed that the sums paid significantly exceeded 'expenses reasonably incurred',[26] but both applied Wall J (as he then was) in *Re C (Application by Mr and Mrs X under Section 30 of the Human Fertilisation and Embryology Act 1990)*[27] to conclude that 'retrospective authorisation was legally possible.'[28]

In the original judgment Hedley J weighed up the competing policy considerations: (I) commercial surrogacy is undesirable and (II) a Parental Order is in the long term best interests of the child. On the facts of the case Hedley J had 'no doubt that the applicants were acting in good faith and that no advantage was taken (or sought to be taken) of the surrogate mother who was herself a woman of mature discretion.'[29]   Therefore, he was able to authorise the payments and make a Parental Order. Nevertheless, Hedley J noted his unhappiness with the process of authorisation which required the court to balance 'two competing and potentially irreconcilably conflicting concepts.'[30]

> It is also almost impossible to imagine a set of circumstances in which … the welfare of any child (particularly a foreign child) would not be gravely compromised (at the very least) by a refusal to make an order.[31]

In other words, public policy concerns with commercial surrogacy will rarely trump the best interests of the child, even where more than reasonable expenses are involved. Both the original and rewritten judgments conclude with some criticisms of the law. In the original judgment Hedley J warns of the obvious difficulties of inconvenience, delay, hardship and expense[32] of international surrogacy. Conflicts of law issues and serious immigration problems are also anticipated.[33] In the rewritten judgment, Bridgeman J also reflects upon these problems.[34]

---

[23] ibid [16] (Hedley J).
[24] Rewritten judgment [22] (Bridgeman J).
[25] ibid [22] (Bridgeman J).
[26] ibid [24] (Bridgeman J) and above n 1 [18] (Hedley J).
[27] *Re C (Application by Mr and Mrs X under Section 30 of the Human Fertilisation and Embryology Act 1990)* [2002] 1 FLR 909.
[28] Rewritten judgment [24] (Bridgeman J) and above n 1 [19] (Hedley J).
[29] ibid [21] (Hedley J).
[30] ibid [24] (Hedley J).
[31] ibid.
[32] ibid [26] (Hedley J).
[33] ibid.
[34] Rewritten judgment [33] (Bridgeman J).

A. The Rewritten Judgment: Maximising the ECHR and UNCRC

Although the original and rewritten judgments reach the same conclusion and award a Parental Order, the latter adopts a more 'substantive children's rights approach'[35] by engaging with European sources of law, and with the United Nations Convention on the Rights of the Child (CRC) which the UK ratified in 1991. According to Bridgeman J, 'European and international law makes us now much more attuned to the rights of children than we were in the twentieth century.'[36] Bridgeman J interprets the twins' Article 8 European Convention on Human Rights (ECHR) right to respect for private and family life using Articles 3, 7 and 8 CRC and concludes that the HFEA 1990 'fails to fulfil our international obligations to safeguard and promote these rights.'[37]

The rewritten judgment uses Article 3 of the CRC to show that courts and legislative bodies must have the best interests of the twins as a 'primary consideration.'[38] By contrast, Hedley J was unable to say that the children's welfare was a 'primary' concern, 'given that there is a wholly valid public policy justification lying behind Section 30(7)',[39] that being the undesirability of commercial surrogacy arrangements. In this respect, the rewritten judgment interprets section 30 more purposively than the original to protect the twin's best interests. Bridgeman J again departs from the original judgment in her engagement with Article 7 of the CRC, which states that every child has a right to be 'registered immediately after birth and shall have the right from birth to a name, the right to acquire a nationality and, as far as possible, the right to know and be cared for by his or her parents'. Clearly, this could be violated where a child is 'marooned stateless' and the UK couple has no right to remain in the foreign jurisdiction.

Furthermore, Article 8 of the CRC, which stipulates that the State has a duty to 'respect the right of the child to preserve his or her identity, including nationality, name and family relations as recognised by law without lawful interference' is used by Bridgeman J to engage with the importance of the intended parents providing their children with information about their origins. This issue is one the original judgment does not engage with. Bridgeman J credits the surrogate as an important figure for the child and their identity, and envisages circumstances where the surrogate can be involved in the child's life: 'It goes without saying that all of us find our lives enriched by healthy relationships, of differing degrees of care and affection, with a wide variety of people.'[40] The rewritten judgment rightly encourages 'full, evidenced, examination and debate' about the complex questions of origin and identity that arise for children born following lawful surrogacy arrangements including 'whether the children's right to respect for a family life includes legal recognition of the place of the surrogate in their family.'[41] In British Columbia for instance, surrogates can be registered on the child's birth certificate alongside the intended parents, providing the

---

[35] J Tobin, 'Judging The Judges: Are They Adopting The Rights Approach In Matters Involving Children?' (2009) 33(2) *Melbourne University Law Review* 579–625.

[36] Rewritten judgment [32] (Bridgeman J).

[37] ibid [27] (Bridgeman J).

[38] ibid [25] (Bridgeman J).

[39] Above n 1 [20] (Hedley J).

[40] ibid [30] (Bridgeman J).

[41] ibid [30] (Bridgeman J).

parties agree beforehand.[42] This approach, which recognises the surrogate's gestational, epigenetic and sometimes genetic ties with the child, is something policy-makers need to look at in the UK.

The main difference between the two judgments is that Bridgeman J undertakes a purposive interpretation of the Parental Order requirements. She relies on section 3 of the Human Rights Act 1998, 'which requires the court to have regard to the intention of Parliament when considering the interpretation of legislation and to adopt any possible construction of legislation compatible with and upholding convention rights.'[43] Interestingly, Bridgeman J talks to the twins directly at the end of her judgment, with the view that they will read the decision one day.[44] This reinforces the children's rights approach that positions the twins at the centre of her decision.

IV. Legal Developments since *Re X And Y (Foreign Surrogacy)*

Since the original judgment, the HFEA 1990 has been amended by the HFEA 2008. Nevertheless, the Parental Order requirements have remained largely unchanged.[45] As a result of the Parental Order Regulations 2010, the courts have read section 54 HFEA 2008 permissively to protect the best interests of the child. By contrast to *Re X and Y (Foreign Surrogacy)*, where Hedley J described the six month limit as 'non-extendable',[46] Munby P read down section 54(3) in *Re X (A Child) (Surrogacy: Time limit)*[47] on the basis that 'given the transcendental importance of a parental order, with its consequences stretching many, many decades into the future' Parliament cannot have intended the difference between six months and six months and one day to be determinative.[48] He found that even if the statute could not be interpreted in this manner, his conclusions could be justified by the requirements of Article 8 of the ECHR. Relying on Theis J in *A v P*[49] Munby P found that the HFEA 2008 must be read down to ensure the child's right to identity, which could only be protected through the making of a Parental Order.[50] The case law is also increasingly taking a permissive approach to section 54(8) in international commercial surrogacy cases, by awarding a Parental Order even where payments have exceeded reasonable expenses.[51]

More recently, the courts have reached their limit in reading down section 54. In *Re Z*[52] the High Court issued a declaration of incompatibility in respect of section 54(1) HFEA 2008, which precludes single parents from applying for a Parental Order. Unlike Bridgeman J's rigorous evaluation of the twins' rights under the CRC and ECHR, Munby P did not

---

[42] P Gerber and P Irving Lindner, 'Birth Certificates for Children with Same-Sex Parents: A Reflection of Biology or Something More?' (2015) 18 (2) *New York University Journal of Legislation and Public Policy* 225–76, 271.

[43] Rewritten judgment [28] (Bridgeman J).

[44] ibid [35] (Bridgeman J).

[45] The only significant change was to allow unmarried and same-sex couples to apply for a Parental Order.

[46] Above n 1 [12] (Hedley J).

[47] *Re X (A Child) (Surrogacy: Time limit)* [2014] EWHC 3135 (Fam).

[48] ibid [55] (Munby P).

[49] *A v P (Surrogacy: Parental Order: Death of Applicant)* [2011] EWHC 1738 (Fam), [2012] 2 FLR 145.

[50] Above n 47 [58] (Munby P).

[51] *J v G* [2013] EWHC 1432 (Fam); *Re C (Parental Order)* [2013] EWHC 2413 (Fam).

[52] *In the matter of Z (A Child) (No 2)* [2016] EWHC 1191 (Fam).

utilise these instruments. In particular, the judgment does not acknowledge that the child, Z, was discriminated against because he was born to a single parent.[53] Instead, Munby J couches the judgment in the intended father's rights to respect for private and family life under Articles 8 and 14 of the ECHR.

The focus on the adult's rights rather than Z's, does not sit easily with the European Court of Human Rights' (ECtHR) approach in *Mennesson v France*.[54] In that case, France refused to register the intended parents as the twins' legal parents because the children were born as a result of a commercial surrogacy arrangement in California. The ECtHR unanimously held there had been no violation of the intended parent's Article 8 right.[55] However, the refusal to recognise the parent-child relationship left the children in a state of 'legal uncertainty' and undermined their identity within French society.[56] Therefore, the ECtHR concluded that the children's (but not the parent's) Article 8 right was violated. Although the decision is more child-centred than *Re Z*, it is questionable whether the parent's Article 8 right should have been disentangled from that of the twins. As Herring argues, 'it is impossible to construct an approach to looking at a child's welfare which ignores the web of relationships within which the child is brought up.'[57] Moreover, because supporting the child also means supporting their care-giver,[58] a truly child-centred 'relational' approach would have found that the parent's Article 8 right, in *Mennesson*, had also been violated. The declaration of incompatibility in *Re Z* is likely to catalyse much needed engagement with these children's rights issues by Parliament.

V. Conclusion

The courts' increasingly permissive interpretation of section 54 may provide some relief from the effects of international arrangements. However, in order to centralise children's rights new surrogacy legislation is required. Unsurprisingly, there is increasing pressure for the law to change.[59] First, the motherhood and fatherhood provisions need to be re-examined because it is not necessarily in the best interests of the child for the surrogate and her spouse or civil partner to be the child's legal parents. Second, the entirety of section 54 HFEA 2008 requires reconsideration. Third, Parliament needs to consider how to regulate international commercial surrogacy and how best to resolve the conflicts of law that arise. The rewritten judgment offers an insight into how a children's rights interpretation of the rights to identity, nationality and respect for private and family life, within the CRC and the ECHR, can guide law reform in this area. As both the original and rewritten judgments emphasise, it is now up to Parliament to reform the law and ensure children's rights are at the centre of surrogacy law in the UK. The declaration of incompatibility issued in *Re Z* could now provide the catalyst for this process.

[53] Art 2 CRC.
[54] *Mennesson v France* (Application no 65192/11).
[55] ibid [102].
[56] ibid [97].
[57] J Herring, 'Farewell Welfare?' (2005) 27(2) *Journal of Social Welfare and Family Law* 159–71, 166.
[58] ibid.
[59] Above n 15. See also, C Fenton-Glynn, 'The Regulation and Recognition of Surrogacy under English Law: An Overview of the Case-law' (2015) 27 *Child and Family Law Quarterly* 83–96.

Family Division of the High Court (England and Wales)

Re X and Y (Foreign Surrogacy)

Bridgeman J:

This judgment, consisting of 35 paragraphs, is being handed down in public on 9 December 2008 and has been signed and dated, and I hereby give leave for it to be reported.

The judgment is being distributed on the strict understanding that in any report no person other than the advocates or the solicitors instructing them (and other persons identified by name in the judgment itself) may be identified by name or location and that in particular the anonymity of the children and the adult members of their family must be strictly preserved.

1.   X and Y are twin baby girls who are the subject of an application for a Parental Order pursuant to section 30 of the Human Fertilisation and Embryology Act 1990 (HFEA 1990). They are much cherished and loved by the applicants (whom I shall refer to as 'Mr W and Mrs W'). Mr and Mrs W, with other routes to parenthood exhausted, entered into an international surrogacy arrangement with a Ukrainian surrogate who then conceived X and Y in IVF treatment using donor eggs and the sperm of Mr W. Until this court made the Parental Order sought by Mr and Mrs W in respect of X and Y these children were, as a result of the application of the laws of the Ukraine and England and Wales, parentless and stateless. This is the first application to come before the courts of England and Wales arising from an arrangement entered into by a British couple and a surrogate abroad. As such, it serves to highlight the extent to which the current statutory provisions fail to address the welfare, interests and rights of children born as a consequence of surrogacy arrangements.

2.   Whilst Mr and Mrs W took all possible steps to secure reliable legal advice, such is hard to come by as a consequence of the prohibition upon the commercial negotiation of surrogacy arrangements in the current law which I outline later in my judgment. The couple entered into an arrangement with a married Ukrainian woman who was offering to carry a child as a surrogate for another. Terms were agreed, to which I shall return, as they are central to the question whether the current law permitted me to make the order with respect to X and Y that Mr and Mrs W sought. Under Ukrainian law, once the Ukrainian surrogate had delivered the babies to the couple, neither the Ukrainian surrogate nor her husband had any rights, duties, powers, authority or responsibilities with respect to the children. Indeed, it may be the case that under Ukrainian law the agreement was enforceable and

they could have been compelled to complete the bargain. Happily, in this instance, the adult parties have all been true to their word so the court is not concerned with a dispute between the adults involved over their parental rights and responsibilities. This is not a case of legal problems caused by deception or change of heart on the part of the surrogate mother (as in the matter of *N (a Child)* [2007] EWCA Civ 1053; *W v H (Child Abduction: Surrogacy)* [2002] 1 FLR 1008). It is the laws of England and Wales together with those of their country of origin, the Ukraine, that made these much loved babies, created by a partnership of five adults, legal orphans.

3.   The Ukrainian surrogate and her husband have no responsibilities towards the babies to whom she gave birth, but neither does the Ukrainian State other than those of basic humanity such as placing the child in basic institutional care. Alarmingly, for a short while, State care of the babies was a genuine prospect given that Mr and Mrs W had no right to remain in the Ukraine once their temporary visa expired. X and Y are not Ukrainian citizens. They have no right to reside in the Ukraine. Under Ukrainian law, Mr and Mrs W are registered as parents on the babies' birth certificates and are their parents. Under Ukrainian law the girls are British nationals. Under English law they are not. Thus, the babies were not only rendered legal orphans they were also stateless. Abandoned by Ukraine law and not embraced by English law. Mr and Mrs W had no right to bring X and Y home, unless possibly Mr W could have sought leave to do so as putative father or relative of his biological children.

4.   A small dose of common sense and humanity prevailed. DNA tests enabled Mr W to establish that he was the biological father of X and Y and the couple were given discretionary leave to enter in order to apply for a Parental Order. It requires little imagination to appreciate the unsettled start to these babies' lives. They are in the loving care of the couple who, in addition to the challenges of first-time parenting of twin babies, have had to deal with an extended stay in Ukraine away from their wider family, in the face of uncertainty over their ability to bring the babies home, arranging DNA testing, fearing whether they had complied with the law and the unknown consequences of having failed to do so.

5.   With the babies in the care of the couple, interim orders were made under section 8 of the Children Act 1989 to enable them to continue to care for and take responsibility for the babies, pending a decision of this court.

6.   In these proceedings, X and Y are represented by the Guardian, who is also the Parental Order Reporter. It is fortuitous that representation of the interests of X and Y has been secured. X and Y are not passive objects of adult choices nor property to be allocated. They are individuals with rights and interests which the law must protect; rights to be loved, cared for, nurtured, rights to an identity, to relationships, to a home, to be protected from harm (Michael DA Freeman, 'Taking Children's Rights More Seriously' (1992) 6 *International Journal of Law and the Family* 52–71, 56). Through these proceedings we have been able to assure the protection of the interests and rights of these two baby girls.

7.   On 5 November 2008 I made the Parental Order sought with respect to X and Y, pursuant to section 30 of the Human Fertilisation and Embryology Act (HFEA 1990). The two issues to be determined before I could make the order were, first, whether the consent of the surrogate's husband was required and, secondly, whether I could retrospectively authorise the expenses paid to the surrogate.

8.   Whilst of fundamental importance to X, Y, Mr and Mrs W, as the first case of an agreement between a British couple and a surrogate overseas to reach the courts, the issues raised are of wider significance. Given the importance of the issues raised by this case for the protection of the rights and interests of children born as a consequence of international surrogacy arrangements, I reserved my reasons to be handed down in writing in this judgment. English law renders surrogacy arrangements unenforceable (section 36 HFEA 1990). In the modern world, however, technology makes it easy to find advertised services overseas and international travel is common place such that the practice of surrogacy will continue and no doubt grow. Across the world there is a range of legislative approaches to the regulation of surrogacy: nations where there is no regulation and others where surrogacy is prohibited. Those who travel abroad to enter into a surrogacy arrangement have to comply with the laws of both the United Kingdom and those of their destination country. Children born as a consequence of such international agreements will be subject to two legal systems which may be incompatible or inconsistent, with alarming consequences for the children who are born and their families.

9.   The law of England and Wales, found in the Surrogacy Arrangements Act 1985 (the 1985 Act) seeks to prevent domestic commercial surrogacy arrangements. Broadly based upon the proposals of the Warnock Committee (Warnock Report, *Report of the Committee of Inquiry into Human Fertilisation and Embryology*, Cmnd 9314, (1984)), the Act was introduced as a panicked response to the birth of Baby Cotton (*Re C (A Minor) (Wardship)* [1985] FLR 846). The primary policy concerns of the legislation are to protect children from commodification and surrogate mothers from exploitation. Critical comment upon the practice of surrogacy often refers to the vulnerabilities of the participants. Here, it is the outmoded state of the current law, which has failed to grapple with the issues of international surrogacy, which placed Mr and Mrs W, X and Y into an uncertain legal, and hence, vulnerable position. We must not permit the rights of children to fall from view by focusing upon the enormous difficulties which the law has caused to this couple despite their best efforts to ascertain their legal obligations and comply with them.

10.   Whilst criminalising commercial arrangements, the law does not prevent couples from entering into unenforceable surrogacy arrangements. Babies, the Warnock Committee emphasised, should not be born 'subject to the taint of criminality' (Warnock Report, *Report of the Committee of Inquiry into Human Fertilisation and Embryology*, Cmnd 9314, (1984), 8.19); after all, the birth of a much loved baby, when all other avenues to parenthood have been exhausted, is to be celebrated. It is not a cause for criminalisation. However, drafters of the reactive 1985 Act thought that the legislation would discourage surrogacy, limiting its occurrence to altruistic agreements made between friends, siblings or other relatives with the consequence that 'the phenomenon of surrogacy [would] go away' (as explained by Michael Freeman, 'After Warnock—Whither the Law?' [1986] *Current Legal Problems* 33, 46). Instead, the practice has grown by crossing national borders. Surrogacy is an ethically controversial practice; international surrogacy raises further complex ethical issues which have not been exposed to full scrutiny or debate. Without meaning to question the integrity of couples who, after trying all the alternatives, find themselves denied the children they so desperately want to love and care for, judges are currently being placed in the difficult position of trying to reconcile implementation of the policy of legislation whilst also fulfilling our duties to protect the interests, welfare and rights of children

born through surrogacy arrangements. Thus judges are being asked to protect children that it was envisaged would, as a result of the legislation, rarely exist, or not exist at all. If international surrogacy is to be an acceptable road to parenthood, a matter upon which I express no view, it seems to me unarguable that the full range of issues needs to be subjected to rigorous examination and debate. It may be that a solution demands an international response such as with the conventions on inter-country adoption and international child abduction. That prospect does not diminish our responsibility to our nation's children.

11.   X and Y have legal rights. Notably they each have a right to respect for their private and family life, as protected by Article 8 of the European Convention for the Protection of Human Rights and Fundamental Freedoms (ECHR), within Schedule 1 to the Human Rights Act 1998. In addition, in 1991, the UK ratified the United Nations Convention on the Rights of the Child (UNCRC) and courts must interpret ECHR rights in harmony with its key principles. While provisions of the UNCRC are not directly incorporated into English law and consequently not enforceable, I bear in mind throughout this judgment the rights therein to nationality (Article 7), to identity (Article 8) and to consider the best interests of these children as a primary consideration (Article 3). The state through this court thus has obligations to these children when deciding the legal relationships which X and Y will have.

12.   The effect of section 27 of the HFEA 1990 is clear. Under English law, at birth and until the making of the Parental Order, the Ukrainian surrogate was the mother of X and Y. Mrs W is not biologically related to the children; she was not their legal mother pursuant to section 27. At that time, and until the making of the Parental Order, Mrs W was not the children's legal mother although she was (and still is) their social and psychological mother.

13.   Who is the father of the twins is determined by section 28 of the HFEA 1990. The Guardian contends that, as the Ukrainian surrogate was married and her husband agreed to the arrangement, the effect of sections 28(2) and (4) was to make the Ukrainian surrogate's husband the father of the children. Miss Lucy Theis QC, on behalf of Mr and Mrs W, argued that these subsections should not be applied extra-territorially and, consequently, Mr W, as biological father, is a legal parent of X and Y.

14.   Sections 27 and 28 of the HFEA 1990 are, however, directed at the parental status of adults undergoing fertility treatment without the additional involvement of a surrogate mother gestating the children. The HFE Bill initially addressed surrogacy only to specify that surrogacy arrangements are unenforceable (which became section 36). A further provision was inserted late into the Bill as a consequence of a complaint by a couple to their MP that they were required to adopt their 'own' child born following a surrogacy arrangement. Section 30 was introduced into the law to permit adults commissioning a surrogacy arrangement to secure the status as parents of any children born in such arrangements. The detailed requirements, which must be fulfilled before the court can make a Section 30 Parental Order, are considered below, taking each, as it applies here, in turn.

15.   The applicants are, as they are required by section 30(1) to be, a married couple.

16.   As proven by the DNA test performed to establish paternity before leave was given for the babies to be brought into the country, Mr W is the biological father of X and Y, as required by section 30(1)(b). If he were not, I could not make a Parental Order even if to do so were, as in this case, manifestly in the interests of the children.

17.   Mr and Mrs W have made the application within six months of birth of X and Y, (section 30(2)).

18.   Mr and Mrs W are domiciled in England and Wales and the temporary leave they have been given has enabled X and Y to have their home with them here, as required by section 30(3).

19.   Mr and Mrs W are both over the age of 18, thus fulfilling section 30(4).

20.   The consent of the Ukrainian surrogate was given six weeks and thus not 'less than six weeks' after the birth of X and Y, thus complying with sections 30(5) and (6).

21.   Thus the majority of the requirements of section 30 are fulfilled in this case. The first issue which remains to be determined is the matter of the consent from the surrogate's husband. Section 30(5) provides as follows:

> The Court must be satisfied that both the father of the child (including a person who is the father by virtue of Section 28 of this Act), where he is not the husband, and the woman who carried the child have freely, and with full understanding of what is involved, agreed unconditionally to the making of the order.

Who, then, in law is the father of the children? That is for this court to determine by application of the provisions of the HFEA 1990, noted above. There is nothing to suggest that Parliament intended the law to apply differently to husbands of surrogates who are of foreign domicile. Indeed, there is nothing to suggest that it even considered the issue.

22.   The plain meaning of the provisions of the HFEA 1990 is that the Ukrainian surrogate's husband is the legal father of the babies. In a case such as this, the law thus permits the surrogate's husband to withhold consent and prevent a parental order being granted to a commissioning couple who wish to take responsibility and care for a child born into a surrogacy arrangement, whilst the laws of his own country relieve him of any responsibility for the children. This is another way in which the current law fails to protect the rights of children who are born in such circumstances. Happily, both the Ukrainian surrogate and her husband have given their consent to the making of an order. The state of the law thus perchance presents no obstacle to the protection of the interests of these babies.

23.   The question is whether the obstacle provided by section 30(7) does so. Section 30(7) provides:

> The court must be satisfied that no money or other benefit (other than for expenses reasonably incurred) has been given or received by the husband or wife for or in consideration of—
>
> (a)   the making of this order,
> (b)   any agreement required by subsection (5) above,
> (c)   the handing over of the child to the husband and the wife or
> (d)   the making of any arrangements with a view to the making of the order unless authorised by the court.

24.   I do not need to go into the detail of the payments agreed between the couple and the Ukrainian surrogate, other than to state that, whilst recognising that the Ukrainian surrogate incurred expenses as a consequence of the pregnancy, the sums paid were significant amounts exceeding reasonable expenses. Therefore, the court must authorise

these payments if a parental order is to be made conferring the legal status as parents upon Mr and Mrs W. This is not a new issue for the courts arising only as a consequence of the international nature of the agreement. The courts have been faced with this issue on a number of previous occasions. The case law permits me to give retrospective authorisation to payments which go beyond reasonable expenses (*Re C (Application by Mr and Mrs X under Section 30 of the Human Fertilisation and Embryology Act 1990)* [2002] 1 FLR 909; *Re Q (Parental Order)* [1996] 1 FLR 369; *Re Adoption Application (Payment for Adoption)* [1987] 3 WLR 31). The Surrogacy Arrangements Act 1985 sought to prohibit commercial surrogacy in which organisations profited but did not prohibit informal arrangements in which reasonable expenses were paid. Section 30(7) envisages that payments may have been made which exceed reasonable expenses but that the requirement for authorisation by the court will prevent those who enter into such agreements from arrangements exploitative of either the commissioning couple or the surrogate.

25.   Regulations require me to place as my first consideration the 'need to safeguard and promote the welfare of the child' (Parental Orders (Human Fertilisation and Embryology) Regulations 1994, (SI No 2767), Sch 1(1)(a)). Article 3 of the UNCRC goes further to provide that with respect to all actions concerning children undertaken by social welfare institutions, courts, administrative authorities or legislative bodies, the best interests of the child is a 'primary consideration'. The Parental Order Reporter informed the court of the couple's commitment to the children with whom they have bonded, their parenting capacities and appreciation for the long term well-being of the children and of the importance of being open about their genetic and gestational origins. The lifelong welfare of the babies so very clearly rests in the loving care of Mr and Mrs W.

26.   It is important to respect the children's rights under the ECHR, including the Article 8 right to respect for a private and family life. X and Y are siblings. X and Y have a family life with Mr and Mrs W; they are biologically related to Mr W. If an order is not made, the fact of that family life will be interfered with as it will not be recognised in law. If an order is not made X and Y will have no legal connection with anyone (except each other). Article 8 imposes a positive obligation upon the State to ensure that de facto relationships are recognised and protected by law (*Marckx v Belgium* (1979–80) 2 EHRR 330, [31]). In circumstances such as these it is a Parental Order which transforms the factual relationship between X and Y and Mr and Mrs W into a legal relationship. A Parental Order will not only ensure that the rights and responsibilities to make decisions about the upbringing of X and Y will rest with their intended parents who have, since birth, taken loving care of them; importantly, it will give to X and Y the security of lifelong belonging in relationship with each other in their family unit. For that reason, the alternatives within the Children Act 1989 of a residence order or special guardianship order, both of which would confer parental responsibility upon Mr and Mrs W but not the legal status as parents, fail to protect the rights of X and Y.

27.   But that is not the end of the matter. I must also have regard to the principles of the UNCRC in my interpretation of Article 8 of the ECHR. Under Article 7 of the UNCRC every child has a right to be 'registered immediately after birth and shall have the right from birth to a name, the right to acquire a nationality and, as far as possible, the right to know and be cared for by his or her parents.' Under Article 8 of the UNCRC the state has a duty to 'respect the right of the child to preserve his or her identity, including nationality, name

and family relations as recognised by law without lawful interference.' In my judgment, the current law does not fulfil these international obligations. However, recognising that as a guiding principle of the UNCRC, Article 3 requires the interpretation of all of the Convention rights in accordance with the best interests of the child, in my judgment the starting point must be to identify the legal parents of X and Y. Mr W is, as noted above, the genetic father of X and Y. Together Mr and Mrs W are their social and psychological parents. It is these latter relationships which are key to the current and future wellbeing of these children and which should be given legal recognition.

28.   As noted at the beginning of my judgment, the children enjoy the protection of their legal rights by virtue of the Human Rights Act 1998 (HRA 1998). Legislation must be read in such a way as to give effect to the provisions of the Human Rights Act 1998 and section 3 of the HRA 1998 requires this court to have regard to the intention of Parliament when considering the interpretation of legislation and furthermore to adopt any possible construction of legislation compatible with and upholding convention rights (*R v A* [2001] UKHL 25 [44]; *Ghaidan v Godin-Mendoza* [2004] UKHL 30 [41–51]). The primary purpose of section 30 is to enable couples who enter into a surrogacy agreement to become the legal parents of the child so that they do not have to adopt the child to whom one or both of them are genetically related (*Re W (Minors)(Surrogacy)* [1991] 1 FLR 385).

29.   Reading Article 8 of the ECHR and Articles 3, 7 and 8 of the UNCRC in order to give a purposive interpretation to section 30 led me to the conclusion that the law should recognise the relationship between X and Y and Mr and Mrs W. Therefore on 5 November I authorised the payment made to the Ukrainian surrogate and made the Parental Order sought. The babies now have legal parents. The couple can now apply for them to have British citizenship.

30.   As noted above, X and Y have their family life with Mr and Mrs W who, as a consequence of the Parental Order, are now their legal parents. But Article 8 of the ECHR requires States to respect not only family life but also private life, including identity. Article 8 of the UNCRC, as noted above, places obligations upon the State to 'respect the right of the child to preserve his or her identity'. Identity is a complex concept which is not defined in law. Samantha Besson has argued that the 'right to know one's *origins* amounts to the right to know one's parentage, ie, one's biological family and ascendance, and one's conditions of birth. It protects each individual's interest to identify where she comes from' (Samantha Besson, 'Enforcing the Child's Right to Know her Origins: Contrasting Approaches under the Convention on the Rights of the Child and the Convention on Human Rights' (2007) 21 *International Journal of Law, Policy and the Family* 137–59, 140). The personal history of the twins, X and Y, includes their birth to a Ukrainian surrogate who conceived them using donated eggs. The existence of X and Y is the result of the combined actions of Mr and Mrs W, the egg donor and the Ukrainian surrogate (and the non-objection of her husband). I am certain that Mr and Mrs W, who have demonstrated such enormous care in their approach to the journey to parenthood and capacity to care since the arrival of X and Y, despite being first time parents confronted by some enormous complications, will demonstrate the same care in their consideration of whether, when and how to provide the children with information about their origins as an integral part of their upbringing. X and Y certainly have an interest in knowing their origins. Whether they are told is currently up to their legal parents who themselves enjoy Article 8 rights to respect for their private

life. The arrangement with the Ukrainian surrogate has blossomed into friendship so, without affecting the security of this family, she may well continue to be part of their lives; no doubt, the extent to which she does so will be determined by all of these responsible adults according to the best interests of the children. It goes without saying that all of us find our lives enriched by healthy relationships, of differing degrees of care and affection, with a wide variety of people. This family are, like others before them, and no doubt many more to follow, entering unchartered waters in navigating the relationships of a number of adults with these children. There are institutions and professionals available to advise, support and guide should that be necessary. The right to respect for a private life includes being able to establish details of an individual's identity (*Gaskin v United Kingdom* (1990) 12 EHRR 36 [39]). I consider there is a further question, upon which I did not hear argument and thus must be fully examined elsewhere, as to whether the children's right to respect for a family life includes legal recognition of the place of the surrogate in their family. As has occurred with adoption and donor conceived children, the complex questions of origin and identity that can arise for children born following lawful surrogacy arrangements need full, evidenced, examination and debate, so all competing rights can be balanced, before clarification in law.

31.   Criticism of the highly unsatisfactory state of the current law of surrogacy has already been made by highly experienced family court judges, distinguished review committees and academic commentators. In a recent case, a very experienced family court judge, McFarlane J, was prompted by the circumstances of the case before him to state, 'given the importance of the issues involved when the life of a child is created in this manner, it is questionable whether the role of facilitating surrogacy arrangements should be left to groups of well-meaning amateurs' (*Re G* [2007] EWHC 2814 [29]). And the judge took the unusual step of ensuring that a copy of his judgment was sent to the Minister of State for Children, Young People and Families. A decade ago, the Brazier Review recommended reform of the law including a new Surrogacy Act, registration of Surrogacy Agencies and a Code of Practice which placed the welfare of the child as the paramount concern of all involved (*Surrogacy: Review for Heath Ministers of Current Arrangements for Payments and Regulation, Report of the Review Team*, Margaret Brazier, Alastair Campbell, Susan Golombok, 1998, Cm 4068, [Executive Summary, 5–7]).

32.   The chair of that review, Margaret Brazier, concluded her subsequent article 'Regulating the Reproduction Business?' (1999) 7 *Medical Law Review* 166–93, with the astute observation, 'the international ramifications of the reproductive business may prove to be a more stringent test of the strength of British law than all the ethical dilemmas that have gone before' (at 193). Furthermore, European and international law makes us now much more attuned to the rights of children than we were in the twentieth century. The current law on surrogacy puts the judiciary in the uncomfortable position of ignoring the policy of the existing legislation in an attempt to fulfil the duty of the State to protect the welfare, interests and rights of children created through assisted reproductive technology and international agreements between adults. I considered it my duty to do so to protect the rights of these twin baby girls.

33.   In recent Parliamentary debates on the Human Fertilisation and Embryology Bill, the government said that it was considering reviewing the law of surrogacy. The Act to which Royal Assent was given on 13 November makes very minor amendments to the terms of

section 30 which are not yet in force. I note that these amendments do not require an application for a Parental Order. Without these proceedings there would have been no consideration of the welfare of these children who, furthermore, would have remained parentless. Not all who enter into surrogacy arrangements are as well informed and careful to understand the legal position as these parents. As is evidenced by this case, the circumstances in which children are born following international surrogacy arrangements raise complex issues of parenting, nationality, origins, identity and relationships. There are issues of the provision of information, legal advice, immigration, registration and of the extra-territorial application of any laws which are not addressed in the current legal framework. It is not for the judiciary to tell Parliament what to do. But we cannot deny that the current law neglects the interests and rights of children which should surely be at the centre of legislation on this matter.

34.   X and Y who are, I must say, delightful babies, are here due to the relentless efforts of Mr and Mrs W and the honourable conduct of the Ukrainian surrogate who carried them. It fell to this court to steer a way through the legislation whilst protecting the rights, interests and welfare of these children. X and Y are at the very beginnings of their journey through life, a start which, through no fault of any of the parties, has been unsettling for all concerned; I share the hope of Mr and Mrs W that X and Y can now enjoy a more stable and secure future.

35.   I reserve my final comments for X and Y in the hope that, at the right time, your parents will show you the judgment of this court which now forms part of your personal history. I want you to know what guided me in making my decision. The law which I have had to apply is very old and was passed without any consideration of the circumstances into which you came into this world. So I thought very carefully about what was best for you and also the rights which the law protects. I could see that your parents, who had tried so hard to become your parents, even when the law and the British authorities caused them problems, are honest, considerate and loving people. I could see that they were already taking good care of you. I hope that my decision has enabled your parents to care for you in the way they intended and that you know, and are proud, of the contributions of both the donor and the surrogate to what makes you both the unique individuals you are.

5

Commentary on *CD v ST*

CONNIE HEALY

I. Introduction

CD v ST was an employment law case,[1] heard by the Court of Justice of the European Union. It focused on the rights of parents whose children are born of a surrogacy arrangement, specifically the right of a commissioning mother, to maternity leave following the birth of her child. Little, if any, consideration was given to the impact of the Court's decision on the rights or best interests of the child. This is not unusual. Children's rights, or even, the *consideration* of children's rights is frequently absent from Court judgments in an EU context. The aim of the re-written judgment in *CD v ST* is to address this anomaly, placing the rights and best interests of the child front and centre. It aims to recognise and uphold the child's rights under Article 24 of the Charter of Fundamental Rights, namely the right to 'care and protection for their well-being'[2] and that the child's 'best interests' is a 'primary consideration' in any decision made.[3]

II. Employment Rights for Modern Day Families

Advances in medicine and, albeit more slowly, developments in the legal recognition of relationships, has meant that the traditional concept of parentage and family based on heterosexual marriage alone is outdated. Expanding the categories of persons eligible to be considered parents will raise employment law issues surrounding the availability of maternity and parental leave. Surrogacy, in particular, has been an emotive topic, leading to differences of opinion from ethical and rights based perspectives: the rights of commissioning parents,[4] and the risk of exploitation for surrogate mothers.[5] Complicating factors also include the fact that it is difficult to get accurate figures on the number of parents opting for surrogacy

---

[1] Case C-162/12 *CD v ST* [2014] ECR I-000.
[2] Art 24 (1) of the Charter of Fundamental Rights.
[3] ibid.
[4] E Caracciolo di Torella and P Foubert, 'Surrogacy, Pregnancy and Maternity Rights: A Missed Opportunity for a More Coherent Regime of Parental Rights in the EU' (2015) (1) *European Law Review* 52.
[5] A Brazier, A Campbell and S Golombok, *Surrogacy: Review for Health Ministers of Current Arrangements for Payments and Regulation* (Cm 4068) (London, HMSO, 1998).

due to differences in the way surrogacy is viewed and recorded or, for example, whether couples have entered into private arrangements.[6] In some jurisdictions, there has been a reluctance by governments to take a stance on the issue for fear of electoral disapproval.[7] This lack of legislation[8] has meant that parents of children born through surrogacy have been left in a 'legal limbo';[9] often, with no option but to fight through the courts to determine their children's identity and nationality and to seek state support and employment rights equivalent to those available to biological and adoptive parents. Crucially, also, their children's rights have been ignored, prejudiced by the circumstances of their conception and birth.

III. Who are Regarded as Parents Under the Present Legal Frameworks?

In most jurisdictions, including England and Wales,[10] the woman who gives birth to the child is automatically considered the mother by law; *mater semper certa est.*[11] This applies irrespective of there being any surrogacy agreement in place.[12] The only concession to intended or commissioning parents in England and Wales is that they are given legal recognition as parents once they comply with the provisions of section 54 of the Human Fertilisation and Embryology Act 2008 (HFEA). As parents by law, therefore, should they be treated differently in relation to employment law protection and support available for biological parents? And, more importantly for the purpose of this commentary, how does this impact on the rights of the child?

IV. Overview of the Judgment in *CD v ST*

The facts of the case are set out in the accompanying judgment. In summary, the case focused on an intended mother's right to paid leave following the birth of her child through

---

[6] *Surrogacy in the UK: Myth Busting and Reform. The Report of the Surrogacy UK Working Group on Surrogacy Law Reform,* (November, 2015).

[7] Several opportunities have arisen and provisions included in heads of a Bill, but the issue has been avoided by successive Governments in Ireland.

[8] Caracciolo di Torella and Foubert, above n 4. The authors note 'that countries broadly fall into three categories: the "surrogacy-friendly," which provide some express provisions to facilitate surrogacy; the "anti-surrogacy," those which prohibit surrogacy for either commercial or altruistic reasons; and finally those which do not have any relevant legislation in place.'; K Horsey and S Sheldon, 'Still Hazy After All These Years: The Law Regulating Surrogacy' (2012) 20 (1) *Medical Law Review* 67, 68 likewise note that '[f]ifteen years on, (from the Brazier Review) the law governing surrogacy remains confused, incoherent, and poorly adapted to the specific realities of the practice of surrogacy.'

[9] *MR and DR (suing by their father and next friend OR) and ors v An t-Ard-Chláraitheoir and ors* [2014] IESC 60. O' Donnell, J [5].

[10] Under the Children and Families Act 2014, ss 120–21, intended parents are entitled to adoptive leave and paid leave for surrogacy, effective April 2015.

[11] s 27 Human Fertilisation and Embryology Act 1990; s 33 Human Fertilisation and Embryology Act 2008.

[12] Most recently *Surrogacy in the UK* above n 6, which noted that: '[t]he law must recognise the correct people as parents of children born through surrogacy. Not to do so is not in children's or families' best interests' 6.

surrogacy. The child was genetically related to CD's partner. She breastfed the baby within one hour of it being born and continued to do so for three months. Approximately four months later, CD and her partner were deemed to have complied with section 54 of the HFEA and were granted a parental order. They were thus the legal parents of the child. However, despite having the requisite contributions to entitle her to paid maternity or adoptive leave under the legislation as it stands, she had not given birth to the child, nor was she in a position to furnish a 'matching certificate', normally available in adoption proceedings.[13]

As CD wished to have a second child through surrogacy she took a case to the Employment Appeals Tribunal, claiming discrimination on the grounds of maternity and pregnancy and/or sex under the Equality Act 2010. In her application, she claimed that her rights under the Employment Rights Act 1996 and the Maternity and Parental Leave Regulations 1999 had been infringed. The Employment Appeals Tribunal filed a request for a preliminary ruling to the Court of Justice of the European Union (CJEU) on the interpretation of Articles 1(1), 2(c), 8(1) and 11(2)(b) of Council Directive 92/85/EEC, otherwise known as the Pregnancy Workers Directive (PWD), Article 2(1)(a) and (b) and (2)(c), claiming discrimination on the grounds of pregnancy and motherhood and Article 14 of Directive 2006/54/EC of the European Parliament (Recast Directive), claiming discrimination on the basis of sex.

The stated purpose of the PWD was to 'implement measures to encourage improvement in the safety and health at work of pregnant workers who have recently given birth *or who are breastfeeding*.'[14] Questions for the court to address, therefore, included whether the Directive provided a right to receive maternity leave to an intended mother who has had a baby through a surrogacy agreement in circumstances where she may breastfeed or does in fact breastfeed.

V. Opinion of Advocate Kokott

AG Kokott issued her opinion on 26 September 2013. She adopted a rights-based approach to the questions posed; acknowledging the need to take a 'functional rather than monistic approach'[15] in cases where the intended mother takes the place of the biological mother. She commented that the PWD was a product of its time; a period when it was not foreseen that women may become mothers in circumstances other than pregnancy.

Central to this was the recognition of the right to family life for intended parents and their children under Article 7 of the Charter of Fundamental Rights of the European Union. Additionally, she recognised the rights of the child under Article 24 of the Charter; the primacy of the child's 'best interests' and the importance of time to bond with its mother

---

[13] The Maternity and Parental Leave etc Regs 1999.

[14] Art 1 Council Directive 92/85/EEC of 19 October 1992 on the introduction of measures to encourage improvements in the safety and health at work of pregnant workers and workers who have recently given birth or are breastfeeding (tenth individual Directive within the meaning of Art 16 (1) of Directive 89/391/EEC). (Emphasis added).

[15] Case C-167/12 *CD v ST* Opinion of Advocate General Kokott delivered on 26 September 2013 [48].

post-birth. Indeed, she acknowledged that such a need may even be greater when the woman has not actually given birth to the child.[16]

On the question as to whether such leave should apply to intended mothers who do not breastfeed, AG Kokott saw no reason to differentiate and focused on the mother-child relationship commenting that:

> Insufficient account would be taken of the objective, enshrined as a fundamental right, of ensuring the unhindered development of the mother-child relationship, if the decisive factor in establishing whether an intended mother is to be granted maternity leave were the way in which the child is fed.[17]

In conclusion, she was of the opinion that such leave should be granted to an intended mother regardless of whether she breastfeeds or bottle feeds the child, once surrogacy is provided for in the Member State and that any national requirements have been satisfied.

This opinion was welcomed by academics[18] and the media.[19] However, on the same day, AG Wahl issued a contrasting opinion in the case of *Z v A Government Department and the Board of Management of a Community School*.[20]

VI. *Z v A Government Department and the Board of Management of a Community School*

The facts of this case were similar. Ms Z suffered from a rare condition; although she had healthy ovaries and was otherwise fertile, she had no uterus and could not support a pregnancy. Ms Z and her husband arranged for a surrogate mother to give birth to their genetic child in California, where surrogacy is permitted. According to Californian legislation, the child was considered the genetic child of the intended parents: there was no mention of the surrogate mother on the child's (American) birth certificate. Ms Z argued that she had been subjected to discrimination on grounds of sex, family status and disability.[21] The Equality Tribunal in Ireland referred the case to the Court of Justice regarding the interpretation of the Pregnant Workers Directive and the Recast Directive respectively.[22]

---

[16] ibid [46].

[17] ibid [62].

[18] Caracciolo di Torella and Foubert, above n 4.

[19] *The Guardian* (26 September 2013), www.theguardian.com/money/2013/sep/26/adoptive-birth-mothers-surrogacy-maternity-leave-ecj.

[20] C-363/12 *Z v A Government Department and the Board of Management of a Community School*.

[21] Arts 1 and 2 Directive 2006/54/EC—equal opportunities of the European Parliament and of the Council of 5 July 2006 on the implementation of the principle of equal opportunities and equal treatment of men and women in matters of employment and occupation (OJ 2006 L 204, 23) and Council Directive 2000/78/EC of 27 November 2000 establishing a general framework for equal treatment in employment and occupation (OJ 2000 L 303, 16), and also the validity of those two directives.

[22] Pregnant Workers Directive 92/85 (OJ L 348). The Recast Directive 2006/54/EC (OJ L 204) of 5 July 2006 on the implementation of the principle of equal opportunities and equal treatment of men and women in matters of employment and occupation replaces the Equal Treatment Directive (76/207/EEC) and the Equal Pay Directive (75/117/EEC). Furthermore, in this case arguments related to disability, were also put forward. It is beyond the scope of this chapter to explore these issues as the re-written judgment focuses on the case of *CD v ST*.

AG Wahl acknowledged the inadequacy of the current framework. He noted that if the objective was to protect the woman's biological condition *and* the special relationship between a woman and her child that 'an appropriate point of comparison seems to be found … in an adoptive mother (or, as the case may be, a parent, male or female) who has *not* given birth to a child.'[23] Specifically:

> [T]he scope of protection afforded by Article 8 of Directive 92/85 could not … be meaningfully limited only to women who have given birth, but would necessarily also cover adoptive mothers or indeed, any other parent who takes full care of his or her new-born child.[24]

However, AG Wahl stated that the EU only requires the Member States to have provisions in place for maternity and/or breastfeeding leave arising as 'a corollary from birth (*and* breast-feeding).'[25] This is a misinterpretation of the PWD which clearly states its purpose as being to 'protect pregnant workers and workers who have recently given birth *or* who are breast-feeding';[26] a breastfeeding worker being defined within 'the meaning of national legislation and/or national practice … who informs her employer of her condition, in accordance with that legislation and/or practice.'[27]

On the issue of whether the applicant should be treated in the same way as an adoptive mother, AG Wahl noted that article 16 of Directive 2006/54 and recital 27 to the preamble in conjunction thereto preserves the freedom of MS to decide whether to grant adoptive or parental leave. This, he decided, meant that adoptive leave could not be used as a comparator, as it does not come within the scope of the Directive. While AG Wahl expressed sympathy for commissioning parents, he did not believe that it

> is for the Court to substitute itself for the legislature by engaging in constructive interpretation that would involve reading into Directives 2006/54 and 2000/78 (or, indeed Directive 92/85) something that is simply not there' and that that would amount 'to encroaching upon the legislative prerogative'.[28]

With two contrasting opinions on the entitlements of intended mothers, the final decision of the Grand Chamber was eagerly awaited with the hope being that the Court would follow the Opinion of AG Kokott.

VII. The Court's Decision

The Court's decision, delivered on 18 March 2014, disappointingly, came to the opposite conclusion. The Court held:

> Maternity leave is 'intended, first, to *protect a woman's biological condition* during and after pregnancy and, second, to protect the special relationship between a woman and her child over the

---

[23] Opinion of Advocate General Wahl delivered on 26 September 2013 Case C-363/12 *Z v A Government Department and the Board of Management of a Community School* [64].
[24] ibid [47].
[25] ibid (emphasis added).
[26] Art 1(1) (emphasis added).
[27] Art 2(C).
[28] ibid [120].

period which follows pregnancy and childbirth, by preventing that relationship from being disturbed by the multiple burdens which would result from the simultaneous pursuit of employment.'

Therefore, in the opinion of the Court, the Directive presupposes that the worker has actually been pregnant and given birth to a child. The Court went on to acknowledge the importance of such leave to the special relationship between a mother and a child;[29] the time for bonding and attachment; but again, presupposing pregnancy and childbirth. The aim: protection from harm in her vulnerable condition. As CD had at no point been pregnant, she was not entitled to maternity leave. The Court failed to give any credence to the fact that Article 2(c) refers to the definition of worker as including someone *who is breastfeeding*; thus ignoring the specific facts of the applicant's case. It also refused to follow the rights-based approach of AG Kokott, or to have any regard for the best interests of CD's child.

VIII. A Children's Rights Perspective

The CJEU is not 'as such, a "human rights court"'.[30] However, as 'the supreme interpreter of EU law, the Court nevertheless has a permanent responsibility to ensure respect for such rights … [and] it is essential for the Court to ensure that it interprets … [the] role and significance of EU fundamental rights.'[31] Additionally, the provisions of the UN Convention on the Rights of the Child had already been referred to and used to support the Court's reasoning in previous decisions, to include C-540/03 *Parliament v Council*.[32] Of particular importance is Article 3 of the Convention; the best interests of the child and subsection 2 thereof which provides that State Parties 'shall take all appropriate legislative and administrative measures'[33] to ensure that the best interests of the child are respected, protected and fulfilled. In interpreting the provisions of the UN Convention on the Rights of the Child (CRC), guidance can be gleaned from General Comments issued by the Committee on the Rights of the Child. General Comment Number 7[34] notes, specifically, that there should be a supportive

> framework of laws, policies and programmes for early childhood which assists (children) in developing strong emotional attachments to their parents or other caregivers, from whom they seek and require nurturance, care, guidance and protection, in ways that are respectful of their individuality and growing capacities.[35]

Being respectful of their 'individuality'; employment law should provide protection to all parents and be cognisant of the importance for every child of forming strong mutual attachments very soon after birth. Underlying the provisions of the CRC and the Charter is

---

[29] *Hofmann v Barmer Ersatzkasse* (C-184/83) [1984] ECR 3047, confirmed in *Kiiski v Tampereen* (C-116/06) [2007] ECR-I-7643.
[30] *Gerardo Ruiz Zambrano v Office national de l'emploi* (C-34/09) ECR-I-01177 AG Sharpston [155].
[31] ibid [155].
[32] C-540/03 *Parliament v Council* [226] ECR I-05769.
[33] Art 3(2).
[34] UN Committee on the Rights of the Child, General Comment No 7 (2005 Implementing the Rights of the Child in Early Childhood).
[35] ibid [6b].

the obligation to consider the 'best interests' of the child. In addressing this issue, the Committee on the rights of the child has acknowledged the best interests principle as being a threefold concept encompassing:

(a) a substantive right;
(b) an interpretative principle: the importance of legal provisions being interpreted in a way which most effectively serves the 'best interests' of a child and,
(c) a rule of procedure to ensure that there is a framework in place to facilitate the assessment and determination of what is in the child's 'best interests'. This includes justification of the decision made and the extent to which the best interests of the child were taken into account.[36]

Viewed from the perspective of Tobin's scale on the extent to which judges take children's rights into account (non-existent to substantive),[37] the recognition given to children's rights or best interests in this case was non-existent. In interpreting the Directive in the light of the questions posed by the referring Tribunal, the Court did not acknowledge the substantive rights of CD's child, nor carry out any assessment or make any determination as to how the Court's decision may impact on the best interests of CD's baby or the group of children born in similar conditions. Tobin, citing Waldron and Dworkin, believes that judges are not as constrained in their interpretation as they might think. Part of their role is to engage in an element of 'moral reasoning.'[38] If judges are children's rights focused, they will find a way to expand their reasoning to incorporate the values underlying the CRC and ensure that the child's rights and best interests are protected.

IX. The Re-written Judgment

The re-written judgment in *CD v ST* does this. It expands the reasoning of the Court to acknowledge the rights of the family and the child under the CRC and the Charter. It accepts that at no point was CD pregnant but holds that in engaging a surrogate she expressed a clear intention and commitment to become a parent. The decision focuses on the *objective* of the Directive: to encourage improvements to the health and safety of workers who are pregnant *or* breastfeeding. In interpreting the Directive as having due regard for the special relationship between a parent (in particular the mother) and child, the re-written judgment refers to an earlier decision of the Court in C-163/82 *Commission v Italy* where the importance of the 'very delicate initial period' when a child is settling in with an adoptive family was accepted.[39] The situation in the case of surrogacy, as with the arrival of all children, is

---

[36] UN Committee on the Rights of the Child, General Comment No 14 (2013 on the right of the child to have his or her best interests taken as a primary consideration (art 3, para 1) www2.ohchr.org/english/bodies/crc/comments.htm [6].

[37] J Tobin, 'Judging the Judges: Are they Adopting the Rights Approach in Matters involving Children' (2009) 33 *Melbourne University Law Review* 579.

[38] ibid 582.

[39] Case 163/82 *Commission v Italy* ECR 3273. See also C-184/83 *Hofmann v Barmer Ersatzkasse* [1984] ECR 3047 [25], to protect health but also to protect the relationship.

equally tenuous. By highlighting the importance of that relationship, the re-written judgment goes further than protecting merely the health and safety of the applicant; it respects her and her child's right to family life, the importance of which has been acknowledged in the European Convention on Human Rights (ECHR), the CRC and the Charter. In doing so, the judgment refers to the child's rights under Article 24 of the Charter and the obligation on private institutions and public authorities to ensure that the best interests of the child is their primary consideration. This should not depend on the circumstances of birth.

On the issue of discrimination, many issues remain to be addressed at national and EU level to break from the traditional stereotypes of the father breadwinner/mother caregiver model.[40] The re-written judgment notes that the aim of the Directive is to cover *minimum* requirements for women who are breastfeeding as a 'specific risk group.' Employers have a duty to adjust working conditions accordingly. Even if mothers are not breastfeeding, time is required to 'protect the special relations between a woman and her child'.[41] Importantly, the Court's re-written judgment notes that the Directive does not preclude Member States from enacting laws to provide maternity leave for commissioning mothers and holds that Member States are now required to do so. The claim regarding discrimination on the grounds of sex is not upheld in this case. Whether commissioning mothers have been discriminated against vis-à-vis adoptive mothers is a matter for individual Member States to decide. The re-written judgment hints that treating commissioning mothers and adoptive mothers differently may amount to discrimination.

X. Conclusion

The Directive does not specify that breastfeeding is an additional requirement; rather it is framed in such a way that breastfeeding is a qualifying factor in itself. In the re-written judgment, the Court held that the Directive should be interpreted such that intended mothers may be protected by the PWD in situations where they are breastfeeding the child. As the Directive applies to the factual circumstances of this case, the provisions of the Charter apply. It was incumbent upon the Court to consider the rights of the child, specifically what was in the child's best interests and the right to family life. This will also have to include intended mothers who, by choice or need, bottle feed their children and as reproductive technologies advance, will have to recognise and accommodate the protection of parents whose children are born through alternative means. Otherwise, as noted by AG Kokott and confirmed by Caracciolo di Torella, insufficient consideration would be given to the *objective* of the Directive, in protecting the mother-child relationship. The re-written judgment is unique in highlighting the intersection between family law (the right to a family life and the best interests of the child) with the importance of ensuing that employment laws are sufficient to protect the health and safety of all workers.

---

[40] G James, 'Forgotten Children: Work–Family Reconciliation in the EU' (2012) 34(3) *Journal of Social Welfare and Family Law* 363, 366.

[41] C-184/83 *Hofmann v Barmer Ersatzkasse* [1984] ECR 3047 [25].

In recent times, there have been many positive initiatives taken by the EU in recognising children's rights and in promoting policies that are mindful of their best interests.[42] However, these can only be achieved if, as Stalford comments, 'the national context in which they are articulated has sufficiently robust mechanisms in place to give them full effect.'[43] The legal framework at EU level and in Member States needs, in so far as is possible, to keep in line with developments in medical technology and modern issues surrounding the rights and duties of natural and social parents. In this specific case, the re-written judgment addresses the issue by applying the Directive to the facts: the mother was breastfeeding. For other cases, however, employment law needs to keep up with the realities of modern life by continuing to respect and protect the importance of appropriate leave for parents and 'risk groups' in society as the accepted definitions of family expand.[44]

---

[42] See for example the Victims Directive 2012/29/EU, http://eur-lex.europa.eu/legal-content/EN/TXT/?qid=14 21925131614&uri=CELEX:32012L0029.

[43] H Stalford, 'The CRC in Litigation under EU Law' in T Liefaard and JE Doek (eds), *Litigating the Rights of the Child* (Dordrecht, Springer, 2015) 220.

[44] Above n 6, at 6.

Court of Justice of the European Union (Grand Chamber)

CD v ST

THE COURT (Grand Chamber),

composed of XX, President, XX, Vice-President, XX, XX and XX (Rapporteur), Presidents of Chambers, XX, XX, XX, XX, XX, XX and E Caracciolo di Torella Judges.

Judgment

1. This request for a preliminary ruling concerns the interpretation of Articles 1(1), 2(c), 8(1) and 11(2)(b) of Council Directive 92/85/EEC of 19 October 1992 on the introduction of measures to encourage improvements in the safety and health at work of pregnant workers and workers who have recently given birth or are breastfeeding (tenth individual Directive within the meaning of Article 16(1) of Directive 89/391/EEC) (OJ 1992 L 348, page 1); Article 2(1)(a) and (b) and (2)(c) and Article 14 of Directive 2006/54/EC of the European Parliament and of the Council of 5 July 2006 on the implementation of the principle of equal opportunities and equal treatment of men and women in matters of employment and occupation (OJ 2006 L 204, page 23).

2. The request has been made in proceedings between Ms D, an intended mother (also referred to as a commissioning mother) who has had a baby through a surrogacy arrangement, and ST, her employer, a National Health Service Foundation Trust, concerning the refusal to grant her paid leave following the birth of the baby.

Legal Context

European Union Law

Directive 92/85

The first, eighth, ninth, fourteenth and seventeenth recitals in the preamble to Directive 92/85 are worded as follows:

Whereas Article 118a [EC] provides that the Council shall adopt, by means of directives, minimum requirements for encouraging improvements, especially in the working environment, to protect the safety and health of workers;

Whereas pregnant workers, workers who have recently given birth or who are breastfeeding must be considered a specific risk group in many respects, and measures must be taken with regard to their safety and health;

Whereas the protection of the safety and health of pregnant workers, workers who have recently given birth or workers who are breastfeeding should not treat women on the labour market unfavourably nor work to the detriment of directives concerning equal treatment for men and women;

…

Whereas the vulnerability of pregnant workers, workers who have recently given birth or who are breastfeeding makes it necessary for them to be granted the right to maternity leave of at least 14 continuous weeks, allocated before and/or after confinement, and renders necessary the compulsory nature of maternity leave of at least two weeks, allocated before and/or after confinement;

…

Whereas, moreover, provision concerning maternity leave would also serve no purpose unless accompanied by the maintenance of rights linked to the employment contract and or entitlement to an adequate allowance.

Article 1(1) of Directive 92/85 states:

The purpose of this Directive, which is the tenth individual Directive within the meaning of Article 16(1) of Directive 89/391/EEC, is to implement measures to encourage improvements in the safety and health at work of pregnant workers and workers who have recently given birth or who are breastfeeding.

Article 2 of that Directive contains the following definitions:

For the purposes of this Directive:

(a) pregnant worker shall mean a pregnant worker who informs her employer of her condition, in accordance with national legislation and/or national practice;

(b) worker who has recently given birth shall mean a worker who has recently given birth within the meaning of national legislation and/or national practice and who informs her employer of her condition, in accordance with that legislation and/or practice;

(c) worker who is breastfeeding shall mean a worker who is breastfeeding within the meaning of national legislation and/or national practice and who informs her employer of her condition, in accordance with that legislation and/or practice.

Article 8 of that Directive, headed 'Maternity leave', provides:

1. Member States shall take the necessary measures to ensure that workers within the meaning of Article 2 are entitled to a continuous period of maternity leave of at least 14 weeks allocated before and/or after confinement in accordance with national legislation and/or practice.

2. The maternity leave stipulated in paragraph 1 must include compulsory maternity leave of at least two weeks allocated before and/or after confinement in accordance with national legislation and/or practice.

Article 10 of Directive 92/85, headed 'Prohibition of dismissal', provides:

In order to guarantee workers, within the meaning of Article 2, the exercise of their health and safety protection rights as recognised under this Article, it shall be provided that:

(1) Member States shall take the necessary measures to prohibit the dismissal of workers, within the meaning of Article 2, during the period from the beginning of their pregnancy to the end of the maternity leave referred to in Article 8(1), save in exceptional cases not connected with their condition which are permitted under national legislation and/or practice and, where applicable, provided that the competent authority has given its consent (…)

Article 11 of that Directive, headed 'Employment rights', provides:

In order to guarantee workers within the meaning of Article 2 the exercise of their health and safety protection rights as recognised under this Article, it shall be provided that:

(2) in the case referred to in Article 8, the following must be ensured:

…

(b)   maintenance of a payment to, and/or entitlement to an adequate allowance for, workers within the meaning of Article 2 (…)

Directive 2006/54

Article 1 of Directive 2006/54 states:

The purpose of this Directive is to ensure the implementation of the principle of equal opportunities and equal treatment of men and women in matters of employment and occupation.

To that end, it contains provisions to implement the principle of equal treatment in relation to:

…

(b) working conditions, including pay;

…

Article 2 of that Directive provides:

1. For the purposes of this Directive, the following definitions shall apply:

(a)   'direct discrimination': where one person is treated less favourably on grounds of sex than another is, has been or would be treated in a comparable situation;

(b)   'indirect discrimination': where an apparently neutral provision, criterion or practice would put persons of one sex at a particular disadvantage compared with persons of the other sex, unless that provision, criterion or practice is objectively justified by a legitimate aim, and the means of achieving that aim are appropriate and necessary;

…

2. For the purposes of this Directive, discrimination includes:

(c)   any less favourable treatment of a woman related to pregnancy or maternity leave within the meaning of Directive 92/85/EEC.

Article 14(1)(c) of that Directive is worded as follows:

There shall be no direct or indirect discrimination on grounds of sex in the public or private sectors, including public bodies, in relation to:

...

(c) employment and working conditions, including dismissals, as well as pay as provided for in Article [157 TFEU].

Charter of Fundamental Rights of the European Union

Article 7 (Respect for Private and Family Life)

Everyone has the right to respect for his or her private and family life, home and communication.

Article 24 (The Rights of the Child)

2. In all actions relating to children, whether taken by public authorities or private institutions, the child's best interests must be a primary consideration.

3. Every child shall have the right to maintain on a regular basis a personal relationship and direct contact with both his or her parents, unless that is contrary to his or her interests.

International Legislation

European Convention on Human Rights

Article 8 ECHR

1. Everyone has the right to respect for his private and family life, his home and his correspondence.

UN Convention of the Rights of the Child

Preamble

The States Parties to the present Convention,

...

Convinced that the family, as the fundamental group of society and the natural environment for the growth and well-being of all its members and particularly children, should be afforded the necessary protection and assistance so that it can fully assume its responsibilities within the community,

Recognizing that the child, for the full and harmonious development of his or her personality, should grow up in a family environment, in an atmosphere of happiness, love and understanding,

...

Have agreed as follows:

...

Article 3

> 1. In all actions concerning children, whether undertaken by public or private social welfare institutions, courts of law, administrative authorities or legislative bodies, the best interests of the child shall be a primary consideration.

> 2. States Parties undertake to ensure the child such protection and care as is necessary for his or her well-being, taking into account the rights and duties of his or her parents, legal guardians, or other individuals legally responsible for him or her, and, to this end, shall take all appropriate legislative and administrative measures.

United Kingdom Legislation

3.   The Human Fertilisation and Embryology Act 2008 provides in section 54 that, on an application made by two people, a court may make an order giving them parental responsibility for a child (a parental order), so that the child is treated in law as the child of the applicants if:

— the child has been carried by a woman who is not one of the applicants, as a result of the placing in her of an embryo or sperm and eggs or her artificial insemination,
— the gametes of at least one of the applicants were used to bring about the creation of the embryo, and
— certain other conditions are satisfied, including the condition that the applicants be husband and wife or in some analogous relationship.

4.   Section 47C of the Employment Rights Act 1996 states that an employee has the right not to be subjected to any detriment by any act, or any deliberate failure to act, by his employer done for a prescribed reason. A prescribed reason is one which is defined by regulations made by the Secretary of State and which relates to, inter alia, pregnancy, childbirth or maternity; ordinary, compulsory or additional maternity leave; and ordinary or additional adoption leave.

5.   Under The Maternity and Parental Leave etc Regulations 1999, an employee is entitled to ordinary maternity leave and to additional maternity leave where certain conditions are satisfied, and the terms and conditions of her employment are protected during maternity leave. These regulations also give the employee the right to return to work after maternity leave and protection against unfair dismissal.

6.   In accordance with Regulation 19 of these Regulations, an employee is entitled under section 47C of the Employment Rights Act 1996 not to be subjected to any detriment by any act, or any deliberate failure to act, by her employer done for the reason, inter alia, that the employee took, sought to take or availed herself of the benefits of, ordinary maternity leave or additional maternity leave.

7.   The Equality Act 2010 states, in particular, that a woman is discriminated against if she is treated less favourably than others on the grounds of her sex, pregnancy or maternity leave.

Children Act 1989

Section 1

When a court determines any question with respect to (a) the upbringing of a child; ... the child's welfare shall be the court's paramount consideration.

The Dispute in the Main Proceedings and the Questions Referred for a Preliminary Ruling

8.   It is apparent from the order for reference that Ms D has been employed by ST since 7 July 2001 at a hospital managed by ST.

9.   Ms D entered into a surrogacy agreement to have a baby; the agreement was compliant with the Human Fertilisation and Embryology Act 2008. The sperm was provided by Ms D's partner but the egg was not Ms D's. Although at no material time was Ms D herself pregnant, by entering a surrogacy agreement, she had expressed a clear commitment to become a parent.

10.   ST has a maternity leave and pay policy and an adoption leave and pay policy which equate to the statutory provisions on paid leave. The policies do not provide for leave and pay for commissioning mothers in cases of surrogacy. ST also has a special leave policy, which does not concern surrogacy. On 15 October 2009, ST's Director of Human Resources stated in reply to a request from a trade union concerning provision for commissioning mothers that, 'on an individual basis, should the need arise, requirements would be addressed by arrangements for maternity leave or adoption [leave]'.

11.   Ms D made an application to her employer for paid leave under its adoption policy. By letter of 14 March 2011, ST informed Ms D that her surrogacy arrangement did not meet the requirements of that policy, as Ms D could not provide a 'matching certificate' issued by an adoption agency, certifying that the future adoptive parent has been matched with a child for adoption.

12.   On the same day, after receiving that letter, Ms D made a formal request to ST for surrogacy leave, which, according to Ms D, equated to adoption leave except for the fact that she could not provide a matching certificate because she was not undergoing adoption proceedings. On 11 April 2011, ST replied that if Ms D was proceeding with adoption she would be entitled to paid leave, but if she was not there was 'no legal right to paid time off for surrogacy'.

13.   On 7 June 2011, Ms D brought an action before the Employment Tribunal, Newcastle upon Tyne, claiming discrimination on the grounds of sex and/or pregnancy and maternity under the Equality Act 2010. She also claimed that the Employment Rights Act 1996 and The Maternity and Parental Leave Regulations 1999 had been infringed. She further claimed that she had been subject to a detriment by reason of pregnancy and maternity and by reason of the fact that she had sought to take ordinary or additional maternity leave.

In addition, Ms D relied on an infringement of Articles 8 and 14 of the European Convention for the Protection of Human Rights and Fundamental Freedoms, signed at Rome on 4 November 1950.

14.   On 10 June 2011, following a further application by Ms D, ST stated that it had a 'residual discretion' to consider the request for paid leave and that, using that discretion, it had decided that the terms of the adoption leave policy should be applied in favour of Ms D, requiring, inter alia, certain documents to be produced. Ms D was therefore granted paid leave under that policy, under the conditions set out in a letter of 29 June 2011.

15.   On 8 July 2011, ST asserted before the Employment Tribunal, Newcastle upon Tyne, that Ms D was not entitled to maternity pay because the right to such pay rests with the child's birth mother.

16.   The baby was born on 26 August 2011. Ms D wished to be present at the birth but the baby's birth was somewhat sudden. Within an hour of the birth, Ms D began to mother and breastfeed the child. She continued breastfeeding the child for three months.

17.   Ms D and her partner applied to the competent court for a parental order under section 54 of the Human Fertilisation and Embryology Act 2008. By order of 19 December 2011, they were granted full and permanent parental responsibility for the child. Ms D and her partner are therefore treated in law as the parents of that child.

18.   In those circumstances, the Employment Tribunal, Newcastle upon Tyne decided to stay the proceedings and to refer the following questions to the Court of Justice for a preliminary ruling:

In each of the following questions:

—   The phrase 'an intended mother who has a baby through a surrogacy arrangement' shall refer to circumstances where the intended mother in question is a worker and has not herself, at any material time, been pregnant, or given birth to the child in question.
—   The phrase 'surrogate mother' shall refer to circumstances where a woman has been pregnant and given birth to a child on behalf of an intended mother.

1.   Do Article 1(1) and/or Article 2(c) and/or Article 8(1) and/or Article 11(2)(b) of [Directive 92/85] provide a right to receive maternity leave to an intended mother who has a baby through a surrogacy arrangement?
2.   Does [Directive 92/85] provide a right to receive maternity leave to an intended mother who has a baby through a surrogacy arrangement, in circumstances where she:

(a)   may breastfeed following birth and/or
(b)   does breastfeed following birth?

3.   Is it a breach of Article 14, taken with Article 2(1)(a) and/or (b) and/or 2(2)(c) of [Directive 2006/54] for an employer to refuse to provide maternity leave to an intended mother who has a baby through a surrogacy arrangement?
4.   Is it by reason of the employee's association with the surrogate mother of the baby a potential breach of Article 14, taken with Article 2(1)(a) and/or (b) and/or 2(2)(c) of [Directive 2006/54] to refuse to provide maternity leave to an intended mother who has a baby through a surrogacy arrangement?

5. Is it by reason of the intended mother's association with the surrogate mother of the baby a potential breach of Article 14, taken with Article 2(l)(a) and/or (b) and/or 2(2) (c) of [Directive 2006/54] to subject an intended mother who has a baby through a surrogacy arrangement to less favourable treatment?

6. If the answer to question 4 is 'yes', is the intended mother's status as intended mother sufficient to entitle her to maternity leave on the basis of her association with the surrogate mother of the baby?

7. If the answer to any of questions 1, 2, 3 and 4 is 'yes':
   (a) Is [Directive 92/85], in the relevant respects, directly effective; and
   (b) Is [Directive 2006/54], in the relevant respects directly effective?'

Consideration of the Questions Referred

The First and Second Questions

19.   By its first and second questions, which it is appropriate to consider together, the referring tribunal asks, in essence, whether Directive 92/85 is to be interpreted as meaning that a commissioning mother who has had a baby through a surrogacy arrangement is entitled to the maternity leave provided for in Article 8 of that Directive, in particular in circumstances where the commissioning mother breastfeeds the baby.

20.   Two preliminary points should be mentioned. First, it should be borne in mind that medical advancements mean that surrogacy is an increasingly common form of medically assisted reproduction and that, despite at the moment being a relatively marginal issue, it is likely to increasingly arise in the future. Second, the twin objective of Directive 92/85 is to encourage improvements in the safety and health at work of pregnant workers and workers who have recently given birth or who are breastfeeding (Case C-460/06 *Paquay* [2007] ECR I 8511, paragraph 27, and Case C-232/09 *Danosa* [2010] ECR I 11405, paragraph 58) and 'to protect the special relationship between a woman and her child' (Case 184/83 *Hofmann* [1984] ECR 3047 paragraph 25; C-116/06 *Kiiski* [2007] ECR I-7643 paragraph 46; and C-5/12 *Betriu Montull*, EU:C:2013:230 paragraph 50).

21.   According to the well-established case-law of the Court, the right to maternity leave is a particularly important mechanism of protection under employment law. It must be stated that the purpose of Directive 92/85, as the first recital in the preamble thereto makes clear, is to establish certain minimum requirements in respect of the protection of pregnant workers and workers 'who have recently given birth or who are breastfeeding'. The eighth recital expressly provides that workers who have recently given birth or who are breastfeeding must be considered a specific risk group and measures must be taken with regard to their safety and health. The wording 'or' implies that there are two situations and women do not have to satisfy both.

22.   Although in the present case it is apparent from the order for reference that Ms D was not pregnant herself at any material time, it is clear that she was breastfeeding. According to the wording of Article 2(c) of Directive 92/85, workers who are breastfeeding mothers are included in the Directive. The rationale of this provision is to protect mothers in this specific case.

23.   The European Union legislature thus considered that the fundamental changes to the living conditions of the persons concerned during breastfeeding constituted a legitimate ground on which they could suspend their employment, without the public authorities or employers being allowed in any way to call the legitimacy of that ground into question (Case C-116/06 *Kiiski*, paragraph 49, and Case C-5/12 *Betriu Montull*, paragraph 48). In this context, Article 8(1) of Directive 92/85 provides that Member States are required to take the necessary measures to ensure that workers are entitled to a continuous period of maternity leave of at least 14 weeks allocated before and/or after 'confinement' in accordance with national legislation and/or practice. As this case expressly relates to a situation described in Article 2(c) of Directive 92/85, the period of leave will take place after confinement.

24.   Furthermore, even if the mother is not breastfeeding, the purpose to protect the 'special relationship' must be intended as a right to facilitate the bond between the mother and the child. This right goes beyond protecting the health and safety of the mother. Such a bond exists regardless of how a child becomes part of the family. The Court has made this clear in previous case law where a 'legitimate concern to assimilate as far as possible the conditions of entry of the child into the adoptive family to those of the arrival of a new born child in the family during the very delicate initial period' (Case 163/82 *Commission v Italy* [1983] ECR 3275 paragraph 16) was upheld. The concern is even greater when the woman has not actually given birth to the child. Thus, whether the mother is biological or not is immaterial. The right to develop a bond between the child and the mother is to be intended as a corollary of the right to family life as expressed in both Article 8(1) of ECHR and Article 7 of the EU Charter of Fundamental Rights (Case C-400/10 PPU *J McB v LE*, ECLI:EU:C:2010:582). Article 8 is a fundamental right and Article 7 of the Charter must be given the same meaning and the same scope (Case C-450/06 *Varec* [2008] ECR I-581, paragraph 48). Article 8 ECHR and Article 7 of the Charter must be interpreted in accordance with the rights of the child. In particular, Article 24 of the Charter, based on Article 3 of the UN Convention on the Rights of the Child, states that in 'all actions relating to children, whether taken by public authorities or private institutions, the child's best interests must be a primary consideration'; this Court has acknowledged the fundamental rights of the child as set out in Article 24 (Case C 491/10 PPU *Andoni Aguirre Zarraga v S Peltz*, paragraph 61) It follows that the best interests of the child must prevail (Case C-195/08 PPU *Rinau*). Accordingly, Member States must enable the creation of the conditions for children to effectively enjoy their rights, *in casu*, the maternity leave of the commissioning mother to enable the two to bond.

25.   Consequently the objectives and the logic of the Directive do not in any way preclude Member States from applying or introducing laws, regulations or administrative provisions which are favourable to the protection of the safety and health of commissioning mothers who have had babies through a surrogacy arrangement, *a fortiori* when they are breastfeeding, by allowing them to take maternity leave as a result of the birth of the child.

26.   In the light of the foregoing considerations, the answer to the first and second questions is that Directive 92/85 must be interpreted as meaning that Member States are required to provide maternity leave pursuant to Article 8 of that Directive to a female worker who, as a commissioning mother, has had a baby through a surrogacy arrangement, especially where, as in this case, in circumstances she is breastfeeding the baby following the birth.

The Third, Fourth and Fifth Questions

27.   By its third, fourth and fifth questions, which it is appropriate to consider together, the referring tribunal asks whether Article 14 of Directive 2006/54, read in conjunction with Article 2(1)(a) and (b) and (2)(c) of that Directive, is to be interpreted as meaning that an employer's refusal to provide maternity leave to a commissioning mother who has had a baby through a surrogacy arrangement constitutes discrimination on grounds of sex.

28.   Article 14(1) of Directive 2006/54 states that there is to be no direct or indirect discrimination on grounds of sex in the public or private sectors, including public bodies, in relation inter alia to employment and working conditions, including dismissals, as well as pay.

29.   As regards discrimination as referred to in Article 2(1)(a) and (b) of that Directive, the refusal to provide maternity leave in the situation outlined by the referring tribunal constitutes direct discrimination on grounds of sex within the meaning of Article 2(1)(a) if the fundamental reason for that refusal applies exclusively to workers of one sex (see, to that effect, Case C-177/88 *Dekker* [1990] ECR I-3941, paragraph 10; Case C-421/92 *Habermann-Beltermann* [1994] ECR I-1657, paragraph 14; and Case C-506/06 *Mayr*, [2008] ECR I-1017, paragraph 50).

30.   Under the national legislation applicable in a situation such as that at issue in the main proceedings, a commissioning father who has had a baby through a surrogacy arrangement is treated in the same way as a commissioning mother in a comparable situation, in that he is not entitled to paid leave equivalent to maternity leave either. It follows from this that the refusal of Ms D's request is not based on a reason that applies exclusively to workers of one sex.

31.   The Court has consistently held that indirect discrimination on grounds of sex arises where a national measure, albeit formulated in neutral terms, puts considerably more workers of one sex at a disadvantage than the other (see, to that effect, Case C-1/95 *Gerster* [1997] ECR I-5253, paragraph 30; Case C-123/10 *Brachner* [2011] ECR I-10003, paragraph 56; and Case C-7/12 *Riežniece* ECLI:EU:C:2013:410, paragraph 39).

32.   As regards the indirect discrimination referred to in Article 2(1)(b) of Directive 2006/54, it must be noted that there is nothing in the file in the case to establish that the refusal of leave at issue puts female workers at a particular disadvantage compared with male workers.

33.   Consequently, the refusal to grant maternity leave to a commissioning mother, such as Ms D, does not constitute direct or indirect discrimination on grounds of sex within the meaning of Article 2(1)(a) and (b) of Directive 2006/54.

34.   However, unfavorable treatment vis-à-vis an adoptive mother cannot be ruled out. It is for the Member States to decide whether an adoptive mother can enjoy the same rights as a biological mother.

35.   Moreover, it is apparent from the answer given to the first two questions that Directive 92/85 requires Member States to provide maternity leave to a female worker who as a commissioning mother has had a baby through a surrogacy arrangement.

36.   Consequently, whilst a commissioning mother cannot be regarded as having been subject to discrimination on grounds of sex for the purposes of Article 2(2)(c) of Directive

2006/54, it is for the Member State to decide whether she has been discriminated against vis-à-vis an adoptive mother.

37.   In the light of the foregoing observations, the answer to the third, fourth and fifth questions is that Article 14 of Directive 2006/54, read in conjunction with Article 2(1)(a) and (b) and (2)(c) of that Directive, must be interpreted as meaning that an employer's refusal to provide maternity leave to a commissioning mother who has had a baby through a surrogacy arrangement does not constitute discrimination on grounds of sex.

…

Costs

Since these proceedings are, for the parties to the main proceedings, a step in the action pending before the national court, the decision on costs is a matter for that court. Costs incurred in submitting observations to the Court, other than the costs of those parties, are not recoverable.

On those grounds, the Court (Grand Chamber) hereby rules:

1. Council Directive 92/85/EEC of 19 October 1992 on the introduction of measures to encourage improvements in the safety and health at work of pregnant workers and workers who have recently given birth or are breastfeeding (tenth individual Directive within the meaning of Article 16(1) of Directive 89/391/EEC) must be interpreted in light of Articles 7 and 24 of the Charter of Fundamental Rights meaning that Member States and Article 8 of the European Convention of Human Rights are required to provide maternity leave pursuant to Article 8 of that Directive to a female worker who as a commissioning mother has had a baby through a surrogacy arrangement, a fortiori in circumstances where she breastfeeds the baby.

2. Article 14 of Directive 2006/54/EC of the European Parliament and of the Council of 5 July 2006 on the implementation of the principle of equal opportunities and equal treatment of men and women in matters of employment and occupation, read in conjunction with Article 2(1)(a) and (b) and (2)(c) of that Directive, must be interpreted as meaning that an employer's refusal to provide maternity leave to a commissioning mother who has had a baby through a surrogacy arrangement does not constitute discrimination on grounds of sex.

[Signatures]

6

Commentary on
Re C v XYZ County Council

BRIAN SLOAN

I. Introduction

Re C v XYZ County Council (hereafter *Re C*)[1] raises a question going to the very core of the propriety of adoption. In essence, should a child (named Elizabeth in the re-written judgment) be legally disconnected from a natural parent (in this case, Elizabeth's mother) who cannot or will not look after her and placed with unrelated, 'better' parents, or should more effort be put into developing the child's relationship with other members of the natural family (in this case, Elizabeth's father, with whom the mother had only a 'one-night stand' and who was unaware of Elizabeth's existence, or the wider family), even if a placement with such people may turn out to be inappropriate? The Court of Appeal's judgment in the case highlights the potential difficulties with an open-textured, welfare-based approach to answering that question, particularly if one factor (in this case the 'no delay' principle) is given priority in the abstract rather than in a fact-specific and contextual fashion. Fenton-Glynn's fictional dissenting judgment demonstrates that a rights-based approach may provide a more helpful framework for answering *Re C*'s question, even if it is still possible to argue over the correct conclusion and even if such a rights-based approach imports a difficult welfare-oriented aspect into its analysis.[2] This commentary sets out the background to the case and compares the approach of Fenton-Glynn with that of the 'majority'. The commentary also explores developments that have taken place since the real judgment was handed down, which variously support and undermine the original decision and the reimagined judgment.

II. Background

The Adoption and Children Act 2002 aimed to bring about 'more adoptions, more quickly' for children who might otherwise remain in foster care,[3] including by making the welfare

---

[1] *Re C v XYZ County Council* [2007] EWCA Civ 1206, [2008] Fam 54.
[2] See, eg, UN Convention on the Rights of the Child, Art 21.
[3] S Harris-Short, 'New Legislation: The Adoption and Children Bill—A Fast Track to Failure?' [2001] *Child and Family Law Quarterly* 405, 407.

of the child potentially to be adopted the paramount consideration[4] rather than merely the 'first' consideration.[5] It also made welfare the governing criterion in most cases for dispensing with parental consent,[6] allowed a child expressly to be placed for adoption by parental consent without the need for a court order,[7] and placed procedural restrictions on parents' ability to oppose the final adoption order.[8] All of these measures had the potential to prioritise the child's welfare as an individual at the expense of her relationship with her natural family. That said, the Act imposed an adoption-specific version of the welfare principle, requiring the court or adoption agency to consider the child's welfare 'throughout his life',[9] including inter alia the effect of ceasing to be a member of the birth family[10] and the child's relationships with relatives (including their ability and willingness to meet the child's needs)[11] as aspects of the child's welfare.

The 2002 Act preserved the principle that the consent to adoption of a father lacking parental responsibility (PR) (who will never have been married to the child's mother) is not even prima facie required (and does not need to be dispensed with).[12] While the approach under the Adoption Act 1976 had been generally to involve such fathers in the process, the de facto relationship between the parents was highly pertinent.[13] *Re C* provided an early opportunity for the Court of Appeal to consider the proper approach to 'unmarried fathers' under the new Act's version of the welfare principle.

The facts of *Re C* were described as 'extraordinary' in the Court of Appeal,[14] although Fenton-Glynn clearly and cogently disagrees with that description in a manner that influences her approach to the case. A 19 year old woman (named 'Rachel' by Fenton-Glynn) became pregnant with 'Elizabeth' after a one-night stand with F. She discovered the pregnancy at a late stage, and did not tell F or her parents about it. Upon Elizabeth's birth, Rachel, who had a career, immediately made it clear that she wished Elizabeth to be adopted because she felt unable to look after the child. She considered her own parents, from whom she was estranged, to be equally incapable of doing so, and denied that her siblings could provide care. Rachel refused to identify F, but gave sufficient information to make him probably identifiable via a local authority (LA)'s independent enquiries. Rachel left the baby in hospital shortly after birth, and the responsible LA sought court guidance on whether they should approach Elizabeth's extended family members, including her maternal grandparents and F (if he could be identified) with a view to finding a home within the family, despite Rachel's wishes.

HHJ Taylor directed that the LA were under a duty to gather 'as much information about the background of the extended family as they are able to do',[15] which would include disclosing the existence of Elizabeth to her extended maternal family and the putative father and

---

[4] Adoption and Children Act 2002, s 1(2).
[5] Adoption Act 1976, s 6.
[6] Adoption and Children Act 2002, s 52.
[7] ibid, s 19.
[8] ibid, s 47.
[9] ibid, s 1(2).
[10] ibid, s 1(4)(c).
[11] ibid, s 1(4)(f).
[12] ibid, s 1(2).
[13] See, eg, *Re H; Re G (Adoption: Consultation of Unmarried Fathers)* [2001] 1 FLR 646.
[14] *Re C*, above n 1, [63] (Thorpe LJ).
[15] ibid, [2].

his family, if he was identifiable. The judge opined that the 2002 Act heralded 'significant changes' in the approach to be taken.[16] He held that the Act's welfare checklist removed the relevant LA discretion under the 1976 Act. Moreover, the judge thought it obvious that Elizabeth's interests would be served by placing her within the family if a suitable person came forward. The Court of Appeal, however, allowed Rachel's appeal and ordered that the children's guardian and the LA should take no steps to identify F or inform him of Elizabeth's birth, or to introduce Elizabeth to the maternal grandparents or assess them as potential carers.

III. The Court of Appeal's Decision and Fenton-Glynn's Dissent Compared

Giving the lead judgment in the Court of Appeal, Arden LJ (with whom Thorpe and Lawrence Collins LJJ agreed) found no duty to make enquiries that did not 'genuinely further the prospect of finding a long-term carer … without delay',[17] and neither F nor the maternal grandparents were considered to be likely carers because there was no reason to doubt Rachel's assessment.

Arden LJ admitted that the paramountcy principle in section 1 of the 2002 Act embraced Elizabeth's interest in retaining her identity, which she apparently equated with the obligation to consider the effect of her ceasing to be a member of the birth family and her relationships with 'relatives'. Both the grandparents and F were considered 'relatives', despite F's ignorance of Elizabeth's birth, but that alone did not generate an obligation to approach them. On Arden LJ's analysis, which elsewhere I have criticised with reference to the range of rights protected by the UN Convention on the Rights of the Child,[18] the birth family were not prioritised by virtue of their status, and the only aspect of welfare emphasised by Parliament was preventing delay.[19] Thus, there could be no absolute duty to make the enquiries. Arden LJ also denied the existence of an 'expectation of disclosure'.[20] While disclosure would be in the child's interests in many cases, in 'exceptional situations' such as this it was appropriate for relatives, including a father, to remain ignorant of a child's birth at the time of adoption.[21] This, she opined, was consistent with the fact that F's consent was not required for the adoption due to his lack of PR. The over-arching consideration was the welfare of the child as an individual. Where a child had never lived with the birth family, the tie was overtaken by the need to find a permanent home. Four month old Elizabeth had formed bonds with her foster parents, and Arden LJ held that there was 'no basis for supposing that [F] could provide a home for E[lizabeth]', and that possibility was 'too intangible'

[16] ibid, [75].
[17] ibid, [3].
[18] B Sloan, 'Conflicting Rights: English Adoption Law and the Implementation of the UN Convention on the Rights of the Child' [2013] *Child and Family Law Quarterly* 40, 52.
[19] Adoption and Children Act 2002, s 1(3).
[20] *Re C*, above n 1, [23].
[21] ibid, [24].

to delay an adoptive placement outside the family.[22] The grandparents' situation similarly militated against delay, particularly since they had not made an application to provide care.

Arden LJ also noted that the Article 8 right to receive information relating to one's identity was within the state's margin of appreciation following *Odièvre v France*.[23] The only such right provided under the 2002 Act related to the adoption file, so no informational right would justify the enquiries, despite the fact that the quality of the information gathered may well decline over time. Further, any benefit that Elizabeth would eventually derive from information about her origins was secondary to, and would delay, the objective of finding a long-term home, notwithstanding the inevitable complexities associated with the concept of identity and the arguable value to the child of knowing that relevant enquiries took place even if they proved fruitless.

Fenton-Glynn agrees that there can be no absolute duty to make the relevant enquiries, and it is certainly true that such a duty would jeopardise individualised decision-making. She also agrees that the natural family are not inherently privileged by the welfare checklist, even if she clearly thinks that their status is more important in the welfare analysis than the 'majority' did. Significantly, however, she takes issue with Arden LJ's assertion that the relevant enquiries must relate solely to finding a long-term carer for Elizabeth. Fenton-Glynn accuses the 'majority' of taking an unnecessarily narrow view of welfare, and considers that the child's prima facie rights to information about her origins (protected by the United Nations Convention on the Rights of the Child (UNCRC)) can also justify the enquiries because of the interdependence of identity and welfare. She also makes use of empirical evidence that is absent from the 'majority' judgments.

Even if the 'majority' are correct that enquiries not aimed specifically at finding a long-term home cannot be justified, Fenton-Glynn is concerned at their over-reliance on the mother's evidence and the absence of any indication about the length of delay that the enquiries would cause, despite her general appreciation of the need to move swiftly. While she is respectful of Rachel's interest in privacy and concurs that Rachel should not be forced to disclose the identity of F, she notes that the LA will be able to make independent enquiries and that Rachel had cited no specific risk to herself or Elizabeth beyond her own view that F was unsuitable.

The 'majority' of the Court of Appeal considered their approach to be compatible with Article 8 of the European Convention on Human Rights, inter alia since F did not have 'family life' with Elizabeth, having neither lived with Rachel nor expressed commitment to Elizabeth. Despite his ignorance of Elizabeth's existence, making it impossible to express such commitment, it was held that preventing F from obtaining the *possibility* of a right with regard to Elizabeth did not violate Article 8. There was therefore no need for a justification under Article 8(2). Fenton-Glynn reluctantly concurs with this conclusion on 'family life', but criticises with reference to 'private life' Arden LJ's assertion that the existence of a right for Elizabeth to be raised by F could be determined only when a final adoption order was to be made, and that a potential right could not require disclosure at this stage. This, on Fenton-Glynn's analysis, failed to put the child at the centre of the decision in question. While she acknowledges that the child's right to respect for her private life is qualified, she

---

[22] ibid, [48].
[23] *Odièvre v France* [2003] 1 FCR 621 (European Court of Human Rights).

convincingly considers that the proportionality requirement would prevent Rachel's views from carrying absolute weight.

Unsurprisingly, Fenton-Glynn concludes that an order similar to the one made at first instance is appropriate, albeit emphasising the need for Rachel to have regard to the extent of Elizabeth's rights and interests, and including assessment of F and the grandparents as potential carers if they are willing to take on the role. Her analysis is much more nuanced and palatable than that of the majority in giving proper consideration to the various rights and aspects of welfare relevant to Elizabeth. She by no means ignores Rachel's interests and does not simply disagree with every conclusion drawn by the 'majority' on principle. This is arguably appropriate in light of the difficult issues raised by Marshall's argument that

> [s]howing care and respect by listening to, and acting upon, a woman's choice not to disclose information concerning the 'father' [sic] and her wider family respects her privacy and confidentiality rights including her health, and possibly her life, and that of the child.[24]

Nevertheless, Fenton-Glynn justifiably stops short of unquestioningly acting upon that choice. She convincingly produces a distinctive judgment with the child at the centre that could not be described (as the majority's approach was) as 'glaringly mother-centred',[25] even if a children's rights approach does not produce unchallengeable conclusions and might have to be relational to some extent.[26]

IV. Responses to, and Developments Since, *Re C*

A. Judicial Interventions

While *Re C* has been subject to academic criticism,[27] the judiciary have been arguably more ambivalent towards cases where its approach (prioritising adoption without delay) would have been pertinent.[28] An example of this ambivalence is *Re A (Father: Knowledge of Child's Birth)*,[29] the facts of which many would more readily describe as 'exceptional' as compared to *Re C*'s. In that case, a mother similarly sought to prevent a father from finding out about the birth and development of their child, whom she intended to relinquish for adoption. The key difference was that the parents were married. After several family members were murdered by the Taliban in Afghanistan, the father suffered from 'Severe Depression with Psychotic Symptoms and Post Traumatic Stress Disorder'.[30] His behaviour was unpredictable, and violent towards his wife and himself. The Court of Appeal (upholding the first

---

[24] J Marshall, 'Concealed Births, Adoption and Human Rights Law: Being Wary of Seeking to Open Windows into People's Souls' [2012] *CLJ* 325, 354.

[25] A Bainham, 'Arguments about Parentage' [2008] *CLJ* 322, 351.

[26] See, eg, the treatment of *Re A (Children) (Conjoined Twins: Medical Treatment)* [2001] Fam 147 (CA) in this volume.

[27] Above n 25. B Sloan, '*Re C (A Child) (Adoption: Duty of Local Authority)*—Welfare and the Rights of the Birth Family in "Fast Track" Adoption Cases' [2009] *Child and Family Law Quarterly* 87.

[28] See, eg, *Re F (A Child) (Placement Order)* [2008] EWCA Civ 439, [2008] 2 FLR 550.

[29] [2011] EWCA Civ 273, [2011] 2 FLR 123.

[30] ibid, [4].

instance decision) nevertheless refused to grant the mother's request. A 'very high degree of exceptionality' was required before such secrecy could be justified,[31] and was not present. Significantly, as the mother's husband the father had both PR for, and 'family life' under Article 8 of the ECHR with, the child. His consent was therefore prima facie necessary before the adoption could proceed, and the judge below failed to see 'how the consent could reasonably be dispensed with if it has never actually been sought'.[32] With reference to the child's welfare throughout his life, the judge also refused to hold that the concealment of the child's existence from the father was in the child's best interests. While the bare result is inconsistent with *Re C* (and consistent with Fenton-Glynn's judgment), the case confirms the impression that the judiciary prefer to attach more importance to the relationship between the parents than the de facto relationship between each parent and the child.

In *Re B (A Child) (Care Proceedings: Appeal)*,[33] however, Lord Neuberger noted and did not expressly disagree with my criticism of *Re C* in light of the UNCRC.[34] Influenced by that Convention, he inspired a more rigorous approach to adoption, asserting that 'adoption of a child against her parents' wishes should only be contemplated as a last resort— when all else fails'.[35] On his analysis, '[a]lthough the child's interests in an adoption case are "paramount" … a court must never lose sight of the fact that those interests include being brought up by her natural family'.[36] The prominence of the UNCRC in Fenton-Glynn's judgment would be appropriate in a 'real' English judgment in light of *Re B* and the Supreme Court's later decision (in a different context) in *R (on the application of SG and others (previously JS and others)) v Secretary of State for Work and Pensions*.[37]

The legacy of *Re B* is demonstrated by *Re B-S (Children) (Adoption Order: Leave to Oppose)* and the case law it produced by imposing exacting standards regarding LA evidence and judicial reasoning inter alia.[38] The Court of Appeal has admittedly 'emphasise[d], with as much force as possible, that *Re B-S* was not intended to change and has not changed the law',[39] and judges have retained scepticism about which placements are likely to be realistic. Moreover, McFarlane LJ may have risked causing confusion in *Re W (A child)* by asserting that there is no 'presumption or right in favour of the natural family' in adoption cases,[40] which seems consistent with Arden LJ's remarks in *Re C*. That said, some recent case law on unmarried fathers is arguably more consistent with Fenton-Glynn's judgment than with the 'majority' approach in *Re C*. In *Re S (Children)*, Macur LJ held that the judge had erred in failing to seek a further assessment of the father as a potential carer for his daughter.[41] Moreover, Holman J declined to make an adoption order in *A and B v Rotherham Metropolitan Borough Council*,[42] where the true genetic father of the relevant child (lacking PR)

---

[31] ibid, [25] (Longmore LJ).
[32] ibid, [7].
[33] [2013] UKSC 33, [2013] 1 WLR 1911.
[34] ibid, [103], citing Sloan, above n 18.
[35] ibid, [104].
[36] ibid, [104].
[37] [2015] UKSC 16, [2015] 1 WLR 1449.
[38] [2013] EWCA Civ 1146, [2014] 1 WLR 563. See, eg, B Sloan, 'Adoption Decisions in England: *Re B (A Child) (Care Proceedings: Appeal)* and Beyond' (2015) 37 *Journal of Social Welfare and Family Law* 437.
[39] *Re R (A Child)* [2014] EWCA Civ 1625, [2015] 1 WLR 3273, [44] (Sir James Munby).
[40] [2016] EWCA Civ 793, [73].
[41] [2014] EWCA Civ 135, [2015] 1 FLR 130.
[42] [2014] EWFC 47, [2015] 2 FLR 381.

came forward only after the adoption application and successfully argued that the child should be placed with the father's sister.

In the post-*Re C* decision in *Anayo v Germany*,[43] the European Court of Human Rights held that a father can have relevant 'family life' with a child where he has not cohabited with the mother but their relationship was not haphazard and he has expressed a desire for contact with the child. While that may still fail to accommodate a father who had only a fleeting relationship with his child's mother and is unable to demonstrate any commitment to the child because (through no fault of his) he is ignorant of the child's existence, the Court held that 'close relationships short of family life' would generally fall within the ambit of private life.[44] Nevertheless, it held in *YC v United Kingdom* that the overall scheme of the 2002 Act is consistent with Article 8 of the ECHR.[45]

In any case, it must be recognised that adoption cases are particularly fact-sensitive, and that *Re C* has not been specifically overruled.

B. Governmental and Legislative Interventions

Schedule 6 to the Welfare Reform Act 2009 could in principle have reversed *Re C*'s effect. Somewhat consistently with several other jurisdictions,[46] it would have obliged mothers not married to the fathers of their children to register those fathers as such, except in limited circumstances.[47] Prima facie, this would have given F PR for Elizabeth,[48] and required his consent to adoption to be given or dispensed with. Schedule 6, however, is apparently not due to be commenced.[49]

Most relevant Government policy and legislation, moreover, has been aimed at increasing and speeding up adoption still further.[50] For example, the Children and Families Act 2014's concept of 'fostering for adoption' effectively requires an LA to consider placing the child with prospective adopters even where it is not yet authorised to place the child for adoption via the birth parents or a court.[51]

Parliament and the Government's general approach appears to endorse Arden LJ's prioritisation of the 'no delay' principle. There may be a tension between the attitudes of the Government and the judiciary to adoption, and Doughty asserts that '[t]here can only be continuing concern about the lack of direction in adoption law'.[52] In any case, the recent

---

[43] *Anayo v Germany* [2011] 1 FLR 1883.

[44] ibid, [58].

[45] [2012] 2 FLR 332. *cf Soares de Melo v Portugal* (Application no 72850/14), 16 February 2016 (European Court of Human Rights).

[46] Austrian Civil Code, Art 163a(1); Paternity Act 1975 (Finland), s 8; Act in Respect of Children No 76/2003 (Iceland), Art 1; Children Act (Denmark), Arts 7–8; Children and Parents Code (1949:381) (Sweden), s 2:4.

[47] Department for Children, Schools & Families, *The Registration of Births (Parents Not Married And Not Acting Together) Regulations 2010: A Consultation* (2009).

[48] Children Act 1989, s 4(1)(a).

[49] J Clifton, 'The Long Road to Universal Parental Responsibility: Some Implications from Research into Marginal Fathers' [2014] *Family Law* 858, 859.

[50] See now Education and Adoption Act 2016; Department for Education, *Adoption: A Vision for Change* (2016); Children and Social Work Act 2017.

[51] Children and Families Act 2014, s 2; see also s 14.

[52] J Doughty, 'Myths and Misunderstanding in Adoption Law and Policy' [2015] *Child and Family Law Quarterly* 331, 353.

judicial approach seems closer to that of Fenton-Glynn's judgment in giving due consideration to a potential adoptee's full range of rights and interests.

V. Conclusion

No doubt the 'majority' of the Court of Appeal in *Re C* genuinely thought that they were
placing Elizabeth at the centre of the decision. Fenton-Glynn much more obviously does
so, however, and she also takes the longer-term view of welfare that the 2002 Act arguably requires, even if it is not possible conclusively to resolve the tensions inherent within
that Act, and whatever the difficulties of rights-based approaches involving very young
children.[53] It is possible that the Court of Appeal's conclusion on the real-life facts was
correct: there may have been particular and verifiable worrying characteristics of F (or the
grandparents) rendering him patently unsuitable to care for Elizabeth, or for Elizabeth
even to know him, such that LA enquiries would have been demonstrably detrimental to
her interests. The difficulty, as Fenton-Glynn elucidates, is that no such specific factors are
alleged on the face of the Court of Appeal's judgments, and the Court refused to allow any
such factors to be properly investigated. It seems unlikely, moreover, that the first instance
judge would have reached his conclusion if relevant concerns were so obvious. The absence
of proper contextual analysis severely limited the utility of the guidance provided by the
'majority' judgment to LAs faced with similar situations, who might now be criticised for
failing to make the very sort of enquiries that the LA in *Re C* were ultimately prohibited
from making. That LA's unsuccessful attempt to appeal *Re C* to the House of Lords suggests
serious dissatisfaction with the Court of Appeal's judgment.[54] In any case, a rights-based
analysis provides a proper basis for consideration that does more to avoid the artificial
prioritisation of certain rights and interests over others in the context of a purely welfare-
oriented approach.

[53] *cf* MDA Freeman, 'Taking Children's Rights More Seriously' (1992) 6 *International Journal of Law, Policy and the Family* 52.
[54] *Re C* [2008] Fam 54, 74.

Court of Appeal (England and Wales)

Re C v XYZ County Council

Dissenting Judgment of Fenton-Glynn LJ:

1.   The case before us concerns the welfare of a four-month old child, whom I shall call Elizabeth. Elizabeth was conceived as a result of a one night stand between her mother, whom I shall call Rachel, and an unidentified man. Rachel was 19 years old at the time, and kept the pregnancy secret from her family and friends. The first time she sought medical help was when she went into labour, and gave birth to Elizabeth. Immediately after the birth, Rachel informed the Local Authority that she did not wish to care for Elizabeth, and would like for her to be placed for adoption.

2.   The questions before the court are whether enquiries should be made to identify Elizabeth's father and inform him of the adoption proceedings, and whether Rachel's family should be assessed as potential carers for Elizabeth.

3.   In deciding whether or not such enquiries or assessments should be made, it is important to recall that the paramount consideration of the court must be Elizabeth's welfare. This is required by the Adoption and Children Act 2002, and is also reflected in Article 21 of the UN Convention on the Rights of the Child. The question that is faced by the court is how her interests are best met, taking into account not only her immediate needs, but her long-term well-being.

4.   The relevant legislation is section 1 of the Adoption and Children Act 2002. This reads:

(1)   This section applies whenever a court or adoption agency is coming to a decision relating to the adoption of a child.

(2)   The paramount consideration of the court or adoption agency must be the child's welfare, throughout his life.

(3)   The court or adoption agency must at all times bear in mind that, in general, any delay in coming to the decision is likely to prejudice the child's welfare.

(4)   The court or adoption agency must have regard to the following matters (among others)—

  (a)   the child's ascertainable wishes and feelings regarding the decision (considered in the light of the child's age and understanding),

  (b)   the child's particular needs,

  (c)   the likely effect on the child (throughout his life) of having ceased to be a member of the original family and become an adopted person,

> (d)   the child's age, sex, background and any of the child's characteristics which the court or agency considers relevant,
>
> (e)   any harm (within the meaning of the Children Act 1989 (c. 41)) which the child has suffered or is at risk of suffering,
>
> (f)   the relationship which the child has with relatives, and with any other person in relation to whom the court or agency considers the relationship to be relevant, including—
>
>> (i)   the likelihood of any such relationship continuing and the value to the child of its doing so,
>>
>> (ii)   the ability and willingness of any of the child's relatives, or of any such person, to provide the child with a secure environment in which the child can develop, and otherwise to meet the child's needs,
>>
>> (iii)   the wishes and feelings of any of the child's relatives, or of any such person, regarding the child.

(5)   In placing the child for adoption, the adoption agency must give due consideration to the child's religious persuasion, racial origin and cultural and linguistic background.

(6)   The court or adoption agency must always consider the whole range of powers available to it in the child's case (whether under this Act or the Children Act 1989); and the court must not make any order under this Act unless it considers that making the order would be better for the child than not doing so.

Decision at First Instance

5.   At first instance, His Honour Judge Taylor decided that under the Adoption and Children Act 2002 the Local Authority had no choice, and were under a duty to inform themselves of as much as possible concerning the background of the child's extended family. He held:

> [O]bviously it will be in the interests of this child to be placed within the family … the reality is—as we all know nowadays—that when children are adopted they come to a time in their lives when they do inquire about their parentage and it would be cruel in the extreme to prevent this child having as much knowledge as possible about her background in the event that she is adopted, even if that information comes without the consent of the mother but as a result of the authorities informing themselves of the relevant information.

6.   On this basis, Judge Taylor gave Rachel 21 days to consider her position, and inform her family and the father herself. If she did not do so, however, he directed the local authority to disclose the existence and identity of Elizabeth to the extended maternal family and, if identified, the putative father and any extended paternal family.

7.   Rachel has appealed.

The Issues for Determination

8.   I concur with the majority of this Court that Judge Taylor misdirected himself as to the obligation to undertake enquiries. It is clear that section 1 of the Adoption and Children Act

contains no duty, save that the court or adoption agency make paramount the consideration of the child's welfare throughout his or her life. While this may indicate that enquiries
should be made in the individual circumstances—a matter that will be discussed below—it
cannot place a duty on the Local Authority that it be done in all cases. However, I disagree
with the basis for this decision, both in terms of the question the Court is called to answer,
and as a consequence, in the ultimate exercise of discretion in relation to Elizabeth.

9.   In her leading judgment, Lady Justice Arden articulates the question before this Court
as follows: does the 2002 Act impose a duty on the local authority to make enquiries about
long-term care for Elizabeth with her mother's family and, if those enquiries did not yield
a long-term carer, with Elizabeth's father, if identified, and his family?

10.   With respect, the question has been formulated too narrowly, and consequently, has
distorted the analysis of the issue. What is required is a holistic understanding of Elizabeth's
interests: the question before the court should be whether the Act imposes a duty to make
enquiries as to the possibility for long-term care with the mother's family, as well as to the
identity of the father. The issue of whether enquiries should be made concerning the father
should not be predicated upon the outcome of enquiries as to the ability of the mother's
family to care for Elizabeth, nor should they be confined solely to whether he would be a
potential long-term carer. Elizabeth's welfare must be interpreted in a much wider manner
than a simple focus on long-term care, to include a more holistic understanding of her best
interests.

11.   This narrow formulation of the issue for decision by the majority comes from a similarly narrow reading of the 2002 Act, namely that enquiries are not in Elizabeth's interests
simply because they would provide more information about her background; enquiries
must genuinely further the prospect of finding a long-term carer without delay. In coming
to this conclusion, Lady Justice Arden relies on the separation of the no delay principle in
section 1(3) from the other welfare considerations in section 1(4), to suggest that this factor
should be elevated above all others in the determination of welfare.

12.   With respect, in circumscribing the analysis in this way, Lady Justice Arden contorts
and subverts the welfare test. The overarching question that must guide the court, including in deciding whether enquiries are warranted, is the best interests of the child. Nothing
more, nothing less. While delay is identified by Parliament as a factor that can cause particular harm, this does not mean that it should dictate the scope of the welfare test. If we look
to the wording of section 1(3), it states that 'in general' delay will be prejudicial, showing
that this is simply one factor to be considered in the context of the child's overall situation,
albeit an important factor. As such, the statutory wording by no means implies that enquiries would only be consistent with best interests if they genuinely furthered the prospect of
finding a long-term carer for the child without delay.

13.   Such an understanding of the issue before the Court reflects a very individualistic
concept of welfare, and fails to take into account the multifaceted nature of Elizabeth's
interests. While Elizabeth was four months old at the time of the hearing, and thus providing stability and security were of increasing importance, to focus only on this matter is to
take a very short-term view of her welfare. The significance of identifying the father goes far
beyond the issue of providing care. While this is of itself of great consequence—especially
as it may open the door for members of the father's family to care for the child—of equal
concern is the child's right to identity.

14.   By failing to take steps to establish the identity of her father, Elizabeth is being denied the opportunity of knowing her biological origins, if she wishes to do so. Studies have shown that a lack of knowledge in this area can have significant implications on a child's emotional and psychological well-being, and in the formation of his or her identity (see, for example, J Triseliotis, *In Search of Origins* (London, Routledge & Kegan Paul, 1973); M Ryburn, 'Adopted Children's Identity and Information Needs' (1995) 9(3) *Children & Society* 41). As such, this must be an important consideration in determining Elizabeth's long-term interests.

15.   This importance of identity, and knowledge of origins, for a child is reflected in the UN Convention on the Rights of the Child (CRC). As an unincorporated international treaty, the CRC is not part of the law of the United Kingdom. However, as Baroness Hale made clear in paragraph 78 of *Smith v Secretary of State for Work and Pensions and Another* [2006] UKHL 35:

> Even if an international treaty has not been incorporated into domestic law, our domestic legisla-
> tion has to be construed so far as possible so as to comply with the international obligations, which
> we have undertaken. When two interpretations … are possible, the interpretation chosen should
> be that which better complies with the commitment to the welfare of children which this country
> made when ratifying the UNCRC.

16.   As such, the provisions of the Convention should be used as an interpretative aid, to shed light on the various factors inherent in the child's best interests.

17.   Article 7 of the Convention requires that every child has the right from birth to know and be cared for by his or her parents, as far as this is possible. These rights—to know one's parents, and to be cared for by them—are joint and severable, and each has important implications for the child's rights. As such, even if there is no possibility of the father pro- viding long-term care for the child, knowledge of origins is important in and of itself. This is further emphasised by Article 8 of the Convention, which protects the right of the child to preserve his or her identity, including nationality, name and family relations without unlawful interference.

18.   The combined effect of Articles 7 and 8 CRC make clear that the child's identity, and knowing who one's parents are, is of fundamental importance, and consequently must be a weighty factor when determining whether further enquiries into the identity of Elizabeth's father are warranted.

19.   Even if Lady Justice Arden is correct, however, and the question to be asked is whether enquiries would genuinely further the prospect of finding a long-term carer without delay, there are two additional issues that arise. The first is how this prospect is evaluated. In deciding whether enquiries would further this aim, the information relied on comes solely from Rachel herself. Lady Justice Arden states that 'there is no basis for supposing that he could provide a home for Elizabeth' [at 46]. With respect, without taking steps to identify him, there is no basis for supposing that he could not do so.

20.   Likewise, in the consideration of the mother's family as carers, emphasis is placed on the information provided by Rachel, and whether she considers that her siblings or parents could offer long-term care. In my view, the opinions of Rachel as to the caring capabilities of her family are of little relevance. Lady Justice Arden emphasises that the Local Authority

must examine what she had said critically, and in this case, there was 'no reason to think that [the information she had given] is materially inaccurate' (at [44]). This is to misconstrue the question that the Local Authority should be asking itself. The role of the Local Authority is not only to check information given to it if there is reason to think it is inaccurate, and to qualify this by 'material' adds an additional burden. This gives a great deal of control to the mother, and restricts the power of the Local Authority unjustifiably. The role of the Local Authority should be to independently check information given to it, especially regarding potential carers for a child. It cannot simply rely on the views or opinions of one individual, but must scrutinise it objectively.

21.   Of course, if Rachel indicates that she does not want her parents to care for Elizabeth then this would be an important and influential factor in the welfare test. Such a placement would involve Elizabeth being cared for within the social and familial sphere of her mother, which could have adverse consequences for Elizabeth's welfare. If Rachel were antipathetic to the placement, it would be doubtful whether Elizabeth's welfare would be furthered, particularly given the possibility of Rachel's disruption. However, where the issue is simply whether Rachel believes that her family would have the capacity to care for the child, this must be approached in a different matter, with Elizabeth's welfare at the forefront of the determination.

22.   The second issue that arises is that there has been no articulation of the length, or cause, of the anticipated delay in identifying the father. An investigation to determine the identity of the father does not have to, and indeed should not, take an inordinate amount of time. This is particularly the case here, as the Local Authority has already indicated that he would be identifiable, even without Rachel's assistance. While an investigation into his ability to care for Elizabeth may be more time consuming this would only follow if he showed an interest in doing so, and it were considered to be in Elizabeth's best interests to undertake such a process. However, in such a situation, the Local Authority would have the advantage of having collected their own information concerning the father, and would no longer be relying purely on the opinions of the mother.

23.   For these reasons, I find that while the majority were correct to find that there is no absolute obligation to make enquiries, they were wrong to confine the duty of the Local Authority to be purely focused on the long-term care of the child. Instead, the question for consideration for the court is, solely and simply: what is in the best interests of the child in this case?

Should the Birth Family be Given Preference?

24.   In light of the misdirection from Judge Taylor, it is for this Court to consider the matter afresh, and come to its own determination as to how to exercise its discretion concerning contacting the mother's family, and taking steps to identify the father. We are in as good a position as the judge to exercise that discretion and accordingly there is no case for remission.

25.   The first issue that should be addressed is whether the biological family—that is, the father, his family or Rachel's family—should be given any preference as potential carers for Elizabeth?

26.   It is clear that section 1 does not privilege care by the birth family over adoption by strangers, simply because they have biological ties to the child. However, it must be a consideration in the welfare determination. Section 1(4)(c) requires that the Court look to the likely effect on the child throughout his or her life of having ceased to be a member of the original family, and having become a member of his or her adoptive family. Importantly, the reference to 'original family' indicates that it is not only those with a legal relationship with the child who must be considered, but all those who could be considered 'family'. Similarly, section 1(4)(f) requires the Court to have regard to the relationship that the child has with relatives, including:

(i)   the likelihood of any such relationship continuing and the value to the child of its doing so;
(ii)   the ability and willingness of any of the child's relatives, or of any such person, to provide the child with a secure environment in which the child can develop, and otherwise to meet the child's needs;
(iii)   the wishes and feelings of any of the child's relatives, or of any such person, regarding the child.

27.   Under section 144, 'relative' is defined to mean 'a grandparent, brother, sister, uncle or aunt, whether of the full blood or half-blood or by marriage', while section 1(8) explicitly provides that this term is not confined to legal relationships. As such, the natural father must also be considered under this section.

28.   Although subsection (i) presupposes that a relationship already exists between the child and the relatives in question, no such precondition exists in relation to the latter two provisions. As such, section 1(4)(f) requires us to consider whether either the mother's family, the father or the father's family would be able to provide a secure environment, or otherwise meet the child's needs. There is no way we can tell whether any such person can provide a secure environment without undertaking such an investigation as to the identity of the father. While this assumes that the information is readily available, the facts suggest that this is indeed the case.

29.   For these reasons, I find that Elizabeth's welfare indicates that appropriate steps should be taken to identify the father, and assess the ability of the wider family to care for the child. Of course, such investigations have to be balanced against the prejudice that is caused, in general, by delay in providing the child with a long-term placement. At four months, Elizabeth is starting to form attachments, and the Local Authority must move swiftly, and keep a keen eye on the time each investigation and evaluation takes, in order to ensure that Elizabeth's best interests are promoted at all times. They must weigh the potential delay caused by each step, anticipating the length of time it will take, and the outcome it will produce for her.

How Far do we Go to Identify the Father?

30.   The question remains: what steps are 'appropriate' in such circumstances? How far should the Local Authority go in its efforts to identify the father? And what role should Rachel's wishes play in this determination?

31.   Our judicial authority on this matter is clear. The Local Authority should not coerce or compel an unwilling mother to name a father, if she does not wish. In *Re L* [2007] EWHC 1771 (Fam), Mr Justice Munby stated that there was 'something deeply unsettling and unat-

tractive' with the proposition that women should be cross-examined for information on the father, and even more so that they should be open to imprisonment for criminal contempt of court for lying about the extent of their knowledge. This approach is both correct, and humane, taking into account the mother's right to privacy.

32.   The importance of allowing a mother a degree of privacy can be seen in the implications not only for the specific individual mother coming before the courts, but also for any woman who finds herself with an unwanted pregnancy. In *Z County Council v R* ([2001] 1 FLR 365), Mr Justice Holman made clear that if this privacy were to be eroded, there would be 'a real risk that more pregnant women would seek abortions or give birth secretly, to the risk of both themselves and their babies'. As such, he identified a strong social need to enable mothers to make discrete, dignified and humane arrangements for the adoption of their children, 'if the mother *for good reason*, so wishes' (my emphasis). This is similar to the argument of the Guardian in this case. While she accepted that there can be no absolute obligation under section 1 to approach the father or the wider family of the child, she argued that there should be an expectation of disclosure, with the circumstances in which this does not occur limited to cases such as those where the life of the child would be at risk.

33.   In their judgments for the majority, Lady Justice Arden and Lord Justice Thorpe refer to this as an 'exceptional' or 'extraordinary' case. With respect, I disagree. Despite the fact that nowadays few mothers give up their babies for adoption at birth, there is little exceptional about this case. The situation of a mother who has a one-night stand and does not disclose the pregnancy to the father because she wants nothing further to do with him is nothing unique. There was no suggestion that there would be a danger to the mother or child—either physical or psychological—should the father be named, and no reason put forward by the mother not to name the father, except that she did not think that he would be a suitable carer. This is for the social services, not the mother, to decide.

34.   While Rachel should not be coerced or compelled to identify the father, the Local Authority should seek to persuade her to do so where possible, over a defined period of time as suggested by Judge Taylor. In doing so, Rachel should be informed of the importance for Elizabeth of having such knowledge, both in terms of her right to identity, and the possibility of kinship care with the father, or the father's extended family.

35.   If Rachel chooses not to provide this information, the Local Authority informs us that, on the basis of the information already given, it is likely that the father could be identified without further assistance from her. In this case, the Local Authority is able to undertake its own discreet enquiries into the matter. Having said this, there is a danger that the Local Authority may draw an incorrect conclusion, which must inform the approach that is taken. Any enquiries should not identify Rachel by name, but instead present the father with the option of a DNA test to determine his parenthood. This allows a balance to be drawn between the right of Rachel to privacy, and the right of Elizabeth to establish her identity, and be cared for by her parent if possible.

The Right to Respect for Private and Family Life

36.   The Court is a public authority for the purpose of section 6 of the Human Rights Act 1998 and we must therefore consider the implications of the European Convention for the Protection of Human Rights and Fundamental Freedoms 1950 (ECHR) on the decision

whether to take steps to identify and contact the father, or assess the wider maternal family as carers. The relevant provision, Article 8, reads as follows:

1. Everyone has the right to respect for his private and family life, his home and his correspondence.

2. There shall be no interference by a public authority with the exercise of this right except such as is in accordance with the law and is necessary in a democratic society in the interests of national security, public safety or the economic well-being of the country, for the prevention of disorder or crime, for the protection of health or morals or for the protection of the rights and freedoms of others.

37.   The Strasbourg jurisprudence has made clear that while the relationship between a mother and child will automatically fall within the scope of Article 8 and respect for family life from the moment of birth (*Marckx v Belgium* (1979–1980) 2 EHRR 330), the relationship between an unmarried father and his child will not be similarly protected. Indeed, in order to establish a potential claim under Article 8, the father will have to demonstrate that he has either made a commitment to the mother or the child herself (*Keegan v Ireland* [1994] ECHR 57).

38.   On the facts as they have been reported by Rachel, the father has neither expressed nor made any commitment to her. Elizabeth was conceived as a result of a one-night stand, and there was no relationship akin to family life with the mother to bring the relationship within the scope of Article 8. Nor does the father have any family life with Elizabeth—he has no knowledge of her existence, and therefore has no possibility of creating such a tie. Indeed, he is precluded from obtaining a right to respect for family life with Elizabeth by the actions of Rachel. This is deeply troubling. It appears both illogical and undesirable that a mother can unilaterally decide whether the father and child's rights are engaged under Article 8. Nevertheless, this remains the result of the well-established Strasbourg jurisprudence.

39.   While it is clear that no family life exists between Elizabeth and her father, what is overlooked by the majority in their judgments is the right of Elizabeth to respect for private life under Article 8. The guardian submitted that Elizabeth has her own Convention right to be brought up by her natural father, and while Lady Justice Arden acknowledges that it could raise a potential issue, she indicates that it would be a matter for the final adoption order, not the present hearing. With respect, this is a fundamental oversight. Elizabeth must be at the centre of our decision-making process, and her rights and interests must be articulated and considered. This is true even if Article 8 does not add anything to the examination of her welfare already being undertaken under section 1. Indeed, Article 8 arguably provides lesser protection than is available under the 2002 Act: while under Article 8, Elizabeth's rights may be qualified by a parent's rights or interests, the position of paramountcy contained in the domestic legislation allows no such qualification. Nevertheless, only to consider the ECHR rights of the father, or indeed the mother, is to relegate Elizabeth to the object, rather than the subject, of these proceedings.

40.   The Strasbourg jurisprudence has recognised that the definition of an individual's identity falls within the scope of Article 8(1), including the identification of a biological parent by a child (see *Mikulic v Croatia* (2002) ECHR 27). This right has always been considered in the context of a child trying to establish whether a known person is their father, rather than the initial step of attempting to identify that individual; nevertheless, it is axiomatic that Elizabeth's rights are engaged under Article 8(1).

41.   Importantly, Article 8(2) permits interference with Elizabeth's rights in this respect if the relevant measure pursues a legitimate aim, and the steps taken are proportionate to achieving this. In this case, the decision not to coerce or compel the mother to identify the father must be seen to pursue the legitimate aim of protecting the rights and interests of the mother to privacy. However, such protection will only be proportionate if the Local Authority seeks to persuade the mother of the importance of Elizabeth's rights in this respect, takes independent steps to verify the information the mother has given them, and attempts to identify the father on that basis, as set out above. It cannot be proportionate to allow the mother's word to be an absolute defence to any attempts to contact the father or provide the child with care within her wider extended family.

Conclusion

42.   Accordingly, I would direct the Local Authority:

—   to take steps to identify Elizabeth's father, if possible. While the mother should not be coerced, the importance of this for Elizabeth's right to identity, and the possibility of a permanent placement with family, should be emphasised to her, and independent steps taken by the Local Authority where the father is identifiable;

—   to assess the father (if identifiable) and the grandparents as potential carers for Elizabeth, if they indicate that they would be willing to undertake this role.

7

Commentary on
Gas and Dubois v France

URSULA KILKELLY

I. Introduction

Gas and Dubois v France[1] concerned the compliance with the European Convention on Human Rights (ECHR) of the decision to deny access to adoption to an unmarried same sex couple in order to grant legal recognition to the relationship between the non-biological parent and the child born to the other parent following donor insemination. The case touched on a range of issues including: the right to marry of same-sex partners, the birth of children following anonymous donor insemination, and the use of adoption to grant legal recognition to family relationships. It followed on from other cases on these issues which have enjoyed varying degrees of success in Strasbourg including: *Schalk and Kopf v Austria* (the right to marriage for same sex couples),[2] and *Fretté v France*[3] and *EB v France*[4] (the right of an individual to adopt regardless of sexual orientation). It was followed by the Grand Chamber judgment in *X and Others v Austria*.[5] The rewriting of the judgment takes place against a backdrop of increased recognition, achieved via litigation and legislative reform, of LGBT rights across Europe and seeks to promote an interpretation of the European Convention on Human Rights (ECHR) that is in line with children's rights.

II. The Judgment of the European Court of Human Rights

The judgment of the European Court of Human Rights in *Gas and Dubois* was handed down on 15 March 2012. It became final, three months later, on 15 June 2012.[6]

[1] *Gas and Dubois v France*, Application no 25951/07, Council of Europe: European Court of Human Rights, 31 August 2010.
[2] *Schalk and Kopf v Austria*, Application no 30141/04, Council of Europe: European Court of Human Rights, 24 June 2010.
[3] *Fretté v France*, 38 EHRR 438, 26 February 2002.
[4] *EB v France*, Application no 43546/02, Council of Europe: European Court of Human Rights, 22 January 2008.
[5] *X and Others v Austria*, Application no 19010/07, Council of Europe: European Court of Human Rights, 19 February 2013.
[6] Above n 1.

The applicants—Valérie Gas and Nathalie Dubois—complained that they had been discriminated against compared with heterosexual couples since no legal means existed in France allowing same-sex couples to have access to second-parent adoption. They relied on Article 14 of the ECHR taken together with Article 8 to say that they had been subjected to discriminatory treatment based on their sexual orientation, in breach of their right to respect for their private and family life.

According to the facts, the applicants have cohabited since 1989 and, on 21 September 2000, Ms Dubois gave birth in France to a daughter, A, conceived in Belgium via anonymous donor insemination. A has lived since her birth in the family home with the applicants. On 22 September 2000, the child's name was entered in the register of births, deaths and marriages and she was formally recognised by her mother on 9 October 2000. In April 2002, the applicants entered into a civil partnership agreement and on 3 March 2006 Ms Gas applied to the Nanterre Tribunal de Grande Instance for a simple adoption order in respect of her partner's daughter after her partner had given her express consent before a notary. Under the French civil code, the simple adoption of a minor results in parental responsibility being shared between a husband and wife (where they are married). In accordance with the Civil Code, the public prosecutor lodged an objection to this application on 12 April 2006. It is relevant also that although parental responsibility can be transferred to a third party under the Civil Code, this does not establish a legal parent-child relationship and it ceases to have effect once the child reaches the age of majority. The law on civil partnership (there is no civil marriage under French law for same-sex partners) has no effect on parental responsibility and the case law of the French courts provided no support to their claim to establish a legal relationship between the child and both parents.

Before the European Court, the applicants illustrated their claim of discrimination with reference to the contrasting situation of a child born by Artificial Insemination by Donor (AID) to a heterosexual couple, where the husband would be entitled to full parental rights and responsibilities via the simple adoption procedure. The response of the state focused on the argument that the relevant legal provisions sought to favour the family relationship based on marriage and were in the interests of the child. Since the measures were equally exclusive of unmarried couples, the state denied that the measures were discriminatory.

The European Court agreed that the matter complained of raised an issue of discrimination on the grounds of sexual orientation under Article 14 taken together with Article 8 of the ECHR. It began by remembering the principles that apply to such cases—in particular, that a difference in treatment of persons in relevantly similar situations will be discriminatory if it has no objective and reasonable justification, ie if it does not pursue a legitimate aim or if there is not a reasonable relationship of proportionality between the means employed and the aim sought to be realised. The state enjoys a margin of appreciation in assessing whether and to what extent differences, in otherwise similar situations, justify different treatment and this is 'usually wide when it comes to general measures of economic or social strategy'.[7] At the same time, the Court reminded that it has held repeatedly that, 'just

---

[7] Citing *Schalk and Kopf v Austria*, above n 2, para 97.

like differences based on sex, differences based on sexual orientation require particularly serious reasons by way of justification'.[8]

The applicants had claimed that they were subjected to discrimination compared with heterosexual couples, whether married or not. In response, the Court noted that as a homosexual couple they were not entitled to marry under French law and it remembered that in *Schalk and Kopf v Austria* the ECHR was found not to impose an obligation to grant same-sex couples access to marriage.[9] Moreover, the Court was not receptive to the applicants' claim that they were not seeking the right to marry but rather sought equal treatment with a married couple in similar circumstances. It reiterated its view that marriage 'confers a special status on those who enter into it' and thus considered that, for the purposes of second-parent adoption, the applicants' legal situation could not be said to be comparable to that of a married couple. Comparing their treatment with an unmarried couple in the same situation, the Court noted that their application for simple adoption would similarly have been refused. It thus rejected that any difference in treatment existed in this context.[10] It concluded by offering an alternative argument, ie that in light of the purpose of simple adoption—which the Court noted is aimed largely at compensating for the failings of the biological parent or parents—there is 'no justification, on the sole basis of a challenge to the application of that provision, for authorising the creation of a dual legal parent-child relationship with A'.[11]

Third party observations were submitted by a range of legal and other interested organisations including the International Federation for Human Rights (FIDH), the International Commission of Jurists (ICJ), the European Region of the International Lesbian, Gay, Bisexual, Trans and Intersex Association (ILGA-Europe), the British Association for Adoption and Fostering (BAAF) and the Network of European LGBT Families Associations (NELFA). Their submissions pointed out that an increasing number of states (in 2011, 10 out of the 47 Council of Europe Member States) allowed second-parent adoption, indicative of a growing consensus that, where a child was being raised within a stable same-sex couple, legal recognition of the second parent's status promoted the child's welfare and the protection of his or her best interests. Based on the UN Convention on the Rights of the Child (CRC) they urged the Court to give priority to the protection of the child's interests in this case.[12] Perhaps surprisingly, this aspect of the judgment has not been the subject of much academic analysis which might, in part, relate to the perception that the judgment concerns LGBT rights, rather than children's rights.[13]

---

[8] Here it referred to its case law including *Karner v Austria*, ECHR 2003-IX, para 37; *L and V v Austria*, ECHR 2003-I, para 45; *Smith and Grady v UK*, ECHR 1999-VI, para 90; and *Schalk and Kopf v Austria*, above n 2, paras 96–97.

[9] *Schalk and Kopf v Austria*, above n 2, paras 49–64.

[10] However, see the later case of *X and Others v Austria*, Grand Chamber, 19 February 2013 on this point.

[11] *Gas and Dubois v France*, above n 1, para 72.

[12] On the CRC issues relating to adoption see the analysis in B Sloan, 'Conflicting Rights: English Adoption Law and the Implementation of the UN Convention on the Rights of the Child' (2013) 25 *Child and Family Law Quarterly* 40.

[13] See for example the analysis of P Johnson, 'Adoption, Homosexuality and the European Convention on Human Rights: *Gas and Dubois v France*' (2012) 75 *MLR* 1123. Of the four points of criticism raised by Johnson only one related to the failure to interrogate the state's reliance on the best interest of the child for the differential treatment complained of.

III. The Rewritten Judgment

The rewritten judgment seeks to recast the judgment of the European Court from the perspective of the rights of the child concerned. It seeks to apply Article 3 CRC ('the best interests of the child') as an interpretive principle ultimately finding, as a result, that the difference in treatment suffered by the applicants violated their European Convention rights under Article 8 together with Article 14. Notwithstanding that the child was not a party to the proceedings, the rewritten judgment concludes that all three were affected by the difference in treatment because the applicants and the child enjoy family life together and the adoption request was aimed at obtaining legal recognition of the family life enjoyed by all three parties.

A number of issues arise with respect to the rewritten judgment including: the status of the child in the proceedings; the extent to which the judgment took account of the child's interests; and the reliance in that regard on the CRC.

A. Reliance on the CRC

To deal with the latter point first, although the rewritten judgment comments on the status of the CRC, especially that it has been ratified by France, the respondent state party in this case, it might have addressed more directly the role of the CRC in the Court's interpretation of the ECHR. It has been argued that the fact that the CRC has been ratified by all states parties to the ECHR enhances it beyond the normal importance given to international treaties in Strasbourg.[14] It might have strengthened the legitimacy and weight attached to the CRC in the revised judgment to draw on this fact, while referencing the other cases in which the best interests principle has been relied upon by the Court.[15]

B. The Child's Status in the Proceedings

With regard to the status of the child in the proceedings, there is no doubt that the issues before the Court in the instant case concerned the child at the centre of the applicants' relationship. Yet, notwithstanding that the negative consequences of the differential treatment complained of were felt most acutely by the child, she was not listed as an applicant. There are no rules regarding the circumstances in which a child will be made a party to proceedings before the Strasbourg court, although the burden would most obviously appear to be on those making the application to list the child formally as an applicant. Rule 44 of the Rules of Court[16] concerning third party intervention do allow for a third party, not otherwise party to the proceedings, to make submissions to the Court, with representation. It is possible therefore that the child's perspective could have been presented to the

---

[14] U Kilkelly, 'The Best of Both Worlds for Children's Rights? Interpreting the European Convention on Human Rights in the Light of the UN Convention on the Rights of the Child' (2001) 23 *Human Rights Quarterly* 308.

[15] See J Eekelaar, 'The Role of the Best Interests Principle in Decisions Affecting Children and Decisions about Children' (2015) 23 *International Journal of Children's Rights* 3.

[16] European Court of Human Rights, Rules of Court, 16 November 2016.

Court via this means, although the initiative for this would not be a matter for the Court. Clearly, the Court is vulnerable to the criticism that it applies one rule to Contracting Parties and one to its own proceedings here. In addition, the European Guidelines on Child-friendly Justice provide that: 'Children should have the right to their own legal counsel and representation, in their own name, in proceedings where there is, or could be, a conflict of interest between the child and the parents or other involved parties.'[17]

The Guidelines further provide that in such cases 'the competent authority' should appoint 'either a guardian ad litem or another independent representative to represent the views and interests of the child'.[18] Although strictly speaking it does not appear open to the Court, under its current Rules of Court, to appoint independent representation to the child, this would have addressed the concern in the judgment, noted at paragraph 60, that 'the child in the present case stands to be most affected by the outcome of the judgment but she has not been made a party to the case'.

C. The Child's Invisibility from the Judgment

Without applicant status or independent representation, the child's perspective is virtually invisible from the Court's consideration of the issues in the case. This is perhaps surprising because even though A was seven years old when the application was lodged, she was aged 12 when the judgment was handed down. By contrast, in other applications concerning the legal relationship between the child and his/her parents, the child was either listed as an applicant or his/her perspective was presented very clearly as part of the complaint to the Court.[19] In such cases, what has proven persuasive before the Court—although admittedly not always resulting in a finding of a violation—is the argument relating to the impact on the child of the failure to grant legal recognition of important social, if not biological, relationships.[20] In fact, the Court has, from a very early point in its jurisprudence, developed a consistent line of argument that reflects the importance of legal ties to children for practical reasons, as well as for reasons associated with their security and the external recognition and indeed validation of their family relationships. This began in the case of *Marckx v Belgium*, in 1979, concerning the relationship between an unmarried mother and her child[21] and it continued in *Johnston v Ireland*, concerning an unmarried couple and their child. Here, the Court found that 'the normal development of the natural family ties between

---

[17] Guidelines of the Committee of Ministers of the Council of Europe on Child-friendly Justice, para 37, available at www.coe.int/en/web/children/child-friendly-justice.

[18] ibid, para 42.

[19] See for example, *Johnston v Ireland* (1986) 9 EHRR 203 where the treatment of the child born to unmarried parents amounted to a violation of all three family members' right to respect for family life. Similarly, the child, born by artificial insemination by donor was listed as an applicant in *X, Y and Z v The United Kingdom* (1997) 24 EHRR 143 and her treatment was an important part of the judgment (although the application for legal recognition of her relationship with her father was ultimately unsuccessful). See the more recent case of *X and Others v Austria*, above n 5.

[20] See for example, A Parkes and S McCaughren, 'Viewing Adoption through a Children's Rights Lens: Looking to the Future of Adoption Law and Practice in Ireland' (2013) 176 *Irish Journal of Family Law* 99, who argue with respect to Gas and Dubois that it is unfair that children who grow up in families with parents of the same sex are denied their rights to the security and permanency of a family unit through the medium of adoption.

[21] *Marckx v Belgium* (1979–80) 3 EHRR 230.

the first and second applicants and their daughter requires … that she should be placed, legally and socially, in a position akin to that of a legitimate child'.[22] It is difficult to argue against the view that to consider otherwise when the child's parents are in a homosexual rather than a heterosexual relationship constitutes an arbitrary difference in treatment of *the child*.[23] The rewritten judgment responds to this precise point by proposing a positive obligation under Article 8 of the ECHR to put in place an appropriate legal regime capable of providing effective legal protection to the child's right to respect for her family life in line with this case-law.

D. The Child's Best Interests

The primary focus of the rewritten judgment is to reshape the judgment from the perspective of the child's best interests. As a result of extensive rewriting, the rewritten judgment reorients the case by placing the emphasis firmly on the child while at the same time remedying other inconsistencies and lack of rigour in the original judgment. The judgment, in the first instance, highlights the relationship between the complaints of the (adult) applicants by drawing on *Johnston v Ireland* to illustrate that the close and intimate relationship between the child and the adult applicants is such that, in failing to respect the right to family life of the child, there is of necessity also a resultant failure to respect the family life of each of the adults. As noted above, the difficulty with this argument is that the child, in *Johnston*, was named as an applicant whereas A was not an applicant in *Gas and Dubois*. Although this underpins the author's decision to make the 'best interests principle' the basis for the judgment, it is arguable that making the child a party, or affording the child independent representation, would have produced a more coherent judgment overall.

At the same time, drawing on the well-established principle of international children's rights law, namely that the best interests of the child are a primary consideration in all actions affecting the child (Article 3 CRC), the rewritten judgment sets out the practical, legal and welfare implications on the child of her parents' inability under the applicable legal regime to acquire full legal recognition of their relationship with her. It takes issue with the claims, too easily accepted by the Court in its judgment, that the state's position— argued to be discriminatory by the parent applicants—was in the interests of the child and in pursuit of the legitimate aim to protect the special status of marriage. The judgment also addresses the inconsistency, especially in this light, of the state's position to permit individuals, whatever their sexual orientation, to adopt children. In taking a children's rights approach, it highlights both the importance of family and family security to the child while also rejecting as contrary to the best interests of the child the state's arguments that appear to deny the rights of this child to protect the theoretical ECHR rights of other children (ie those born in marriage). Overall, the children's rights judgment both refocuses the case of *Gas and Dubois* firmly on the child concerned, and in doing so it remedies the weak and incoherent reasoning on which it is based, offering a coherent, child-rights framework for the resolution of the issues raised.

---

[22] *Johnston v Ireland*, above n 19, para 74.
[23] For some further analysis of the case law on legal recognition of family ties see U Kilkelly, 'Protecting Children's Rights under the ECHR: The Role of Positive Obligations' (2010) 61(3) *Northern Ireland Law Quarterly* 245.

IV. Conclusion

It is clear that states, as well as the Court, struggle with the parameters of differential treatment with regard to family life based on marriage, especially where children are concerned. There is an acceptance, on the one hand, that states are entitled to treat married parties differently from those who are not married, even where marriage is not available or not equal (as in the case of same sex-relationships). The rewritten judgment shines a light on this ambiguity from the child's perspective highlighting, ultimately, that it is not relevant to children whether their parents are same or opposite sex, married or not. All children are entitled to equal treatment and equal protection of the law and this is the important dimension brought by the introduction of Article 3 UNCRC into the rewritten judgment. At the same time, as both the original and the rewritten judgment make clear, even where judgments affect children directly, they are not always a party to the proceedings such that their interests are not independently represented. As long as these structural barriers remain, limitations on respect for children's rights will persist.

European Court of Human Rights

Gas and Dubois v France

The European Court of Human Rights (Fifth Section), sitting as a chamber composed of Lydia Bracken and Judges U, V, W, X, Y and Z delivers the following judgment.

The Facts

I. The Circumstances of the Case

...

8. Ms Valérie Gas ('the first applicant') has cohabited since 1989 with Ms Nathalie Dubois ('the second applicant'). The latter gave birth in France on 21 September 2000 to a daughter, A, conceived in Belgium via anonymous donor insemination. A does not have an established legal tie to her father, who acted as an anonymous donor in accordance with Belgian law.

9. The two applicants subsequently entered into a civil partnership agreement which was registered on 15 April 2002 with the registry of the Vanves District Court.

10. In March 2006, the first applicant applied for a simple adoption order in respect of her partner's daughter. In a judgment of 4 July 2006, the tribunal de grande instance observed that the statutory conditions for adoption were met and that the applicants were actively and jointly involved in the child's upbringing, providing her with care and affection. However, the court rejected the application on the grounds that the requested adoption would have legal implications running counter to the applicants' intentions and the child's interests because, pursuant to Article 365 of the Civil Code of France (see paragraph 19 below), had the simple adoption taken place, parental responsibility would have been transferred to the adoptive parent thus removing the birth mother's parental status.

II. Relevant Domestic Law and Practice

...

19.   Where the adoptee is a minor, simple adoption results in all the rights associated with parental responsibility being removed from the child's father or mother in favour of the adoptive parent. The legislation provides for one exception to this rule, namely where an individual adopts the child of his or her spouse. In this case, the husband and wife share parental responsibility. Hence:

> Article 365 of the Civil Code

> All rights associated with parental responsibility shall be vested in the adoptive parent alone, including the right to consent to the marriage of the adoptee, unless the adoptive parent is married to the adoptee's mother or father. In this case, the adoptive parent and his or her spouse shall have joint parental responsibility, but the spouse shall continue to exercise it alone unless the couple make a joint declaration before the senior registrar of the tribunal de grande instance to the effect that parental responsibility is to be exercised jointly.

...

A. *The Court's Assessment*

i. Applicability of Article 14 taken in conjunction with Article 8

58.   The applicants in the present proceedings alleged that they had been subjected to discriminatory treatment based on their sexual orientation in that the first applicant was refused a simple adoption order in respect of the child of the second applicant. They argued that this refusal breached Article 14 of the Convention, taken in conjunction with Article 8.

59.   The Court notes at the outset that Article 8 does not guarantee either the right to found a family or the right to adopt (see *EB v France* (2008) 47 EHRR 21). Nevertheless, the Court observes that examination of the applicants' specific case leads to the conclusion that they have a 'family life' within the meaning of Article 8 of the Convention. The notion of 'family life' under this Article is not confined to families based on marriage. On the contrary, it encompasses relationships where the parties, whether of the same or opposite sex, are living together in a committed relationship. Children born to such relationships are part of the family unit from the moment of birth (*Schalk and Kopf v Austria* (2011) 53 EHRR 20 at paragraph 91). In the instant case, the applicants have lived together in an intimate and committed relationship for over 20 years and have both acted as parents to the child, A, since her birth. It follows that this family enjoys a 'family life' for the purposes of Article 8.

60.   The Court observes that the child in the present case stands to be most affected by the outcome of the judgment but she has not been made a party to the proceedings.

61.   The Court notes that the human rights of children and the standards to which all States must aspire in realising these rights for all children are set out in the United Nations Convention on the Rights of the Child 1989 (UNCRC) (*Sahin v Germany* (2003) 36

EHRR 43). The UNCRC entered into force on 2 September 1990 and has been ratified by 193 countries, including France.

62.   Article 3(1) of the UNCRC provides that the best interests of the child must be a primary consideration in all actions concerning children. This provision expresses one of the fundamental values of the UNCRC and is regarded as one of the four general principles for interpreting and implementing all of the rights of the child contained therein. In cases of adoption, the best interests principle is to be applied as the paramount consideration (Article 21).

63.   The Committee on the Rights of the Child has explained that every action taken on behalf of the child has to respect the best interests of the child. This obligation extends to legislative bodies such that every law, regulation or rule that affects children must be guided by the 'best interests' criterion (Committee on the Rights of the Child, *General Comment No 12 (2009). The right of the child to be heard*, CRC/C/GC/12 (Geneva, 2009) at paragraphs 70–72).

64.   The Court has endorsed and applied the best interests principle on a number of occasions (*Elzholz v Germany* (2002) 34 EHRR 58; *Hoppe v Germany* (2004) 38 EHRR 15; *Yousef v Netherlands* (2003) 36 EHRR 20). The Court accepts that the principle is to be applied as the paramount consideration which means that if any balancing of rights is necessary the child's rights must prevail (*Yousef v The Netherlands*, cited above). Further, the Court notes that the principle is not only a substantive right, but also a fundamental, interpretive legal principle and a rule of procedure. As a rule of procedure, the principle requires States parties to introduce steps to ensure that the best interests of the child are taken into consideration.

65.   In the present case, the Court must therefore apply the best interests principle as an interpretive principle notwithstanding that the child is not a party to the proceedings. This is necessary in so far as the outcome will affect the child's upbringing. In line with Article 21 of the UNCRC, the best interests of the child must be paramount in cases of adoption. This means that what is best for the child must be the determining factor for this Court in considering whether Article 14 of the Convention, taken in conjunction with Article 8, is applicable in this case. The child and the applicants enjoy family life together and the complaint directly affects all three as it concerns the legal recognition of that family life. It follows that the complaint must be interpreted and determined in line with the child's best interests.

66.   In order for an issue to arise under Article 14, there must be a difference in the treatment of persons in relevantly similar situations. Article 14 must also be interpreted in light of the best interests principle under Article 3(1) UNCRC and therefore the Court must examine the treatment of the child in this case.

67.   The Court concludes that Article 14 of the Convention taken in conjunction with Article 8 applies to the facts of the present case.

ii. Compliance with Article 14 taken in Conjunction with Article 8

a. *Difference in Treatment*

68.   In light of the above considerations, the first issue to be addressed is whether the child of the applicants, A, has been subject to differential treatment when compared to a child who is raised by a parent and his or her opposite-sex spouse. The Court finds weight

in the applicants' submission that the child, A, was treated differently. A child of married opposite-sex parents can acquire two legal parents through simple adoption by the social parent whereas the child in the present case cannot. The effect of this is to prevent the first applicant, who cares for the child on a daily basis, from participating in the child's everyday life (such as in relation to school enrolment and monitoring the child's progress in school). She is also legally incapable of protecting the child in more serious circumstances (such as a road traffic accident). By contrast, a child of a married opposite-sex couple can benefit from the protection of two legal parents through the simple adoption procedure in the same circumstances.

69.   Furthermore, the Court notes that in the event of the death of A's birth mother, she would become an orphan and could be placed in the care of a guardian or a foster family. By contrast, a child of an opposite-sex married couple who has been subject to a simple adoption order would be entrusted to the care of her second legal parent.

70.   The Court has previously found that similar difficulties, which arose in the context of a social parent who could not be recognised as a legal parent, were surmountable as they did not cause undue hardship to the child (*X, Y and Z v United Kingdom* (1997) 24 EHRR 143). However, that finding was made in the context of a system which allowed for parental responsibility to be acquired by the social parent through application for a joint residence order. Parental responsibility gave the social parent the necessary legal tools to care for the child.

71.   In the present case, the Court notes that a mechanism, namely the delegation of parental responsibility, is available to the applicants to overcome, or at least minimise, the disadvantages experienced by the child in this case. Article 377-1 of the Civil Code allows for an order to be made that one or both parents are to share the exercise of their parental responsibility in whole or, in part, with a third party. This measure makes it possible to regulate the relationship between the child, the parents and third parties, whether they be grandparents, step-parents or live-in partners.

72.   Although the delegation of parental responsibility is available to same-sex couples in France, the Court of Cassation subsequently tightened up the conditions to be met for the granting of an application to delegate parental responsibility. In a recent case concerning same-sex partners, the application by a woman to delegate parental responsibility to her female partner, with whom she had lived as a couple since 1989 and entered into a *pacte civil de solidarité* with in 1998, was refused on the basis that it was not shown that the measure was 'essential' (Court of Cassation, First Civil Division, 8 July 2010, published in the Bulletin).

73.   The case law of the Court of Cassation shows that, although the delegation of parental responsibility to a same-sex partner of a parent is possible in France, it is not readily available. Further, although the extension of parental responsibility to the partner gives him or her many of the legal tools necessary to properly care for the child of the partner, it does not fully integrate the child into the new family. It does not give rise to inheritance obligations or legal relationships with members of the extended family, and it ceases to operate once the child reaches the age of majority. By contrast, simple adoption creates a secure and life-long family relationship between the adult and the child.

74.   The best interests principle is designed to be flexible so that the interests of individual children can be protected. Although the delegation of parental responsibility will be

sufficient to secure the child's best interests in many cases, it will not be the most appropriate solution in every situation. Mechanisms other than the extension of parental responsibility must, therefore, be considered when determining the best interests of the child. In order to be considered, those alternatives must be available in the first place.

75.   The Court is of the opinion that there is no doubt that the applicable legislation creates a distinction between the children of same-sex relationships and those of married opposite-sex relationships. The former are legally disadvantaged in a number of areas by virtue of the fact that their parents are unable to access simple adoption (see paragraphs 68 and 69 above). Thus, there is plainly a difference in treatment between the child of the applicants and the child of a married opposite-sex couple. That difference is inseparably linked to the fact that the applicants are part of a same-sex couple, and is therefore based on their sexual orientation.

b. Legitimate Aim and Proportionality

76.   The Court recalls that the pertinent issue in this case is whether the difference of treatment complained of is justified from the vantage point of the child's best interests. The Court observes that the community, as a whole, has an interest in maintaining a coherent system of family law which places the best interests of the child at the forefront (*X, Y and Z v United Kingdom*, cited above). The Court therefore has to examine whether the refusal to allow the first applicant to obtain a simple adoption order in respect of the child of her partner served a legitimate aim and whether it was proportionate to that aim from the perspective of the best interests principle.

77.   The Government submitted that the difference in treatment did not give rise to any objective discrimination because Article 365 of the Civil Code applied in an identical fashion to all unmarried couples, regardless of the composition of the couple. According to the Government, the exception created, whereby the spouse of the parent may adopt a child in a manner which does not affect the parent's parental responsibility, was designed to safeguard children's interests. In the Government's submission, marriage remained an institution which ensured greater stability within couples than other types of union. Moreover, in the case of the break-up of a marriage, the family judge automatically became involved, whereas the termination of a civil partnership did not have any implications in terms of family law. As such, the Government argued that by restricting simple adoption to married couples, the regime which was created provided a stable framework for children's care and upbringing.

78.   The Court notes that the protection of the interests of the child is undoubtedly a legitimate aim. Thus, the decision to exclude same-sex partners from the simple adoption process served a legitimate aim. It remains to be ascertained whether, in the circumstances of the case, the principle of proportionality was adhered to.

79.   The Court reiterates that the Contracting State enjoys a margin of appreciation in assessing whether and to what extent a difference in treatment is justified. The breadth of the State's margin of appreciation under Article 8 of the Convention depends on a number of factors. On the one hand, where there is no consensus within the Member States of the Council of Europe on the issue to be determined (such as in the instant case where only 10 of the 47 Council of Europe Member States currently allow for simple adoption), the

margin afforded to the Respondent State will be wider (*X, Y and Z v United Kingdom*, cited above; *Fretté v France* (2004) 38 EHRR 21).

80. On the other hand, the margin allowed to the State will normally be restricted where the case concerns a particularly important facet of an individual's existence or identity (*Evans v United Kingdom* (2008) 46 EHRR 34). Furthermore, where the difference in treatment is based on sex or sexual orientation, the margin afforded to the State is narrowed and there is a burden on the State to show that the difference in treatment is necessary to achieve the stated legitimate aim (*Karner v Austria* (2004) 38 EHRR 24). In the instant case, it is for the Government to show that the protection of the child's interests requires the exclusion of same-sex couples from the simple adoption process.

81. The Government argued that civil partnerships lack the stability of marriage and that this justified the restriction of simple adoption to married couples. The Court notes that marriage confers a special status on those who enter into it. The exercise of the right to marry is protected by Article 12 of the Convention and gives rise to social, personal and legal consequences (*Schalk & Kopf v Austria,* cited above).

82. Marriage is not, however, a guarantee of stability. The law cannot force any couple to stay together and, in any case, the Court notes that divorce is available under French law. Furthermore, the Court notes that the applicants in the instant case are legally prevented from accessing marriage. They have nonetheless demonstrated their commitment to one another by entering into the only legally recognised union which is available to them, a *pacte civil de solidarité.*

83. The Court recalls that the marital status of a child's parent or parents cannot be used to justify discrimination against him or her (*Marckx v Belgium* (1979–80) 2 EHRR 330; *Mazurek v France* (2006) 42 EHRR 9). Such discrimination can only be lawful where particularly convincing and weighty reasons are advanced to justify the difference in treatment (*Inze v Austria* (1988) 10 EHRR 394). The principle of non-discrimination is also expressly recognised in Article 2 of the UNCRC. Article 2 is one of the four general principles of the UNCRC and so must be applied to guide the interpretation and application of all other rights of the child, including the best interests principle enshrined in Articles 3 and 21.

84. In the Court's view, the Government has not adduced any convincing evidence to justify the difference in treatment experienced by the child. It has not been shown that partners in a civil partnership are less capable of providing for a child's interests than a married couple, nor has it been shown that same-sex relationships are less stable than marital relationships. Accordingly, the discrimination against the child in the present case cannot be justified solely by reference to the special status of marriage.

85. Having regard to the considerations set out above, the Court finds that the Government has failed to adduce particularly weighty and convincing reasons to show that the exclusion of same-sex couples from the simple adoption process is necessary for the protection of the interests of the child. The distinction is therefore incompatible with the Convention.

86. Although the child is not a party to the instant proceedings, the Court considers that, because the applicants and the child enjoy family life together and the adoption request was aimed at obtaining legal recognition of that family life, all three are directly affected by the difference in treatment in issue. It would be artificial to only consider the applicants'

rights under Article 14 of the Convention, taken in conjunction with Article 8, given that the enjoyment of their rights is inextricably joined to the enjoyment of the child's rights. It follows that there has been a violation of Article 14 of the Convention, taken in conjunction with Article 8, when the situation of the child is compared with that of a child of a married opposite-sex couple.

c. Positive Obligation

87.   In addition to the above, the Court notes that although the essential object of Article 8 is to protect the individual against arbitrary interference by the public authorities, there may also be positive obligations inherent in an effective 'respect' for family life (*Johnston v Ireland* (1987) 9 EHRR 203). As far as those positive obligations are concerned, the Contracting Parties enjoy a wide margin of appreciation in determining the steps to be taken to ensure compliance with the Convention, having regard to local circumstances.

88.   Certain factors have been considered relevant for the assessment of the content of those positive obligations on States (see *X and Y v the Netherlands* (1986) 8 EHRR 235). In the present case, the relevant factors include the impact on an individual of a situation where there is discordance between social reality and the law, the coherence of the administrative and legal practices within the domestic system and the impact of the alleged positive obligation at stake on the State concerned (see *Goodwin v United Kingdom* (2002) 35 EHRR 18).

89.   The Court observes that in contrast to individual adoptions or joint adoptions, which are usually aimed at creating a relationship with a child previously unrelated to the adopter, simple adoption serves to confer rights vis-à-vis the child on the partner of one of the child's parents who has usually been acting in the capacity of a de facto parent for some years. The Court has often stressed the importance of granting legal recognition to de facto family life (*Emonet v Switzerland* (2009) 49 EHRR 11).

90.   In the instant case, the Court notes that the first applicant has jointly raised and cared for the child from birth. She is clearly a suitable adoptive parent. To exclude her from the simple adoption process simply by virtue of her sexual orientation surely defeats the social purpose of simple adoption which is to offer security, stability, commitment and support to children. The best interests of the child are to be paramount in cases of adoption (Article 21 UNCRC) and must be assessed on a case-by-case basis. In the instant case, the Court is satisfied that this individualised assessment cannot be achieved because the national court is forced to refuse any application for simple adoption by the gay or lesbian partner of a legal parent, even where the simple adoption would clearly be in the best interests of the child. This situation is plainly contrary to the best interests principle and cannot be reconciled with Articles 3 and 21 UNCRC.

91.   In this case, simple adoption would formalise the existing family relationship between the first applicant and the child. Legal recognition of this relationship would have a profoundly positive effect on the child's life as she could then benefit from the protection of two legal parents rather than just one. Simple adoption would give the first applicant important decision-making rights and responsibilities in respect of the child; it would generate inheritance obligations; and it would create legal relationships between the child and members of the first applicant's extended family. The simple adoption would create a permanent, lifelong relationship between the first applicant and the child and it would demonstrate to

the child that the first applicant is fully committed to her. In these circumstances, the Court is of the view that it would clearly be in the best interests of the child for the simple adoption to take place.

92.   The circumstances of this case demonstrate that the exclusion of same-sex couples from the simple adoption process leaves their children in a vulnerable position since they are denied many of the protections which are afforded to the children of opposite-sex relationships. Children must be given the opportunity to obtain the security of having a legal relationship with both of their parents, whatever the gender of those parents may be.

93.   In this regard, the Court is not convinced that the extension of parental responsibility to the first applicant would alleviate the difficulties encountered. The Court notes that there are significant differences between the nature of legal parentage (which would flow from the simple adoption) and that of parental responsibility. Although the extension of parental responsibility to the first applicant would give her many of the legal tools required to properly care for the child, that mechanism does not create a lifelong family relationship and it does not create any legal ties with the adult's extended family. Full family integration is only possible where the first applicant is recognised as a legal parent of the child. In addition, legal parentage gives rise to a number of practical legal benefits, in areas such as succession law and immigration, which the extension of parental responsibility alone does not.

94.   Furthermore, as was previously noted, the delegation of parental responsibility to the gay or lesbian partner of a legal parent in France is not readily available. The delegation is determined on a case-by-case basis and it is only permitted where it is shown that the delegation is 'essential', which sets a high threshold for the application. In these circumstances, the Court is not satisfied that the existence of that mechanism alone provides an effective 'respect' for the family life of the child in the instant case.

95.   The Court also notes that the French law on adoption lacks coherence. Under French law, single gay and lesbian persons are permitted to adopt and the Court reiterates from its case law that sexual orientation cannot be a bar to raising a child. Furthermore, the fact that an individual is living with a partner of the same sex is not a justification for discriminatory treatment (*Salgueiro Da Silva Mouta v Portugal* (2001) 31 EHRR 47; *EB v France*, cited above). These points further call into question the legitimacy of the Government's claim that same-sex couples should be excluded from utilising simple adoption so as to protect the child's interests.

96.   The Court reiterates that 'respect' for family life implies the existence in domestic law of legal safeguards that render possible, as from the moment of birth, the child's integration in his or her family (*Marckx v Belgium*, cited above). Hitherto, this principle has only applied where there is a biological connection between the child and the adult (*X, Y and Z v United Kingdom*, cited above). The Convention is, however, a living instrument which is to be interpreted in the light of present-day conditions (see *EB v France*, cited above and *Goodwin v United Kingdom*, cited above). While there is no European consensus on the question of simple adoption or the legal recognition of same-sex parenting, the Court recalls that this case concerns the position and interests of the child. In this regard, the Court notes that all of the Member States of the Council of Europe are parties to the UNCRC. Therefore, there is a European consensus concerning the principle of non-discrimination (Article 2), the best interests principle (Articles 3 and 21) and the child's right to know and be cared for by his or her parents (Article 7).

97.   Taking these factors into account, the Court finds that a distinction cannot legitimately be made between 'respect' for the family life of a child of a married opposite-sex couple and that of a child of a same-sex couple.

98.   The child in the present case is being raised by the two applicants but the law prevents her from acquiring a permanent legal relationship with the first applicant. In this situation, there is clearly discordance between social reality and the law. It is a situation which cannot be said to adhere to the best interests principle as the child is prevented from enjoying a legal relationship with the first applicant who cares for her on a daily basis. The Court is not satisfied that any coherent reasons have been put forward as to why the first applicant should not be permitted to become the child's legal parent through the simple adoption process.

99.   Having regard to the particular circumstances of this case, the absence of an appropriate legal regime reflecting the family life of the applicants and the child, A, amounts to a failure to respect that family life (*Johnston*, cited above). The current regime fails to adhere to the best interests principle. The Court again notes that the close and intimate relationship between the child and the first and second applicants is such that, in failing to respect the right to family life of the child, there is of necessity also a resultant failure to respect the family life of each of the latter (*Johnston*, cited above).

100.   It is not the Court's function to indicate which measures France should take in this connection; it is for the State concerned to choose the means to be utilised in its domestic law for the performance of its obligation under Article 53.

For these Reasons, the Court:

1.   *Declares*, the application admissible;
2.   *Holds*, that there has been a violation of Article 14 of the Convention taken in conjunction with Article 8 when the situation of the child is compared with that of a child of a married opposite-sex couple;
3.   *Holds*, that a positive obligation arises under Article 8 of the Convention that an appropriate legal regime must be put in place to respect the family life of the applicants and the child.

8

Commentary on *P-S (Children)*

DAVID LANE

I. Introduction

This commentary provides an outline of the original decision in *Re P-S (Children) (Care Proceedings: Right to give evidence)*[1] and explains the rules relating to the child's party status and attendance at court. It then explains and reflects upon how Jane Williams' re-written judgment differs in its approach. The re-written judgment is much more respectful of the child's view, an approach which aligns with a number of academic and judicial views.

II. Original Judgment

The subject of the proceedings in *Re P-S* was a 15 year old boy M, who did not wish to remain in foster care but to return to live with his mother. The local authority's view was that this would not be in M's best interests since his mother had previously attempted to leave the country without making adequate care arrangements for her children. An application for a Care Order was made under section 31 of the Children Act 1989. Details of the case background are outlined in the re-written judgment, and thus only a brief outline follows.

M sought and was granted separate legal representation as he did not feel his guardian (whose role is to advise the court on a child's best interests) was representing satisfactorily his true wishes and feelings. Initially, M did not wish to attend the final hearing but did wish to meet the judge to express directly the strength of his feelings. M met with the trial judge in the presence of the guardian and his solicitor during the first part of the final hearing. However, the judge did not afford M an opportunity to express his wishes and feelings, and limited her communication with M to an explanation of the court process and task.

During the second part of the final hearing M applied to give evidence via video link. His application was refused. The trial judge felt that the detriment to M, particularly in terms of him feeling responsible for the final decision of the Court, outweighed the benefit of his evidence to the Court. A Care Order was made in respect of M.

---

[1] *Re P-S (Children) (Care Proceedings: Right to give evidence)* [2013] EWCA Civ 223, [2013] 1 WLR 3831.

The Court of Appeal unanimously upheld the trial judge's decisions both in respect of M's application to give evidence and in respect of the Care Order. In his judgment on the application to give evidence, Sir Alan Ward's reasoning encompassed a wide range of statutory and non-statutory provisions and relevant case law pertinent to the application including section 1(3) of the Children Act 1989,[2] Article 6 of the European Convention on Human Rights, as scheduled to the Human Rights Act 1998,[3] and Article 12 of the United Nations Convention on the Rights of the Child.[4] The main case law referred to was *re W (Children) (Abuse: Oral Evidence)*.[5] Whilst the party status of the child[6] was acknowledged in Sir Alan Ward's judgment, it was held that the relevant provisions did not give M the right to express directly his views to the Court. M's very strong views were already known to the Court and acknowledged by the trial judge. The current model of children being represented by a guardian and a specialist solicitor was seen as meeting the requirements under Article 12 United Nations Convention on the Rights of the Child (CRC).[7] Sir Alan Ward agreed with the trial judge that the harm to M of giving evidence far outweighed the benefit to the judge,[8] as M would feel responsible for the final decision. In relation to the Care Order application, based on the known history of parenting, his lordship also agreed that there was no realistic prospect of either of M's parents having the capacity to meet his needs.

The original judgment highlights vividly the very real tensions that exist between the requirements of children's welfare as contained in the welfare checklist of the Children Act 1989 and a children's rights perspective. M's story in his own words was considered to be of less value to the Court than those recorded in formal submissions and reports. Baroness Hale, writing extra-judicially, observes that in her experience children frequently have important things to say and she maintains that, '[i]t is a big mistake to think that children's views can be effectively communicated through the adult parties to any dispute'.[9] She includes among the advantages of judges meeting with children, the need to see children as real people and not to just view them merely as subjects of proceedings and to find out more about their wishes and feelings directly, rather than just relying on second or third hand information, which is the case currently in most public law cases.[10] Raitt, in a research study with members of the Scottish judiciary, found it was possible for a judge to 'simply encourage a child to talk about their wishes and feelings without rehearsing the options or presenting stark choices'.[11] Of course the starting point for considering what might be achieved when children are the subject of legal proceedings is the legal framework within which the child's wishes and feelings are presented to the court, to which we now turn.

---

[2] The Children Act 1989, s 1(3): the welfare checklist, which includes the wishes and feelings of the child.
[3] European Convention on Human Rights, Art 6 right to a fair trial.
[4] UN Convention on the Rights of the Child 1989, Art 12 child's right to express a view.
[5] *Re W (children) (abuse: oral evidence)* [2010] 1 FCR 615, [2010] 2 All ER 418.
[6] The child is automatically a party to care proceedings under FRR 2010, r 12.3(1) of the Family Procedure Rules 2010, SI 2010/2955 (FPR 2010).
[7] *Re W (children) (abuse: oral evidence)* [2010] 1 FCR 615, [2010] 2 All ER 418, at para 26.
[8] ibid, at para 41.
[9] B Hale, 'Can you Hear me Your Honour?' [2012] *Family Law* 31.
[10] B Hale's address to the Association of Lawyers for Children 2015—'Are We Nearly There Yet?'
[11] FE Raitt, 'Hearing Children in Family Law Proceedings: Can Judges make a Difference?' (2007) 19 *Child and Family Law Quarterly* 214.

A. The Party Status of the Child

In care proceedings, the child is automatically a party. The Children Act 1989 and the Family Proceedings Rules (FPR) provide how, in practice, effect is given to that party status, bearing in mind that a child may be a party from as early in life as the day of the child's birth. Section 41 of the Children Act 1989 requires the appointment of a guardian—who in practice in England will be commissioned by the Children and Family Court Advisory and Support Service (CAFCASS) and in Wales, will be a Welsh family proceedings officer acting on behalf of the Welsh Ministers. The court may appoint a solicitor to represent the child. A child of sufficient maturity and understanding may instruct a solicitor independently.

Since the Children Act 1989 became law in October 1991 there has existed a presumption that children and young people who are subject to care and adoption proceedings do not attend court.[12] As a consequence of this presumption, children are not routinely asked about their views on participating directly in proceedings, including meeting with the judge, because the child's part in the proceedings for the most part is mediated through their guardian.

Under section 95 of the Children Act 1989 the court may order the child concerned to attend as prescribed by rules of court. FPR 12.14 provides that any party must attend the proceedings, but the proceedings or any part of them will take place in the absence of a child pursuant to FPR 12.14(3) if the court considers it in the interests of the child, having regard to the matters to be discussed or the evidence likely to be given, and the child is represented by a guardian or solicitor.

III. The Re-written Judgment

The re-written judgment differs significantly from the original judgment. It gives greater relevance to, and places more weight on, the European Convention on Human Rights (ECHR) and CRC, leading to a more young person-centred outcome, with Williams J allowing the appeal in respect of M's application to give evidence and in respect of the care order application. The young person's voice is placed at the centre of their proceedings. M is 15 years old and has been considered capable of independently instructing his own legal representative. The judgment quite rightly highlights the consequence were any other party to these proceedings to be prevented from being heard in person. As Lundy observes, '[i]t is difficult to imagine egregious breaches of children's rights in situations where they have been fully and effectively involved in determining the issues which affect them'[13] while Griffiths and Kandel make the point that, '[w]hether we recognise children's agency or not has a profound effect on the kinds of legal narratives we expect to emerge when the child's voice speaks directly or indirectly and is heard in a legal proceeding'.[14] While the trial judge

---

[12] Now FPR 2010, r 12.14(3).

[13] L Lundy, 'Mainstreaming Children's Rights in, to and through Education in a Society Emerging from Conflict' in M Freeman (ed), *Children's Rights: Progress and Perspectives: Essays from the International Journal of Children's Rights* (Boston, Martinus Nijhoff, 2011).

[14] A Griffiths and RF Kandel, 'Legislating for the Child's Voice: Perspectives from Comparative Ethnography of Proceedings Involving Children' in M Maclean (ed), *Making Law for Families* (Oxford, Hart Publishing, 2000).

in this case followed the 2011 guidance,[15] weighing up the relevant evidence and welfare considerations in relation to M, the spirit of the principles of justice and fairness contained in Article 6 of the ECHR[16] were very much diluted, particularly in relation to M's full party status. It seems that all parties, except the child, are given the opportunity to express a view about whether the child should meet the judge. Children meeting judges is almost wholly dependent on the judge receiving a request for such a meeting from the child's guardian or their solicitor or the child's Local Authority social worker. The 2011 guidance is firmly entrenched in the protective mode of the welfare paradigm, in which adults' views determine the best interests of children.[17] It is a paradigm where the rights of children are relegated to a status that is inferior to adults' '*superior*' knowledge and wisdom and are seen by the judicial system as being appropriately accommodated through proxy accounts.

The re-written judgment states that the child is entitled to a 'fair and public hearing' (paragraph 28) and points out that a hearing would not be fair if the child's case is not heard. The judgment reframes both the guidance on hearing children directly and the Court's thinking in this case by focusing on the potential harm that M might suffer should he be prevented from expressing his views directly. There may already be some indication of a similar judicial shift in thinking in a more recent case, *Re R*, in which Briggs LJ commented:

> The risk of harm which the process may cause to this bright and articulate fourteen year old does not seem to me to be more substantial than the risk of long-term harm at being denied the opportunity to have her evidence properly weighed in the determination by a court of matters of the utmost importance to her.[18]

Re R was a case in which allegations of sexual abuse were made against the father of a 14 year old girl, who wished to be heard directly in legal proceedings. She had not made any allegations against her father. The common element in M's case and in *Re R* is the strength of feeling expressed in relation to the young people's need to express their views directly to the court, yet the outcomes were very different.

A. The Voice and Dignity of the Child

The re-written judgment allows the appeal in respect of M giving oral evidence, giving real effect to Articles 3 *(best interests)* and 12 *(right to express a view)* of the UN Convention along with Article 6 of the ECHR *(right to a fair trial)* (paragraph 31). This approach ameliorates the position, as identified by Michael Freeman, that '[f]or too long [children] have been regarded as objects of concern (sometimes worse, as objects), rather than as persons, and even today they remain voice-less, even invisible, and it matters not that the dispute is about them'.[19]

---

[15]   Family Justice Council, *Guidelines in Relation to Children Giving Evidence in Family Proceedings* (2011) 1.
[16]   ECHR Art 6 right to a fair trial.
[17]   J Fortin, 'Children's Rights: Are the Courts Now Taking them More Seriously?' (2004) 15 *King's College Law Journal* 253, 272.
[18]   *Re R* [2015] EWCA Civ 167, para 36.
[19]   M Freeman, 'The Value and Values of Children's Rights' in A Invernizzi and J Williams (eds), *The Human Rights of Children—From Visions to Implementation* (Abingdon, Routledge, 2011).

Carol Smart makes the point that having a voice and an environment where that voice is heard is considered in developed societies as a basic human right.[20] Courts are not particularly welcoming of children and therefore it is difficult to see a space within the current system where children can give expression to their true voice. This is particularly important when a child's views are at odds with their court appointed guardian. This space needs to be created within the legal process and the judicial system itself to enable children to speak if they wish, with confidence. Being excluded or prevented from expressing strongly held views can only undermine a child's dignity and confidence. Direct participation within the current system is often very much seen as consisting of a one-off brief meeting with the judge, lasting on average no more than 15 to 20 minutes, yet in practice even such meetings are rare. As Tobin has argued, this reflects an incidental rights approach, wherein children's rights are on the periphery of the judicial process.[21] M's meeting with the trial judge did not enable him to express his strongly held views. This space is dominated by the children's guardian and legal representative (Children Act 1989, section 41) and the child's Local Authority social worker. According to Connolly and Morris, this can lead to risk aversion, where professionally-driven rather than child-centred practices take priority and professional voices prevail and dominate proceedings to the exclusion of the child.[22]

B. Formality, Rules and Procedures—are we Forgetting the Child as a Person with Rights?

The re-written judgment places much importance on the centrality of the young person's position in these proceedings and on the application of both the letter and spirit of Articles 3 and 12 of the UN Convention and Article 6 of the ECHR. It highlights the narrow legal interpretation of M's rights in the original trial and re-focuses on justice and fairness for M throughout, as a person with full party status. According to the European Network of Councils for the Judiciary, the ability to listen is considered one of the core judicial values.[23] In contrast, the 2010 Guidelines place emphasis on the judge having the opportunity to explain to the child what's going on in the process, not on the child having an opportunity to speak and the judge to listen.[24] In this case, the level of participation afforded to M is superficial at best. The re-written judgment asserts that the original trial placed insufficient value on M's dignity and integrity, in contrast to the UN Convention, particularly Articles 3 and 12, and Article 6 of ECHR. Fortin maintains that courts are not familiar with organising the evidence within a rights-based structure and states that, '[a]lthough complicated,

---

[20] C Smart, 'From Children's Shoes to Children's Voices' (2002) 40 *Family Court Review* 318.

[21] J Tobin, 'Courts and the Construction of Childhood: A New Way of Thinking' (2012) 14 *Law and Childhood Studies: Current Legal Issues* 1, 25.

[22] M Connolly and K Morris, *Understanding Child and Family Welfare: Statutory Responses to Children at Risk* (London, Palgrave, 2012).

[23] European Network of Councils for the Judiciary, *Judicial Ethics—Principles, Values and Qualities* (Working Group Judicial Ethics 2009–2010), www.encj.eu.

[24] Family Justice Council, *Guidelines for Judges Meeting Children who are subject to Family Proceedings* (2010) 1.

the advantage of such a strategy is that it might produce a deeper analysis of the child's own position',[25] making the proceedings much more young person-centred.

In respect of the Care Order, the re-written judgment quite rightly allows the appeal. It reflects the consistent approach adopted in this judgment in relation to M's right to express his views, having full party status within these proceedings. It is also consistent with the principles of fairness and justice, otherwise an assumption is being made that nothing M might say could change the decision. Such an assumption disrespects and pre-judges M's views regarding this application.

For Smart, '[b]eing able to hear what children have to say does change things. At the very least, we have to be able to stand in children's shoes if we are going to be able to hear their voices'.[26] It seems reasonable to suggest that judges who have so much power over children's lives are very unlikely to be able to stand in their shoes without having had the opportunity of face-to-face meetings with the child.

IV. Concluding Comments

The current system favours mediation of children's views through the guardian and the child's Local Authority social worker. McFarlane LJ has observed that, 'the previous culture and practice of the family courts remains largely unchanged with the previous presumption against children giving evidence remaining intact'.[27] The Family Justice Council however has made it clear in their guidance on judges meeting children that the main purpose of such meetings is to 'enable children to feel more involved and connected with proceedings in which important decisions are made in their lives and to give them an opportunity to satisfy themselves that the Judge has understood their wishes and feelings ...'.[28] The re-written judgment embodies the spirit of this guidance and upholds M's legal rights.

[25] J Fortin, 'Accommodating Children's Rights in a Post Human Rights Act Era' (2006) 69 *The Modern Law Review* 313.
[26] Smart, above n 20.
[27] *Re E* [2016] EWCA Civ 473, paras 48, 56.
[28] ibid, 1.

Court of Appeal (Civil Division)
(England and Wales)

P-S (Children)

Williams LJ:

1.   The appellant, M, was 15 years old when he applied through solicitors and counsel separately representing him for leave to attend court to give evidence in care proceedings to which he was a party. Other parties were the Local Authority, M's younger half-brother A and their Mother. The Local Authority sought care orders in respect of both boys. M wished to return to the care of his Mother and in his application stated that 'he does not feel that the strength of his feelings [are] being sufficiently understood and wishes an opportunity to attend before the learned judge to express himself in person in his own words so that his case is fully advanced.' On 21 November 2011 Her Honour Judge Parry sitting in the Swansea County Court dismissed M's application. On 24 November 2011 she ordered that both boys be placed in care. With permission granted by Thorpe LJ, M appeals against both the dismissal of his application to give evidence in the case and against the care order.

2.   Mr David Blake, M's counsel, submits that 'this case raises a novel point of principle as to whether a young person who has been afforded full independent party status should be heard orally as any other party would "fairly" expect to be and a general point of interest as to what is the right test for whether a child should be heard on questions of wishes, feelings and indeed future intentions when they are competent to express them.' He goes further and submits that 'M does have a "right" to give evidence or there is at least a presumption in favour.' In the appeal against the care order 'the general point … is essentially should the elements of the welfare checklist be weighted with a rebuttable presumption in favour of wishes and feelings being complied with, where the young person is fast approaching majority?'

The background

3.   M was born on [a date in] 1996 in Romania of Romanian parents. His Mother settled in the Republic of Ireland and was granted Irish citizenship. M's father played no part in the proceedings and there was no evidence about him. When in Eire, Mother met Mr S, a Nigerian citizen. A was born of this relationship on [a date in] 2011.

4.   The Mother, M and A came to Wales in September 2009, where they came to the attention of the Local Authority Social Services. On 28 May 2010, while the children were in school, the Mother attempted to leave Wales for Eire without having made proper arrangements for the care of the children. She was arrested and charged with neglect though eventually acquitted. The children were received into care and placed with foster parents. An application for a care order was issued on 24 June 2010 and a guardian duly appointed to both M and A. Contact ceased at the end of July 2010 because the Mother refused to agree to the Local Authority's requirement that she would not discuss the case with the children. M then tried twice to run away to re-join his Mother, on the second occasion being removed by the police after they forced entry in to the Mother's home. M's initial foster placement with A broke down but M is reported to have settled well with new foster parents.

5.   In July 2011 M met his guardian and her solicitor and asked for separate representation. On 26 July 2011 the judge so ordered and appointed a solicitor to represent him. In a position statement settled by his solicitor, dated 31 July 2011, M said, 'I do not wish to remain where I am and I strongly desire to return home.' He said he wished to meet with the judge to convey to her how he felt. The Mother made an application for both M and A to give oral evidence. That application was dismissed.

6.   The final hearing commenced on 1 August 2011. M was represented by counsel. At the end of the second day, HHJ Parry saw M in her room in the presence of his solicitor and the guardian. In her judgment of 21 November 2011, the judge explained that she did not use the meeting as an opportunity to ascertain M's wishes and feelings, 'because those wishes and feelings were already perfectly obvious from formal reports that the Court had received from the Guardian and the fact that he now wished to have separate representation …' Instead, she explained to M the task of the Court in trying to achieve a welfare outcome for children that reflects their wishes and feelings, and that the Court has to look at the whole picture, all the evidence that is available about the child and about the people who are looking after him and who want to look after him. She did not 'discuss any issues evidentially with him, such as the reasons why he does not see his mother and the reasons why he apparently absconded to her care in early December 2010'. In taking this approach the judge applied the Guidelines issued by the Family Justice Council in 2010, which state that a meeting out of court between the judge and the child is not to be used for the gathering of evidence. However it is clear that the judge did, as a result of that meeting, form some impression of M, since she noted that M was reasonably subdued during the meeting, but became animated 'when talking about matters that are far removed from the heavy emotional baggage which must constitute his day-to-day life and his feelings about his brother and mother'.

7.   The next day the hearing was adjourned for some three weeks to 26 August to hear the guardian and for closing submissions to be made. On 26 August A's father attended court and in view of his albeit belated interest the matter was further adjourned for a further three months, to 21 November 2011.

8.   On 16 November 2011 M applied for permission to attend to give evidence by video link 'so that the strength of my feelings can be made clear to everyone'. He explained that he would be 'extremely distressed if told that I was to be forced to remain in foster care and I would struggle greatly to accept this outcome'. He also said that 'I have had thoughts of running away as sometimes I have felt that people are not taking me seriously. These have

occurred quite often, including quite recently, but in the last few weeks I have been a little more optimistic and hope that the court will grant my wishes. I would feel devastated if I were told I could not return.' M's application was heard on 21 November 2011. The Local Authority and guardian indicated that they did not wish to cross-examine M, and M's Mother indicated that the only question she would be seeking to ask him through her counsel would be about the likelihood of him running away from his placement should a care order be made.

9.   The judge dismissed the application and continued to hear the care proceedings, in which A's father offered himself as a carer for the children either jointly with the Mother or in the alternative by himself. The Mother seemed willing to care for the children jointly with A's father but without any Local Authority intervention. The Local Authority was successful in its application.

The judgment on M's giving evidence

10.   The judge based her dismissal of M's application to give evidence as follows. First, the Mother had always displayed her own emotions openly in court whether represented or not and there was a severe risk she would make an extreme emotional outburst which it would be impossible to control. M would be 'available to Mother' in the court precincts, with 'real potential detriment to M in terms of his coming to give evidence'. Second, M would want to do what he thought right by his Mother and would want to put right matters over which he had no control and for which he was not responsible. He would 'assume a responsibility for the outcome of this case' which would be enormously harmful to him. If he felt he had failed, there was a prospect that his relationship with his carers and guardian would be damaged. Third, she doubted whether M would communicate anything that would assist her in the determination of the relevant issues: she had already accepted that M would be bitterly disappointed if he could not return to his mother. She concluded that 'the additional benefit to the determination of the relevant issues of M giving evidence is significantly outweighed by the very real potential detriment'. M should not 'be placed in the invidious position of giving evidence when the giving of that evidence may make matters significantly harder for him should the case go against his express wishes'. Any 'short-term emotional harm' resulting from the rejection of the case put on his behalf, was a reflection of the reality that 'there is rarely a perfect outcome to proceedings involving children'.

The judgment on the care application

11.   The judge accepted the evidence relating to the Mother's inadequate parenting and neglect. As to the welfare stage, the judge held there was 'simply no material' permitting a conclusion that the children could be safe in the care of their Mother or that a repetition of the past problems could be avoided. A's father, M's step-father, had no real understanding of the difficulties nor had he been prepared to gain insight during the short period that he had been involved in the proceedings. Neither the mother and father/step-father jointly, nor either of them solely, could provide the parenting that both A and M needed.

12.   Turning to M's wishes and feelings, the judge accepted that 'M has strong feelings' and felt that the professionals misunderstood him and misinterpreted his apparent compliance with the arrangements made for his welfare. She accepted that M had thought of running

away and that what he had written was what he wanted the court to hear of his wishes and feelings. However, she said that the court must 'assess and interpret his wishes and feelings in the light of other welfare concerns', specifically her conclusion about the capacity of the parents to meet 'M's global welfare needs'. She referred also to the evidence of a clinical and counselling psychologist which indicated that M's anxiety about himself translated into anxiety about his Mother because of the role he had played in the family, that in the psychologist's view, M would not run away and that in the current foster placements there was 'a degree of containment and flexibility' in which M would feel safe albeit remaining concerned about his Mother. The judge concluded that the expert evidence gave rise to a suggestion that M's expressed wishes and feelings could not outweigh her clear conclusion on the danger to M's welfare if he returned to his mother—so his evidence could not, in her view, affect the outcome.

13.   After the judge had concluded her *ex tempore* judgment, Mr Blake made further submissions and asked the judge to amplify her reasons for refusing to adopt M's wishes about his long term care. She acknowledged the need to balance the expressed wishes and feelings of the child against circumstances likely to prevail if the child's wishes are acted upon. There was no need to 'place any gloss on the s 1(3) "checklist"'. In this case, she said, 'the risk of harm from Mother is overwhelming'.

Discussion on the issue of M giving evidence

14.   Section 96 of the Children Act 1989 makes special provision about children's evidence. Subsection (1) has the effect that if a child understands the nature of the oath, the child can give evidence in the normal way. Subsection (2) provides that where the court is not satisfied that the child understands the nature of the oath, the child's evidence may be heard if the judge considers that the child understands the duty to speak the truth and has sufficient understanding. Section 96 also provides for the admissibility of hearsay evidence. Family Proceeding Rule (FPR) 22.1 gives the court power to control evidence by giving directions as to the issues on which it requires evidence, the nature of that evidence and the way in which the evidence is to be placed before the court. The general rule is that any fact which needs to be proved by the evidence of witnesses is to be proved at the final hearing by the oral evidence.

15.   That is the legislative framework. As for its application, the leading authority is *ON v W (Children) (Family Proceedings: Evidence)* [2010] UKSC 12, [2010] 1 WLR 701, in which a 14 year old girl was being called to give evidence about alleged abuse relevant to the threshold stage. There are significant differences between that case and M's, but the principles set out by Lady Hale are still pertinent. Her Ladyship said that the object was to achieve a fair trial in the determination of the rights of all the people involved. When considering whether a child should be called to give evidence, the court had to weigh the advantages that will bring to the determination of the truth and the damage it may do to the welfare of that or any other child. The hearing, she said, cannot be fair to children unless their interests are given great weight. Lady Hale set out various factors which the court would need to take into account when carrying out the balancing exercise. These included the child's own feelings about giving evidence, the age and maturity of the child and 'the general evidence of the harm which giving evidence may do to children, as well as any features which are

particular to this child and this case'(at paragraph 26). The risk, and therefore the weight to be attached to the several factors, would vary from case to case. But she predicted that 'the consequence of the balancing exercise will usually be that the additional benefits to the court's task in calling the child do not outweigh the additional harm that it will do to the child.' (at paragraph 30).

16.   The Court of Appeal in that case (hereafter, *Re: W* [2010] EWCA Civ 57) had invited the President of the Family Division to consider the issue of children giving evidence in family proceedings. Lord Justice Thorpe's working party of the Family Justice Council did so, and produced Guidelines in December 2011. The resultant 2011 Guidelines drew heavily on the Supreme Court's decision in *Re: W*. The Guidelines state that there is no presumption or starting point against children giving evidence in family proceedings and that the court's 'principal objective' should be achieving a fair trial. The essential balancing exercise requires the court to weigh the possible advantages to the 'determination of the truth' against the possible damage to the child, having regard to a number of factors. Understandably, given the provenance of the Guidelines, the factors include many which have relevance only to the 'proof of abuse' cases. However some of the factors and the Guidance generally are helpful in dealing with the issue of whether the child should give evidence at the disposal stage when the question is what the welfare of the child demands.

17.   Thorpe LJ remarked in *Re: H (Abuse: Oral Evidence)* [2011] EWCA Civ 741, [2012] 1 FLR 186 at [8], that Lady Hale's guidance in *Re: W* essentially requires a measured balance between the demands of justice and the needs of child welfare. That reduction should I think be seen in the context of the 'proof of abuse' cases, of which *Re: H* was another example. In those cases, 'justice' is a shorthand for fairness to an alleged abuser, and 'child welfare' is a shorthand for the risk of the child being traumatised by having to give evidence and be cross-examined about the alleged abuse. I would not accept, as a general proposition, that justice and child welfare are opposing aims, and I am sure that is not what Thorpe LJ intended to be understood.

18.   I turn now to the features which importantly distinguish M's case from cases like *Re: H* and *Re: W*, where the child would be a witness of facts as to alleged past abuse and would face cross-examination in court on difficult and painful issues. M's evidence would not be about what had happened, but about what should happen. M, a child of relatively mature years, sought to address the court about his own welfare interest, on which he took a different view from the guardian and the Local Authority. Neither the Local Authority nor the guardian wished to challenge M's evidence and on behalf of the Mother it had been indicated that questioning would be limited to one issue only, which was whether he might run away again. It would be wrong to assume that the 'general evidence of harm' to children from giving evidence (paragraph 26 of Lady Hale's judgment above) has the same purchase in M's situation. Furthermore, in M's case and others like it, the 'general evidence' about the impact of direct participation must nowadays, in my view, include evidence about ensuring respect for the rights of children in proceedings which affect them.

19.   At about the time the Children Act 1989 was passed, the Convention on the Rights of the Child ('the Convention') was adopted by the United Nations General Assembly. The Convention was ratified by the United Kingdom in 1990 and is the most widely ratified human rights treaty ever. It contains some 42 substantive articles containing requirements

for States Parties to recognise a wide range of rights and to take actions. The Convention has not been made a part of Anglo-Welsh law but under a canon of construction well-established in that law, it may be invoked to point to a construction most in line with the UK's international obligations. (*Smith v Secretary of State for Work and Pensions and Another* [2006] UKHL 35 per Lady Hale at paragraph 78.)

20.   This approach applies throughout England and Wales, but in Wales, where M's case was heard, there is an additional aspect which, whilst not in force at the time, will apply in family proceedings, when the Rights of Children and Young Persons Measure (Wales) 2011 comes fully into force. Section 1 of the Measure requires the Welsh Ministers, 'when exercising any of their functions' to have due regard to the requirements of Part 1 of the Convention and specified articles of the Optional Protocols which have been ratified by the UK Government. Welsh Ministers, not the courts, are subject to this duty of due regard, but in Wales, it is the function of Welsh Ministers, exercised in practice by the Welsh family proceedings officers, to exercise the 'CAFCASS' functions in family proceedings. Accordingly this legal duty to have due regard to the Convention applies to the exercise of those functions in Wales. This will affect the court's approach to evidence; especially when considering any argument that due regard has not been given to the requirements of the Convention. Had the 2011 Measure been in force at the time of the hearing in M's case, this would have been an additional argument at his disposal, upon which the court would have had to adjudicate.

21.   Even at the time of M's case, the Convention had already been recognised as having effects on the exercise of judicial discretion in family proceedings: see Thorpe LJ in *Mabon v Mabon* [2005] EWCA Civ 634, [2005] Fam 366, at paragraph 32. Certain of the Convention's requirements have been identified by the UN Committee on the Rights of the Child ('the UN Committee') as being of particular and general importance. These include Article 3, paragraph 1 of which requires that in all actions concerning children undertaken by courts of law (and other institutions), 'the best interests of the child shall be a primary consideration', and Article 12, which requires States Parties to 'assure to the child who is capable of forming his or her own views the right to express those views freely in all matters affecting the child, the views of the child being given due weight in accordance with the age and maturity of the child'. The UN Committee has made it clear that Articles 3 and 12 are interdependent. A best interests determination which fails to respect the child's Article 12 rights would be incompatible with the Convention, however well-intended and attentive to the child's other needs. Equally, a mechanism for 'hearing the child' which failed adequately to protect the child's best interests would be non-compliant.

22.   Apart from these requirements of the Convention, there is the well-established right to a fair hearing guaranteed by Article 6 of the ECHR and enforceable under the Human Rights Act 1998. No person, however young, is excluded from its protection. Furthermore, as pointed out by Munby J in *CF v Secretary of State for the Home Department* [2004] EWHC 111 (Fam) at paragraph 158, the child, as well as the parent, has the right to respect for private and family life under Article 8 ECHR, including the procedural aspects recognised in *W v United Kingdom* (1987) 10 EHRR and *McMichael v United Kingdom* (1995) 20 EHRR 205. Section 3 of the HRA 1998 requires the court 'so far as possible' to interpret legislation compatibly with the ECHR Convention rights, and the common law requires that if more than one interpretation is possible, the more UN Convention-compliant inter-

pretation should be preferred. This points inescapably to the conclusion that in proceedings which may result in interference with a child's private and family life, the child has the right to be heard, express views and have due weight attached to them in accordance with the child's age and understanding.

23.   Still, this does not answer the question of *how* the child's views will be heard. Paragraph 2 of Article 12 contemplates that this may be 'either directly, or through a representative or an appropriate body, in a manner consistent with the procedural rules of national law', so the representative participation supplied by the 'tandem' model appears on the face of it compatible with the Convention. This is the view taken by many commentators, for example Professor Jane Fortin (*Children's Rights and the Developing Law* 3rd edition (Cambridge, Cambridge University Press, 2009) Chapter 7). Plainly, however, this can only be the case *if* those exercising discretion—judicially, professionally or administratively—act in a manner which is compatible with the holistic interpretation required by the Convention.

24.   The UN Committee's General Comment on Article 12 at [43] prefers the child being heard under conditions of confidentiality, not in open court—a preference that would of course be satisfied by the closed character of care proceedings, from which the public are excluded. Further, it is clear that it may be enough that an intermediary hears the child's views and reports them to the judge: it does not seem essential that the judge must hear directly from the child. But the question in this case is what approach must be taken by a court where the child party's views are at odds with those of the court-appointed intermediary and the child party, being of sufficient age and understanding to instruct a solicitor independently, wants to participate directly and give evidence in the case. Mr Blake argues that in this situation, the child has a right to give evidence. To this, the Local Authority replied that no-one has 'the right to give evidence' in family proceedings, the question of what evidence is required to determine the case being under the control and direction of the court. Quite so, but that is not the point: the point is how the court should exercise that power.

25.   As in most cases involving the exercise of discretion, there is a balance to be struck between the benefits and the burdens. That is what the judge sought to do, but in my view she erred: as to the relevance of one factor, as to the weight to be attached to others, and in omitting relevant factors. Her view that M would not be able to convey anything she did not already know was not a relevant consideration. Whether or not, technically, anyone has a 'right to give evidence' in family proceedings, it is inconceivable that an adult party would be prevented from doing so simply because the court already knows the position that party wishes to convey. There is no justification for distinguishing between adult and child parties in this regard except by reference to the child's best interests. As to that, the judge erred when she preferred Dr Street's opinion and the 'general evidence' of harm to children from giving evidence to what M himself might tell her directly. She erred in finding that the impact on M of an outburst from his mother would be uncontrollable, since M had requested the use of a video link rather than being physically present in court. Crucially, she did not consider the potential harm to M from not being allowed to give his evidence. This was the final hearing which would determine whether he could, in the immediate future, live with his mother. He was 15, had been granted the facility of separate representation and had clear views which he wanted to convey directly, not through intermediaries. It seems to me

curious that when we recognise that adult parties, excluded from a private meeting between the judge and child, may feel an injustice has been done to them, we should fail to recognise that children may also feel an injustice has been done to them if they are excluded from the process. I note that social research on this issue (for example, Judith Masson and Maureen Winn-Oakley, *Out of Hearing: Representing Children in Court* (Chichester, Wiley and Sons, 1999)) suggests that such feelings of injustice are in practice often experienced by children in family proceedings.

26.   Accordingly, I would allow the appeal on this point. Where a party, of any age, to family proceedings is competent and wishes to give evidence, the effect of Articles 6 and 8 ECHR, and additionally in the case of a child, Articles 3 and 12 of the UNCRC, is that in practice they do enjoy that right. The judge must still control the proceedings, but judicial discretion must, as Thorpe LJ recognised in *Mabon v Mabon* quoted above, be exercised in such a way as to give effect to these fundamental human rights requirements.

Discussion of the issue of weight to be attached to the mature child's views

27.   I have concluded that M had, effectively, the right to give evidence, and in light of that conclusion I cannot assume that his evidence would have made no difference to the court's decision on the welfare test. To do so would be to fall in to the same error as the trial judge. Accordingly, the appeal against the care order must also be allowed. In the event that the case comes again before the court of first instance, there is then the question of the weight to be attached to M's views. Mr Blake argues that there is a rebuttable presumption in favour of a mature child's preferred outcome at the welfare stage. There is merit in this argument, since, as with the question of direct participation in the proceedings, we have to recognise that the law is on the move in terms of recognition of the capacity and agency of the child. As I have already explained, this affects our interpretation of the rules and the exercise of discretion in family proceedings.

28.   On balance, however, I decline to take that further step. The weight to be given to the wishes, feelings and views of the child will vary from case to case. It may be the determinative factor in a particular case but section 1(3) of the Children Act 1989 cannot be construed so as to read into it a hierarchy of weight amongst the factors there listed. Each and all of the factors should also be interpreted in light of the fundamental human rights requirements to which I have referred. But as to the weight to be attached to them, each case is fact sensitive.

9

Commentary on the Judgment of the *Hoge Raad* of the 5th December 2014

TON LIEFAARD AND MARIELLE BRUNING

I. Introduction

The rewritten judgment of the Netherlands Supreme Court of 5 December 2014 revolves around the right to be heard and the right to effective participation of children in civil proceedings. The core legal issue concerns a minor's right to access all files relating to the case in connection with his[1] right to be heard as recognised under Dutch law and in Article 12 of the UN Convention on the Rights of the Child (CRC). In its original judgment, the Netherlands Supreme Court ('*Hoge Raad*'[2]) touches upon the legal capacity of minors under the Dutch Code of Civil Procedure, the role of the guardian *ad litem* in Dutch family law proceedings concerning parental custody and the right of minors to access information including case files as part of their right to access to justice.

This commentary starts with a few general remarks regarding the position of minors in Dutch family law (section II), followed by some critical reflections on the original judgment (section III). This helps to understand the rewritten judgment. The commentary closes with some concluding observations (section IV).

II. Dutch Family Law and the Procedural Position of the Minor

Under Dutch Family Law a minor is a person under the age of 18,[3] in line with the CRC. Minors lack legal capacity.[4] Only their parents or legal guardians can initiate legal

---

[1] This commentary refers to the minor or the child in the masculine form.

[2] The Netherlands Supreme Court 5 December 2014, ECLI:NL:HR:2014:3535 (also: original judgment).

[3] Art 1:233, Dutch Civil Code ('*Burgerlijk Wetboek*').

[4] Dutch law provides that minors lack legal capacity unless the law provides otherwise; see for some exceptions MMC Limbeek and MR Bruning, 'Chapter 6. The Netherlands. Two Decades of the CRC in Dutch Case Law' in T Liefaard and JE Doek (eds), *Litigating the Rights of the Child. The UN Convention on the Rights of the Child in Domestic and International Jurisprudence* (Dordrecht, Springer, 2015) 92–93. Under Dutch administrative law and criminal law the minor has a stronger position.

proceedings and act as an independent party. As bearers of parental responsibility, they are responsible for the minor's legal representation in civil matters.[5] In case of a conflict of interests between the minor and his legal representative, the court can appoint a guardian *ad litem* ('*bijzondere curator*')[6] who can instigate and represent the child in civil legal proceedings. The rewritten judgment provides relevant background information in sections 6 to 13. It is important to highlight that in some family law matters, Dutch law provides minors with the possibility to approach the court informally and ask for a specific decision. This informal access to court is available in matters related to custody after divorce and contact between a minor and a parent.[7]

Despite their legal incapacity, minors are interested parties in all family proceedings,[8] which include proceedings concerning child protection measures such as a family supervision orders. Moreover, they have the right to be heard in court proceedings if they are 12 years or older and not regarded legally incompetent to express their will.[9] A minor younger than 12 can, upon his request, be heard if the court finds him competent, but he has no *right* to be heard under the Dutch Code of Civil Procedure. It is safe to assume that, in practice, requests like these are rare. In addition, children under the age of 12 are not invited to participate in the court procedure.[10]

III. Commentary

A. General Observations

In the present case, the mother of a child lodged an appeal before the Netherlands Supreme Court complaining that the District Court had denied her child the right to access all case files.[11] It was argued that unlimited access to files was necessary to assess whether the minor wanted to exercise his right to be heard in court.[12] The Supreme Court upheld the judgment of the lower courts and ruled (in paragraph 3.8) that a competent ('*oordeelsbekwame*') minor's effective enjoyment of the right to be heard can require that he must be informed about the content of the files relevant for the court procedure. In case a minor does not have legal capacity on the basis of a specific legal provision[13] or does not have a right to access certain files on the basis of Article 811(d) Code of Civil Procedure, he can be represented by his legal representatives and access the files through them. If the

---

[5] Art 1:245 (4) Dutch Civil Code.

[6] Art 1:250 Dutch Civil Code.

[7] Art 1:251a (4) Dutch Civil Code and Art 1:377g Dutch Civil Code.

[8] Art 798 (2) Code of Civil Procedure.

[9] Art 809 Dutch Code of Civil Procedure; see further The Netherlands Supreme Court, 1 November 2013, *NJ* 2014/24 annotated by SFM Wortmann.

[10] MP de Jong-de Kruijf and KAM van der Zon, 'Hoger beroep tegen een uithuisplaatsingsbeslissing en de rol van de minderjarige' (2015) *Trema* 298–307.

[11] Art 290 Dutch Code of Civil Procedure provides that each interested party has the right to access files (and receive a copy) related to the legal matter. This also applies to interested parties in family law matters (art 798 Code of Civil Procedure).

[12] See original judgment, para 3.4 with reference to paras 2.1.2 and 2.3.1.

[13] Note that minors in general lack legal capacity, but that Dutch law provides for many exceptions to this rule; see eg E Jansen, 'De eigen(aardige) procesbevoegdheid van de minderjarige' (2016) *Nederlands Juristenblad* 1563.

minor thinks that his interests are not represented well, he can access a court and request the appointment of a guardian *ad litem*. Consequently, the Supreme Court ruled that the right to access justice, as laid down in Article 6(1) European Convention on Human Rights (ECHR) and Article 12 CRC, has been sufficiently safeguarded, provided that the child can access justice effectively.

Regardless of these conclusions, it was noteworthy that—unusually—the Supreme Court gave extensive reasoning for its decision and referenced a wide range of legal *and* non-legal sources (including a report of the Children's Ombudsman).[14] This is to be commended, since Dutch courts, particularly the Supreme Court, tend to be brief and lack the narrative found in many common law judgments.[15]

This commentary provides four points of criticism, which have laid the foundations for the rewritten judgment: the structure of the judgment and the confusion caused by the Supreme Court's reasoning; the limited reference to international human rights law; the court's role in developing and forming the law (*'rechtsvormende taak'*); and the court's approach to the child as a rights-holder.

B. Structure and Accessibility of the Judgment

The rewritten judgment first of all restructures the arguments of the Supreme Court and brings it back to the core question: can the child effectively exercise his right to be heard and participate effectively in court proceedings affecting him without having direct access to files, that is: without representation by parents, legal guardian or guardian *ad litem*? Bearing in mind the structure of the original judgment, the rewritten judgment elaborates on the right to be heard, on the right to information and the right to access files, and on the right to effective participation and right to personal autonomy as recognised under international law (ECHR and CRC).[16] The first two parts connect directly to the reasoning of the Supreme Court in the original judgment. The third part, which to a large extent concentrates on 'the right to personal autonomy', provides an additional, but in our view essential element of the rewritten judgment. In doing so, the rewritten judgment has tried to connect better to the core of the complaints, to move away from the confusion caused by the Supreme Court and to make the judgment more accessible.

The structure of the original judgment is rather confusing and therefore not very accessible.[17] Although the Supreme Court elaborated extensively on the legal incapacity of minors and recognised the minor as an interested party (contrary to the Court of Appeal), for its main conclusions it zoomed in on the right of minors to be heard under Dutch law and observes that neither Article 6 ECHR nor Article 12 CRC stipulate that the right to

---

[14] Wortmann criticises the Supreme Court for this; The Netherlands Supreme Court, 5 December 2004, *NJ* 2015/57 annotated by SFM Wortmann.

[15] The Supreme Court's judgment can be considered part of an evolving line of jurisprudence in which the legal position of minors in civil proceedings is addressed in a more elaborated manner. The judgment was preceded by the judgment of 1 November 2013 on the right to be heard; The Netherlands Supreme Court, 1 November 2013, *NJ* 2014/24 annotated by SFM Wortmann.

[16] See ECtHR Judgment of 3 September 2015, Application No 10161/13 (*M and M v Croatia*), para 171. This right is as such not recognised under the CRC.

[17] See also The Netherlands Supreme Court, 5 December 2004, *NJ* 2015/57 annotated by SFM Wortmann.

be heard can be enjoyed effectively only if the minor has direct access to all case files. It concludes that because parents, legal guardians or a guardian *ad litem* can represent the child de facto and de jure, he can effectively access justice.

C. Reference to International Human Rights Law

The rewritten judgment elaborates extensively and almost exclusively upon the implications of international human rights law. This relates to the second point of criticism: the limited reference to international human rights law, confined to a narrow articulation in the conclusion of the requirements under Article 12 CRC and Article 6 ECHR (holding that these provisions do not require direct access to all case files). It is rather unfortunate, particularly in light of the monistic tradition of the Netherlands,[18] that the Supreme Court does not provide a comprehensive analysis of the legal status of minors in Dutch family law proceedings, based on *both* Dutch law and international law. This rather marginal approach is characteristic for the Supreme Court[19] and disregards the wealth of case law and international standards in which the right to be heard, the right to participate effectively in judicial proceedings and the right to personal autonomy have been developed, far beyond the simple wording of the provisions.

The rewritten judgment acknowledges the relevance of this comprehensive set of human rights and standards (including ECHR jurisprudence, the general comments of the UN Committee on the Rights of the Child and the Council of Europe's Guidelines on child-friendly justice). One could question the legal validity of the reference to General Comment Number 12 in paragraph 16 of the rewritten judgment. A general comment is 'soft law', a recommendation by the UN Committee on the Rights of the Child, on how state parties should implement the CRC. However, general comments provide an authoritative interpretation of the CRC and, indeed, they are now cited in case law, including that of the European Court of Human Rights.[20] Although this is a rather new and modest development, it justifies the use by the Supreme Court of general comments when interpreting Dutch law under the CRC. The same can be argued with regard to the reference to the Council of Europe's Guidelines on child-friendly justice.[21]

D. Competence to Develop and Form the law

Even though the rewritten judgment shows that the Supreme Court could have found reason in international legal standards to strengthen the legal position of minors in Dutch

---

[18] JH Gerards and JWA Fleuren, *Implementatie van het EVRM en de uitspraken van het EHRM in de nationale rechtspraak. Een rechtsvergelijkend onderzoek* (Nijmegen: Radboud Universiteit Nijmegen / WODC, Ministerie van Veiligheid en Justitie, 2013). See arts 93 and 94 of the Dutch Constitution. Limbeek and Bruning point at the 'long-established rule in Dutch case law', based on a 'principle [that] derives from the presumption that the Netherlands, by ratifying a treaty, intends to fulfil its treaty obligations' (Limbeek and Bruning, above n 4, 91). In addition, the self-executive force of Art 12 CRC as well as Arts 6 and 8 ECHR is beyond any doubt.

[19] See Limbeek and Bruning, above n. 4.

[20] See eg ECtHR, Judgment of 3 September 2015, Application No 10161/13 (*M and M v Croatia*).

[21] T Liefaard, 'Child-Friendly Justice: Protection and Participation of Children in the Justice System' (2016) 88(4) *Temple Law Review* 905–927.

civil law, one could question the competence of Dutch courts to develop and form the law in such a way. This should be understood in light of the civil law tradition of the Dutch legal system. The primacy of (comprehensive) law making lies with the legislator, the Dutch Parliament ('*Staten-Generaal*'). There is no system of 'precedent' in the Netherlands and courts do not have an active role in law making. Strictly, court judgments are not a source of law.[22] At the same time it can be argued that the judiciary, in particular the Supreme Court,[23] has a role to play in the development and forming of law, as well as in the promotion of the unity of the case law.[24] This seems particularly true if the courts have found an inconsistency between Dutch and international law and the legislator fails to act upon it.[25] In contrast to the original judgment, where the Supreme Court did not explicitly require[26] the Dutch legislator to take action to strengthen the legal position of minors, the rewritten judgment concludes, because of the tension between international human rights and Dutch law, that

> it is not beyond the powers of the judiciary to conclude that every child requesting access to files who is capable of forming his or her views has the right to access to all relevant files as part of the right to be heard in child protection proceedings.[27]

E. Child as a Rights Holder

The fourth point of criticism concerns the Supreme Court's disregard for the recognition of the child as a rights holder under international law, in particular under the CRC. In contrast, the rewritten judgment places the child as a rights holder at the core of its reasoning. It starts with the right to be heard.

i. *The Right to be Heard*

In the rewritten judgment, the Supreme Court reflects on the Dutch rule that minors under the age of 12 do not have the right to be heard. It questions the validity of this in light of Article 12 CRC and the interpretation provided by the CRC Committee in General Comment Number 12. The rewritten judgment acknowledges that Article 12 CRC's requirement that every child 'capable of forming his or her own views' has the right to be heard should not be seen as a limitation, but as an obligation to presume that a child has the capacity to

---

[22] CH van Rhee and W van der Woude, 'Judicial Rulings with Prospective Effect' in LPW van Vliet (ed), *Netherlands Reports to the Nineteenth International Congress of Comparative Law. Vienna 2014* (Cambridge-Antwerp-Portland, Intersentia, 2015) 13. See also J Uzman, T Barkhuysen and ML van Emmerik, 'The Dutch Supreme Court. A Reluctant Positive Legislator?' (2010) 14(3) *Electronic Journal of Comparative Law* 1–35.

[23] The Netherlands Supreme Court is responsible for hearing appeals in cassation, the aim of which is 'to promote legal uniformity and the development of law' (www.rechtspraak.nl/English/Judicial-system/Pages/Supreme-Court.aspx) and examines the legality of the lower courts.

[24] This seems particularly true if the courts have pointed at an inconsistency between Dutch law and international law and the legislator fails to act upon it. In such a situation, it cannot be excluded that the Supreme Court does step in; Gerards and Fleuren, above n 18, 37.

[25] Gerards and Fleuren above n 18, 37.

[26] The Court of Appeal had ruled that it would go beyond the competence of the court to strengthen the legal position of minors in Dutch civil law on the basis of international discussions and international standard-setting.

[27] Para 26 of the rewritten judgment.

express his or her own views and that it is not up to the child to prove that he has the capacity. It also acknowledges that the age limit of 12 is on strained terms with the CRC Committee's recommendation against setting age limits, which can find support in the European Court of Human Rights ruling in *Pini and others v Romania*[28] that age limits can impede a child's expression of their own views in court proceedings. Of course, the setting of age limits serves certain legal interests, including the principle of legality, legal certainty and equality, but the feasibility of an age limit of 12 years can be questioned under Article 12 CRC and that is one of the assumptions underlying the rewritten judgment.

The conclusion in the rewritten judgment that Dutch law is in violation of international law (see paragraph 17) is rather firm. It is unlikely that the actual Supreme Court will ever go this far for two reasons: first, it might question to what extent Article 12 CRC really stands in the way of setting an age limit of 12 years of age, with the opportunity to hear children who are younger. This position can find support in the fact that neither Article 12 CRC, nor the case law of the European Court of Human Rights, stipulate that minors must be heard directly by the court.[29] The child may be heard indirectly, even though the CRC Committee recommends to hear the child directly and that it is up to the child to decide if he wants to be heard directly or not.[30] And second, the rewritten judgment assumes that the Supreme Court sets aside Dutch legislation, which has been part of the Dutch Civil Code for a long period of time. As mentioned earlier, it is questionable whether the Supreme Court would go beyond using international law as a tool for interpretation of Dutch law at this point.

ii. Effective Participation: Right to Information and Access to All Files

Later, the rewritten judgment elaborates on the right to information as part of the minor's right to be heard. Again with reference to the CRC Committee's General Comment Number 12, it can be argued that access to information[31] is an important prerequisite for the effective exercise of the right to be heard.[32] This also finds support in academic literature.[33] In paragraph 48 of General Comment Number 12 the CRC Committee observes that '[t]he child's right to be heard … [requires] … providing children with access to appropriate information …'. However, General Comment Number 12 primarily refers to general information on how to access courts, how to participate in court proceedings and on what to expect from the child's participation. The question remains whether the importance of the right to information for the effective realisation of the right to be heard implies that a

[28] ECtHR, Judgment of 22 June 2014, Application No(s) 78028/01 and 78030/01 (*Pini and Others v Romania*), para. 157.
[29] ECtHR, Judgment of 8 July 2003, Application No(s) 30943/96 (*Sahin v Germany*), para 73.
[30] UN Committee on the Rights of the Child, *General Comment No 12: The Right of the Child to be Heard*, UN Doc CRC/C/GC/12, 20 July 2009, para 25.
[31] See also art 17 CRC (right to access information) and art 13 CRC (right to seek, receive and impart information).
[32] UN Committee on the Rights of the Child, above n 30.
[33] See eg G Lansdown, 'The Realisation of Children's Participation Rights. Critical Reflections' in B Percy-Smith and N Thomas (eds), *A Handbook of Children and Young People's Participation. Perspectives from Theory and Practice* (London/New York, Routledge, 2011) 11–23 and L Lundy, '"Voice" is Not Enough: Conceptualising Article 12 of the United Nations Convention on the Rights of the Child' (2007) 33(6) *British Educational Research Journal* 927–42.

child has the right to access all files. This touches upon the question how to make the right to effective participation 'practical and effective', which is connected to both the right to be heard and the right to a fair trial, as laid down in Article 12 CRC and Article 6 ECHR, respectively.

In order to avoid that the right to effective participation in judicial proceedings affecting the minor becomes illusory or merely tokenistic, access to adequate information is key.[34] This has also been confirmed by the Council of Europe's Guidelines on child-friendly justice,[35] which assumes that adequate information is crucial for effective participation and underscores the importance of providing information directly to the child.[36] The guidelines built on the case law of the European Court of Human Rights under Article 8 ECHR and Article 6 ECHR. Under these human rights provisions, the European Court has ruled that the child's right to be heard must be factored in and implies that domestic courts have to take into account the wishes expressed (directly or indirectly) by the child when deciding, for example, on access and custody rights,[37] or matters related to adoption.[38] The European Court of Human Rights has also dealt with effective participation of children under Article 6 ECHR's right to a fair trial, albeit primarily in the context of the administration of juvenile justice.[39] 'Effective participation' in this context 'presupposes that the accused has a broad understanding of the nature of the trial process and of what is at stake for him or her'.[40] It is not necessary that the accused should 'understand or be capable of understanding every point of law or evidential detail'.[41] Even though this does not rule out that a minor could participate effectively without having understood all the details of the case, it does show that it is the child that has the right to participate effectively in judicial proceedings affecting him. This finds support in the principle of 'equality of arms', which has been recognised by the European Court under Article 6 ECHR's right to a fair trial. The rewritten judgment explains in paragraph 29 that under this principle, a child, who is capable of forming his own views, like parents who are confronted with child protection proceedings, should have access to files.[42] The child's right to a fair trial includes the right to such procedural guarantees, enabling him to overcome his weaker position and the inequalities between him and the state.

The conclusion that a child only has limited access to case files can therefore be problematic in light of the meaning of the participation rights in the CRC, as well as the child's right to a fair trial and right to effective participation as part of that. This brings us to the third and most important point of criticism, which is related to the conclusion of the Supreme Court—in the original judgment—that the child is dependent upon his legal representative or a guardian *ad litem* in his access to files. Such a conclusion is on strained terms with the recognition of the child as a rights holder in the first place.

---

[34] Lundy, ibid.

[35] Adopted on 17 November 2010 at the 1098th meeting of the Ministers' Deputies.

[36] See Pt IV, Guideline 48 and Pt IV, Guideline 3.

[37] See eg ECtHR, Judgment of 8 July 2003, Application No(s) 30943/96 (*Sahin v Germany*); see further U Kilkelly, 'The CRC in Litigation Under the ECHR' in Liefaard and Doek, above n 4, 199ff.

[38] ECtHR, Judgment of 28 October 2010, Application No 52502/07 (*Aune v Norway*).

[39] See Kilkelly, above n 37.

[40] ECtHR Judgment of 15 June 2004, Application No 60958/00 (*SC v UK*) para 29.

[41] ibid.

[42] ECtHR Judgment of 21 September 2016, Application No 12643/02 (*Moser v Austria*).

iii. *Legal Status of Children under International Law; Personal Autonomy*

The rewritten judgment of the Supreme Court above all recognises that children have to be seen as rights holders; they have the right to have rights.[43] This recognition is one of the major achievements with the adoption of the CRC. And article 12 CRC, typified as one of the four general principles of the CRC,[44] can be seen as one of 'the most notable improvements and innovations' of the CRC, particularly in this regard.[45] Another crucial article underscoring the child as bearer of human rights is article 5 CRC. At first it seems to be about the rights and responsibilities of parents and others responsible for the child, including the extended family, but in fact it is this provision that underscores that it is the child that owns his rights. Parents (and others) can guide the child in the 'exercise of his or her rights', but this must be done in a manner that takes into account the child's 'evolving capacities'. The rewritten judgment underscores that a similar reasoning can be found in the case law of the European Court of Human Rights[46] with reference to personal autonomy of the child. In light of this, distinctions between children on the basis of their age and maturity can be justified, but this does not affect the rights ownership of the child. Moreover, a complete denial of legal capacity seems hard to reconcile with the CRC and the Supreme Court's original reasoning should be questioned for this very reason. Of course, one should acknowledge, as mentioned earlier, that it is the Dutch legislator who has decided not to grant children legal capacity and that it would probably go too far, in the context of the Dutch legal tradition, to expect the Dutch Supreme Court to set aside Dutch law on the basis of the CRC. The Dutch Constitution does, however, give the Supreme Court the power to do so. In addition, it can be argued that Dutch law does grant the child access to justice, formally and informally, in a wide variety of ways.[47] A fundamental denial of the child's capacity does not seem to fit here either.

Finally, it is important to note that the Supreme Court in its rewritten judgment observes that the margin of appreciation doctrine does allow for a system in which the child's request to access all files can be balanced against other interests. However, since the Netherlands does not provide for such a system, it acted in violation of Article 8 ECHR, in conjunction with the CRC.[48]

IV. Conclusions

The rewritten judgment should be seen as an aspirational document. If the Dutch Supreme Court were to adopt an approach like this it would be ground-breaking. However, given the

---

[43]   M Freeman, 'The Human Rights of Children' (2010) 63(1) *Current Legal Problems* 18.

[44]   UN Committee on the Rights of the Child, *General Comment No 5 (2003): General measures of implementation of the Convention on the Rights of the Child,* 27 November 2003, CRC/GC/2003/5.

[45]   N Cantwell, 'The Origins, Development and Significance Of the United Nations Convention On The Rights Of The Child' in S Detrick (ed), *The United Nations Convention on the Rights of the Child: A Guide to the 'Travaux Preparatoires'* (Dordrecht, Nijhoff, 1992) 28.

[46]   ECtHR, Judgment of 3 September 2015, Application No 10161/13 (*M & M v Croatia*). See also para 27ff of rewritten judgment.

[47]   Jansen, above n 13.

[48]   Rewritten Judgment, para 31.

legal tradition in which the Court operates, it is not likely that this will happen (soon). At the same time, it is important that the Supreme Court shows more willingness to take into account international standards, beyond the ECHR and the case law of the ECtHR, and make more explicit why (or why not) this justifies a critical reflection upon Dutch law. Such an approach can be very well defended in the Netherlands' monistic tradition and would connect much better to increasing efforts of European courts and also domestic courts to incorporate international children's rights in regional and domestic jurisprudence.[49]

---

[49] Liefaard and Doek, above n 4; see also European Union Agency for Fundamental Rights and Council of Europe, *Handbook on European Law Relating to the Rights of the Child* (Luxembourg, Publications Office of the European Union, 2015).

The Netherlands Supreme Court

Hoge Raad

Judgment of MR Bruning and T Liefaard

The Circumstances of the Case

Background

1.   Parents J and T divorced on 2 March 2011. They have four children; the oldest child, daughter H, was born in 2001. Since the divorce, the parents shared parental responsibility. H lived with her maternal grandfather as an informal arrangement. The father, J, filed a request to the District Court of Limburg on the 24 January 2013 for a family supervision order for his four children aimed at solving the conflict with regard to access to and contact with his children. On 8 February 2013, H's attorney filed a request to the District Court to access all files on behalf of H, who was 11 years old at the time. Her request was declined. According to Article 811 of the Dutch Code of Civil Procedure (CCP) only minors of 12 years and older have the right of access to all files in the procedure, provided that they are regarded as having intellectual capacity to oversee the consequences of their choices.

Appeal Proceedings

2.   At the District Court hearing the children's judge heard J and his attorney, T and her attorney, H's grandfather as foster parent of H, the Child Protection Agency and the social services responsible for the family supervision order. Daughter H was allowed to be present at the hearing without being heard since she was not a party to the proceedings. Only minors of 12 years of age or older who have intellectual capacity to oversee the consequences of their choices are invited to be heard at court hearings; H was 11 years old at the time of the hearing. On 27 February 2013 the District Court issued a family supervision order for the four children in favour of the father's wish for the duration of 12 months.

3. On the 22 May 2003, H lodged an appeal at the Court of Appeal of 's-Hertogenbosch with her mother acting as her legal representative. H submitted that the District Court's decision of issuing a family supervision order for the four children should be set aside. H also complained that she had not been permitted access to all relevant files. Furthermore, she argued that the children's judge was incorrect in failing to postpone the hearing until she had been given access to all files, and that she had not been heard in court to express her views. The Court of Appeal invited H, by then 12 years old, to be heard in court, but H failed to show up. Instead H's attorney was heard by the Court of Appeal. On the 9 January 2014, the Court of Appeal dismissed H's appeal, reasoning that courts are not permitted to guarantee the child's right to be heard, to have access to all files and to strengthen the child's procedural rights in line with international developments and relevant international treaties if this goes against Dutch law. It is up to the legislator to decide upon such matters. According to Dutch law (Article 811 of the CCP) only minors of 12 years of age or over who are not intellectually incapable have the right to be heard in court. In addition, minors are not independent parties to civil proceedings according to Dutch law. Therefore minors do not have an independent right of access to all procedural files; they have to be represented by parents, legal guardians or by a guardian *ad litem*.

Complaints

4. On behalf of H, the mother, T, filed an appeal at The Netherlands Supreme Court (Hoge Raad). She complained that the District Court had unjustly and without giving sufficient reasoning ruled that H was an interested party in family court proceedings, but not a legal party to the proceedings as follows from Article 1:234 Dutch Civil Code (CC) in conjunction with Article 798 CCP and therefore did not have the right to access to all files. She also challenged the District Court's argument that the judiciary is not competent to better guarantee children's procedural rights in child protection proceedings since this is the competence of the legislator and that the *trias politica* forbids the court to take over the legislator's role of implementing children's rights in Dutch law.

5. Furthermore, it was argued that the District Court's way of hearing daughter H was in violation of Article 12 of the Convention on the Rights of the Child (CRC), General Comment Number 12 of the Committee on the Rights of the Child (the right of the child to be heard, 2009), Article 6 European Convention of Human Rights, Articles 24 and 47 of the Charter of Fundamental Rights of the European Union and the Guidelines of the Committee of Ministers of the Council of Europe on Child-Friendly Justice. Although the District Court invited daughter H to be heard, without the right of access to all the relevant files prior to being heard H could not participate adequately in the proceedings. According to the appellants the right to be heard includes the right to be informed, and thus the right to access all relevant files prior to the hearing. Without access to the relevant files H did not have effective access to court. Consequently, the District Court's judgment was wrong and in breach of international children's rights, according to the appellants.

Judgment

Legal Capacity

6.   According to Article 798 CCP minors are interested parties in all family proceedings, including child protection proceedings. However, according to the Dutch legislator, minors (ie children under the age of 18) lack legal capacity and need parents or other legal guardians or a guardian *ad litem* to initiate proceedings and to be an independent party to the proceedings. Therefore minors of 12 years of age or older who have intellectual capacity to oversee the consequences of their choices are invited to be heard at court hearings but need representation to take legal action and cannot initiate proceedings or appeal to court independently. Although the minor's legal position in family proceedings has been repeatedly debated in recent decades (eg *Parliamentary Documents II* 1989/90, 21 309; *Parliamentary Documents II* 1990/91, 21 309, No. 5), the legislator has clearly decided that there is no reason to change this concept of legal incapacity of minors in family proceedings.

7.   According to the Dutch legislator, in principle the minor's best interests will be sufficiently represented by his parents or other legal guardians. When the child's interests conflict with the interest of his legal representative (parent or legal guardian) and this causes a serious conflict of interests, for example with regard to the education and upbringing of the child, access to court is guaranteed through the appointment of a guardian *ad litem*. The court can appoint a guardian *ad litem* ex officio. The minor can also request the appointment of a guardian *ad litem*.

8.   In 1991, the legislator made clear that minors do not have the legal capacity to initiate family proceedings; minors are not legal parties to proceedings and need to be represented by their parents or other legal guardians or by a guardian *ad litem (Parliamentary Documents II* 1991/92, 22 487, No. 3, p 7). In order to strengthen the legal position of minors in civil proceedings, the legislator has chosen to improve the minor's possibilities to be represented by a guardian *ad litem* in cases where the minor's best interests cannot be represented by a parent or other legal guardian, for example in the situation of a conflict of interest.[1]

9.   In 2003, the legislator again took the same position in response to a research report focused on the legal position of minors and the guardian *ad litem*.[2] The legislator stated that the current possibilities of representation by a guardian *ad litem*, when there is a conflict of interests between the minor and his parents or other legal guardians, were sufficient and it was unnecessary to introduce an independent legal position in civil proceedings for minors. According to the legislator the current system sufficed in which parents or other legal guardians represent their child unless there is a conflict of interest. In the legislator's opinion in 2003 the child's legal position did not need to be strengthened and was sufficiently protected.[3]

[1] *Parliamentary Documents II* 1991/92, 22487, No. 3, p 7.
[2] Verweij-Jonker Instituut, *Minderjarige als procespartij? Een onderzoek naar de bijzondere curator en een formele rechtsingang voor minderjarigen*, Utrecht: 2003, *Kamerstukken II* 2003–2004, 29 200 VI, No. 116.
[3] *Parliamentary Documents II* 2003/04, 29200 VI, No. 116, p 3.

The Right to be Heard

10.   Minors of 12 years or older, who are not intellectually incapable, have the right to be heard in court in civil law proceedings (Article 809 CCP). Minors who are under the age of 12 can be permitted by the court to be heard. The court has discretionary power to decide whether a minor under the age of 12 will be heard or not, and how this will be done.

Appointing a Guardian Ad Litem

11.   In 2012, the Dutch Children's Ombudsman expressed his concerns about the effectiveness of the possibility of appointing a guardian *ad litem*.[4] In reply to the recommendations of the Dutch Children's Ombudsman, the State Secretary of Security and Justice explained that case law has shown that a 'serious conflict of interests' required for the court appointment of a guardian *ad litem* does not need to be interpreted strictly, but can also have a wider meaning.[5] One could speak of a 'serious conflict of interests' requiring the appointment of a guardian *ad litem* not only when the parents and the child obviously have direct conflicting interests, but also when parents are incapable of overseeing the issues concerning the child or to objectively present those issues. In other words, the threshold for the appointment of a guardian *ad litem* should be considered low. Divorce or separation conflicts between two ex-partners can already lead to the assumption of such a 'serious conflict of interests' that requires the appointment of a guardian *ad litem* for the child.

12.   One of the Dutch Children's Ombudsman's recommendations concerned the development of guidelines about the appointment of a guardian *ad litem* (based on Article 1:250 CC). These guidelines have been developed and launched in 2014 by the judiciary[6] and encompass the principle that when a conflict between two parents or legal guardians exists, this gives reason to appoint a guardian *ad litem*, even when there is no direct serious conflict between the child's best interests and the interests of both parents or legal guardians.

13.   In other words, the threshold to appoint a guardian *ad litem* is lowered and the new guidelines give guidance to a broader interpretation of the legal requirements for the appointment of a guardian *ad litem* in which the conflict of interests does not necessarily have to involve the child's direct interests, but can also involve a conflict of interests between both parents that influences the child's best interests. This has broadened the possibility to appoint a guardian *ad litem* for the child.

Complaints

14.   The central question in this case is whether Article 6(1) of the European Convention on Human Rights (ECHR) and Article 12 of the UN Convention on the Rights of the Child (CRC) or any other binding international document imply that the right to be heard can only be guaranteed effectively when a minor has the right to independent access to all relevant files in the proceedings in which he will be heard.

[4] Dutch Children's Ombudsman, *De bijzondere curator, een lot uit de loterij?*, The Hague 2012.
[5] *Parliamentary Documents II* 2012/13, 31 753, No. 56.
[6] *Werkproces benoeming bijzondere curator ogv art 1:250 BW*, Den Haag: Raad voor de Rechtspraak 2014.

The Court's Assessment

The Right to be Heard

15.   Under Dutch Law, minors have the right to be heard when they are 12 years or older *and* are not regarded as intellectually incapable. Furthermore, although a minor is not legally capable to access court and initiate civil proceedings, he has the right to legal representation in civil court proceedings by a guardian *ad litem* in cases where his parents or legal guardian cannot act as representatives. Children under the age of 12 do not have the right to be heard, but only have the right to *request* to be heard. The Court has the discretionary power to decide whether children under the age of 12 will be heard in such cases.

16.   Article 12 CRC provides:

> 1. States Parties shall assure to the child who is capable of forming his or her own views the right to express those views freely in all matters affecting the child, the views of the child being given due weight in accordance with the age and maturity of the child.
>
> 2. For this purpose, the child shall in particular be provided the opportunity to be heard in any judicial and administrative proceedings affecting the child, either directly, or through a representative or an appropriate body, in a manner consistent with the procedural rules of national law.

General Comment Number 12 on the right of the child to be heard, drawn up by the UN Committee on the Rights of the Child (UN Doc CRC/C/GC/12) serves as an interpretative tool for Article 12 CRC. It states in section 20 that:

> States parties shall assure the right to be heard to every child 'capable of forming his or her own views'. This phrase should not be seen as a limitation, but rather as an obligation for States parties to assess the capacity of the child to form an autonomous opinion to the greatest extent possible. This means that States parties cannot begin with the assumption that a child is incapable of expressing her or his own views. On the contrary, States parties should presume that a child has the capacity to form her or his own views and recognize that she or he has the right to express them; it is not up to the child to first prove her or his capacity.

In section 21, it is stated:

> The Committee emphasizes that article 12 imposes no age limit on the right of the child to express her or his views, and discourages States parties from introducing age limits either in law or in practice which would restrict the child's right to be heard in all matters affecting her or him.

17.   In light of this interpretation by the UN Committee on the Rights of the Child, the current Dutch practice of hearing children only when they are 12 years or older, with a discretionary power to hear the child who is under 12 years of age, but without a right for children under 12 years of age to be heard in civil proceedings, constitutes a violation of Article 12 CRC. Children are to be considered as rights-holders and in principle every child has the right to be heard without (legal) limitations.

18.   The Court notes that not only does Article 12 CRC give rise to a child's right to be heard in court when capable of forming his or her own views, but also the European Court of Human Rights has made clear that age limits can be no impediment for children who have reached an age at which it could reasonably be considered that their personality is sufficiently formed and they have attained the necessary maturity to express their opinion (ECtHR 22 June 2004, *Pini and Others v Romania*, application number(s) 78028/01 and

78030/01, paragraph 157), even when legal age limits hinder the child from being heard. The Court therefore concludes that every child who is capable of forming his or her own views should have an effective possibility to be heard in court and should be informed about his or her right to be heard.

The Right to be Informed

19.   The right of the child to be heard (Article 12 CRC) includes the right to be informed. As General Comment Number 12 CRC states in section 41 with regard to preparing a child to be heard:

> Those responsible for hearing the child have to ensure that the child is informed about her or his right to express her or his opinion in all matters affecting the child and, in particular, in any judicial and administrative decision-making processes, and about the impact that his or her expressed views will have on the outcome. The child must, furthermore, receive information about the option of either communicating directly or through a representative. She or he must be aware of the possible consequences of this choice. The decision maker must adequately prepare the child before the hearing, providing explanations as to how, when and where the hearing will take place and who the participants will be, and has to take account of the views of the child in this regard.

20.   Furthermore, General Comment Number 12 refers to the relationship between Article 12 CRC and Article 17 CRC: the child's right to information (sections 80 and 82):

> Article 13, on the right to freedom of expression, and article 17, on access to information, are crucial prerequisites for the effective exercise of the right to be heard. These articles establish that children are subjects of rights and, together with article 12, they assert that the child is entitled to exercise those rights on his or her own behalf, in accordance with her or his evolving capacities …

> Fulfilment of the child's right to information, consistent with article 17 is, to a large degree, a prerequisite for the effective realization of the right to express views. Children need access to information in formats appropriate to their age and capacities on all issues of concern to them. This applies to information, for example, relating to their rights, any proceedings affecting them, national legislation, regulations and policies, local services, and appeals and complaints procedures. Consistent with articles 17 and 42, States parties should include children's rights in the school curricula.

21.   The question arises whether the child's right to information (Articles 17 and 13 CRC) as part of the right to be heard (Article 12 CRC) includes the right to access to all relevant procedural files, or whether it is primarily focused on informing the child about his right to be heard, the context of the hearing, and the way in which he or she is to be heard, etc. The Court notes that to limit the child's right to information in the latter way reflects a tokenistic approach that does not fulfil the principle of the child as a rights-holder. It also follows from General Comment Number 12 that basic rules of fair proceedings, 'such as the right to a defence and the right to access one's own files' (section 38) should be complied with by States parties of the CRC. This not only expresses the importance of the child's right to access to all files as a prerequisite of the child's right to be heard, but stresses the necessity to comply with the child's right to access to all files before being heard. This approach is reinforced by the Guidelines on Child-Friendly Justice, adopted by the Committee of Ministers of the Council of Europe in November 2010 and is firmly grounded in the case law of the European Court of Human Rights under Articles 8 and 6 ECHR (see also below under 26). These assume that 'information' is a prerequisite for the effective enforcement of the right

to be heard and for effective participation, as one of the fundamental principles of child-friendly justice (see eg Part IV, Guideline 48). Moreover, the Guidelines underscore the importance of providing information directly to the child (Part IV, Guideline 3): 'As a rule, both the child and parents or legal representative should directly receive the information. Provision of information to the parents should not be an alternative to communicating the information to the child.'

22.   The Court therefore considers that children who are capable of forming their own views should have the possibility to access all files upon request before deciding about being heard. Children's right of access to files as a first step towards guaranteeing their right to be heard as is stated in Articles 12 in conjunction with Article 13 and Article 17 CRC overrides Dutch legislation in which no such right is guaranteed.

The Right to Access Files as a Prerequisite to Exercising the Right to be Heard

23.   Dutch minors are not considered as independent parties to family proceedings according to Dutch law, even in child protection cases that deal with their best interests. They are represented by their parents or other legal guardians. When a conflict of interests between parents and child occurs, the child can be represented by a court appointed guardian *ad litem*. Children lack legal capacity, but participate in child protection proceedings by way of being heard in court when they are 12 years or older. The question arises whether this form of indirect participation in child protection proceedings responds to a sufficient, effective and meaningful implementation of the right to information and the right to participate in the proceedings.

24.   According to the CRC, children are fully autonomous rights-holders that have the right to participate in proceedings and the right to be heard. According to General Comment Number 12 CRC (section 35),

> [a]fter the child has decided to be heard, he or she will have to decide how to be heard: "either directly, or through a representative or appropriate body." The Committee recommends that, wherever possible, the child must be given the opportunity to be *directly* heard in any proceedings (emphasis added).

25.   According to the UN Committee, it is therefore the child's own decision how to be heard. In the current case, girl H decided at the age of 11 years old that she wanted to be heard directly, and not through representation by her parents or a guardian *ad litem*. She argued that she was an independent party to the proceedings who had the right to access to all relevant files before she could decide about whether or not to be heard. Her parents were divorced and the supervision order was requested in order to resolve conflicts between H's parents. Therefore a conflict of interests can be assumed. In the light of Article 12 CRC and General Comment Number 12 CRC H's right to independent access to all relevant files as an independent party can be assumed. According to section 135 (Conclusions) of General Comment Number 12 of the CRC, 'achieving meaningful opportunities for the implementation of article 12 will necessitate dismantling the legal, political, economic, social and cultural barriers that currently impede children's opportunity to be heard and their access to participation in all matters affecting them'.

26.   Dutch law precludes minors under 12 years of age from being an independent party to the proceedings and to have an independent right to access to all relevant files.

The Dutch legislator decided in 1991 and in 2003 that changes are neither needed nor wanted. Nevertheless, in light of articles 93 and 94 of the Dutch Constitution, Article 12 CRC can be regarded as directly applicable and therefore it is not beyond the powers of the judiciary to conclude that every child requesting access to files, who is capable of forming his or her views, has the right to access to all relevant files as part of the right to be heard in child protection proceedings. If a child decides that he or she prefers to access all relevant files independently this should be determinative and should be guaranteed. Without the possibility to access all files at the child's request, hearing the child can become a superficial exercise and a meaningless experience for the child.

27.   The child's right to participate effectively in child protection proceedings also flows from Article 8 ECHR, which concerns the right to respect for family and private life and which includes a child's right to personal autonomy. The European Court of Human Rights has emphasised that the child's right to personal autonomy is exercised through the child's right to be heard in any judicial proceedings. In any proceedings affecting children's rights under Article 8 ECHR the decision-making process must be fair and children should be, just like parents, sufficiently involved in the decision-making process.

> This right to personal autonomy—which in case of adults means the right to make choices as to how to lead one's own life, provided that this does not unjustifiably interfere with the rights and freedoms of others—has a different scope in the case of children. They lack the full autonomy of adults but are, nevertheless, subjects of rights … This circumscribed autonomy in case of children, which gradually increases with their evolving maturity, is exercised through their right to be consulted and heard. As specified in Article 12 of the Convention on the Rights of the Child (…), the child who is capable of forming his or her own views has the right to express them and the right to have due weight given to those views, in accordance with his or her age and maturity, and, in particular, has to be provided the opportunity to be heard in any judicial and administrative proceedings affecting him or her (ECtHR 3 September 2015, *M&M v Croatia*, Appl No 10161/13, par 171).

28.   In other words, the right to respect for private life includes the child's right to personal autonomy and this means that Member States must guarantee that children are sufficiently involved in the decision-making process. The European Court on Human Rights reiterates that whilst Article 8 contains no explicit procedural requirements, the decision-making process must be fair so as to afford due respect to the interests safeguarded by Article 8. It is established in case law of the European Court of Human Rights that parents must have been sufficiently involved in the decision-making process, with a view to establishing whether their rights under Article 8 have been violated.[7] Having regard to Article 12 of the CRC and in particular point 32 of the General comment number 12 of the Committee on the Rights of the Child, the European Court of Human Rights finds in *M & M v Croatia* that the same considerations apply *mutatis mutandis* in any judicial or administrative proceedings affecting children's rights under Article 8 of the present Convention.

29.   Procedural guarantees for parents and children who are involved in child protection proceedings cannot only be derived from Article 8 ECHR, but also from Article 6

[7] See eg ECtHR 21 September 2006, *Moser v Austria*, appl no 12643/02; ECtHR 17 December 2002, *Venema v The Netherlands*, appl no 35731/97.

ECHR, guaranteeing a fair trial, including procedural safeguards. One of the elements of the broader concept of a fair trial concerns the equality of arms principle. This principle requires that each party should be afforded a reasonable opportunity to present his or her case under conditions that do not place him or her at a substantial disadvantage vis-à-vis his or her opponent (ECtHR 21 September 2006, *Moser v Austria*, application number 12643/02, paragraph 86). In child protection proceedings one can often speak of a weaker party, eg parents and children who are often unrepresented, and a stronger party, eg the responsible authorities. Therefore, according to the equality of arms principle, parents should have access to files (ECtHR 21 September 2006, *Moser v Austria*, application number 12643/02, paragraph 86). The Court notes that the same considerations apply *mutatis mutandis* for any child who is capable of forming his or her own views in any child protection proceedings. According to the Court the child's right to a fair trial includes the right to procedural guarantees to overcome inequalities between the child and responsible authorities and this right encompasses the right to access his or her files upon request.

30.   The Court notes that H was not heard because she argued that she could not decide on her wishes to be heard unless she was given access to all relevant files. According to H, the right to be heard and participate in the proceedings entail the right to information as an independent rights-holder. The Court finds that children who are capable of expressing their views have the right to participate effectively. Being heard should be a meaningful exercise and this starts with access to files on request in order to make an informed decision about exercising the right to be heard. Furthermore the right to be heard includes an obligation to give the expressed views of the child due weight in accordance with the age and maturity of the child (Article 12(1) CRC). Children participating in child protection proceedings who are capable of expressing their views have to be recognised as active agents in their own lives, entitled to be listened to, respected and granted increasing autonomy in the exercise of rights.

31.   The Court concludes that H's right to respect for family and private life (Article 8 ECHR), which has been interpreted as extending to the right to personal autonomy, was not respected since she was not given independent access to all relevant files in order to decide about her wishes of being heard and this constituted a violation of both Article 6 and Article 8 ECHR. The obligations under Articles 6 and 8 ECHR, taking into account the margin of appreciation of the State, include a system in which the child's request to access to all relevant files is balanced against other interests and thus the principle of proportionality can be applied under the specific circumstances of the case (see ECtHR, 7 July 1989, *Gaskin v UK* application number 2/1988/146/20). The Court finds that a system lacking such mechanism is in breach of Article 8 ECHR.

Judgment

32.   For these reasons, the Court holds:

—   that there has been a violation of Article 12 of the CRC as regards H's right to be heard;

—   that there has been a violation of Article 6 of the ECHR as regards to H's right to participate effectively in the child protection proceedings by a refusal of an independent
right to access to all relevant files;

—   that there has been a violation of Article 8 of the ECHR as regards H's right to respect
for private and family life on account of the child protection proceedings and her non-
involvement in the decision-making process caused by a refusal of an independent
right to access to all relevant files.

This judgment has been delivered by [vice-president], as chair and [Justice 1], [Justice 2],
[Justice 3] and [Justice 4], and delivered in open court by [vice-president] on 5 December
2014.

10

Commentary on
AAA v Associated Newspapers Ltd

THOMAS DC BENNETT

I. Introduction

Once upon a time there was a larger-than-life political figure who (allegedly) fathered a child as a result of an extra-marital sexual liaison. His name cannot be revealed, for legal reasons. But, as the Court of Appeal helpfully noted in *AAA*,[1] many of the details surrounding this affair can be read about in Sonia Purnell's book, *Just Boris*.[2] Owing to the (supposedly) high degree of public interest in this man's extra-marital activities, the *Daily Mail* decided to publish the allegation pertaining to the fact of the child's paternity. It also decided to spice-up its story by publishing a photograph of the child, in order to show that the child bore a striking physical resemblance to her (alleged) father. (The hair is, apparently, unmistakeable.)

Today, many of us are familiar with the fall-out from celebrity sex scandals, which are often drawn to public prominence by the tabloid press and social media. Many quickly become subject to legal proceedings even before they break as the figure concerned seeks to prevent publication by obtaining an injunction. Where this sort of proceeding arises, the court must weigh up the interests on each side (celebrity privacy versus the public interest in knowing about the allegations) and endeavour to 'balance' them.[3] Of course, it is a 'balance' in name only; the winner in this 'balance' takes all.[4] But the 'balance' metaphor conjures up the ancient image of the 'scales of justice'. And this image encourages us to think about such cases in a purely bilateral way: the celebrity versus the press. However, where the desire to expose a miscreant public figure's misdeeds can be satiated only by intruding significantly upon the privacy of his (alleged) infant child, the bilateral image is a fundamental distortion of reality. The publication of such information clearly has an impact upon persons beyond the two key players.

---

[1] *AAA v NGN Ltd* [2013] EWCA Civ 554 [54].

[2] S Purnell, *Just Boris: A Tale of Blond Ambition* (London, Aurum Press Ltd, 2012).

[3] *Re S (A Child) (Identification: Restrictions on Publication)* [2004] UKHL 47, [2005] 1 AC 593 [17] (Lord Steyn).

[4] P Wragg, 'Protecting Private Information of Public Interest: *Campbell's* Great Promise, Unfulfilled' (2015) 7(2) *Journal of Media Law* 225.

AAA was an action for damages and injunctive relief in the tort known as 'misuse of private information' (MPI).[5] It was brought not by the (alleged) father but by the (anonymised) child against Associated Newspapers Ltd in an attempt to protect her own privacy interests. The claimant sought an injunction (to prevent further publication) in respect of the allegations (ie the (alleged) fact of her paternity) and the photograph of her, and damages in respect of those matters that had, by the time the action was commenced, already been published by the defendant. The (alleged) father was not a party to the action at all.

The injunction was sought on the basis that photographs are 'particularly intrusive'.[6] Moreover, the decision to reveal to the child the fact of her (alleged) paternity was characterised by the claimant as a classic example of private information regarding which a claimant is entitled to exercise autonomy (and, in the case of a small child, to have that autonomy exercised by an adult).

At first instance, the case was heard by Davies J in the High Court. The claimant was awarded damages for the publication of the photograph (and the defendant agreed not to republish it). However, the Court found the defendant justified in publishing the (alleged) fact of her paternity. Whilst the claimant had a reasonable expectation of privacy in respect of both the photograph and the (alleged) fact of her paternity, that expectation was to be accorded a reduced weight in the 'balance' against the public interest. The reduction in weight resulted from certain actions of the child's mother (whereby she had been indiscreet, having discussed the child's paternity with friends and, on one occasion, with a man who turned out to be a high-ranking figure at *Condé Nast*). With the weight accorded to the child's privacy reduced, the 'balance' favoured publication of the (alleged) fact of her paternity (but not of the photograph).

The claimant appealed, arguing that Davies J had been wrong to find her privacy interest to carry reduced weight. For if Davies J was right, the result would seem to indicate that, under English law, a parent can effectively 'waive' the privacy right of the child. This was made all the more serious by virtue of the fact that privacy is a human right guaranteed by Article 8 of the European Convention on Human Rights (ECHR): if a parent's indiscretion could 'waive' it, this would place an onerous restriction on a fundamental right. The Court of Appeal, however, upheld the first instance decision and it is that ruling which is the subject of the rewrite that follows.

II. The Rewritten Judgment

The English law of privacy is underdeveloped and, consequently, riddled with inconsistencies and idiosyncrasies. *AAA* is worthy of detailed scrutiny because it sits at the confluence of a number of these problems and allows us to critique the way in which privacy law has developed. In a short commentary, not all of the issues worthy of study can be flagged up.[7] So I highlight one major point that is brought into the foreground by Hughes'

---

[5] The nomenclature comes from *Campbell v MGN Ltd* [2004] UKHL 22, [2004] 2 AC 457 [14] (Lord Nicholls).

[6] *Douglas v Hello! Ltd* [2005] EWCA Civ 595, [2006] QB 125 [84].

[7] The difficulties that courts have encountered in privacy cases in endeavouring to accommodate the 'best interests of the child' within MPI methodology is an issue I have written about elsewhere. See TDC Bennett, 'Privacy, Third Parties and Judicial Method: *Wainwright's* Legacy of Uncertainty' (2015) 7(2) *Journal of Media Law* 251, 264–66.

rewritten judgment: the issue of parental 'waiver' and the relevance of the claim's contextual background.

Hughes has rewritten the judgment of the Court of Appeal. The determinations of fact made by Davies J are not readily challengeable (despite clear concerns over the judge's grasp of the chronology of events[8]). Nevertheless, the rewritten judgment is highly critical of Davies J's treatment of the 'waiver' issue, reversing her on that point. This treatment of the 'waiver' issue helpfully brings into focus different methodological perspectives on the case. For Hughes' fictive judge focuses heavily on the substantive (privacy) right of the child and the apparent absurdity in allowing the unwise actions of a parent to derail the rights-claim. Yet the methodology adopted by the High Court which had the effect of reducing the weight accorded to the child's claim is both broadly reflective of tort methodology across the board and, seemingly, an inevitable consequence of the doctrine known as 'indirect horizontal effect'.

A. Horizontal Effect

Human rights law is typically considered to be an aspect of public law. The ECHR is binding only upon state actors, whilst section 6 Human Rights Act 1998 (HRA) creates statutory obligations to protect Convention rights that are binding only upon public bodies. Yet owing to the doctrine of 'indirect horizontal effect' (which describes how the HRA operates in disputes between individuals and/or bodies corporate), the medium through which individuals resolve privacy claims against each other or against bodies corporate is private law, not public law. In other words, one cannot bring a claim against a company alleging a human rights violation per se. Instead, one must bring a claim at common law to protect an existing common law right (eg a right to the non-misuse of one's private information). The court which hears the case is a public body that is bound by the HRA to protect Convention rights. But it will discharge that obligation not by automatically ruling in the claimant's favour, but by developing the common law incrementally in order to ensure that both parties' Convention rights are accorded sufficient protection 'indirectly' by the common law to discharge the UK's Convention obligations.[9]

Unfortunately, the common law develops rather haphazardly in a piecemeal fashion. It is shaped solely by the circumstances that are brought before the courts. The methodology the courts use to decide these cases is the methodology of the particular common law cause of action being pleaded. Thus in a misuse of private information case, the courts will first ask whether the claimant had a 'reasonable expectation of privacy' in respect of the information complained of ('Stage 1'). If such a reasonable expectation is found to exist, the courts will move to 'Stage 2': the 'ultimate balancing test'.[10] At Stage 2, the courts will endeavour to 'balance' the competing interests of the parties in a fact-sensitive exercise involving 'an intense focus on the comparative importance of the specific rights being claimed'.[11]

---

[8] See para 32 of the rewritten judgment.
[9] G Phillipson and A Williams, 'Horizontal Effect and the Constitutional Constraint' (2011) 74(6) *MLR* 878.
[10] *Re S (A Child)*, above n 3 [17].
[11] ibid.

B. Fact-sensitivity in Tort Law

Fact-sensitivity is not only required in MPI cases (by virtue of the 'intense focus' mandated by *Re S*); it is a hallmark of English tort law generally. For individuals cannot claim private law rights in a vacuum; rights at common law arise out of particular circumstances and fact patterns.[12] The right to privacy, whilst rather abstract in the language of the Convention, has been developed in a far more concrete fashion in England. This is perhaps most apparent when one considers that the common law in England has long rejected a broad 'right to privacy'[13] in favour of more narrowly focused rights (eg to confidentiality,[14] to non-misuse of private information,[15] to freedom from the intentional infliction of psychiatric harm[16]).

The 'waiver' issue comes to the fore at paragraph 25 of the rewritten judgment. Hughes' fictive judge asserts that: (a) it would be 'unconscionable' if the human right of one person could be waived by the actions of another, (b) that there is no basis for departing from that position simply because the claimant is a child, and (c) that to suggest otherwise is to undermine the fact that the child has her own rights under international and domestic law.

Hughes' fictive judge's view is that, if the substance of my human rights is to be taken seriously, it ought to make no difference what someone else has said or done in respect of them. For if another person is able to say or do something that ends up derailing my claim—because I no longer have a sufficiently strong reasonable expectation of privacy—then my rights have been, in substance, 'waived'.

The ECHR makes no distinction on its face between adults' and children's rights. Indeed, the Strasbourg Court has held that a new-born infant has full privacy rights under Article 8.[17] But the common law of England—the only mechanism open to us for the securing of Convention rights against private parties—does. Consider the case of *Dobson v Thames Water*—a case in the tort of nuisance.[18] In that case, a child was denied damages for nuisance whilst his parents were permitted to recover. The reason was that the common law does not permit claims for private nuisance to be brought by children since they cannot have a legal interest in the affected land. The Court of Appeal found that this did not give rise to a breach of its obligations to secure protection for the child's Article 8 interests because the damages awarded to the parents would cover any loss of amenity suffered by the child as well. Consider what would have happened, however, had the parents *not* pursued a claim in respect of their own suffering. Inevitably, the child would have had no remedy. The parents would, in a sense, have 'waived' the child's right to non-interference with his family life by deciding against bringing their own claim.

This approach is not limited to nuisance cases. In *O v A*, the Court of Appeal rejected a claim in negligence by the child of a well-known performing artist.[19] The child sought

---

[12]   See eg *Qualcast (Wolverhampton) Ltd v Haynes* [1959] AC 743, 755 (Lord Keith of Avonholm).

[13]   *Wainwright v Home Office* [2003] UKHL 53, [2004] 2 AC 406.

[14]   *Stephens v Avery* [1988] FSR 510.

[15]   *Campbell*, above n 5.

[16]   *Wilkinson v Downton* [1897] 2 QB 57; *Rhodes v OPO (O v A)* [2015] UKSC 32, [2015] 2 WLR 1373.

[17]   *Reklos v Greece* [2009] EMLR 290.

[18]   *Dobson v Thames Water Utilities Ltd* [2007] EWCA Civ 28, [2009] 3 All ER 319.

[19]   *O v A (previously OPO v MLA)* [2014] EWCA Civ 1277, [2015] EMLR 4.

to restrain the publication of the defendant's autobiography (which contained graphic accounts of sexual abuse the defendant had suffered). The claim was brought on the basis that, if the claimant read it, he might be caused severe psychological distress. The Court of Appeal essentially held that parents are immune from suit in negligence in respect of decisions made pertaining to their offspring's upbringing. Whatever one makes of that ruling (and it is certainly a questionable reading of negligence law generally), we may at the very least take it as authority for the proposition that a parent may not be sued for making the decision to publish a book that might distress their child. Once more the parent might be said, in this sense, to have 'waived' the child's right to freedom from psychological distress.

C. An Alternative Perspective on 'Waiver'

O and *AAA* could, however, be seen as cases where the parent's actions form part of the contextual background to which the court has regard when focusing intensely on the rights-claim. If this were so, then we would have cause not to regard these as instances of 'waivers' at all. Tort claims are brought into focus by examining them against the factual backdrop against which they arise. What is unique about the reasonable expectation of privacy of a young child is that it must be attributed to the child; it is a constructive expectation. This is because young children may not be able to hold, and certainly are in no position to articulate, an *actual* expectation of privacy. In circumstances where the parents take steps to shield the child from intrusion, the courts see this background as enhancing privacy.[20] Since, logically, the background might go the other way (as in *AAA*), Hughes' fictive judge is pressed into an attack on this aspect of *Murray* (at [25]). Such an attack, however, downplays the relevance of the contextual background. Hughes' judgment argues that *Murray* is wrong on this point. In the alternative, she argues that if *Murray* is indeed binding, its precedential effect should be limited to 'cases concerning photographs of a child in a public place.'[21]

This approach to the use of precedent is reminiscent of Perry's 'weak Burkean conception' of adjudication.[22] A court adjudicating in the weak Burkean mode regards precedent as binding only when the outcome it prescribes is itself desirable.[23] Since Hughes' fictive judge finds that the effect that *Murray* would, if followed, have on *AAA* is undesirable—leading as it does to this apparent 'waiver' of her privacy—she is not minded to apply it. Such an approach, however, if consistently adopted, risks diminishing the value of precedent. For 'it obviously takes very little to overcome the binding force of an earlier case.'[24] The courts might then, in short order, find themselves mired in Tennyson's 'wilderness of single instances'.[25]

---

[20] *Murray v Express Newspapers plc* [2008] EWCA Civ 446; [2009] Ch 481.

[21] Para 26.

[22] SR Perry, 'Judicial Obligation, Precedent and the Common Law' (1987) 7(2) *OJLS* 215.

[23] According to Perry, the weak Burkean conception of adjudication 'would regard a court as being bound by a previous decision, itself decided on the basis of a balance of reasons, only until such time as it was convinced both that the balance of reasons had been wrongly assessed on the prior occasion, and that the correct assessment in fact led to the opposite result.' See ibid 221–22.

[24] ibid.

[25] Lord Alfred Tennyson, *Aylmer's Field* (1793).

There are other reasons why the relevance of the contextual background is important. It may play a role in establishing harm—normally a pre-requisite for liability in tort (although this has never been conclusively analysed by the courts). Stage 1 of the MPI methodology goes some way to fulfilling the harm requirement; only if there is a reasonable expectation of privacy to violate can harm be thereby occasioned. This is certainly imperfect. For as Eric Descheemaeker has observed, there is no consensus in MPI doctrine as to when harm is occasioned (that is, whether it is contingent upon, or inherent within, the violation of the privacy right itself).[26] Assuming, however, that there must be some sort of harm in order for an act to be tortious, and further that (like most of English tort law) MPI follows what Descheemaeker terms a 'bi-polar' model of harm (that is, harm being causally contingent upon a rights violation), it makes sense to regard the establishment of a reasonable expectation of privacy as a necessary first step in setting the scene for harm to be occasioned.[27] With that in mind, it becomes apparent that the contextual background is relevant to determining whether there is something worth protecting present. For this reason, the courts refuse relief for the publication of trivial information—a certain threshold of sensitivity must be reached before a reasonable expectation of privacy can be established.[28] Likewise, where information has already appeared in the public domain such that there can be no reasonable expectation that it will be kept private, we might rationalise the courts' refusal to provide relief on the basis that further publication will not engender any further harm. (Incidentally, the courts' approach to interim injunctions in MPI fits very well with this rationalisation, since they will be granted even where information is already in the public domain if they can serve the useful purpose of preventing some further harm).[29]

The contextual background thus provides the backdrop against which the rights-claim can be elucidated and considered. In the view of Davies J, the mother in *AAA* has acted in a way that impacts upon the background to the claim to such an extent that some of what may harm the child (in terms of revelations) has already occurred in a non-tortious fashion. The weighting Davies J attached to the mother's actions in calculating their impact upon the child's claim might be criticised, but the overarching method is entirely consistent (formally) with generally applicable tort methodology. Hughes' preferred approach issues a broader challenge to established tort method. Therein lies the value of this rewrite.

III. The Value of the Rewritten Judgment

It may or may not be desirable that the actions of parents in situations such as these are considered by the courts as part of the background against which the rights-claim is judged. But that is a normative issue—one which Hughes' rewritten judgment brings into the foreground. For the doctrine of indirect horizontality places us in a situation where the only available mechanism for the determination of Article 8 (privacy) claims between non-state

---

[26] E Descheemaeker, 'The Harms of Privacy' (2015) 7(2) *Journal of Media Law* 278.
[27] ibid 279.
[28] *Weller v Associated Newspapers Ltd* [2014] EWHC 1163 (QB) [27].
[29] *CTB v News Group Newspapers Ltd* [2011] EWHC 1326 (QB) [19].

actors is tort law. Tort comes with its idiosyncrasies—including its heavy fact-sensitivity and its determination to focus closely on the contextual background to the claim.

The desirability of the result—the apparent 'waiver' of the child's rights—is inseparable from the model of application (indirect horizontality) that the courts have given to the HRA. Criticism of the former must entail criticism of the latter. Hughes' judgment thus does contemporary domestic human rights scholarship a significant service by pointing out a consequence of indirect horizontality that, despite the seemingly exhaustive debate that ensued around the HRA's possible models of application in the early 2000s, seems not to have been foreseen.

We are now at a point where the government of the day[30] plans to introduce legislation to repeal the HRA and replace it with a 'British Bill of Rights'. Although it seems unlikely that the content of the rights contained in the new Bill will emanate from the ECHR, the Bill will still have to grapple with the issue of horizontality. This is because its purpose will be to impose higher-order rights norms onto lower-order private law. The model of horizontality that is to be adopted ought to form part of the debate when it becomes time to draft the new Bill. And the case of *AAA* is particularly prescient, for it highlights some of the less foreseeable consequences of the indirect horizontal method. Given this, and the implications for the substance of children's rights that inevitably flows from making these—often disconnected—methodological decisions, the timing of this rewritten judgment could not be more appropriate.

---

[30] As of April 2017.

Court of Appeal (England and Wales)

AAA v Associated Newspapers Ltd

Hughes LJ

Introduction

1.   This case concerns the right to privacy of an infant. It arises from a series of publications by the *Daily Mail* containing photographs of the claimant (who was less than a year old at the time of publication) and speculation that she was conceived during an affair with a prominent married British politician.

2.   Due to the child's age it was not possible for her to give evidence. These proceedings were brought on her behalf by her maternal step-grandfather, and the child's mother, nanny and grandparents gave evidence. This was proper. The child's rights are not, however, contingent upon the views and conduct, whether satisfactory or otherwise, of her family or carers. The trial judge has made her findings of fact and they bind us; however, as a Court of Appeal we have the advantage of looking at matters of principle at a stage removed from individual witnesses.

The factual background

3.   On 16 July 2010 the *Daily Mail* published an article about the claimant's alleged paternity. It was salacious in tone, conveyed the fact that the mother's friends gossiped and joked about the paternity, and that the mother had been shocked to discover that the named politician may be the father of her daughter. It included a photograph of the child on an outing with her mother in central London.

4.   Prior to that publication this information was not in the public domain.

5.   The Daily Mail subsequently published a further eight articles, three of which included the photograph and all of which included details about her paternity.

6.   It was alleged at trial that following the publication, photographers and reporters camped outside the claimant's home for 12 days. The defendant disputed this and no clear picture emerged because evidence advanced by the claimant's mother and nanny was found to be unreliable. What is apparent, however, is that the child was relocated with the assistance of a private security team to her grandmother's house in Kent in an attempt to protect her from the media.

Decision of Nicola Davies J

7.   At trial Nicola Davies J awarded £15,000 damages for repeated publication of the photograph and accepted an undertaking from the defendant concerning future publication of photographs.

8.   She dismissed the claim in respect of publication of the child's alleged paternity. Her reasoning was, first, that although the child had a reasonable expectation of privacy, that expectation was lowered by virtue of comments that her mother had made about the child's paternity at a party and when later interviewed for an article published in *T* magazine. Second, that the public interest in disclosing the information outweighed the claimant's reduced expectation of privacy. Finally, she refused to grant an injunction restraining further publication of the child's paternity on the ground that this information was now in the public domain such that an injunction would serve no real purpose.

The grounds of appeal

9.   The claimant appeals against: (i) the dismissal of her claim for damages in respect of the publication of her alleged paternity and (ii) the refusal to grant an injunction.

10.   There are four grounds of appeal.

a)   The judge failed to make any, or any proper, assessment of the claimant's best interests regarding media attention and media publication of information or speculation concerning her paternity and related private information.

b)   The judge was wrong to hold that two factors weakened the claimant's expectation of privacy. These factors were (i) the events at a house party attended by the mother during the weekend of 26 June 2010; and (ii) the interview published in *T* magazine in September 2010.

c)   The judge wrongly held that the claimant's expectation of privacy (weakened as she held it to be) was outweighed by the public interest in the recklessness of the father.

d)   The judge was wrong to hold that there was a public domain defence for publication of subsequent articles and that an injunction preventing further publication of information about the claimant's paternity would serve no real purpose.

The first ground of appeal: Failure to consider the claimant's best interests

11.   To determine whether this should succeed it is necessary to examine what a proper assessment of a child's best interests should entail, and the relationship between that assessment and the enquiry into whether the child had a reasonable expectation of privacy. The general approach to a child's best interests was summarised by Lord Kerr in *ZH (Tanzania) v Secretary of State for the Home Department* [2011] UKSC 4, [2011] 2 AC 166 at paragraph 46:

> 46. It is a universal theme of the various international and domestic instruments to which Lady Hale has referred that, in reaching decisions that will affect a child, a primacy of importance must be accorded to his or her best interests. This is not, it is agreed, a factor of limitless importance in the sense that it will prevail over all other considerations. It is a factor, however, that must rank higher than any other. It is not merely one consideration that weighs in the balance alongside other competing factors. Where the best interests of the child clearly favour a certain course, that course

should be followed unless countervailing reasons of considerable force displace them. It is not necessary to express this in terms of a presumption but the primacy of this consideration needs to be made clear in emphatic terms. What is determined to be in a child's best interests should customarily dictate the outcome of cases such as the present, therefore, and it will require considerations of substantial moment to permit a different result.

12.   This was cited in *K v News Group Newspapers* [2011] EWCA Civ 439, [2011] 1 WLR 1827, at [19] where Ward LJ described it as the proper approach in the context of an application for a privacy injunction. He suggested that in privacy cases this required the courts to 'accord particular weight to the Article 8 rights of any children likely to be affected by the publication, if that would be likely to harm their interests'.

13.   The use of a best interests approach in privacy cases raises important issues that require further consideration.

14.   Nicola Davies J approached the matter as follows: (i) the claimant had a reasonable expectation of privacy in relation to her paternity; (ii) respect for this expectation was in her best interests; and (iii) considerable weight was to be attached to her best interests.

15.   Unfortunately, the best interests argument was not argued satisfactorily at trial and there appears to have been some uncertainty as to the basis for it, in particular, whether this required the child's best interests to be a 'primary consideration' as required by Article 3 UN Convention on the Rights of the Child (UNCRC), or a paramount consideration as required by the Children Act 1989 (at [57], [104], [114]). Ultimately, Nicola Davies J concluded that the child's interests were not a 'paramount consideration' (at [114]) and presumably intended to follow the UNCRC 'primary consideration' route (albeit that the legal basis for this is not clearly established in the judgment). In future cases it will be important to determine the precise basis for introducing a best interests approach and the standard that should apply. We have elected to leave that matter here and have accepted Nicola Davies J conclusion that the child's best interests should have been a primary consideration. Our reasons for this are: (i) the use of the primary consideration approach has not been contested by the applicants; (ii) we have concluded that the applicant succeeds on the primary consideration approach and if she succeeds on that basis she would also succeed on a paramount consideration approach; and (iii) the fundamental problem for this appeal, is that regardless of whether the child's best interests were a primary consideration or a paramount consideration they should have been considered independently of the reasonable expectation of privacy analysis. It is the latter problem that is the focus of our judgment.

16.   Ward LJ in *K v News Group Newspapers*, and Nicola Davies J at trial, took the view that the starting point is that judicial scales are tipped in favour of the child's interests. We have, however, considered whether a child's best interests approach necessitates more than this and requires a different approach for privacy cases concerning children. We have concluded that it does.

17.   Although *K* could be read as simply giving greater weight to the child's reasonable expectation of privacy, 'best interests' and 'reasonable expectation of privacy' are not synonymous, even if they raise issues under the same Convention right. They have different points of enquiry and purposes. The best interests approach examines the child's welfare; whereas the reasonable expectation of privacy test is a way of determining whether the

applicant's privacy right is engaged. The two may often point in the same direction, but this will not necessarily be the case as the 'best interests' approach focuses entirely upon the child's welfare and takes a broader look at welfare beyond protecting the child's privacy, whereas the reasonable expectation of privacy test takes into consideration factors beyond the interests of the child, and focuses exclusively upon what is private. It should not therefore be assumed that giving weight to a child's *expectation* of privacy is sufficient to satisfy the best interests test.

18.   We propose that the correct approach is as follows: (i) does the claimant have a reasonable expectation of privacy? (ii) if the answer to (i) is yes and the claimant is a child then the court should apply a best interests approach, which necessitates a *broader look at the implications for the child's welfare*; and (iii) in determining whether publication should be permitted there must be a countervailing reason of considerable force that would outweigh the welfare of the child.

19.   This is particularly important in light of the suggestion that the child's reasonable expectation of privacy is diminished as a result of disclosures made by a parent. This is contrary to the best interests approach, which was introduced to protect the welfare of the child regardless of the actions and wishes of parents. The best interests approach may also necessitate giving greater consideration to the consequences of publication and future publications than would ordinarily occur under the reasonable expectation of privacy test.

20.   There is no reason to doubt that Nicola Davies J attached considerable weight to the claimant's best interests. However, the case was litigated in a manner that resulted in an inappropriate meshing of best interests and reasonable expectations of privacy arguments. This led her to conclude that due to the child's mother's disclosures the weight to be attached to the claimant's expectation of privacy (and therefore her best interests) was reduced. As discussed below, we are of the view that such disclosures are not relevant to a child's reasonable expectation of privacy, but even if they were, they were certainly not relevant to an assessment of a child's best interests. We have therefore concluded that where best interests arguments are raised they should be considered independently of the reasonable expectation of privacy test and on that basis the first ground of appeal should succeed. It is not necessary, however, to determine the case on this basis as we have allowed the appeal on other grounds.

The second ground of appeal: The judge was wrong to hold that the reasonable expectation of privacy was weakened by the two events

The relevance of parental conduct to a child's right to privacy

21.   This raises the important question of the relevance of the mother's disclosures to the child's expectation of privacy. It has been assumed since *Murray v Express Newspapers plc* [2008] EWCA Civ 446 that parental conduct is relevant.

22.   *Murray* was an application for summary judgment. It concerned the publication of a photograph of the infant son of JK Rowling on a family outing with his mother. The photograph was published alongside a story about JK Rowling. There was no story relating to the child akin to the publication in this case; essentially the case concerned the right of a child to privacy in public places. At first instance the judge held that the claim should be

struck out. The Court of Appeal overturned this. The passage that is alleged to be relevant here is paragraph 37:

> The question whether a child in any particular circumstances has a reasonable expectation of privacy must be determined by the court taking an objective view of the matter including the reasonable expectations of his parents in those same circumstances as to whether their children's lives should remain private … The court can attribute to the Appellant reasonable expectations about his private life based on matters such as how it has in fact been conducted by those responsible for his welfare and upbringing.

23.   Nicola Davies J sought to apply this and concluded at paragraph 116:

> The claimant's mother is an intelligent professional woman. She chose to speak and act as she did. In my view, the result has been to compromise the claimant's reasonable expectation of privacy upon the issue of her paternity. I do not find that the claimant has no reasonable expectation, rather the weight to be attached is of a lesser degree than would have been the case had nothing been said or permitted to be said upon this matter.

24.   In principle this Court is bound by an earlier decision of the Court of Appeal. Lord Greene MR set out the circumstances in which we may depart from a decision in *Young v Bristol Aeroplane Co Ltd* [1944] 1 KB 718, 729. There are a number of reasons why we believe that we are not bound by this particular dictum from *Murray*. First, *Murray* was an application for summary judgment. Second, the Court of Appeal did not find that the claimant's reasonable expectation of privacy was lowered as a result of his mother's conduct; the statement was therefore *obiter*. Third, *Murray* is inconsistent with the child's right to privacy under Article 8 ECHR and under Article 16 United Nations Convention on the Rights of the Child. Fourth, *Murray* is inapplicable to the facts of this case. The third and fourth points require further elaboration.

25.   The child has her own rights under Article 8 ECHR. Whether or not the holder of a right waives his or her rights by his or her own conduct (the so called doctrine of waiver) is contentious and is for another day. What is clearly unconscionable is that the human right of one person can be waived by the conduct of another. There is no basis for departing from that simply because the claimant is a child. To suggest otherwise is to undermine the fact that the child has her own rights under international and domestic law. The Court of Appeal in *Murray* was therefore wrong to suggest that the courts can 'attribute to the Appellant reasonable expectations about his private life based on matters such as how it has in fact been conducted by those responsible for his welfare and upbringing' (at [37]).

26.   If, however, contrary to our view, *Murray* is binding, it should be strictly limited to what was contemplated in *Murray*, namely cases concerning photographs of a child in a public place. It is therefore inapplicable to the publication of other types of information. The information in this case was sensitive information about the child's biological origins and family life. This must be contrasted with the facts of *Murray*, which concerned an anodyne photograph of the infant on an outing with his mother. The Court's suggestion that the conduct of the child's parents may be relevant must be seen in the context of that enquiry. It was not considering whether a child may have a right to privacy vis-à-vis sensitive private information, but rather whether the child would have a right to restrict photographs in cases where the child's parents have courted publicity by disseminating the child's

image. The fact that the Court of Appeal in *Murray* only contemplated a lowered expectation of privacy vis-à-vis photographs taken in public places is apparent in its reasoning at paragraphs [37] and [38]:

> 37. In the case of a child the position is somewhat different from that of an adult. The judge recognised this in [23] of his judgment, where he said this, albeit in the context of a somewhat differently formulated test discussed by Lord Hope at [100] in *Campbell*:

> '... *The question whether a child in any particular circumstances has a reasonable expectation for privacy must be determined by the Court taking an objective view of the matter including the reasonable expectations of his parents in those same circumstances as to whether their children's lives in a public place should remain private.* Ultimately it will be a matter of judgment for the Court with every case depending upon its own facts...*The Court can attribute to the child reasonable expectations about his private life based on matters such as how it has in fact been conducted by those responsible for his welfare and upbringing.*' (emphasis added)

> 38. Subject to the point we made earlier that we do not share the judge's view that the proceedings are artificial, we agree with the approach suggested by the judge in that paragraph. '*Thus, for example, if the parents of a child courted publicity by procuring the publication of photographs of the child in order to promote their own interests, the position would or might be quite different from a case like this, where the parents have taken care to keep their children out of the public gaze.*' (emphasis added)

Thus even if *Murray* is binding it is inapplicable here. We now turn to consider the facts.

Country weekend party

27.   The mother was invited to a house party on the weekend of 26 June 2010. At the party she had a conversation with the managing director of a major magazine group during which she revealed the child's father.

28.   In examining the relevance of these facts the trial judge focused upon whether the mother regarded the child's paternity as confidential and whether this was a confidential conversation. These were the wrong questions. In determining whether the child had a reasonable expectation of privacy the mother's views on confidentiality (a different concept to privacy) were not relevant.

The article in T magazine

29.   In October 2010, *T* magazine published an interview with the mother, which contained references to her relationship with the politician and the alleged paternity.

30.   The interview was conducted on 21 September 2010.

31.   After examining this material Nicola Davies J concluded that:

> [T]he claimant's reasonable expectation of privacy is affected by her mother's conduct of what is her private life. The fact that her mother contrary to advice from solicitors acting on behalf of her daughter chose to go ahead with an article which she knew would contain information about her daughter and speculation as to her daughter's paternity demonstrates an ambivalence on her part, to the matters which are at the core of this application.

32.   This assessment was wrong for the following reasons. First, as discussed above, the mother's attitude is no basis for waiving the claimant's right. The judge focused entirely upon the mother's conduct and motive; this was an irrelevant consideration, which dominated the judge's analysis to the exclusion of proper consideration of the child's right. Second, all of these events took place after the publication on 16 July 2010 and are therefore irrelevant to the child's expectation of privacy at the relevant time. The mother's subsequent behaviour (whether right or wrong) cannot be invoked to recalibrate the child's expectation of privacy retrospectively.

33.   We therefore allow the appeal on this ground.

The third ground of appeal: Challenge to the judge's balancing of the rights under article 8 and 10 of the ECHR

34.   When balancing the two rights the judge stated at [118] that the 'test required to justify publication is a high one, "exceptional public interest"', but that it was 'undisputed that there is a public interest in the professional and private life of the claimant's supposed father'. There were two reasons for this. The first was his professional position as a prominent politician. The second was that 'the claimant is alleged to be the second such child conceived as a result of an extramarital affair of the supposed father' which 'goes to the issue of recklessness on the part of the supposed father, relevant both to his private and professional character, in particular his fitness for public office'. Consequently the publication was justified at [119].

35.   The claimant argues that any public interest in the father's infidelities and philandering could be fully served by discussion and criticism of the alleged affair and his other affairs, without any need to identify the claimant. The deputy editor of the *Daily Mail* was cross-examined on this issue.

> It could be, but there is an additional element to this, which is the charge against [the father] which has been levelled in relation to this case and previously, which is of recklessness. Self-evidently it is possible to have an extra marital affair and ensure that there is not a child. Extreme recklessness of this type was already on [the father's] record, as we all know. There was a previous affair which resulted in the lady concerned having an abortion. That caused him great personal and professional discomfort, and this story appeared to suggest that history in his case was repeating itself, which made explaining the child's part in the story and indeed demonstrating that the child looked an awful lot like [the father] very important.

36.   The trial judge accepted that argument. She did not, however, spell out what she meant by 'recklessness' as fully as she might have done.

37.   It is clearly established that a balancing exercise between articles 8 and 10 of the European Convention on Human Rights (ECHR) conducted by a first instance judge is analogous to the exercise of a discretion. The balancing exercise requires a detailed appreciation of the evidence before the trial judge. She had the advantage of seeing and hearing the witnesses and making an assessment of them. Accordingly, an appellate court should not intervene unless the judge has erred in principle or reached a conclusion which was plainly wrong or outside the ambit of conclusions that a judge could reasonably reach: see, for example, *Lord Browne of Madingly v Associated Newspapers Limited* [2007]

EWCA Civ 295, [2008] QB 103 at [45], and *JIH v News Group Newspapers Ltd* [2011] EMLR 15, Lord Neuberger MR at [26].

38.   The Court of Appeal may, however, intervene where the first instance judge has taken into account irrelevant considerations in evaluating the claimant's right or in assessing the public interest. Moreover, the Court may also intervene where the trial judge has failed to adopt the proper mechanism for evaluating competing rights. Although there may well be a public interest in examining the father's conduct, this does not mean that there is a public interest in revealing the identity of the child. It was the revelation of this information that was contested by the claimant and the judge should therefore have asked whether the public interest required the disclosure of the child's identity; the proportionality test demands this.

39.   The judge erred in: (i) assuming that the public interest in discussing the conduct of the politician required the revelation of the child's identity and (ii) in failing to consider the argument that revealing the child's identity was a disproportionate interference with Article 8 (2) ECHR.

40.   We therefore allow this ground of the appeal.

The fourth ground of appeal: The Judge was wrong to hold that an injunction restraining publication of the private information would serve no useful purpose

41.   The judge refused to grant the injunction on the basis that the information was already in the public domain. Her reasons were first, that this story was going to be published; if the defendant had not done it, another newspaper would. Second, that no one can stop the claimant's mother's ex-boyfriend speaking to the press. She was further influenced by the fact that the claimant had delayed bringing proceedings and what she referred to as 'the troubling matter' of the claimant's mother's interview with the magazine.

42.   The claimant argues that before the *Daily Mail* publication nothing had appeared in the media about the claimant, it was that publication that opened the floodgates and many of the later publications explicitly refer to the *Daily Mail* article. The claimant also submits that the fact that the information was in the public domain should not be accorded much, if any, weight because: (i) it was the defendant who put it in the public domain in the first place; and (ii) if the injunction was granted, the information would fade from the public mind, so that the injunction would serve a real purpose. We accept both of those submissions.

43.   The judge rejected the contention that all subsequent publications resulted from the first article. Her reasoning was that it was 'clear that other newspapers were working on similar information at the same time'. We accept the trial judge's finding of fact; however, multiple violations of a child's right (whether connected or independent of one another) do not provide a satisfactory basis for refusing an injunction.

44.   Although the extent to which information is in the public domain is relevant to the utility or futility of an injunction, and therefore whether it would amount to a dispro-portionate interference with freedom of expression, the courts are entitled to consider further press intrusion and have granted an injunction on that basis: see *CTB v News Group Newspapers* [2011] EWHC 1326 where Eady J refused to vary an injunction after

information had been made publicly available. His reasons were that with 'each exposure of personal information or allegations, whether by way of visual images or verbally, there is a new intrusion and occasion for distress or embarrassment' at [24]. That for 'so long as the court is in a position to prevent *some* of that intrusion and distress, depending upon the individual circumstances, it may be appropriate to maintain that degree of protection' at [25]. That the desire of newspapers to 'publish more about this "story", with a view to selling newspapers and perhaps achieving other commercial advantages, demonstrates that coverage has not yet reached saturation point', and therefore judicial intervention is not 'wholly futile'. Finally, he stated that the question to ask in these cases 'is whether there is a solid reason why the claimant's identity should be generally revealed in the national media, such as to outweigh the legitimate interests of himself and his family in maintaining anonymity' at [26]. Applying this to the facts he found that the claimant and his family would 'be engulfed in a cruel and destructive media frenzy' if the injunction were varied and thus he declined to do so.

45.   Although Eady J was considering whether to vary an existing injunction, similar considerations apply here. There is a solid reason for protecting the claimant from further intrusions during her childhood.

46.   The 'fade factor' carries some weight in this case, but there are some hurdles. First, much that has been published in relation to the claimant's paternity remains available online and is also included in a book. Second, the permanent injunction would only restrain the defendant from referring to the information, although many other media organisations have published the same thing. We are nevertheless convinced that the injunction would serve a genuine purpose. It would preclude the defendant from publishing 'details of her name, addresses of her home, nursery and school.' It also includes restraint of 'any particulars reasonably likely to lead to her identification in conjunction with information concerning the claimant's paternity'. Although the injunction cannot undo the existing disclosures it can mitigate their effects by precluding the defendant from publishing her future whereabouts, in particular her home, nursery and school.

Conclusion

47.   For all these reasons we allow this appeal. The judge carefully considered the issues and reached a conclusion, but that conclusion is not beyond challenge. First, the judge wrongly conflated the child's best interests with whether or not she had a reasonable expectation of privacy. The former focuses upon the child's welfare, the latter upon the child's right to privacy. Second, the judge erred in lowering the child's expectation of privacy based upon the conduct of the mother. The conduct of the mother is irrelevant to the assessment of the child's right. In any event some of the alleged conduct took place after the relevant disclosure. Third, the judge erred in focusing upon the public interest in discussing the conduct of the child's alleged father. The core information, namely that the father had an adulterous affair, deceiving both his wife and the mother's partner resulting in the birth of a child was a public interest matter which the electorate was entitled to know when considering his fitness for high public office. This did not, however, necessitate revealing the identity of the claimant. In balancing the child's right against the public interest, the relevant question was whether the revelation of the child's identity was necessary to the assessment of

the father's character. It was not. Finally, the judge erred in declining the application for the injunction. Although some information is in the public domain an injunction will serve a genuine purpose in protecting the child as she grows up by precluding the defendant from reporting the addresses of her home, nursery and school. The child's interest in privacy in those environments outweighs the defendant's right to freedom of expression vis-à-vis the publication of such details.

Appeal allowed.

Part III

Children's Rights and Medical Decision-making

11

Commentary on *Re W (A Minor)* (*Consent to Medical Treatment*)

EMMA NOTTINGHAM

I. Introduction

In *Re W (A Minor) (Consent to Medical Treatment)*[1] the Court of Appeal grappled with the difficult subject of children's refusal of medical treatment, in circumstances in which an adolescent's refusal would result in her irreparable harm or death. The reasoning which led the Court to authorise treatment in the face of the young person's refusal to consent, has been the subject of extensive academic commentary and, in some instances, strong criticism from a children's rights perspective. Gilmore LJ's rewritten judgment, while acknowledging the force of much of the Court's reasoning on the case law and statutory provisions, adopts a stronger children's rights perspective, which seeks to give greater respect to the child's autonomy interest in the Court's process of determining where the young person's welfare lies. While the rewritten judgment may address some of the criticisms of the original judgment, disagreements as to how adolescent autonomy and welfare are to be mediated run deep, and Gilmore LJ's departure from the more paternalistic approach taken in the original judgment is unlikely to be universally welcomed. In what follows, the original decision in *Re W* and essential background are first explored, before comparing Gilmore LJ's approach with the original judgments.

II. The Autonomy of Children Prior to *Re W*

Prior to *Re W*, the House of Lords in the landmark case *Gillick v West Norfolk and Wisbech Area Health Authority*[2] held that a child under the age of 16 could give a valid consent to medical treatment. Lord Scarman stated that:

> [A]s a matter of law the parental right to determine whether or not their minor child below the age of 16 will have medical treatment terminates if and when the child achieves a sufficient understanding and intelligence to enable him or her to understand fully what is proposed.[3]

---

[1] *Re W (A Minor) (Consent to Medical Treatment)* [1993] Fam 64. For comment, see J Eekelaar, 'White Coats or Flak Jackets? Doctors, Children and the Courts—Again' (1993) 109 *LQR* 182; H Houghton-James, 'The Child's Right to Die' [1992] *Family Law* 550; N Lowe and S Juss, 'Medical Treatment—Pragmatism and the Search for Principle' (1993) 56 *MLR* 865; J Masson, '*Re W*: Appealing from the Golden Cage' (1993) 5(1) *Journal of Child Law* 37.
[2] *Gillick v West Norfolk and Wisbech Area Health Authority* [1986] 1 AC 112.
[3] ibid, 188–89.

The test for establishing a child's power to consent to medical treatment, with reference to this passage, is now referred to in shorthand form as '*Gillick* competence'.[4] *Gillick's* acknowledgement that parental rights are not absolute and that a child under 16 could, if competent, consent to medical treatment, was heralded as a victory for children's rights. However, the extent to which the case recognised the child's autonomy interest prompted greater debate. Perhaps most radically, John Eekelaar's influential interpretation, drawing largely on Lord Scarman's opinion, concluded that the case meant that when a child reaches capacity, a parent cannot impose a conflicting view, even if that view was contrary to the parental view of the child's best interests.[5]

A minor's refusal of medical treatment was considered by the Court of Appeal post-*Gillick*, but prior to *Re W*, in *Re R (a minor)(wardship: consent to treatment)*.[6] In that case a 15 year old girl with a psychiatric illness was found not to be *Gillick*-competent and the Court of Appeal in Wardship held that it was in her welfare to have her anti-psychotic medicine administered contrary to her expressed wish. More controversially, it was held obiter that the wishes of a competent minor could be overridden by the Court. Further, Lord Donaldson MR made other obiter comments on the relationship between the child's and parents' powers of consent, concluding that the 'parental right' that Lord Scarman had been referring to in *Gillick* was a 'right to determine'. This, he explained, is wider than a right to consent:[7]

> In a case in which the '*Gillick* competent' child refuses treatment, but the parents consent, that consent *enables* treatment to be undertaken lawfully, but in no way determines that the child shall be so treated. In a case in which the positions are reversed, it is the child's consent which is the enabling factor and again the parents' refusal of consent is not determinative.[8]

This case received strong criticism and was the start of what has been perceived by some commentators as the 'retreat from *Gillick*'.[9]

III. The Original *Re W* Judgment

Re W concerned a 16 year old girl, referred to by the Court as 'J', who suffered from anorexia nervosa and who was in local authority care. The local authority applied for permission to move the girl to a specialist treatment unit and to give her medical treatment without her consent, should it become necessary to do so. In spite of the fact that she was found to be of sufficient understanding and intelligence to consent to treatment and refused to consent, Thorpe J granted permission. J appealed. The Court of Appeal held that an emergency

---

[4] The phrase '*Gillick* competent' was used by Lord Donaldson in *Re W (A minor) (Medical Treatment)* [1993] Fam 64, 77.

[5] J Eekelaar, 'The Emergence of Children's Rights' (1986) 6 *OJLS* 161. For criticism, see S Gilmore, 'The Limits of Parental Responsibility' in R Probert, S Gilmore and J Herring, *Responsible Parents and Parental Responsibility* (Oxford, Hart Publishing, 2009).

[6] *Re R (a minor)(wardship: consent to treatment)* [1992] Fam 11.

[7] ibid, 23E–H.

[8] ibid.

[9] G Douglas, 'The Retreat from *Gillick*' (1992) 55(4) *MLR* 569, 576.

order should be made in respect of J without her consent as, shortly before the appeal hearing, J's weight had dropped and there was a risk that her capacity to have children in later life would be seriously at risk and that a little later her life itself might be in danger. For this reason, Lord Donaldson MR, in his leading judgment, held that J's wishes were not of any weight due to 'the threat of irreparable damage to her health and risk to her life.'[10]

As J was 16 years old, she had a statutory power to consent to medical treatment as set out in section 8 of the Family Law Reform Act 1969.[11] This raised a question for the court as to whether section 8 gave adolescents aged 16 and 17 complete autonomy in the sphere of medical decision-making. If it did, the Court would be precluded from use of its inherent jurisdiction, because of the House of Lords' ruling in *A v Liverpool City Council*,[12] that the inherent jurisdiction cannot be used in an area reserved to others by statute. Lord Donaldson MR and Balcombe LJ concluded that section 8 was limited in its scope, conferring merely a power to consent to treatment, and thus the inherent jurisdiction was available to the Court.

In addition, their lordships interpreted section 8 as preserving parental power to consent to an adolescent's medical treatment. Developing his comments in *Re R*, Lord Donaldson explained that a doctor requires only one valid consent as a legal 'flak jacket' to protect against a claim in battery.[13] This 'flak jacket' could be the consent of a minor over 16, a '*Gillick* competent' minor, or a person with parental responsibility and, as long as a doctor had the consent of one of these parties, the minor could be lawfully treated. There could be concurrent consents from parent and child and only one is needed for treatment to lawfully take place. Thus, if a child refuses treatment, even if he or she is competent or over the age of 16, his or her refusal could be overridden by parental consent.[14]

The main issue in *Re W*, however, was whether Thorpe J was correct to exercise the High Court's inherent jurisdiction to authorise the treatment. The Court of Appeal was clear that if consent cannot be obtained from parent or child, the Court could use its inherent jurisdiction to act in the best interests of the child.[15] All three judges commented upon the extent to which the child's wishes should be balanced against their best interests. Lord Donaldson suggested that 'good parenting' involves 'giving children as much rope as they can handle without the unacceptable risk that they will hang themselves'.[16] Balcombe LJ stated that, in exercising the inherent jurisdiction, the court should 'ascertain the wishes of the child and will approach its decision with a strong predilection to give effect to the child's wishes.'[17] Nolan LJ stated that '[d]ue weight must be given to the child's wishes.'

[10] *Re W*, above n 1, 80.
[11] '(1)The consent of a minor who has attained the age of 16 years to any ... medical treatment, which in the absence of consent would constitute a trespass to the person, shall be as effective as it would be if he were of full age; and where a minor has by virtue of this section given an effective consent to any treatment it shall not be necessary to obtain any consent for it from his parent or guardian; ... (3) Nothing in this section shall be construed as making ineffective any consent which would have been effective if this section had not been enacted.'
[12] *A v Liverpool City Council* [1982] AC 363.
[13] Above n 1.
[14] *Re W*, above n 1, 67.
[15] ibid 79, 81.
[16] ibid 81.
[17] ibid 88.

However, he also stated that 'the court is not bound by them'.[18] Although there was some suggestion that weight should be given to the child's wishes, the judges agreed that the court should invoke its inherent jurisdiction if the child would suffer irreparable harm if their wishes were adhered to and that this would reflect the child's best interests. As we shall see, crucial to the difference between Gilmore LJ's re-written judgment and the original judgments is how the best interests (welfare) of the child is to be interpreted in light of the child's competence to decide an issue.

IV. Rewritten Judgment of Gilmore LJ

There are several features of Gilmore LJ's judgment which seek to emphasise that the court is dealing with a person with rights. Gilmore LJ names the child 'Jenny', in order to 'remind the court and those reading this judgment that we are dealing with the life of a young person whose personhood and full range of interests warrant our very careful attention and utmost respect.'[19] The acknowledgment of personhood is further reflected in the use of the language 'young person', which contrasts with the original *Re W* judgment in which the judges mostly adopt the word 'minor'.

Gilmore LJ agreed with the judges in the original judgment that an emergency order should be made in respect of Jenny without her consent. However, his reasons differed from the original judges. Gilmore LJ makes a distinction between consent and refusal of treatment and reaches the conclusion that the Court was not apprised fully of Jenny's ability to refuse medical treatment:

> [T]here is an important difference between not assenting to treatment, that is, not saying 'yes' to treatment in the sense of fully understanding what is proposed but declining treatment, and by contrast, positively taking a decision to refuse treatment, having considered fully what is involved in such a refusal and its consequences.[20]

This interpretation has previously been explored by Gilmore and Herring.[21] They argued that there are two different ways of saying 'no' to treatment:[22] first, a rejection of proposed treatment, where the child understands what is proposed by way of treatment, but declines to provide consent; and second, a refusal of treatment, where the child makes a decision not to have any treatment with a full understanding of the consequences of a failure to treat. In adopting this approach, Gilmore LJ maintains that the implications of this distinction are that different questions need to be asked. The second question 'may require a higher level of understanding than simply understanding what is proposed by way of treatment, particularly where the refusal will lead to irreparable harm or death.'[23] He suggests that this

---

[18] ibid 94.

[19] Re-written judgment at 220.

[20] ibid at 222.

[21] S Gilmore and J Herring, '"No" is the Hardest Word: Consent and Children's Autonomy' (2011) 23 *Child and Family Law Quarterly* 3.

[22] S Gilmore, 'Children's Refusal of Medical Treatment: Could *Re W* be Distinguished?' (2011) *Family Law* 715.

[23] Re-written judgment at 222.

approach is in line with the view of Ward J in the earlier case of *Re E (A Minor)(Wardship: Medical Treatment)*[24] where E, a boy who was almost 16 years of age, and who was being treated in hospital for leukaemia, refused to consent to any blood transfusions due to his religious beliefs as a Jehovah's Witness. Ward J found that the boy had 'no realisation of the full implications ... as to the process of dying.'[25] Gilmore LJ would maintain that this is a refusal of treatment question and therefore different to the question of a child choosing whether or not to assent to a particular treatment (eg a blood transfusion). Gilmore LJ observes that the Court heard expert evidence only on Jenny's capacity to consent to treatment, not her ability to refuse treatment. Gilmore LJ therefore concurs in the Court's making of the emergency order not only because of 'the imminent danger to Jenny's health' but also because he found that the 'Court was not fully apprised of Jenny's capacity fully to refuse treatment.'[26] Gilmore LJ makes clear that a preferable situation—had it not been an emergency—would have been to remit the case to the judge to assess Jenny's capacity to understand the consequences of refusal of treatment.[27]

However, Gilmore LJ agreed with Lord Donaldson that there could be concurrent powers of consent from both parent and child; providing clarification on how this approach is compatible with the opinions of the majority of the House of Lords in *Gillick*. He emphasised that this interpretation is in line with Lord Fraser's opinion in *Gillick* that the consent of parents should normally be sought, despite a finding that a child is *Gillick*-competent. He further identified that Lord Scarman cited section 8 of the Family Law Reform Act 1969 several times in his judgment,[28] and that there was nothing in Lord Donaldson's interpretation of section 8 which was incompatible with Lord Scarman's opinion. Like Lord Donaldson, Gilmore LJ saw section 8(1) and (3) as compatible with the view that parental consent could remain valid, even if a child of 16 could also consent.

Nonetheless, the interpretation provided by Gilmore LJ is different from the original judges and better justifies the dichotomy between the law on consent and refusal. Nonetheless, this interpretation—put forward previously by Gilmore and Herring[29]—has come under sharp scrutiny from Cave and Wallbank, who clearly doubt the effectiveness of this approach when applied in a clinical setting.[30] They interpret *Gillick* differently and suggest that it 'requires the minor to fully understand the implications of her decision, which might involve more than one treatment. Equally, there might be more than one decision about the same treatment.'[31] They have therefore rejected the idea of concurrent consents as one which would not address the disparity between how consent works in law and practice.[32] Gilmore and Herring have disagreed with Cave and Wallbank's interpretation of *Gillick*

[24] *Re E (A Minor)(Wardship: Medical Treatment)* [1993] 1 FLR 386. For discussion see D Archard and M Skivenes, 'Hearing the Child' (2009) 14(4) *Child and Family Social Work* 391.

[25] *Re E*, ibid 391.

[26] Re-written judgment at 221–2.

[27] ibid at 226.

[28] *Gillick*, above n 2, at 188–89.

[29] Gilmore and Herring, above n 21.

[30] E Cave and J Wallbank, 'Minors Capacity to Refuse Treatment: A Reply to Gilmore and Herring' (2012) 20(3) *Medical Law Review* 423, 423.

[31] ibid, 448.

[32] ibid, 424. But see S Gilmore and J Herring, 'Children's Refusal of Treatment: The Debate Continues' [2012] *Family Law* 973.

and stated that there is 'nothing in *Gillick* to suggest that what the child must understand is anything other than what is being proposed by the doctor by way of treatment.'[33] Further they suggested that the 'full understanding' required by the Cave and Wallbank analysis will mean that there will be some instances where young people will not be competent to consent to relatively straightforward procedures, purely because they do not fully understand the consequences of not receiving treatment.[34] Gilmore and Herring use the example of a nine year old child being found to lack capacity for having a plaster put on a grazed knee simply because she does not fully understand what may happen if she doesn't not have a plaster put on her knee (such as the danger and consequences of septicaemia).[35] In the re-written judgment, Gilmore LJ uses the case of *Re E* to illustrate this point

Gilmore LJ disagreed with the original judges' approach to the use of the Court's inherent jurisdiction. His view was that '[i]f she is found to be fully competent to refuse treatment, then in my judgment no court should impose treatment upon her, whether in an emergency or otherwise.'[36] He made it clear that it is possible to respect a competent child's autonomous wishes as well as protecting the child's welfare and asserted that 'the welfare principle must be interpreted in a way that reflects an adolescent's evolving capacities for autonomous decision-making, in the sense that it recognises that it is in a person's best interests to respect their autonomy.'[37] Thus, where a child is fully competent to take a decision to refuse treatment, parental responsibility is then extinguished within that sphere of decision-making and cannot be used to override the young person's competent decision.[38] This will reflect the child's best interests in this circumstance.[39]

In assessing competency, Gilmore LJ noted that although young people have the technical ability to make decisions, 'the court will also need, … carefully to consider whether the young person truly has the necessary maturity and independence of judgment …'[40] A possible difficulty with this might lie in the need for 'independence of judgment' as it is unrealistic to expect anyone, even an adult, to make decisions that are entirely free from the influence of others. However, Gilmore LJ is probably simply emphasising that if a child is subject to undue influence, this can impede independent decision-making. He further stated that, '[t]his will require an individualised assessment of the unique situation of the particular young person',[41] especially where there is a significant risk of death or permanent physical or mental impairment. But, where, a child demonstrates a real understanding of the implications of her decision to refuse treatment, under Gilmore LJ's approach she may well be allowed to die. This may invite disagreement from those who believe that a child should be protected until they reach adulthood, when they will then be able to have their autonomous decision upheld by the law.

---

[33]   Gilmore and Herring, ibid, 976.
[34]   ibid, 977.
[35]   ibid.
[36]   Re-written judgment at 226.
[37]   ibid at 224.
[38]   ibid.
[39]   ibid.
[40]   Re-written judgment at 225. There are similarities here with the reasoning in *AC v Manitoba (Director of Child and Family Services)*, 2009 SCC 30, [2009] 2 SCR 181.
[41]   Re-written judgment at 225.

Finally, in the rewritten judgment, Gilmore LJ addresses the stigma of mental health and disagrees with Lord Donaldson that the inherent jurisdiction should be used in favour of the mental health legislation.[42] He further highlighted the importance of taking account of the nature of anorexia nervosa, with expert opinion, in considering whether to impose treatment.[43]

V. Conclusion

Since the original *Re W* judgment the legal children's rights framework has seen further development. Decisions like *Re Roddy (A Child)(Identification: Restriction on Publication)*,[44] *R(Axon) v Secretary of State for Health and Family Planning Association*[45] and *Mabon v Mabon*[46] all acknowledge adolescent autonomy. There have also been at least two known instances where the refusal of treatment by a young person has been accepted and the issue has not gone to court.[47]

Rewriting this judgment has provided an opportunity to offer greater respect to a young person and has provided a better rationale for how the autonomy of a young person can still be respected if they refuse treatment, even if the outcome of the case is that their wishes are ultimately overridden. The rewritten judgment also offers a way to distinguish *Re W* so that in future a young person could refuse medical treatment.[48] This should address some of the extensive criticism that the original judgments received about the recognition of a young person's rights and autonomy.[49] However, it could still be open to the criticism that the law is requiring a higher standard of competency for young people's refusals of treatment than it is for adults. Gilmore LJ's judgment might also sit uncomfortably with advocates of a paternalistic approach to children's rights and those who want to protect children from refusing treatment if it will lead to irreparable harm or death, regardless of their competence.[50] If Gilmore LJ's approach is to be accepted or adopted in future, we need to be ready to acknowledge the autonomy of children to an extent that might result in irreparable harm or death.

---

[42]   This point has been discussed by Phil Fennel, 'Informal Compulsion: The Psychiatric Treatment of Juveniles under Common Law' (1992) 14(4) *Journal of Social Welfare and Family Law* 31; Douglas, above n 9.

[43]   Re-written judgment at 225.

[44]   *Re Roddy (A Child)(Identification: Restriction on Publication)* [2004] 2 FLR 949.

[45]   *R(Axon) v Secretary of State for Health and Family Planning Association* [2006] EWHC 37.

[46]   *Mabon v Mabon* [2005] EWCA Civ 634.

[47]   'Teenage Jehovah's Witness refuses blood transfusion and dies' *The Telegraph* www.telegraph.co.uk/news/health/news/7734480/Teenage-Jehovahs-Witness-refuses-blood-transfusion-and-dies.html and 'Girl wins right to refuse heart' *BBC News* http://news.bbc.co.uk/1/hi/england/hereford/worcs/7721231.stm.

[48]   Gilmore, above n 22.

[49]   L Edwards, 'The Right to Consent and the Right to Refuse; More Problems with Minors and Medical Consent' [1993] *Juridical Review* 52; J Fortin, 'Children's Rights and the Use of Physical Force' [2001] *Child and Family Law Quarterly* 243; K Mason, 'Master of the Balancers; Non-Voluntary Therapy under the Mantle of Lord Donaldson' [1993] *Judicial Review* 115; J Murphy, 'W(h)ither Adolescent Autonomy?' [1992] *Journal of Social Welfare and Family Law* 529.

[50]   Jane Fortin has acknowledged the importance of protecting adolescents from making life-threatening decisions on the basis of their best interests, in spite of their level of competency in J Fortin, 'Children's Rights- Flattering to Deceive' (2014) 26 *Child and Family Law Quarterly* 51.

Court of Appeal (England and Wales)

Re W (A Minor)
(Consent to Medical Treatment)

Gilmore LJ:

This case concerns a 16 year old young woman, Jenny, who is in the care of a local authority, and who suffers from anorexia nervosa. 'Jenny' is not her real name, which cannot be disclosed, but the use of a forename (rather than an initial to preserve anonymity) should at least serve to remind the Court and those reading this judgment that we are dealing with the life of a young person whose personhood and full range of interests warrant our very careful attention and utmost respect. Lord Donaldson of Lymington MR has already set out the sad history which led to Jenny's receipt into the care of the local authority and her struggles with her illness, and I need not repeat it.

It suffices to note that, against a background of Jenny's increasing weight loss, the local authority applied for, and was granted, leave to apply for an order under the inherent jurisdiction of the High Court for leave to move Jenny to a named treatment unit or such other establishment as the Official Solicitor might approve; and leave to give her medical treatment without her consent. The matter came before Thorpe J, who found that 'There is no doubt at all that [Jenny] is a child of sufficient understanding to make an informed decision.' This finding was based upon the evidence of Dr G, a consultant psychiatrist, who was 'convinced that she has a good intelligence and understands what is proposed as treatment'. Dr G noted that Jenny was 'adamant that under no circumstances would she consent to further use of a nasogastric tube'. Thorpe J held that, despite the refusal of consent of a child of sufficient understanding to make an informed decision, he had jurisdiction, and authorised the removal of Jenny to, and her treatment at, a specialist London unit. Jenny now appeals to this Court.

During the course of the hearing before this Court, however, we were informed that Jenny had not taken food for nine days. Agreed medical opinion advised that, should she continue in this way, within a week her capacity to have children in later life would be seriously at risk and later her life itself might be in danger. In those circumstances, I concurred in the Court's making of an emergency order permitting Jenny to be treated, if necessary without her consent. My reasons for doing so were the imminent danger to Jenny's health at a time when, in my opinion, and as I shall seek to show, this Court was not fully apprised of Jenny's capacity fully to refuse treatment. My reasons for making the emergency order differ from those of Lord Donaldson of Lymington MR and Nolan LJ. First, with respect,

I cannot agree with Nolan LJ's view that in making the emergency order we answered the first question of principle raised by the appeal, and decided that the Court has the power in its inherent jurisdiction to override Jenny's refusal to undergo the necessary treatment. Second, I cannot agree with Lord Donaldson's view that at the emergency stage Jenny's wishes were no longer of any weight.

The question now arises on this appeal whether Thorpe J had jurisdiction to authorise treatment in the circumstances which existed at the time of his order, and, if so, whether he was correct to do so.

The first issue is whether section 8 of the Family Law Reform Act 1969 precludes intervention by a court. Counsel argued that this provision conferred upon a child over the age of 16 an absolute right to refuse medical treatment, and that under the rule in *A v Liverpool City Council* [1982] AC 363, a court cannot exercise discretion within an area committed by statute to another. So far as material, section 8 provides:

> (1) The consent of a minor who has attained the age of sixteen years to any ... medical ... treatment which, in the absence of consent would constitute a trespass to his person, shall be as effective as it would be if he were of full age; and where a minor has by virtue of this section given an effective consent to any treatment it shall not be necessary to obtain any consent for it from his parent or guardian ...

> (3) Nothing in this section shall be construed as making ineffective any consent which would have been effective if this section had not been enacted.

For the reasons given by Lord Donaldson of Lymington MR and Balcombe LJ, this argument cannot be sustained. Section 8 is limited in its scope and focus. Its purpose, as illustrated by the *Report of the Committee on the Age of Majority* (Cmnd 3347), the Latey Report, is to permit the child's acquisition of a statutory power to consent to medical treatment, without preventing parental consent remaining effective. This interpretation is confirmed by the words 'it shall not be necessary to obtain any consent from his parent' in (1) and the wording of (3). The idea that there can be concurrent powers of consent inhering in parent and child is also consistent with a passage in the opinion of Lord Fraser of Tullybelton in *Gillick v West Norfolk and Wisbech Area Health Authority and Another* [1986] 1 AC 112 (*Gillick*) in which, after recognising that a child under 16 may be competent to consent to medical treatment, his Lordship goes on to say: 'Of course the consent of the parents should normally be asked, but they may not be immediately available.' (at page 169).

The conclusion that both parent and child can hold powers of consent concurrently is, in my judgment, also not inconsistent with any other passages in their Lordships' opinions in *Gillick*. Lord Scarman in *Gillick* cited section 8 at several points before concluding as follows:

> In the light of the foregoing, I would hold that as a matter of law the parental right to determine whether or not their minor child below the age of 16 will have medical treatment terminates if and when the child achieves a sufficient understanding and intelligence to enable him or her to understand fully what is proposed. ([1986] 1 AC 112, at pages 188–89)

I share the view expressed by Lord Donaldson of Lymington and Balcombe LJ that Lord Scarman meant that, upon the child's acquisition of capacity to consent, the parents lost their exclusive power to determine the issue of the child's medical treatment because the medical treatment could then lawfully be carried out with the child's consent in the face of parental refusal. Such an interpretation is entirely consistent with the interpretation that the Court has given to section 8 of the Family Law Reform Act 1969. In any event, in my judgement the passage from Lord Scarman's opinion set out above cannot be interpreted as providing a common law rule binding on this Court that a *Gillick* competent child acquires complete autonomy in the field of medical treatment. *Gillick* was not a case in which the welfare of a particular child was before the court, nor was it a case about *refusing* consent to medical treatment. *Gillick* was concerned with consenting *to* medical treatment, and it is quite clear, in my judgement, from the words in the above passage that Lord Scarman is concerned with whether or not the child *will* have medical treatment. In my judgement, Lord Scarman is not considering whether the child will not have treatment since that was not the House's focus in *Gillick*. As Lord Scarman himself acknowledged, *Gillick* was 'the beginning, not the conclusion, of a legal development in a field glimpsed by one or two judges in recent times … but not yet fully explored' ([1986] 1 AC 112, at page 176).

While it will be clear that I agree with much of Balcombe LJ's judgment, there is one important aspect of his judgment with which I respectfully disagree, namely the view that in logic 'there can be no difference between an ability to consent to treatment and an ability to refuse treatment.' It is clear from *Gillick* that in order to consent to medical treatment a child must be capable of understanding what is proposed. The simple opposite of consenting to treatment is refusing to consent to the treatment, that is understanding what is proposed but not giving one's assent to the treatment. In my judgement, there is an important difference between not assenting to treatment, that is, not saying 'yes' to treatment in the sense of fully understanding what is proposed but declining treatment, and, by contrast, positively taking a decision to refuse treatment, having considered fully what is involved in such a refusal and its consequences. In my judgement, the latter is a different question and (depending upon the circumstances) may require a higher level of understanding than simply understanding what is proposed by way of treatment, particularly where the refusal will lead to irreparable harm or death. This certainly seems to have been the view of Ward J in *Re E (A Minor) (Wardship: Medical Treatment)* [1993] 1 FLR 386, in which he set a very high level of understanding when considering whether a 15 year old boy, A, was competent to refuse a blood transfusion, where such refusal would likely lead to the boy's death. His lordship considered carefully the child's situation and understanding, and concluded, at page 391:

> I find that A is a boy of sufficient intelligence to be able to take decisions about his own well-being, but I also find that there is a range of decisions of which some are outside his ability fully to grasp their implications. Impressed though I was by his obvious intelligence, by his calm discussion of the implications, by his assertion even that he would refuse well knowing that he may die as a result, in my judgment A does not have a full understanding of the whole implication of what the refusal of that treatment involves …

> I am quite satisfied that A does not have any sufficient comprehension of the pain he has yet to suffer, of the fear that he will be undergoing, of the distress not only occasioned by that fear but also—and importantly—the distress he will inevitably suffer as he, a loving son, helplessly watches his parents' and his family's distress. They are a close family, and they are a brave family, but I find that he has no realisation of the full implications which lie before him as to the process of dying. He may have some concept of the fact that he will die, but as to the manner of his death and to the extent of his and his family's suffering I find he has not the ability to turn his mind to it nor the will to do so. Who can blame him for that?'

The above analysis of the difference between refusing to assent to treatment and taking a positive decision to refuse treatment (and the possible different levels of understanding required, and recognised in law) lends some support to the interpretations given above to section 8 of the Family Law Reform Act 1969 and to this Court's interpretation of Lord Scarman's opinion in *Gillick*. It supports the view that concurrent consents in parent and child can occur when the child has power to consent, but not full capacity to understand fully what is involved in refusing treatment such as wholly to extinguish parental responsibility in relation to the issue. This, it seems, is the position, according to Ward J's assessment, in which the young man, A, who was the subject of the case, *Re E*, found himself. There is no doubt that the young man, A, was capable of consenting to a blood transfusion. He had the necessary intelligence and understanding of what was proposed in order to consent to such treatment as required by their Lordships in *Gillick*. However, Ward J found that, despite A's capacity to consent, he did not have capacity to refuse the treatment. In such a case, in my judgement, parental responsibility may then be exercised to provide a valid consent to treatment, in order to protect the child in light of his or her lack of full capacity.

However, what of the child who is fully competent to refuse, as seemingly envisaged by Ward J in *Re E*? (I expressly leave open the question whether a future Court of Appeal would take the same approach to ascertaining capacity as taken by Ward J, requiring as he did an understanding of the manner of a person's death, which might be said to expect a standard which many adults might not be capable of achieving). While, as explained above, *Gillick* is not strictly binding in this case, in my judgement this Court should nevertheless recognise the general principle espoused by Lord Scarman in that case (with which Lord Bridge of Harwich expressly agreed), namely that 'parental right yields to the child's right to make his own decisions when he reaches a sufficient understanding and intelligence to be capable of making up his own mind on the matter requiring decision' (see [1986] 1 AC 112, at page 186). It is of note that, although this Court has interpreted section 8 of the Family Law Reform Act 1969 as not conferring on children complete autonomy in the sphere of their medical treatment, subsection (3) of section 8 proclaims only that *nothing in this section* shall be construed as making ineffective any existing consent, and cannot constrain the development of the common law. In my judgement, therefore, this Court should recognise, as Lord Donaldson of Lymington MR does *obiter* in his judgment, that there may be occasions on which a child's refusal to consent to medical treatment might be overruled by consent provided by a person with parental responsibility for the child. However, the Court should also acknowledge that where a child is fully competent to take a decision to refuse treatment, parental responsibility is then extinguished within that sphere of decision-making and cannot be used to override the young person's competent decision.

The central issue in this case, however, is whether the Court has power to override the decision of a competent young person in the exercise of its *parens patriae* jurisdiction. The *parens patriae* jurisdiction might be said to be analogous to the parental role in exercising parental responsibility, the Court arguably stepping into the shoes of parents as the judicial parent, although, as Lord Donaldson of Lymington MR rightly observes, the Court's jurisdiction is somewhat wider and is theoretically limitless. For my part, however, the issue in this case is not so much about the theoretical extent of the jurisdiction, but about how far the jurisdiction should extend in practice.

The law assumes that adults are the best judges of their own interests. In matters concerning an adult's own welfare, only if it is positively shown that an adult lacks capacity to take a decision will the law intervene to protect the adult concerned. This Court cannot, of course, adopt the same assumption of capacity, or indeed exactly the same rights-based approach, in respect of persons under the age of 18. This is because Parliament enjoins the Court under section 1(1) of the Children Act 1989, in exercising its inherent (or indeed any other) jurisdiction in matters with respect to a child's upbringing, to consider the child's welfare as its paramount consideration. In the case of every child in respect of whom this Court is asked to exercise its inherent jurisdiction, there must therefore be a careful consideration of the child's welfare. In my judgement, however, a young person's interest in competent decision-making can only properly be respected within this statutory decision-making framework if the range of interests that children might plausibly claim as matters going to the promotion of their welfare is fully appreciated. As John Eekelaar observed in his seminal article on children's rights ((1986) *Oxford Journal of Legal Studies* 161), there are, perhaps, three main categories of interests which children might plausibly claim; their basic (survival) interest; their developmental (or educational) interest; and their autonomy interest. As Eekelaar pointed out, in general the autonomy interest might be ranked subordinate to the basic and developmental interests because of the risk that exercise of autonomy may prejudice the basic and developmental interests, but the autonomy interest may be reconciled with the other interests through the acquisition of full capacity (as assumed in the case of adults). It seems to me that Lord Bridge of Harwich's agreement with Lord Scarman's general principle in *Gillick* that parental right yields to the child's right, and Lord Bridge's agreement also with Lord Fraser in that case that the solution in the particular context in *Gillick* depended upon an assessment of the child's best interests, is perhaps only fully compatible on the basis that the child's autonomy interest and the child's welfare are in some sense reconcilable.

In my judgement, therefore, I can see no reason why those three interests, which are all relevant considerations going to the child's welfare, should not in principle be reconciled in the case of the fully mature adolescent in entirely the same way that the law reconciles them for the adult who is assumed to have full capacity. When applied to adolescents, therefore, in my judgement the welfare principle must be interpreted in a way that reflects an adolescent's evolving capacities for autonomous decision-making, in the sense that it recognises that it is in a person's best interests to respect their autonomy. If, after a careful analysis of the young person's ability to exercise mature, true, stable and independent judgement, the court is persuaded that the necessary level of judgement exists, it seems to me to follow that the adolescent's views ought to be respected as conducing to his or her welfare. In other words, in my judgement, the distinction between the child's welfare and the child's interest in autonomous decision-making collapses altogether at the point at which there is judicial determination that the child is fully autonomous in a particular sphere of decision-making with which the court is concerned. The result must, of course, be expressed in the terms of the child's welfare because of the welfare focus of the statutory decision-making criterion.

In practice, assessing whether the adolescent is making a maximally autonomous choice in his or her welfare may not be an easy task. Nonetheless, however difficult that assessment may be, in my judgement respect for the child's autonomy interest requires a thorough assessment of whether the young person's decision represents a mature autonomous decision such that it can be said to conduce to the young person's welfare to respect that decision.

In my judgement such an assessment will need to be mindful that adolescent choices may be particularly prone to defects in decisional autonomy, and that there may be a number of subtle factors potentially profoundly affecting an adolescent's ability to make mature, stable and independent choices. Where a refusal of treatment carries a significant risk of death or permanent physical or mental impairment, a careful and comprehensive evaluation of the maturity of the adolescent will necessarily have to be undertaken to determine whether the decision reflects a real understanding and appreciation of the decision and its potential consequences. Young people may have the technical ability to make complex decisions, and be viewed as competent according to developmental and cognitive criteria, but a court will also need, in my judgement, carefully to consider whether the young person truly has the necessary maturity and independence of judgement to make an autonomous choice. It will be for the court to decide, in the context of all the circumstances of the case, quite what is required for the court to be satisfied that the child is exercising an autonomous choice. This will require an individualised assessment of the unique situation of the particular young person, his or her lifestyle, family relationships and broader social relationships in their potential impact upon the young person's ability to exercise independent judgement. The adolescent may, for example, in the context of family relationships be influenced by feelings of loyalty or guilt; or he or she may be rebelling, or reacting to family conflict. The young person may also be influenced by opinions in his or her wider circles, such as cultural or religious influences. As in this case, the court may also need to be mindful of whether the adolescent has any emotional or psychiatric vulnerabilities, in particular whether any illness or vulnerabilities have an impact upon the young person's decision making ability.

In relation to the last point, I wish to record my respectful disagreement with Lord Donaldson of Lymington's suggestion that the exercise of the inherent jurisdiction may be preferable to use of relevant mental health legislation for reasons of avoiding stigma to a young person. In my judgement, if a child is suffering from a mental illness such that a relevant provision of the Mental Health Act 1983 applies, then the Act ought probably to be invoked to assist the child concerned. Presumably that is what Parliament envisaged. Stigma is not addressed by hiding mental illness under the cloak of the use of the inherent jurisdiction. It is time that it is recognised that mental illnesses, like physical illnesses, are just that, illnesses that require treatment. In many cases, particularly in the cases of young persons, an illness, whether physical or mental, is not the fault of the young person. That message is not aided by suggesting that the inherent jurisdiction should be used simply to avoid a stigma. In addition, as I have stated above, the mental illness (if any) of a young person is an important factor going to consideration of his or her competence to take a decision and, where appropriate, requires careful assessment by a mental health professional. Thus the impact of Jenny's anorexia nervosa (whether or not it can be characterised as falling within the Mental Health Act 1983) is something which any future court will need to consider very carefully in its impact upon Jenny's decision-making capacity. The nature of that illness may also be relevant to consideration of whether the court should impose its own view over the young person's view in the case. As I understand this illness, it is a feature sometimes of it that the young person concerned engages in control over his or her eating as a means of maintaining some control over his or her life, where he or she may feel that there has been a loss of control of his or her autonomy in other areas of life. This is a matter which will need carefully to be considered in a future case in light of expert evidence. In other words, the court may need carefully to consider whether the imposition of the court's view may upset a very delicate balance in the treatment of the individual concerned, and possibly exacerbate the symptoms of the illness. I say no more on the matter in this case since, as I emphasise, that is a matter for the courts in future, with the aid of expert opinion.

It will be clear that I disagree with the approaches to the exercise of the inherent jurisdiction advocated by the Master of the Rolls and Balcombe and Nolan LJJ. In my judgement the idea that one should merely give competent children as much rope as they can handle without the unacceptable risk that they will hang themselves; or that one should approach the matter merely with a predilection to giving effect to the child's wishes; or that one should defend the child's right to make his or her own decision, but not when the decision may lead to irreparable harm or death, risks merely paying lip-service to the competent child's autonomy. This Court should put in place a more rigorous and more principled approach to determination of the best interests of the child, which takes full account of the child's autonomy interest.

So how is this case to be disposed of? It will be recalled that the evidence of Dr G, Consultant Psychiatrist, showed only that Jenny had capacity to understand what was proposed by way of treatment. No court has received evidence in this case as to Jenny's capacity to refuse treatment. I concurred in the emergency order made by this Court because of the imminent danger to Jenny, and the fact that, in my judgement, this Court did not have at its disposal the necessary information to make a judgement on whether Jenny had capacity to refuse treatment. Had we not felt compelled to dispose of this case earlier by way of an emergency order, I would therefore have remitted the case to the judge in order to assess her capacity fully to understand the consequences of refusal of medical treatment. Should Jenny recover, as indeed I hope she will, a full assessment of her capacity to refuse should be carried out. If she is found to be fully competent to refuse treatment, then in my judgement no court should impose treatment upon her, whether in an emergency or otherwise.

In future cases, in my judgement the court must ensure that any assessment of the paramountcy of the child's welfare takes full, and careful, cognisance of the interests of the child in competent decision-making. The very important point, on which emphasis I would wish to leave this judgment, is that, in any such decision, there must not simply be a predilection to giving effect to the young person's wishes, overridden by 'welfare considerations' where the judge so adjudges. Rather, an assessment of welfare which carefully (indeed meticulously) engages with the competent child's interests is required. We must recognise that if, after such meticulous engagement, the court concludes that the child is mature in the full sense required by the court's assessment, and thus fully competent to refuse medical treatment, such a decision represents the outcome of an assessment of the child's best interests in the case. Accordingly, the court should conclude that the child's welfare dictates that such a competent child be permitted positively to take a decision not to have the treatment offered, or indeed any treatment, and to accept (perhaps endure) the consequences of a total failure to treat. Even in cases in which the child is not adjudged to be fully competent, a judge should carefully consider whether it is truly in the interests of an adolescent to be forced to endure treatment against his or her will. If treatment is to be imposed, the court should also give anxious and careful attention to ensuring that the dignity of the child is protected as far as possible in such a case.

In summary, the court's message should be clear that the adolescent who is adjudged to be fully competent to take decisions in this sphere (a matter which, I emphasise, requires great caution and very careful evaluation) should be accorded the same respect for his or her autonomy interest as English law accords to an adult who is regarded as so fully competent. In all cases, even those in which the child is adjudged not to be competent to refuse treatment, the court's focus in exercising its inherent jurisdiction should, as far as possible, be focused upon respect for the child's wishes, feelings and dignity.

In conclusion, I would hold that Thorpe J erred in his exercise of the inherent jurisdiction because his lordship did not have at the material time sufficient information as to Jenny's capacity to refuse medical treatment, information which was essential to a fully informed judgement as to whether treatment should be authorised, applying her welfare as the paramount consideration. His lordship's analysis of welfare therefore failed fully to respect Jenny's autonomy interest in the process of determining her welfare. Had this Court not been confronted by the emergency situation outlined above, I would therefore have allowed this appeal.

12

F v F

JULIE DOUGHTY

I. Facts and Issues

In *F v F*[1] Mr F sought a declaration and specific issue order that his daughters, L (aged 15) and M (aged 11), receive the MMR (measles, mumps, rubella) vaccination. Neither L nor M wanted the vaccine, and the applications were opposed by their mother, Mrs F. A specific issue order is 'an order giving directions for the purpose of determining a specific question which has arisen, or which may arise, in connection with any aspect of parental responsibility for a child'.[2] L was vegan and part of her objection was that the vaccine contains gelatine.

The MMR vaccination is administered in two doses, one when the child is a year old and one before the child starts school. It protects against contracting measles, mumps (both of which can lead to life-threatening complications) and rubella (which can affect the development of an unborn baby). It was introduced as a routine combined vaccine in 1988. Older children or adults who are not immune can be vaccinated later, or can have a top-up if they missed the second dose. Government guidance in England is that children should be vaccinated, although this has remained voluntary. Several other jurisdictions have made vaccination compulsory, by way of refusing welfare benefits or school places to non-immunised children.

L had received one vaccination but the younger child, M, had received none; L therefore had a higher level of immunity. It was not until early 2013 (the parents having separated in 2011) that Mr F took action to remedy what he later indicated was his reluctant participation in the joint decisions. He explains that he was spurred to action by the widely-reported outbreak of measles in south Wales early in 2013, which highlighted that a proportion of the population was unprotected against the infections.

The case was heard on 31 July 2013, and judgment handed down in private on 5 September 2013. Theis J made the declaration sought by the father, and directed the parties' lawyers to agree the terms of an order. She also suggested that L and M meet a specialist paediatrician to answer any questions they may have. The rewritten judgment retains much of Theis J's original text but reaches a different conclusion with respect to 15 year-old L. In doing so, it emphasises young people's rights to autonomy and participation in decisions made about them.

---

[1] *F v F* [2013] EWHC 2683 (Fam), [2014] 1 FLR 1328.

[2] Children Act 1989, s 8. Specific issue orders have been used to address a range of questions, including in the context of children's medical treatment, HIV testing, circumcision and sterilisation: see *Re C (HIV test)* [1999] 2 FLR 1004; *Re J* [2001] 1 FLR 571; *Re HG (Specific issue: sterilisation)* [1993] 1 FLR 587.

II. Context

The case attracted predictable mainstream media coverage and, for that reason, it may be that Theis J preferred to keep details about the family to the minimum. The preamble of reporting restrictions to protect the identity of the children reflects the standard rubric attached to judgments in the family jurisdiction, where the child's right to privacy is at the forefront of judicial thinking. Thus the young people are not named in the judgment. Although this provides some protection, it has been argued that the fact that they are being read about by strangers, outside their control, is still sufficient to be an intrusion on their privacy.[3] Although protection of the children's privacy is a laudable aim, there is little background material in the original judgment, which places some constraints on re-writing.

The brevity of the published judgment, only 25 paragraphs, means that general knowledge of the controversy surrounding the MMR is assumed. While Theis J outlined the position in paragraphs 3 and 4, reproduced in the rewritten judgment, the level of public debate is not evident from the judgment. This is because the judge's focus is required to be on the best interests of L and M, not on wider policy considerations.[4] More comprehensive coverage of the background is given in Cave's 2014 case comment, and a wealth of information is available in an earlier judgment, *Re C (Welfare of Child: Immunisation)*[5] (which runs to 384 paragraphs). However, some readers may find it helpful to read more widely about the high levels of concern that were generated by the discredited Wakefield paper.[6] The parents' initial delay in having the children immunised is stated in evidence to be a consequence of the Wakefield scandal.

The case before Theis J was indeed whether vaccination was in the best interests of these two young people, but policy and publicity had played a part in these parents finding themselves in dispute and may well have been a direct influence on the young people themselves. It will be argued that they were also an indirect influence on the judge.

III. Responses to the Judgment

Academic criticism has been made of the absence of expert medical evidence adduced in *F v F*.[7] However, it is clear from *Re C (Welfare of Child: Immunisation)*,[8] the leading judgment relating to MMR and which concerned children aged 10 and four, that vaccination

---

[3] J Doughty, 'Opening up the Family Courts: What Happened to Children's Rights?' (2010) 10 *Contemporary Issues in Law* 50–75.

[4] As required by House of Lords authority: see *Re B (A Minor) (Wardship: Sterilisation)* [1988] AC 199.

[5] *Re C (Welfare of Child: Immunisation)* [2003] EWHC 1376 (Fam), [2003] 2 FLR 1054.

[6] See, for example, S Heawood, 'Why I wish my daughter had been vaccinated' *The Guardian* (24 April 2013).

[7] LA Barnes McFarlane, 'F v F: MMR Vaccine—Welfare Need or Welfare Norm?' (2014) 18 *Edinburgh Law Review* 284–89.

[8] *Re C (Welfare of Child: Immunisation)* [2003] EWHC 1376 (Fam). See case comments by K O'Donnell, '*Re C (Welfare of Child: Immunisation)*– Room to Refuse? Immunisation, Welfare and the Role of Parental Decision Making' (2004) 16 *Child and Family Law Quarterly* 213 and R Huxtable, '*Re C (A Child) (Immunisation: Parental Rights)* [2003] EWCA Civ 114 [2004]' (2003) 26 *Journal of Social Welfare and Family Law* 69–77.

is the accepted norm where the court is called on to intervene in the exercise of parental responsibility.[9] As neither Mrs F nor the CAFCASS guardian applied for any expert evidence regarding the health or wellbeing of L and M themselves, Theis J had little scope for departing from that position.[10] Commentary also noted the narrowness of the decision in not making any explicit order that the children be physically taken to be treated.[11] (Orders to that effect had been made in *Re C*). In the absence of an appeal, it is assumed that in *F v F*, agreement between the parents was eventually reached.

F v F attracted negative coverage in the mainstream media. This gave the impression that the children were to be forcibly injected, using phrases such as 'A judge has ruled that sisters aged 15 and 11 must have the MMR vaccine …'[12] and 'Girls aged 15 and 11 forced to have MMR jabs by High Court judge …'[13] The *Telegraph* subsequently reported that Mrs F might be committed for contempt of court because the girls had not been inoculated by the deadline set by the judge.[14] A lawyer wrote on a human rights blog that 'The High Court has ruled that two sisters must receive the MMR vaccine against their wishes and the wishes of their mother.'[15] Unless the reader links to the judgment itself,[16] the non-coercive nature of the best interests declaration and the judge's intention that the parties will come to an agreement will be bypassed.

Despite the fact that Theis J's judgment reflects what may objectively be the correct view, that the health benefits to a child of receiving the vaccination normally outweigh any disadvantages (a view in line with the father's standpoint, whatever his motivation), it is still arguable that the court's approach to respecting L and M's interests was lacking. Was the right balance between rights and welfare achieved? The rewritten judgment offers an alternative approach, which addresses troubling aspects of this tension.

IV. Adolescent Autonomy and Medical Treatment

Ten years earlier, in *Re C*, Sumner J had this to say about the views of the children at the centre of the dispute:

> I have regard in particular to the wishes and feelings of F to the extent she can at 10 years of age understand the issues with which I am concerned. The fact that she is in favour of one injection and against MMR are factors. Her views on MMR are influenced by her mother's unreasoning and rigid

---

[9] The declarations made in that case, that it was in the best interests that both children be immunised, and orders made to that effect, were upheld by the Court of Appeal. See *Re B* [2003] EWCA Civ 1148.

[10] The CAFCASS guardian, named as Ms Vivian in the judgment, is a social work practitioner appointed by the court. Information about this role is available at www.cafcass.gov.uk/children/family-court-after-separation.aspx.

[11] J Herring, 'An Injection of Sense' (2013) 163 *New Law Journal* 9–10.

[12] Available at http://www.bbc.co.uk/news/health-24493422.

[13] G Rayner, 'Girls aged 15 and 11 forced to have MMR jabs by High Court judge after parents disagree over vaccine' *Daily Telegraph* (11 October 2013).

[14] G Rayner, 'Mother could be back in court after failing to give girls MMR jab on judge's orders' *Daily Telegraph* (14 October 2013).

[15] R English, 'Court orders MMR vaccine for children' UK Human Rights Blog (18 October 2013) http://ukhumanrightsblog.com/2013/10/18/court-orders-mmr-vaccine-for-children/.

[16] Available to the public on BAILII at www.bailii.org/ew/cases/EWHC/Fam/2013/2683.html.

approach. As she will accept the court's decision I largely discount her concerns. C is too young at 4 to have her wishes taken into account.[17]

One could perhaps in passing note that under section 1(3) of the Children Act 1989, the court must *consider* the ascertainable wishes and feelings of the child, albeit in light of his or her age and understanding. Thus Sumner J might better have expressed this by saying that little weight was being given to the wishes of the child in light of C's age and understanding, rather than entirely not taking the child's wishes and feelings into account.

Sumner J had relied on the evidence of the CAFCASS officer to convey the children's views. The facts of *F v F* can be distinguished because, unlike the 10 year old's mother in *Re C*, Mrs F was not found to have had undue influence on her daughters. It is encouraging from a children's rights perspective that Theis J appears to have taken the views of M (aged 11) about medical treatment relatively seriously. (In contrast, in a recent case relating to medical treatment, the views of a 10 year old were considered solely on the basis of his age, rather than any assessment of the level of his understanding).[18]

The principles governing the *consent* of children and young people aged under 16 to medical treatment are still those developed in *Gillick v West Norfolk & Wisbech Health Authority* (*Gillick*),[19] although the extent to which these apply to *refusal* of medical treatment is still hotly debated.[20] Taking up the opportunity for NHS provision, and encouragement, of inoculation is a matter of consent. Theis J made no explicit reference to *Gillick* because, in a specific issue application, the court is making a decision about the child's welfare, and only one factor in reaching this is the ascertainable wishes and feelings of the child. As noted above, these are to be taken into account whether or not the child is competent. The competent child does not have a right that transcends other factors in determining her welfare. In the spirit of *Gillick*, however, the court should have respect for the autonomy rights of a 15 year old. Findings on *Gillick* competence in the rewritten judgment are therefore helpful in demonstrating this. It is, of course, clear that Theis J had regard to the young people's views, as conveyed in the evidence of the CAFCASS guardian. Moreover, (as discussed below) she met them herself. For the judge to take as her starting point that a 15 year old has capacity is welcome. However she concludes:

> Obviously in reaching this decision I am aware this is against the girls' wishes, but that it not the only factor. It is of course an important factor, particularly bearing in mind their ages but the court also has to consider their level of understanding of the issues involved and what factors have influenced their views. In this case I do not consider there is a balanced level of understanding by them of the issues involved, the focus has been on the negative aspects in a somewhat unfocussed way.[21]

In other words, any presumed capacity of a 15 year old was rebutted by a judicial conclusion that her view had been arrived at through an unbalanced process, because of flaws in

---

[17] *Re C (Welfare of Child: Immunisation)* [2003] EWHC 1376 (Fam), [2003] 2 FLR 1054 [311].
[18] Mostyn J in *A NHS Trust v Mr M, Mrs M, JM (A Child) (By his Guardian), A local authority* [2015] EWHC 2832 (Fam), [2016] 2 FLR 235 at 13; 'In this case, J, aged 10, is not '*Gillick*-competent'.
[19] *Gillick v West Norfolk & Wisbech Health Authority* [1986] AC 112 (*Gillick*).
[20] J Fortin, 'The Gillick Decision—Not Just a High Watermark' in S Gilmore, J Herring and R Probert (eds), *Landmark Cases in Family Law* (Oxford, Hart Publishing, 2011); J Herring, R Probert and S Gilmore, *Great Debates in Family Law* (London, Palgrave Macmillan, 2012) ch 3. See further the re-written judgment and commentary in this volume on *Re W (A Minor)*.
[21] *F v F* n 1 above [22(4)].

her level of understanding and alignment with the views of her primary carer. In contrast, such a conclusion could not be drawn in the case of someone aged 16 or over, unless all practicable steps had been taken to help them make a decision, without success.[22] In her evidence, Ms Vivian is regretful that L and M have undertaken their own research and not developed a balanced picture, but we do not know what steps have been taken to assist their decision making.[23] The rewritten judgment takes a proactive approach to maximising L and M's potential to achieve capacity.

Theis J's conclusion regarding L's lack of balance can be contrasted with the observations by Hedley J in *L v P* of the 'unwisdom' of exercising compulsory powers regarding medical intervention against the will of older children, in a case where he held that the substantial part of a 15 year old's reasoning was rational and cogent and reflected a degree of understanding that compels respect.[24] Although L's precise date of birth is not given (probably as a safeguard against risk of jigsaw identification), if she was 15 in July 2013, it may only have been a matter of months before she could make her own decision about inoculation. This is therefore a puzzling response to a decision taken by an adolescent, described as 'charming, intelligent, articulate and thoughtful'[25] even if her argument was less persuasive than the child in *L v P*. Perhaps Theis J was hopeful that L would be swayed by judicial authority toward accepting the injection, the CAFCASS officer having stated that the sisters knew the ultimate decision would be taken by a judge.[26]

Despite the disavowal of wider policy considerations, might Theis J have been wary of attracting headlines along the lines of 'Judge agrees with objections to MMR'? The anti-vaccination movement continues to be influential and it would be difficult for a judge entirely to ignore the risks of being seen by campaigners to side with Mrs F. One gets the impression that the judgment was written primarily for Mrs F, whose anxieties, the guardian believed, were affecting her children.

V. Judicial Conclusion on L and M's Reasoning

Theis J concluded that, despite being acutely aware of L and M's wishes and feelings, these had to be balanced with factors that had affected their views. These were:

(1)   Their lack of understanding of why their father had changed his mind stemmed from a lack of mature understanding about changing circumstances. There is little in the judgment to explain why Mr F changed his mind but this may well have followed a high-profile GP-led vaccination programme in April 2013.[27]

---

[22]   s 1(3) Mental Capacity Act 2005.

[23]   *F v F* n 1 above [14].

[24]   *Mr L v Mrs P* [2011] EWHC 3399 (Fam) [2013] 1 FLR 578 at [25]. The child did not consent to having a DNA test in an application brought by her father under s 55A Family Law Act 1986 for a declaration that he was not, in fact, her father.

[25]   *F v F* n 1 above [6].

[26]   *F v F* n 1 above [14].

[27]   Public Health England press release, 25 April 2013. www.gov.uk/government/news/national-mmr-vaccination-catch-up-programme-announced-in-response-to-increase-in-measles-cases.

(2)   They were being unrealistic about the issue of the ingredients and the consequences of not being vaccinated. This is from the guardian's evidence, which tended to merge the perceived gaps in each sister's understanding, for example, that they envisaged that if they became ill, there would be other non-animal-based medicine available. Although Theis J tries to avoid being disrespectful of L's vegan views, she accepts the guardian's and Mr F's views that these are vague. The rewritten judgment is more realistic in its appreciation of the range of research about choices in a vegan lifestyle that intelligent teenagers could easily access on the internet.

(3)   They could not avoid being over-influenced by their mother's views. Despite Mrs F claiming not to have a view on the vaccine itself, the guardian reported that she was anxious and that the daughters were sensitive to this.

VI. Differentiating between the Respective Needs and Wishes of the Two Children

In the original judgment, Theis J made a declaration that it was in the best interests of both children to have the injection but a different position is taken in the rewritten judgment. Although having the injection would be in L's medical interests, having it against her wishes would not be in her best interests. If L is to adjust her position after the judicial determination, she would have more respect for a process that clearly identified her objective best interests, while at the same time, respected her autonomy. The rewritten judgment emphasises that with autonomy comes the responsibility of taking serious decisions— 'responsibility for taking risks that affect her own life and living with consequences of her choices.'[28]

We know something of L's reasons but less about M's. In the original judgment, the reasons are presented in summaries of the evidence given to the court by the father, the mother and the CAFCASS guardian; a traditional analysis of adult applicant, adult respondent and finally the independent analysis which includes the children's rights and welfare. In the rewritten judgment, we are assisted by the parental views being condensed, followed by specific sections on the views and then the needs of each of the two children.

Mrs F stated that she had no strong views herself but the sisters were settled in their beliefs and should not be forced to do something differently 'without positive reassurance … and the recording of ingredients'. She (Mrs F) felt a responsibility to put the girls' views across strongly or they would be traumatised and their relationships with both parents would suffer. She claimed to identify strongly with their need to have enough weight given to their wishes. Mr F did not think L's views about the ingredients outweighed parental responsibility to look after children's welfare and that as a parent he had balanced L's view against the risks of the sisters being infected and thought the latter was greater. He said that M's view was strongly influenced by L.

The guardian reported that L said she would be upset to think animal products were in her body. Although the judgment states that the guardian's report sets out L and M's wishes

---

[28] Rewritten judgment para 35.

comprehensively, and her oral evidence is summarised (paragraph 15) there is no further evidence about why L or M object to having the vaccine, such as possible side effects.

The rewritten judgment challenges the perception of L's views and fears as vague and immature. It argues that concerns over the ingredients and independent research could be perceived as evidence of a considered and thoughtful approach to vaccination. The same opportunity does not arise in respect to M whose views are sparsely evidenced and articulated. The rewritten judgment therefore accepts Theis J's assessment of M's limited understanding of the issues and also raises the issue of M's heightened risk because, unlike L, she has not had the first of the two inoculations. The result is a differentiated outcome for L and M and much of the judgment is given over to explaining the reasons for this to them.

VII. L and M's Participation in the Court Process

As the rewritten judgment points out,[29] this is the first time a court decided on the issue of a parental vaccination where the child was old enough to express a view. Therefore, Cave begins her analysis with the UN Convention on the Rights of the Child and the evolving capacity of the child, while explaining that the child's views are not determinative because they are one factor in the section 1(3) welfare checklist. She goes on to cite *Mabon v Mabon* in emphasising the Article 12 right of 'articulate teenagers' to participate in court proceedings.[30] This practice is reflected in Theis J having met the sisters with Ms Vivian. Since *F v F*, policy encourages judges to meet children in section 8 cases but such a meeting cannot be for the purpose of obtaining evidence.[31] Theis J is clear that the purpose of the meeting was about process only. However, the sisters may have wondered what their participation contributed, as the judge indicates that even if their views were better informed, it would still be in their best interests to have the vaccinations.

The rewritten judgment, however, would give the young people concerned a greater sense of agency in participation, having paid closer attention to the perceived medical benefits and the emotional needs of each of them within, rather than alongside, their expressed views. While there is much to applaud in the original judgment, where some efforts were made to engage with the young people's views, the alternative judgment provides scope for a more positive outcome for both these young people, their family relationships, and a wider message to other families about the weight that will be given to teenagers' rights to consent to treatment.

---

[29] Rewritten judgment para 20.
[30] *Mabon v Mabon* [2005] EWCA Civ 364, [2005] Fam 366.
[31] www.transparencyproject.org.uk/the-final-report-of-the-vulnerable-witnesses-and-children-working-group/.

High Court of Justice Family Division (England and Wales)

F v F

Cave J:

[This judgment retains the original judge's expression of the facts, issues and evidence in this case in paragraphs 1 to 7 and 9 to 15 below, although the order of the paragraphs has been changed. The part of the decision as to disposal in paragraphs 41 to 43 is also from the original judgment. Other parts of the judgment have been re-written].

Introduction

1. This matter concerns an application by Mr F (hereinafter referred to as the father) for a declaration and a specific issue order concerning his daughters L and M, who are now 15 years and 11 years respectively. He seeks an order that they both receive the MMR vaccination. This is opposed by their mother, Mrs F (hereinafter referred to as the mother).

Background

2. The parents were married in 1996, the marriage broke down in 2009 and they separated in January 2011. L and M remain living with their mother but have contact with their father on alternate weekends, half the school holidays and occasional weekdays. Agreement regarding financial matters was reached in December 2012 and the decree absolute made in January 2013.

3. L was inoculated, by agreement between the parents, soon after her birth. In 1998 there was great public debate about the MMR vaccine. Much of the controversy surrounded the research paper, published in the Lancet, by Dr Andrew Wakefield, which cast doubt on the vaccine's safety and the risks said to be attached to administering it, particularly in relation to the possibility of autism. As a consequence of this the parties decided, in consultation with their GP, that L should not receive her booster and M has had no vaccinations at all.

4.   The father now states he was a reluctant participant in the joint decision not to inoculate. Dr Wakefield's research paper was later discredited. The Lancet subsequently retracted Dr Wakefield's paper and his research was not approved by the General Medical Council. The NHS, General Medical Council, Chief Medical Officer and the World Health Organisation all recommend that children should have this vaccine. He is concerned that the consequences of contracting measles, mumps and rubella are serious. He states the need for the children to have protection has been brought into sharper focus following the recent outbreak of measles in Wales.

5.   On 25 January 2013 the father's solicitors wrote to the mother seeking her agreement to the girls being vaccinated, failing which it was indicated he would apply to the court. That agreement was not forthcoming and the father issued this application on 5 April 2013. Following initial directions by the District Judge the matter was listed before me on 25 April 2013. I made directions, including the filing of a CAFCASS report setting out L and M's wishes and feelings. I made further directions on 6 June 2013 listing the matter for hearing on 31 July 2013 and making directions for L and M to discuss this issue with their GP, which took place on 16 July 2013. They came and met me on 25 July 2013 together with Ms Vivian, an officer in the High Court team of the Children and Family Court Advisory and Support Service ('CAFCASS'). Ms Vivian filed an addendum report on 26 July 2013, together with a note of our meeting. Both parties have filed updating statements.

6.   The meeting I had with L and M was to enable me to explain my role, the process by which decisions are made and that the decision in circumstances such as this is my responsibility. The questions they asked me were perceptive and well targeted. They both wanted to understand what would happen.

7.   The matter was listed for hearing before me on 31 July 2013. In addition to the written material I have, which includes two statements from each parent, I heard the oral evidence from both parents and Ms Vivian. At the conclusion of the hearing I reserved judgment as this not only gave me an opportunity to consider the matter but, in addition, the parents agreed that it was preferable for there to be a delay in the decision to enable both parents to enjoy their respective summer holidays with L and M.

The Parental Viewpoints

8.   Though this case involves a parental dispute, the parental viewpoints are pertinent only insofar as they are relevant to the welfare of L and M.

9.   In her oral evidence the mother stated the decision not to inoculate the children was a joint decision taken by both parents following their experience of L's first vaccinations; she considered it was their joint view that they don't always work and there may be side effects. She denied any influence on the children's views. Until this recent application she said both girls had been brought up in a family where there was a consensus between the parents regarding vaccinations.

When asked about what her opposition was to the vaccinations she said:

> Parents have a choice to do what they feel in their hearts they really believe. I feel both children have grown up in a frame of mind which they were settled in and supported in the same outlook

and are now forced to take a different view without more positive reassurance and help given and the recording of ingredients [of the vaccine] is unsatisfactory. They have a right to be informed.

10.   In relation to the suggestion by the father that the girls need to be protected from the risk of getting either measles, mumps or rubella she said from the NHS guidelines the risk of complications from these diseases is higher if the immune system is compromised in some way; L and M are healthy active children which she considers lowers the risk. If the father's application was granted she said she would feel she had 'not been able to put their [the children's] views across enough'. In cross examination she said she 'had no view' on whether the MMR vaccination was effective as she was not trained in reading statistics. In relation to any health benefits of the vaccination being given she said 'I have my doubts, [which] led me and Mr F to come to the decision [not to have the vaccinations] … we both had doubts and these outweighed our perceived benefits.' When pressed about the health benefits to the girls having the vaccination she considered the children have to have a say. She accepted the girls would have seen her distressed by the father's behaviour and this application, which she described as 'bullish'. She considers the girls will feel they have let her down if the application is granted. She said that is because 'they will feel they were not able to articulate how it affects our lives. I have one chance to get it right.'

11.   The mother submits if their will is overborne they will suffer harm, they will be traumatised, their sense of personal autonomy will be undermined, their relationship with their father may suffer and they may feel they have let the mother down and might feel resentment and confusion at not having been listened to.

12.   The mother's opposition to L and M receiving these vaccinations can be summarised as follows:

(1)   She is ambivalent as to the benefits of the vaccine and remains concerned about any possible side effects;
(2)   She questions the father's change in position bearing in mind what she considered was the parties agreement that the girls should not be vaccinated;
(3)   She is concerned about the impact of the vaccination being undertaken against the girls wishes, in particular L who has had psychological problems including anxiety issues for which she has received counselling;
(4)   L is a vegan and part of her objection is based on the content of the vaccine which includes animal based ingredients (eg gelatine).

13.   In his oral evidence the father was concerned about the focus by the girls on the ingredients of the vaccine; he said they are a distraction to the benefits. He acknowledged the girls are angry with him regarding this application, they think he is trying to exert control on the mother and using them as a vehicle to do this. He regards his relationship with his daughters as being 'solid and strong', although he accepted this issue has caused difficulties in his relationship with them in the short term. His concern, he said, is the risks to them of getting any of the diseases if they do not have the vaccination. It was the Wakefield research that caused the parents to decide not to have any further vaccinations. He said he had always been pro-vaccine but in the light of the position at the time following L's birth they agreed not to give L any further vaccinations and M had none. He was asked about the delay and timing of this application, bearing in mind the parent's relationship broke down in 2009. He said the mother was aware he was unhappy about the situation. He accepted he could have made

this application earlier, when the children were younger, but said the Swansea outbreak exacerbated the issue for him. He denied he reacted to what was termed tabloid hysteria.

14. Whilst it is correct the parents presented a united front in relation to their decision about booster injections for L and no vaccinations for M; that has to be looked at in the context of the information that was available at the time. The father suggests the landscape is different now, the combination of the Wakefield evidence being discredited and the recent outbreak of measles has made him re-consider his previous opposition to the vaccinations.

15. The father submits it is in the interest of both girls to receive the vaccine. It is, he feels, more likely than not that the girls' wishes and feelings have been shaped by their mother's views. He submits M's understanding of the importance of the vaccine is limited and unbalanced. In relation to L he accepts her understanding is perhaps greater but lacks balance as to the risks and consequences of getting the diseases.

16. The father believes M to be strongly influenced by L. He is not convinced that L fully understands the risks of contracting the diseases. He respects L's views as a vegan, but in his view, the risks of contracting the diseases outweigh the risk to L's emotional well-being if she is required to have the vaccination.

17. The father's argument for L and M receiving these vaccinations can be summarised as follows:

(1)   Vaccination will reduce the risk of L and M's contracting the diseases;
(2)   L and M are not able to make properly informed and voluntary decisions;
(3)   L and M's health needs outweigh their expressed concerns.

Legal Framework

18. Section 1(1) of the Children Act 1989 provides that L and M's welfare is the paramount consideration. The court is guided by the welfare checklist in section 1(3) Children Act 1989.

19. In *The NHS Trust v A (a child) and Ors* [2007] EWHC 1696, Holman J set out 10 guiding propositions at paragraph 40. An objective test applies:

> v. That test is the best interests of the patient. Best interests are used in the widest sense and include every kind of consideration capable of impacting on the decision. These include, non-exhaustively, medical, emotional, sensory … and instinctive … considerations.

The court must balance all the conflicting considerations in a particular case.

20. Despite the individual and public health benefits that flow from vaccination, the UK does not operate a policy of compulsion. Childhood vaccinations require a valid consent. In the case of children, the decision of whether or not to vaccinate is generally left to parents. Where those with joint parental responsibility disagree over vaccination of their children, neither should make the decision alone. In such cases, the court will determine whether vaccination is in the child's best interests. The court will not rule out invasive and preventative healthcare in the best interests of the child purely on the basis of opposition from one of the parents (*Re C (Welfare of Children: Immunisation)* [2003] 2 FLR 109).

21.   Twice, the court has considered parental disputes about their children's vaccination. In *Re C (Welfare of Children: Immunisation)* [2003] 2 FLR 1095 the Court of Appeal upheld the decision of Sumner J to order two mothers to have their children vaccinated with the MMR in line with the fathers' wishes. Vaccination was in the best interests of those children. Thorpe LJ rejected the 'repeated categorisation of the course of immunisation as non-essential invasive treatment. It is more correctly categorised as preventative healthcare' (paragraph 22). In *LCC v A, B, C and D* [2011] EWHC 4033 parents opposed the vaccination of their four children who were the subject of care proceedings. Theis J found that vaccination was in the children's best interests, stating (at paragraph 16):

> a. Measles, mumps and rubella are serious infections, each of which carried an appreciable risk of dangerous complications in healthy individuals. Vaccination is the only practical way to prevent an individual from contracting infection, and all the evidence is that it is effective and has a very low level of side effects, which are generally mild and transient …

> d. With due consideration for established contraindications to vaccination in an individual case, it is otherwise in every child's interest to be protected against measles, mumps and rubella with the MMR vaccine.

22.   In this case the court must consider the hearing of the young people's wishes when determining their best interests in a parental vaccination dispute. In *Gillick v West Norfolk & Wisbeck Area Health Authority* [1986] AC 112 Lord Scarman at page 253 recognised the validity of a minor's consent to treatment in the child's best interests provided the minor 'understand[s] fully what is proposed'. Subsequent cases, notably *Re R (A Minor)* [1991] 4 All ER 177, have determined that a minor under the age of 16 cannot necessarily refuse treatment that is in their best interests.

The Importance of L and M's Views

23.   The welfare checklist requires that regard must be had to the 'ascertainable wishes and feelings of the child concerned (considered in the light of his age and understanding)'. In determining best interests the court should refer to the UN Convention on the Rights of the Child, ratified in 1991, which recognises the evolving capacities of children to make decisions (Article 12) and their rights to freedom of thought, conscience and religion (Article 14). L and M's wishes and feelings are not, however, determinative of their best interests. It is for this court to balance the various factors in the welfare checklist and this can lead to an outcome which conflicts with young people's expressed wishes and desires.

24.   The mother submits that L and M are mature minors with clearly expressed views. She argues that considerable weight should be attached to L's views in particular due to her age and understanding. The Court of Appeal in *Mabon v Mabon & Ors* [2005] EWCA Civ 634 called for greater acknowledgement of autonomy rights protected by both Article 8 of the European Convention on Human Rights and Article 12 of the Convention on the Rights of the Child. Thorpe LJ stated at paragraph 28:

> Unless we in this jurisdiction are to fall out of step with similar societies as they safeguard Article 12 rights, we must, in the case of articulate teenagers, accept that the right to freedom of expression and participation outweighs the paternalistic judgment of welfare.

25. Assessing 'the wishes and feelings' of L and M involves consideration of their ages and levels of understanding. In my meeting with L and M I found them to be 'charming, intelligent, articulate and thoughtful'. Both have intimated that they do not want to receive the vaccination. Both are aware of their parents' respective views and have had access to information gleaned through independent research and a conversation with their GP. L, aged 15, is a vegan and high on her list of concerns is the presence of animal products in the vaccine. M, aged 11, also objects to immunisation. She is aware of her sister's and parents' views.

26. The CAFCASS officer has discussed with L and M the reasons for their opposition to vaccination. She considers that M may be influenced by her mother and sister and might lack a full understanding which prevents her from reaching her own view. L is particularly concerned about the ingredients of the MMR vaccine, saying she would 'be so upset if that was in my body'. We should be slow to dismiss L and M's fears as immature or unfounded. Concern over the ingredients of medicines is not uncommon. For example, Public Health England has published advice on ingredients in medicinal products to inform faith groups.

27. The CAFCASS officer feels that L and M lack a full appreciation of the vaccine and its likely effects. This lack of information is the cause of fear and anxiety that is exacerbated by the mother's concerns. It was for this reason that I gave direction for L and M to discuss matters with their GP. In the case of adults, section 1(3) of the Mental Capacity Act 2005 states that:

> A person is not to be treated as unable to make a decision unless all practicable steps to help him to do so have been taken without success.

If we are to take seriously the views of young people and optimise their participation in decisions made about them, then they must be given every practicable opportunity to understand the relevant information upon which they base their views. Discussion with an independent expert enhanced L and M's ability in this regard.

28. The fact that L and M share the mother's view does not automatically render her influence 'undue', just as it would not if they happened to share their father's view. L in particular has articulated reasoning quite separate to her mother's.

29. L is a mature and thoughtful young person and her response is considered. Her understanding of the risks and benefits of vaccination is not complete, but neither does it fall below the levels of most adults' understanding. M is younger and has struggled to assert a line of reasoning independent of her sister's and mother's. Nonetheless, she has, in line with her sister, independently researched the issue and discussed matters with her GP.

L and M's Physical and Emotional Needs

30. In *LCC v A, B, C and D* parents sought to rely on unfounded evidence that vaccination posed an unacceptable risk to the children concerned. Vaccination was ruled in *LCC* to be in the children's best interests. The dispute before us today is subtly different. Both parties had the chance to present expert evidence, which was not taken up. Though ambivalent as to the benefits of vaccination, the mother does not rely on evidence that vaccination poses a medical risk to L and M. The medical position as set out in the case of *LCC* (at paragraph 21

above) is not disputed. The issue in this case is not whether vaccination is in L and M's medical interests but whether compulsory vaccination in opposition to their wishes is in their best interests.

31.   In order to balance the medical benefit to L and M in receiving the MMR vaccination against the risks to their emotional interests, it is important to put the medical benefits into context. The Department of Health recommends vaccination with the MMR before the first birthday with a follow up vaccination before starting school. This protects young children from a health risk which they are incapable of appreciating or guarding against. That these recommendations were not followed in L and M's case is lamentable, but the joint decision was one which the parents were entitled to make. This is so even though the risks of serious adverse effects if measles is contracted are most serious in under 5 year olds. L and M are now 11 and 15 respectively and the risks associated with developing measles, mumps or rubella are lower. This is especially so for L who is likely to have immunity as a result of the first MMR vaccination given to her as a baby. Up to one in 10 children are not fully immune after the first injection and the second dose reduces this to one in 100. The risks rise again in early adulthood, especially in relation to rubella contracted during pregnancy. But this future risk is not a relevant consideration today as L and M would be free to reassess the risks as young adults and decide accordingly.

32.   The court has shown willing to overrule the views of mature minors to sustain their life or health. In *Re R (A Minor) (Wardship: Consent to Medical Treatment)* [1992] Fam 11, Lord Donaldson at para 25 said (obiter) that a decision to refuse treatment made by a child under the age of 16 could be overridden provided another valid source of consent could be found. Treatment of a 15 year old girl suffering from acute psychiatric problems was sanctioned despite her refusal to consent. *Re R* caused considerable academic controversy because it conflicts with the legal principle that decisions to refuse intervention should be respected where that individual is making an informed and voluntary decision. Contravention of this principle harms the individual's autonomy interests. I would be wary of applying the rule in *Re R* to overrule a competent minor whose life or health would not be put at serious risk if their views are upheld. It is worthy of note that the Department of Health already requires the assent of minors undergoing the HPV vaccination at age 12 to 13 in addition to parental consent (NHS, *The HPV Vaccine* 2012 leaflet for girls and parents). This is the case whether or not the young person is assessed as 'Gillick competent'.

Determining Best Interests

33.   There is a strong public interest in encouraging parents to vaccinate their children. MMR vaccine uptake is still recovering from the effects of media coverage of an alleged link between the MMR vaccine and autism and Crohn's disease in the late 1990s. Measles, mumps and rubella are dangerous diseases for both the patient and others who will come into contact with the patient, especially those whose immunity is compromised by virtue of

illness or age. But the public health benefits of the MMR are not at issue today. The court is concerned exclusively with the welfare interests of L and M.

34.   In reaching my decision I have considered the welfare checklist in section 1(3) of the Children Act 1989. The NHS advises that children receive the vaccine even though it is accepted there are risks of side effects of the vaccine. The risks associated with contracting the diseases the MMR vaccine aims to prevent are potentially very serious. When L and M were babies and unable to decide for themselves, their parents opted not to vaccinate them. Now that L and M are capable of forming an opinion, their views are a relevant consideration. Through the medium of CAFCASS, L and M have made their views known to the court.

35.   This is the third case of its kind to come before the court. In previous cases the clear medical evidence of benefit of the MMR was indicative of the best interests of the children. In this case, best interests must encompass L and M's emotional needs in light of their objections to vaccination. Each case is different and my decision does not dictate how the issue should be decided in future cases.

Decision: L

36.   I have reached the conclusion that whilst it is in the medical interests of L to receive the MMR vaccine it is not in her best interests to receive it against her will. L is a mature and intelligent young person and I am satisfied that she is Gillick competent. I very much hope that she will decide in due course to consent to inoculation so as to protect her from potentially dangerous diseases and also to protect those with whom she comes into contact. In this case L carries responsibility for the taking of risks affecting her own life, and living with the consequences of her choices.

37.   It is not in her best interests to undergo vaccination against her will for the following reasons:

(1)   Whilst the medical benefits of vaccination outweigh the risks of the procedure, overall the benefits do not outweigh the harms associated with requiring her to undergo vaccination against her will. Each case must be assessed on its merits and each will be different. The medical benefits of vaccination are mitigated in L's case by virtue of her current levels of immunity which flow from the first inoculation given to her as a baby; and by virtue of the fact that complications arising from measles, mumps and rubella are most prevalent in those under 5 and over 20. There remains a risk of serious harm, but the risk of that harm eventuating between now and adulthood is low.

(2)   The risks to L's emotional needs are heightened by the strength of her views and her maturity. She has researched the matter and considered it carefully. L has had access to independent advice from her GP. It is important that direction and guidance provided by parents and also by this court takes into account L's capacities to exercise rights on her own behalf.

(3)   The assessment of best interests incorporates L's emotional needs which will not be served by vaccination against her will. L has had psychological problems in the past including anxiety. L has acknowledged that she would 'be so upset if that [vaccine] was in my body'. Compulsion is likely to disempower L and exacerbate her anxiety.

38.   Accordingly the father's application with respect to L is rejected.

Decision: M

39.   The balance sheet must be applied to L and M individually. Though M is close to her sister and shares some of her views, her interests are nonetheless distinct and separate from her sibling's.

40.   M did not receive the first MMR inoculation as a baby and so lacks immunity. Though intelligent, and mature for her age, it is not clear that M fully understands the implications of her refusal and the influence of her sister and mother have a bearing on her decision. It is my conclusion that in this case M, aged 11, is not 'Gillick-competent' and it is in her best interests to receive vaccination.

41.   I will make a declaration that it is in the interests of M to receive the MMR vaccination and that she should do so before 11 October 2013 on a date to be arranged by the parents together with the GP. I agree it would be helpful for M to have a meeting with a paediatrician who has an expertise in vaccinations to answer any questions M has. This should be someone whose identity is agreed by both parents with an agreed letter of instruction and the appointment should take place by 27 September 2013. I give permission for that paediatrician to see this judgment and the two CAFCASS reports. This will enable M to have a more balanced picture about the risks and deal with any questions they have.

42.   The parents' legal representatives should agree an order to submit for my approval by 16 September 2013. If there remains any dispute on the terms of any order proposed I can either resolve that by the parties agreeing I can do that by considering written representations on 16 September 2013 or the matter can be listed for a short directions appointment before me on 18 September 2013 at 9.45 am with a time estimate of 30 minutes.

43.   I know this issue is felt deeply by the parents, but I have every confidence, that despite their differences, they will be able to manage their parental responsibility in such a way that will ensure the strong and secure relationships that exist between each parent and L and M will remain in place.

44.   I recognise that the different outcomes for L and M, who have both expressed serious reservations about vaccination, may be difficult for them to comprehend. This judgment is written with them in mind so that they might better understand how the legal framework has applied in each of their cases and in particular how it balances their rights to health protection with their rights to make autonomous decisions.

13

Commentary on *Re T (A Minor)* *(Wardship: Medical Treatment)*

I. Introduction

Re T (A Minor) (Wardship: Medical Treatment)[1] is an English case from 1996 about a 17 month old baby boy suffering from biliary atresia, a life-threatening liver defect. After undergoing an unsuccessful operation at the age of three and a half weeks, his doctors came to the conclusion that only a liver transplant could prolong his life beyond the expectancy of 24 to 30 months. The three doctors who gave evidence before the High Court of England and Wales were unanimous in their opinion that the transplant's 'prospects of success were good and that this operation was in the best interests of the child'.[2] However, the boy's parents, both medical professionals who moved to an unnamed Commonwealth country with their sick baby, refused to consent to this procedure. They both preferred that their son live the rest of his short life without what they argued is the pain involved with a transplant and the treatment that follows. In the High Court, Connell J accepted the local authority's wardship application, ruling that the parents' objection was unreasonable under the circumstances, and that the possibility of prolonging the child's life should take precedence. The Court consequently provided the doctors with the permission to perform the surgery. The parents appealed.

In its decision, the Court of Appeal reversed the High Court's judgment. The Court ruled that the welfare principle in the Children Act 1989 should be examined in broad terms, which goes beyond the reasonableness of the parents' decision,[3] or the doctors' clinical opinions. The Court ruled that when assessing the child's welfare, it is not only the operation's chances of success and a pro-life presumption that should be taken into account, but also the need for post-operative care, which under the circumstances would require the child's mother either to relocate back to England alone, or ask the child's father to resign from his current employment and move with them back to England. As the revised judgment suggests, in allowing the appeal, the Court of Appeal gave more weight to the parents' wishes[4] over the medical opinion and the child's right to life.

---

[*] I would like to thank Angela Kintominas for her excellent research assistance.
[1] *Re T (A Minor) (Wardship: Medical Treatment)* [1997] 1 WLR 242, CA.
[2] ibid, 246.
[3] Primarily the mother, as she was not married to the father, who therefore had no parental responsibility.
[4] P Alderson, 'Commentary on the "Family Rule"' (1999) 25 *Journal of Medical Ethics* 497, 497.

A. The Application of the Best Interests Principle

The decision carries a number of legal and ethical difficulties, and the revised judgment provides an alternative approach, adopting a children's rights perspective.

The original judgment was decided under the framework of the Children Act 1989. Section 1(1) states that whenever a court is considering a matter with respect to the child's upbringing, as it does in wardship applications, the child's welfare shall be the 'paramount consideration'. In comparison to Article 3 of the UN Convention on the Rights of the Child (CRC), which the United Kingdom has signed and ratified, English law gives greater weight to child welfare. Article 3 states that in all matters concerning children, the child's best interests shall be 'a primary consideration'. But as the revised judgment demonstrates, the main issue in this case was not necessarily the weight given to welfare, but rather the interpretation of the welfare principle itself. This commentary will highlight the main difficulties with the ways in which *Re T* interprets the 'child welfare'/'best interests of the child' principle, and will contextualise the revised judgment in a broader child-centred approach to decisions concerning children's health.

The fundamental problem with the Court of Appeal's interpretation of the welfare principle is that it does not focus on the child himself, but rather conflates the child's and the mother's interests. Indeed Butler-Sloss LJ states that: 'The mother and the child are one for the purpose of this unusual case' and the decision of the court to consent to the operation jointly affects the mother and son and it also affects the father. The welfare of the child 'depends upon his mother'.[5] By failing to differentiate between the child's rights and interests, and the mother's wishes and interests, the Court inherently undermines the protection of the child's best interests,[6] and agency. T's parents are not the subjects of this case but rather interested parties. It is not their future and life, including their inherent right to life (CRC, Article 6(1)) at stake, but rather their child's life.[7]

In contrast to the Court of Appeal's parent-centred approach, the revised judgment adopts a child-centred approach. It focuses concretely on the child's interests in the context of whether he should undergo this life-saving operation or not, a discussion that should also take into account the child's right to life, survival and development (CRC Article 6). In determining that the child's welfare will be best served if he undergoes the operation, the Court takes into account the interests of others, including the interests of the parents, but gives them a lesser weight. In that sense, and in accordance with the CRC, other factors that should be taken into account are not only parental wishes, but also the parents' duties vis-à-vis their child, primarily their duty to care for their child's development (Article 18 CRC). This element is one of the changes that a children's rights approach introduces, reshaping parent-child relationships under the law.

The Court of Appeal was right to say that the best interests principle is not a one dimensional concept,[8] and that it should be examined from a broader perspective. Therefore, the

---

[5] Above n 1, 251.

[6] S Michalowski, 'Is It in the Best Interests of a Child to Have a Life-Saving Transplantation—Re T (Wardship: Medical Treatment)' (1997) 9 *Child and Family Law Quarterly* 179, 186.

[7] *cf* L Cherkassky, 'Children and the Doctrine of Substituted Judgment' (2014) 14 *Medical Law International* 213, 219.

[8] M Freeman, *Commentary on the United Nations Convention on the Rights of the Child—Article 3* (Leiden, Brill, 2007).

Court was also right to ask what will happen after the operation. Adopting a broad view about the meaning of the best interests principle has been seen as a 'refreshing' move.[9] However, the original judgment does not identify all the components of the best interests principle, nor the weight that should be given to them in the balancing exercise, as the revised judgment demonstrates.[10]

Instead of encompassing other medical, emotional and welfare issues concerning the child,[11] the Court collapsed the mother's interests onto the child's interests, asking what bearing the operation will have on the mother. Thus, the Court included factors that are not intrinsic to the child's interests. Hardship following a liver transplant is a valid consideration, but it is the hardship that the child will suffer, including the child's pain and need of constant care and medication, which should be taken into account as part of the child's best interests assessment.[12] Constructing the child and the mother as one enabled the Court of Appeal to minimise the conflicts between their interests. The re-written opinion observes that the Court of Appeal erred in its over-identification of the child's and mother's interests.

The meaning of the best interests principle goes beyond the question of life and death, and includes, for example, the child's 'emotional, psychological and social interests',[13] and the child's wishes and feelings.[14] These are factors that neither the High Court nor the Court of Appeal say anything about. As Bridgeman notes, while the original judgment mentions the parents' profession, preferences, concerns and wishes, it includes no reference to the boy's personality:

> We learn nothing of C's current status of health or his ability to cope with medical intervention. There is no reference to his personality, character, or spirit, all those aspects which make him a unique individual and which are relevant to determination of his best interests.[15]

Lord Freeman's re-written opinion acknowledges that T, who is a toddler, cannot express his opinion on questions of life and death.[16] However, Freeman is at pains to point out that even very young children's feelings can be ascertained.

A guardian ad litem was appointed to protect the child's interests, thus respecting to some extent the child's right to participate in decisions concerning his life (Article 12 CRC). However, it appears from the original judgment that the guardian did not meet the child in person, had no first hand impression of him, his behaviour in the shadow of his liver condition, or of his interaction with his mother, etc. As such, one should wonder whether the guardian was able truly to fulfil the child's right to participation and separate

---

[9] A Grubb, 'Medical Treatment (Child): Parental Refusal and Role of the Court—Re T (A Minor) (Wardship: Medical Treatment)' (1996) 4 *Medical Law Review* 315, 319.

[10] J Bridgeman, 'Critically Ill Children and Best Interests' (2010) 5 *Clinical Ethics* 184, 186.

[11] See R Heywood, 'Parents and Medical Professionals: Conflict, Cooperation, and Best Interests' (2012) 20 *Medical Law Review* 29, 44.

[12] M Davis, 'Selective Non-Treatment of the Newborn: In Whose Best Interests—in Whose Judgment' (1998) 49 *Northern Ireland Legal Quarterly* 82, 91.

[13] Bridgeman, above n 10, 185.

[14] CRC, *General Comment 14—the Best Interests of the Child* (29 May 2013) UN Docs CRC/C/GC/14.

[15] J Bridgeman, *Parental Responsibility, Young Children and Healthcare Law* (Cambridge, Cambridge University Press, 2007) 128.

[16] But see P Alderson et al, 'The Participation Rights of Immature Babies' (2005) 13 *International Journal of Children's Rights* 31–50. See also a recent study suggesting that babies have logical reasoning before the age of one. RP Gazes et al, 'Transitive Inference of Social Dominance by Human Infants' *Developmental Science* (published online November 16 2015), doi: 10.1111/desc.12367.

representation. If a guardian's role is reduced to mere gesture, this undermines a child's inherent dignity and dismisses the need to recognise every child, including babies, as agents of their own rights.

B. Parental Autonomy and Children's Rights

The original judgment in *Re T* focuses on the parents' autonomy, and upholds the view that parental discretion and family 'privacy' preclude the state from intervening in parents' decisions concerning their children. This approach is based on the presumption that 'when family integrity is broken or weakened by state intrusion, [the child's] needs are thwarted and [their] belief that [their] parents are omniscient and all-powerful is shaken prematurely.'[17] The Court of Appeal's decision also implies that the post-operative support that the mother would be required to provide 'mean[s] that mother and child should be regarded as one for the purposes of deciding where the best interests of the child lay.'[18] This approach contradicts a child rights approach, because it inherently dismisses the child's agency and is disrespectful to the child's human dignity. The revised judgment corrects this misperception, and instead offers the alternative standpoint which focuses on the rights and interests of the child.

The Court of Appeal gives significant weight to the mother's concerns about the post-operative care that the child will need. By contrast, the re-written opinions conclude that overemphasising these logistical considerations led the Court to the wrong conclusion that it is legitimate to allow a child to die, rather than to ask his parents (or indeed others, including if necessary the state) to care for him,[19] in order to fulfil parental duties to protect the child's rights and development (Article 18 CRC). As Fortin has argued, the decision suggests that the child's best interests are to die, primarily due to his parents' objection to the procedure.[20]

From the point of view of the child, it does not matter whether his parents' refusal to consent to his liver transplant arises from their preference that he lives a short but relatively painless life, their own personal comfort, or, as in the case of other parents, their religious beliefs (for example, Jehovah Witnesses who refuse to consent to blood transfusions).[21] All of those justifications might be sufficient to deny the child from a life-saving treatment from the point of view of the *parent*, and at times judges might consider them to be reasonable grounds as well.[22] But at the end of the day, respecting parental autonomy in cases such as this results in the unnecessary, early death of a child, in circumstances in which life-saving medical treatment is available. As the revised judgment demonstrates, examining this situation from the point of view of the *child* leads to the conclusion that parental autonomy cannot prevail.

[17] J Goldstein, A Freud and A Solnit, *The Best Interests of the Child* (Free Press, New York 1988) 9.
[18] Davis, above n 12, 88.
[19] ibid, 82.
[20] J Fortin, 'Re C (Medical Treatment)' (1998) 10 *Child and Family Law Quarterly* 411, 416.
[21] *Re S (a Minor) (Medical Treatment)* [1993] 1 FLR 376, *Re O (a Minor) (Medical Treatment)* [1993] 2 FLR 149. But see *Birmingham Children's NHS Trust v B & C* [2014] EWHC 531 (Fam) where the judge order that a baby will receive blood transfusion despite his parents' objections.
[22] The doctrine of the reasonable parent was rejected by the Court of Appeal in the case of *Re T*.

Analysing the original and re-written judgments using the lenses of the capability approach exposes further shortcomings of the original judgment and some further advantages of the revised one. The parents' request to deny the child the possibility to live and to grow up can be framed as a request to deny the child the capability to develop and be free,[23] and to realise his rights to life and development.[24] The parents' wish deprives the child of an available function (the choice to live and to cope in the aftermath of a liver transplant) and therefore is inherently disrespectful to his human dignity and agency. Asking the Court to favour the parents' request over the child's life situates the child's life as a life of unfreedom,[25] and of no hope. A somewhat progressive children's rights perspective might, based on Articles 4 and 18 of the CRC, ascribe the latter as the duty of parents. And where parents fail to meet their duties, the state, via the judiciary, is obligated to step in and facilitate the protection and realisation of the child's right to live.

Some commentators have argued that only considering the medical opinion which recommended the liver transplant to determine the child's best interest is also wrong, as it essentially leaves the decision with the doctors instead of with the court.[26] This is a somewhat simplistic representation of the judicial decision-making process, as the revised judgment demonstrates. The doctors' opinion is evidence before the Court, but it is the judge who decides how much weight it should have. As the original judgment shows, the Court should identify the relevant law, and is free to weigh up other factors against the medical opinion, within the boundaries of the law. Both the original and the revised judgment considered the doctors' opinion in context, and the difference between the two judgments lies with the way in which each one defines and interprets this context. The revised judgment focused on the child's welfare and rights and considered the high chances of success as supporting evidence to the need and, indeed, the Court's duty, to protect the child's rights to life and development. One might assume that, in a situation where the doctors are unanimous, a patient should undergo a certain procedure in order to survive, and that the court has no other choice but to adopt their position, despite parental objection, but this is incorrect. Expert testimony can be contradicted by another expert testimony, or can be rejected by the patient (if the patient is an adult or deemed of sufficient intelligence and understanding to make a decision).[27] But in the case of *Re T*, there are no such exceptional circumstances. In that sense, *Re T* is not different from any other case where the parents disagree with the doctors' recommendations, but with one striking difference: a treatment that can prolong the child's life is available, and the disagreement with this course of treatment does not derive from religious convictions. In *Re Wyatt (a child) (medical treatment: parents' consent)*,[28] for example, a baby, Charlotte, was born at 26 weeks' gestation weighing about 458 grams, had multiple medical problems, and did not respond to stimulation. The dispute was whether if Charlotte stopped breathing again she should be ventilated, which would cause her further pain and distress. Charlotte's parents, who are devout Christians, believed that Charlotte could respond to their love and that their child was not ready to die.

[23] A Sen, *Development as Freedom* (Oxford, Oxford University Press, 1999).
[24] N Peleg, 'Reconceptualising the Child's Right to Development: Children and the Capability Approach' (2013) 21 *The International Journal of Children's Rights* 523–42.
[25] ibid, 530.
[26] Heywood, above n 11, 34.
[27] *Gillick v West Norfolk and Wisbech Area Heath Authority* [1986] AC 112.
[28] *Re Wyatt (a child) (medical treatment: parents' consent)* [2004] EWHC 2247.

The professionals caring for her argued that she was severely brain damaged and highly unlikely to live for more than a few more months whatever was done for her. The Court concluded that at that point it was not in her best interests to require that doctors accede to her parents' wishes and ventilate her should she stop breathing.

The Court of Appeal's different approach in *Re T* is arguably due to the 'exceptional circumstances' of this case.[29] But it seems that the only 'exceptional' circumstances in *Re T* are the parents' profession. The Court of Appeal repeatedly mentions that the parents are healthcare professionals who specialise in treating children, and therefore gives more weight to their position than to the positon of the medical experts. But these two points of view— the medical professions on the one hand, and the parents on the other hand—should not have been weighed against each other in this way, as the revised judgment articulates so eloquently. The parents are not expert witnesses, but rather interested parties in this case, and it is their decision that the Court of Appeal has been asked to revoke. It is therefore rather odd that while the Court of Appeal declares that it does not evaluate the reasonableness of the parents' decision, it uses their professional knowledge as a means to rebut the medical experts' testimony. The revised judgment remedies this error and introduces an appropriate analytical process, where the parents' objection is considered in the context of the need and, indeed, the Court's duty under the Children Act 1998, to ensure the child's welfare.

One might argue that the Court of Appeal's analysis is not wrong if seen through the public interest prism. Huxtable, for example, argues that the parents' mental health, their need to leave their job and relocate back to England, and the autonomous wishes for the child's future were respected for good reason.[30] But as the revised judgment points out, the case of *Re T* is not about the convenience of the parents, nor about their quality of life. It is about the quality of life of T, and moreover, his right to life itself.

The original decision was handed down before the Human Rights Act 1998 was enacted. However, this law, which incorporated the European Convention on Human Rights (ECHR) into UK domestic law, might have changed the way in which the Court of Appeal decided this case. This is primarily due to two reasons. First, both the child and his parents can claim that their human rights ought to be protected—either the child's right to life (Article 2 of the ECHR), or the parents' 'right to respect for private and family life' (Article 8 ECHR)—thus framing the case in human rights terms, and not only as a case of parental rights and T's best interest. Second, the interpretation of the best interest principle could change in a way that could 'ensure adequate protection for children'.[31] While the principle of the best interests of the child is a well-established principle in English law irrespective of international law, and while it is not an explicit consideration under the ECHR, the European Court of Human Rights (ECtHR) has nonetheless interpreted Article 8 in a way that includes the need to protect children's best interests as part of protecting the right to privacy and family life.[32] Thus, Article 8 of the ECHR could be used as a vehicle to consider children's 'best interests' in broad human rights terms, rather than in a paternalistic welfare term.

---

[29] See, for example, Heywood, above n 11, 32.

[30] R Huxtable, 'Autonomy, Best Interests and the Public Interests: Treatment, Non-Treatment and the Value of Medical Law' (2014) 22 *Medical Law Review* 459, 483.

[31] H Stalford, *Children and the European Union* (Oxford, Hart Publishing, 2012) 38.

[32] *Sahin v Germany* (30943/96) [2003] ECHR 340; *Sommerfeld v Germany* (31871/96) [2003] ECHR 341.

The revised judgment ends with a child-friendly version. This is another example of applying a child-centred approach. A judgment that deals with, and in this case determines, a child's life, should respect his human dignity and make the judgment—and its reasons—available to him. This can be done in different forms. For example, the court can write a letter to the child, invite the child to the court for a face-to-face meeting, or, as the revised judgment did, provide a child-friendly version of the judgment itself. In a somewhat cynical comment, the revised judgment suggests that at least one judge considered that a cartoon version of a judgment might be a step too far in terms of departing from the common law tradition of how judgments should look like. I, however, do not find this so ridiculous. This case deals with a young baby, and maybe a cartoon style judgment is the most child-friendly mode of communication for him.

House of Lords

Re T (A Minor)
(Wardship: Medical Treatment)

Lord Y and Lady Z (respectively):

I have had the advantage of reading in draft the opinion of my noble and learned friend, Lord Gilmore and, for the reasons that he gives, I too would allow this appeal and restore the order of Connell J.

Lord Gilmore:

My Lords,

This case illustrates vividly how easy it may be for a court to lose sight of protection of a child's fundamental interests, even when applying, as Parliament has said it must, the child's welfare as its paramount consideration. The case raises a point of general public importance, namely whether it is correct for the court to conflate the interests of parent and child when applying section 1(1) of the Children Act 1989.

The facts of this case are fully set out in the judgments of the courts below (see *Re T (A Minor) (Wardship: Medical Treatment)* [1997] 1 WLR 242, CA) and require only brief repetition here. T is a toddler some months short of his second birthday. He suffers from a life threatening liver condition known as biliary atresia. Leading specialists involved in this case are of the unanimous opinion that without a liver transplant he is unlikely to survive beyond the age of two-and-a-half years. A transplant is likely to be successful, although of course a donor organ must first become available. There is consensus amongst the medical experts that it is in this child's best interests to have a transplant. However, T's mother and father, who are themselves health care professionals with experience of caring for sick children, are opposed to the transplant operation. The case is complicated by the fact that T and his parents are out of the jurisdiction, T having been taken against medical advice to a distant Commonwealth country, AB.

At first instance Connell J held, in light of the medical evidence, that the mother was acting unreasonably in refusing her consent, and ordered her to return to England with her son and present him to hospital so that further investigations could be undertaken with a view to a liver transplant. On the mother's appeal, the Court of Appeal (Butler-Sloss, Waite and Roch LJJ) correctly held that Connell J's approach constituted an error of law, and that his lordship should simply have applied the child's welfare as the paramount consideration as enjoined by section 1(1) of the Children Act 1989. The Court of Appeal, exercising discretion afresh, allowed the mother's appeal. It held that while there is a strong presumption in favour of prolonging life, that should not always prevail over other considerations. The Court held in all the circumstances of the case that it was not in this child's best interests to have the operation against the wishes of a devoted, caring mother who was well informed as to the consequences of the operation. The Official Solicitor, acting as the child's guardian, now appeals to this House.

My Lords, with great respect to the Court of Appeal in what was clearly a very difficult case, I have reached the firm conclusion that the Court of Appeal erred in its interpretation of section 1(1) of the Children Act 1989 and was plainly wrong in its balancing of the welfare considerations. In my opinion, the circumstances of this case came nowhere near to displacing a strong presumption in favour of prolonging life in the court's application of the welfare principle.

The Court of Appeal found that Connell J had failed to give adequate weight to factors which ought to be fed into the welfare test. In particular, his lordship had paid insufficient attention to 'the enormous significance of the close attachment between the mother and baby' and whether it was in the best interests of the baby for the court to direct the mother to 'take on this total commitment' where she did not agree with the proposed course. In reaching its different view, however, in my opinion the Court of Appeal erred in the other direction, that is in over-identifying the interests of the mother with the child. Indeed, at one point Butler-Sloss LJ went so far as to say: 'This mother and this child are one for the purpose of this unusual case...'. In some cases, of course, these interests do coincide, and fortunately so since there are limits to what the state can do. But there are cases where there is conflict between the interests and/or the views of the mother and the child, and this case was one of them.

The Court of Appeal's conflation of the child's and mother's interests was an error of principle. It operated with the implicit assumption that if the parents were not prepared to bring up the child, then he should be left to let nature take its course, because he could not be raised by anyone else. This is tantamount to regarding the child as the property of his parents. It fails to capture the child's interests as distinct from those of his parents as required by the paramountcy given to the child's welfare in the Children Act 1989. It also fails to appreciate the significance of the UN Convention on the Rights of the Child 1989. It does not engage at all with earlier case law, such as the 'Baby Alexandra' decision (*Re B* [1981] 3 FLR 117). There the clear assumption was that if parents abandoned a sick child, the local authority would receive her into care.

The Court of Appeal also erred in placing undue weight on the parents' professional perspective. It concluded that this gave greater credibility to their judgement, whereas I incline to the view that, given their professional knowledge and experience, the parents' professional conclusion should better have appreciated the medical benefits to the child of the proposed transplant operation. There was a great danger in the Court of Appeal's approach of mixing up the parents' personal and professional viewpoints.

My Lords, for these reasons I would allow this appeal. The question arises whether we should remit the case for re-hearing or whether, as the Court of Appeal did, we should exercise our discretion afresh on the evidence available. In my opinion, we are in no worse a position than the Court of Appeal was to do so, and we should adopt the latter approach, particularly in the circumstances of this case where the clock is ticking with respect to this child's health chances. I have carefully considered the medical opinion concerning the likely successful outcome of a transplantation operation, the views of the parents as a very important factor in so far as they bear upon the child's welfare, and the very strong interest that this child has in remaining alive. I also bear in mind the complication that the parents are outside the jurisdiction. Applying the child's welfare as the paramount consideration to all of the facts of this case, I am firmly of the view that the child's best interests compel the chance to have a transplant operation. Thus by a different route and on different reasoning, I reach the same conclusion as Connell J and would restore his order.

On Lord Freeman's recommendation, a 'child-friendly' opinion of the majority in this case has been appended to our opinions, explaining briefly, in language which we hope a child can understand, our reasons and conclusion. Counsel informed us that there was (until now) no precedent in this jurisdiction for this practice. Indeed opinion among your Lordships was divided as to the propriety of writing such a parallel opinion. One of us thinks that it is an unnecessary concession to 'political correctness', and wonders how long it would be before we started presenting our opinions in the format of cartoons! However, I am of the view that in decisions affecting a child, and where a judge deems it appropriate, there may be considerable value in conveying the decision in part in language which children can understand.

Lord Freeman:

I have had the advantage of reading in draft the opinion of my noble and learned friend Lord Gilmore. For the reasons he gives, I too would allow this appeal. However, I wish to add several observations and comments of my own on the subject of this case and on the issue of children's rights more generally. It is well known that, prior to my appointment to the House, I was an academic specialising in children law, with a particular focus on children's rights. Let me say first that the issues in this case have not been previously discussed by me, but sitting in this case has now given me the opportunity to think out the implications of my theoretical writing to the problem. My general thoughts in relation to this case are as follows: to deny the very independence of children's rights, submerging them in the rights of a parent, undermines children's dignity, their very personhood. Respect for a child and the love of a child presuppose a child's independent existence. As Janusz Korczak, the great advocate of children's rights, once said, just because the child doesn't know anything does not justify treating him or her with indifference (see Janusz Korczak, *The Child's Right to Respect* (translated by EP Kulawiex, Lanham, MD, University Press of America, 1922). I wish to draw attention to some aspects of this case which raise issues of respect for children's interests.

Lord Gilmore has drawn attention to the danger of treating children as the property of their parents. On this point, I wish, with respect, to draw attention to Lord Justice Waite's use of language in the Court of Appeal. In his lordship's opinion, 'in the last analysis the best interests of every child includes an expectation that difficult decisions affecting the length and quality of its [sic] life will be taken for it [sic] by the parent to whom its [sic] care has been entrusted by nature'. I have deliberately appended *sic*, because calling a child an 'it' gives the game away. It constitutes the textual abuse of childhood in the English-speaking world. To use 'it' may be grammatically correct but the word dehumanises the person who is the subject of these proceedings. The child is a person, not a mere object of concern.

It is clear that T is not in a position to make a decision for himself. However, I wish to emphasise that judges must not lose sight of the fact that even very young children are capable of expressing their feelings. Counsel referred us to a most interesting, emerging body of research on the participation rights of premature babies (see P Alderson and C Goodey, 'Theories of Consent' (1998) 317 *British Medical Journal* 1313), which suggests that even the most fragile of newborns are capable of expressing their feelings, even though they cannot communicate their views. There seems to have been little focus in these proceedings on the feelings of this toddler.

The child's right to make his or her own decision when of sufficient intelligence and understanding to do so was in principle recognised in *Gillick v West Norfolk and Wisbech Area Heath Authority* [1986] AC 112. Contrary to the views of some commentators, *Gillick* is in my opinion a case about children's rights. In future case law, therefore, where appropriate, decision-making should be grounded in that general principle rather than approaches that are not so explicitly child rights-orientated. These remarks are of course obiter, but I take this opportunity to offer them as guidance to courts in the future.

In this case we are confronted by the resurgence of lines of reasoning which not only antedate *Gillick* but arguably turn the clock back to a time when children were the property of their parents. By the early 1960s this had, with the help of (now discredited) pseudoscience, transmogrified into a so-called justification based on the blood-tie (see the nadir of this in *Re C (MA)* [1966] 1 WLR 646). We need to exercise caution in relying on such evidence since children, in particular, often suffer as a result of the conclusions drawn from 'junk science' of this nature.

The dominant trend now is away from parents' rights in the direction of parental responsibility (see eg, Children Act 1989, section 3), and children's rights with the near universal ratification of the UN Convention on the Rights of the Child. The UN Convention on the Rights of the Child 1989 provides radical new recognition of the personality of children. Although the UK government ratified this with great enthusiasm—the Prime Minister of the day going so far as to refer to children as 'our sacred trust'—it has not been incorporated into English law. In my opinion, the provisions of the Convention should, where relevant, be a more prominent focus for domestic jurisprudence as an important source for ensuring that the rights of children are not overlooked. What a pity that some states, including the USA, have not even ratified the Convention, a matter all the more poignant when their leading legal and political philosopher, Ronald Dworkin, sees rights as 'trumps' (See R Dworkin, *Taking Rights Seriously* (1977) ix).

In the context of the case under consideration, another right which children ought to possess is the right to die with dignity. This, and many other issues affecting children, are probably matters which should be left to the legislature. However, an important point which must not be lost in legislation which concerns children, is that rights codified ought to be those which children themselves might plausibly claim, not those foisted upon them by civil servants and parliamentarians whose experiences are remote from the everyday lives of children. Children's confidence will be regained and retained when there is mutual trust. The importance of a democratic environment for children (such as children's parliaments) cannot be exaggerated. Give children responsibilities and they will learn to act responsibly. We also need what I believe will in time come to be known as 'child-friendly justice'.

In line with such an ethos, on my initiative, and with the support of the majority of this House, we offer as an appendix to our opinions the following 'child-friendly judgment' which, as Lord Gilmore points out, is written in language which, we hope, will be accessible to children. I hope very much that this practice will be adopted in other suitable cases.

Appeal allowed. Order accordingly.

Child-friendly explanation of the House's opinion

This is a case of a little boy aged two who needed a liver transplant operation. Otherwise, very sadly he would die. He had already had an operation and the little boy's mother did not want him to have to go through another operation. She was worried about the pain he might suffer. The boy's doctors all said that the transplant had a good chance of success and that he could grow up to become an adult. The boy's mother, however, wanted her little boy to have a shorter, happy life, without the operation. The House of Lords had to decide whether the boy should have the operation or not. There were lots of things to consider, especially the views of the boy's mother and of his doctors.

When a judge has to decide a case like this about a child's upbringing, Parliament has told the judge that the child's welfare (well-being and happiness) is the only thing that matters. In this case, the House of Lords looked at all the things that had happened and what the boy's mother, father and doctors thought, and in the end said that the boy should have the operation.

14

Commentary on *Re A*
(Conjoined Twins)

JONATHAN HERRING

In ethical analysis a distinction is commonly drawn between utilitarianism and deontology, or in legal terms, between rights-based approaches and welfare-centred approaches. In fact, few people are pure utilitarians or pure deontologists; and few legal systems adopt solely a rights-based or welfare-based approach. The decision in *Re A (Conjoined Twins)*[1] is a particularly fine example of how these different approaches can be used in one case.

I. The Facts of *Re A*

Jodie and Mary were born as conjoined twins in August 2000. Mary's heart and lungs did not work and the blood was pumped around her body by the heart in Jodie's body. Mary's brain was poorly developed. The medical opinion at the time of the court hearing was clear that if separation did not take place then either both twins would die or Mary would die first, necessitating an emergency separation with a 60 per cent chance of mortality for Jodie. If separation were carried out soon then there was only a six per cent chance of mortality. However, separation would inevitably lead to Mary's death. The parents, who were devout Roman Catholics, refused to consent to the procedure because they believed the procedure would infringe Mary's right to life.

St Mary's Hospital initiated proceedings in the High Court to declare that separation of the twins was lawful. This was granted at first instance by Johnson J and upheld on appeal.

II. The Court of Appeal Decision

The judgments of the Court of Appeal are complex and the judicial reasoning differs. This makes a summary of the case problematic. Fortunately, the judgments adopt a similar structure to their analysis. They first look at the case from a criminal law perspective to

---

[1] *Re A (Conjoined Twins)* [2001] Fam 147.

determine whether the separation of the twins would be legally permissible or not. They then decide whether the declaration should be made, which was perceived as a matter of family or medical law, based on the best interests of the girls.

From a criminal law perspective, the difficulty was that at first sight the separation appeared to be murder: the operation would cause the death of Mary and, while not the purpose of the doctors, they were aware it was an inevitable result and so can be taken to have intended it. Several arguments were used in the judgments to explain that the procedure was not murder. Johnson J at first instance held that the operation would be an omission. That was an argument which found little favour in the Court of Appeal with Ward LJ describing it as 'fanciful'.[2] In the Court of Appeal their lordships seemed to accept the ingredients of a murder charge were made out but that a defence could be made out on the basis of necessity (Brooke LJ) or 'quasi self-defence' (Ward LJ).[3]

Having decided the operation was permissible under criminal law, the Court then had to determine whether or not to make the declaration applying a best interests test. As the procedure would save Jodie it was unproblematic to find the procedure to be in her best interests. The difficulty was explaining how the operation was in Mary's interests. Johnson J at first instance placed particular weight on the fact that Mary's life would be short and painful and continued life would be a disadvantage. This argument found some favour with Walker LJ in the Court of Appeal, who put it in terms that the operation would restore Mary's dignity. However, it was rejected by Ward and Brooke LJJ. While Mary's life would be short there seemed little evidence she was in such pain and that her life was harmful to her. Ward LJ and Brooke LJ preferred to emphasise that the case required a weighing up of the best interests of both twins. Weighing their interests up it was found that Jodie's benefit of a chance of life, outweighed the harm to Mary of losing her short life.

Following the Court of Appeal decision the separation was performed in November 2000. As expected Mary died in the operating room. Jodie made excellent progress and was able to return to Gozo (her place of origin) in 2001.

III. Alghrani LJ's Judgment

Alghrani LJ sees the doctrine of double effect as providing the most effective way of finding the separation permissible under criminal law. This issue received very little attention in the Court of Appeal, where it seemed to be taken for granted that intention to kill could be found if the operation succeeded. However, even if there is no intention found under the doctrine of double effect, the possibility of manslaughter still exists and so, as Algrhani LJ indicated, a protection of life defence may be required.

Alghrani LJ's revised judgment in *Re A* is highly alert to the difficulties in applying a rights-based analysis to the situation at hand. Her judgment is explicit in its consideration of the rights of the twins both as individuals and as a conjoined entity. Her judgment

---

[2] ibid, 189H.
[3] ibid, 204B.

also offers a more sustained consideration of the rights of the parents than the original. In the original judgment the rights of the parents, particularly their role in the future care of the children, were somewhat side-lined. Alghrani LJ correctly emphasises the importance of looking to the future and what the family life for the parents and Jodie would be like if the operation were performed. While ultimately the Alghrani judgment determines that the rights of parents cannot prevail, in articulating and giving careful consideration to their arguments she acknowledges the importance of the role the parents must play in the future.

Underpinning Alghrani LJ's judgment is a concern with the individualised nature of rights. In this commentary I want to explore those concerns a little more. The judgment of Alghrani LJ seems to focus on the difficulty, on the facts of the case, of using traditional rights language, although I suggest the problems are more wide-ranging than simply their application to conjoined twins.

IV. Concerns over Rights

The decision in *Re A (Conjoined Twins)* is a fine example of a case where the judiciary moved uncomfortably between utilitarian and deontological approaches. The language of rights and welfare is used in the judgment with a degree of uncertainty as to how the arguments fit together. The traditional legal and ethical tools of analysis do not seem to provide a straightforward answer to the dilemma facing the Court.

This is not surprising. It has been a longstanding and powerful critique of rights analysis that it tends to promote individualistic values.[4] Hard cases are presented as those involving a deep clash between each person's individual rights. In this case the right to life of Mary versus the right to bodily integrity of Jodie.

Individualised rights or welfare analysis obviously lacks fit in a case such as *Re A* where the interests and bodies of the twins were entwined in a highly visible way. Alghrani LJ's judgment acknowledges this and adopts a more relational approach. This is one that can recognise our interconnection; relationships; and mutuality.[5] The central themes of that critique are as follows.

First, the rights that are commonly promoted by lawyers are those that seek to protect the individual from outside intrusion. Rights are there to keep other people out: the rights of privacy, autonomy and bodily integrity being perhaps the three prominent rights. This individualised understanding of rights is backed up by an image of the autonomous individual, driven by self-centred values, being self-sufficient and with bounded bodies. This image may appeal to some, but those who would emphasise the interconnected and relational sense of the self, find such an understanding of rights as unrealistic and somewhat counterproductive.

---

[4] J Herring, 'Forging a Relational Approach: Best Interests or Human Rights?' (2013) 13 *Medical Law International* 32.
[5] ibid.

Second, the traditional presentation of rights leads to unhelpful analysis in difficult cases. Rights tend to pit the claims of one person against another, with no ready route to resolving them, as the original judgment in *Re A* so powerfully demonstrates. Brooke LJ described the case as one where 'there are conflicting rights of apparently equal status and conflicting philosophies as to the priority, if any, to be given to either.'[6] Indeed, as a result he departs from rights language and resolves the case on the basis of the 'lesser of two evils' defence of necessity. Particularly in disputes over the upbringing of children, the fluid, messy, ongoing nature of relationships cannot fully be captured by models of rights based on interactions between strangers.

Third, traditional versions of rights tend to abstraction. It assumes that we can determine and understand our claims in universal terms. The rights I have against one person are the same as the rights I have against another. They are rights against the world. Again there are contexts in which this might be appropriate. However, in many contexts the meaning, value and understanding of rights differ. The rights to bodily integrity of a disabled person might, for example, have a different meaning for them as compared to an able bodied person. Conceptions of autonomy for a toddler are very different from an adult. As Carol Smart puts it: 'the rights approach takes and translates personal and private matters into legal language. In so doing, it reformulates them into issues relevant to law rather than to the lives of ordinary people'.[7] Often the rights a child has will, therefore, be different from those some adults have, not because they are children per se, but because of the nature of the relationships within which they live.

Fourth, rights tend to focus on the right at a particular time and consider whether any interference is justified at that point in time. There is no room for a relational approach which acknowledges that in intimate relationships the rights of each party are constantly being interfered with. A decision which may appear to be an unjustified interference with rights at one point in time can appear more justified when looked at in the context of the whole relationship.

From a relational perspective, a final concern with traditional versions of rights is that they downplay or even ignore the importance of responsibilities. Rights fail to place value on issues such as commitment and obligation. This is why Alghrani LJ's judgment is correct to discuss the ongoing relationship between the parents and Jodie and the obligations that flow from that. While rights can be seen as imposing an element of obligation, namely to respect the rights of others, that does not capture the kinds of relational obligations which may require a person to forgo their own rights as part of a caring relationship.

Relational theorists have, not surprisingly, preferred to produce new ways of looking at legal issues, and turned to, for example, an ethic of care.[8] However, Alghrani LJ's judgment does not seek to present a grand picture of a new model of rights or to abandon rights in favour of a more relationally-friendly terminology. She largely sticks to the traditional tools, but is open to presenting and using them in a more relational way. Given the political power of rights discourse there may be some benefit in this approach.

---

[6] *Re A (Conjoined Twins)* [2001] Fam 147, 230d.
[7] C Smart, 'Children and the Transformation of Family Law' in J Dewar and S Parker (eds), *Family Law Processes, Practices, Pressures* (Oxford, Hart Publishing, 2003) 238–39.
[8] V Held, *The Ethics of Care* (Oxford, Oxford University Press, 2006).

V. *Re A* and problems

The decision in *Re A (Conjoined Twins)* provides a good example of relational critique of rights. Many of the problems highlighted with rights generally are revealed in the original judgment.

First, despite the twins' relationship being so co-dependent, they are presented as two separate individuals. This leads to some extraordinary passages. Lord Justice Ward, for example, states:

> Mary … is alive because and only because, to put it bluntly, but nonetheless accurately, she sucks the lifeblood of Jodie … Mary's parasitic living will be the cause of Jodie's ceasing to live. If Jodie could speak, she would surely protest, 'Stop it Mary, you are killing me'. Mary would have no answer to that.[9]

This view of one twin being parasitic on the other and their dignity only being found in the separation of their bodies, only makes sense with the traditional image of rights based on the immutabilities and separateness of bodies. I would suggest the joining together of interdependent bodies is entirely natural. At the most biological level our bodies are entirely dependent on a wide range of non-human bacteria and 'parasites', without which we would not be able to live.[10] In a wider sense, our bodies and selves are deeply vulnerable and we are entirely dependent on others to meet our social, emotional and physical needs.[11] Mary is no more a parasite on Jodie, than any of the rest of us are on our planet or each other.

Second, we see the individualised values in an assessment of Mary's best interests. Ward LJ is adamant the operation cannot be in her best interests:

> [the operation] is not in her [Mary's] best interests … It cannot be. It will bring her life to an end before it has run its natural span. It denies her inherent right to life. There is no countervailing advantage for her at all. It is contrary to her best interests. Looking at her position in isolation and ignoring, therefore, the benefit to Jodie, the court should not sanction the operation on her.[12]

This is an approach Alghrani LJ's judgment does not adopt. Yet, it must be acknowledged that it is based on a particular vision of best interests and what is a good life. Charles Foster and I[13] have argued that wellbeing involves the values of altruism, virtue and relationality. Mary giving up her life to keep her sister alive may exhibit these values. She is living in line with her responsibilities. Indeed many of the great heroes whose lives we celebrate are those who have given up their lives for others. From such a perspective it is not implausible to see the operation as very much in Mary's welfare. Indeed to deny her the possibility of acting in the way virtue would require might be said to be a serious interference of her rights and causing her a serious harm.

---

[9] *Re A (conjoined twins)*, above n 1, 197E.

[10] J Herring and P-L Chau, 'My Body, Your Body, Our Bodies' (2007) 15 *Medical Law Review* 34.

[11] For development of this idea see J Herring, *Vulnerable Adults and the Law* (Oxford, Oxford University Press, 2016) ch 2.

[12] *Re A (conjoined twins)* [2000] 4 All ER 961, 1004.

[13] C Foster and J Herring, 'Welfare means Relationality, Virtue and Altruism' (2012) 32 *Legal Studies* 480.

VI. A Relational Approach

A relational approach seeks to promote values which support and uphold relationships, rather than individual freedom.[14] That is because identity is found by and through relationships with others. We define ourselves by our relationships. We are dependent on each other for our physical and emotional wellbeing. We are all profoundly dependent on others for our physical and psychological well-being. Part of our vulnerability leads from our embodiment. We like to present our bodies as self-contained and secure structures. In fact our bodies are leaky and in a constant change of flux. Our bodies are insecure and vulnerable. Models of autonomy and independence do not work as we are not in reality free to 'live our lives as we choose' because we are constrained by the responsibilities, realities and relationships which embed our lives. This is clearly true of children, but it is just as true of adults. The day-to-day reality of our lives, especially our intimate lives, are not understood as constant clashes of individual rights or interests, but rather as a working through of relationships. The muddled give and take of everyday caring life where sacrifices are made and benefits gained, without them being totted up on some giant familial star chart, chimes more with everyday life than the image of independent interests and rights. In intimate relationships, we do not break down into 'me' and 'you'.

A relational approach starts with responsibilities and connection as a norm. The question is not 'is there a good reason to restrict my freedom', but rather 'is it possible to have some freedom, given the responsibilities of those I am connected to'.[15] Responsibilities therefore can be seen not as the corollary of rights, but rather rights are the tools we need to be able to carry our responsibilities. It is the performance of our relational responsibilities which should be key, not the maintenance of our freedoms. As Jennifer Nedelsky argues:

> The relational approach redresses this historical imbalance by making clear that what rights in fact do and have always done is construct relationships—of power, of responsibility, of trust, of obligation. Legal rights *can* protect individuals and the values that matter to them, but they do so by structuring the relations that foster those values. Thus all rights, the very concept of rights, are best understood in terms of relationship.[16]

VII. Applying a Relational Approach to *Re A*

A relational approach enables us to recognize that in *Re A (Conjoined Twins)* we do not have a case of conflict between two people. Rather we have a relationship marked by profound interconnection. There is no question of elevating bodily independence as a goal for them, as that is not who they are. Nor is it a matter of giving each the autonomy to make a decision as to how they wish to live their lives, as their lives and autonomies are intertwined. The language of a relational approach would focus on the rights and responsibilities that arise

---

[14] See J Herring, *Caring and the Law* (Oxford, Hart Publishing, 2013) for a full development of this argument.
[15] ibid, ch 2.
[16] J Nedelsky, *Law's Relations* (Oxford, Oxford University Press, 2012) ch 6.

from their relationship. Mary, in such an approach, is not a parasite, but living together with Jodie. Theirs is the closest of relationships and greatly to be valued, not seen as a monstrosity.

The question then would not be put just in terms of rights of bodily integrity or autonomy, but in terms of what obligations Mary and Jodie owed each other. What sacrifices could they expect from each other? What relational values would they live by? What kinds of rights do they need to reflect these obligations and values? These would be put in terms of their very particular relationship between them and not in abstract terms. Here we might draw on how other conjoined twins understand their relationship and obligations.

This would include not only their relationship with each other, but also the special relationship they would have with their parents and those involved in caring for them. It would acknowledge that the twins' lives are mixed up with their parents; that if the operation went ahead it would be likely that Jodie's wellbeing would be dependent on her parents' love and care. Indeed it would be possible to write a relational rights judgment not authorising the operation. That might be based on an argument that Jodie would wish their relationship to continue as it is until they both die. However, a relational approach could also justify performing the operation. We might assume that Mary would reasonably prefer saving her sister's potentially long life over her own, given her own inevitable imminent death. The fact that in her death she would give life to her sister, gives her death a value and meaning of its own.

VIII. Conclusion

Ward LJ opens his judgment by referring to the situation before the courts as 'quite unique'. This observation is used to explain why the case is complex and the traditional legal tools do not operate well. However, it has been argued that the interconnection between Jodie and Mary is found in many family and medical cases. Far from being some kind of monstrosity, they exhibit most fully the mutuality which is at the heart of all of us.[17] Alghrani LJ's judgment is more alert to the relational context. It seeks to use traditional tools of analysis to consider these. However, in this commentary it has been suggested that the approach reflected in her judgment can be used beyond the specifics of the case. We can then develop a relational understanding of rights which rests on the values that underpin us all, both children and adults. One that recognises the importance of the relational context we live in and the values we live our relationships by.

---

[17] M Shildrick, 'Transgressing the Law with Foucault and Derrida: Some Reflections on Anomalous Embodiment' (2005) 40 *Critical Quarterly* 30.

Court of Appeal (England and Wales)

Re A (Conjoined Twins)

Alghrani LJ

This is an appeal against the decision of Mr Justice Johnson to grant declaratory relief to the respondent hospital, permitting it to carry out surgery to separate babies, Jodie and Mary, who are ischiopagus tetrapus conjoined twins. The medical evidence is that Jodie, the stronger twin, sustains the life of Mary, the weaker twin, by circulating oxygenated blood through a common artery, and that Mary's heart and lungs are too deficient to oxygenate and pump blood through her own body. If they are not surgically separated, Jodie's heart will eventually fail and they will both die within a few months of their birth. Whilst the surgery will end Mary's life, the doctors believe separation surgery is the best way to proceed, as it will ensure Jodie's survival. The appellant parents of the children, who oppose the surgery and do not consent to it, contend that Mr Justice Johnson erred in holding: (i) the surgery was in Mary's best interests; (ii) the surgery was in Jodie's best interest; and (iii) the separation surgery was lawful.

Like my learned colleagues, I too would dismiss the appeal, albeit for different reasons. I shall first explain why, in my judgment, it is in both Jodie and Mary's best interests that the surgery be performed, whether they are viewed as separate entities, or the issue is approached from a perspective that regards the conjoined twins as a joint entity. Given the parents' vehement objections to the surgery, it is also necessary to address the scope and limitations of parental authority. Finally, I shall set out my reasoning on the legitimacy of the proposed surgery.

1. Best interests

The question of best interests can be approached in two ways: the first is to consider Jodie and Mary as two separate entities and to assess and weigh each child's best interests against the other's—this has been the approach of my learned colleagues. The second option is to approach the conjoined twins as a joint entity with mutual interests.

Separate Entities

Jodie, the stronger twin, sustains the life of Mary, the weaker twin, by circulating oxygenated blood through a common artery. If separated, Jodie has a reasonably good prospect of a long and reasonably normal life. It seems self-explanatory why Jodie's best interests would dictate intervention to protect her from the inevitable death that not performing the surgery will cause.

If Mary is approached as an individual entity, Mary's medical situation is bleak: Mary's heart and lungs are too deficient to oxygenate and pump blood through her own body and Jodie is sustaining her life. If the surgery is performed, Mary will be anaesthetised against all pain, and death will be mercifully quick; she will die in minutes. Evidence was given that, if not, and the sisters remain fused, Mary will have a 75 per cent or more chance of developing hydrocephalus which would be 'extremely difficult' to treat because of the way the twins are conjoined. The effect of untreated hydrocephalus will be to increase brain damage. She is at risk of suffering epilepsy. Lack of sufficient oxygen will progressively cause cellular damage and brain damage. There is great uncertainty as to the extent to which she suffers pain. Owing to the strain on Jodie, if they remain conjoined, both will die within a few months of their birth.

The surgery holds no therapeutic benefit for Mary, in that she will die. However, 'best interests' is not limited to therapeutic benefit. In *Re MB* (1997) 38 BMLR 175 Butler-Sloss LJ affirmed 'best interests' are not limited to 'medical best interests' (at 188). Mary, like Jodie, also has a right to life under Article 2 of the European Convention on Human Rights (ECHR), which we must consider since the Human Rights Act 1998 will be in force in 10 days' time, and under Article 6 of the UN Convention on the Rights of the Child 1989 (UNCRC). As this court confirmed in *Re C (a minor) (wardship: medical treatment)* [1990] Fam 26 CA, however, a dying baby's life does not have to be extended by artificial means, at whatever cost. Article 3 of the ECHR, which protects against inhumane and degrading treatment, lends support to the argument that a child has a right to die with dignity. Not proceeding with the separation surgery will mean the siblings will continue to be conjoined, resulting in both dying. In the present situation each does not have an equal prospect of living, and Mary's life is less sustainable than Jodie's.

In my judgement, this Court should also be mindful that Mary could derive some benefit from allowing her to save the life of her sister. In *Re Y* [1997] 2 WLR 556 the court was asked to consider whether donation of bone marrow was in the 'best interests' of an incompetent donor, where the only benefit that would flow would be to the recipient, her terminally ill sibling. In that case, the child's best interests were expansively interpreted to include 'emotional, psychological and social benefit'. Mr Justice Connell, noting that this was 'a close knit' family, declared that the treatment would be lawful in this instance. Mr Justice Connell explained ([1997] 2 WLR 556: 559) that:

> The test to be applied in a case such as this is to ask whether the evidence shows that it is in the best interests of the defendant for such procedures to take place. The fact that such a process would obviously benefit the plaintiff is not relevant unless, as a result of the defendant helping the plaintiff in that way, the best interests of the defendant are served.

Furthermore, in *Re Y*, Mr Justice Connell stated that the 'defendant would give her consent to the proposals if she was in a position to do so …' Applying this approach, in my judgement Mary's interests might be served in knowing that, in circumstances of her own inevitable death, she helped save her sister's life. If Mary was old enough to be asked whether she would consent to the separation surgery, which would allow her twin sister to live, the only alternative being that both would die in a few months, one may plausibly conclude she would give her consent.

Best Interests of the Conjoined Twins as a Combined Entity

If Jodie and Mary are approached as two distinct children, each a rights holder with detached interests, the Court has the difficult task of balancing one child's best interest and right to life against those of another child and rights bearer. However, the reality is that Mary and Jodie are not physically independent of each other; they are conjoined. To consider their best interests in isolation from each other and as physically distinct individuals is thus somewhat artificial and detracts from the real and difficult decision facing the Court. Approaching the problem contextually with the twins as a combined entity allows the Court to examine their situation jointly as a conjoined common problem for both. This is preferable to narratives that position each twin as a problem and adversary of the other; it is to see them rather as conjoined twins who both face a common dilemma in the resolution of which they have a joint interest.

In my judgement, this approach, which conceives of Jodie and Mary as a joint entity, allows the Court to act in the best interests of both twins, rather than balancing one's rights against the other. It also avoids rhetoric that pits the children's interests against each other, with Mary being depicted as the weaker, parasitical twin, sucking the life out of Jodie. Mary did not deliberately attach herself to Jodie in the manner of a parasite; the twins were born conjoined. Their common problem can be solved by surgical separation. Despite the limited therapeutic benefit to Mary, it would allow her to die with dignity and give her conjoined twin a chance at life. Each is valued equally, but as only one is capable of survival, intervention to that end is in the best interests of both. Approaching the 'conflict' from this angle recognises the co-dependent relationship that Jodie and Mary both share and the significance of their relationship with each other as conjoined twins. Mary has an interest in sustaining the life of her conjoined twin, given the closeness of their relationship and in face of her own unavoidable death. In my judgement, the harm brought upon Mary should not be looked upon in isolation from the benefit brought to Jodie and the fact she is the only one of the two that has a life capable of being sustained.

The Court must not recoil from its duty in this case. The exercise of that duty to both children entails preferring intervention/separation that will allow one child to live, which is preferable to the alternative that both children will die.

2. Scope and limits of parental authority

The parents' objections, which are two-fold, stem from both their religious beliefs and their concerns that they cannot meet the medical aftercare Jodie might need. In evidence, the parents stated that they feel they know what is best for their children and as such should be able to make decisions about their care:

> We do not understand why we as parents are not able to make decisions about our children, although we respect what the doctors say to us and understand that we have to be governed by the law of England.

With this in mind, I shall now address the point about parental authority and its rightful limits. Parents with parental responsibility are given much discretion over their children's upbringing regarding everyday affairs. In *Re KD* [1998] 1 AC 806, 902, Lord Templeman stated: 'The best person to bring up a child is the natural parent. It matters not whether the parent is wise or foolish, rich or poor, educated or illiterate, provided the child's moral and physical health are not endangered.' In the same case Lord Oliver explained:

> parenthood, in most civilized societies, is generally conceived of as conferring on parents the exclusive privilege of ordering, within the family, the upbringing of children of tender age, with all that entails. This is a privilege which ... would be protected by the courts.

Whilst the parents' wishes are of utmost importance, parental rights are not absolute and exist for the benefit of the child (*Gillick v West Norfolk and Wisbech Area Health Authority and Department of Health and Social Security* [1985] 3 All ER 402). Whilst parents are given freedom in how they raise their children and this falls under the umbrella of respecting one's private and family life (under Article 8 ECHR), it is expected that parental liberty will be exercised in a way that maximises the child's potential to develop to an age of maturity, in a manner that best allows them to flourish. In any court proceedings regarding a child's care and upbringing, section 1 of the Children Act 1989 mandates that the welfare of a child is the paramount consideration in any court proceedings about his/her care and upbringing. Article 3.1 UNCRC also requires that the best interests of the child shall be 'a primary consideration' in all actions concerning children.

If a child requires medical treatment, a parent who has parental responsibility within the meaning of section 3 of the Children Act 1989 can consent to medical treatment on behalf of their child. When a child is sick and his/her health is in question, rights bestowed upon children support the maintenance of life in children unless it is clearly against their interests to do so. Article 6 UNCRC demands that states 'recognise that every child has the inherent right to life'. Article 2 ECHR also provides that 'everyone's right to life shall be protected by law'. Article 3 ECHR offers protection against inhumane and degrading treatment. The rights of the children must be taken into consideration and protected by the parents when making decisions about their medical treatment.

McHugh J, in a case before the Australian High Court, examined the source of the common law power of parents in *Secretary, Dept of Health and Community Services v JWB and SMB* (1992) 175 CLR 218:

> It follows that the common law gives this power to parents simply because it perceives them to be the most appropriate repository of such power. Both the interests of the child and the interests of society require that, wherever possible, a child should not be deprived of medical treatment that is for his or her benefit.

McHugh J rejected the view that the power was derived from a 'natural right of almost absolute control' over the child, as inconsistent with current 'social and judicial recognition of children as persons with independent rights' (at 314). Given the unique position of children in society, duties owed to them need to be prioritised, as rights of parents are rightly subjugated to their duties towards their children. Lord MacDermott in *J v C* [1970] AC 668 at 710–11 affirmed this when he stated that treating the child's welfare as the first and paramount consideration (as then required by section 1 of the Guardianship of Minors Act 1971, and now simply the paramount consideration as set out in section 1 of the Children Act 1989):

> connotes a process whereby when all the relevant facts, relationships, claims and wishes of the parents, risks, choices and other circumstances are taken into account and weighed, the course to be followed will be that which is most in the interests of the child.

Once a case on a matter with respect to a child's upbringing is before the court, this is the approach which English law applies. Accordingly, the parents' views, while important, are only relevant in so far as they bear upon the child's welfare. The court's jurisdiction may take a variety of forms; it could arise, under its inherent jurisdiction, under section 8 of the Children Act 1989 or, as in the present case, in wardship.

The wardship jurisdiction is vested in the court under section 41 of the Supreme Court Act 1981 (and Rsc Ord 90) and was described by Latey J in *Re X (a minor) (wardship: restricted on publication)* [1975] 1 ALL ER 697 at 700–01 as follows:

> What then are the origin and function of the wardship jurisdiction? In my understanding they are these. All subjects owe allegiance to the crown. The crown has a duty to protect its subjects. This is and always has been especially so towards minors, that is to say now, the young under the age of 18. And it is so because children are especially vulnerable. They have not formed the defence inside themselves which older people have, and therefore need, especial protection. They are also a country's most valuable asset for the future. So the crown as parens patriae delegated its powers and duty of protection to the courts.

The central focus then turns to the scope and limits of parental power. Parental authority when not exercised in accordance with a child's welfare can be challenged and even overridden by the courts. In delineating the limits of parental authority and whether the courts can override the parents' refusal to consent to the proposed operation, I now turn to their objections:

I. Religious Objections

I start firstly with the parents' firm opposition to the proposed surgery predicated on their religious beliefs. As devout Roman Catholics, they argue that the proposed separation surgery is going against God's will and that, instead, it is preferable for nature to take it course:

> We cannot begin to accept or contemplate that one of our children should die to enable the other to survive. That is not God's will. Everyone has the right to life so why should we kill one of our daughters to enable the other to survive. That is not what we want and that is what we have told the doctors treating Jodie and Mary.

Supported by advice from the Church, they would prefer nature to take its course and stated in evidence: 'We have faith in God and are quite happy for God's will to decide what happens to our two young daughters'. As parents, they are entitled to a private and family life and to raise their children in accordance with their beliefs. Article 8 ECHR provides that 'Everyone has the right to respect for his private and family life, his home and his correspondence'. Article 9 ECHR provides that everyone has the right to 'freedom of thought, conscience and religion; this right includes freedom to ... manifest his religion or belief in worship, teaching, practice and observance'. Consideration has been accorded to the parents' religious wishes and the written submissions from The Pro-Life Alliance, and the Archbishop of Westminster in support of them and their decision. Notwithstanding this, the Court has to decide this appeal by reference to legal principle and not by reference to religious teaching or individual conscience. Whilst this Court must also respect the parents' rights under Articles 8 and 9 ECHR, these rights are not absolute; both are subject to 'limitations as are prescribed by law ... and are necessary in a democratic society in the interests of public safety, for the protection of public order, health or morals, or for the protection of the rights and freedoms of others' (Article 8(2) and 9 (2)). Here the limitation is that parental exercise of these rights in objecting to the proposed surgery endangers the health and life of the conjoined twins, and conflicts with Jodie's and Mary's ECHR rights under Articles 2, 3 and 8. The parents' Article 8 and 9 rights do not justify or invest in them the right to reject lifesaving treatment for their children when one of them (Jodie) has a life that is sustainable. As suggested in *Johansen v Norway* (1997 23 EHRR 33), the court 'will attach particular importance to the best interests of the child, which depending on their nature and seriousness, may override those of the parent'.

This is not to dismiss the genuinely held beliefs of the parents, but where religious beliefs conflict or jeopardise a child's life, the duty towards a child must prevail. There is much authority on this: in both *Re O (A Minor) (Medical Treatment)* [1993] 2 FLR 149 which involved a three month old very low weight premature baby, and *Re R (A Minor) (Blood Transfusion)* [1993] 2 FLR 757 which involved a 10 month old baby suffering from leukemia, the courts overrode the parents' objections to blood transfusion based on their Jehovah's Witness beliefs. The courts did so on grounds that refusal of a blood transfusion was not in the best interests of their children.

This conflict must be determined by what is in the best interests of the conjoined twins. In reaching my assessment that surgery is in their best interests, I have acknowledged the fact that should the separation surgery be permitted, Jodie, the surviving twin, may live to be raised in a religious community that may not support the heroic efforts undertaken to ensure her survival. However, this consideration must be subjugated to ensuring her health and survival, so that when she reaches an age of maturity she can reconcile this with her own chosen beliefs. I reaffirm the widely-held consensus that parents are free to practise whatever religious beliefs they wish to, provided that, in so doing, they do not cause harms to others. They cannot make martyrs of their children and, on this point, I refer to the well-known quote of Justice Holmes in the United States Supreme Court in *Prince v Massachusetts* 321 US 158 (1944):

> Parents may be free to become martyrs themselves. But it does not follow they are free, in identical circumstances, to make martyrs of their children before they have reached the age of full and legal discretion when they can make that choice for themselves.

II. Aftercare

The parents' second point, about which they have been very candid, is their concerns they may not be able to meet Jodie's aftercare needs, in that there is a high chance Jodie might be left with a significant disability. In evidence they stated that in the remote town of their home country there are few, if any, facilities. They claimed this would make it extremely difficult for them to cope with a disabled child and also for that disabled child to have 'any sort of life at all'. They were open about their limitations in their statement to the Court:

> [W]e have to be realistic and look at what we as parents can offer to our daughter and what care and facilities are available to her in our homeland. They are virtually nil. If Jodie were to survive she would definitely need specialist medical treatment and we know that cannot be provided. Jodie would have to travel, on many occasions, possibly to England to receive treatment. It concerns us that we would not have any money for this treatment and we do not know if this is something (our) government would pay for. This has meant that we have also had to give very careful consideration to leaving Jodie in England, should she survive, to be looked after by other people. We do not know

if other people would be willing to look after such a seriously disabled child, but we do know that this is something that if we had any other choice we would not even give it consideration … We do not want to leave our daughters behind, we want to take them home with us but we know in our heart of hearts that if Jodie survives and is seriously disabled she will have very little prospects on our island because of its remoteness and lack of facilities and she will fare better if she remains in this country.

Determining best interests in view of parental concerns regarding the significant role they will have to play in Jodie's aftercare undermines earlier principles from case law that parental autonomy is not absolute and the right to live or die does not rest solely in the parents' hands. That a child's rights are not subsumed within the rights of the parent was confirmed in *Re C (HIV test)* [1999] 2 FLR 1004 where an application was made by a local authority that a baby be subjected to an HIV test, notwithstanding the vehement opposition of her parents. Mr Justice Wilson noted the case was not about the rights of the parents; the baby had rights of her own and the father was incorrect in his contention that the rights of the baby were subsumed within the rights of the parent.

In the present case it is the children's rights that must be the ultimate deciding factor in whether or not the surgery should be performed. Parental refusal to consent to life-saving treatment owing to parental fear that they cannot look after a disabled child does not justify withholding consent to treatment and allowing two children to die when one can be saved. There are two authorities that are relevant on this point. In the case of *Re B* [1981] 1 WLR 1421 the Court sanctioned, contrary to the parents' wishes, a life-saving operation for a newly born baby who suffered from Down's Syndrome. The parents wished to withhold treatment from their child against medical advice that their baby, Alexandra, was in need of the life-saving surgery. The Court of Appeal upheld the physicians' request for surgery against parental wishes, concluding that the infant's life was not 'demonstrably so awful' that she should be allowed to die. The Court noted that if the parents did not want to care for the child the local authority would easily be able to find foster parents to do so. In *Re J (a minor) (wardship: medical treatment)* [1991] Fam 33 this court (upholding the trial judge) authorised non-resuscitation (on a future emergency) of a six-month-old child who had been born very prematurely and had suffered very severe brain damage. The question was whether any continued life for the child with treatment would be intolerable. Whilst there is a chance Jodie may survive with a significant disability, the Court has not heard evidence that her life would not be 'demonstrably awful' or 'intolerable'.

Thus, whilst the Court must note the parental concern in the present case that they may not be able to meet the long-term physical, psychological or economic burdens of caring for Jodie should she survive with a disability, this does not minimise the duties owed to the child. For the aforementioned reasons, I am in agreement with the High Court that the operation is in the best interests of both twins when conceived of as a joint entity. Post-surgery, if Jodie survives with a severe disability and the parents can not meet her needs, the state will assume responsibility and place Jodie with foster or adoptive carers (as it does in other unfortunate cases where disabled children cannot be looked after by their parents). Parental limitations in caring for disabled children cannot dictate that the child's death is preferable.

This is not to criticise the parents or their concerns. The parents find themselves in a position that no parent would ever want to be in and they obviously love their children very much. In reaching an alternative assessment of what is in their best interests, the Court does not detract from the respect owed to the parents, or undermine the authority vested in them. Owing to the special position children hold in society and the duty imposed on the state to protect such children in matters of life and death such as this, or where medical decisions are irreversible or have serious consequences, it is understandable that they be reviewed by an impartial and objective authority such as the court. Parents, by virtue of the closeness of their relationship, may be overwhelmed by the magnitude of decision and their emotions which may cloud their judgement of what is in the children's best interests.

3. *Lawfulness of the separation surgery*

Separate to the question of what is in the best interests of the children, is the question of whether the proposed surgery to separate the twins would be lawful. Separation surgery that is intended to bring about the death of Mary, or where it is an inevitable and foreseen consequence, would be homicide in the absence of a legal defence. This present conflict stems from the law's recognition of the conjoined twins as two separate autonomous right bearers, and as such reveals limitations of rights discourses in the present context.

I concur with my learned colleagues that the trial judge erred in law in equating the proposed surgical operation with the discontinuance of medical treatment (such as disconnecting a heart-lung machine). The proposed operation represents a positive act that will involve a number of invasions of Mary's body before the positive step is taken of clamping the aorta and bringing about Mary's death. This differs from the discontinuance of artificial feeding sanctioned by the House of Lords in the *Bland* case, which was regarded as an 'omission' as opposed to a 'positive act'. However, I am in agreement with my learned colleagues that, in the circumstances, there are valid legal defences that legitimise such action. The acknowledgment that both lives are of equal value in the eyes of the law does not detract from the fact that only one of those lives is sustainable.

Legitimacy for sanctioning the surgery that will end Mary's life could be grounded on an invocation of a 'quasi self–defence argument'. Necessity in the *R v Dudley and Stephens* (1884) 14 QBD 273 sense arises where A kills B to save his own life. My personal reservations for relying on this defence stem from the fact that the threat to Jodie's life is posed by the circumstances, rather than an act or threat by Mary on Jodie in conventional self-defence terms. Regarding the conjoined twins as a combined entity and acknowledging the inter-connection of their existence allows the avoidance of such individualistic narratives that portray Mary as a killer, sucking the lifeblood out of Jodie. Anatomically, the configuration of the conjoined twins' bodies is not an interference with Jodie on Mary's part. Historically they have always been conjoined; Mary and Jodie were born sharing a common artery in which Mary is a passive recipient of oxygenated blood. The twins came into being conjoined and were created that way endangered. The sisters are formed in a way that threatens them both. This defence is more persuasive if Jodie is acting in self-defence against a culpable or 'wrongful act' which connected her to Mary. In the present circumstances there is no wrongful act; nature has connected the sisters, conjoined as they are. Furthermore, to focus on culpability (with distinctions between culpable and non-culpable) does not tell us of the conditions in which A constitutes an unjust threat to B. Whilst the sisters came into being with a conjoined circulatory system, it could, however, be argued there is a legal obligation imposed by Article 2 of the ECHR to preserve life where it is sustainable, that this justifies the intervention by a third party to protect the life of Jodie, thus rendering the separation permissible.

In my judgement, the doctrine of double effect (*R v Adams* [1957] Crim LR 365) may offer a more plausible defence in the present circumstances. The 'double effect' principle works when doctors are treating one patient administering pain-killing drugs for the sole good purpose of relieving pain, yet appreciating the bad side effect that it will hasten the patient's death. The separation surgery could be deemed lawful as Mary's death is an unintended consequence and not the primary purpose of the surgery; an adaptation of the defence of double effect. In order to save Jodie's life, the surgery would clamp the common artery, which would kill Mary. This turns on whether killing Mary was also intended by the clamping. If the twins are regarded as a combined entity, with mutual rights and interests, as opposed to two separate individuals, the doctrine of double effect is useful since the surgery would benefit and harm the same entity, but enable the survival of one of the conjoined twins, Jodie.

Whilst this is a deeply troubling and unprecedented case, ultimately the Court has to decide this appeal by reference to legal principle. Whilst I cannot emphasise enough how much I sympathise with the plight of the parents and the choice they have been asked to make, I cannot agree that their decision opposing the surgery is in the children's best interests. For the aforementioned reasons I have set out why, in my judgement, it is in both Jodie and Mary's best interests that the surgery be performed, whether they are viewed as separate entities, or the issue is approached from a perspective that regards the conjoined twins as a joint entity. I have also set out why I am of the view that the proposed surgery to separate the sisters can be lawfully carried out. For these reasons, I too would dismiss the appeal.

Part IV

Children's Rights and Public Authorities

15

Commentary on *R (on the Application of Castle) v Commissioner of Police for the Metropolis*

FIONA DONSON

I. Introduction

R (On the Application of Castle) v Commissioner of Police for the Metropolis[1] is a largely overlooked case but one which raises important issues regarding children's political rights and the role of the UN Convention on the Rights of the Child (CRC) in domestic law. The backdrop to the case is the highly controversial decision by the 2010 Coalition Government to increase University fees in England from £3000 per year to a maximum of £9000 a year. Unsurprisingly, it led to demonstrations drawing participants from both current students and those who would be affected by the fee hike in the future, ie school children. The three applicants—Sam (16), Rosie (14) and Adam (16)—participated peacefully in a demonstration against education cuts held in London on 24 November 2010.

Central to the case was the police decision to 'kettle' protesters during the protest on the basis of violent and unruly behaviour.[2] Kettling is an established policing tactic designed to take control of a crowd, gather intelligence and make arrests.[3] However, it is controversial, not least because it is indiscriminate in nature, results in the denial of free movement, the denial of access to food and toilets and increased tension and related violence amongst demonstrators. The experience of being kettled is distressing for all involved. However, the impact on vulnerable individuals, including children, is recognised as being particularly terrifying.[4]

---

[1] *R (On the Application of Castle) v Commissioner of Police for the Metropolis* [2011] EWHC 2317 (Admin), [2014] 1 All ER 953.

[2] ibid, para 18.

[3] P Joyce et al, *Palgrave Dictionary of Public Order Policing, Protest and Political Violence* (London, Palgrave Macmillan, 2014) 154.

[4] The UK Parliament Human Rights Joint Committee criticised the operation of the 10 November kettle on the basis of a number of factors including the effect on vulnerable individuals. Human Rights Joint Committee, *Facilitating Peaceful Protest*, HL Paper 123, HC 684 (London, Stationery Office, 2011), www.publications.parliament.uk/pa/jt201011/jtselect/jtrights/123/12304.htm.

The House of Lords had found in *Austin v Commissioner of the Police for the Metropolis*[5] that lengthy kettling in unpleasant conditions did not amount to the deprivation of liberty under Article 5 of the European Convention on Human Rights (ECHR).[6] This decision was controversial because the Court adopted a proportionality approach to Article 5 right to liberty, which is not explicit in the Article itself (unlike Articles 9–11), and failed to provide any criteria by which the legality of police action could be assessed.[7] The *Austin* decision limited the ability of the young applicants in *Castle* to challenge the legality of the use of the kettle on Article 5 grounds. Instead, Sam, Rosie and Adam argued that the police had failed in their duty under section 11 of the Children Act 2004 to 'make arrangements to safeguard and promote' the welfare of children, and that it was this breach of duty that rendered the containment unlawful.

The underlying tension that exists between the Article 5 ECHR liberty provisions and a finding that the authorities are entitled to seek to prevent violence through the use of kettling, specifically in relation to the children participating in the demonstration, is not directly addressed in either the original or the rewritten judgment. Instead the focus is on whether the police acted in accordance with their wider duties particularly under section 11 Children Act 2004. The interpretation of section 11 therefore is significant—what are the duties of the police when children are involved in a protest? The case also demands a consideration of the widely overlooked right of children to political engagement. This requires a widening of the concept of welfare of such children in the context of the case as moving beyond protection and welfare to include the promotion and protection of children's political rights. Daly LJ's rewritten judgment seeks to focus the *Castle* case into a reworked consideration of these multiple children's rights dimensions.

II. Interpretation of Section 11 of the Children Act 2004 in Light of Article 3(1) of the Convention on the Rights of the Child

Section 11 of the Children Act 2004 places a duty on the police to make 'arrangements to safeguard and promote' the welfare of children. This should include adequate preparation and training which, in the context of this case, relates to the operation of protest policing and the use of containment measures. Welfare is understood here to be broad in nature and includes children's health and development which, in turn, can include physical, intellectual, social, emotional and behavioural development.[8]

---

[5] *Austin v Commissioner of the Police for the Metropolis* [2009] UKHL 5, [2009] 1 AC 564.

[6] As a result, the authorities were not required to justify the decision to contain on the basis of the 'permitted purposes' contained in Art 5.

[7] D Mead, 'Kettling Comes to the Boil before the Strasbourg Court: Is It a Deprivation of Liberty to Contain Protests *en masse*?' [2012] *CLJ* 472, 473; D Mead, *The New Law of Peaceful Protest* (Oxford, Hart Publishing, 2010).

[8] See *Castle*, above n 1, para 36, quoting 'Every Child Matters, Change for Children', para 2.7 which states:

> In this guidance, welfare is defined, as in the Children Act 1989, in terms of children's health and development, where health means 'physical or mental health' and development means 'physical, intellectual, emotional, social or behavioural development'.

Given that section 11 'falls far short of the requirements in Article 3(1)'[9] of the Convention on the Rights of the Child (CRC) the question of whether it should be interpreted in conformity with that article is critical to the *Castle* decision. It is well established that the CRC may be used to interpret ECHR provisions, particularly Article 8, engaged via the Human Rights Act (HRA).[10] However, beyond this context the interpretive role of Article 3 is not entirely clear.[11] The controversial dissenting judgment by Lord Kerr in *SG*[12] that Article 3(1) is directly enforceable in domestic law has so far found no support from other members of the judiciary.[13]

Lady Hale, in the *Nzolameso* case,[14] noted that the courts have not yet directly considered the question as to whether statutory obligations should be interpreted in line with Article 3(1) irrespective of whether a claim under the Human Rights Act 1998 (HRA 1998) arises, leaving the matter open to be heard at a later date. Daly LJ, in her re-written judgment, steps into that space to consider just this point; indeed she concludes that it is 'appropriate for the court to interpret [section 11] in line with Article 3.'[15]

The rewritten judgment is, therefore, focused on this and related questions; Daly LJ does not consider the duty of the police under section 6 of the HRA 1998. However, the judgment draws on the ECHR in order to interpret the CRC as well as considering the interrelationship between the two.[16] In doing this the judgment provides an interesting reversal of the normal approach to this relationship which is usually focused on the role of the CRC in developing an understanding of the ECHR.[17] Daly LJ thus provides important support for the wider utility of the CRC in interpreting domestic legislation; something that could be critical to embedding it within domestic law if the HRA 1998 is repealed.

The case also illustrates the importance of counsel in developing children's rights focused arguments. Where a judge is not presented with such arguments s/he may be hamstrung in their reasoning or at least unable to develop the law innovatively (as alluded to by Lady Hale in *Nzolameso*).[18] However, Daly had the benefit of seeing the skeleton arguments used in the *Castle* case which directly engaged with children's rights. Her conclusions relating to the role of Article 3(1) CRC in interpreting section 11 were, therefore, based on the claimants' argument and legitimately developed in her judgment.

---

[9] R Taylor, 'Putting Children First? Children's Interests as a Primary Consideration in Public Law' (2016) 28(1) *Child and Family Law Quarterly* 45, 50.

[10] Daly LJ, para 12 referencing Lady Hale in *ZH (Tanzania) v SSHR* [2001] UKSC 4, [2011] 2 AC 166.

[11] A cautious recognition in relation to Art 14 ECHR can be found in *Mathieson v Secretary of State for Work and Pensions* [2015] UKSC 47, [2015] All ER (D) 90 (Jul).

[12] *R (SG) v Secretary of State for Work and Pensions (Child Poverty Action Group Intervening)* [2015] UKSC 16, [2015] All ER (D) 197 (Mar).

[13] See discussion in Taylor, above n 9, 56–57.

[14] *Nzolameso v Westminster City Council* [2015] UKSC 22, [2015] All ER (D) 35 (Apr), paras 28–29.

[15] Daly LJ, para 12.

[16] Daly LJ, para 18.

[17] U Kilkelly, 'The Best of Both Worlds for Children's Rights? Interpreting the European Convention on Human Rights in the Light of the UN Convention on the Rights of the Child' (2001) 23(2) *Human Rights Quarterly* 308.

[18] 'We have not heard argument on the interesting question of whether, even where no Convention right is involved, section 11 should nevertheless be construed consistently with the international obligations of the United Kingdom under article 3 of the UNCRC. That must be a question for another day', above n 14 at 29.

III. The Right of Children to Participate in Political Activity

While the Divisional Court judgment focused primarily on children's rights arising from Article 3(1) CRC it is important to note that this is too narrow an approach. Adopting a narrow welfare-based best interests approach to a case such as *Castle* results in courts failing to understand the wider role that children's rights play. As Fortin notes, a paternalistic approach to best interests prevents courts from recognising children as rights holders.[19] This, in turn, is not in line with the UN Committee's guidance which stresses that the 'best interests' principle must be viewed in light of the wider rights contained in the CRC.[20]

Castle illustrates the need for courts to recognise that the concept of 'welfare' is not limited to Article 3(1) CRC but involves other rights including the rights of children to engage in *political* activity. Articles 12 and 15 of the CRC provide for the rights of children to be heard and to peaceful assembly.[21] However, as Daly has observed in her academic writing, little discussion has taken place to date regarding the rights of children to protest.[22] This case focuses attention on the risks involved in children's participation in protests. In turn, as Daly points out, it is important to acknowledge the state's positive obligations to facilitate that participation, not least in ensuring the safety of children in the protest space:

> Article 15 of the CRC … means that children have the right to protest safely and that state obligations will involve specific consideration for one's status as a child along with the safety issues that this consideration entails. Children simultaneously need recognition of autonomy rights and protection of their vulnerabilities …[23]

Historically this has not happened. The experiences of the applicants in *Castle* highlight the failure of police forces to develop training and protocols to deal systematically with the rights and needs of children in protests, while the Divisional Court decision ignores the political rights of the children. The ongoing failure to recognise children as rights holders in the context of political activism diminishes any attempt to meet the required positive obligations in relation to Article 15. Daly LJ challenges this approach in her judgment, recognising that the involvement of young citizens in political demonstrations is beneficial to them and their wider community.[24]

Indeed, the treatment of children in the context of political activism has important consequences. The negative experiences of Sam, Rosie and Adam, both in the demonstration itself and following the outcome of their judicial review application, has a chilling effect on their political activism. We need to recognise the role children's rights can play in facilitating the development of children into citizens. Indeed, Buss highlights this in her analysis of US Supreme Court decisions dealing with school protests which 'emphasized the connection between children's treatment at the hands of school authorities and their emerging

---

[19] J Fortin, 'Are Children's Interests Really Best? *ZH (Tanzania) v Secretary of State for the Home Department*' (2011) 74 *MLR* 932.

[20] UN Committee on the Rights of the Child (CRC), *General comment No 14 (2013) on the right of the child to have his or her best interests taken as a primary consideration (Art 3, para 1)*, 29 May 2013, CRC/C/GC/14.

[21] As do Arts 10 and 11 ECHR.

[22] A Daly, 'Demonstrating Positive Obligations: Children's Rights and Peaceful Protest in International Law' (2013) 45 *George Washington International Law Review* 763.

[23] ibid.

[24] Daly LJ, para 16.

understanding of their rights as citizens'.[25] Daly LJ recognises these dangers in her judgment and acknowledges the responsibility of the state to help develop children as active citizens rather than deterring them from exercising their political rights.

IV. Case Narrative/Linguistics

The Divisional Court judgment is striking in its narrative and linguistic tone. The description of the events of 24 November 2010 is told by the Court almost exclusively from the perspective of police evidence put before the Court. The Court adopts a largely uncritical view of the policing of the protest accepting the official version of the events.

Also significant is the specific use of 'young people' by the Divisional Court rather than 'children' which comes from the terminology adopted by the police throughout the protest. Statements regarding police attempts to identify children in the kettle referred to school uniforms and 'small children'. Underlying this language is a distinction between children in need of protection and young people/adolescents who are to be treated as adults. This is heightened by the use of language describing (university) students as 'targeting' schools to 'persuade' children to join the protest, portraying children as passive objects or even as victims being radicalised rather than as being capable of acting as independent political thinkers and actors.[26]

Daly LJ's judgment provides an important restatement that all under 18-year olds should be included in the police duty under section 11 regardless of the context. She stresses that 'adolescents are children'[27] and that under-18 year olds should be 'considered inherently vulnerable'.[28] Recognising that all participants under 18 are children rather than some older children or adolescents being treated as adults leads, in turn, to the development of a responsibility on the part of the police to develop a better approach to demonstrations involving children; one that is required by international human rights standards.

V. Interpretation of Section 11 of the Children Act 2004 in the Context of *Castle*

The Divisional Court judgment found that the Metropolitan Police Commissioner was under a duty to make 'arrangements to safeguard and promote' the welfare of the children in its policing of the protest. However, the Court went on to conclude that that duty had been met in the circumstances of the case, finding that it was reasonable for the police not to make any specific arrangements for children beyond a general statement reminding police

---

[25] E Buss, 'What the Law Should (And Should Not) Learn from Child Development Research' (2009) 38 *Hofstra Law Review* 13, 30, referencing *New Jersey v TLO*, 469 US 325, 334 (1985) (quoting from the judgment in *West Virginia State Board of Education v Barnette*, 319 US, 637 (1943)).

[26] *Castle*, above n 1, para 14.

[27] Daly LJ, para 27.

[28] Daly LJ, para 28.

commanders 'of the need to protect the vulnerable'.[29] The Court concluded that section 11 did not require the police to undertake specific planning to ensure children were protected even when kettling was likely.

That conclusion arises out of a deferential approach adopted by the Court to police planning and implementation, despite evidence that both were flawed. The Court is naïve both in terms of the responsibility of the police as well as the likelihood of operational chaos in relation to complex public order situations. The dynamic nature of protest operations does not reduce the police obligation to make sufficient preparations. On the contrary, it demands a higher level of planning to ensure that the complexity and chaos of events on the ground do not overtake the planning. The Court failed to recognise this and, although the police emphasis on public order is not surprising in the context, it is disappointing that the Court found itself unable to balance this with the child rights elements of the case.

Daly LJ delivers an alternative decision that concludes that the section 11 duty was breached by the Police Commissioner on the 24 November 2010. As noted above, she uses the CRC to interpret section 11 concluding that the duty on the police to promote and protect children's welfare encompasses both the promotion and protection of child safety *and* the promotion and protection of their political rights in a way that is 'effective'—'that police action cannot disregard children's vulnerabilities in a way that disproportionately harms their rights in a demonstration.'[30]

Having found that the section 11 duty goes beyond a basic Article 3 CRC approach, Daly LJ then considers the scope of the duty. Specifically she notes the difference between the duty to 'have regard to' the making of arrangements promoting and safeguarding welfare within section 11 and the duty to consider as a primary consideration the best interests/welfare of the child.[31] She concludes that while the 'child's best interests does not necessarily take priority over other important factors, weighty reasons are required for choosing the outcome which does not accord with children's best interests'.[32] She goes on to conclude that applying Article 3 to section 11 results in there being a 'duty on police … [re] safeguarding and promotion … [and] children's welfare as a primary consideration in the discharging of their functions'.[33]

Finally Daly LJ considers whether police preparation for the protest and the operation on the day were adequate. She concludes that the police should have assumed that the protest would attract more children than normal given the subject matter of the demonstration. Having said that, however, she notes that the police should assume that children will be present at any demonstration given they have the right to participate in political life in this way.[34]

In addition Daly LJ finds that section 11 places a statutory obligation on the police to ensure appropriate planning and training on children's welfare. Despite consideration by the police of vulnerable people at the protest Daly LJ regards the events of 24 November 2010 as identifying serious flaws, not least the lack of clear guidance as to the police duty

[29] *Castle* judgment, above n 1, para 64.
[30] Daly LJ, para 20.
[31] Daly LJ, para 21.
[32] Daly LJ, para 22.
[33] Daly LJ, para 23.
[34] Daly LJ, para 25.

to all under-18 year olds. Underlying her conclusions is the lack of understanding of the definition of a child by the police both at a planning level and in relation to the operation of the kettle. Daly ultimately concludes that senior police officers failed to make plans for the management of children in the protest and adequately to consider their responsibility to children involved in the demonstration.

Having found that the police authorities had failed to meet their duty at the protest, Daly LJ concludes by issuing a declaration that the planning and operation around the protest unlawfully failed to take account of the presence of children at the event, breaching section 11 of the Children Act 2004.

VI. Conclusion

Daly LJ's judgment is important in illustrating the potential scope for developing a children's rights approach embedded in national legislative provisions where ECHR/HRA rights are not directly at stake. It also brings much needed reflections on the role of children's political rights and their significance in relation to children's development.

The conclusion that the police had a duty not only to promote children's safety but also their political rights is important given the potential tension in meeting both. This is illustrated in situations where police make use of their welfare obligations and powers actively to deter children's engagement in demonstrations. For example, Leicester police have on two occasions distributed leaflets telling young people that under section 46 of the Children Act 1989 they have the power to remove under 18 year olds from a demonstration if they were considered to be at risk of harm.[35] Such actions are not primarily oriented to upholding children's rights but instead seek to disenfranchise children. A judgment such as Daly LJ's, which upholds children's rights to engage in political demonstrations and recognises them as being central to our democratic values, is invaluable in helping public authorities strike the right balance between public order and children's rights in such circumstances.

---

[35] V Swain, 'Report on the policing of the EDL and Counter Protests in Leicester on October 9th 2010' (Netpol, 2011) available at https://netpol.org/wp-content/uploads/2012/07/report-on-the-policing-of-the-english-defence-league-and-counter-protests-in-leicester-on-october-9th-2010.pdf, at 7, and Netpol, 'Report on the policing of the EDL and Counter Protests in Leicester on 4th February 2012' (Netpol, 2012), available at https://netpol.org/wp-content/uploads/2012/12/Report-on-the-Policing-of-the-EDL-and-Counter-Protests-in-Leicester2012.pdf, at 5.

Divisional Court (England and Wales)

R (on the Application of Castle) v Commissioner of Police for the Metropolis

Daly LJ

I. Introduction

1. Police have a duty when discharging their functions to have regard to the need to safeguard and promote the welfare of children under section 11 of the Children Act 2004. This duty exists in the context of public order policing as it does in other contexts where police interact with children in the course of their duties. The claimants, Adam Castle, Rosie Castle and Sam Eaton, aged 16, 14 and 16 years respectively, seek a declaration that the defendants, the Metropolitan Police, breached this duty to children in its action in respect of a public demonstration on 24 November 2010. The claimants argue that the police unlawfully failed to take into account that many of the demonstrators on that day would be children and that, when the tactic of containment was used, there should have been a plan in place to release them. They have sought a declaration to this effect and also seek damages and costs from the Court.

II. Background to the instance of containment

2. On 24 November 2010, the claimants took part in a demonstration in London against education cuts (ie the proposed increase in university fees and the abolition of the Educational Maintenance Allowance). The rally, which included school and university students, teachers and parents, started at Trafalgar Square and the demonstrators then marched to Whitehall.

3. In the course of the day, although the vast majority of demonstrators were peaceful, some caused unrest. Incidents reported in the police log include the damaging of a police vehicle, fighting and the throwing of missiles. Some of the crowd departed from the arranged route. At about 12.32pm the defendant's senior tactical commander at the event, Chief Superintendent Michael Johnson, authorised the containment of the demonstrators, the entry in his log recording: 'Containment of large group 3–5,000 to take place

in Whitehall between Parliament Square and Trafalgar Square'. Some demonstrators were ultimately contained for seven or eight hours in very uncomfortable conditions.

4.   At 1.07pm the instruction was given that 'vulnerable persons' were to be identified 'if possible'. Some school students were permitted to leave the cordon and late in the day (5.37pm), a police helicopter was ordered to search the crowd for 'vulnerable children'. The claimants state, however, that they themselves were not permitted to leave when they asked police whether they could do so. They were contained until 7pm (Rosie) and 8–8.30pm (Adam and Sam).

5.   Conditions in the cordon were near freezing. At approximately 4pm a toilet was provided, although it is agreed it was not sufficient for the numbers in the cordon. There was no provision of food and water. The claimants left the cordon shivering and distressed (as did many of those released, according to the police log), and state that they no longer feel able to participate freely in peaceful protest for fear of being contained again.

6.   This is a judicial review of the decision to contain and procedural aspects of engaging in containment. The ground of review is that the police failed in their duty under section 11 and the claimants argue that this renders the containment unlawful.

III. Legal issues

7.   I shall proceed to consider the meaning and scope of section 11 of the Children Act 2004, and whether the duty therein was breached by the police in this instance. In interpreting the *meaning* of section 11 of the Children Act 2004, I shall consider Article 3 of the UN Convention on the Rights of the Child (UNCRC)—the principle of the best interests of the child. To understand Article 3 of the UNCRC, other rights enshrined in the UNCRC must be considered and, in this instance of containment, children's assembly and association rights (UNCRC Article 15) inform the analysis. Section 11 and specifically the meaning given to 'welfare' should also be interpreted in a way compatible with the European Convention on Human Rights (ECHR) as per section 3 of the Human Rights Act 1998. The *scope* of section 11—the duty to 'hav[e] regard to' the need to safeguard and promote the welfare of children—will also be informed by Article 3 of the UNCRC. Finally, this legal analysis will be applied to the facts of this case.

1. The Legality of Containment

8.   Containment, popularly referred to as 'kettling', is a tactic used by police to manage demonstrations. It involves the containment or cordoning of demonstrators in a confined space for periods of time.

9.   It is a controversial method, but it has been upheld as lawful in certain circumstances. In *Austin v Commissioner of the Police of the Metropolis* [2008] EWCA Civ 989 it was held that where there is a breach of the peace or an imminent threat of such, containment will be a proportionate interference with the rights under the common law and ECHR Article 5 (freedom from arbitrary detention) of third parties, where they are innocent bystanders/protestors (rather than the instigators of disorder).

10.   The claimants concede in the present case that the occasion to utilise the tactic of containment had arisen as it was reasonable to conclude that a breach of the peace was

imminent. They submit, however, that the defendant's officers failed to plan for and mitigate the containment of innocent third party children, breaching section 11 of the Children Act 2004. To address this claim, I must determine the extent of the duty owed to children by police authorities under section 11 of the Children Act 2004 when they seek to uphold public order at lawful demonstrations.

11.   The defendant has a duty, by virtue of section 11 of the Children Act 2004, to have regard to the need to safeguard and promote the welfare of children. This duty applies to authorities in England and reads:

> 11.   Arrangements to safeguard and promote welfare
>
> (1) This section applies to each of the following— ...
> (h)   The police authority and chief police officer of police for a police area ...
>
> (2) Each person and body to whom this section applies must make arrangements for ensuring that—
> (a)   their functions are discharged having regard to the need to safeguard and promote the welfare of children ...

I will now interpret what that provision means, how far the duty extends, and how the duty applies in this case.

2. The Meaning of Section 11 Children Act 2004

i. Section 11 and the Relevance of the UNCRC

12.   Although the UNCRC has not been incorporated into domestic law, it is used as a basis on which to develop the common law and to interpret the rights under the ECHR. The concern here is the extent to which the UNCRC is relevant in interpreting statutes and in particular, its relevance in interpreting section 11 of the 2004 Act. Where legislation is ambiguous, international treaties, including the UNCRC, can be relied upon to interpret the relevant provision. Article 3(1) of the UNCRC, which enshrines the principle of the best interest of the child, states:

> In all actions concerning children, whether undertaken by public or private social welfare institutions, courts of law, administrative authorities or legislative bodies, the best interests of the child shall be a primary consideration.

Section 11 of the 2004 Act is 'clearly inspired by our international obligations under UNCRC' (*Re E Children* [2011] UKSC 27 at paragraph 12). It is appropriate for the Court to interpret this statute in line with Article 3 of the UNCRC for the following reasons:

1.   First, (as noted above) in *ZH (Tanzania)* Lady Hale stated that section 11 of the 2004 Act gives effect to the spirit, if not the precise wording, of Article 3(1) of the UNCRC (*ZH (Tanzania) v Secretary of State for the Home Department* [2011] UKSC 4 at paragraph 23). The intention of Parliament in bringing into effect section 11 of the 2004 Act was to introduce a provision that reflected Article 3(1). It would, therefore, be in accordance with Parliamentary intent for this Court to interpret section 11 in accordance with Article 3(1).
2.   Second, it is and always has been legitimate for this Court to draw on international treaties when interpreting ambiguous legislation. In Section 11 of the 2004 Act, the terms 'have regard to' and 'promote and safeguard welfare' remain undefined. It is open to this Court to draw on the UNCRC in order to interpret these ambiguous terms.

3.   Third, the principle of promoting and safeguarding children's welfare (or, the 'best interest principle' in the language of UNCRC Article 3[1]) is a—if not *the*—key right for children. It helps to ensure that their interests are adequately considered in order to 'compensate' them for their lack of power in other regards. There is no reason why this right, developed to mitigate against the lack of specific regard for children in other legal frameworks (including the ECHR itself), should not also, like ECHR rights, be interpreted in line with the principal international treaty for children, the UNCRC. This is a natural progression of this Court's approach to interpreting ECHR rights.

For these reasons, it is open to this Court to interpret the obligation under section 11 in a way that conforms with the UK's obligations under the UNCRC.

ii. Definition of 'Safeguarding and Promoting the Welfare of Children'

13.   In order to determine how police should engage in 'safeguarding and promoting the welfare of children' we must consider how 'welfare' is to be defined. A definition is not provided in section 11, though section 10 refers to a framework of co-operation between authorities for improving the 'well-being' of children in the area. Well-being for this purpose is defined as (a) physical, mental and emotional well-being; (b) protection from harm and neglect; (c) education, training and recreation; (d) the contribution made by children to society; and (e) social and economic well-being. This is quite general, but more insight is provided by 'Every Child Matters, Change for Children'—one of a suite of five documents issued by the Secretary of State to guide application of the 2004 Act. In the guidance document (chapter 2, paragraphs 7–9) it is explained that the scope of 'welfare' is quite broad:

> The term 'safeguarding and promoting the welfare of children' is well understood within the context of the Children Act 1989 which provides the statutory framework for safeguarding and promoting the welfare of children in need. In this guidance, welfare is defined, as in the Children Act 1989, in terms of children's health and development, where health means 'physical or mental health' and development means 'physical, intellectual, emotional, social or behavioural development'.

The interpretation of the section 11 term 'welfare of children' encompasses not just the physical and mental health needs of children to remain safe, then, but also other development needs of a 'social or behavioural' nature. This approach is in line with a modern approach to children's rights and interests, ensuring that they have the necessary protection for all the areas of life in which they engage, rather than simply aiming to keep them physically safe, which would be a very limited approach. It can be read to include the need for children to develop their personalities and experiences through safely engaging in activities with friends, communities and even in political activities. The section 10 reference to 'the contribution made by children to society' points to this relatively clearly. This definition of 'welfare' is still somewhat ambiguous, however, when attempting to apply this duty to the present case, which concerns the policing of a demonstration. As noted above it is legitimate to draw upon the UNCRC where this is the case.

CRC Other Provisions

14.   In the UNCRC, Article 3 uses the term 'best interests' rather than 'welfare' or 'well-being'. 'Best interests' is still an indistinct term. However we have the benefit of the other 41 substantive provisions of the UNCRC to aid in the interpretation of how to define it. We

must draw upon these other provisions because it is envisioned in Article 3 that this will occur; respecting the rest of the children's rights in the UNCRC is clearly in children's best interests (*General Comment No 5: General Measures of Implementation of the Convention on the Rights of the Child* [2003], paragraph 12). As noted above, the best interest principle aims to 'compensate' children for their vulnerability and lack of power, not just on matters of physical safety, but in all areas, including their political participation.

iii.   Section 11 and Children's Political Rights

A.   Further Consideration of the Welfare/Political Rights Link

15.   The need to consider the meaning of 'welfare' in context means protecting children and their development (see consideration of 'Every Child Matters, Change for Children' above at paragraph 14). This necessarily means protecting their rights, and their development as rights-holders, in the specific context of this case where the duty to children in the policing of a demonstration is under consideration. Therefore 'welfare' must be considered in relation to the other rights in the UNCRC, not just those relating to protection per se, but also those relevant to children's involvement in a demonstration context. These include political rights such as the right to freedom of association and assembly, rights which facilitate children's enjoyment of their citizenship.

Value for Democracy of Children's Political Activities

16.   Public order issues may arise in the context of political demonstrations. However, the value of such activities for democracy and the development of society should be acknowledged. 'One of the features of a vigorous and healthy democracy is that people are allowed to go out onto the streets and demonstrate' (Lord Hope in *Austin*, at paragraph 1) and this right applies to children to the extent that it does to adults. The engagement of the claimants as young citizens is nothing but commendable. The involvement of under-18s in political demonstrations and other activities not only benefits them as a group; they can also provide communities and countries with impetus for social change. It is a vital way for under-18s to be heard, particularly as they do not have the right to vote. It is something to be encouraged, as well as a right owed to children under common law and international human rights law. The claimants are politically active young people who were seeking to exercise their lawful right to demonstrate. The claimants' representatives submit that the claimants wish to go to university in due course and will, therefore, be directly affected by the proposed increase in university fees. These young people are also very aware of social justice issues and are greatly concerned by the effect of the proposed changes on students from disadvantaged backgrounds. They wished to voice their opposition to the proposed changes and, together with thousands of other school, college and university students nationwide, took part in this national day of action involving demonstrations throughout the country.

Welfare Rights can be Interpreted as Protecting Political Rights

17.   The importance of interpreting the 'welfare' or 'best interest' principle as requiring protection of political rights is emphasised by the prominence of political rights for children in the UNCRC. The right of children to be heard and to participate in matters

affecting them (Article 12 of the UNCRC) is one which is recognised internationally. It is also recognised in the laws of England and Wales in, for example, section 1(3) of the Children Act 1989. UNCRC Article 12 has clearly heralded a new era of explicit legal recognition for the autonomy rights of children, not only in matters concerning their personal interests but in the political arena also. This is of crucial importance because, as noted above, children are so often powerless in such matters, not least because they are excluded from the right to vote. Other activities must compensate for this, activities such as engaging in public events like demonstrations.

18.   The UNCRC encompasses numerous political rights for children, mirroring provisions in general 'adult' instruments including the ECHR. Of primary relevance in this case is UNCRC Article 15: 'States Parties recognize the rights of the child to freedom of association and to freedom of peaceful assembly.' UNCRC Article 15 acknowledges that, like adults, children can and will engage in activities in their communities that may be social, cultural or political. Such activities may take many forms, including the form of political demonstrations. This provision mirrors closely ECHR Article 11 (Freedom of assembly and association) which reads: 'Everyone has the right to freedom of peaceful assembly and to freedom of association with others, including the right to form and to join trade unions for the protection of his interests.' There is no 'UNCRC Court' and so no judicial jurisprudence from the UNCRC. Although the inter-relationship between the UNCRC and ECHR has usually been to use the UNCRC to inform the content of the ECHR rights for children, the ECHR jurisprudence can also be used to interpret the content of the UNCRC where it is the meaning of the UNCRC (rather than the ECHR) that is relevant to the legal issue in question. I shall engage with the latter here.

B. 'Promoting' Welfare—Positive Obligations

19.   As argued by the claimants, under ECHR Article 11 states have a positive obligation to facilitate the right (*Aldemir v Turkey*, Application No 32124/02, 18 December 2007, paragraphs 41–43; *Oya Ataman v Turkey*, No 74552/01, 5 December 2006, paragraph 16) and particularly states must promote the *effective* enjoyment of Article 11. In *Baczkowski and Others v Poland* (Application No 1543/06, 3 May 2007, paragraph 64), the European Court of Human Rights held:

> A genuine and effective respect for freedom of association and assembly cannot be reduced to a mere duty on the part of the State not to interfere; a purely negative conception would not be compatible with the purpose of Article 11 nor with that of the Convention in general. There may thus be positive obligations to secure the effective enjoyment of these freedoms … This obligation is of particular importance for persons holding unpopular views or belonging to minorities, because they are more vulnerable to victimisation.

This word 'effective' is of crucial importance here; a right on paper is not effective if it is not enjoyed in practice, and this often becomes most relevant for groups with particular needs and characteristics, like children. Because of children's vulnerabilities, extreme conditions, such as hours of containment in freezing temperatures into the night, will be more frightening and harmful for them than they will be for adults. If a failure by authorities to account for these characteristics leads to a disproportionate effect on children of various policing policies, then it cannot be said that authorities have met their positive obligations to facilitate children's right to *effective* enjoyment of freedom of assembly and association. This is supported by the statutory language of section 11 of the Children Act 2004 in the inclusion of the words '*promote*' welfare – implying a positive obligation. Thus 'promoting' children's welfare includes promoting their rights under the UNCRC including their political rights. This requires facilitating children's development as active democratic citizens. As part of this, police must operate on the understanding that children, as opposed to adults, have distinct needs which must be considered in advance of policing operations.

20.   Using the UNCRC to determine the meaning of section 11 in this context, then, means an examination of the requirements of the duty on police to promote and protect children's welfare, where it is understood that these duties include not simply promoting and protecting children's safety, but also promoting and protecting their political rights to the extent necessary for effective enjoyment by this particularly vulnerable group. This must be 'effective' in that police action cannot disregard children's vulnerabilities in a way that disproportionately harms their rights in a demonstration.

3. The Scope of the Section 11 Duty

21.   I now turn to the scope of the duty in this case. This requires examination of the difference between the duty to '*have regard* to' making arrangements that promote and safeguard children's welfare (section 11) and the duty to consider children's welfare/best interest (the term 'best interest' is more commonly used here—see eg ZH (Tanzania)) as a '*primary consideration*' (Article 3).

22.   The child's best interests as '*the* primary consideration' is the standard used, for example, in a decision about where a child should live on family breakdown (in accordance with the Children Act 1989, section 1). Typical decisions where children's best interests are '*a* primary consideration', on the other hand, are where a child is seeking leave to remain in the UK, or decisions where a child has been accused of a crime. The best interest of the child is one, albeit important, factor, amongst others. Although it can be overridden by other factors such as state security, it remains highly important. Lord Kerr, in expressing his agreement with the judgment of Lady Hale in *ZH (Tanzania)* held in paragraph 45 that, in such a case, the best interest of the child is not a factor of limitless importance, trumping all other factors. He qualified this with the statement:

> It is a factor, however, that must rank higher than any other. It is not merely one consideration that weighs in the balance alongside other competing factors. Where the best interests of the child clearly favour a certain course, that course should be followed unless countervailing reasons of considerable force displace them.

Therefore, although the child's best interests does not necessarily take priority over other important factors, weighty reasons are required for choosing the outcome which does not accord with children's best interests.

23.   Next it must be determined whether the section 11 term 'having regard' for the promotion and safeguarding of children's welfare creates a weaker duty than holding these matters as 'a primary consideration'. It has been outlined above that 'welfare' in section 11 is to be defined according to UNCRC Article 3. This must also mean that section 11 can be interpreted in accordance with Article 3 in *how* it is used—ie, treating children's welfare as a

primary consideration. So 'having regard' in section 11 must be read as '*having regard to the need to make arrangements to treat as a primary consideration the promotion and safeguarding of the welfare of the child*'. The duty on police must be the safeguarding and promotion of children's welfare as a primary consideration in the discharging of their functions, such as on the occasion in question. Although the safeguarding and promotion of children's welfare will not necessarily prevail against all other factors, it should be considered a factor of considerable importance (*ZH (Tanzania)*).

4. What Does the Duty Mean in this Case?

24.   In light of the meaning and scope of the duties outlined above, I now turn to the specifics of what should have been expected from police in advance of and during this event in order to meet the obligations presented by the Children Act 2004.

24.   The claimants argue that the police unlawfully failed to take account that many of the demonstrators on that day would be children, and that when the tactic of containment was used there should have been a plan in place to release them. First, this necessitates examination of the advance planning for the event. It should have been assumed by police that this particular event would attract more children than other demonstrations, given it concerned education. Yet police should assume that children may be at any demonstration, as is their right, and in accordance with the section 11 duty, must plan for this.

25.   The section 11 statutory guidance 'Every Child Matters, Change for Children' emphasises that section 11 requires each police force to ensure awareness by police officers and staff at all levels 'of their statutory requirements to promote and safeguard the welfare of children' including through the preparation of appropriate policing plans and appropriate training of all staff. I turn to copies of the training presentation for senior officers with which I have been presented. It is specified in the presentation that where containment is deemed necessary, the Metropolitan Police policy is 'to allow vulnerable or distressed persons or those inadvertently caught up in the police containment to exit'. Amongst the duties of the supervising officer responsible for the containment is communication to his officers of the 'the legal basis for containment, location of release points and release protocols …' The discretion as to *whom* to release rests upon those officers engaged with the containment. The discretionary release protocol applies to 'non-violent persons, accredited media, vulnerable persons, those requiring medical attention, [and] those entering the criminal justice system'. This is the policy under which police Commanders were acting on 24 November 2010.

26.   The defendant's senior tactical commander at the event, Chief Superintendent Michael Johnson, comments at paragraph 20 of his witness statement that he has specifically received training on containment and dealing with vulnerable persons, and he considers children to fall within that category. He states:

> This duty sits alongside those of the MPS [defendants] towards any groups who may be regarded as vulnerable, such as the elderly and disabled but this extends much wider than this; for example, to those who have an illness or even become cold if wearing just a T-shirt in cold conditions. It is for an officer to use his individual discretion, depending on the circumstances presented at the time.

The broad definition of 'vulnerable' here is commendable. However it is perhaps its breadth which is in part responsible for the failure to release the claimants and many other under-18s during this instance of containment. Chief Superintendent Michael Johnson did not make specific plans for the management of children. He simply reminded his commanders of the need to protect the vulnerable, and it was seemingly left to commanders to determine whether all those under the age of 18 are necessarily vulnerable. This resulted in an ad hoc approach to the management of children on the day; apparent in the fact that the focus appeared to be on younger children (the log refers to police searching for 'obvious small children'). In practice, police then failed to include adolescents in the definition of vulnerable people, in spite of the fact that all under-18s are technically children for most purposes.

27.   It is clear, therefore, that children as a distinct group were given little explicit consideration in the planning for the use of containment on 24 November 2010. The duty to children, which involves positive obligations to consider children's safety and other (eg political) rights means that special arrangements for under-18s should be put in place in police planning for all demonstrations, and that all police are trained on their duty to children in that context. The planning should involve specific plans for releasing under-18s. The training should include reference to 1) police duties to have regard for children's welfare as a primary consideration; and 2) the fact that 'welfare' includes political rights, rights which require additional attention because children are a vulnerable group. This additional attention involves recognition that adolescents are children.

IV. Conclusion

28.   The welfare of the child need not trump all other considerations. Therefore it is not the case that containment is necessarily unlawful because of the duty to children. However, section 11 of the Children Act 2004 requires that the principle of the best interest of the child must be given explicit consideration in planning and training. The experience of the claimants, contained for seven or eight hours, demonstrates that on paper there is a duty to children, but in reality it has been interpreted as nothing but the need to provide the most cursory consideration of their needs. This means that children do not effectively enjoy their ECHR Article 11 right. Children were simply categorised with the generally 'vulnerable', with the police on the ground left to determine whether in fact an under-18 is a vulnerable child. Under-18s are indeed to be considered inherently vulnerable, and without a clear acknowledgement of this in police training from the level of Chief Superintendent downwards, the approach taken on 24 November 2010 is likely to continue. The fact that these children have no wish to demonstrate again is evidence of the possible outcomes where the duty under section 11 (as interpreted in this judgment) is not complied with. If the implementation of the duty is not effective for many children, as it was not for the claimants, then the duty is not being met.

29.   Sceptics may wonder why it is necessary to be concerned over the transient discomfort and distress of a few demonstrators. However, the failure adequately to account for under-18s in the planning of policing major events is unlawful, and in any case the conditions involved—being out late in the evening, freezing, without water or toilets—appear quite distressing. It is contrary to the importance we place on democracy if the result of

policing tactics is to deter under-18s from engaging in political demonstrations on the basis that their youth, and the vulnerabilities that accompany it, will not be accounted for.

30.   Police authorities did not abide by their duties to plan for children in containment and to train police officers accordingly. Accordingly, I am issuing a declaration that the defendant's advance planning for the events of 24 November 2010 unlawfully failed to take account of the fact that many of the demonstrators on that day would be children and was consequently in breach of section 11 of the Children Act 2004.

16

Commentary on *Collins v Secretary of State for Communities and Local Government*

STEPHEN COTTLE

I. Introduction

This case of *Collins*[1] concerned the unsuccessful appeal of a decision made by a Planning Inspector appointed by the Secretary of State. The appeal was made by an extended family of Irish Travellers that included 39 children against the refusal of planning permission to remain living on land which they owned. Planning permission would facilitate the children's access to education and healthcare by providing for the extended family a safe, secure and settled place to live, as opposed to a precarious and vulnerable roadside existence.

Following an unsuccessful challenge of the decision in the High Court, the claimant then appealed to the Court of Appeal on the basis that the judge had failed adequately to consider, under Article 8 of the European Convention on Human Rights (ECHR), the best interests of the child pursuant to Article 3 of the UN Convention on the Rights of the Child (CRC).[2] The problem with the decision of the Court of Appeal was that, even though no one had even requested the Planning Inspector to identify the interests of the children and to address which outcome would be in their best interests—and so no best interests determination was carried out—the Court nevertheless decided that in substance the Secretary of State had lawfully complied with his duty under Article 3 of the CRC.

II. The Wider Context

Irish Travellers comprise a separate ethnic group and are a national minority for the purpose of the Framework Convention for the Protection of National Minorities ratified by

---

[1] *Collins v Secretary of State for Communities and Local Government* [2013] EWCA Civ 1193; [2013] PTSR 1594.
[2] As per *ZH (Tanzania) v Secretary of State for the Home Department* [2011] 2 AC 166.

the UK government on 15 January 1999. The European Court of Human Rights accepted in *Chapman v UK*[3] that occupying a caravan was an integral part of the Applicant's ethnic identity (as a Gypsy). That is also the case for the extended Collins family. This means that measures affecting the ability to station their caravans engage Article 8 of the ECHR. Planning control therefore has a wider impact than on the right to respect for the home. Such measures also affect a Gypsy or Irish Traveller's ability to maintain their ethnic identity and to 'lead her private and family life in accordance with that tradition'.[4] Importantly, the Grand Chamber in *Chapman* went on to identify a positive obligation imposed by virtue of Article 8 to facilitate the Gypsy way of life.[5]

A Ministerial Progress Report concerning inequalities experienced by Romany Gypsies and Irish Travellers was published in 2012. The report shows that the positive obligation to facilitate the Gypsy way of life is very far from being met. It contains appalling statistics demonstrating the worst outcomes of any group:-

(i)   In 2011 just 12 per cent of Gypsy, Roma and Traveller pupils achieved five or more good GCSEs, including English and mathematics, compared with 58.2 per cent of all pupils;[6]

(ii)   There is an excess prevalence of miscarriages, stillbirths and neonatal deaths in Gypsy and Traveller communities;[7]

(iii)   Studies consistently show differences in life expectancy of over 10 per cent less than the general population, although a recent study stated that the general population were living up to 50 per cent longer than Gypsies and Travellers.[8] Research also shows that the health of Gypsies and Travellers starts to deteriorate markedly when individuals are over 50;[9]

(iv)   Around 20 per cent (3000) of traveller caravans are on unauthorised sites;[10]

(v)   Gypsies and Travellers living on unauthorised sites can face additional difficulties accessing health and education services and the precarious nature of their homes can further exacerbate inequalities and stifle life chances;

(vi)   Studies[11] have reported that Gypsy and Traveller communities are subjected to hostility and discrimination and in many places, lead separate, parallel lives from the wider community.[12]

[3] *Chapman v UK* (2001) 33 EHRR 18.

[4] ibid at [73].

[5] ibid at [96].

[6] Department for Education.

[7] G Parry et al, *The Health Status of Gypsies and Travellers in England* (Sheffield, University of Sheffield, 2004).

[8] J Barry, B Herity and J Solan, *The Travellers' Health Status Study, Vital Statistics of Travelling People* (Dublin, Health Research Board, 1987); M Baker, *Leeds Baseline Census* 2004–2005 Gypsies and Travellers (Leeds, Leeds Racial Equality Council, 2005).

[9] J Richardson, J Bloxsom and M Greenfields, *East Kent Sub-Regional Gypsy and Traveller Accommodation Assessment Report (2007–2012)* (Leicester, De Montfort University, 2007).

[10] Progress report by the ministerial working group on tackling inequalities experienced by Gypsies and Travellers, published by DCLG in April 2012; See also July 2016 Traveller Caravan Count that shows that 3481 out of 21,419 traveller caravans were then on unauthorised sites.

[11] See for example, M Greenfields, R Home, S Cemlyn et al., *West of England—Gypsy Traveller Accommodation (and Other Needs) Assessment 2006–2016* (High Wycombe, Buckinghamshire Chilterns University College, 2007).

[12] CRE *Common Ground*, 2006, at 13. This reported a scrutiny exercise of all English Local Authorities by the Commission for Racial Equality, mainly carried out during 2005.

The problem for Romany Gypsies and Irish Travellers in the UK, and equally for their children, is that the discrimination they face seems to be the last acceptable face of racism. Imagine, if you can, for one moment that the words 'Gays', 'Sikhs' or 'Disabled' were used instead of the word 'Travellers' in the following newspaper articles: 'Traffic disruption as 800 attend … funeral' 'Winning the war against …' '… need to clear off' 'Blitz on … invasions'. Hence there is still resonance in Vaclav Havel's observation made in December 1993 that Gypsies are the litmus test of civil society.

The national shortage of sufficient accommodation is well known. Municipal sites that are well run, are over-subscribed. This, combined with the blocking up of traditional stopping places derived from historic routes, leaves a sizeable percentage of the ethnic community with no lawful stopping places. The settled communities' experience of unlawful encampments in inappropriate locations breeds a vicious circle[13] that can only be halted by a duty to provide sites, something the Welsh National Government has recently enacted.[14] Prejudice against Irish Travellers and stereotyping of what a new site will mean, fuels opposition to new site provision.

Annual enforcement costs in relation to unauthorised sites, spent by public authorities year in, year out, appears to outstrip the cost of making adequate site provision sufficient to meet the accommodation needs of those with no lawful stopping place. The reason appears to be because it is politically unattractive or a vote loser to support a new site. This means that, if policies strictly limit new residential development in the countryside aimed at avoiding adverse impact on the character of the area, often it may seem to those seeking permission for a Travellers' site that there is simply nowhere to go that would accord with development plan policy and so gain planning permission. Inside settlement boundaries the potential development value of land for residential use makes purchase unaffordable. Due to the absence of policies specifying locations where planning permission would be granted, the starting point is that an application for planning permission for a Travellers' caravan site does not accord with the planning framework. Conflict with development plan policies is why planning permissions for Traveller sites are refused.

There is however, a residual discretion to grant planning permission even if development does not meet the criteria of the policies of the local or national development plan.[15] This discretion allows the decision-maker to have regard to such matters as the general need for sites, the lack of anywhere else to go to, health need and rights under the ECHR. Getting planning permission depends on showing that there is sufficient justification for departing from the local council's policies and in areas of particular planning restraint this can be a formidable hurdle. Demonstrating justification for departing from the adopted local planning policy is where achieving an outcome that is in the best interest of the child comes in.

III. The History of Proceedings in the *Collins* Case

The family arrived on the land in 2009 and made an application for planning permission for change of use of the site to use it for the stationing of caravans for residential occupation

---

[13] Depicted in the CRE Report *Common Ground* 2006, ibid, at 223.
[14] Housing (Wales) Act 2014, pt 3.
[15] Planning and Compulsory Purchase Act 2004, s 38(6).

by Gypsy-Travellers. On 2 June 2010, the Council refused the application. On 27 July 2010, the Council issued an enforcement notice alleging use of the site as a residential caravan site in breach of planning control. The matters went on appeal, under sections 78 and 174 of the Town and Country Planning Act 1990 respectively, to the Secretary of State and from his adverse decision by sections 288 and 289 to the High Court.

The High Court challenge, despite being unsuccessful on the facts, was something of a breakthrough on the law.[16] Even though they lost, the High Court decision in *Collins* was the first to establish the requirement to give effect to Article 3.1 of the CRC in a planning context. The decision meant that the underlying requirement identified in *ZH (Tanzania)* to give effect to Article 3.1 of the United Nations Convention on the Rights of the Child,[17] should be applied to a planning decision taken by the Secretary of State—who was not subject to the duty imposed on local authorities by section 11(2)(a) of the Children Act 2004.[18] Subsequent decisions followed.[19] This however, merely led to changes in decision-writing, with a paragraph purposefully dedicated to the issue, rather than any marked change in outcomes.

The matter then went to the Court of Appeal. The issues before the Court of Appeal included: what should a decision-maker be evaluating when considering best interests?; what weight should be attributed to achieving the outcome that represented the child's best interest?; should best interests be considered first?; and what did Article 12 of the CRC add if the decision-maker already knew that the parents wanted planning permission instead of having to leave the land? The Court of Appeal decided that despite the fact that the decision-maker was not even requested to address which outcome would be in the best interests of the children, that in substance the Secretary of State had lawfully complied with his duty under Article 3 of the CRC.

The result was a disappointment and clearly wrong. In practice, there is now the danger that if a decision-maker is understood to have been aware of the effect of a decision upon the children, for example that a life by the roadside makes it difficult to maintain schooling, that awareness is wrongly accepted as enough to comply with the UNCRC; merely having regard to such effects is not the same as carrying out a best interests assessment that involves an understanding that no other factor should be given more weight than achieving the outcome that is in the best interests of the child. In the leading judgment it was said:

> Nobody concerned in the case was thinking at the material time about the way in which the best interests of the children should be addressed; and whilst the question is one of substance, not form, I feel cautious about concluding that the decision-maker happened nonetheless to adopt the correct approach in substance. I have been troubled in particular about whether the best interests of the children can be said to have been identified as such and to have been kept at the forefront of the mind as a primary consideration in reaching the decision. In the end, however ... I accept that

---

[16] *Elizabeth Collins v Secretary of State for Communities and Local Government & (2) Fylde Borough Council* [2012] EWHC 2760 (Admin). This case took place before publication of the CRC's General Comment No 14 (2013) on the right of the child to have his or her best interests taken as a primary consideration (art 3, para 1).

[17] Above n 2.

[18] '(2) Each person and body to whom this section applies must make arrangements for ensuring that–

   (a)   their functions are discharged having regard to the need to safeguard and promote the welfare of children'.

[19] *AZ v Secretary of State for Communities and Local Government* [2012] EWHC 3660 (Admin); *Stevens v Secretary of State for Communities and Local Government* [2013] EWHC 792 (Admin).

in substance the Secretary of State was of the view that the best interests of the children coincided with those of their families as a whole and lay in remaining on the site.[20]

The history of proceedings then took a few more turns. In February 2014 there was an unsuccessful attempt to persuade the Supreme Court to entertain an appeal regarding the status of the factors identified by the 'UNHCR Guidelines on Determining the Best Interests of the Child' and whether failure to address those interests[21] was not in accordance with the law. But the Supreme Court refused permission observing that their Lordships were not persuaded that it would eventually result in a different outcome, even if they were addressed.

In 2014 the local planning authority Fylde Borough Council decided to use direct action and to enter the land to carry out works necessary to comply with the enforcement notices. That decision was challenged by judicial review on the heels of a second application for planning permission, this time for a smaller site with fewer caravans involved. Permission to apply for judicial review was allowed in April 2015 because it was decided that the Council had failed to address the planning merits of the recent planning application. Fylde Borough Council took another decision to clear the land taking into account what had been said and a second judicial review against that decision was issued. This claim included the argument that it was disproportionate to evict before the planning merits had been clarified especially because by then the date for a further planning appeal before the Secretary of State had been set. The Court was told that the Council would not seek to evict before the Secretary of State had promulgated his decision. Just as well, because on 3 August 2016 the Secretary of State granted permanent planning permission. At long last the Collins family had won! The decision-maker said 'It is clear that a roadside existence would be the worst possible outcome for these children, and that their best interests would be served by having a settled family base, such as would be available at the appeal site'.[22] Due process had been achieved by obtaining, after a long legal battle, an opportunity for the merits of the case to be properly ventilated. But the fact some of the extended Collins family are now living on the land with permanent planning permission does not overcome the inadequacies of the Court of Appeal's decision.

The *Collins* case established that best interests are a material consideration in a planning decision that significantly affects the welfare of affected children. The case shows that the principle explained in *ZH* extends beyond statutory references to the welfare of the child[23] so that the obligation to apply the CRC arises whenever a public authority is poised to take a decision in which a child's Article 8 rights are at stake. But a better understanding of what comprises a lawful best interest determination was not advanced. *Collins* had the opposite effect. Moreover, the case set the clock back as regards Article 12, instead deciding: 'It is highly unlikely that a planning decision-maker (or, as here, an inspector appointed to hold a public inquiry and make recommendations to the Secretary of State) will need to hear directly from any children affected by the decision'.[24]

---

[20] Above n 1, at paras 41 and 42.

[21] Which go beyond educational need.

[22] Para 56 of Planning Inspectorate decision Appeal Ref: APP/M2325/W/15/3026000; Land known as Angel Lane Caravan Park, off Fairfield Road, Hardhorn, Poulton-le-Fylde, Lancashire FY6 8DN.

[23] As contained in Children Act 2004, s 11(2)(a).

[24] Above n 1, at para 15.

The existing planning case law does not spell out what a decision-maker is legally required to do in order to give effect to Article 3 of the CRC. Furthermore, it is clear that those involved in planning decisions are a long way behind in recognising the force and purpose of Article 12.

IV. What the Rewritten Judgment does differently

The Court of Appeal judgment has fallen to be re-written because the judgment missed the opportunity to spell out the need to very sharply focus on the interests of the children in order to arrive at a considered and reasoned explanation for giving substantial weight to achieving the outcome that was in the best interests of the children on the site. The Court of Appeal also failed to recognise the difference between whether or not (for the purposes of Article 3 of the CRC) the best interests were treated as a primary consideration and the (different) issue of whether or not in terms of participation and the opportunity to be heard, Article 12 was complied with. The importance of Article 12 should not have to be rehearsed but the Planning Court has yet to accept that the methodology for hearing the views of the child is critical to facilitating the role of children in all decisions affecting their lives. Town and Country planning in England has a long way to go because it fails to recognise that an assessment of best interests 'must respect the child's rights to express his views'.[25] Applying Article 3 without ensuring that those old enough can express their views consistently with Article 12, deprives the decision-maker of the necessary, and potentially vital, information required to identify the child's interests. Failure to comply with Article 12 is not just a hollow breach of the CRC, it is a recipe for ill-informed decision-making and means the decision-maker is blind to the matters that a child might raise and the importance (or lack of it) that she or he attaches to them. Being able to participate before an adverse decision is reached is a fundamental feature of the procedural safeguards inherent in Article 8. Hence even though Article 12 is freestanding, it should be considered alongside Article 3 of the CRC.

The re-written judgment remedies these omissions. There are two points that should be taken from the re-written judgment. First, if a planning judgment (on proportionality) does not properly reflect the factors in operation in a case involving serious impact on affected children, then it will be unlawful. The interests affecting the child need to be properly explored[26] as do the views of those able to express them. Second, the weight to be given to achieving the outcome that represents the best interests of the child is not to be left to the discretion of the decision-maker. Substantial weight to achieving the outcome that would be in the best interests of the child should be given before the overall balancing exercise is embarked upon. Their importance does not fluctuate depending on the harms caused by any given site. When there is a range of factors for and against refusing or granting planning permission, the question of what weight to attribute to each will influence the cumulative

---

[25] CRC's General Comment No 14 (2013) on the right of the child to have his or her best interests taken as a primary consideration (art 3, para 1) at para 43.

[26] The Court of Appeal in the *Collins* case rejected submissions made on the strength of the factors listed at the end of Annex 9 to the UNHCR Guidelines on Determining the Best Interests of the Child.

weight of the factors on each side of the equation; hence the potency of children's best interests as an influential factor to the outcome in a given case. Hence also the need for a proper
understanding of what goes into an assessment of best interests.

Whereas the Court of Appeal had stated that drawing on the factors listed under section
1 of the Children Act 1988 or listed in Annex 9 of the CRC Guidelines sought to 'bring
into this area a greater degree of elaboration than in my view is appropriate' the re-written
judgment has pragmatically sought to provide a go-to list of relevant factors. The re-written
judgment is an example of placing the children's interests at the heart of the case from the
outset, including steps to ensure hearing the views of the child and highlighting procedural opportunities to ensure transparency. It therefore provides a welcome insight into
the content and weight of best interests and how they can be applied in planning decisions.
The impact of the re-written judgment on planning applications when the Article 8 rights
of a child are at stake, would be to restore the correct legal position by proper compliance
with Articles 3 and 12 of the CRC. It means that the decision should be arrived at on a more
informed basis and where the best interests of the child clearly favour a certain course,
'that course should be followed unless countervailing reasons of considerable force displace
them'.[27]

---

[27] *ZH (Tanzania)* above n 2 at para 46.

Court of Appeal (Civil Division) (England and Wales)

Collins v Secretary of State for Communities and Local Government

Hoffman LJ

Introduction

1. Elizabeth Collins and her children are members of a community of four closely related families who consider themselves an extended family. This community of 78 people includes 39 children. With the exception of two Scottish Travellers, they are all Irish Travellers. In the tradition of Traveller communities the families live in mobile caravans. These are located on about 2.4 hectares of land near Hardhorn, Fylde. This land is occupied without appropriate planning permission. Fylde Borough Council, the local planning authority, has issued an enforcement notice (27 July 2010) requiring the Community to leave the land.

2. An application for planning permission for residential use of the land has been made (14 December 2012), and refused. Ms Collins appealed to the Secretary of State against the refusal. A Planning Inspector was appointed to hold an inquiry. The Inspector recommended that the appeal should be dismissed and the enforcement notice upheld. The Secretary of State agreed (18 August 2011). Ms Collins then appealed to the High Court against the refusal of planning permission and the Secretary of State's decision to uphold the enforcement notice (under sections 288 and 289 of the Town and Country Planning Act 1990 respectively). Ms Collins was unsuccessful and so renews her appeals to this Court. The question that is to be decided today is whether the Secretary of State took proper account of the best interests of the children in this case in reaching his decision.

The children in this case

3. At the heart of this case are 39 children who will all be affected by the planning decision. Eviction from the Hardhorn site will expose the Community to an uncertain existence. In the Fylde area there is no official site where the families concerned may lawfully relocate their homes. It is likely they will have to resort to a precarious roadside existence. In these

circumstances there is a real risk that the children's education will suffer, as might their health. This is what the Inspector says at paragraph 122 of his report:

> it is very likely that if the travellers were obliged to leave the appeal site with no alternative site to go to there would be serious disruption to the education of the 22 children currently attending school. It is also likely that the education of those on school waiting lists would be disrupted ... A roadside existence would make access to health care considerably more difficult, with the potential for a harmful effect on the health of some members of the group, including those with significant existing medical conditions.

4.   This raises serious concerns about the situation of the children. I will return to consider the Inspector's findings shortly.

Children's best interests in planning cases

5.   The best interests of the child should be a primary consideration in planning decisions that affect children. This is not in dispute. However, it is worth explaining why the best interests of the child should be integral in all planning decisions that affect children.

6.   The United Kingdom is party to the United Nations Convention on the Rights of the Child (UNCRC). Article 3.1 of the UNCRC establishes as a right the 'best interests principle', which reads:

> In all actions concerning children, whether undertaken by public or private social welfare institutions, courts of law, administrative authorities or legislative bodies, the best interests of the child shall be a primary consideration.

7.   The United Kingdom is party to the European Convention on Human Rights (ECHR). Article 8.1 of the ECHR reads:

> Everyone has the right to respect for his private and family life, his home and his correspondence.

8.   A number of authorities consider the relationship between ECHR article 8.1 and UNCRC article 3.1. In *Beoku-Betts v Secretary of State for the Home Department* [2008] UKHL 39 the House of Lords held that where ECHR article 8.1 is engaged, the relevant decision-making authority should take into account the right to respect for family life of all family members who might be affected by the decision. In *ZH (Tanzania) v Secretary of State for the Home Department* [2011] UKSC 4 and *H(H) v Deputy Prosecutor of the Italian Republic, Genoa* [2012] UKSC 25, the Supreme Court held that where ECHR rights are those of a child the decision-maker should take into consideration the best interests of the child as a primary consideration in accordance with UNCRC article 3.1.

The issues

9.   In my judgement, in any planning case in which the best interests of the child are to be taken into account, the decision-maker must first assess what is in the best interests of the child or children involved. This assessment is then to be taken into account in the planning decision. Therefore two questions need to be addressed:

[i]   What is the correct approach to assessing the best interests of the child?
[ii]   Once determined, how are the best interests of the child to be taken into account as a primary consideration in planning cases?

What is the Correct Approach to Assessing the Best Interests of the Child?

10.   I do not think it controversial to suggest that the concept of the best interests of the child is inherently flexible. It needs to be in order to make it suitable to the range of situations in which decisions are taken that impact on the lives of children. The Committee on the Rights of the Child is preparing guidance on the best interests principle. When this is available it is likely to provide invaluable assistance to planning decision-makers and I would anticipate that they will take this guidance fully into account.

11.   A preliminary issue is whether the decision-maker is required to assess the best interests of a child or group of children. UNCRC article 3.1 may be read as applying to either or both situations. In cases involving individual children, it will be what is in the individual child's best interests that will be taken into account. Where a decision affects a community—as here—the decision-maker will need to take into account the best interests of children as a group. In these circumstances the decision-maker should remain sensitive to the possibility that one or more children may be affected differently, in which case their best interests will need to be separately taken into account.

12.   In order to assess a child's or children's best interests a decision-maker must be furnished with relevant evidence. Although planning is an area where Parliament has entrusted much to the planning authorities I see no reason why the courts should not offer guidance on considerations to be taken into account. In matters of fundamental human rights the courts have a unique responsibility to safeguard individual rights, and judges should not shirk their responsibility to assist planning decision-makers to understand their human rights obligations. To do less would be an abdication of responsibility.

13.   The European Court of Human Rights has observed that the ECHR cannot be interpreted in a vacuum, but should be interpreted in harmony with rules of international law and in particular rules concerning the protection of human rights (Baroness Hale, in *ZH (Tanzania)* at paragraph 21, citing *Neulinger v Switzerland* (2010) 28 BHRC 706). The Supreme Court has recognised the relevance of UNCRC article 3.1 where ECHR article 8.1 rights belong to children. There seems to me no reason why the obligation to take article 3.1 into account does not extend to all other rights guaranteed to children under the UNCRC. This is the implication of the United Kingdom's freely accepted human rights obligations.

14.   In planning cases, evidence about the likely impact of planning decisions will often come from those affected. In *Stevens v Secretary of State* [2013] EWHC 792 (Admin) Hickinbottom J states that the interests of a child's carer and the best interests of the child are likely to coincide in planning cases, and that the carer will usually be in the best position to put forward evidence as to the impact a decision may have on any child (at paragraph 58). I disagree. The decision-maker should not assume that the views of the child's carers coincide with the views of the child. In *D (A Child) (Abduction: Rights of Custody)* [2006] UKHL 51, Baroness Hale said:

> [57] … there is now a growing understanding of the importance of listening to the children involved in children's cases. It is the child, more than anyone else, who will have to live with what the court decides. *Those who do listen to children understand that they often have a point of view which is quite distinct from that of the person looking after them.* (emphasis added)

15.   *D (A Child)* was about custody rights, but Baroness Hale's observation holds true in planning cases. Children's views can, and often do, differ from those of the adults that care for them. As the Committee on the Rights of the Child said in General Comment No 12 (2009) on the Right of the Child to be Heard at paragraph 36:

> there are risks of a conflict of interest between the child and their most obvious representative (parent(s)).

And as Baroness Hale observed in *ZH(Tanzania)* at paragraph 37, after noting what was said by the Committee:

> Children can sometimes surprise one.

16.   The views of the child's carers are relevant to inform the assessment of the child's best interests, but these should not be assumed as the views of the child. This risks overlooking the child's opinion and is a potential breach of UNCRC article 12.1 which guarantees any child capable of forming their own views the right to express those views freely in all matters affecting them, and for due weight to be given to their views in accordance with their age and maturity. In my judgement, the child's right to be heard in planning cases is integral to the assessment of their best interests and should not be circumscribed in the manner contemplated in *Stevens*.

17.   The child's wishes and feelings should be sought wherever possible from the child. This does not mean that the decision-maker needs to hear directly from the child, or every child, in every case. For example, where a planning decision affects very young children, or many children, it may be appropriate to consider different mechanisms for receiving their views. Alternative methods for receiving the views of the child include: social inquiry reports, health professional or educationalist reports, or through representatives. I do not go so far as to suggest that social inquiry reports should be routine in planning cases involving children as His Honour Judge Thornton QC did in *Sedgemoor District council v Hughes* [2012] EWHC 1997 (QB). Instead, the question of how the views of the child (or children) are received should be decided on a case-by-case basis, with social inquiry or welfare reports as options.

18.   I agree with Mr Cottle, who represents Ms Collins, that useful guidance on relevant considerations in the best interests assessment may be found in section 1 of the Children Act 1989, and in statutory guidance issued under section 11 of the Children Act 2004. Neither of these statutes applies in planning cases, but I see no good reason why sensible guidance given in one context should not inform procedure in another. With this in mind I take the view that the following considerations are likely to be relevant to any assessment of a child's best interests in planning cases:

— The ascertainable views, wishes and feelings of the child or children concerned.
— The child's physical, emotional and educational needs.
— The likely effect on the child of any change in their circumstances.
— The age, sex, background and any characteristic of the child.
— The prevention of impairment of health and development of the child.
— The provision of safe and effective care for the child.
— Enabling the child to have optimum life chances and to enter adulthood successfully.

19.   Having regard to the child's UNCRC rights more widely I would add that planning decision-makers should also take into account:

— The importance of family life to children's well-being (UNCRC, article 5 and article 9).
— The need to ensure non-discrimination in the implementation of human rights (UNCRC article 2, ECHR article 14).

20.   None of the above is to be read as a closed or prescriptive list of relevant considerations. There may be good reason for some considerations to be omitted in some cases although in my view this should be the exception. Decision-makers may also need to take into account other considerations. For example, Annex 9 of the United Nations High Commissioner for Refugees Guidelines on Determining the Best Interests of the Child lists a number of useful considerations, although these are primarily intended as guidance in the context of children as refugees and asylum seekers.

21.   The contours of what is in the best interests of the child may be complex. The decision-maker may be required to consider factors that pull in different directions. They will need to take all relevant considerations into account and exercise judgement to arrive at an assessment of what is in the best interests of the child in a particular planning context. In many cases the planning decision will be limited to whether or not to grant planning permission. In these circumstances the planning decision-maker will need to assess whether planning permission is, or is not, consistent with the best interests of the child. This will involve an aggregation of factors weighing in favour of the alternatives, and a careful balancing of the arguments and considerations in play. What is vitally important is that once an assessment of what is in the best interests of the child has been made it is kept to the forefront of the decision-maker's mind.

22.   Planning decision-makers might think the above approach too onerous. I think not. Can there be a more pressing duty on a public authority than the human rights of children? Planning decisions have potentially serious consequences for children, in the present and in the future, and so it is entirely sensible for the courts to provide guidance to assist planning decision-makers to meet the weighty duty that rests on their shoulders.

How Should the Best Interests of the Child be taken into Account as a Primary Consideration in Planning Cases?

23.   Once a planning decision-maker has assessed what is in the best interests of the child in a given planning context they have to take this assessment into account in the decision-making process. There is no dispute about the relevant statutory framework. In short, by virtue of section 70, Town and Country Planning Act 1990, in planning cases where ECHR article 8.1 is engaged and UNCRC article 3.1 is in play, both are material considerations in the planning decision-making process.

24.   Hickinbottom J deals with the relevance of the best interests assessment in planning cases in *Stevens* at paragraphs 59 to 66. The starting point is that the assessment of what is in the best interests of the child is to be taken as a primary consideration, but is not itself determinative of the planning issue (*Stevens* at paragraph 59). This is consistent with the Supreme Court authorities (see for example: Lady Hale in *ZH* at paragraph 26; Lord Kerr in

H(H) at paragraph 145). In my judgement the correct approach thereafter is for the plan-ning decision-maker to determine whether the best interests of the child in any given case should be overridden by other material considerations, taken separately or cumulatively. What is to be firmly borne in mind by the decision-maker when reaching their decision is that no other consideration is to be taken as inherently more important than the best interests of the child.

25.   There is some suggestion in *Stevens* that the weight given to the child's best interests at different stages in the planning decision-making process may vary, depending on other considerations taken into account (*Stevens*, eg at paragraph 63). This would seem to permit a lesser weight to be attached to what is assessed to be in the best interests of the child, depending on the weight attached to other considerations (ibid). In my opinion, and with great respect, if this is what was intended in *Stevens*, the judge has fallen into error at this stage. What is apparent from *ZH* and *H(H)* is that other material considerations, whether taken separately or cumulatively, can override or outweigh what is in the best interests of the child in planning cases. As Baroness Hale put it in *ZH* at paragraph 26:

> Provided the tribunal did not treat any other consideration as inherently more significant that the best interest of the children, it could conclude that the strength of other considerations outweighed them.

26.   A planning decision-maker may reach a decision which conflicts with what has been assessed to be in the best interests of the child. However, this can only be justified where other material considerations, taken separately or cumulatively, override or outweigh the best interests of the child.

27.   Where a planning decision is made which is contrary to what has been assessed to be in the best interests of the child the decision-maker must provide compelling reason(s) for the decision. I use the phrase 'compelling good reason' but I do not intend to establish a formal test. What is important is that what is in the best interests of the child is made clear in emphatic terms. This is what Lord Kerr conveys in strong language in *ZH* at paragraph 46, in a passage cited by Lady Hale in *HH* at paragraph 14, referring to the best interests of the child:

> This is not, it is agreed, a factor of limitless importance in the sense that it will prevail over all other considerations. It is a factor, however, that must rank higher than any other. It is not merely one consideration that weighs in the balance alongside other competing factors. Where the best interests of the child clearly favour a certain course, that course should be followed unless coun-tervailing reasons of considerable force displace them. It is not necessary to express this in terms of a presumption but the primacy of this consideration needs to be made clear in emphatic terms. What is determined to be in a child's best interests should customarily dictate the outcome of cases such as the present, therefore, and it will require considerations of substantial moment to permit a different result.

28.   In the light of my analysis so far I derive a number of propositions on the application of the best interests principle in planning cases:

i.   Planning decision-making will often engage ECHR article 8 in a way that requires the rights of children to be taken into account.

ii.   Where the ECHR article 8 rights are those of children, they must be interpreted in the light of UNCRC article 3 requiring the child's best interests to be taken into account as a primary consideration.

iii.   In the circumstances described in (ii) above, the decision-maker is required to assess what is in the best interests of the child in any given case (being the best interests of a group of children, or of individual children, or both).

iv.   The decision-maker should not assume that the interests of the child's carer will coincide with those of the child, or that the carer will properly represent the best interests of the child (although the views of carers as to what is in the best interests of their child should be taken into account).

v.   The decision-maker should give careful consideration as to how to receive the views of the child or children involved in the case about the planning decision.

vi.   The decision-maker should take appropriate steps to ensure that all relevant considerations are taken into account in the assessment of what is in the best interests of the child: the decision-maker should begin with the factors set out above at paragraphs 18 and 19 but these should not be regarded as a prescriptive or closed list of relevant considerations.

vii.   Although a primary consideration, what is in the best interests of the child is not determinative of the planning issue.

viii. The best interests of the child must remain a primary consideration and at the forefront of the decision-maker's mind throughout the planning decision-making process; no other material consideration is to be regarded as inherently more important than the best interests of the child.

ix.   Other material considerations, taken separately or cumulatively, can override or outweigh the best interests of the child but this can only be decided after a careful balancing of interests in each case. The decision-maker should provide compelling good reason(s) for a planning decision that is contrary to the best interests of the child.

29.   Whether the decision-maker has properly performed the exercise of determining the best interests of the child is a question of substance, not form. In *R (Baker) v Secretary of State for Communities and Local Government* [2008] EWCA Civ 141 the Court of Appeal considered the discharge of the public authority equality duty under section 71 of the Race Relations Act 1971 (superseded by section 149 of the Equality Act 2010). At paragraph 38 in *Baker* Dyson LJ held that it would be good practice for a decision-maker to make reference to any relevant statutory duty, observing that this is more likely to ensure that relevant factors are taken into account. The same may be said of planning decisions where the decision-maker is under an obligation to take the best interests of the child into account. If the decision-maker fails to refer to this obligation in the course of coming to their decision the court may nevertheless find that they took the best interests of the child into account in substance. However, in my view the court should be very reluctant to arrive at this inference unless there is clear and compelling evidence to support it.

30.   It seems to me that it would be good practice for the planning decision-maker to include the following in any report or decision letter:

—   Confirmation that the best interests of the child have been taken into account as a primary consideration.

— A list of factors that influenced the assessment of a child's best interests, and the importance attached to these considerations.
— What the decision-maker determines as being in the best interests of the child in the particular case, and why the decision-maker believes this to be the case.
— If the final planning decision is not consistent with what is assessed to be in the best interests of the child, what other material considerations have been taken into account and why it is that these are seen as sufficiently compelling to override the best interests of the child.

Application

31.   Although the Inspector's report refers to a number of considerations familiar in a planning context (at paragraph 83), there is no mention of the best interests of the children concerned.

The Inspector's Report

32.   I have already made reference to an important finding from the Inspector's report at paragraph 3 above, concerning the children's health and education. Health is dealt with in the context of access to health services for the Community as a whole. The findings are wholly inadequate. A number of questions were not asked and therefore remain unanswered. For example: how will the problem of access to health services affect children of different ages (what are the ages of the children)? Are there any specific health issues affecting the children, or individual children? Will these be made worse by the consequences of the decision? Although the Inspector refers to evidence from Ms Hartley on the possible harmful effect of an adverse planning decision on members of the Community with pre-existing 'significant' medical conditions, there is no indication whether this includes children.

33.   On the issue of education, a vitally important aspect of children's lives and futures, the Inspector finds that there would be serious disruption to the education of the 22 children attending school (at paragraph 122). This is worrying, but again leaves many questions unanswered. Can the problems be managed in the short, medium or longer term? Does the disruption affect any child approaching important examinations in a particularly adverse way? Do any of the children have special educational needs? To my mind these sorts of questions require answers if the best interests of the children concerned are to be properly understood. Why is there no report from the children's school or Local Education Authority? Was one requested? A separate issue raised by the Inspector's findings on the issue of education is: what about the 17 children not in education? What is the likely affect of refusal of planning decision on their lives and futures? They seem to have been overlooked in the report, or their interests have been treated as concurrent with the interests of adults involved—which amounts to the same thing.

34.   Paragraph 118 of the Inspector's report identifies problems of disadvantage and marginalisation, high levels of discrimination, harassment, a lack of sites and insecure, unhealthy living conditions that affect, in particular, Irish Travellers. The Inspector says nothing about how this affects the children in the Community, for example, whether this makes it more difficult to gain access to essential services or prejudices their access to and/ or their participation in education.

35.   I have one final observation on the manner in which the Inspector arrived at the findings in his report. At no point is there any suggestion that the children at the heart of the case were consulted, either directly or indirectly through representatives. I am concerned that this Court is once again being asked to decide a case which is all about children, the outcome of which will have a significant impact on their lives, without any evidence from the children themselves. Regrettably the voice of the child (or children) in this case about children is in fact the voice of the adults involved. When will those who make potentially life-changing decisions recognise the value of hearing from those children who will have to live with the consequences of their decisions?

36.   In my judgement the decision-making process was defective because the best interests of the children, not having been properly assessed, could not thereafter be properly taken into account as a primary consideration. I therefore conclude that the Inspector did not, as a matter of substance, take into account all relevant considerations in order to assess what is in the best interests of the children in this case.

37.   Having reached the conclusion set out in the previous paragraph there is no need for me to consider how the Inspector weighed the best interests of the child alongside other material planning considerations. However, as the issue is likely to reoccur in future cases I will say something about this. The Inspector sought to attach weight to the various material considerations. He attached significant weight to the consideration of education and moderate weight to the consideration of access to healthcare. In my judgement this is only a partial assessment of the best interests of the children concerned. The Inspector should have taken into account the various considerations identified as affecting the children to arrive at an overall assessment of what is in their best interests. He should then have treated this assessment as a primary consideration to be weighed in the balance alongside other material considerations. The significance of the different considerations contributing to the overall assessment of best interests, and the impact of these considerations on the children concerned, will naturally influence any decision about whether or not other material considerations are capable of outweighing the best interests of the child. However by treating each consideration relevant to the best interests determination separately, the Inspector undermined the intended effect of the best interests principle (discussed above at paragraphs 25 and 26), and failed to give proper recognition to the cumulative impact of best interests considerations. If the matter had fallen to be decided on this issue, I would have concluded that the best interests of the child had not been properly taken into account.

The Secretary of State's Decision

38.   Apart from some minor points of difference the Secretary of State agreed with the Inspector's findings. For this reason, I conclude that the Secretary of State did not, as a matter of substance, take into account all relevant considerations that should have been taken into account in order to assess what is in the best interests of the children concerned. I further conclude that the decision-making process adopted by the Secretary of State was defective because the best interests of the children concerned, not having been properly determined, could not be properly taken into account as a primary consideration.

Additional comments

39.   It is settled planning law that where the court is asked to review a planning decision this is to be conducted on the basis of *Wednesbury* unreasonableness. The parameters of this sort of judicial review are well-established. The court will confine itself to a review of the correctness of the decision-making process, and will only interfere with the decision on the merits if the decision may be said to be irrational. The authorities are well known (eg *Tesco Stores v The Environment Secretary* [1995] 1 WLR 759).

40.   A new basis of review has emerged which addresses the possibility of human rights violation by public authorities based on the principle of proportionality. The contours of proportionality may be derived from the decision of the House of Lords in *Huang v Secretary of State for the Home Department; Kashmiri v Secretary of State for the Home Office* [2007] UKHL 11. It is widely acknowledged that this is a different basis of review than the *Wednesbury* unreasonableness/irrationality approach. It enables the court to conduct a much more searching examination of the way in which a decision-maker reaches a decision. It is a more rigorous form of review which is justified by the importance of human rights to individuals and to communities.

41.   The Courts are a vital bulwark of children's human rights. With this in mind, and having regard to the importance of fundamental rights, I see no reason why proportionality review should not be the practice of the courts in planning cases involving children's human rights. If the evidence were otherwise, and I had been required to determine whether the best interests of the child had been properly taken into account alongside other considerations, I would have been very open to argument that the proportionality principle should have governed my decision.

42.   Finally, there is an obvious gap in planning guidance. The Secretary of State should, as a matter of urgency, prepare guidance for planning authorities on the determination of the best interests of the child and how this is to be taken into account in planning decisions. I would respectfully suggest that the propositions I have set out in my judgment might provide some insight into the content of any such guidance.

Conclusion

43.   For the reasons given above I allow the appeal. Accordingly:

(i)   The decision of the Secretary of State will be set aside.
(ii)   Case remitted to the Secretary of State for reconsideration.

17

Commentary on *Government of the RSA & Ors v Grootboom & Ors*

AOIFE NOLAN

I. Introduction

Grootboom is probably the best-known socio-economic rights decision.[1] In it, the Constitutional Court engaged with the complex and highly politicised issue of housing in post-Apartheid South Africa, a society of gross inequality, and adopted a model of judicial assessment of state compliance with socio-economic rights—reasonableness review—that has had enormous comparative[2] and international influence.[3] While the impact of the decision in terms of advancing enjoyment of the constitutional right to have access to adequate housing was limited and did not fully resolve the situation faced by the entire community who brought the case,[4] the ruling is regarded as a key judicial refutation (indeed, perhaps *the* key judicial refutation) of long-standing—and incorrect—assertions about the non-justiciability of socio-economic rights.[5] However, *Grootboom* has not been lauded as a *children's* socio-economic rights decision. Rather, the Constitutional Court was criticised for its failure to adequately reflect a constitutional schema within which children's rights appeared to impose more direct and immediate obligations on the state than those of others. The rewritten judgment addresses this criticism head-on, putting children's rights back at heart of the *Grootboom* decision.

---

[1] *Government of the RSA & Ors v Grootboom & Ors* [2000] ZACC 19. Unlike other well known cases where children's socio-economic rights were at issue (for instance, *Brown et al v Board of Education of Topeka et al*, 347 US 483 (1954) ('*Brown I*'), *Grootboom* was decided expressly on the basis of socio-economic rights standards.

[2] For more on the comparative influence of the reasonableness review standard in an African context, see D Chirwa and L Chenwi, *The Protection of Economic, Social and Cultural Rights in Africa* (Cambridge, Cambridge University Press, 2016).

[3] See, eg, Art 8(4) of the Optional Protocol to the International Covenant on Economic, Social and Cultural Rights.

[4] See M Langford, 'Housing Rights Litigation: *Grootboom* and Beyond' in M Langford, B Cousins, J Dugard and T Madlingozi (eds), *Socio-economic Rights in South Africa: Symbols or Substance?* (New York, Cambridge University Press, 2014) 63.

[5] For a discussion of such assertions, see A Nolan, B Porter and M Langford, *The Justiciability of Social and Economic Rights: An Updated Appraisal*, NYU Centre for Human Rights and Global Justice Working Paper Series No 15/2007.

II. The *Grootboom* Case

At the time of *Grootboom*, South Africa was experiencing a housing crisis, largely attributable to the apartheid policy of influx control which sought to limit African occupation of urban areas[6] and the critical housing shortage inherited by the new democratic government.[7]

Government of the RSA & Ors v Grootboom & Ors concerned 900 persons (of whom 510 were children) who had been evicted from private land onto which they had moved due to the 'intolerable conditions under which they were living while waiting in the queue for their turn to be allocated low-cost housing'[8] and they subsequently settled on a sports field. The community approached the Cape of Good Hope High Court seeking an order directing the state to, inter alia, provide adequate and sufficient basic temporary shelter and/or housing for the applicants and their children, pending their obtaining permanent accommodation. The action centred on the constitutional right of everyone to have access to adequate *housing* and the constitutional right of children to *shelter* (sections 26[9] and 28[10] of the Final Constitution of South Africa respectively).

A. High Court Decision

With regard to 'everyone's' rights under section 26, Davis J in the High Court stated that the government had produced clear evidence that a rational housing programme had been initiated and that such programme had been designed to solve a pressing problem in the context of scarce financial resources, thus following the Constitutional Court's approach in the 1997 health rights case of *Soobramoney v The Minister of Health, Kwazulu Natal*.[11] For this reason, he concluded that it could not be said that the respondents had not taken reasonable legislative and other measures within their available resources to achieve the progressive realisation of the right to have access to adequate housing.[12]

In considering section 28(1)(c), Davis J reasoned that parents bore the primary obligation to provide shelter for their children, but that the state had an obligation to do so if

---

[6] P De Vos, 'The Right to Housing' in D Brand & C Heyns (eds), *Socio-economic Rights in South Africa* (Pretoria, PULP, 2005) 85.

[7] For an overview of housing policy prior to *Grootboom*, see S Liebenberg, *Socio-Economic Rights: Adjudication under a Transformative Constitution* (Cape Town, Juta, 2010).

[8] Per Yacoob J, Constitutional Court *Grootboom*, above n 1, para 3.

[9] '(1) Everyone has the right to have access to adequate housing. (2) The state must take reasonable legislative and other measures, within its available resources, to achieve the progressive realisation of this right. (3) No one may be evicted from their home, or have their home demolished, without an order of court made after considering all the relevant circumstances. No legislation may permit arbitrary evictions.'

[10] '(1) Every child has the right— ... (b) to family care or parental care, or to appropriate alternative care when removed from the family environment; (c) to basic nutrition, shelter, basic health care services and social services; ... (2) A child's best interests are of paramount importance in every matter concerning the child. (3) In this section "child" means a person under the age of 18 years.'

[11] *Soobramoney v The Minister of Health, Kwazulu Natal* 1998(1) SA 765(CC).

[12] *Grootboom v Oostenberg Municipality and Other* ('*Grootboom HC*'), Case No 6826/99, 17 December 1999, at 13–14.

parents could not.[13] Relying on the dictionary definition of 'shelter', Davis J continued to say that such shelter to be provided was significantly more rudimentary than a house and fell short of adequate housing.[14] He emphasised that while the provision of shelter to children should be of such a nature that their parents may join them, 'this does not mean that the parents become the bearers of a constitutional right which expressly provides that the children have such right.'[15] Davis J concluded that 'an order which enforces a child's right to shelter should take account of the need of the child to be accompanied by his or her parent. Such an approach would be in accordance with the spirit and purport of section 28 as a whole',[16] including the right to family care and the best interests principle set out in section 28(2). He pointed out that section 28(1)(c) is drafted as an unqualified constitutional right[17] and that, unlike the section 26 right to access adequate housing, the right to shelter has not been made subject to a qualification of availability of financial resources.[18] Accordingly, the question of budgetary limitations was not applicable to the determination of rights in terms of section 28(1)(c).[19]

Davis J held that, under section 28(1)(c), the applicant children were entitled to be provided with shelter, that their parents were entitled to be accommodated with their children in that shelter and that the state was obliged to provide the children, and their accompanying parents, with such shelter until the parents were able to do so.[20] He also granted a supervisory order, requiring the respondents to report back to the Court on the implementation of the order and allowing the applicants to deliver their commentary on the state's report.[21]

B. Constitutional Court Decision

In its decision 10 months later, the Constitutional Court differed from the High Court in its findings in relation to both sections 28 and 26. With regard to section 28, the respondents and amici in *Grootboom* had argued that the right enshrined in section 28(1)(c) was a more basic, attenuated form of the right set out in section 26, that the state was obliged to provide to all children on demand. The Constitutional Court rejected both this argument and the High Court's construal of section 28. The Constitutional Court stated that, on the High Court's reasoning, parents with their children have two distinct rights: the right of access to adequate housing under section 26, and a right to claim shelter on demand under section 28(1)(c). Yacoob J, who delivered the judgment, argued that this produced an anomalous result as people with children would have a direct and enforceable right to housing under section 28(1)(c), while those who have none, or whose children are adult, would not, no matter how old, disabled or otherwise deserving they may be: 'The carefully constructed

---

[13] ibid at 16.
[14] ibid.
[15] ibid at 19.
[16] ibid.
[17] ibid at 21.
[18] ibid at 22.
[19] ibid.
[20] ibid at 26–27.
[21] ibid at 27.

constitutional scheme for progressive realisation of socio-economic rights would make lit-tle sense if it could be trumped in every case by the rights of children to get shelter from the state on demand.'[22] The Constitutional Court seemed particularly concerned at the notion that children could become stepping-stones to housing for their parents instead of being valued in their own right.[23]

With regard to the relationship between section 28 and section 26, the Court stated that the obligation created by section 28(1)(c) can properly be ascertained only in the context of the rights and, in particular, the obligations created by sections 25(5), 26 and 27 of the Constitution.[24] Having rejected the view that the Constitution drew a distinction between 'housing' on the one hand and 'shelter' as a rudimentary form of housing on the other,[25] the Constitutional Court ruled that there was 'an evident overlap between the rights created by Sections 26 and 27 and those conferred on children by Section 28'.[26] This overlap was not consistent with the notion that section 28(1)(c) creates separate and independent rights for children and their parents.[27]

The Court held that it followed from section 26(1)(b) that the Constitution contem-plates that a child has the right to parental or family care in the first place, and the right to alternative appropriate care only where that is lacking:

> Through legislation and the common law, the obligation to provide shelter in ss (1)(c) is imposed primarily on the parents or family and only alternatively on the state. The state thus incurs the obligation to provide shelter to those children, for example, who are removed from their families.[28]

This passage suggests that section 28(1)(c) does not create any primary state obligation to provide shelter (or basic nutrition, basic health care services or social services) on demand to parents and their children if children are being cared for by their parents or families.

With regard to the obligation owed by the state in relation to children who are being cared for by their parents or families, the Constitutional Court stated that the state must provide the legal and administrative infrastructure necessary to ensure that children are accorded the protection contemplated by section 28:

> This obligation would normally be fulfilled by passing laws and creating enforcement mechanisms for the maintenance of children, their protection from maltreatment, abuse, neglect or degrada-tion, and the prevention of other forms of abuse of children mentioned in s 28.[29]

The state is also required to fulfil its obligations to provide families with access to land, housing and health care, food, water and social security in terms of sections 25, 26 and 27.

The Constitutional Court's conclusions in relation to the positive obligations imposed by section 26 were more cheering, albeit not from a child-specific perspective.[30] Having

---

[22] *Grootboom*, above n 1, para 71.
[23] ibid.
[24] ibid at para 74. S 25 sets out the right to property, while S 27 sets out rights related to health care, food and water and social security.
[25] ibid at para 73.
[26] ibid at para 74.
[27] ibid.
[28] ibid at para 77. See also ibid at para 79.
[29] ibid at para 77.
[30] For the Court's findings vis-à-vis negative obligations, see *Grootboom*, above n 1, para 34.

rejected the notion of a minimum core obligation on the state to provide a basic level of services to every individual in need (which had been argued by the amici),[31] the Court held that the real question in a challenge based on a failure to fulfil the positive duties under section 26(2) was whether the legislative and other measures taken by the state were 'reasonable'. In specifying the criteria for such, the Court made clear that it required more of state programmes, that they be rational.[32] The Court held that the state had failed to satisfy its obligation under section 26(2) to devise and implement, within its available resources, a comprehensive and co-ordinated programme to progressively realise the right of access to adequate housing. This was due to the fact that the state housing programme failed to make reasonable provision within its available resources for people in the Cape Metropolitan area with no access to land, no roof over their heads, and who were living in intolerable conditions or crisis situations.[33]

The Court's decision in *Grootboom* in relation to section 28 was the subject of much criticism. It was asserted, inter alia, that the judgment sent the message that children's claims do not have to be accorded priority,[34] and that it limited the state's obligation under section 28 to those children who lack a family environment. This might result in (a) a disproportionately large proportion of state socio-economic support for children having to be channelled towards foster grants or subsidies for such children, and (b) encouraging parents to abandon their responsibilities and leave their children at the doorstep of the state.[35] Certainly, the Court adopted an approach that was a significant departure from the ordinary understanding of the wording of section 28 in the context of the constitutional schema more generally.

The Constitutional Court has subsequently responded to these criticisms, to make clear that its construal of section 28 did not mean that 'the state incurs no obligation in relation to children who are being cared for by their parents or families'[36] and that 'the state is obliged to ensure that children are accorded the protection contemplated by section 28 that arises when the implementation of the right to parental or family care is lacking'.[37] Thus, section 28 is not limited to instances in which children lack a family environment or are physically separated from their families. However, the Court did not change its reasoning in *Grootboom* so as to conclude that children had a direct individual entitlement to services in circumstances where their parents could not afford them.

[31] See para 10 of General Comment No 3 on the nature of States parties obligations (art 2(1) of the Covenant) UN doc E/1991/21, for an explanation of the concept of the minimum core.
[32] The Constitutional Court's criteria for a 'reasonable' government programme to give effect to s 26 are set out in paras 39–44 of the judgment.
[33] *Grootboom*, above n 1, para 52.
[34] J Sloth-Nielsen, 'What is Left for the Right? Children's Right to Social Services, Social Security, and the Primary Prevention of Child Abuse in South Africa: some Conclusions in the Aftermath of Grootboom' in P Van der Auweraert, T De Pelsmaeker, J Sarkin and J Vande Lanotte (eds), *Social, Economic and Cultural Rights: An Appraisal of Current European and International Developments* (Antwerp, MAKLU, 2002) 315 at 336.
[35] J Sloth-Nielsen, 'The Child's Rights to Social Services, the Right to Social Security, and Primary Prevention of Child Abuse: Some Conclusions in the Aftermath of Grootboom' (2001) 17 *SAJHR* 210 at 229–30.
[36] *Minister of Health and Others v Treatment Action Campaign and Others (No 2)* (CCT8/02) [2002] ZACC 15, para 77.
[37] ibid, para 79.

III. The Rewritten Judgment

Pillay's rewritten judgment immediately identifies the core issue from a child rights perspective post-*Grootboom:* the relationship between the general socio-economic rights protected in the Constitution and those specifically held by children.[38] This is an appropriate starting point given that it was a strongly contrasting approaches in terms of defining that relationship which resulted in the very different rulings of the High Court and the Constitutional Court in *Grootboom*. The rewritten judgment implicitly justifies this approach by emphasising the high proportion of children amongst the Wallacadene community, as well as by highlighting the particular vulnerability of children vis-à-vis other members of society and the especially important implications that the realisation (or not) of their socio-economic rights will have in terms of their life chances.[39] While Pillay is in agreement with the Constitutional Court's findings with regard to Section 26, she disagrees that section 28(1)(c) does not create a right to shelter for children that is independent of the general right to have access to adequate housing in section 26(1). In doing so, Pillay reaches the same point as the High Court though adopting different reasoning to get there.

The rewritten judgment starts by asking the crucial question of why, if section 28 does not furnish children with a right to shelter, separate to and different from the general right of access to adequate housing, was it included in the Constitution? Like Davis J in the High Court, the author focuses on the difference in wording between the sections and the lack of express qualification of section 28(1)(c) rights in terms of resources or progressive realisation. She argues that, with section 28(1)(c), the state intended to establish a 'floor or minimum level of socio-economic provision, below which parents in the first place, and the state in the alternative, cannot go'[40] and that this provision for children reflects their special vulnerability as a social group and highlights their status as bearers of rights within the Constitution.[41]

The rewritten judgment also addresses head-on the Constitutional Court's 'child rights as trumps or stepping stones' claims. Again looking to the wording of section 28, as supported by international law sources,[42] Pillay argues that 'shelter' and 'adequate housing' are not synonymous and that 'an immediate and urgent right to shelter for children' does not entitle parents to jump the housing queue for adequate housing;[43] rather it provides a guarantee to children (who the author contestably describes as 'the *most* vulnerable members of society')[44] that 'their basic need to be protected against the elements will be met until more permanent accommodation is available'.[45]

---

[38] Rewritten judgment, para 1.

[39] For a consideration of the particular position of children relative to other social groups in relation to socio-economic rights, see A Nolan, *Socio-economic Rights, Democracy and the Courts* (Oxford, Hart Publishing, 2011) Ch 1.

[40] Rewritten judgment, para 12.

[41] ibid.

[42] ibid para 13.

[43] ibid para 14.

[44] Emphasis added. For more on this point, see Nolan above n 39.

[45] Rewritten judgment, para 14.

Pillay is to be commended for reiterating the different purposes of sections 28(1)(b) and (c) and highlighting the crucial importance of supporting families to meet children's socio-economic rights-related needs. As the judgment notes, this is necessary in order to ensure that parents struggling to make ends meet are not pushed to abandon their parental responsibilities to state institutions and to ensure that poverty does not give rise to parental neglect or abuse resulting in the break-up of families in order to ensure child protection.[46] This was an issue that was inadequately considered in the Constitutional Court's judgment.

The rewritten judgment also includes a child rights issue that was not considered by either the High Court or the Constitutional Court, specifically that mediation did not take place and highlighting the importance that mediation should allow for the views of the children to be heard and considered, as far as is feasible.[47] In doing so, Pillay cites Article 12 of the Convention on the Rights of the Child (CRC). While this is a desirable addition to the judgment from a child rights perspective, it is notable that the child's right to be heard is not included in the 1996 Constitution and that, as a result, the courts' failure to address children's participation rights beyond specific contexts is not particularly surprising[48] (albeit that they could have done so through section 39 which requires the courts to consider international law including the CRC). However, awareness of child participation rights has increased significantly since 2000 (as has the Constitutional Court's jurisprudence on 'meaningful engagement' between parties in the context of socio-economic rights cases)[49] and such a statement might well appear if *Grootboom* were decided now. Pillay's commitment to ensuring children's ability to participate in matters affecting them to the greatest extent possible is reflected in her excellent child-friendly judgment, which will serve as an important human rights education resource for children in South Africa and beyond.

IV. Conclusion

The housing crisis (comprising backlogs, evictions, removals and inadequate housing, amongst other issues) is still a reality in South Africa.[50] From a child rights perspective, the UN Committee on the Rights of the Child expressed concern in 2016 that the lack of affordable and adequate housing was resulting in the creation of informal settlements, and the practice of forced evictions from such settlements persisted.[51] Unlike at the time of the *Grootboom* decision, judicial application and enforcement of housing rights is now a common occurrence: in a 2016 report, the Socio-economic Rights Institute, a leading

---

[46] Rewritten judgment, paras 12 and 18.

[47] Rewritten judgment, para 8.

[48] See ss 28(1)(h) and 35.

[49] See, eg, B Ray, *Engaging with Social Rights: Procedure, Participation and Democracy in South Africa's Second Wave* (Cambridge: Cambridge University Press, 2016).

[50] L Chenwi, 'Implementation of Housing Rights in South Africa: Approaches and Strategies' (2015) 24 *Journal of Law and Social Policy* 68, 69.

[51] CRC, Concluding Observations: South Africa (2016), UN Doc, para 57(b). The Committee called on the state to take effective measures to ensure access by all children to adequate and affordable housing. Ibid at para 58(b).

South African housing rights NGO, stated that access to adequate housing enshrined in section 26 is 'undoubtedly the most fiercely contested and frequently litigated socio-economic right'.[52] It is thus clear that children's housing rights remain a burning issue in a South African context—and so too does the role of the courts in relation to such rights. Without suggesting that law as mediated by judges can constitute a panacea to complex and multifaceted problems like homelessness and inadequate housing supply, one might well wonder whether things might be different—for families with children at least—if the Constitutional Court adopted an approach closer to that of the rewritten judgment back in 2000.

---

[52] SERI, 'Evictions and Alternative Accommodation in South Africa 2000–2016: An analysis of the jurisprudence and implications for local government' (2016), available at www.seri-sa.org/images/Jurisprudence_Revised_2016_Final_to_print.pdf, 3.

Constitutional Court of South Africa

The Government of the Republic of South Africa & Rs v Grootboom & Ors

Pillay J:

Dissenting judgment

Introduction

1.   The inclusion of a range of justiciable socio-economic rights is one of our Constitution's most celebrated features. The provisions enshrining rights of access to healthcare services, sufficient food and water, social security and adequate housing are a reminder of the profound toll that apartheid took on South African lives. For black people in South Africa, apartheid meant not just the deprivation of their political freedoms—their dignity, liberty and access to justice; it also entailed systematic socio-economic exploitation. The Constitution's socio-economic provisions are an acknowledgement of that fact and an attempt to remedy it. For the first time, this Court has been required to pronounce on the interpretation and application of the right of access to adequate housing in section 26(1). This right is raised alongside children's right to shelter, protected in section 28(1)(c). Thus, the case also invites the Court to consider, for the first time, the relationship between the general socio-economic rights protected in the Constitution and those specifically held by children. For these reasons, this case is a highly significant one in our constitutional history.

2.   For the group of people who initiated this case, the respondents before this Court, the case is important in a much more direct way. For them, this case is about the conditions in which they live, their personal safety, health and comfort. It will determine where they will sleep, cook, eat and communicate with those people closest to them. The majority of the respondents[1] in this case are children. Of these 510 children, 276 are infants. These children are amongst the most vulnerable members of our society. The extent to which their socio-economic rights are realised will have a deep and lasting impact upon their lives. The respondents had been living in an informal settlement called Wallacedene, located in Oostenberg on the eastern margin of the Cape Metropolitan area, for varying periods of time. Conditions at Wallacedene were appalling. The respondents had no access to water, refuse removal or sewerage services. Only five per cent of the shacks had electricity. The settlement was partly waterlogged and perilously close to a major road. Both the safety and health

---

[1]   510 children and 390 adults.

of those living at Wallacedene—particularly the children who are especially susceptible to these dangers—were placed at risk by the conditions under which they were living. From September 1998, the respondents began to leave Wallacedene in the hope that they could find somewhere better to live. They moved onto a plot of unoccupied land and called the settlement 'New Rust', 'rust' meaning 'rest' in Afrikaans. But the land was privately-owned and ear-marked for a housing development. The respondents were evicted. Some are now sheltering in a community hall, others in a sports field. They are, as Davis J put it in the High Court judgment, 'truly homeless'.[2] Relying on their rights in sections 26(1) and 28(1) (c) of the Constitution, they have approached the courts for a remedy to their predicament.

3.   The majority, per Yacoob J, find that the housing programme at issue in this case is unreasonable because it contains no provision for temporary relief for people in desperate need, that is those 'who have no access to land, no roof over their heads, for people who are living in intolerable conditions and for people who are in crisis because of natural disasters such as floods and fires, or because their homes are under threat of demolition'.[3] I am in agreement with this conclusion. However, in the process of reaching this conclusion, the majority judgment also concludes that section 28(1)(c) does not create a children's right to shelter that is independent of the general right of access to adequate housing in section 26(1). I find I am unable to agree with this aspect of the decision for the reasons set out below.

Facts and Background

4.   The facts are set out in detail in the judgment of Yacoob J. I summarise the main points for ease of reference here. The first respondent, Mrs Irene Grootboom, brought the application before the High Court on behalf of all the respondents. The appellants represent those responsible for housing at all levels of government. As noted above, the respondents had all lived for varying periods of time in an informal housing settlement called Wallacedene. Many of the respondents were on a waiting list for low-cost housing. Some of them had been on the list for as long as seven years. The respondents' living conditions in Wallacedene were deplorable and this drove them to leave the settlement. However, the land they moved on to was privately owned and the owner began eviction proceedings. The respondents did not vacate the land after the first eviction order as they had nowhere else to go. They could not return to Wallacedene where their shacks had been occupied by others in need of a place to live.

5.   Renewed eviction proceedings resulted in an order for eviction to take place on 19 May 1999. The Magistrate's Court granting the order directed that mediation take place between the parties so that alternative land could be identified for the temporary occupation of the respondents. No mediation took place and the respondents were evicted from their homes in New Rust on 18 May 1999, a day early. Shacks were bulldozed and possessions destroyed, a process that must have been extremely frightening for those present at the time and which

---

[2] The High Court judgment is reported as *Grootboom v Oostenberg Municipality and Others* 2000 (3) BCLR 277 (C).

[3] At pars. 52 and 69 of the majority judgment.

showed a lack of respect for the dignity of all the occupants of the New Rust settlement. Yacoob J notes in his judgment for the majority that the evictions were conducted prematurely and in an inhumane manner which was 'reminiscent of apartheid-style evictions'. This is a view with which I am in complete agreement. However, the validity of the eviction order itself has not been challenged by the respondents.

6.   Following their eviction, the respondents moved onto a sports field adjacent to Wallacedene but their temporary plastic structures failed to provide protection against the winter rains. They instituted an urgent application before the High Court for the protection of their rights as set out in sections 26(1) and 28(1)(c). The matter was set down for hearing at a later date. In the interim, Josman AJ ordered the appellants to make the Wallacedene Community Hall available for the temporary accommodation of the respondent children, each child to be accompanied by an adult or parent if the child required parental supervision. The matter was then heard by Davis J who handed down judgment on 17 December 1999. It is that judgment which was appealed before this Court and which the majority has set aside. Davis J held that, as there was a rational housing programme designed to progressively realise the right of access to adequate housing in place, there was no violation of section 26. I agree with the majority that this aspect of the High Court judgment should be set aside. Davis J went on to find a violation of section 28(1)(c) and, unlike the majority, this is a conclusion I have also reached.

7.   Before setting out my reasons for these conclusions, it is appropriate to highlight the complex circumstances in which the case has arisen. As noted by Yacoob J, there is a critical housing shortage in the country. This shortage is a legacy of apartheid. Under the racist system of 'influx control', people classified as African were formally excluded from the Western Cape and provision for family housing for African people in this part of the country was frozen in the 1960s. At the same time, dispossession of farming land from African people in the rural areas meant that they continued to move to urban areas in search of work. Informal housing settlements began to mushroom around the Cape Peninsula. The housing shortage is a formidable problem which the new, democratically-elected government has sought to address over the past six years. The housing programme which is currently in place has significant merit and the complexity of the problem should not be under-estimated. The conditions under which respondents have been living are dreadful but they represent a very small percentage of people living in similar conditions who are also in need of housing. Like the respondents, these people have been on a waiting list for housing for varying periods of time. However, it is also important to bear in mind that the respondents are no longer in any kind of housing settlement—formal or informal. It is unclear whether they knew that the land they were moving on to was privately owned. But it is undisputed that they now find themselves living either on the Wallacedene sports field or in the adjacent community hall in a situation of extreme vulnerability.

8.   Another aspect of this case worth mentioning at the outset relates to the issue of mediation. It is a great pity that the mediation ordered by the magistrate did not take place as much of the hardship resulting from the manner in which the eviction took place could have been avoided through mediation. Furthermore, in cases such as these, where the rights of children are implicated, it is important that mediation or engagement of any kind between the parties allows for the views of the children to be heard and considered, as far

as is feasible. This participatory right is protected under Article 12 of the UN Convention on the Rights of the Child:

> 1. States Parties shall assure to the child who is capable of forming his or her own views the right to express those views freely in all matters affecting the child, the views of the child being given due weight in accordance with the age and maturity of the child.

As the reasons for mediation not taking place here are unclear, there is not much more to be said on the matter. However, it is worth emphasising for future mediation processes with respect to evictions that the views of children should be sought and considered together with those of the adults involved.

Section 28

9.   Relevant parts of section 28 provide:

> (1) Every child has the right …

> (b)   to family care or parental care, or to appropriate alternative care when removed from the family environment;

> (c)   to basic nutrition, shelter, basic health care services and social services …

> (2) A child's best interests are of paramount importance in every matter concerning a child.

The majority have held that '[t]he obligation created by section 28(1)(c) can properly be ascertained only in the context of the rights and, in particular, the obligations created by sections 25(5),[4] 26(2) and 27(2)[5] of the Constitution'.[6] The majority judgment rejects the finding of Davis J in the High Court that section 28(1)(c) creates distinct socio-economic rights for children and that these rights are not subject to the qualifications or internal limitations present in the general socio-economic rights clauses. As acknowledged by Davis J, it would not be in the best interests of the children to be separated from their parents and the result of the application of section 28(1)(c) would be that the respondent children are entitled to shelter with their parents. Thus, Yacoob J states that the High Court's reading of the relevant sections produces the perplexing result that people with children have an immediately enforceable right to shelter under section 28(1)(c) as well as a right of access to adequate housing under section 26, which is subject to the limitations of progressive realisation and availability of resources. According to the majority:

> The carefully constructed constitutional scheme for progressive realisation of socio-economic rights would make little sense if it could be trumped in every case by the rights of children to get shelter from the state on demand. Moreover, there is an obvious danger. Children could become stepping stones to housing for their parents instead of being valued for who they are.[7]

---

[4] 'The state must take reasonable legislative and other measures, within its available resources, to foster conditions which enable citizens to gain access to land on an equitable basis'.

[5] Sections 26(1) and 27(1) are identically worded: 'The state must take reasonable legislative and other measures, within its available resources, to achieve the progressive realisation of this right.'

[6] At par. 74 of the majority judgment.

[7] At par. 71 of the majority judgment.

These are important concerns, which I address further below. Nevertheless, it is my opinion that the majority's approach to the interpretation of section 28 is problematic for several reasons, to which I now turn.

10.   The majority judgment raises the question of what the purpose of section 28(1)(c) is. If it does not provide children with a right to shelter, separate to and different from the general right of access to adequate housing in section 26, why was it included in the Constitution? The majority suggest that section 28(1)(c) exists to provide details of the kind of care required under section 28(1)(b) when children are removed from the family environment. According to Yacoob J, these two sections must be read together. The obligation to provide children with shelter rests primarily on the parents and only alternatively on the state. Section 28 'does not create any primary state obligation to provide shelter on demand to parents and their children if children are being cared for by their parents or families'.[8] Rather, the obligation to provide shelter applies when children are, for instance, removed from their families.[9] The state does have obligations with respect to the socio-economic welfare of children who live with their parents but these are to be fulfilled through the general socio-economic provisions in the Constitution—the rights of everyone to have access to adequate housing, health care services, food, water and social security on a programmatic basis and according to the resources available to the state under sections 26 and 27.[10]

11.   But this narrow reading of section 28(1)(c) is not consistent with the protection of children's rights within the Constitution. Unlike the general socio-economic rights clauses in the Constitution, section 28(1)(c) contains no internal limitations related to resources or the progressive realisation of the right. Furthermore, the socio-economic rights protected in the section are restricted forms of the rights to housing, adequate health care, sufficient food and social security mentioned elsewhere in the Constitution. The section acknowledges that, where other sections in the Constitution are aimed at progressively realising fuller claims to socio-economic rights,[11] section 28(1)(c) is intended to prioritise the immediate realisation of a more attenuated form of these rights for children. As stated by Pierre De Vos:

> [T]he Constitution enunciates the rights of children as clear, near-absolute core entitlements that are necessary to provide the basic subsistence needs of children, the most vulnerable group in any state. These rights have been worded in a precise and restrictive way, first by referring to 'basic' nutrition and health care services, and secondly by restricting the right holders to children.[12]

12.   In light of this, it is inescapable that the drafters of section 28(1)(c) intended to spell out, with respect to children, a floor or minimum level of socio-economic provision, below which parents in the first place, and the state in the alternative, cannot go. This provision for children reflects their special vulnerability as a social group and highlights their status as bearers of rights within the Constitution:

> Children as bearers of rights, after all, are different. Not only are they physically and economically vulnerable and powerless (as may be the case with other recipients, of international human rights

---

[8]   At par. 77 of the majority judgment.
[9]   Ibid.
[10]   At par. 78 of the majority judgment.
[11]   Sections 26(1) and 27(1).
[12]   'Pious Wishes or Directly Enforceable Human Rights? Socio-Economic Rights in South Africa's 1996 Constitution' 1997 (13) *South African Journal on Human Rights* 67 at 88.

protection, such as refugees, ethnic or racial minorities, arrested persons, and so on), but they are also politically voiceless; they do not, and cannot, constitute a political constituency, able to gain ground through political action.[13]

By finding that the basic socio-economic claims of children living with their parents are subject to progressive realisation by the state and restricted by the resources available to the state, irrespective of whether the parents are able to provide for the essential needs of their children, the majority have read into section 28(1)(c) limitations that are simply not present in the text or warranted by the South African context. The reform of childcare legislation in this country in the mid to late 1990s was motivated by a desire to move away from an approach that was overly interventionist and that favoured the removal of children from family structures to state institutions.[14] The interventionist approach fails to adequately acknowledge the extent to which poverty, rather than parental neglect and abuse, is a driving factor in children's maltreatment. An approach that does not make it a priority to provide parents with the material assistance they need to meet the essential socio-economic needs of their children does nothing to ensure that families remain together.

13.   The concerns that the interpretation proposed here effectively means that children's socio-economic rights trump those of adults, however vulnerable those adults may be and that children could come to be seen as vehicles through which parents can 'jump the queue' for housing provision, are important and need to be addressed. It is important to note that the right protected in section 28(1)(c) is a right to shelter, not to adequate housing. The majority have held that there is no real distinction between housing and shelter in the Constitution.[15] I cannot agree. The term 'shelter' in section 28(1)(c) must be read in the context of the surrounding terms, all of which refer to a basic form of fuller socio-economic rights protected in the Constitution. There was no need to include the word 'basic' as a qualification of 'shelter' as shelter *is* a basic form of housing. This interpretation is supported by General Comment 4 on the right to housing issued by the Committee on Economic, Social and Cultural Rights. The state has not ratified the International Convention for Economic, Social and Cultural Rights (ICESCR). South Africa is, thus, not bound by the provisions of the ICESCR but, because it has signed the ICESCR, it has a customary international law obligation not to defeat the object and purpose of the treaty. Moreover, section 39 of the Constitution requires that courts take both binding and non-binding international law into account when interpreting the Bill of Rights.[16] Thus, the ICESCR and General Comments of the Committee on Economic, Social and Cultural Rights, although not binding on the state, are nonetheless important tools in the interpretation of sections 26 and 28.

14.   Whilst the Committee acknowledges that certain forms of shelter could constitute adequate housing for the purposes of the ICESCR, it also notes that:

> [T]he right to housing should not be interpreted in a narrow or restrictive sense which equates it with, for example, the shelter provided by merely having a roof over one's head or views shelter

---

[13] J Sloth-Nielsen 'Chicken soup or chainsaws: some implications of the constitutionalisation of children's rights in South Africa' (1996) *Acta Juridica* 6 at 6–7.

[14] South African Law Commission First Issue Paper on the Review of the Child Care Act (Issue Paper No 13) May 1998 (Chapter 1).

[15] At par. 73 of the majority judgment.

[16] See also *S v Makwanyane and Another* 1995 (3) SA 391 (CC), 1995 (6) BCLR 665 (CC) at par. 35.

exclusively as a commodity. Rather it should be seen as the right to live somewhere in security, peace and dignity.

According to the General Comment, 'whether particular forms of shelter can be considered to constitute "adequate housing" for the purposes of the Covenant' depends on a range of factors including legal security of tenure, affordability and cultural adequacy.[17] Thus, whilst adequate housing always includes the provision of shelter, shelter does not necessarily amount to adequate housing. An immediate and urgent right to shelter for children does not entitle parents to jump the housing queue for adequate housing. It merely provides a safety net for the most vulnerable members of society, children—an assurance that their basic need to be protected against the elements will be met until more permanent accommodation is available.

15.   An approach that recognises that the state's obligations are not limited to circumstances in which children are removed from the care of their parents is also consistent with the principal international instrument dealing with children's rights, the Convention on the Rights of the Child (CRC), which South Africa ratified in 1995. Section 28 is one of the means through which the state is attempting to meet its obligations under this Convention. The CRC is therefore a key resource for interpreting section 28. Article 27(1) of the CRC deals with the right of every child to an adequate standard of living. As indicated in the majority judgment, Article 27(2) places the primary responsibility to secure 'the conditions of living necessary for the child's development' on the parent(s) or those with parental responsibility for the child. However, Article 27(2) limits this obligation to what is within the abilities and financial capacities of the primary duty-bearers. Furthermore, Article 27(3) provides:

> States Parties, in accordance with national conditions and within their means, shall take appropriate measures to assist parents and others responsible for the child to implement this right and shall in case of need provide material assistance and support programmes, particularly with regard to nutrition, clothing and housing.

The assistance referred to in this Article clearly applies both to situations where a child has been removed from the parents' care and in circumstances where the child remains with the parent(s) but where they are unable to provide nutrition, clothing and housing without material state assistance. The latter situation perfectly describes the plight of the respondent parents and children with respect to housing in this case. There is a strong imperative in the CRC to assist parents who do not have the resources to provide for the material needs of their children.[18]

16.   On this interpretation, sections 28(1)(b) and 28(1)(c) fulfil different purposes and are to be read independently of each other. Section 28(1)(b) indicates that parents or families are primarily responsible for their children but that state care is to be made available as an alternative. Section 28(1)(c) refers to the basic rights to which every child is entitled— whether this is provided by their families or through the state. The section cannot be interpreted simply as a delineation of what a child who is removed from the family environment

---

[17] At par. 8.
[18] The right of a child to 'to know and be cared for by his or her parents' as far as is possible is protected in Article 7(1) of the CRC.

is entitled to. It is important to emphasise that 'basic nutrition, shelter, basic health care services and social services' protected under section 28(1)(c) do not equate to 'a standard of living adequate for the child's physical, mental, spiritual, moral and social development' which is referred to in Article 27(1) of the CRC. The latter is a much fuller right. Children who are removed from their families are, in the first place, entitled to the basic, unqualified level of protection described in section 28(1)(c). But this is not all they are entitled to. In the South African context, there has historically been little or no reintegration of children into a family environment once they have been placed into the care of the state.[19] It is hoped that legislative reform will lead to a change in this situation. But it is still the case that children who are removed from the family setting may be in the care of the state for long periods of time. These children are entitled to more than the most basic standard of living. They are entitled to an adequate standard of living, allowing for their full development, to the extent that the state can afford to provide it. It follows from this that, if the South African Constitution provided for the socio-economic rights of children in section 28(1)(c) alone, it would not be meeting its obligations under the CRC. But the Constitution does more than this. It also provides to 'everyone', including children, the rights of access to adequate housing, healthcare services, food, water and social security in sections 26 and 27 to be progressively realised by the state to the extent possible within its available resources.

17.   The majority judgment expresses concern that granting a distinct right to shelter to children—and by necessary implication, their parents—could have the unintended consequence of children being valued as vehicles through which to access housing rather than as worthy of love and protection in their own right. But the alternative proposed in Yacoob J's judgment, that is that section 28(1)(c) applies only in circumstances where children are removed from the family environment, may have the different, unintended consequence that parents struggling to make ends meet are pushed to abandon their parental responsibilities to state institutions, knowing that their children will at least be entitled to basic care in such institutions. Moreover, as noted by Davis J,

> [T]he children … in the present case are in fact homeless, or will be when the order granted by Josman AJ is lifted, and thus in need of shelter. The same may not always be the case with children who belong to and live with squatter families. The parent applicants in the present case are unable to provide the requisite shelter for their children, which it is their primary duty to provide. Again, the same may not always be the case.[20]

Each case will be different and will have to be decided in the context of the particular facts. In light of the circumstances of this case, the relevant constitutional provisions and international law, I have come to the conclusion that the rights of the respondent children to shelter in section 28(1)(c) have been infringed. Thus, whilst I agree with the order handed down by the majority, I would add to it the following:

Section 28(1) (c) of the Constitution requires the state to devise a housing programme that ensures the immediate realisation of the rights of all children to shelter.

[19] Inter-Ministerial Committee on Young People at Risk, *In whose Best Interests: A Report* on *Places of Safety, Schools of Industry and Reform Schools* (Department of Welfare, 1996).
[20] Supra n 4.

I include below a child friendly version of my dissenting opinion so that the many children who are affected by it and who may come to read this can fully understand the reasons for my conclusions.

Child-friendly judgment

This story is about a group of people, Mrs Grootboom and her neighbours, who do not have a proper place to live. They are a big group of people—900 altogether—and most of them are children. At the moment, some of these people are living on a sports field and others are living in a community hall. In South Africa, there are not enough proper homes for people in the cities where most people have to come to work. A proper home keeps the people who live in it safe from bad weather and gives them a space of their own to cook, eat, learn, play, sleep and be with their family. The people who have been in charge of this country for about the last six years—who are called the government—have been trying to build enough houses for everyone. But there are many people like those in this case who have been waiting for these new houses for a long time. Mrs Grootboom and the others used to live in shacks which they built themselves in a place called Wallacedene. They hoped that they would be able to move out of Wallacedene as soon as the new houses were built. But, as time went by, they found it very difficult to stay in Wallacedene. This was because they did not have water, lights and proper toilets. So they moved to another place called New Rust. But they could not stay at New Rust because houses were being built there for other people who were also waiting to move to a new place. Mrs Grootboom and the others were forced to leave New Rust and their shacks were destroyed. They could not go back to Wallacedene because other people had moved there and there was no more space.

In South Africa, there is a very important book called the Constitution that tells us how to make sure that everyone is treated fairly, and the courts make sure that the rules in the Constitution are followed. Mrs Grootboom and the others have asked this Court to use the rules in the Constitution to order the government to give them a clean place to live where they will be protected from wind and rain while they wait for proper houses to be built. All of the judges who make decisions in this Court agree that the government must give Mrs Grootboom and the others a place to live while they wait for houses to be built. This is because the Constitution rule-book says that everyone should have a proper house. The judges all agree that the government is trying to make sure that everyone who needs it will get a house. But the government also needs to make sure that when people like Mrs Grootboom are pushed out of their homes, they have a safe and warm place to stay while they wait for a house.

Our Constitution also says that if children can't have a nice house right now, they should at least be living in a place that will keep them safe, warm and dry in the meantime. And, because children need their parents there to take care of them, it is best for children and their parents to stay together. Mrs Grootboom and the others in this case say that the place to keep the children safe, warm and dry should be big enough so that the grown-ups who look after them—mums, dads, grandparents—can live with the children. Most of the judges don't think that the rules allow them to give special treatment to grown-ups who have children. They are worried that this would be unfair to people who don't have children. They think that it is important to wait your turn. I disagree with the other judges. I think that the Constitution says that children are extra-important and must be protected because they are not as powerful as grown-ups. Children are not as powerful as grown-ups because they are not very big or strong, they do not have their own money and they cannot help to decide who runs the country.

Most of the judges are also worried that, if children are given a place to stay right now, people will think of children as a way of getting a house and will not love these children just for who they are. I do not agree with this because I think that parents want and love their children but sometimes need help to take care of them. The extra protection for children in our Constitution is there to help them and their children.

18

Commentary on *Valsamis v Greece*

JENNY DRISCOLL

I. Introduction

Valsamis is a case in which the apparent triviality of the facts and of the punishment giving rise to the application belie the complexity and importance of the principles and competing rights which are engaged. The Valsamis family were Jehovah's Witnesses. Their daughter, Victoria, was 12 at the time of the incident. At her parents' request, Victoria had been exempted from school religious education lessons and attendance at Orthodox mass. The additional request that Victoria be excused from attending the National Day Parade (commemorating the outbreak of war between Greece and Italy in 1940) in October 1992, on the basis that pacifism was central to her religious beliefs, was refused. She did not attend and was given a one-day suspension from school as a punishment. The applicants (Victoria and her parents) alleged breach of Protocol 1, Article 2 (P1-2) of the European Convention on Human Rights (ECHR) in respect of the parents and of Articles 9 and 3 in relation to Victoria herself. The claim in relation to ECHR Article 3, which prohibits 'torture or inhuman and degrading treatment or punishment', was dismissed unanimously in both the original and revised judgments on the basis that the minimum level of severity required for a breach was not met, and will not be further considered.

P1-2 was drafted at a time when the protection of religious freedom was an acute concern after the events of the Holocaust during World War II.[1] It provides that 'No person shall be denied the right to education' and stipulates that 'In the exercise of any functions which it assumes in relation to education and to teaching, the State shall respect the right of parents to ensure such education and teaching in conformity with their own religious and philosophical beliefs.' There are therefore circumstances in which it may conflict with Article 14 of the UN Convention on the Rights of the Child (CRC), which instructs states to 'respect the right of the child to freedom of thought, conscience and religion', and ECHR Article 9(1) which reads:

> Everyone has the right to freedom of thought, conscience and religion; this right includes freedom to change his religion or belief and freedom, either alone or in community with others and in public or private, to manifest his religion or belief in worship, teaching, practice and observance.

---

[1] U Kilkelly, The Child and the European Convention on Human Rights (Ashgate, Dartmouth, 1999).

Under Article 9(2),

> Freedom to manifest one's religion or beliefs shall be subject only to such limitations as are prescribed by law and are necessary in a democratic society in the interests of public safety, for the protection of public order, health or morals, or for the protection of the rights and freedoms of others.

An identical provision is to be found in the CRC Article 14.3.

II. The Original and Revised Judgments

The original case appears to have been presented and decided by the majority judges on the assumption that the interests of Victoria and her parents were identical. The Court held by a majority of 7:2 that there had been no violation of P1-2 in respect of the parents. The Court expressed surprise that attendance at the National Day Parade should be compulsory on a school holiday but did not regard the parade as offending 'the parents' pacifist convictions to the extent prohibited' by P1-2.[2] Rather, such events served pacifist objectives as well as the national interest, and the presence of the military in itself did not affect this finding. As a result, the school's actions did not violate Victoria's freedom to manifest her religion either.

The original majority judgment in *Valsamis* adopts an 'incidental' rights approach, in which, while identified in the judicial process, children's rights are marginalised.[3] Indeed, despite Victoria being a party to the case, *Valsamis* almost qualifies under Tobin's 'invisible' rights approach, in that it 'affirms and embraces a vision of children in which they are primarily seen as an extension of their parents'.[4] Aoife Daly, who describes the case as 'an unfortunate judgment from a children's rights perspective', points out that the court's failure to consider Victoria's claims independently of those of her parents is 'particularly difficult to justify' given that only she endured the stigma of punishment.[5] Judge Lundy corrects this fundamental flaw by considering the claims of Victoria and her parents separately. She draws on the wording used by the partially dissenting judges (Thór Vilhjálmsson and Jambrek), who considered that there had been a breach of both P1-2 and Article 9. In a succinct summary in relation to Victoria's Article 9 claim, they concluded:

> Victoria Valsamis stated that the parade she did not participate in had a character and symbolism that were clearly contrary to her neutralist, pacifist, and thus religious, beliefs. We are of the opinion that the Court has to accept that and we find no basis for seeing Victoria's participation in this parade as necessary in a democratic society, even if this public event clearly was for most people an expression of national values and unity.[6]

---

[2] *Valsamis v Greece* Application No. 21787/93 (18 December 1996), (1997) 24 EHRR 294 at 316.

[3] J Tobin, 'Judging the Judges: Are they Adopting the Rights Approach in Matters Involving Children?' (2009) Legal Studies Research Paper No 456 33(2) *Melbourne University Law Review* 579–625. Tobin identifies a spectrum of judicial approaches to children's rights, ranging from the 'invisible' to the 'substantive', and including 'incidental', 'selective', 'rhetorical' and 'superficial'.

[4] ibid at 594.

[5] A Daly, 'Demonstrating Positive Obligations: Children's Rights And Peaceful Protest In International Law' (2013) 45 *The George Washington International Law Review* 763–812 at 803.

[6] *Valsamis v Greece*, above n 2 at 322.

Judge Lundy, however, goes further in her conclusion that Victoria's own rights under P1-2 (to education) were also breached, an issue not considered in the original judgment because the question had not been put before the Court. In her judgment, Judge Lundy places direct reliance on the CRC Articles 12 (respect for the child's views) and 5 (provision of parental guidance in accordance with the child's evolving capacities) in relation to the breach of ECHR Article 9; and on the CRC Articles 3 (the child's best interests) and 29 (the aims of education) in relation to P1-2. Arguably, in this regard, Judge Lundy takes a far bolder approach than the European Court of Human Rights would have done in 1996, or indeed, is likely to do now. Although the Court now draws more often on the provisions of the CRC as persuasive authority,[7] Kilkelly has expressed the view that it is 'essential for the integrity of the Strasbourg system that references to the CRC are limited to where they are appropriate to guide its interpretation, for example where such guidance is lacking in either the ECHR or its case law'.[8] She has also observed in 2015 that 'explicit references to Article 12 within the ECHR case law have been very limited'.[9] Nonetheless, Judge Lundy's finding that the requirement of the Greek national curriculum of enforced attendance at the National Day parades breaches the aims of education as set out in Article 29(1)(c) CRC is a significant one.

Central to the achievement of the aims of Article 29, which also include 'The development of respect for civilizations different from his or her own' (29(1)(c)) and 'preparation of the child for responsible life in a free society, in the spirit of understanding, peace, tolerance, equality of sexes, and friendship among all peoples, ethnic, national and religious groups and persons of indigenous origin' (29(1)(d)), is an inclusive approach to education. The original judgment in *Valsamis*, by punishing Victoria for upholding her religious beliefs, threatens to marginalise minority religious groups further. In contrast, the revised judgment, in respecting Victoria's ECHR Article 9 rights, would enable her to remain fully engaged with the mainstream school community without violating her principles. Allowing plurality of religious expression is an important means by which schools may promote mutual tolerance through enabling all children to understand and respect beliefs and values that differ from those underpinning their own upbringing.

Judge Lundy, like the dissenting judges, proceeds on the basis that Victoria's beliefs were genuinely held. She finds that a child of 12 'will ordinarily be in a position to express and understand the basis for a religious belief' (paragraph 15). Yet she also deplores the school's failure to take adequate steps to clarify Victoria's views pursuant to Article 12 of the CRC, which requires states to 'assure to the child who is capable of forming his or her own views the right to express those views freely' and to give 'due weight' to those views according to 'the age and maturity of the child'. In the absence of independent investigation of Victoria's views, arguably this reasoning overlooks the restricted and socially isolating upbringing which may be experienced by children within the Jehovah's Witness community,[10] as well as

---

[7] J Fortin, *Children's Rights and the Developing Law* 3rd edn (Cambridge, Cambridge University Press, 2009).

[8] U Kilkelly, 'The Best of Both Worlds for Children's Rights? Interpreting the European Convention on Human Rights in the Light of the UN Convention on the Rights of the Child' (2001) 23 *Human Rights Quarterly* 308–26 at 326.

[9] U Kilkelly, 'The CRC in Litigation Under the ECHR' in T Liefaard and JA Doek (eds), *Litigating the Rights of the Child: The UN Convention on the Rights of the Child in Domestic and International Jurisprudence* (Dordrecht, Springer, 2015) 207.

[10] NS Hookway and D Habibis, 'Losing my Religion: Managing Identity in a Post-Jehovah's Witness World' (2015) 51(4) *Journal of Sociology* 843–56.

evidence that Victoria's views were no more than a mirror of her parents. The parents based their argument on the fact that Victoria was simply obeying their instructions and should not therefore be held responsible for her actions. The opinion of the Commission records that: '[t]hey emphasise that it was they who, because of their philosophical and religious convictions, instructed their child to behave in a way for which she was later criticised.'[11] Judge Lundy herself acknowledges that it was the *parents'* decision to withdraw Victoria from school on the day of the parade (paragraph 42).

III. A Children's Rights Dilemma: Respect for a Child's Beliefs in the Context of their Religious Upbringing

The question of the extent to which a child is in a position to choose to follow any particular religion or none is important because underlying theories of moral rights is the notion that everyone is entitled not only to equality of dignity and concern but also to autonomy.[12] The significance of freedom of thought in the protection of human rights is that it represents a 'fundamental area of the individual's autonomy': '[w]hat freedom of religion or belief protects is, precisely, the right to choose the truth(s) in which one is willing to believe.'[13] Consequently, protection of the freedom is a matter of public, not just private, interest in a democratic society and although the external dimension of religious freedom (*forum externum*), comprising freedom to manifest one's beliefs, may be limited, the internal dimension (*forum internum*), recognising freedom to hold whatever beliefs one chooses, is absolute,[14] and it is this which underlies the Court's interpretation of P1-2, in upholding the prohibition on state religious indoctrination of children through the education system. But in relation to children, the parents' P1-2 rights must be balanced against the child's Article 9 right to *choose* her own beliefs, fulfilment of which requires that her religious convictions are grounded in a deliberate and free choice made in the context of knowledge of the plurality of beliefs, including non-beliefs. The facts of *Valsamis* therefore raise the critical question as to society's expectations upon parents and the state in preparing young people for autonomy of thought as well as action in adulthood, by enabling them to adopt their own values and beliefs. The following section briefly considers the role of the state, through education—defined by the European Court of Human Rights as 'the whole process whereby, in any society, adults endeavour to transmit their beliefs, culture and other values to the young'[15]—in assuring to the child an 'open future',[16] in the current context of greater religious and cultural diversity, and political concerns about religious extremism, coinciding, in the UK, with a focus on greater parental choice in education.

---

[11] *Valsamis v Greece*, above n 2 at 304 [para 32].
[12] M Freeman, *The Moral Status of Children: Essays on the Rights of the Child* (The Hague, Martin Nijhoff Publishers, 1992).
[13] J Martinez-Torron, 'The (Un)protection of Individual Religious Identity in the Strasbourg Case Law' (2012) 1(2) *Oxford Journal of Law and Religion* 363–85 at 375.
[14] Martinez-Torron, ibid and see eg *Kokkinakis v Greece* 260-A Eur Ct HR (series A) (1993), (1994) 17 EHRR 397.
[15] *Campbell and Cosans v UK* Series A no 48 (1982) 4 EHRR 293 at para 33.
[16] J Feinberg, 'The Child's Right to an Open Future' in W Aiken and H La Follette (eds), *Whose Child? Children's Rights, Parental Authority and State Power* (Totowa, NJ, Rowman and Littlefield, 1980) 124–53.

IV. The Implications of the Judgment 20 Years On

Valsamis was heard at a time before the radicalisation of children became a widespread and high-profile concern. But the events of recent years have served to bring issues of the competing interests of the state and parents in relation to the upbringing of children, and particularly their religious and philosophical convictions, to the fore. The 'Trojan Horse' scandal in the UK provides a good example of these issues. It concerned allegations that a group of Salafi Muslims planned to take control of the governing bodies of targeted schools in Birmingham in order to impose an intolerant Islamic ideology on staff and students. While almost no direct attempts to radicalise the young people in the schools concerned were revealed upon investigation, an inquiry found 'clear evidence' of influential post-holders in schools in Birmingham who endorsed or did not challenge extremist views.[17]

The incident occurred in the context of a proliferation of faith schools as a consequence of a government policy designed to encourage parental and community (including religious) groups to set up new schools, designated 'free' schools, which, while funded by central government, have a significant degree of independence from local authority control. This policy reflects neoliberal discourses which promote the 'marketisation' of education, in which parents are designated as consumers in relation to their child's education. While its philosophical roots may be very different, this agenda accords with that of P1-2 and indeed goes beyond the state's obligations under that provision, which does not demand delivery by the state of specific types of religious or philosophical instruction to meet parental requirements, only that the state *not* impose a particular way of thinking on children.[18] Moreover, although the state is not required to fund institutions to cater for parents' particular beliefs and values, freedom to set up independent schools is acknowledged as an important principle of international law as contributing to cultural plurality.[19]

A report on the 'Trojan Horse' schools found that, although the conservative religious practices promoted by the schools involved were supported only by a minority of parents, they nonetheless served to deny the pupils suitable preparation for life in a multi-cultural society,[20] in breach of the aims of education set out in the CRC Article 29. There were also instances of gender discrimination, endorsing Carolyn Hamilton's point that while '[a]llowing a child to be educated within … an ideological, social and educational enclosure undoubtedly upholds the principle of pluralism, and defends the right of the community to continue and perpetuate its way of life … it does not provide equality of opportunity,'[21] in accordance with CRC Article 2.

---

[17] P Clarke, *Report into Allegations Concerning Birmingham Schools Arising from the 'Trojan Horse' Letter* (2014) HC 576 at 95.

[18] C Evans, *Freedom of Religion under the European Convention on Human Rights* (Oxford, Oxford University Press, 2001).

[19] See R Andar and I Leigh, *Religious Freedom in the Liberal State* 2nd edn (Oxford, Oxford University Press, 2013); Evans, ibid.

[20] Clarke, above n 17.

[21] C Hamilton, 'The Right to a Religious Education' in A Bainham and D Pearl (eds), *The Frontiers of Family Law* (Chichester, John Wiley & Sons, 1995) 239.

V. Conclusion

Although the revised judgment in *Valsamis* successfully reaches a more just conclusion for the child involved through adopting a children's rights approach, it is perhaps time for international law to respond to changing social conditions by reconsidering the appropriate balance between the rights of children and their parents in the arena of freedom of religious thought. Although P1-2 requires the state to have regard to pluralism and objectivity when imparting religious or philosophical knowledge,[22] Fortin argues that the law as it stands allows parents to 'exploit their own position as rights-holders under the ECHR in an attempt to influence their children's education'.[23] And although the child is ostensibly given individual rights to freedom of religious belief and to 'seek, receive and impart information and ideas of all kinds' in Articles 14 and 13 of the CRC respectively, both Belgium and the Netherlands entered declarations in respect of these provisions when ratifying the CRC, indicating their objection that the rights awarded were too weak.[24] The CRC also presents the preservation of familial, cultural or religious traditions as aspects of *children's* rights, as demonstrated by Articles 29(1)(c) and 30 (which requires States Parties not to deny the rights of child members of ethnic, religious or linguistic minorities or of indigenous groups 'in community with other members of his or her group, to enjoy his or her own culture, to profess or practise his or her religion, or to use his or her own language'). Guidance is needed on how these provisions should be interpreted and on balancing children's rights to religious freedom against parents' P1-2 rights. Currently, insufficient weight is accorded to the child's right to an education that enables her to choose for herself her values and beliefs.

---

[22] *Kjeldsen, Busk Madsen & Pederson v Denmark*, ECtHR, 7 Dec 1976, Series A no 23, (1976) 1 EHRR 711.

[23] Fortin, above n 7, at 413.

[24] Belgium's declaration comments that the right of the child to freedom of thought, conscience and religion implies freedom to choose their religion or belief; the Netherlands' declaration claims that children should have the freedom to have or adopt a religion or belief of their choice as soon as a child is capable of making such a choice in view of his or her age and maturity.

European Court of Human Rights

Valsamis v Greece

The European Court of Human Rights, sitting … as a chamber composed of the following Judges: Laura Lundy and Judges U, V, W, X, Y and Z, delivers the following judgment.

As to the Facts

I. Circumstances of the Case

1.   The three applicants are Jehovah's Witnesses. Elias and Maria Valsamis are the parents of Victoria, who was a pupil in the last three years of state secondary education at a school in Athens. Pacifism is a fundamental tenet of their religion and forbids any conduct or practice associated with war or violence, even indirectly. It is for this reason that Jehovah's Witnesses refuse to carry out their military service or to take part in any events with military overtones.

2.   On 20 September 1992 Mr and Mrs Valsamis submitted a written declaration in order that their daughter Victoria, who was then 12 and in the first three years of secondary education at a school in Melissia, should be exempted from attending school religious education lessons, Orthodox Mass and any other event that was contrary to her religious beliefs, including national holiday celebrations and public processions.

3.   Victoria was exempted from attendance at religious education lessons and Orthodox Mass. In October 1992, however, she, in common with the other pupils at her school, was asked to take part in the celebration of the National Day on 28 October, when the outbreak of war between Greece and Fascist Italy on 28 October 1940 is commemorated with school and military parades. On this occasion school parades take place in nearly all towns and villages. The school and military parades are only held simultaneously in a small number of municipalities.

4.   Victoria informed the headmaster that her religious beliefs forbade her joining in the commemoration of a war by taking part, in front of the civil, Church and military

authorities, in a school parade that would follow an official Mass and would be held on the same day as a military parade.

According to the applicants, the school authorities refused to accept her statement. In the Government's opinion, it was imprecise and did not make clear the religious beliefs in question. At all events, her request to be excused attendance was refused but she nevertheless did not take part in the school's parade.

5.   On 29 October 1992 the headmaster of the school imposed a disciplinary sanction on her, for her failure to attend, of one day's suspension from school. That decision was taken in accordance with Circular no C1/1/1 of 2 January 1990 issued by the Ministry of Education and Religious Affairs (see paragraph 6 below).

II. Relevant Domestic Law and Practice

6.   Circular no C1/1/1 of 2 January 1990 issued by the Ministry of Education and Religious Affairs provides:

> Schoolchildren who are Jehovah's Witnesses shall be exempted from attending religious-education lessons, school prayers and Mass.
>
> …
>
> In order for a schoolchild to benefit from this exemption, both parents (or, in the case of divorced parents, the parent in whom parental authority has been vested by court order, or the person having custody of the child) shall lodge a written declaration to the effect that they and their child (or the child of whom they have custody) are Jehovah's Witnesses.
>
> …
>
> No schoolchild shall be exempted from taking part in other school activities, such as national events.

7.   The relevant Articles of Presidential Decree no 104/1979 of 29 January and 7 February 1979 are the following:

> Article 2
>
> 1. The behaviour of pupils inside and outside the school shall constitute their conduct, irrespective of the manner—by act or by omission—in which they express it.
>
> Pupils shall be required to conduct themselves suitably, that is to say in accordance with the rules governing school life and the moral principles governing the social context in which they live, and any act or omission in contravention of the rules and principles in question shall be dealt with according to the procedures provided in the educational system and may, if necessary, give rise to the disciplinary measures provided in this decree.

The disciplinary measures laid down in Article 27 of the same decree are, in increasing order of severity, a warning, a reprimand, exclusion from lessons for an hour, suspension from school for up to five days and transfer to another school.

> Article 28 paragraph 3
>
> Suspended pupils may remain at school during teaching hours and take part in various activities, under the responsibility of the headmaster.

III. Relevant International Texts

A. *The United Nations Convention on the Rights of the Child 1989*

8.   This treaty (hereafter, 'the UN Convention'), adopted by the General Assembly of the United Nations on 20 November 1989, has binding force under international law on the Contracting States, including all of the Member States of the Council of Europe.
     Article 3(1) of the UN Convention states:

> In all actions concerning children, whether undertaken by public or private social welfare institutions, courts of law, administrative authorities or legislative bodies, the best interests of the child shall be a primary consideration.

Article 5 of the UN Convention states:

> States Parties shall respect the responsibilities, rights and duties of parents or, where applicable, the members of the extended family or community as provided for by local custom, legal guardians or other persons legally responsible for the child, to provide, in a manner consistent with the evolving capacities of the child, appropriate direction and guidance in the exercise by the child of the rights recognized in the present Convention.

Article 12 of the UN Convention states:

> 1. States Parties shall assure to the child who is capable of forming his or her own views the right to express those views freely in all matters affecting the child, the views of the child being given due weight in accordance with the age and maturity of the child.

> 2. For this purpose, the child shall in particular be provided the opportunity to be heard in any judicial and administrative proceedings affecting the child, either directly, or through a representative or an appropriate body, in a manner consistent with the procedural rules of national law.

Article 29(1) of the UN Convention states:

> 1. States Parties agree that the education of the child shall be directed to:

> (a)   The development of the child's personality, talents and mental and physical abilities to their fullest potential;
> (b)   The development of respect for human rights and fundamental freedoms, and for the principles enshrined in the Charter of the United Nations;
> (c)   The development of respect for the child's parents, his or her own cultural identity, language and values, for the national values of the country in which the child is living, the country from which he or she may originate, and for civilizations different from his or her own;
> (d)   The preparation of the child for responsible life in a free society, in the spirit of understanding, peace, tolerance, equality of sexes, and friendship among all peoples, ethnic, national and religious groups and persons of indigenous origin;
> (e)   The development of respect for the natural environment.

9.   The UN Committee on the Rights of the Child has given guidance as to the meaning and interpretation of Article 29(1) in its General Comment (No 1) on the Aims of Education (CRC/ C/GC/ 1).

As to the Law

10.   The applicants complaint relates to the penalty of one day's suspension from school that was imposed on the pupil, Victoria, who had refused to take part in the school parade on 28 October, a national day in Greece. The child's application relates to Article 2 of Protocol No 1 (P1-2) and Articles 3 and 9, (article 3 and article 9). The parents' application relates only to P1-2.

11.   The child and her parents are joint applicants in the case. While the wishes and interests of parents and children on issues of religious belief and education often align or overlap, that is not necessarily the case. The Court deems it important that the rights of the child are considered separately and are not subsumed within a consideration of the rights of her parents. The complaints by the child are considered first, followed by a consideration of the complaint by the parents.

I. Alleged Violation of Article 9 of the Convention (Article 9)

12.   Miss Valsamis relied on Article 9 of the Convention (article 9), which provides:

> 1. Everyone has the right to freedom of thought, conscience and religion; this right includes freedom to change his religion or belief and freedom, either alone or in community with others and in public or private, to manifest his religion or belief, in worship, teaching, practice and observance.

> 2. Freedom to manifest one's religion or beliefs shall be subject only to such limitations as are prescribed by law and are necessary in a democratic society in the interests of public safety, for the protection of public order, health or morals, or for the protection of the rights and freedoms of others.

13.   Miss Valsamis stated that the parade had a character and symbolism that were clearly contrary to her neutralist, pacifist, and thus religious, beliefs. She asserted that Article 9 guaranteed her right to the freedom not to manifest, by gestures of support, any convictions or opinions contrary to her own. She disputed both the necessity and the proportionality of the interference, having regard to the seriousness of the penalty, which stigmatised her and marginalised her.

14.   The government has argued that the applicant's reasons for objecting to participation in the parade, set out in a letter written to the school principal, were unclear and 'muddied'. The Court notes, with concern, the limited efforts undertaken by the school to ascertain Victoria's views on what was an issue of conscience. The Court considers that, in determining what Victoria's beliefs were and why and how strongly they were held, it was important to seek her views on these directly. Article 9 should be interpreted in line with Article 12 of the UN Convention which requires states to assure to the child who is capable of expressing a view the right to have the view given due weight in accordance with her age and maturity. It is the Court's view that further efforts should have been made to ensure that Victoria was in a position to fully and freely explain the reasons why she considered herself unable to

take part in the parade. This is particularly important in instances where there is a possibility that the child's views may differ from those of his or her parents. Even though this does not appear to be the case in this instance, it is important that opportunities are provided for the child whose parents have requested an exemption from core educational activity to be heard independently on the issue.

15.   The Court accepts that it was the child's genuine belief that participating in the parade was against the tenets of her religious convictions and that it was not possible for her to take part. That view should have been given due weight in accordance with her age and maturity. We consider that a child of 12 years of age will ordinarily be in a position to express and understand the basis for a religious belief and to identify practices which contravene it. We consider that the child's perception of the symbolism of the school parade and its religious and philosophical connotations has to be accepted by the Court unless it is obviously unfounded and unreasonable.

16.   The Court does not consider that the opinions held by the applicant were obviously unfounded and unreasonable. The government argued that there was nothing in the parade that would contravene pacifists' convictions. However, the parade commemorates the outbreak (and not the cessation) of a war. Moreover, while the school parade may have been separate from the military parade, the associations are apparent and participating children would be required to walk past military personnel. The parents were of the view that participation in the parade was inconsistent with their beliefs as Jehovah's Witnesses and had clearly discussed and communicated that to the applicant. The Court is of the view that, in these circumstances, the obligation to parade in this instance would require the applicant to act against her conscience and religion.

17.   The Court finds no basis to consider that punishing Victoria for her refusal to take part in this parade was necessary in a democratic society 'in the interests of public safety, for the protection of public order, health or morals, or for the protection of the rights and freedoms of others.' Even if this public event was for most people an expression of national values and unity, there are no grounds for arguing that the child's right to freedom of conscience should be limited on the basis that her participation in this event was necessary in a democratic society. Nor does her non-participation in any way interfere with the rights of others.

18.   The Court deems it necessary to comment on the suggestion that the exemptions granted from religious education and the Orthodox Mass were in some way sufficient accommodation for her religious beliefs. The implication is that sufficient ground had been ceded to the child in terms of respecting her beliefs and that this request was a step too far. The Court rejects the suggestion that an exemption from one activity might cover accommodation of belief for other different actions by the state. Each request for exemption needs to be considered on its own merit and the fact that she had been permitted to withdraw from other school activity is not relevant to the consideration of the issue in this case. The Court does, however, acknowledge that there might be rare exceptions to this. One example is a situation where the requests for exemptions are so extensive that their combined effect would be to undermine the child's right to an effective education. That is not the case in this instance.

19.   The Court finds that there has been a breach of Article 9 of the Convention (article 9).

II. Alleged Violation of Article 2 of Protocol No 1 (P1-2)

20.   The first applicant alleges that she was the victim of a breach of (P1-2), which provides:

> No person shall be denied the right to education. In the exercise of any functions which it assumes in relation to education and to teaching, the State shall respect the right of parents to ensure such education and teaching in conformity with their own religious and philosophical convictions.

The Court notes the broad approach to what constitutes 'education' and, in particular, that it applies to the imposition of disciplinary penalties (*Campbell and Cosans v United Kingdom*, judgment of 25 February 1982, Series A no 48, page 16). These are an integral part of the process whereby a school seeks to achieve the object for which it was established, including the development and moulding of the character and mental powers of its pupils (see the *Campbell and Cosans* judgment, page 14, and paragraph 33).

21.   The Court observes that there were other disciplinary sanctions open to the school principal and that these included the options of a reprimand and a warning. The Court considers that Article 3(1) of the UN Convention is relevant to the interpretation of what constitutes a denial of the right to eduction under P1-2. A suspension from school is a matter that affects the child and her best interests should have been a primary consideration in the decision to impose it. States have a wide degree of discretion in determining what disciplinary sanctions are appropriate in schools. However, in general terms, the Court expresses doubt as to whether a suspension from school is an appropriate disciplinary sanction for a child's failure to attend school. In many cases, that will amount to a further reduction in a child's opportunities to receive education and in cases of persistent absenteeism would appear to be not only counterproductive but also a denial of the child's right to education under Article 2 of the First Protocol.

22.   In this instance, the Court cannot identify a process where the child's right to education and her best interests were considered by those making the decision to suspend her. The Principal appears to have responded to Circular no C1/1/1 of 2 January 1990 issued by the Ministry of Education and Religious Affairs which provides:

> Schoolchildren who are Jehovah's Witnesses shall be exempted from attending religious-education lessons, school prayers and Mass. …

> No schoolchild shall be exempted from taking part in other school activities, such as national events.

While this is only guidance from the Ministry and does not bind the school in law, it appears that the school did not exercise any discretion in this instance and did not grant the child an exemption from the parade. At no stage does there appear to have been consideration of the best interests of the child in the decision to impose a temporary suspension for failure to attend the parade.

23.   The Court acknowledges that states are given a large degree of discretion and that 'the setting and planning of the curriculum fall in principle within the competence of the Contracting States. This mainly involves questions of expediency on which it is not for the Court to rule and whose solution may legitimately vary according to the country and the era' (see the *Kjeldsen, Busk Madsen and Pedersen* judgment of 7 December 1976, Series A no 23, page 26, paragraph 53).

24. The Court, in interpreting what constitutes education and its scope and, consequently, what may constitute a denial of education under P1-2, takes cognisance of Article 29(1) of the UNCRC which defines the agreed aims of education. National curricula should not contravene these agreed aims. In particular, it notes that Article 29(1) (c) requires education to be directed to:

> The development of respect for the child's parents, his or her own cultural identity, language and values, for the national values of the country in which the child is living, the country from which he or she may originate, and for civilizations different from his or her own …

The Committee on the Rights of the Child has observed in General Comment no 1 on the Aims of Education, at paragraph 17, that:

> The aims and values reflected in this article are stated in quite general terms and their implications are potentially very wide ranging. This seems to have led many States parties to assume that it is unnecessary, or even inappropriate, to ensure that the relevant principles are reflected in legislation or in administrative directives. This assumption is unwarranted.

25.   In this instance, the National Day parade is one part of the state's efforts to promote 'national values' on a day of significance to many Greeks. It is not for the Court to rule on the expediency of other educational methods which, in the applicants' view, would be better suited to the aim of perpetuating historical memory among the younger generation. However, the state, in ensuring access to education that meets the aims of education set down in Article 29(1) of the UN Convention, also has an obligation to ensure that the education provided is directed towards respect for the child's own identity and culture and promotes respect for the child's parents.

26.   The Court considers that the blanket approach to national events in Circular No C/1/1/1 does not allow for full consideration of cases where the child seeks an exemption based on conscience or religious belief. While it is appropriate for the state to give schools guidance on this, it should be made clear that schools have a discretion to grant exemptions on an individual basis. The guidance should advise schools to give the child the opportunity to be heard, ensure that the child's best interests are a primary consideration and attempt to ensure that the education that the child receives provides an appropriate balance between promoting respect for national values and the child's values and right to receive an education that does not undermine respect for his or her parents.

27.   The Court finds that there has been a breach of Article 2 of Protocol 1 of the Convention.

III. Alleged Violation of Article 3 of the Convention (Article 3)

28.   Miss Valsamis went on to allege, without giving any particulars, that her suspension from school was contrary to Article 3 of the Convention (article 3), which provides:

> No one shall be subjected to torture or to inhuman or degrading treatment or punishment.

29.   The Government did not express a view.

30.   The Court reiterates that ill-treatment must attain a minimum level of severity if it is to fall within the scope of Article 3 (article 3) (see, in particular, the *Ireland v the United Kingdom* judgment of 18 January 1978, Series A no 25, page 65, paragraph 162, and the *Campbell and Cosans* judgment cited above, pages 12–13, paragraph 27–28).

31.   The Court has previously observed that there is always some sort of humiliation involved in a punishment and that this does not mean that it will inevitably be 'degrading'. In this case, the Court notes, the penalty of suspension is of limited duration and does not require the exclusion of the pupil from the school premises (Article 28 paragraph 3 of Decree no 104/1979—see paragraph 7 above). The Court acknowledges that the applicant is a child and the punishment will have been implemented in a public institution. It also recognises that there will be an additional degree of humiliation related to the fact that she was disciplined for acting in accordance with her conscience rather than for more typical misbehaviour. However, the Court has not heard any suggestion that the suspension was carried out in a manner that was intended to or had the effect of stigmatising the child for her beliefs or marginalising her from her peers. The Court accepts that the suspension has caused the child some distress and humiliation but does not consider that it amounts to torture, inhuman or degrading treatment.

32.   In conclusion, there has been no breach of Article 3 of the Convention (article 3).

IV. Alleged Violation of Article 2 of Protocol No 1, Second Sentence (P1-2)

33.   The second and third applicants alleged that they were the victims of a breach of Article 2 of Protocol No 1 (P1-2), which provides:

> No person shall be denied the right to education. In the exercise of any functions which it assumes in relation to education and to teaching, the State shall respect the right of parents to ensure such education and teaching in conformity with their own religious and philosophical convictions.

34.   The second and third applicants alleged that there is a breach of this Article (P1-2) where pupils, like their daughter Victoria, are forced as part of their school duties to take part in organised events imbued with a symbolism that is contrary to the most deeply held religious and philosophical convictions of their parents. This applies even more where the events are held in a public place, outside school, on a national holiday with the intention of delivering a message to the community concerned. According to Mr and Mrs Valsamis, the pupils are thus obliged to show publicly, by their acts, that they adhere to beliefs contrary to those of their parents.

35.   The Government contested the parents' submission, arguing that the school parade on 28 October had no military overtones such as to offend pacifist convictions.

36.   The Court reiterates that 'the two sentences of Article 2 [of Protocol No 1] (P1-2) must be read not only in the light of each other but also, in particular, of Articles 8, 9 and 10 of the Convention (article 8, article 9, article 10)' (see the *Kjeldsen, Busk Madsen and Pedersen v Denmark* judgment cited above, page 26, paragraph 52).

37.   As the Court observed in its judgment of 25 May 1993 in the case of *Kokkinakis v Greece* (Series A no 260-A, page 18, paragraph 32), Jehovah's Witnesses enjoy both the

status of a 'known religion' and the advantages flowing from that as regards observance. Mr and Mrs Valsamis were accordingly entitled to rely on the right to respect for their religious convictions within the meaning of this provision (P1-2).

38.   The Court reiterates that Article 2 of Protocol No 1 (P1-2) enjoins the state to respect parents' convictions, be they religious or philosophical, throughout the entire state education programme (see the *Kjeldsen, Busk Madsen and Pedersen* judgment cited above, page 25, paragraph 51). That duty is broad in its extent as it applies not only to the content of education and the manner of its provision but also to the performance of all the 'functions' assumed by the state. The verb 'respect' means more than 'acknowledge' or 'take into account'. In addition to a primarily negative undertaking, it implies some positive obligation on the part of the state (see the *Campbell and Cosans* judgment cited above, page 17, paragraph 37).

39.   The Court has also held that 'although individual interests must on occasion be subordinated to those of a group, democracy does not simply mean that the views of a majority must always prevail: a balance must be achieved which ensures the fair and proper treatment of minorities and avoids any abuse of a dominant position' (*Young, James and Webster v the United Kingdom* judgment of 13 August 1981, Series A no 44, page 25, paragraph 63). The second sentence of P1-2 thus plays a role in enabling a pluralistic approach to education systems which is important in democratic societies.

40.   The government has argued that such commemorations of national events serve, in their way, both pacifist objectives and the public interest. The presence of military representatives at some of the parades which take place in Greece on the day in question does not mean that the parades are celebrating or endorsing war. However, Victoria Valsamis stated that the parade had a character and symbolism that were clearly contrary to her neutralist, pacifist, and thus religious, beliefs. As the Court has observed above, the parade commemorates the commencement of a war (not its cessation) and there are obvious associations with the military.

41.   Furthermore, the Court notes the parents' right 'to enlighten and advise their children, to exercise with regard to their children natural parental functions as educators, or to guide their children on a path in line with the parents' own religious or philosophical convictions' (see, mutatis mutandis, the *Kjeldsen, Busk Madsen and Pedersen* judgment cited above, page 28, paragraph 54). The interpretation of this is aided by a consideration of Article 5 of the UNCRC which gives parents the right and duty to provide guidance to the child in the exercise of his or her rights. This is an important provision which reinforces the significant role of parents in providing the child with guidance in line with their 'evolving capacities'.

42.   The Court reiterates that the parents' right to have their child educated in accordance with their religious and philosophical convictions must not interfere with the child's right to an education (*Kjeldsen, Busk Madsen and Pedersen* judgment cited above). It observes that the failure to attend the Saturday parade will have a minimal impact on her education overall. The parents' decision to withdraw her, in this instance, will not impact adversely on her enjoyment of her right to education. Nor will it have had any adverse impact on the education of the other children in her class. In contrast, the child's experience of being asked to act in contravention of her parents' wishes and values and her own, and subsequently punished for non-compliance, has the potential to cause significant distress and stigma to both parents and the child.

43.   In conclusion, there has been a breach of the parents' right under the second sentence of Article 2 of Protocol No 1 (P1-2).

Child-Friendly Summary

Victoria was a 12 year old girl attending school in Greece. She and her parents are Jehovah's Witnesses. This is a religion that supports 'pacifism'. This means that they do not want to be involved in any activities that relate to war or the military.

All the children in Victoria's school were required to take part in a parade which marked Greece's National Day. This is on the date that Greece began a war. Victoria and her parents thought that it was not possible for her to take part in this because of her beliefs.

Victoria and her parents asked her school principal if she could be allowed to stay away from the parade. The Principal said no. Victoria did not go to the parade and the Principal gave her a suspension from school for one day.

Under the European Convention on Human Rights, children have a right to education, a right to freedom of religion and belief and a right not to treated in a way that is degrading. The United Nations Convention on Children's Rights can also be used by courts to interpret and understand these rights. It gives children a right to have their views heard and for their best interests to be considered when decisions are taken about them.

Victoria complained to the court that the suspension for not taking part in the parade was not in accordance with her rights to freedom of religion and education. She also argued that it was degrading for her to be punished for this.

The government argued that there was nothing about participating in the parade that could offend Victoria and her parents as the event was not about war.

The Court looked at all of the arguments. We found that the decision to suspend her did not comply with her right to freedom of religion and that it was reasonable for her to hold the views that she did about the parade.

We also found that the decision to suspend her breached her right to education and that her best interests were not considered properly when the school made the decision.

We advised that governments need to find ways of ensuring that education allows children to develop respect for national values and children's own values and respect for their parents.

We considered that Victoria would have felt embarrassed and upset at the punishment but that it was not so severe that it can be considered 'degrading'.

We found that there was a breach of Victoria's parents' right to have their daughter educated in accordance with their religious beliefs.

19

Commentary on *R (on the Application of Begum) v Governors of Denbigh High School*

NUNO FERREIRA[*]

I. Background to *Begum*

It is more than 10 years since the decision of the House of Lords (HL, as it was then) in *Begum*,[1] but it remains as contentious and relevant as ever. In *Begum*, religion, age, gender, culture and socio-economic background conflate, raising issues of equality, tolerance, autonomy, diversity and respect.[2] The decision alerts us to the way in which a range of socio-cultural variables affect children's lives.

Shabina Begum started Denbigh High School in 2000, aged 11. The school catered to a student population ethnically, religiously and culturally diverse, and so adopted its uniform policy after wide consultation with the community and religious leaders.[3] One of the uniform options for girls included the shalwar kameeze and headscarf.[4] After two years of abiding by the school's uniform policy, Begum went to school one morning, accompanied by her older brother and his friend, dressed in a jilbab, a long coat-like garment.[5] The brother and his friend requested, in allegedly rather forceful terms, that Begum be allowed to attend school wearing the jilbab, thus in contravention of the school's uniform policy.[6]

---

[*] Fieldwork has been carried out by the authors of the dissenting judgment and of this commentary, consisting of two interviews: one on 24 February 2016 with Shabina Begum, and one on 12 November 2015 with Cherie Booth QC, Shabina's counsel. Ethics approval to carry out these interviews was granted by the University of Liverpool on 5 October 2015 (Reference No. SLSJSTAFF15-1602). The authors would like to express their gratitude to the interviewees for their generous participation in this work.

[1] *R (on the application of Begum) v Governors of Denbigh High School Governors* [2006] UKHL 15; [2007] 1 AC 100.

[2] H Cullen, 'Commentary on R (on the application of Begum) v Governors of Denbigh High School' in R Hunter, C McGlynn, and E Rackley (eds), *Feminist Judgments: From Theory to Practice* (Oxford, Hart Publishing, 2010) 329–35 at 329.

[3] Above n 1 at [6]–[7].

[4] *R (on the application of Begum) v Governors of Denbigh High School Governors* [2004] EWHC 1389 (Admin), [2004] ELR 374 [26], [41].

[5] Above n 1 at [10].

[6] ibid.

The Department for Education and Skills (DfES) guidance (the Guidance) at the time encouraged schools to accommodate the needs of different cultures, races and religions, explicitly 'allowing Muslim girls to wear appropriate dress'.[7] The school was of the opinion that its policy conformed with such guidance and did not believe it was under an obligation to accede to Begum's request. The school thus asked Begum to change clothes to adhere to the school's uniform policy. Begum did not follow these instructions and initiated a judicial review of the school's decision.

II. The Judicial Decisions

Begum claimed that her freedom of religion (protected under Article 9 of the European Convention on Human Rights (ECHR)) and right to education (protected under Article 2 of First Protocol to the ECHR) had been violated. In the High Court Bennett J refused both claims.[8] He relied especially on the 'contracting out' doctrine, developed by the European Court of Human Rights (ECtHR), which established that individuals contract out of the right to manifest their religious beliefs in certain ways when they engage with particular employment relationships or roles—in this case, the role of pupil at a particular school— that are not compatible with those religious manifestations.

Begum appealed. Contrary to the High Court, the Court of Appeal found that Begum had in effect been excluded from school and that there had been an insufficient assessment of Begum's right to religious freedom.[9] The Court of Appeal held that the school should have carried out a much more detailed analysis of the requirements in Article 9 ECHR, including the scope of justification of interferences under Article 9(2).[10] This type of detailed analysis, however, was criticised by scholars as an excessive and inappropriate burden on schools,[11] and undue judicialisation of public decision-making.[12] The school was not satisfied either and appealed.

In 2006 came the final stage of this four year judicial saga: in a decision led by Lord Bingham of Cornhill, the House of Lords (HL) reversed the Court of Appeal's decision for unduly burdening the school with a detailed assessment of the issues raised under Article 9[13] and determined that the school had acted lawfully. Although only two members of the Court found that Article 9 ECHR had been engaged (Lord Nicholls and Baroness Hale of Richmond), all five members found that there had been no violation of Begum's religious freedom, as any interference could be justified under Article 9(2) ECHR and was within the UK's margin of appreciation. The overall tone of the decision is respectful of and deferential to Begum's religious beliefs,[14] but that was not enough to deprive the school of

---

[7] Department for Education and Skills, *Uniform Guidance 0264/2002*; above n 4 at [22].

[8] Above n 4.

[9] *R (on the application of Begum) v Governors of Denbigh High School Governors* [2005] EWCA Civ 199; [2005] 1 WLR 3372.

[10] ibid [81].

[11] T Poole, 'Of Headscarves and Heresies: The Denbigh High School Case and Public Authority Decision-Making under the Human Rights Act' (2005) *PL* 685.

[12] M Malik, 'House of Lords, Regina (SB) v Governors of Denbigh High School [2006] UKHL 15' in Hunter, McGlynn and Rackley, above n 2, 336–45.

[13] Above n 1 at [28]–[29].

[14] ibid [21], per Lord Bingham.

its autonomy in uniform policy matters. There was no violation of Begum's right to education either, as there was no intention to exclude Begum and the onus was on her to secure
admission to another school.[15]

III. A Children's Rights Critique of *Begum*

The alternative, dissenting opinion written by Moscati adopts a children's rights perspective in substance, as well as a child-friendly tone. The *Begum* decision was not indifferent to
children's rights; Baroness Hale's opinion highlighted the need to ensure that adolescents
are able to develop their own moral and religious views.[16] Nonetheless, even Baroness Hale
concluded that any interference with Article 9 ECHR could be justified in order to promote
a sense of community and cohesion.[17] Children of school age are thus expected to postpone
a fuller assertion of their rights and beliefs until they leave school.

The re-written opinion explicitly uses the UN Convention on the Rights of the Child
(CRC) as the fundamental framework to reach an appropriate—the best possible—
outcome. Although not domestically incorporated into UK law, the UK Supreme Court has
applied CRC norms in its decisions, albeit via the ECHR and Human Rights Act 1998.[18] The
legal tools used by the judiciary in these cases were already available to the House of Lords
in *Begum,* and thus to Moscati in the re-written dissenting opinion, particularly in terms
of placing considerable importance on a child claimant's best interests when carrying out a
proportionality exercise.

The HL considered three key arguments: first, whether Begum 'contracted out' her right
to manifest her religion by having enrolled at the school in question; second, the potential
effect that allowing Begum to wear the jilbab could have on other female pupils; third,
whether Begum acted on her free will.

A. Contracting Out One's Right to (Express One's) Freedom of Religion

Following Lord Bingham's famous 'no more, no less' approach in relation to the application of the ECHR in the UK context,[19] the HL relied on the broad margin of appreciation
afforded by the ECtHR case law,[20] even though that case law and the 'no more, no less'
approach are wholly criticisable.[21] In justifying any interference with Begum's freedom
of religion, Lord Bingham highlighted that: Begum and her family had chosen a school

---

[15] ibid [36].

[16] ibid [93]. See also N Ferreira, 'Putting the Age of Criminal and Tort Liability into Context: A Dialogue
between Law and Psychology' (2008) 16/1 *International Journal of Children's Rights* 29.

[17] ibid [97]–[98].

[18] *ZH (Tanzania) v Secretary of State for the Home Department* [2011] UKSC 4, especially at [23]; *R (on the
application of SG) and Others v Secretary of State for Work and Pensions* [2015] UKSC 16, especially at [83] ff.

[19] See, for example, N Ferreira, 'The Supreme Court in a Final Push to Go Beyond Strasbourg' (2015) PL 367.

[20] *Sahin v Turkey,* Application No 44774/98, 10 November 2005, unreported.

[21] See, for example, K Altiparmak and O Karahanoğullari, 'After Şahin: The Debate on Headscarves Is Not Over,
Leyla Şahin v Turkey, Grand Chamber Judgment of 10 November 2005, Application No 44774/98' (2006) 2(2)
European Constitutional Law Review 268; and J Marshall, 'Freedom of Religious Expression and Gender Equality:
Şahin v Turkey' (2006) 69/3 *Modern Law Review* 452; and on the 'no more, no less' approach, see Ferreira,
above n 19.

outside their own catchment area; she knew from the start that that school did not allow the jilbab; there were three other schools in the area that did allow the jilbab; and the school had taken immense pains to devise a uniform policy that 'respected Muslim beliefs … in an inclusive, unthreatening and uncompetitive way'.[22] The HL thus found that Begum was free to change her beliefs, but as a consequence it would not have been too much of an inconvenience to require her to change schools.[23]

Although it is true that the ECtHR's case law places emphasis on choice and voluntariness through its 'contracting out' doctrine, both the ECtHR and UK courts recognise that there are limits to this doctrine when the consequences become unreasonable.[24] Baroness Hale's Opinion in *Begum* also suggests that the 'contracting out' doctrine may not be appropriate in the context of compulsory education, as often it is not the child choosing the school and there may not be any alternative for the child due to a range of difficulties (lack of own transport, lack of financial means, etc).[25] Indeed, Begum confirms that:

> once I lost my case in the High Court the Local Education Authority (LEA) helped me to get into a school which was very far from my house. It used to take me 1 hour and 20 minutes to get there by bus. … and that school was [a] very under-achieved school.[26]

Similarly, Cherie Booth QC states that:

> I also felt that some of the judges were extremely insensitive to the reality of what this choice was … it completely underestimates how a family basically on benefits, how can she just get to another school, it was her nearest and local school, to go anywhere else would be a lot more costly …[27]

These difficulties are compounded by gender, age and religious dimensions, as being a Muslim female adolescent could render the range of options more limited.[28]

In contrast to the rewritten feminist judgment of *Begum* (which, despite advocating a more critical use of the 'contracting out' doctrine, shared the outcome of the HL judgment),[29] the children's rights judgment focuses squarely on Begum's status as a school-age female, Muslim child. By contextualising more thoroughly Begum's experience and what could be expected of Begum in her circumstances, Moscati reaches the conclusion that there has been an unjustified interference with Begum's religious freedom: Begum had not 'contracted out' her right to express her religion.

B. A Balancing Rights Exercise

The second key argument in *Begum* was the school's claim that allowing Shabina to wear the jilbab might result in other female pupils who did not wish to wear the jilbab feeling pressured to do so.[30] Baroness Hale also accepted that 'protecting the rights and freedoms

---

[22] Above n 1 at [25] and [34].
[23] ibid. At [41] Lord Nicholls of Birkenhead, however, finds that it may have not been so easy for Begum to move to another school.
[24] See *Darby v Sweden* (1991) 13 EHRR 774, *Copsey v WWB Devon Clays Ltd* [2005] EWCA Civ 932, [2005] ICR 1789.
[25] Above n 1 at [92].
[26] Interview with Shabina Begum on 24 February 2016.
[27] Interview with Cherie Booth QC on 12 November 2015.
[28] Above n 12 at 339 ff.
[29] Above n 2 at 329–35.
[30] Above n 1 at [18].

of others' was a legitimate aim of the school's uniform policy, but rightly asks whether the policy was proportionate to that aim.[31] She concludes that the policy was proportional, thus lawful.

Tobin found this decision struck the right balance between restricting Begum's right and the protection of the freedom of religion of the other children not directly involved with the proceedings.[32] This is, however, contentious, as it seems to place too much emphasis on the rights of children who are not involved with the proceedings who had not been affected by the proceedings and who would not necessarily suffer any detriment even if the HL had found in favour of Begum. On this matter, Begum states the following:

> I find this really absurd, patronising, when someone says 'maybe other girls can feel pressured to doing that'. When we have a problem in society, when girls have been pressured to do things that they don't want to do, the solution isn't to prevent other people … stopping other people from practising their religion, because these things do happen, girls may feel pressured even to wear the headscarf. And to tackle that you have groups, you have mediation, you talk to them, you give children, girls, men, women, everyone the confidence to do what they want in society, freedom to do what they want … You can't infringe somebody's rights just because somebody else feels threatened.[33]

Similarly, Cherie Booth QC rightly points out that:

> [When] hearing French feminists [saying] 'I'm offended, or I'm frightened when I see a woman wearing [the veil], covered up in the street', … I'm thinking, 'well, on what basis is my fear or my offence a reason to restrict the other person's religious belief?'[34]

More fundamentally, the whole basis for such concerns seems to be unfounded, as Begum asserts that:

> I honestly believe that [the claim that other pupils felt threatened] was false, because I remember at that time I had a petition among the other girls about who wants to wear the jilbab and a lot of girls [said] they would wear it … a lot of children, when [they] go to college [they] wear the jilbab. So, if people felt threatened, why don't they feel threatened when they go to college?[35]

Law should rightly protect children from any sort of oppression and maximise their autonomy, but that should not be done for the sake of unsubstantiated limitations to those children's rights and freedoms or at the expense of the actual exercise of another child's substantive right. Consequently, the re-written judgment concentrates on actual limitations to Begum's rights, not hypothetical and unfounded violations of other pupils' rights.

C. Questioning Begum's Autonomy

The third key argument in the HL relates to the extent to which this challenge to the school's uniform policy was genuinely dictated by Begum's own religious beliefs or whether it had been instigated by Begum's older brother, who acted as her litigation friend. Bennett J wondered why it was the brother, and not Begum herself, presenting the evidence

---

[31] ibid [94].
[32] J Tobin, 'Courts and the Construction of Childhood: A New Way of Thinking' in M Freeman (ed), *Law and Childhood Studies: Current Legal Issues* vol 14 (Oxford, Oxford University Press, 2012) 10–11.
[33] Above n 26.
[34] Above n 27.
[35] Above n 26.

regarding her change of views on the required dress code.[36] Moreover, the brother apparently stated that he was not prepared to let his sister attend school without wearing a long skirt.[37] Begum's autonomy was thus questioned in several, intertwined ways throughout this judicial saga.

Some have attempted to explain the brother's role on the basis that Begum's father had died many years before and the mother did not speak English.[38] Begum's own account of the facts is refreshingly prosaic:

> [My family] were very scared and nervous [about starting a lawsuit]. Some of them didn't support me … I am not sure why my brother keeps being mentioned because obviously I had to take an adult with me when I go to see a lawyer and I speak with somebody. When I spoke with the Head Teacher I had to take my brother with me obviously because I was scared of them saying something to me, I had to. But ultimately between me and my brother, I know that this was my decision and what I wanted to do.[39]

On Begum's autonomy, Cherie Booth QC asserted the following:

> I was trying to be satisfied in my own mind that she knew what she was doing and she wanted to do this … but I was pretty quickly convinced that she was quite a determined young woman and she definitely knew in her own mind that it was her religious beliefs that she wanted to express … There was an assumption there that this wasn't Shabina's choice, and … how do they know that? They didn't know that, they never met her.[40]

With regard to Begum's autonomy in relation to the procedures (ie the scope for Begum to steer the judicial proceedings and make her voice heard in court), it is in the nature of judicial review cases—such as *Begum*—to generally only rely on written statements;[41] hence Begum was not heard by the courts involved in this case. Furthermore, children filing judicial claims in England and Wales are represented by litigation friends.[42] Although the courts in this case cannot be reproached for either of these procedural obstacles, more care could have been taken to ensure that Begum's voice—through her litigation friend and/or counsel—was acknowledged and respected.

With regard to the autonomy of Begum's decision (ie the scope for Begum to reach her own decisions and act upon them), the fact that Begum's older sister had always abided by the school's uniform policy also suggests that Begum's desire to wear a jilbab was an individual, genuine wish, unrelated to that of her relatives.[43] One may always suggest that Begum was, nevertheless, led (perhaps unconsciously) to this choice of dress code owing to her personal, family or community circumstances and (limited?) range of choices. This phenomenon—termed 'adaptive preferences'—may well be detrimental to (fuller) individual autonomy,[44] but may not justify paternalistic judicial reactions. All individual decisions are—to a greater or lesser extent—a product of compromises with other individuals, one's family context, socio-economic background, gender, religion, age, etc. That relational dimension of one's decisions may qualify the extent of one's autonomy, but may not

[36] Above n 4 at [68].
[37] Above n 1 at [11], [81].
[38] Above n 2 at 331.
[39] Above n 26.
[40] Above n 27.
[41] Treasury Solicitor's Department, *The Judge over Your Shoulder* 4th edn (London, 2006) 35.
[42] Rule 21.2 of the Civil Procedure Rules.
[43] Above n 1 at [9].
[44] B Colburn, 'Autonomy and Adaptive Preferences' (2011) 23(1) *Utilitas* 52.

disqualify one from taking decisions unless there is strong and clear evidence of oppressive practices.

The re-written judgment thus highlights Begum's right to participation under Article 12 CRC. Indeed, it ensures that Begum's voice is heard and carefully considered. Cherie Booth QC also argues that the House of Lords should have guaranteed greater respect for Begum's autonomy: 'I think there should be more of an acknowledgement of Shabina as an individual, who had made an individual choice'.[45] A focus on Begum's rights—including to participation—would not, in itself, require that the re-written judgment found in favour of Begum. Indeed, a 'substantive children's rights approach'[46] to cases involving not only children but other actors as well (for example, the state) does not necessarily require a decision in favour of the children in question, as the outcome may tip in favour of the rights and interests of others. Moreover, the right to participation does not require that a child's views be determinative, but simply avoids that children's voices be silenced or subject to interpretation of other individuals.[47] Still, according to a children's rights-based approach, it would have been appropriate for the Court not only to respect Begum's (procedural) right to participation to its fullest, but also to focus on the actual harm caused to Begum's rights, thus enhancing her (substantive) autonomy.

IV. Conclusion

The decision in *Begum* and its critique are linked to a certain vision of what schools should be entitled to impose in terms of uniforms, of what pupils should be allowed to claim in terms of education, and of what individuals—in particular girls—should be allowed to demand in terms of religious dress. Yet, for Begum, it was all quite straightforward:

> This case was about my education—I wanted to study, I wanted to go to school. While doing that I wanted to practise my religion and I felt the school didn't accept me; didn't accept me as a person and accept me to practise my religion.[48]

The Department of Education reacted to the decision in *Begum* by publishing revised Guidance on school uniforms soon after the judgment, expressly referring to the jilbab as an acceptable (but not necessarily allowed) form of dress in schools.[49] The current version of the Guidance may also be interpreted as leading to the same outcome, always with the school being entitled to reach its own reasoned uniform policy.[50] The decision in *Begum* can thus be said to have led to the clarification of the policy in this field. Although the final outcome was certainly unfavourable to Begum, she can at least have the satisfaction of having enacted her citizenship through the courts, thus overcoming to some extent children's limited democratic voice.[51]

---

[45] Above n 27.

[46] Above n 32 at 12.

[47] J Tobin, 'Understanding a Human Rights Based Approach to Matters Involving Children: Conceptual Foundations and Strategic Considerations' in A Invernizzi and J Williams (eds), *The Human Rights of Children: From Visions to Implementation* (Farnham, Ashgate, 2011) 61, at 71.

[48] Above n 26.

[49] Above n 2 at 335.

[50] Department for Education, *School Uniform: Guidance for Governing Bodies, School Leaders, School Staff and Local Authorities*, September 2013.

[51] A Nolan, 'The Child as "Democratic Citizen"—Challenging the "Participation Gap"' (2010) Winter *PL* 767.

House of Lords

R (on the Application of Begum) v Head-teacher and Governors of Denbigh High School

Baroness Moscati

My Lords

1.   Shabina Begum asserts that the head-teacher and governors of Denbigh High School have unlawfully excluded her from school and, in so doing, have limited her freedom to manifest her religion as protected under article 9 of the European Convention on Human Rights (ECHR); and infringed upon her right to education under article 2 of the First Protocol to the ECHR (A2P1). Bennett J, ruling on the respondent's application for judicial review at first instance, rejected both of these contentions: [2004] EWHC 1389 (Admin); [2004] ELR 374. The Court of Appeal (Brooke, Mummery and Scott Baker LJJ) reversed the decision, and confirmed that Shabina was excluded (unlawfully) from school: [2005] EWCA Civ 199; [2005] 1 WLR 3372. The head-teacher and governors of Denbigh High School (appellants) contend that the Court of Appeal was wrong.

2.   I agree with my noble and learned friends Lord Nicholls of Birkenhead (paragraph 41) and Baroness Hale of Richmond (paragraph 92) that there was an interference with Shabina Begum's freedom of religion under article 9(1) of the ECHR. I disagree, however, with their Lordships that the school's interference was justified and that Shabina's right not to be denied education under A2P1 was not violated. I therefore would not allow this appeal.

3.   As my noble and learned friend Lord Bingham of Cornhill points out (paragraph 2), it is important to recognise that this case concerns a particular pupil and the extent to which schools in the UK should be able to decide dress code issues.

4.   However, I think that it must be emphasised that this is a case about children: a particular child—Shabina, the other children attending Denbigh High School, and also all the children who will read this judgment and those who inevitably will be affected by our decision.

5.   Therefore, in deciding this appeal it is important to remind ourselves that the UN Committee of the Rights of the Child recommends that judges—including members of this Appellate Committee—consider 'how children's rights and interests are or will be affected by their decisions and actions' (General Comment No 5: General Measures of

Implementation of the Convention on the Rights of the Child (Articles 4, 42 and 44(6)), 34th session [12] UN Doc CRC/GC/2003/5 (2003)). The need for consciousness of the interests which children might plausibly claim has received significant support within academic literature: eg John Eekelaar, 'The Emergence of Children's Rights' (1986) 6 *Oxford Journal of Legal Studies* 161.

The facts

6.   To explain the above conclusions I must refer to some of the facts of the case. My noble and learned friend Lord Bingham of Cornhill has comprehensively set out all the facts and therefore I shall offer here a condensed version of those I consider more relevant.

7.   The respondent Shabina Begum, now aged 17, was born in the UK to parents who came from Bangladesh. Shabina is Muslim. At the time of the relevant events she lived with her mother (who did not speak English and has since died), one older sister, and one older brother (Rhaman) five years older than Shabina, who is now her litigation friend.

8.   In September 2000, at the age of nearly 12, Shabina joined her elder sister at Denbigh High School in Luton. The school offered three uniform options, including the shalwar kameeze and headscarf. The shalwar kameeze is a combination of the kameeze, a sleeve-less smock-like dress with a square neckline, revealing the wearer's collar and tie, with the shalwar, loose trousers, tapering at the ankles.

9.   On 3 September 2002 Shabina (then aged nearly 14) went to school with her brother and another young man, and Shabina's brother asked that Shabina be allowed to wear the jilbab. The jilbab is a long coat-like garment covering the entire body. The assistant head decided that Shabina should wear the correct school uniform and told her to go home, change and return to school wearing it. For Shabina, this was equivalent to being expelled, since she could not accept attending school any more without wearing the jilbab.

10.   The school made several failed attempts in writing and over the telephone to convince Shabina to come back to school and on 27 September 2002 they referred the matter to the Education Welfare Service (EWS).

11.   Shabina instructed solicitors who on her behalf wrote to the head-teacher, the gover-nors and the Local Education Authority (LEA), contending that Shabina had been 'excluded/suspended from school because she refused to remove her Muslim dress comprising of a headscarf and long over garment.' The letter contended that Shabina believed that it was an absolute obligation on her to wear that dress and she was not prepared to take it off. It also alleged that the school's decision to exclude Shabina breached her rights under UK and European human rights law. Articles 9, 8 and 14 (ECHR) and A2P1 were set out and reasons given explaining why the school's actions had breached Shabina's human rights.

12.   Shabina's solicitor and the head-teacher obtained opinions from imams regarding Muslim dress code for women and, in September 2003, a statement made by the Muslim Council of Britain on the 'dress code for women in Islam' was forwarded to the school, advising that: there was no recommended style; modesty must be observed at all times; and trousers with long tops for school were 'absolutely fine.' However, as Brooke LJ rightly points out in his judgment (*R (on the application of Begum) v Governors of Denbigh High School Governors* [2005] EWCA Civ 199 [paragraph 31]) there was no expert evidence

before the court, only an exchange of letters between one source and another, which did not offer a conclusive answer.

13.   In October 2003, a committee of the school's governors met, considered this matter and upheld the decision of the school. Shabina was urged to return to school, or to seek a place at another school. It must be said, however, that there is some confusion regarding the number of viable alternative schools available to Shabina.

14.   Shabina issued her claim for judicial review on 13 February 2004. Since then, according to the appellants, a number of Muslim girls at the school have said that they do not wish to wear the jilbab and fear they will be pressured into wearing it. The head-teacher also asserted that several children expressed their concerns that the jilbab might become the school uniform, and the school would be favouring a particular religion (*R (on application of Begum) v Governors of Denbigh High School Governors* [2004] EWCH 1389 paragraph 82). However, the head-teacher also clearly says that she and her staff did not consider it appropriate to survey the students directly about their feelings. Therefore, the opinions and feelings of the other individuals concerned by this matter cannot be verified by this House, and this raises questions about the presumptions upon which the case has been decided in the lower courts. I elaborate on this further below.

Questions

15.   There are three key questions to be addressed. The first is whether, in the circumstances I have described, Shabina was excluded from the school in the sense of section 52(10) of the Education Act 2002. The second question is whether there was an interference with Shabina Begum's freedom of religion under article 9(1) of the ECHR and, if so, whether the interference by the school was justified. The third question is whether Shabina's right to education was infringed as a result of her being deemed to have been excluded from school.

The applicable law: the ECHR and the United Nations Convention on the Rights of the Child (1989) (UNCRC)

16.   Article 9 ECHR provides:

> 1. Everyone has the right to freedom of thought, conscience and religion; this right includes freedom … to manifest his religion or belief, in worship, teaching, practice and observance.

> 2. Freedom to manifest one's religion or beliefs shall be subject only to such limitations as are prescribed by law and are necessary in a democratic society in the interests of public safety, for the protection of public order, health or morals, or for the protection of the rights and freedoms of others.

17.   A2P1 reads:

> No person shall be denied the right to education. In the exercise of any functions which it assumes in relation to education and to teaching, the State shall respect the rights of parents to ensure such education and teaching in conformity with their own religious and philosophical convictions.

18.   The case before this House concerns a child, and when children's rights are under consideration then not only the ECHR but also the UNCRC, the authoritative children's human rights treaty, deserves analysis. I had the advantage of reading the draft speeches of

my noble and learned friends and, with respect, insufficient attention has been given to the rights and principles enshrined in the UNCRC.

19.   The United Kingdom ratified the UNCRC in 1990. Although the UNCRC does not bind UK courts, it is used to interpret the law, where possible, in matters concerning children. This is well acknowledged by courts in the UK (see, eg *Payne v Payne* [2001] EWCA Civ 166, [2001] Fam 473 at 487 per Thorpe LJ at paragraph 38; *R (Howard League for Penal Reform) v Secretary of State for the Home Department* [2002] EWHC 2497 (Admin) per Munby J at paragraph 51; and *R (Williamson) v Secretary of State for Education and Employment* [2005] UKHL 15, per Baroness Hale at paragraphs 80–81). In particular, Munby J points out that

> neither the UN Convention nor the European Charter is at present legally binding in our domestic law and they are therefore not sources of law in strict sense. But both can, in my judgment, properly be consulted insofar as they proclaim, reaffirm or elucidate the content of those human rights that are generally recognized throughout the European family of nations, in particular the nature and scope of those fundamental rights that are guaranteed by the European Convention.

20.   This approach follows that of the European Court of Human Rights (see, eg *V v United Kingdom* (Application no 24888/94) [1999] ECHR 171 at paragraphs 73, 76 and 97; *T v United Kingdom* (Application no 24724/94) [1999] at paragraphs 44, 75, and per Lord Reed's concurring opinion), where the UNCRC informs the interpretation of children's ECHR rights. In my respectful opinion, this approach taken by the European Court of Human Rights (ECHR) is relevant to the decision in this case, and accordingly, pursuant to section 2 of the Human Rights Act 1998, this House is obliged to take the ECHR jurisprudence into account in determining a question which has arisen in respect of a Convention right.

21.   The UNCRC rights to participation and respect for the views of the child (article 12); to freedom of thought, conscience and religion (article 14); and to education (article 28) are particularly relevant here. In addition, the UNCRC recognises that children grow, learn, develop their ideas and personalities and, therefore, parents, guardians and any other person responsible for the child shall provide guidance and direction in a manner 'consistent with the evolving capacities of the child' (article 5).

22.   The right to participation is central in this case, although I note this has been absent from consideration in these proceedings and in the decision made by the school.
   Article 12 of the UNCRC reads:

> 1. States Parties shall assure to the child who is capable of forming his or her own views the right to express those views freely in all matters affecting the child, the views of the child being given due weight in accordance with the age and maturity of the child.

> 2. For this purpose, the child shall in particular be provided the opportunity to be heard in any judicial and administrative proceedings affecting the child, either directly, or through a representative or an appropriate body, in a manner consistent with the procedural rules of national law.

23.   As explained by G Lansdown, *Promoting Children's Participation in Democratic Decision-Making* (Florence, UNICEF Innocenti Research Centre, 2001) page 2,

> article 12 introduces a radical challenge to traditional attitudes, which assume that children should be seen and not heard … the right to be heard extends to all actions and decisions that affect

children's lives—in the family, in the school, in local communities ... it is not sufficient to give children the right to be listened to. It is also important to take what they have to say seriously.

24.   Furthermore, as the Warnock Report (1978) suggested at paragraph 1.4, education pursues two aims:

[T]o enlarge a child's knowledge, experience and imaginative understanding, and his [sic] awareness of moral values and capacity for enjoyment; and secondly to enable him [sic] to enter the world after formal education is over as an active participant in society and a responsible contributor to it, capable of achieving as much independence as possible.

25.   The Committee on the Rights of the Child also specifies that the right to education is interconnected with other rights and, in particular, the right to participation, and adds that 'children do not lose their human rights by virtue of passing through the school gates. Thus, for example, education must be provided in a way that respects the inherent dignity of the child and enables the child to express his or her views freely in accordance with article 2(1) and to participate in school life' (General Comment No 1, *The Aims of Education*, UN Doc CRC/GC/2001/1 (2001) para 8). According to the facts of this case Shabina and the other children of the school were not consulted or involved in any consultative process regarding the issues we are discussing in this case.

Exclusion from school

26.   The first question to consider is whether Shabina was excluded (unlawfully) from school.

27.   In this context, the 'exclusion' referred to is 'exclusion on disciplinary grounds' (section 64(4) of the Schools Standards and Framework Act 1998 ('the 1998 Act') and section 52(10) of the Education Act 2002 ('the 2002 Act')). The Department of Education and Skills (DfES) Circular 10/99 gives special guidance to schools in relation to exclusions specifying that '[e]xclusion should not be used for breaching school uniform [norms]' (6.4).

28.   It is clear from the agreed facts that the school did not intend to exclude Shabina in the statutory sense of the word, nor did it believe that it was doing so. However, I agree with Brooke LJ in his judgment *R (on the application of Begum) v Governors of Denbigh High School Governors* [2005] EWCA Civ 199 (paragraph 24) that, in effect, the school did exclude Shabina when she was told 'to go home and change and return wearing correct school uniform' (in appealed decision *R (on the application of Begum) v Governors of Denbigh High School Governors* [2004] EWHC 1389 (Admin) paragraph 3.5). The basis for such request is not evident from the facts. First, as suggested by Bennett J at paragraph 79 of his judgment *R (on the application of Begum) v Governors of Denbigh High School Governors* [2004] EWHC 1389 (Admin), the school did not have a policy stating that if a pupil came to school dressed contrary to the uniform policy, he or she would be sent home to change and then return to school; nor was there a policy stating that if the pupil refused to change into the school uniform, he or she might not be allowed to return to school.

29.   Second, at paragraph 26 of his judgment Bennett J reports that Ms Spencer, the solicitor instructed by Shabina, proposed to the school two options for Shabina: 1) to attend the school wearing the jilbab, but to be educated in the Inclusive Learning Room away from the main school community; 2) to attend school wearing clothing that accorded with her

beliefs by adopting simple adjustments to the school uniform. She would still wear a white shirt and tie, but her arms and legs would be covered by one dark garment in the school's uniform colours. The school did not consider these options. However, in the past the wearing of headscarves had been allowed and the facts do not provide evidence for why the school did not adopt the same approach regarding the jilbab.

30.   Therefore, the school had the opportunity to accommodate Shabina's request, but did not. Research shows that schools often use 'unofficial exclusion', with children being sent home (see A Steer (Chairman) (2005) *Learning Behaviour: The Report of the Practitioners' Group on School Behaviour and Disciplines* DFS paragraphs 144–45). This seems to me to be what happened here and, therefore, in my view the school de facto excluded Shabina.

Article 9: Interference and justification

31.   I do not agree that Shabina's right to religion was not infringed. According to article 9 ECHR and article 14 UNCRC, children are entitled to freedom of thought, conscience and religion and that freedom protects both the right to hold a belief and the right to manifest a belief. Restrictions to the manifestation of a held belief must be prescribed by law and only when necessary for public safety, for the protection of public order, health or morals, or for the protection of the rights of others. Finally, article 9 (1) recognises that religious choices can change.

32.   I turn first to the authenticity of Shabina's belief. It is important to recognise at the outset that this case concerns a determined young woman who knows her religious beliefs and wishes to express them. Based on the proceedings before the Court of Appeal and in the words of Ms Booth QC who was instructed by Shabina, it is evident that Shabina is an intelligent and articulate young woman who has matured her religious beliefs as part of her own identity. It might be difficult to accept—even for judges, as case law on blood transfusion shows (see C Bridge, 'Religion, Culture and Conviction—the Medical Treatment of Young Children' (1999) 11 *Child and Family Law Quarterly* 1)—that children can have strong religious views and follow a religion freely and consciously without being encouraged or forced by adults. Shabina seems to be one of those children. Allowing Shabina the freedom to make her own decisions and to live by them is an important part of the role of the law and of this Court, in securing the conditions that allow children to develop their potential as rights-holders (G Lansdown, *The Evolving Capacities of the Child* (Florence, UNICEF Innocenti Research Institute, 2005).

33.   There are two issues here to consider. First, Shabina's right to be heard in the proceedings and by the school according to article 12 UNCRC. In my respectful opinion, given Shabina's age and understanding, the most appropriate way of hearing her views would be directly. The second issue is the weight that children's (religious) views should have. I elaborate further on this below.

34.   Lord Nicholls of Birkenhead has stated in *R (Williamson and others) v Secretary of state for Education* [2005] 2 AC 246, paragraph 22, that: (a) 'when the genuineness of a claimant's professed belief is in issue in the proceedings, the court will inquire into and decide this issue as an issue of fact', (b) 'the court is concerned to ensure an assertion of religious belief is made in good faith "neither fictitious, nor capricious and that it is not an artifice"',

(c) 'emphatically it is not for the court to embark on an inquiry into the asserted belief and judge its validity by some objective standard such as the source material upon which the claimant founds his [sic] belief or the orthodox teaching of the religion in question or the extent to which the claimant's belief conforms to or differs from the views of other professing the same religion', and (d) 'the relevance of objective factors such as source material is, at most, that they may throw light on whether the professed belief is genuinely held.'

35.   Applying those factors to Shabina's case, I have little doubt that as she got older she changed her views on religious dress and now genuinely believes that her religion requires her to wear the jilbab. I therefore agree with Brooke LJ at paragraph 78 of his judgment that the school did not attribute Shabina's 'beliefs the weight they deserved' and this happened, in my view, because Shabina was not heard. Indeed, as Bennett J at paragraph 68, referring to the statement given by Shabina's brother, points out:

> it might have been expected that it would be the claimant herself who would have given that evidence. One wonders why it should have been her brother who articulated what the claimant was perfectly capable of saying herself. Nevertheless, Mr Birks did not suggest that I should find that the claimant's motives and beliefs were anything other than completely genuine.

Too much emphasis has been put on the role that Shabina's brother had in this case when, in fact, he was simply acting as litigation friend.

36.   What relevance does not giving weight to Shabina's views have on the interference with her right protected by article 9? It is for the law to support children in becoming competent individuals and for the courts as well, when children's rights are involved, to first ascertain that children's views have not been constrained by their contexts and social expectations. Although not considered by the courts below, *Gillick v West Norfolk and Wisbech Area Health Authority* [1986] AC 112 is the authority showing that due consideration must be given to a competent child's decisions, an obligation which in my view was not respected in this case. There is no doubt that Shabina has a genuinely held belief and that in her view this should be manifested through the wearing of the jilbab. I regret therefore that we did not hear more from Shabina herself on this. Of course this is not the individual judges' fault, but a negative consequence of the way the judicial review system is set up and the way judicial procedures generally exclude children's voices, raising in my view serious concern of access to justice.

37.   It is true that Shabina knew that her older sister had gone to Denbigh High School and had agreed to abide by the school policy on dress code, thus wearing the shalwar kameeze quite happily. However as my noble and learned friend Baroness Hale eloquently suggests, adolescence is a time of changes and physical, cognitive and psychological developments which happen at different times and at different rates for different people. Likewise, Shabina with time developed a more personal understanding of her beliefs and chose to wear a religious dress with which she felt more comfortable to express her religion. Shabina changed her opinion regarding some aspects of her beliefs, and in so doing was exercising her right as protected by article 9. Her changed opinion was the consequence of Shabina's evolving capacity to learn and which is protected under article 5 UNCRC, and which families, schools and the law must take into account. If we accept this, as I do, then we acknowledge that Shabina not only has the right to change her mind,

but also that it would be inappropriate in particular for a child to choose between religion and education. Nonetheless, it is clear that Shabina's article 9 right was engaged. The refusal of the school to consider the proposed alternatives constituted exclusion and thus interference with her article 9 right. We have now to consider whether such interference was justified.

Justification

38.   I am in no doubt that this interference with article 9 was not justified. Under article 9(2), a limitation of or interference with the right is justified only where it is: (a) prescribed by law and (b) necessary in the interests of public safety, for the protection of public order, health or morals, or for the protection of the rights and freedoms of others.

39.   Regarding article 9(2)(a), it is true that the governors of the school were entitled to, and did, publish a clear uniform policy. However, as explained above, the policy did not prescribe that pupils not wearing the uniform would be sent home. A school policy inspired by the principles of the rule of law and children's rights should clearly define the circumstances under which the policy would be held to be violated and the consequences of failure to comply with it. Children should be given the opportunity to make an informed choice about the school's uniform. Based on the policy of the school, Shabina could not imagine that exclusion would be an option. Moreover, it has been suggested that Shabina had the choice to attend another school (Bennett J paragraph 60). However, as I explained earlier, there are doubts about the viability of the alternatives offered to Shabina and I agree with my noble and learned friend Lord Nicholls of Birkenhead that 'this may over-estimate the ease with which Shabina could move to another school and under-estimate the disruption this would be likely to cause to her education.' In fact, as I have explained earlier, the school had the option to accommodate Shabina's manifestation of religious belief, but decided not to do so.

40.   I shall now turn to article 9(2)(b). It has been suggested that if Shabina succeeds in her claim, other children might be affected. That argument again raises questions about the participation of children in decisions regarding their upbringing and the weight given to children's views and wishes. It also does not take into account the view expressed by the European Court of Human Rights in *Serif v Greece* (2001) 31 EHRR 561 at paragraph 53:

> [I]t is possible that tension is created in situations where a religious or any other community becomes divided, [the Court] considers that this is one of the unavoidable consequences of pluralism. The role of the authorities in such circumstances is not to remove the cause of tension by eliminating pluralism but to ensure that competing groups tolerate each other.

This approach was not followed in the case before this House, because of the assumption that other children might feel pressurised.

41.   First, as my noble and learned friend Lord Bingham of Cornhill suggests in his opinion, the head-teacher and her assistant were concerned that the acceptance of the jilbab as a permissible variant of the school uniform would lead to the differentiation between Muslim groups. We know from the facts above that some parents expressed their worry about the jilbab. However, I am inclined to agree with my noble and learned friend Baroness Hale in *D (A Child) (Abduction: Rights of Custody)* [2006] UKHL that the decision-maker should

not assume that the views of the child's carers coincide with the views of the child. Moreover, Thorpe LJ in *Mabon v Mabon* [2005] EWCA Civ 634, at paragraph 28, stressed that

> unless we in this jurisdiction are to fall out of step with similar societies as they safeguard article 12 rights [UNCRC], we must, in the case of articulate teenagers, accept that the right to freedom of expression and participation outweighs the paternalistic judgment of welfare.

42.   In addition, the head-teacher felt that adherence to the school uniform policy was necessary to promote inclusion and social cohesion. However, on the basis of paragraph 82 of the decision of the High Court, it seems that such assumptions draw upon teachers' reports based on the views of a few students; the school felt that surveying all the students directly was not appropriate. Therefore, without direct consultation, there is no evidence that the wishes of the other pupils have been explored sufficiently to justify refusing Shabina's request. Without direct consultation it is not possible in my view to sustain the head-teacher's claims that others will feel pressured to wear the jilbab.

43.   Instead, a school decision, informed by an inclusive participatory process involving the other pupils and Shabina, would have been more respectful of Shabina's and the other children's rights and interests, and would have potentially led to another outcome in this case. This conclusion is reinforced by the fact that there is no uniformity of views on what is the appropriate dress for Muslim women (as evidenced by the competing views received by the school from the imams it consulted). And it is in these regards that the procedure followed by the school to assess the proportionality of their decision was mistaken.

44.   In doing so, the school struck a dangerous balance between individual rights (Shabina's rights) and the rights of some other pupils. It is crucial to point out that '[e]duca- tion must enable [pupils] to understand and respect different cultural values and traditions and the processes of cultural change and development. The engine of cultural change is the human capacity for creative thought and action' (National Advisory Committee on Crea- tive and Cultural Education (1999), 'All Our Futures: Creativity, Culture and Education'). Moreover, it is the role of education (article 29 UNCRC) to promote

> [t]he preparation of the child for responsible life in a free society, in the spirit of understanding, peace, tolerance, equality of sexes, and friendship among all peoples, ethnic, national and religious groups and persons of indigenous origin.

45.   In light of this, I conclude that the interference was unjustified.

Article 2 of the first protocol to the ECHR

46.   As I have found in favour of Shabina on article 9, my discussion of A2P1 is brief. Shabina contends that the school violated her right to education. I agree with my noble and learned friend, Lord Nicholls of Birkenhead, that the ease with which Shabina could move to another more suitable school was over-estimated and that the disruption that this would be likely to cause to her education was under estimated.

47.   According to the agreed facts, the school attempted several times to convince Shabina to go back to school. However, as explained above, and from the facts, there is no evidence that suitable schools were available.

48.   Therefore, on the plain facts, Shabina's right to education was infringed.

Conclusion

49.   In conclusion, Shabina was excluded by the school and, therefore, her rights to manifest her religion or belief and to education were unjustifiably infringed. I would dismiss this appeal.

20

Commentary on *S v Special Educational Needs and Disability Tribunal and Oxfordshire County Council*

SEAMUS BYRNE

I. Introduction

The intersection of education and disability is one wherein a number of profound and competing issues arise from a children's rights perspective. Although the non-discriminatory delivery of available, accessible, acceptable and adaptable[1] education is well-anchored in international human rights law, the concretisation of this right in the lives of children who suffer from a disability is less assured.[2] Traditionally regarded as 'objects of charity and passive recipients of welfare',[3] the rights of disabled persons are becoming more centralised within the human rights sphere, after a somewhat protracted voyage.[4] Resource allocation and public spending[5] often impact the domestic provision of much needed resources for the furtherance of children's rights, including education.[6] These issues are crystallised in *S*.[7] In his re-written fictitious appellate judgment, Lord Justice Harris centralises, engages and elaborates on the relevant children's rights principles within the adjudicative function of the Court of Appeal, and overturns the decision of the High Court on a point of law.

---

[1] See Committee on Economic, Social and Cultural Rights, (1999) General Comment No 13: The Right to Education (Art 13) & Preliminary report of the Special Rapporteur on the right to education, Ms Katarina Tomasevski, submitted in accordance with Commission on Human Rights resolution 1998/33, (13 January 1999) E/CN.4/1999/49.

[2] According to UNICEF (2013) children with disabilities often experience problems accessing basic services such as education and health and are disproportionally vulnerable to abuse, neglect and violence. See UNICEF (2013) Factsheet: Children and Disabilities and WHO *World Report on Disability* (2011).

[3] UNICEF (2007) *Promoting the Rights of Children With Disabilities* at 5.

[4] See generally, G Quinn, 'A Short Guide to the United Nations Convention on the Rights of Persons with Disabilities' (2009) 1 *European Yearbook on Disability Law* 89.

[5] See *R (on the application of SG and others (previously JS and others)) (Appellants) v Secretary of State for Work and Pensions (Respondent)* [2015] UKSC 16.

[6] For example, see *A v Essex County Council and National Autistic Society (Intervener)* wherein Lord Philips states that 'A2P1 does not impose a positive obligation on contracting states to provide effective education for children who have special educational needs' [2010] UKSC 33 at para 81.

[7] *S v Special Educational Needs and Disability Tribunal and Oxfordshire County Council* [2005] EWHC 196 (Admin).

II. Background

The applicant appealed pursuant to section 11 of the Tribunals and Inquiries Act 1992 against a decision of the Special Educational Needs and Disability Tribunal (SENDIST), which had refused his appeal against the decision of Oxfordshire County Council, the local education authority (LEA), to carry out a statutory assessment of his daughter's (C's) special educational needs (SEN).[8] A key issue was whether C's exceptional ability combined with her emotional, social and behavioural difficulties warranted a statutory assessment of her SEN which could have led to a confirmed placement at an independent residential school at the LEA's expense, as distinct from a mainstream local authority day school. At the time of the first instance appeal and the subsequent re-written appellate hearing, the law in England governing SEN was found in Part IV of the Education Act 1996 (hereafter the 1996 Act) and its associated regulations.[9] Having SEN hinged on whether the child had a learning difficulty calling for special educational provision to be made for him or her.[10] The Act defined 'learning difficulty' with reference to having a greater difficulty in learning than the majority of children of the relevant child's age[11] or a disability which either prevented or hindered him or her from making use of the educational facilities, of a kind generally provided for children of their age in schools within the LEA's area.[12] Special educational provision was defined to include educational provision which was additional to, or otherwise different from, the educational provision made generally for children in schools maintained by the local education authority (other than special schools).[13]

The kind or level of special educational provision required might require determination, in some instances, by the LEA (a body replaced since 2010 by the 'local authority' per se). It would hinge on a formal assessment of the child's needs by the authority.[14] If, post-assessment, the LEA decided that the special educational provision needed determination, it was required to make a statement of SEN[15] specifying the nature and type of SEN required[16] and also the type of school (or in some cases the name of the school) appropriate to meet the SEN of the child.[17] Parents had a right of appeal against a refusal of a request to assess or a decision not to make a statement.[18] In the present case, the refusal by Oxfordshire County Council to assess, and its subsequent affirmation by the SENDIST, prompted the appeal to the High Court.

---

[8] The law relating to statutory assessments has since been changed and is now governed by the Children and Families Act 2014 in England only. In Wales the process continues to be governed by the Education Act 1996 and in Northern Ireland by the Special Educational Needs and Disability (NI) Order (SENDO) 2005. In Scotland, the law is governed by the Education (Additional Support for Learning) (Scotland) Act 2004.

[9] Special Educational Needs Code of Practice (November 2001).

[10] s 312(1) 1996 Act.

[11] s 312(2)(a) 1996 Act.

[12] s 312(2)(b) 1996 Act.

[13] s 312(4) 1996 Act.

[14] s 323 1996 Act.

[15] s 324 1996 Act.

[16] s 324(3)(b) 1996 Act.

[17] s 324(4)(a) 1996 Act.

[18] s 325 and s 329 1996 Act.

III. First Instance Determinations

The appellant's appeal was dismissed by Elias J in the High Court in a judgment given on 4 February 2005. Elias J first rejected the contention that the SENDIST had insufficient regard to the evidence before it and the contention that its decision 'was against the weight of evidence'.[19] While noting that the preponderance of psychological evidence presented to the tribunal favoured the appellant's daughter's education outside the maintained sector and within the more structured confines of a residential school, the judge held that the tribunal was entitled to look at her recent school reports, which were 'better than expected', and to also 'use its own knowledge and experience when assessing the evidence'.[20]

Second, Elias J agreed with the tribunal that 'exceptional ability' did not amount to a SEN for the purposes of the 1996 Act. While urged to adopt a more expansive and functionalist perspective which would bring those with exceptional ability within the ambit of the Act's (section 312) definition of SEN, the judge found the language of section 312 to be not 'sufficiently flexible to give effect to any such change'[21] while noting that 'disability' was not the appropriate word for someone with the benefit of high intelligence.

Third, Elias J held that the appellant's claim, while engaging European Convention on Human Rights (ECHR) Article 2 Protocol 1 (A2P1) (Right to Education), did not transgress Article 14 (the non-discrimination provision) read with it. The difference in treatment between the 'less able' and the 'exceptionally able' did not require objective justification because they were not sufficiently analogous groups and because there were 'obvious social and economic reasons why it may be thought desirable to use resources to help the less able but not the most able'.[22] Further, even if such justification *was* needed, it could 'readily be established'.[23]

Having regard to the ruling, a number of anomalies emerge from a children's rights perspective. First, while domestic law concerning education does not, on the basis of ECHR jurisprudence, guarantee the child the best possible or highest level of instruction,[24] nor oblige a local authority in the delivery of special educational provision 'to provide a child with the best possible education',[25] the United Nations Convention on the Rights of the Child (CRC) in Articles 28 and 29 mandates a holistic educative approach[26] to develop the child's talents and abilities to their fullest potential so as to enable them to 'participate fully and responsibly in a free society'.[27] Similarly, Article 23 extends this obligation to disabled children as well as encouraging their 'active participation' in the community including the receipt of education directed towards their 'fullest possible social integration and individual development'.[28] However, in the determination of the adequacy of the maintained sector for

[19] Above n 1 at para 16.
[20] ibid.
[21] ibid, para 26.
[22] ibid, para 38.
[23] ibid, para 39.
[24] *Belgian Linguistics Case* [1968] 1 EHRR 252.
[25] See *R v Surrey CC ex P C* (1984) 83 LGR 219 & *S v SEN Tribunal* [1995] 1 WLR 1627.
[26] See Committee on the Rights of the Child (2001), General Comment No 1, *The Aims of Education*.
[27] ibid, para 14.
[28] Art 23 (3) CRC and see also the UN Convention on the Rights of Persons with Disabilities.

C's educational needs, the Court appears to have failed to consider either the views of the child regarding her preferred option or which system would likely be in her best interests'[29] as to promote and further her development and growth. Rather, the Court agreed with the SENDIST that her needs could be sufficiently accommodated for in the maintained sector. This approach conforms to the narrow obligation to provide education, as opposed to the best possible education as envisaged by the CRC.

Second, issues arise from the finding that 'exceptional ability' was not a disability within the definitional parameters of the 1996 Act. Admittedly, while the 1996 Act overtly encases a narrow and prescribed version of disability in terms of reduced or prevented access to standard educational facilities for children of the same age in schools within the LEA's area, the Court's failure to adopt an expansive and functionalist interpretation of disability was clearly rooted in the constricted statutory classification of disability then persisting, which as construed by Elias J meant 'want of an ability, not excess of it'.[30] While he was obviously mindful to operate within the confines of the prevailing statutory regime, a failure to engage with the specificities of 'exceptional ability' and to consider the concurrent and often detrimental socio-emotional difficulties which accompany it is apparent.[31] Moreover, the Court could have reached an alternative outcome if it had considered such difficulties and aligned them with what would be in C's best interests. While not as such amounting to a disability, the consequential effects of exceptional ability could and should have played a more prominent role in the judicial determination as to whether C's needs could be best accommodated in the maintained sector, and if considered in light of the psychological evidence adduced at the tribunal, could have resulted in a different outcome.

IV. The Court of Appeal Judgment

Harris's fictitious 2006 Court of Appeal Judgment is instituted on three separate grounds of appeal, examined below for their compatibility with the children's rights framework at the time. Subsequent statutory and jurisprudential developments in this area of law are also assessed.

A. Exceptional Ability

Harris agrees with Elias J that the possession of an 'exceptional ability' does not in itself constitute a 'disability' for the purposes of the 1996 Act. Central to both is an appreciation of the narrow and somewhat limited statutory definitions which prevailed in 2005. Harris refers to the fact that despite the CRC mandating an approach to the development of the child which is holistic and all-inclusive,[32] such an approach is at variance with the statutory

---

[29] See Art 3 CRC which guarantees the child the right to have his/her best interests taken as a primary consideration in all matters affecting them.

[30] Above n 1 at para 26.

[31] See L Vaivre-Douret, 'Developmental and Cognitive Characteristics of 'High-Level Potentialities' (Highly Gifted) Children' [2011] *International Journal of Paediatrics* Article ID 420297.

[32] Harris judgment at para 10.

espousals regarding disability and in particular the Disability Discrimination Act 1995.[33] The 1995 Act aligned disability with a physical or mental impairment which resulted in a 'substantial and long term effect' on the 'ability to carry out normal day to day activities' and thus this Act, and the definition of disability therein, is inseparable from the enunciation of disability in the 1996 Act, on which SEN provision was dependent.

The adherence of both judgments to the statutory definitions of disability exposes the tension between the aims of the CRC on the one hand and the concretisation of those aims within the domestic legal framework on the other hand. While the CRC, in terms of both education and disability rights, enunciates a broad, purposive approach, the domestic implementation of these rights is much narrower in scope, content and practice. Specifically, in the context of SEN provision:

> [T]his does not oblige the local education authority to make available the best possible education, Parliament has imposed an obligation to meet the needs of the child and no more.[34]

B. Discrimination Contrary to Article 14 ECHR

Extending only to the Convention rights, freedoms and protocols (including A2P1 which secures the right to education), Article 14 prohibits discrimination on a range of defined grounds[35] in addition to other undefined grounds which fall under the umbrella term 'other status'. Both the first instance appeal and the imagined appellate judgment agree that the appellant's claim engaged A2P1 and thus the question of whether the difference in treatment can be justified arises.

In contrast to Elias J's approach (above), Harris's judgment, in addressing whether the 'less able' and 'exceptionally able' are analogous for the purpose of Article 14, refers to the pronouncement of Baroness Hale in *Ghaidan*[36] that unmarried same-sex couples and opposite sex-couples were in comparable situations and thus he holds that the difference in treatment warrants justification.[37] In so doing, he observes that the failure of the lower court to do so constituted an error of law, sufficient to set aside the judgment. In upholding the condition for the advancement of economic reasons pertaining to the difference in treatment, Harris rules that in light of such differential treatment and their consequential effects, Elias J 'ought to have adjourned'.[38]

In adopting a more holistic and complete approach to the provision of education for both the less able and the exceptionally able, unconstrained by the Education Act 1996, Harris' Court of Appeal judgment states that 'the justification for the difference of treatment should relate to the overall level of provision by the state to meet educational needs within each of the respective groups'.[39] Underpinning this decision lies the acknowledgement that common to both groups is the acceptance that both require additional measures

---

[33] This Act has now been revoked and replaced by the Equality Act 2010 but is still applicable in Northern Ireland.

[34] *S v SEN Tribunal* [1995] 1 WLR 1627 at para 1638 (C).

[35] Such grounds include sex, race, colour, language, religion, political or other opinion, national or social origin, association with a national minority, property and birth.

[36] *Ghaidan v Godin-Mendoza* [2004] UKHL 34.

[37] Harris judgment at paras 46–47.

[38] Harris at para 47.

[39] Harris at para 46.

and needs to reach their full potential. The re-written judgment adopts an all-inclusive approach to the delivery of the right to education consistent with the CRC, including its stated objective for education relating to '[t]he development of the child's personality, talents and mental and physical abilities to their fullest potential'.[40]

C. Article 12 UNCRC

The re-written judgment also addresses the question of the voice of the child at the centre of the dispute pursuant to Article 12 CRC. In mandating that the views of the child are heard and given due weight in accordance with the child's age and maturity,[41] Article 12 represents the acceptance of children as rights-holders who are entitled to have a say in matters affecting their rights and are permitted to participate in the realisation of those rights, including education. In his consideration of whether the lower court accorded sufficient weight, if any, to the views of the child, Harris expounds the legal and procedural significance of obtaining the child's views within an educational context.[42] In alluding to the Code of Practice[43] which encased the right of the child to express their views and on examining European human rights jurisprudence pursuant to Articles 6 and 8 of the ECHR,[44] Harris LJ engages with the procedural and substantive elements of Article 12 CRC, interlocking them within the adjudicative fabric of his judgment.

Indeed, the Children Act 1989 commands a court, when considering the making of a public or private law order pertaining to the upbringing of a child, to have regard 'to the ascertainable wishes and feelings of the child concerned'.[45] Similarly, *in Re L (A Child) (Contact: Domestic Violence)*[46] a case preceding both judgments and concerning four simultaneous appeals against the refusal to permit parental contact against a background of domestic violence, Dame Elizabeth Butler-Sloss P in quoting from *Contact and Domestic Violence— The Expert's Court Report* stated that: 'the older the child the more seriously they should be viewed and the more insulting and discrediting to the child to have them ignored'.[47]

Although such sentiments were expressed within a family law context, the underpinning ethos is upheld in the Harris judgment, thereby rectifying the evident anomaly in the first instance appeal whereby the Court, in determining the future of the education of the appellant's daughter and in also applauding her academic success to date, failed to make reference to her opinions, wishes or feelings.[48] In his re-written appellate judgment, Harris corrects this procedural irregularity by engaging with Article 12 CRC. Despite holding that it was unclear whether the High Court took account of or attached any weight to the views of the child,[49] such interrogations were unnecessary as the decision had already been set aside.

---

[40] Art 29(1)(a) CRC.
[41] See Art 5 CRC and G Landsdown, 'The Evolving Capacities of the Child' (UNICEF Innocenti Research, 2005).
[42] Harris judgment at para 49.
[43] ibid.
[44] Harris judgment at paras 51–52.
[45] s 1(3) Children Act 1989.
[46] *Re L (A Child) (Contact: Domestic Violence)* [2001] FAM 260.
[47] ibid at 271 (H).
[48] Harris judgment at para 53.
[49] ibid.

V. Developments since *S*

Since 2005, the legal, social and political landscape has altered considerably and children now occupy a terrain which hitherto was both unfamiliar and at times inaccessible. Legislative[50] and jurisprudential developments at both national and international level have resulted in the acceptance of children's rights principles as indispensable to the adjudicative process.[51]

Moreover, the enactment of the Children and Families Act (CFA) 2014 Part 3 (which sets out a new framework for SEN in place of Part IV of the 1996 Act) obliges local authorities to have regard to the views, wishes and feelings of children in the performance of their responsibilities[52] and to consult the child's parent (or young person (aged 16–24 inclusive) him/herself) when considering carrying out an Education, Health and Care (EHC) assessment.[53] Furthermore, the 2014 Act also makes provision for the young person concerned to request an EHC needs assessment,[54] which represents a profound departure from the old 1996 Act which circumscribed such requests to the preserve of parents or the local authority.

VI. Conclusion

That more attention has been allotted to the position of children and their rights within the decision-making process is beyond doubt. The application of children's rights principles has, however, been slow to emerge in the jurisprudence in the SEN field. Harris' Court of Appeal judgment, in overturning the High Court's decision, demonstrates the potency and influence which an observance of children's rights principles can have on the decision-making process. In its recognition of the need to engage with and consider the voice of the child, or to seek justification for the difference in treatment between the 'less able' and the 'exceptionally able', the re-written judgment has carefully re-configured the outcome and confirms the plausibility and credibility of judicial pronouncements through children's rights standards.

---

[50] For example, see s (55) Borders, Citizenship and Immigration Act 2009 and Pt 1, Ch 2 Protection of Freedoms Act 2012.

[51] For example see Art 24 of the EU Charter of Fundamental Rights. See also, T Liefaard and J E Doek (eds), *Litigating the Rights of the Child: The UN Convention on the Rights of the Child in Domestic and International Jurisprudence* (Dordrecht, Springer Science & Business Media, 2015).

[52] s 19(a) CFA 2014.

[53] s 36(4) CFA 2014.

[54] s 36(1) CFA 2014.

Court of Appeal (England and Wales)

S v Special Educational Needs and Disability Tribunal and Oxfordshire County Council

Harris LJ

The proceedings

1.   This appeal concerns the education of C, a child of exceptional ability. On 4 February 2005 Elias J dismissed C's father's appeal against the decision of the Special Educational Needs and Disability Tribunal (SENDIST) refusing to overturn the decision by the second respondent, Oxfordshire County Council ('Oxfordshire'), not to conduct a statutory assessment of C's special educational needs (SEN) ([2005] EWHC 196 (Admin)). Permission to appeal to this court was granted on several grounds, pursued further by the appellant.

2.   At issue are three important matters: (i) whether C has SEN for the purposes of the Education Act 1996 (the 1996 Act) section 312; (ii) whether there was unlawful discrimination against her contrary to Article 14 of the European Convention on Human Rights (ECHR) read with Article 2 of the First Protocol (A2P1); and (iii) whether there was an alleged failure to ensure that C's views were heard and given the degree of consideration required by Article 12 of the UN Convention on the Rights of the Child (UNCRC).

3.   *R (CES (A Minor) (by her father and friend NS)) v Oxfordshire* [2004] EWHC 133 (Admin) (*CES*), a decision on the appellant's judicial review challenge to a refusal to meet the cost of educating C privately, is not the subject of the current appeal.

The Law

A. The Education Act 1996

4.   The main obligations of local education authorities (LEAs) in England towards children with SEN are in Part 4 of the 1996 Act. Section 313 provides that LEAs, school governing bodies, and the SENDIST must have regard to a code of practice made by the Secretary of State, currently the *Special Educational Needs Code of Practice* (2001) (section 313(2) and (3)).

5.   Under section 312(1) a child has SEN if 'he has a learning difficulty which calls for special educational provision to be made for him'. (Part 4 uses gender specific language

but applies to both genders.) In the case of a child aged at least two, 'special educational provision' is 'educational provision which is additional to, or otherwise different from, the educational provision made generally for children of his age in schools maintained by the [LEA] (other than special schools)' (section 312(4)(a), as amended).

6.   The definition of 'learning difficulty' is of particular importance in this case. Under section 312(2) a child aged five or over has such difficulty if:

   (a) he has a significantly greater difficulty in learning than the majority of children of his age, [or]

   (b) he has a disability which either prevents or hinders him from making use of educational facilities of a kind generally provided for children of his age in schools within the area of the [LEA].

7.   There are separate obligations on local education authorities for assessing the child's needs (section 323). Where, in the light of the assessment, an authority considers it is necessary to determine the special educational provision which the child's needs call for, it must make a 'statement' setting out such provision and other prescribed matters (section 324).

B. The ECHR

8.   Under the ECHR, A2P1:

   No-one shall be denied the right to education. In the exercise of any functions which it assumes in relation to education and to teaching, the State shall respect the right of parents to ensure such education and teaching in conformity with their own religious and philosophical convictions.

The right in the first sentence is a right of the child himself or herself: *Campbell and Cosans v United Kingdom* (1982) Series A no 48, 4 EHRR 293 at [40]; and see U Kilkelly, *The Child and the European Convention on Human Rights* (Aldershot, Ashgate/Dartmouth, 1999) 64.

9.   As with other Convention rights, the right must be available on an equal basis—that is, without discrimination on a prohibited basis. Article 14 provides for the enjoyment of the Convention's rights to be:

   [S]ecured without discrimination on any ground such as sex, race, colour, language, religion, political or other opinion, national or social origin, association with a national minority, property, birth or other status.

To invoke Article 14 the facts must fall within the ambit of and engage a substantive Convention right. See, for example, *Petrovic v Austria* (2001) 33 EHRR 307 at 319 [28]. Discrimination will not violate Article 14 if it has an objective or reasonable justification which, in turn, is dependent on it having a legitimate aim being pursued in a way that is proportionate to it; see, *Belgian Linguistics (No 2)* Series A no 6 (1979–80) 1 EHRR 252.

C. The UNCRC

10.   The UNCRC recognises the right to education in Article 28, while Article 29 specifies the matters towards which education should be directed. They include: 'The development of the child's personality, talents and mental and physical abilities to their fullest potential' (Article 29(1)(a)). States Parties must undertake appropriate measures for implementa-

tion of the Convention rights; and, regarding economic, social and cultural rights, do so, inter alia, 'to the maximum extent of their available resources': Article 4. Enjoyment of all UNCRC rights must be ensured without discrimination on grounds which include disability: Article 2.

11.   Article 3(1) enshrines the important principle, that in 'all actions concerning children, whether undertaken by public or private social welfare institutions, courts of law, administrative authorities or legislative bodies, the best interests of the child shall be a primary consideration'.

12.   Also highly important is Article 12(1), requiring States Parties to 'assure to the child who is capable of forming his or her views the right to express those views freely in all matters affecting the child, the views of the child being given due weight in accordance with the age and maturity of the child'. Article 12(2) provides that 'the child shall in particular be provided with the opportunity to be heard in any judicial and administrative proceedings affecting the child, either directly, or through a representative or an appropriate body, in a manner consistent with the procedural rules of national law.'

13.   Disabled children's interests are specifically recognised by Article 23. States Parties must recognise their need for special care and to ensure the extension to them and their carers, 'subject to available resources', of appropriate assistance in light of their condition and the parents' or carers' circumstances. Assistance must be provided without charge, where possible, and designed to ensure effective access to and the receipt of, inter alia, education 'in a manner conducive to the child's achieving the fullest possible social integration and individual development' (Article 23(3)).

14.   The relevance of the UNCRC's requirements to the application of the ECHR has been recognised by the European Court of Human Rights: see *V v United Kingdom* (Application no 24888/94) [1999] ECHR 171 at [73], [76] and [97]. Moreover, while the UNCRC is not binding on UK courts, judges have acknowledged the importance of its principles, particularly where key issues affecting children's welfare are at issue: see, *Re H (a minor) (blood tests: parental rights)* [1996] 4 All ER 28, per Ward LJ at [42] and *R (Williamson) v Secretary of State for Education and Employment* [2005] UKHL 15, per Baroness Hale at [80]–[82]. The fundamental principle within the SEN Code (1:5), that a child with SEN 'should have their needs met', could be said to reflect the idea that meeting them upholds the child's 'best interests' as per Article 3 UNCRC, although the law nevertheless permits resource limitations to set a threshold of support.

The factual background

15.   C was born in 1989. Since the age of five she has been brought up by her father. From September 1995 until 1998 she had a statement of SEN due to her emotional and behavioural difficulties. The local authority assessed C to have, when aged just 10 and-a-half, an overall IQ of 138 and a reading age of 17.

16.   C's secondary education started in September 2000. At first, she attended a local authority girls' school with a grammar stream. But she found her schoolwork too easy, began to arrive late at school and became inattentive towards her homework. By 2001/02 her father's relations with the school were deteriorating. He moved her in September 2002 to a small independent school as a weekly boarder. She joined year 10, a year above her

age group. She made progress and appeared to cope well, receiving one hour per week of psychotherapy.

17.   In 2003 Oxfordshire refused a request for a statutory assessment of C. The SENDIST dismissed an appeal against that decision. That SENDIST decision is not connected to the present proceedings.

18.   By spring 2004 C was experiencing problems due to her mother's re-involvement in her life, contrary to a court order, and C's difficult relationship with her school 'house mother'. C's school work was adversely affected and she was temporarily excluded. She nevertheless gained two A*, six A and two B grade GCSEs. In September 2004 her father moved C to a different independent school, as a full time boarder, for sixth form studies. According to the head teacher, C was a very able but difficult and disruptive pupil and needed special provision.

19.   C's father again sought a SEN statutory assessment of C with a view to a statement showing C's present school as the specified placement. He considered that her considerable psychological problems, due to high intelligence, meant that no local authority day school could meet her needs. Oxfordshire decided that C's emotional, social and behavioural needs were insufficient to necessitate a statutory assessment or a statement. C's father appealed.

20.   The SENDIST upheld Oxfordshire's decision. It considered that no new needs had been identified: C's GCSE results had been better than her school had predicted; there was no additional need for C to have a residential placement; and there were no circumstances justifying the making of a statement. The tribunal also rejected the idea that C's exceptional ability could amount to a learning difficulty.

21.   As Elias J rightly reminded the parties, the tribunal's role was not to determine the best form of education for C but rather to decide whether a statutory assessment was needed. In doing so, it had to determine whether appropriate arrangements were in place to meet C's SEN. Elias J had to consider whether its conclusion was one the tribunal had been entitled to reach or whether it had erred in law.

The high court's decision

22.   Elias J found that the tribunal had approached its task correctly and had reached a rational and lawful decision. It had not had regard to irrelevant considerations. It had not viewed C's exceptional ability as compensating for other difficulties. Rather, it had merely inferred that her results 'suggested that her social, behavioural and emotional needs were perhaps less disabling than had originally been anticipated'. The appellant has not renewed this *Wednesbury*-based challenge; but, in any event, we find no obvious basis for it.

23.   Elias J also found that the tribunal had not erred in concluding that exceptional ability did not, in itself, constitute a 1996 Act learning difficulty. C did not have a 'disability' for section 312 purposes. Despite increased societal recognition of the needs of very able children since the legislation was enacted, the language of section 312(2) was 'not sufficiently flexible to give effect to any such change' in interpretation. 'Disability' meant 'want of an ability, not excess of it'.

24.   As to whether the capacity of very able children to learn quickly prevented them from having a learning difficulty, per section 312(2)(a), Elias J considered the subsection had not

been intended to cater for 'high flyers' (as he put it) since Parliament could otherwise have made that plain in the Act. As to the idea that exceptional ability prevented or hindered a child from making use of 'facilities of a kind generally provided for children of his age' (per section 312(2)(b)), while the teaching might not stretch or sufficiently stimulate the exceptionally able child and could mean not receiving education appropriate to his/her needs, that was 'not the same as saying that he is prevented or hindered from taking advantage of such facilities as are provided for him'.

25.   As regards discrimination under ECHR Article 14 read with A2P1, Elias J considered that A2P1 was engaged and exceptionally abled children were discriminated against under the 1996 Act. He accepted, for argument's sake, that exceptional ability constituted an Article 14 'status'. But a difference in treatment between the very able and the not very able did not, he believed, require specific justification, because their situations were insufficiently analogous, although if justification was needed it 'could readily be established'. While supporting highly intelligent children so they could fully exploit their talents was a legitimate aim, there were 'obvious social and economic reasons' for targeting resources on the less able but not on the most able. He thus resisted the call to construe section 312 to include exceptionally abled children via the power in section 3 Human Rights Act 1998.

Appeal grounds

26.   The appellant contends, first, that Elias J erred in holding that exceptional ability was not a SEN for 1996 Act purposes. Particularly in view of the considerable recognition now given by education bodies and professionals to the needs of exceptionally able children and their problems within mainstream education, such children should be considered to have learning difficulties requiring special educational provision. Further, under the now widely accepted social model of disability, exceptional learning ability could be classifiable as a form of disability.

27.   Second, it is argued that a failure to construe exceptional ability in either such ways has resulted in discriminatory treatment under ECHR Article 14 read with A2P1 for which there is no reasonable justification. The social and economic justification falls away when one considers the respective numbers of children in each category, even allowing for any average cost differences between the categories for the provision needed. The 1.45 million children in England with SEN constitute 18 per cent of the school population (Department for Education and Skills, *Special Educational Needs in England* January 2005 SFR 24/2005 (2005)); the number of 'gifted and talented' children is almost certainly very much smaller (although there is no official headcount). The government asked schools to identify the top five per cent of children in the ability range to join the National Academy for Gifted and Talented Youth, a provider of summer school placements to 100,000 children to date, although arguably not all of these children would necessarily *require* special provision. Either way, the difference in numbers in each category is considerable.

28.   The third contention is that in determining whether proper regard was given by the tribunal to all relevant considerations, Elias J failed to test whether or to what extent it heard C's views and gave them due weight; and, furthermore, he failed to indicate what weight, if any, he gave C's views in reaching his own decision. It is argued that particularly having regard to C's age and high intelligence, both such failures indicated non-compliance with UNCRC Article 12 and constitute procedural unfairness.

Analysis

Giftedness as a SEN under the 1996 Act

29.   Before Elias J's ruling, while the issue of whether exceptional ability could in itself give rise to SEN had arisen in several cases (see *R v Secretary of State for Education ex parte C* [1996] ELR 93; *R v Portsmouth City Council ex parte F* [1998] ELR 619; *CES* (see [4] above)), it had not received a definitive judicial determination. For that reason, little turns on Elias J's failure to refer to those previous cases. Given the lack of clarification around the issue, it was however important that Elias J was able to reach some conclusions on it. The question thereafter, is whether his conclusions were correct.

30.   First, was Elias J right that a high level of ability cannot in itself constitute SEN for section 312 purposes, whether on the basis of having a 'learning difficulty' or a 'disability'? We can assume that any provision for a child of exceptional ability and on account of that ability, which is outside the standard schooling arrangements for the majority of local children of his/her age, should be considered special educational provision.

31.   Elias J was unwilling to strain the interpretation of 'learning difficulty' to include highly able children, particularly as Parliament did not identify such children when considering the legislation. He was also unpersuaded that he should adopt the kind of purposive approach applied to the definition of 'family' by the House of Lords in *Fitzpatrick v Sterling Housing Association Ltd* [2001] 1 AC 27 in holding that a homosexual partner of a deceased tenant was entitled to succeed to the latter's tenancy on the basis of being a member of his 'family' for the purposes of the Rent Act 1988. Should this Court feel similarly constrained?

32.   It is first necessary to observe that over the years there have been many criticisms of the definition of SEN and how it categorises children. For example, the Commons Education and Skills Committee commented recently (*Special Educational Needs* (HC 478-I (2006), at [34]) that the premise of there being 'a single category of children with SEN—is fundamentally flawed'. It also noted (at paragraph [36]) that SEN 'exist across the whole spectrum of classes and abilities. Indeed … there is a particular category of "gifted and talented" children who are defined as having [SEN]'. While the legislation may not have been intended to support 'high flyers', their apparent omission may have been the result of oversight rather than a deliberate decision.

33.   However, government policy to extend support for gifted children is occurring outside the SEN framework, being 'integral to [the Government's] core strategies to improve teaching and learning' which include, among other things, 'a dedicated strand' of the Excellence in Cities programme for targeting support to raise pupil achievement levels (HC Deb, 8 September 2003 volume 410 c129W, per D Miliband, Minister for Education). The Government's *Five Year Strategy for Children and Learners* (2004) promised extra support for gifted and talented pupils (particularly from disadvantaged backgrounds), who have 'not been well served by the system in the past' (Chapter 5 [15]).

34.   Yet, no specific legislation regarding the gifted and talented has been set in place. There is, however, a proposed reform under the Education and Inspections Bill 2006 before Parliament. LEAs would have to exercise their relevant functions with a view to 'promoting the fulfilment by every child concerned of his educational potential'. The possible impact and enforceability of this new duty does not require this Court's consideration, but in any event it has the look of a 'target duty' (per Woolf J in *R v ILEA ex parte Ali and Murshid*

[1990] 2 Admin LR 822) rather than a mandatory duty (see *R v East Sussex County Council ex parte T* [1998] AC 714).

35.   Against such a background, one can see why the hopes of a parent of an exceptionally able child may be pinned on the SEN legislation. Elias J's view that the absence from it of any specific reference to children of exceptional ability evidenced a lack of Parliamentary intent to cater for such a characteristic is only partly supported by Parliamentary discussions around 'learning difficulty', to which reference may be made under the *Pepper v Hart* doctrine.

36.   The starting point is the Education Act 1981. Its definition of SEN was similarly based around 'learning difficulty'. In the House of Lords there was a concern that the 'significantly greater difficulty in learning than the majority of children of his age' test failed to cater for children falling behind others of a similar level of ability, whether 'low, average, or high' (HL Deb 6 July 1981 volume 422 col 459 per Lord Alexander of Potterhill). Lord Radnor's proposed amendment aimed to ensure that highly able children failing to realise their potential due to learning problems would be judged against others within their ability range rather than against the majority of children in their age group. For the Government, Baroness Young, however, explained that learning difficulty should be a flexible concept that avoided creating 'special categories of children with particular learning difficulties' which the Warnock Report (*Report of the Committee of Enquiry into the Education of Handicapped Children and Young People*, Cmnd 7212 (1978)) wished to avoid. She nevertheless sought to reassure the House that the children Lord Radnor was concerned about would be covered by the statutory definition (HL Deb 6 July 1981 volume 422 col 459). The Radnor amendment was withdrawn. The Warnock Committee did not in fact consider that the problems facing highly gifted children fell within their remit (op cit, [1.2]).

37.   When an Education Bill was before Parliament in 1993 a proposed amendment supporting the needs of highly able children sought to replace 'learning difficulty' with 'particular need' (Standing Committee E, 26 January 1993, cols 1051–52).[1] The Minister, however, considered the new phrase too broad and an unnecessary change to the well-established terminology; and the national curriculum would provide the framework for identifying 'the needs of particularly able or gifted children and to stretch and explore their abilities to the maximum within the 10-point scale of achievement ...' (col 1054). Gifted pupils were expected to benefit from non-statutory special arrangements a number of schools made. Although the amendment was defeated, the debate offers clear evidence of Parliament's intention *not* to include exceptional ability in the SEN legislation.

38.   With regard to the disability head of 'learning difficulty', there is scope for a wider interpretation due to a shift towards the well-established 'social model' of disability, which looks at the extent of a person's limitation or disadvantage within society as a consequence of their mental and/or physical state or condition. It focuses on how disabled people experience long-term disadvantage in their daily lives and how the barriers which create it can be addressed: see, J Swain et al, *Controversial Issues in a Disabling Society* (Buckingham, Open University Press, 2003) 23–25. Unlike the 'medical model', which focuses on particular

---

[1]   At http://data.parliament.uk/assets/standingcommittees/SC1992-1993V006P0/SC1992-1993E19930126am.xml.

forms of disablement and the extra needs that arise (or are assumed to arise) from them, the social model references the social context within which the disability is experienced. In the social setting of a school, an exceptionally able child may be at a relative disadvantage, in comparison to a majority of others, in securing maximum benefit from the provision made.

39. The social model, while not viewed uncritically by some (see for example T Shakespeare and N Watson 'The Social Model of Disability: An Outdated Ideology' (2002) 2 *Research in Social Science & Disability* 9–28), is reflected in the UNCRC. Article 23 is clearly directed towards maximising the 'active participation' of children with disabilities 'in the community' and in ensuring that they receive education in a manner conducive to their 'achieving the fullest possible social integration and individual development' (Article 23(3)). There is also the draft UN Convention on the Protection and Promotion of the Rights of Persons with Disabilities, which refers to securing disabled persons' full participation in the community and would require the education of disabled children to be directed towards realisation of their fullest potential in terms of personality, talents and mental and physical abilities. No definition of disability is included in the Convention, but the draft's Preamble notes that disability 'is an evolving concept' and 'results from the interaction between persons with impairments and attitudinal and environmental barriers that hinders their full and effective participation in society on an equal basis with others'. This patently reflects the social model.

40. Construing disability in this way does not, however, sit well with the Disability Discrimination Act 1995. The SENDIST's joint jurisdiction over disability discrimination complaints and SEN appeals supports a common interpretation. The 1995 Act's definition is based on a physical or mental 'impairment' having a 'substantial and long term effect' on the 'ability to carry out normal day-to-day activities': section 1(1). For a child, participation in schooling is a normal day-to-day activity. But can exceptional ability be considered an 'impairment'? The official guidance which courts and others must take into account (section 3(3), as amended), provides that physical or mental impairment 'should be given its ordinary meaning': *Disability Discrimination Act. Guidance on matters to be taken into account in determining questions relating to the definition of disability* (2005), [A3]. On that basis, there is no reason to disagree with Elias J's view, reflecting the ordinary meaning of 'impairment', that 'disability' in the present context means 'want of an ability, not excess of it'.

41. Even adopting the broader definition would still leave the question of whether C's disability prevents or hinders her from making use of the kind of educational facilities generally provided for children of her age (per the 1996 Act, section 312(2)(b)). Elias J concluded that while C would soon 'exhaust the benefit' of the school's provision, and by being insufficiently stretched intellectually may not have her needs fully met, she was not being prevented or hindered from taking advantage of such facilities. This Court, however, finds some disagreement with the judge. If C had exhausted the benefit of the available provision, her frustration could well hinder her by adversely affecting her continuing ability to make use of the facilities. One must, however, acknowledge the absence of factual evidence of that effect here, at least with reference to C's recent educational experience. In the event, nothing turns on this matter in view of the Court's conclusion that C did not have a disability.

42. Therefore, this Court agrees with Elias J that C did not, due to her high ability level, have SEN by virtue of a learning difficulty or disability.

The ECHR

43.   There is common ground that C's claim engaged A2P1 and that, on the Strasbourg case law, this is sufficient to bring Article 14 into play (see [9] above). The parties also agree that pupils of exceptional ability have 'some other status' under Article 14, even though Elias J only hesitantly accepted that position.

44.   In *Ghaidan v Godin-Mendoza* [2004] UKHL 34, Baroness Hale of Richmond (at [141]–[142]) regarded unmarried same-sex and opposite sex-couples as being in an analogous situation for Article 14 purposes. However, could the same be said of exceptionally able children and children of limited learning capacity? If it could, the relative disadvantage of the former under Part 4 of the 1996 Act requires specific justification in order to avoid inconsistency with Article 14.

45.   This Court does not agree with Elias J that a reasonable person would not regard distinguishing between the two groups of children by providing extra resources for the less able group to require specific justification. Government seems to recognise that both groups of children face a reduced likelihood of realising their full potential through education if additional provision is not made for them. Both are less likely than the general majority to realise their potential via standard educational provision alone. Of course, the ways in which each of these groups is supported by the system differs greatly and this is the basis for the ECHR discrimination claim.

46.   Therefore, specific justification for the difference in treatment is required. Elias J considered that if that were so, such justification could readily be shown given the purpose of the legislation. Nevertheless, was he right to limit his consideration of Article 14 compliance to the context of inclusion in and exclusion from the relevant provisions? This argument is based on the promise the 1996 Act offers of extra resources to support the education of a child with SEN. Yet, the non-inclusion of children of exceptional ability does not, of itself, necessarily imply that their needs are less significant or deserving of support. It could merely suggest that, as the evidence indicates, Part 4 was not considered an appropriate framework for support. On that basis, the justification for the difference in treatment should relate to the overall level of provision by the state to meet educational needs within each of the respective groups. Of course, resource constraints may justify the targeting of specific areas of need and thus, in the current instance, children with reduced capability.

47.   No such justification was, however, sought by Elias J. But for his view that no justification was required he would have been prepared to adjourn the proceedings so the Secretary of State could make representations on economic justification. Since, in this Court's view, specific justification *was* required, he ought to have adjourned. His failure to do so constituted an error of law. His decision must therefore be set aside.

48.   It is necessary to add, for completeness' sake, that since the right to education is engaged the Court could utilise its power under section 3 Human Rights Act 1998 to counter the apparent legislative omission in the SEN legislation in order to correct a denial of the right. The section 3 power was, for example, used in *Ghaidan v Godin-Mendoza* [2004] UKHL 34 in construing as 'spouses' members of an unmarried same-sex couple. That was, per Lord Rodger of Earlsferry (at [128]), a 'modest ... extension' which would 'not contradict any cardinal principle' of the relevant legislation. In the present case, however, constituting giftedness as a 'difficulty in learning' would seemingly involve a more substantial extension.

Furthermore, in view of the state's margin of appreciation—particularly as regards alloca-tion of resources across the education system (see *Belgian Linguistics* above)—the right to education per se was almost certainly not being denied.

Article 12 UNCRC

49. The Article 12 UNCRC obligations ([12] above) are particularly significant in the education context. The importance of hearing from children and enabling their views to inform decision-making is increasingly acknowledged within the education sphere (see, R Davie et al, *The Voice of the Child* (London, Falmer Press, 1996)). The SEN Code of Practice includes a general principle that 'the views of the child should be sought and taken into account' ([1:5]). Citing Article 12, it states:

> Children and young people with special educational needs have a unique knowledge of their own needs and circumstances and their own views about what sort of help they would like to help them make the most of their education. They should, where possible, participate in all the decision-making processes that occur in education including the setting of learning targets and contributing to ... discussions about choice of schools ... They should feel confident that they will be listened to and that their views are valued.

50. The SENDIST is required to have regard to this principle in the Code. Although the procedural regulations (Special Educational Needs Tribunal Regulations 2001 (SI 2001/600), as amended) could go further to support it, they nevertheless: enable the par-ent's case statement to include the child's views (regulation 9(1)); require the LEA to state in its response the child's views concerning the issues raised by the appeal or the reasons why they have not been ascertained (regulation 13(2)); permit the child to be present at the hearing (regulation 30(2)(a)), unless justice requires exclusion (regulation 30(4)(b)); and enable the child to be permitted to give evidence and address the tribunal on the subject matter of the appeal (regulation 30(7)). What they fail to do, however, is impose a specific obligation reflecting the Article 12 requirements (see N Harris, *Special Educational Needs and Access to Justice* (Bristol, Jordan Publishing, 1997) 150).

51. Does, however, the ECHR require consideration to be given to the child's views in this context? The Article 6 'right to a fair trial in civil proceedings' has not yet been held to embrace a right of a child to be heard therein (see A Bainham, *Children: the Modern Law* 3rd edition (Bristol, Family Law, 2005) 599) and, in any event, education appeals may not be considered civil proceedings for Article 6 purposes (see *Simpson v UK* (Application no 14688/89) (1989) 64 DR 188, but cf *S, T and P v London Borough of Brent* [2002] EWCA Civ 693).

52. Article 8, however, has been held to require the child's views to be heard in certain circumstances, although states have a margin of appreciation and in any event the matter has yet to be determined definitively (see U Kilkelly, above, 117–20). In *Sahin v Germany* (Application no 30943/96) (8 July 2003), for example, Article 8 was invoked over a domestic court's failure in a child custody case to elicit the child's views. Some education issues may engage Article 8: see *Costello-Roberts v United Kingdom* [1994] ELR 1 and *The Queen (O) v St James RC Primary School Appeal Panel* [2001] ELR 469. Nevertheless, in *Belgian Linguistics* ([9] above, The Law, part I.B at [7]) the Court of Human Rights held that Article 8 'by itself in no way guarantees either a right to education or a personal right of parents

relating to the education of their children: its object is essentially that of protecting the individual against arbitrary interference by the public authorities in his private family life'.

53.   Therefore the ECHR may not advance the appellant's case on this issue. Nevertheless, C is a highly intelligent child in her mid-teens with strong views on her education, which were explicitly taken into account in the earlier litigation: *CES* at [19]. In the present case, however, Elias J made no reference to her views. Consequently it was unclear whether account was taken of them or, if it was, what weight or significance the judge attached to them. Moreover, if those views were absent there is no indication that he made enquiry as to the reason why. Furthermore, there is nothing to indicate whether the judge considered whether C's views were presented to the SENDIST and, if they were, how the tribunal dealt with them.

54.   Despite these criticisms, it is unclear that there has been an error of law arising from these failures. The point is somewhat speculative; and since the Court has already concluded that Elias J's decision should be quashed on the Article 14 point above it is unnecessary to explore it further.

Conclusion

55.   Therefore, in light of the Court's conclusion on the Article 14 issue, the appeal is allowed and the decision of the lower court is quashed. The matter is remitted to the SENDIST for fresh determination and for the question of justification to be properly examined on the facts. The Court urges that C's views should, consistently with Article 12 UNCRC, play a part in the determination to be made.

21

Commentary on *Canadian Foundation for Children, Youth and the Law v Canada (Attorney General)*

LUCINDA FERGUSON

I. Introduction

Physical punishment[1] of children can occur at the hands of the state—in school, care or other institutional settings—or private individuals—parents, other family members and individuals involved in raising the child. Legal systems must choose whether to directly regulate physical punishment. If not specifically regulated, the general law—child protection, criminal, contract and tort law—applies. Specific regulation can increase the legal justification or excuse beyond that which would otherwise trigger state intervention. An absolute ban has the appearance of specific regulation but simply means that the general law applies.[2]

As at 30 November 2016, 51 states prohibit all forms of physical punishment of children in all settings.[3] Canada and the UK have ratified but not incorporated the Convention on the Rights of the Child (CRC).[4] Despite legal challenges, both jurisdictions continue to prefer specific regulation in the form of particular defences,[5] 'reasonable correction'[6] and 'reasonable punishment'[7] respectively, which heighten the legal protection against criminal law liability for the use of physical punishment. Section 43 of the Canadian Criminal Code[8]

---

[1] I adopt this terminology to cover the full range of acts: 'corporal punishment' is sometimes understood to refer to only severe acts, hence the language itself incorporates a *de minimis* exclusion. See J E Durrant, R Ensom, and Coalition on Physical Punishment of Children and Youth, *Joint Statement on Physical Punishment of Children and Youth* (Coalition on Physical Punishment of Children and Youth, 2004) 2.

[2] As I discuss below in relation to the language of 'children's rights' and 'rights for children', however, the expressive aspect of an absolute ban may be critical.

[3] Global Initiative to End Corporal Punishment of Children, 'States which have prohibited all corporal punishment', online: www.endcorporalpunishment.org/progress/prohibiting-states/.

[4] United Nations' Convention on the Rights of the Child (20 November 1989), 1577 UNTS 3.

[5] This is to be distinguished from general law defences, such as the posited *de minimis* defence to common law liability in criminal law, discussed below.

[6] Criminal Code, RSC 1985, c C-46, s 43.

[7] Children Act 2004, c 31, s 58.

[8] Criminal Code, above n 6.

explicitly 'justifie[s]'[9] the reasonable use of force by way of correction in the context of assault under section 265 of the Criminal Code. As written, the Canadian defence applies to schoolteachers,[10] parents and persons standing in the place of parents, whereas the UK defence has been legislatively excluded from application to schools[11] and childminders.[12]

II. The Original Decision in *Canadian Foundation for Children, Youth and the Law v Canada (Attorney General)*[13]

The Supreme Court of Canada's decision in *Canadian Foundation* remains the leading authority on the interpretation of section 43. The case involved a constitutional challenge,[14] driven by Ailsa Watkinson, who secured funding from the Court Challenges Program and approached the Foundation to take the case forward to court.[15] There was widespread media coverage as the case progressed through the various levels of hearing and appeal[16] and, as demonstrated by the large number of organisations that sought to act as interveners,[17] significant issues of public policy were at stake.

A. Issues before the Supreme Court of Canada

The appellant, the Foundation, sought a declaration that section 43 infringed three sections of the Canadian Charter of Rights and Freedoms.[18] In particular, the Foundation argued

---

[9] s 43 reads as follows:

> Every schoolteacher, parent or person standing in the place of a parent is justified in using force by way of correction toward a pupil or child, as the case may be, who is under his care, if the force does not exceed what is reasonable under the circumstances.

[10] As discussed below, judicial interpretation of the Canadian statutory defence in *Canadian Foundation* brings it into line with the UK's legislative position.

[11] Education Act 1996, c 56, s 548, as substituted by School Standards and Framework Act 1998, c 31, s 131(1).

[12] Day Care and Child Minding (National Standards) (England) Regs 2003, para 5 (SI 2003/1996).

[13] *Canadian Foundation for Children, Youth and the Law v Canada (Attorney General)* 2004 SCC 4.

[14] A constitutional challenge without facts might be a missed opportunity—both to demonstrate respect for children through participation and to make more likely child-centred reasoning and a better outcome for children. Children value participation: C Marshall, B Byrne and L Lundy, 'Face to Face: Children and Young People's Right to Participate in Public Decision-making' in T Gal and B Faedi Duramy (eds), *International Perspectives and Empirical Findings on Child Participation: From Social Exclusion to Child-Inclusive Policies* (Oxford, Oxford University Press, 2015) 357–80. Participation can enable children to develop as rightsholders: E Buss, 'What the Law Should (and Should Not) Learn from Child Development Research' (2009) 38 *Hofstra Law Review* 13–68. But the missed opportunity was not necessarily for a 'children's rights' approach. In *R (Williamson) v Secretary of State for Education and Employment and Others* [2005] UKHL 15, Baroness Hale highlighted the need for children's participation and inclusion, but did so within an approach that saw children as holding 'rights' rather than 'children's rights': [71].

[15] A M Watkinson, 'Human Rights Legislation, Court Rulings, and Social Policy' in A Westhues (ed), *Canadian Social Policy: Issues and Perspectives* 4th rev ed (Waterloo ON, Wilfred Laurier Press, 2006) 69–89, 79.

[16] See, for example, C Robertshaw, 'Spare the law and kill the child' *Globe and Mail* (18 April 2002), online: www.theglobeandmail.com/globe-debate/spare-the-law-and-kill-the-child/article754215/.

[17] Watkinson, above n 15, 79.

[18] Part 1 of the Constitution Act, 1982, being Schedule B to the Canada Act 1982 (UK) 1982, c. 11.

that section 43 infringed: section 7, the right to life, liberty and security of the person, of which a person cannot be deprived except in accordance with principles of 'fundamental justice', because it failed to give procedural protections to children, did not further the 'best interests' of the child, and was both overbroad and vague; section 12, the right not to be subjected to cruel and unusual treatment or punishment, because physical punishment fell within the terms of section 12; and section 15(1), the right to equality before the law, because it denied children the legal protection against assaults that was accorded to adults. The Foundation further argued that, if section 43 infringed any of those sections, such infringement could not be saved by section 1 of the Charter as a 'reasonable limit[] prescribed by law as can be demonstrably justified in a free and democratic society'.

Both the Ontario Supreme Court[19] and Court of Appeal[20] rejected the Foundation's contentions and held that section 43 was constitutional.

B. The Supreme Court's Reasoning

The Supreme Court of Canada held, by a majority, that section 43 did not unjustifiably infringe sections 7, 12, or 15(1) of the Charter and dismissed the Foundation's appeal.

There are four substantive judgments: a majority (McLachlin CJ, with whom Gonthier, Iaccobucci, Major, Bastarache and LeBel JJ agreed); a partial dissent (Binnie J); and two dissents for different reasons (Arbour J; Deschamps J).

A majority of seven (McLachlin CJ's majority judgment and Binnie J) held that section 43 did not infringe the section 7 right to life, liberty and security of the person.[21] The majority demarcated a clear, protected space for physical punishment of children by first 'reading down' section 43 and establishing 15 qualifications on the substantive defence, intended to clarify the requirement that the punishment be 'reasonable under the circumstances'[22] and that, in direct contradiction of the wording of section 43, teachers were outwith the scope of the defence.[23] Only then, after creating a prospective interpretation that ignored the significant evidence of prior inconsistency in practice,[24] did McLachlin CJ ask whether section 43 was unconstitutional for vagueness.[25] As Arbour J commented, 'it is useful to note how much work must go into making the provision constitutionally sound and sufficiently precise'.[26] Whilst 'unusual', the majority's 'aggressive' 'reading down' has been characterised as an 'increasingly familiar strategy ... to cure elements of residual unconstitutionality'.[27] Arbour J dissented and relied solely on this ground to conclude

---

[19] *Canadian Foundation for Children, Youth and the Law v Canada (Attorney General)* [2000] OJ No 2535 (Ont SCJ).

[20] *Canadian Foundation for Children, Youth and the Law v Canada (Attorney General)* [2002] OJ No 61 (Ont CA). Goudge JA gave the judgment of the court.

[21] *Canadian Foundation*, above n 13, [70.1] (McLachlin CJ), [130.1] (Binnie J).

[22] ibid [39]–[40] (McLachlin CJ).

[23] ibid [40] (McLachlin CJ).

[24] Arbour J convincingly demonstrates the inconsistent meaning given to 'reasonable' in the prior body of case law: ibid [181]–[182] (Arbour J).

[25] ibid [42] (McLachlin CJ).

[26] ibid [190] (Arbour J).

[27] J Cameron, 'From the *MVR* to *Chaoulli v Quebec*: The Road Not Taken and the Future of Section 7' (2006) 34 *Supreme Court Review* 105–65, 128.

that section 43 of the Criminal Code was unconstitutional.[28] Whilst Deschamps J agreed with Arbour J's reasoning on this point, she preferred to resolve the constitutionality of section 43 under section 15(1).[29]

The same majority of seven held that section 43 did not infringe the section 12 right to be free from cruel and unusual treatment or punishment.[30] Neither Arbour J nor Deschamps J considered it necessary to decide this point.[31]

A majority of six (McLachlin CJ's majority judgment) held that section 43 did not infringe the section 15(1) right to equality before the law.[32] Arbour J did not consider it necessary to decide this point.[33] Deschamps J, dissenting, relied solely on this ground to conclude that section 43 was unconstitutional.[34] Binnie J purported to agree with Deschamps J on this issue, albeit it for somewhat different reasons.[35] He dissented in part, in relation to teachers, but not parents or persons standing in the place of parents.[36] In respect of the latter, he reasoned that the prima facie infringement of section 15(1) was justified under section 1.[37]

Arbour and Deschamps JJ proposed striking down as the appropriate remedy.[38] In his partial dissent in respect of teachers, Binnie J proposed only a declaration of unconstitutionality.[39] Advocating the repeal of section 43 does not necessarily entail supporting a complete ban on all forms of physical punishment.[40] There are relevant defences in the general law, namely *de minimis* and necessity. Even in the absence of such defences, a complete ban does not necessarily mean that there can be no overlooked physical punishment. The interpretation of the section 265 offence of assault leaves space for declaring the definitional threshold not met in particular cases; thus, a child may be physically punished without triggering a legal response.

On the basis of the general law defences, Arbour J reasoned that she had 'come to a conclusion which may not be very different from that reached by the Chief Justice'.[41] Given her dissent on the basis of section 7, she was suggesting that courts would likely reach similar outcomes in future cases whether 'reading down' section 43 or prima facie criminalising all instances of physical punishment subject to the applicability of the *de minimis* and necessity defences. But this outcome-oriented construction of 'rights' may pay insufficient attention to rights' expressive function.[42]

---

[28]   *Canadian Foundation*, above n 13 [211.2] (Arbour J).
[29]   ibid [213], [246.1–2] (Deschamps J).
[30]   ibid [70.3] (McLachlin CJ), [130.3] (Binnie J).
[31]   ibid [211.3] (Arbour J), [246.3] (Deschamps J).
[32]   ibid [70.5] (McLachlin CJ).
[33]   ibid [211.5] (Arbour J).
[34]   ibid [246.5–6] (Deschamps J).
[35]   ibid [73] (Binnie J).
[36]   ibid [129], [130.6] (Binnie J).
[37]   ibid [130.6] (Binnie J).
[38]   ibid [194] (Arbour J), [242] (Deschamps J).
[39]   ibid [129] (Binnie J).
[40]   Sweden, for example, adopted a two-stage approach to parents: first, it removed the defence in 1966; then, in 1979 it introduced an explicit ban. See S Janson, B Långberg, and B Svensson, 'Sweden: A 30-Year Ban on Physical Punishment of Children' in J E Durrant and A B Smith (eds), *Global Pathways to Abolishing Physical Punishment: Realizing Children's Rights* (Abingdon, Routledge, 2011) 241–55, 245–47.
[41]   *Canadian Foundation*, above n 13, [131] (Arbour J).
[42]   Though note that elsewhere I argue the expressive and procedural aspects of rights are contingent on outcomes, including potential for better outcomes for children. See L Ferguson, 'Not Merely Rights for Children but Children's Rights: The Theory Gap and the Assumption of the Importance of Children's Rights' (2013) 21 *International Journal of Children's Rights* 177–208.

Academic criticism of the Court's decision has been wide-ranging, extending from targeting the Court's remedial reinterpretation of section 43 to preserve its constitutionality[43] to focusing on its failure to clarify whether there is in fact a *de minimis* defence in criminal law.[44]

III. Grover J's Reimagined Dissent

In order to hold section 43 constitutional, the majority of the Court must demonstrate that it does not unjustifiably infringe any of the three proposed sections of the Charter. To conclude that section 43 is unconstitutional, the dissent need only show that one of the three sections has been unjustifiably infringed.

In focusing on section 15(1), Deschamps J centred on the issue of equality between children and adults, and thereby put the larger, political debate at the centre of the case. The difficulty with taking such a stance is that the physical punishment of children was a 'controversial social issue'[45] and 'divisive'.[46] Canadian public sentiment at the time of *Canadian Foundation* is characterised by complexity, and divergence between individuals' attitudes and behaviours. In 2004, Durrant et al reported research from 1988 that found that more than 75 per cent of parents surveyed believed 'that physical punishment is harmful to children and unnecessary'.[47] Yet, they also noted 2003 research findings that 70 per cent of surveyed mothers of preschool children in Manitoba reported that they had used physical punishment, one in three of whom stated that they used it at least weekly.[48] Similarly, Rosborough cites a public opinion survey from 2002, which found that 70 per cent of Canadian parents were opposed to a legal ban on physical punishment.[49] This demonstrates the difficulties for Grover J to ground her reimagined dissent in section 15(1).

In relying on section 7, Arbour J arguably sought to avoid taking a stance on that issue. Perhaps because of the technical nature of the section 7 route to unconstitutionality, Grover J instead holds section 43 unconstitutional for unjustifiably infringing section 12. Whilst she does not frame her analysis as addressing section 7, she agrees with Arbour J's reasoning against first 'reading down' section 43 before assessing its constitutionality.[50] She also endorses an enlarged role for the *de minimis* and necessity defences.[51] Dissenting on section 7 grounds also invites taking a view on children's 'best interests' as a principle of 'fundamental justice';[52] this treats children as distinct from adults. Within the terms of her

---

[43] See, for example, Cameron, above n 27, 128.

[44] See, for example, S Anand, 'Reasonable Chastisement: A Critique of the Supreme Court's Decision in the "Spanking Case"' (2004) 41 *Alberta Law Review* 871–78 (not paginated). See also M E Rosborough, *The 'Spanking Defence': Canadian Foundation for Children, Youth and the Law v Canada and the Future of Reasonable Correction of Children by Force in Canada*, LLM Thesis (University of Alberta, 2011) 108, 117–21.

[45] *Canadian Foundation*, above n 13, [185] (Arbour J).

[46] Anand, above n 44.

[47] Durrant et al, above n 1, 3.

[48] J E Durrant, L Rose-Krasnor and A G Broberg, 'Maternal Beliefs about Physical Punishment in Sweden and Canada' (2003) 34 *Journal of Comparative Family Studies* 586–604, 593.

[49] Rosborough, above n 44, fn 391 and corresponding main text.

[50] Rewritten judgment [26] (Grover J).

[51] ibid [20] (Grover J).

[52] *Canadian Foundation*, above n 13, [7] (McLachlin CJ); see also [10].

section 12 argument, Grover J instead focuses on human dignity, a concept applicable to children and adults alike.[53] The section 12 route enables Grover J to approach the issue of physical punishment on the assumption of the equal status of children and adults, albeit in terms of human rights (or 'rights for children'), rather than children's rights.[54]

IV. Critique of Grover J's Reimagined Dissent

There are two perspectives from which Grover J's judgment should be evaluated: first, the extent to which the detail of the section 12 argument is successful; and, second, the value of assuming the equal status of children and adults.

A. The Detail of the Section 12 Reimagined Dissent

It is undisputed that teachers are state actors. The success of Grover J's section 12 argument requires her to satisfy three points: first, that parents are also state actors;[55] second, and relatedly, that the state's role here comprises positive action; and third, that section 12 is applicable outside of the criminal context. This is an ambitious argument, aimed at dispelling the common assumption that there is anything truly private in the familial context so as to secure full protection for children regardless of the setting.

The usual view is that the state simply provides a defence for the use of physical punishment by others. If parents are state actors, however, parents' positive actions thereby become the active state imposition[56] of physical punishment. This is an unconventional perspective and likely to be controversial. For example, shortly after its judgment in *Canadian Foundation*, the UK House of Lords in *R (Williamson) v Secretary of State for Education and Employment and Others*[57] demarcated schoolteachers as outwith the defence available to parents, and rejected the argument that there could be any circumstances in which teachers could exercise a parent's right to use physical punishment, even if the parents explicitly sought to delegate it.[58]

Grover J contrasts the exercise of a parental liberty right with the delegated exercise of state power, and argues that both teachers and parents physically punish children via the latter.[59] Hill has previously set out a broader account on identical lines.[60] There are two critical difficulties with this argument. First, in vital respects, Grover J elides the more

---

[53] Rewritten judgment [18] (Grover J).
[54] L Ferguson, 'The Jurisprudence of Making Decisions Affecting Children: An Argument to Prefer Duty to Children's Rights and Welfare' in A Diduck, N Peleg and H Reece (eds), *Law in Society: Reflections on Children, Family, Culture and Philosophy—Essays in Honour of Michael Freeman* (Leiden, Brill, 2015) 141–89, 143–44. See also Ferguson, above n 42, especially 179–92.
[55] Rewritten judgment [5]–[13] (Grover J).
[56] See D Newman, 'Cruel and Unusual Punishment' in *Halsbury's Laws of Canada—Constitutional Law (Charter of Rights)* (LexisNexis Canada, 2014 reissue) HCHR-94.
[57] Above n 14.
[58] ibid [12]–[13] (L'Nicholls).
[59] Rewritten judgment [7] (Grover J).
[60] B J Hill, 'Constituting Children's Bodily Integrity' (2015) 64 *Duke Law Journal* 1295–362, 1305 (positing parents as exercising state power via delegation).

straightforward position of teachers with the 'more complex'[61] family setting involving parents.[62] Grover J acknowledges 'the State has afforded parents ... a certain constitutional scope of private activity',[63] yet does not consider the implications of this point for her assertion that 'the parent, parental delegate or teacher acts as an agent of the State'.[64] In agreeing with Binnie J that teachers using physical punishment are not exercising a parental liberty interest and acting *in loco parentis*,[65] this invites Binnie J's solution, whereby parents' use of physical punishment *can* be so grounded. Whereas the phrasing of section 43 treats a 'schoolteacher' as a distinct category from both a 'parent' and a 'person standing in the place of a parent', Grover J posits that 'the separate listing ... is *not* to distinguish a separate status/ grounding.[66] Yet, the distinctiveness of parents' position is reinforced by the Supreme of Canada's reasoning in *Ogg-Moss v R.*[67]

Second, there is no Canadian or persuasive comparative authority that treats the parental use of physical punishment as positive state action. Whilst Grover J cites Supreme Court of Canada decisions, none substantiate this point without requiring further assumptions. For example, in his majority concurring judgment in *B (R) v Children's Aid Society of Metropolitan Toronto*,[68] La Forest J reasoned that '[the parental] liberty interest is not a parental right tantamount to a right of property in children'.[69] But this only supports the case against the section 43 defence on the assumption that the use of physical punishment does, as Grover J asserts, 'render children akin to property',[70] the case for which remains to be made.

In terms of comparative sources, Grover J cites *Campbell and Cosans v United Kingdom*[71] regarding the limits of teachers' and parents' 'parental liberty right'.[72] *Campbell* cannot ground that contention since the European Court of Human Rights (ECtHR) itself states both that it sees teachers' and parents' 'power of chastisement' as separately grounded and that neither is in the form of delegated state power.[73] Further, Grover J suggests that the ECtHR in *A v United Kingdom (Human Rights: Punishment of Child)*[74] held that the *stepfather's actions* violated the child's Article 3 ECHR right.[75] In fact, the unjustifiable violation was the *state's failure to adequately prevent or respond* to the stepfather's actions.[76]

Grover J draws on the US case law discussed by Hill.[77] In particular, she cites the US Supreme Court's decision in *Ingraham v Wright*[78] to evidence that teachers exercise delegated

[61] *Williamson*, above n 14, [84] (Baroness Hale).
[62] For example, rewritten judgment [5]–[7] (Grover J), though note the additional, separate discussion of parents ([12]–[14]) and teachers ([15]).
[63] ibid [12] (Grover J).
[64] ibid [5] (Grover J). In respect of parents in particular: 'I hold that parents as section 43 'persons-in-authority' act as delegates of the State in exercising authority under shield of section 43': [12].
[65] ibid [9] (Grover J).
[66] ibid [9] (Grover J) (emphasis in original).
[67] *Ogg-Moss v R* [1984] 2 SCR 173, especially 190–92 (Dickson J).
[68] *B (R) v Children's Aid Society of Metropolitan Toronto* [1995] 1 SCR 315.
[69] *B (R)* [85] (La Forest J).
[70] Rewritten judgment [12] (Grover J).
[71] *Campbell and Cosans v United Kingdom* Application no 7511/76; 7743/76) (23 February 1982) (ECtHR).
[72] Rewritten judgment [12] (Grover J), citing *Campbell and Cosans*, ibid [36].
[73] *Campbell and Cosans*, ibid [12].
[74] *A v United Kingdom (Human Rights: Punishment of Child)* [1998] 2 FHR 959 (ECtHR).
[75] Rewritten judgment [10] (Grover J).
[76] *A v UK*, above n 74, [24].
[77] Hill, above n 60.
[78] *Ingraham v Wright* 430 US 651 (1977) (US Supreme Court).

state power[79] but, for the purpose of her argument in respect of parents, overlooks that the court in *Ingraham* distinguished between parents and teachers.[80] Hill recognises that the argument that parents exercise delegated state power is both doctrinally and conceptually difficult,[81] though finds it ultimately compelling.[82]

But the view that parental decision-making is simply the delegated exercise of state power contains no natural limits. It treats all individuals' actions not prohibited by the state and/or protected by a state defence as state action, and suggests that there is no scope for any private domain of family life. Families are afforded a measure of protection from state interference because they are 'irreplaceable' in modern liberal society;[83] 'different families are tolerated only so long as their adult members discharge the morally fundamental duty to provide adequate care for children'.[84] This is evidenced by the existence of a threshold for child protective intervention. Hill is correct that Foucault 'demonstrates the pervasiveness of state power and its implications',[85] but recognising that state power permeates familial relationships does not make parents state actors for legal purposes. Recognising that the state permits parents a 'privileged sphere'[86] of familial interactions, and a measure of protection from state interference does not mean that parental action within that protected domain is state action for legal purposes *qua* exercise of delegated state power. In this way, the doctrinal concern over identifying state action in the family context collapses into the conceptual concern over the state's scrutiny of the limits of any private domain.

Through the existence of a legal regime, the state regulates all individual actions and inactions, whether through positive intervention or lack of intervention. Individuals' actions qualify as the exercise of delegated state power only if these individuals are acting *qua* the state. Individuals acting within the private family sphere, which is protected by the state from state interference, are not. The state action is in the provision of the defence, not the underlying physical action protected by the defence.[87] Otherwise, a victim of domestic violence who is able to rely on the defence of diminished responsibility is thereby an agent of the state, rather than a victim. The conceptual argument cannot be sustained.

The third matter on which Grover J's argument turns is that, contrary to the general understanding, section 12 is applicable outside of the criminal context.[88] Drawing on the open-textured language of the section itself, Grover J asserts that section 12 is not restricted to penal sentencing and the judicial context.[89] Outside of sentencing, however, section 12 case law remains confined to issues of criminal process, prison treatment, and immigration.[90]

---

[79]   Rewritten judgment [16] (Grover J).

[80]   *Ingraham*, above n 78, 662, as cited ibid.

[81]   Hill, above n 60, 1336 ff.

[82]   Hill contends that it does not make sense that the US courts have constitutionalised children's right to bodily integrity in the abortion context: above n 60, 1314. Yet, as Hill notes, that right is underpinned by both autonomy and protection against bodily harm understood in terms of best interests: ibid 1317–18. In other contexts such as physical punishment, however, it is not clear that those twin concerns of autonomy and best interests similarly combine to exclude any space for parental decision-making.

[83]   D Archard, *The Family: A Liberal Defence* (London, Palgrave Macmillan, 2010) 117.

[84]   ibid 118.

[85]   Hill, above n 60, 1347.

[86]   J Eekelaar, *Family Law and Personal Life* (Oxford, Oxford University Press, 2006) 82.

[87]   In her reimagined dissent, Grover J confounds the distinction ([10]), discussed above at n 75–n 76 and corresponding main text.

[88]   See also *Ingraham*, above n 78 and corresponding main text.

[89]   Rewritten judgment [22] (Grover J).

[90]   Newman, above n 56.

In arguing for broader application, Grover J cites *Kindler*,[91] a case concerned with extradition for criminal proceedings, and *Rodriguez*,[92] a case in which the Supreme Court assumed that section 12 could apply more broadly only so as to enable it to determine whether the section could have been infringed in any event. In addition, the majority in the US case of *Ingraham*,[93] a case on which Grover J relies elsewhere, held that the ban on 'cruel and unusual punishment' did not apply to the non-criminal context.[94]

In addition to these three context-specific hurdles to sustaining her section 12 argument, Grover J must also demonstrate that either any physical punishment or at least that which exceeds *de minimis* falls within the terms of 'cruel' or 'unusual' treatment or punishment. From her reference to 'especially that beyond *de minimis*', it is unclear whether Grover J regards the failure to criminalise all physical punishment as unconstitutional or *only* that which meets a *de minimis* threshold.[95] Grover J relies on their conclusion to contend that that majority's definition is 'circular'.[96] In their judgment, however, the majority first determined that the conduct covered by section 43 was 'reasonable' within the terms of section 7, and then were logically bound to conclude that section 12 could not be violated:

> Conduct cannot be at once both reasonable and an outrage to standards of decency. Corrective force that might rise to the level of 'cruel and unusual' remains subject to criminal prosecution.[97]

Whilst ambitious, there are thus significant difficulties to sustaining the detail of Grover J's section 12 argument. Yet, as discussed above, there is clear strategic value in the attempt to make the section 12 case rather than rely on either section 15(1) or section 7.

B. The Assumption of Equal Status

None of the Court's judgments referred to children's rights. The ongoing availability of particular defences to the physical punishment of children stands in stark contrast to the increasing use of children's rights to frame legal regulation, as well as the evaluation thereof.[98] This makes the physical punishment of children a critical site for determining what it means for children to be rightsholders, whether of (human) rights for children or children's rights.

Insofar as children should be seen as holding human rights just as adults because they 'are entitled to the same moral consideration as adults',[99] this is a powerful point in favour of Grover J's approach. She justifies reasoning in terms of human rights on the basis that 'there are currently few if any instances of recognised arguably non-derogable specific "children's rights"'.[100] Whilst that is not itself an obstacle to adopting a children's rights approach, one might wonder if reclaiming the equalising status of human rights is more desirable. This is

---

[91] *Kindler v Canada (Minister of Justice)* [1991] 2 SCR 779, cited [23] (Grover J).
[92] *Rodriguez v British Columbia (Attorney General)* [1993] 3 SCR 519, cited [22] (Grover J).
[93] *Ingraham*, above n 78.
[94] ibid 664.
[95] Rewritten judgment [17], [18] (Grover J).
[96] ibid [23] (Grover J).
[97] *Canadian Foundation*, above n 13, [49] (McLachlin CJ).
[98] For example, consider the increasing use and importance of variously-titled children's or child rights impact assessments in respect of proposed legislation and budgetary reform.
[99] S Brennan and R Noggle, 'The Moral Status of Children: Children's Rights, Parents' Rights, and Family Justice' (1997) 23 *Social Theory and Practice* 1–26, 2.
[100] Rewritten judgment [29] (Grover J).

especially so, given that children are rightsholders under the Charter,[101] which suggests it should be necessary to either assume the equal applicability, or at least justify the unequal applicability of rights to children and adults. Otherwise, the majority's decision may be seen as realising the risk that a human rights model can 'descend into the co-option or appropriation of a rights based approach by existing power structures'.[102]

One might wonder if the similar consequences of the decision of the European Court of Human Rights in *A v UK*[103] are at least in part attributable to the human rights basis of the reasoning. Whilst the ECtHR held that the UK government owed the child a positive obligation to provide practical and effective state protection against treatment or punishment contrary to Article 3 ECHR,[104] the decision related only to that specific case[105] and the ECtHR stressed that only physical punishment of 'sufficient severity'[106] would infringe Article 3. Insofar as the ECtHR held Article 3 violated and the majority of the Supreme Court did not hold the Charter infringed, the outcomes reached differ. Yet, the consequences for future cases are nearly identical; the limits introduced by section 58 of the Children Act 2004 can be neatly contrasted to McLachlin CJ's15 qualifications.[107] Might a distinctive children's rights model have been more robustly applied?

Would reframing the legal issue in terms of children's rights be more likely to invert the premise of the section 43 debate than a human rights perspective? The current approach to physical punishment unjustifiably assumes children should be treated differently to adults, and *then* considers arguments for equal treatment. Given that, as Grover J argues, children hold the same human rights as adults in this context, why do we not assume equal treatment and *then* consider whether we have sufficient justification for othering children? Approaching the issue in terms of children's and adults' equal (human) rights for children ought to highlight the unjustified disparate starting-points. Yet, the *different* language of children's rights is sometimes the critical impetus for truly *equal* treatment. Further, the Committee on the Rights of the Child has suggested that

> [t]he distinct nature of children, their initial dependent and developmental state, their unique human potential as well as their vulnerability, all demand the need for more, rather than less, legal and other protection from all forms of violence.[108]

To the extent that a children's rights approach prioritises children's interests,[109] the Committee's analysis supports the *different* language of children's rights in order to achieve *different*, better protection for children.

---

[101] As under the European Convention on Human Rights, children are not explicitly mentioned in the Charter. Charter rights are treated as extending to children yet, in practice, they are of limited application.

[102] J Tobin, 'Understanding a Human Rights Based Approach to Matters Involving Children: Conceptual Foundations and Strategic Considerations' in A Invernizzi and J Williams (eds), *The Human Rights of Children: From Visions to Implementation* (Abingdon, Routledge, 2011) 61–98, 90.

[103] *A v UK*, above n 74.

[104] Convention on Human Rights and Fundamental Freedoms, Rome 4 XI 1950 [ECHR].

[105] *A v UK*, above n 74, [19].

[106] ibid [23].

[107] *Canadian Foundation*, above n 13, [40] (McLachlin CJ).

[108] United Nations' Committee on the Rights of the Child, *General Comment No 8 (2006): The right of the child to protection from corporal punishment and other cruel or degrading forms of punishment (arts 19; 28, para 2; and 37, inter alia)*, CRC/C/GC/8 [21].

[109] For a detailed argument to this effect, see L Ferguson, 'The Case for Treating Children as a "Special Case"' in E Brake and L Ferguson (eds), *Philosophical Foundations of Children's and Family Law* (Oxford, Oxford University Press, 2017) (forthcoming).

Finally, in relation to the human dignity basis for Grover J's argument, it is noteworthy that, post-*Canadian Foundation*, it has been rejected as an aspect of the legal test for section 15(1) due to the excessive burden it placed on claimants.[110] Might this also cast doubt on its value for Grover J's section 12 argument?

V. Government Commitment to Change

Grover J's reimagined dissent supports the existing dissenting judgments in *Canadian Foundation* and completes the trio of Charter arguments whereby the Supreme Court could have concluded that section 43 was unconstitutional. This is vital because of the harms of physical punishment. In 2012, drawing on 20 years of research, Durrant and Ensom concluded that 'no study has found that physical punishment enhances developmental health'.[111] Watkinson comments that, whilst 'the result was not what [she] had hoped for, it still reaped some benefits'[112] and highlights the extent to which the decision increased public awareness of the empirical evidence.[113] To the extent that social attitudes have changed, however, it is not clear that they changed as a result of *Canadian Foundation*. In 2012, Bell and Romano found that, of the 818 non-parents they surveyed, 'individuals were more or less evenly divided as to whether the law giving parents the right to use reasonable force in disciplining their children should be upheld or removed'.[114] In particular, 38.6 per cent held favourable views towards section 43 and 25.8 per cent were favourable towards 'spanking' generally.[115]

In his judgment in the Ontario Superior Court of Justice, McCombs J reviewed approaches taken in other jurisdictions, including the UK government's response to the European Court of Human Rights in *A v UK*, and concluded that they revealed 'a consensus that the most appropriate way of addressing this issue is to develop educational and other social programs designed to change social attitudes, rather than to expand the reach of criminal law'.[116] But the Canadian government did not initiate any such public education campaign in response to the Court's decision in *Canadian Foundation*.[117]

---

[110] *R v Kapp* 2008 SCC 41 [20]-[21] (McLachlin CJ, Abella J).

[111] J Durrant and R Ensom, 'Physical Punishment of Children: Lessons from 20 Years of Research' (2012) 184(12) *Canadian Medical Association Journal* 1373–77, 1373. A minority of scholars do persist in arguing to the contrary. See, for example, J M Fuller, 'The Science and Statistics Behind Spanking Suggest that Laws Allowing Corporal Punishment Are in the Best Interests of the Child' [2015] 42 *Akron Law Review* Issue 1, Article 7.

[112] Watkinson, above n 15, 78.

[113] ibid 81 (citing Durrant et al, above n 1).

[114] T Bell and E Romano, 'Opinions About Child Corporal Punishment and Influencing Factors' (2012) 27(11) *Journal of Interpersonal Violence* 2208–29, 2221.

[115] ibid 2217–18.

[116] *Canadian Foundation* (Ont SCJ), above n 17, [104] (McCombs J). This also accords with emerging evidence from Sweden regarding the difficulty of educating parents in the context of a pre-existing ban, which can cause professionals to worry about stigmatising parents and parents to be concerned about the ramifications of 'confessing' that they need support: Pernilla Leviner, 'The Swedish Prohibition against Corporal Punishment from a Comparative Perspective—Effects and Challenges' (2015) 61 *Scandinavian Studies in Law* 219–46, 243.

[117] A McGillivray and C Milne, 'Canada: The Rocky Road of Repeal' in Durrant and Smith, above n 40, 98–111, 105.

If the harm is clear, and progress with social attitudes is slow, can we justify waiting for social change? That difficult question looks to have been avoided. In December 2015, Prime Minister Trudeau affirmed the Liberal government's commitment to implement every one of the 94 recommendations made by the Truth and Reconciliation Commission on Indian residential schools.[118] This has critical, broader ramifications as recommendation 6 is to repeal section 43.[119] Canada thus stands on the verge of equal treatment and respect for children and adults in the law on assault. The language of 'reasonable correction' will lose its power; in turn, children will gain theirs.

---

[118] J Smith, 'Liberal government commits to repealing "spanking law"' *OurWindsor.ca* (21 December 2015) online: www.ourwindsor.ca/news-story/6203504-liberal-government-commits-to-repealing-spanking-law-/.

[119] Truth and Reconciliation Commission, *Canada's Residential Schools: Reconciliation—The Final Report of the Truth and Reconciliation Commission of Canada, Volume 6* (Truth and Reconciliation Commission of Canada 2015) 224, online: www.myrobust.com/websites/trcinstitution/File/Reports/Volume_6_Reconciliation_English_Web.pdf.

Supreme Court of Canada

Canadian Foundation for Children, Youth and the Law v Canada (Attorney General)

Grover, J (Dissenting)

1.   Section 43 of the *Criminal Code* RSC 1985, c C-46 (the *Code*) provides the following defence to assault of a child (with the elements of assault being set out at section 265 of the *Code*):

> PROTECTION OF A PERSON IN AUTHORITY: Every schoolteacher, parent or person standing in the place of a parent is justified in using force by way of correction toward a pupil or child, as the case may be, who is under his care, if the force does not exceed what is reasonable under the circumstances (*Criminal Code*, RSC 1985, c C-46, section 43).

2.   At issue in this appeal is the constitutionality of the section 43 defence provision under the *Canadian Charter of Rights and Freedoms* (the *Charter*).

3.   The appellant sought a declaration that section 43 of the *Code* violates sections 7, 12 and 15(1) of the *Charter*. The trial judge and the Court of Appeal rejected the appellant's position and declined to issue the requested declaration. The majority of this Court upholds the constitutionality of section 43 and dismisses the appeal. By contrast, I hold that section 43 is unconstitutional and would therefore allow this appeal. In reaching that conclusion, I find that section 43 constitutes a violation of section 12 of the *Charter* and that this is sufficient to render section 43 of the *Code* unconstitutional.

Reasoning on section 12 of the charter

4.   Section 12 of the *Charter* provides that: 'Everyone has the right not to be subjected to any cruel and unusual treatment or punishment.' As the majority of this Court (at paragraph 47) sets out, in order to show a section 12 *Charter* violation 'the Foundation must show both (a) that section 43 involves some treatment or punishment by the State ... and (b) that such treatment is "cruel and unusual"'. In my respectful view, the majority sidestepped the key issues involved in determining whether section 43 violates section 12 of the *Charter* by: (i) simply accepting as a given that parents administering corporal punishment by way of correction to their children do so as private actors, (ii) declining to answer the question as to whether teachers administering 'corrective' corporal punishment to their

students act in *loco parentis* or as State actors and (iii) holding that the section 43 reference to 'reasonable force' precludes cruel and unusual treatment of the child as lawful while, at the same time, conceding that 'borderline' cases will occur in that regard and erroneously accepting that the latter is legally supportable.

A. Section 43 'Persons-in-Authority' as Delegates of the State

5.   Section 43 of the *Code*, unlike most other defences, designates categories of persons as 'persons-in-authority'. This Court has set out the legal meaning of 'persons-in-authority' in Canadian law as a person allied with the State: 'acting in concert with … or as … agent' of the State (*R v Hodgson*, [1998] 2 SCR 449; paragraph 47); an 'actual person in authority' being an '"instrumentality" of the state' (*Hodgson, supra* at page 454). Here the parent, parental delegate or teacher acts as an agent of the State in applying force to a child as 'reasonable correction' where that 'person-in-authority' is protected from successful prosecution by section 43 of the *Code*.

6.   While parents, their delegates and teachers commonly wield authority over children in their charge, this is not what qualifies them as actual 'persons-in-authority' in the sense of that legal term as used in section 43 of the *Code*:

> The important factor to note … is that there is no catalogue of persons, beyond a peace officer or prison guard, who are automatically considered a person in authority solely by virtue of their status. A parent, doctor, teacher or employer all may be found to be a person in authority if the circumstances warrant, but their status, or the mere fact that they may wield some personal authority … is not sufficient to establish them as persons in authority (*Hodgson, supra* at paragraph 36).

Rather it is their close connection to or their alliance with the State for a certain purpose that renders them actual 'persons-in-authority' (*Hodgson, supra* at page 454). Further, the section 43 'persons-in-authority' are such only in relation to the application of alleged corrective force to the child, what would otherwise be considered private activity (ie administration of corporal punishment to the child). Such activity thus attracts *Charter* scrutiny but not all of their private activity does so (*Eldridge v British Columbia Attorney -General* [1997] 3 SCR 624 at paragraph 44): 'Just as Governments are not permitted to escape *Charter* scrutiny by entering into … "private" arrangements, they should not be allowed to evade their constitutional responsibilities by delegating the implementation of their policies and programs to private entities' (*Eldridge, supra* at paragraph 42); '[I]t is a basic principle of constitutional theory that since legislatures may not enact laws that infringe the *Charter*, they cannot authorize or empower another person or entity to do so' (*Eldridge, supra* at paragraph 35); '[T]he Charter applies to private entities in so far as they act in furtherance of a specific governmental program or policy. In these circumstances, while it is a private actor that actually implements the program, it is government that retains responsibility for it' (*Eldridge, supra* at paragraph 42). See also *Re Blainey and Ontario Hockey Association et al* [1986] OJ No 236; 26 DLR (4th), 728 where the Court held (at paragraph 27) that: 'there can exist a relationship between "government" and private citizens and organizations so that the actions of the citizen or organization can be considered "actions of government" for the purposes of the Charter.' Here the State specifically authorises parents, their substitutes and schoolteachers by law as 'persons-in-authority' (delegates of the State) to implement the government policy of purportedly moulding children into good citizens by use of reasonable force by way of correction, including corporal punishment.

7.   Where a government interest involves the delegation of a public function (here the behavioural guidance aspect of education) in part to the private sector it attracts *Charter* scrutiny ('It may be that if the state were to abandon in whole or in part an essential public function to the private sector, even without an express delegation, the private activity could be assimilated to that of a state actor for *Charter* purposes' (*R v Buhay*, [2003] 1 SCR 631, 2003 SCC 30, at paragraph 31). That the corporal punishment is administered by parents (their delegates) or schoolteachers does not render it an expression of a parental liberty interest as opposed to treatment by the State subject to *Charter* scrutiny. Further, the act of a person triggered at least in part by personal motive (here a parent, parental substitute or schoolteacher administering corporal punishment to a child in their charge) but, at the same time, prescribed by law in furtherance of a government interest, involves conduct that is properly open to scrutiny under the *Charter* as a State action (*R v Lerke*, 1986 ABCA 15, paragraphs 22–23).

8.   Only a person-in-authority in respect of a particular child, who is 'in charge' of *that* child, is likely, if so inclined, to use corporal punishment against *that* child given the section 43 *Code* shield applicable in their case while other adults are less likely to do so in respect of that specific child. Such a change in the material nature and quality of the interaction is an additional indicator that the section 43 designated 'person-in-authority' is acting as an agent of the State in applying corporal punishment to the child (Compare *R v Broyles* [1991] SCR 595 at page 608).

9.   I hold that the separate listing of parents, persons standing in the place of parents and schoolteachers in section 43 is *not* to distinguish a separate status/grounding for this State-conferred authority for parents and their substitutes as compared to teachers. Thus, while I agree with Binnie J (at paragraph 125) that schoolteachers under section 43 are not acting in *loco parentis* ('While at one time teachers were regarded as parent-type figures, section 43 itself draws a distinction between a "person standing in the place of a parent" and a teacher'), I disagree that parents, relying on their authority under section 43 of the *Code*, are acting in their private capacity in the exercise of a parental liberty right. Instead I find that each of the categories of persons listed in section 43 of the *Code* (as a 'person-in-authority') acts as an agent of the State under the authority of and for the purposes of section 43.

10.   Certain European Court of Human Rights (ECHR) cases have also affirmed that treatment by the State can involve administration of corporal punishment to a child by a parent or schoolteacher under colour of law: In *A v the UK* [1998] 2 FLR 959 (ECHR), the beating of a boy by his stepfather under the authority of the 'reasonable chastisement' statute was held to be a violation *by the State* of the child's fundamental rights under Article 3 of the European Convention on Human Rights on the particular facts of the case. In *Costello-Roberts v the United Kingdom* [1993] 89/1991/341/414, the Court held (at paragraph 28) that: 'in the present case, which relates to … school discipline, the treatment complained of although it was the act of a headmaster of an independent school, is none the less such as may engage the responsibility of the United Kingdom under the Convention if it proves to be incompatible with Article 3 or Article 8 or both …' and (at paragraph 27) 'the State cannot absolve itself from responsibility by delegating its obligations to private bodies or individuals'.

11.   Contrast *Campbell and Cosans v the United Kingdom* [1982] (ECHR), Application no 7511/76; 7743/76, Chamber Judgment, where the Court held that: (i) the authority of

parent or schoolteacher to administer moderate corporal punishment to a child in their charge as 'discipline' (at paragraphs 12 and 15) and an aspect of education (at paragraph 33) derived under Scottish law, at the time of the case, from the common law and not statute and that (ii) this did not therefore represent a delegation of State authority (at paragraph 12). However, in my view, corporal punishment of the child by a parent (parental substitute) or schoolteacher based only on the authority of the common law still constitutes treatment by the State. This is the case in that in a democracy the State must meet its obligation to enforce only common law that is 'reasonable': 'The *Charter* applies to the common law' (*RWDSU v Dolphin Delivery Ltd* [1986] SCR 573, page 574. See also *R v Golden* [2001] 3 SCR 679, 2001 SCC 83) on the Court finding that authority under the common law as exercised by agents of the State must be in a reasonable manner respectful of the person's human dignity. In Canada, the *Charter* acts as a check on the compatibility of the common law as enforced with democratic values that call for respect of human rights.

12.   *Parents:* I hold that parents as section 43 'persons-in-authority' act as delegates of the State in exercising authority under shield of section 43. The majority holds (at paragraph 48), in contrast, that 'Corrective force by parents in the family setting is not treatment by the State …' Blackstone considered the use of so-called reasonable force applied by the parent to the child 'by way of correction', including in the form of corporal punishment, as an aspect of lawfully fulfilling the parental duty of meeting the child's educational needs and as an aspect of the parental liberty right (*Commentaries on the Laws of England*(Clarendon Press, Oxford, 1765) Book I, chapter 16). However, the social science consensus is that greater than *de minimis* corporal punishment causing injury constitutes abuse while corporal punishment produces only short term compliance and is hence not educational/corrective (*Children Youth and the Law v the AG of Canada* [2002] ON CA, at paragraph 8, items 5 and 7)). I do not dispute that the State has afforded parents and their delegates, in the normal course, a certain constitutional scope of private activity: Section 7 of the *Charter* protects a parent's liberty interest in raising his or her child and making autonomous private decisions regarding education and other matters consistent with parental values including but not limited to parental religious beliefs and cultural mores ((*B(R) v Children's Aid* [1995] 1 SCR 315 at page 317). Such a right is affirmed also at Articles 14(2), 18(1) and 29 (1)(c) of the UN Convention on the Rights of the Child (CRC) which Canada ratified in 1991 (see *Baker v Canada* [1999] 2 SCR 817 at page 861 affirming that though the CRC 'has no direct application within Canadian law' (at paragraph 69), 'international human rights law … is a critical influence on the interpretation of the scope of the rights included in the *Charter*' (at paragraph 70)). However, at the same time the ' liberty interest is not a parental right tantamount to a right of property in children …' (*B(R) v Children's Aid supra* at page 318). In my view, the administration of corporal punishment to a child by a parent or parental delegate: (i) renders the child akin to property (compare *A v Israel* Supreme Court of Israel, 25 January, 2000, at page 39, paragraph 29 CrimA 4596/98) and (ii) lies beyond the scope of the parental liberty interest and also the authority of someone acting in *loco parentis* (Compare *Campbell and Cosans supra* at paragraph 36 where the Court held that the parental liberty right referenced in Article 2 of the First Protocol to the European Convention for the Protection of Human Rights and Fundamental Freedoms must relate to 'such convictions as are worthy of respect in a "democratic society" … and are not incompatible with human dignity' such as the Court held was the case with a parental *objection* to the use of corporal punishment at home and at school).

13.   I respectfully disagree with Binnie J's non-empirical supposition (at paragraph 125) that 'Less harm may flow from discipline inflicted by a parent' than by a teacher. I hold instead that the outcome may, depending on the circumstances, be no less harmful if the corporal punishment is administered by a parent as compared to a teacher. Further, while Binnie J finds (at paragraph 125) that: 'The pupil-teacher relationship is closer to the master-apprentice relationship for which section 43 protection was abolished by Parliament in 1955', in my view the application of corporal punishment by a parent (or schoolteacher) sets up a situation of similar rights denial for the child treated as property. This defeats the presumption that grounds the parental liberty interest in the first instance, namely that parents will act in the best interests of their children. Section 43, in my view, is thus incompatible with the notion of the *Charter* as a 'living document' incorporating the modern recognition of children as constitutional rights holders.

14.   *Teachers:* I hold that schoolteachers as section 43 'persons-in-authority' act as delegates of the State in exercising authority under shield of section 43. This Court has previously held that teachers are agents of the State in carrying out the government education objective and that, in acting as delegates of the government, their actions as school officials are subject to *Charter* scrutiny: See *R v M (MR)*, [1998] 3 SCR 393 at page 394 and *R v M (MR) Supra* at page 398. Here the majority acknowledges (at paragraph 48) that since 'Teachers … may be employed by the state' this raises 'the question of whether their use of corrective force constitutes "treatment" by the State'. Yet, the majority maintains (at paragraph 49) that: 'It is unnecessary to answer this question since the conduct permitted by section 43 does not in any event rise to the level of being "cruel and unusual", or "so excessive as to outrage standards of decency" …' At the same time, the majority 'read down' section 43 of the *Code* in respect of teachers' authority to apply corporal punishment to a child: 'corporal punishment by teachers is unreasonable' (at paragraph 38). The majority (at paragraph 40) expounds on the point as follows: 'Teachers may reasonably apply force to remove a child from a classroom or secure compliance with instructions, but not merely as corporal punishment'.

15.   We are also left with no answers from the majority as to whether parents who employ corporal punishment as discipline in home schooling their children are thereby:(i) applying 'treatment by the State' and, if so, (ii) whether corporal punishment in the latter context is also to be considered 'unreasonable'.

16.   Certain case law from the United States explicitly refers to the government's alleged legitimate interest in the 'reasonable' corporal punishment of children at school (*Baker v Owen* 423 US 907 [1975]; Affirmed 395 Fed Supp 294; *Gonyaw v Gary* [1973] United States District Court, D Vermont 361 F Supp 366). See also *Ingraham v Wright* 430 US 651 [1977] where the Court held that teachers are not acting in *loco parentis* when administering so-called reasonable corporal punishment to their student at page 662:

> Although the early cases viewed the authority of the teacher as deriving from the parents, the concept of parental delegation has been replaced by the view … that the State itself may impose such corporal punishment as is reasonably necessary 'for the proper education of the child' …

Mr Justice Black's Dissenting Opinion in *Tinker v Des Moines School District*, 393 US 503 (1969) at page 524 sets out the State interest in discipline of the child as follows: 'School discipline, like parental discipline, is an integral and important part of training our children to be good citizens-to be better citizens'. The US cases contrast with *Seven Individuals v Sweden*, European Commission on Human Rights, Decision on Admissibility, Application no 811/79, 13 May 1982, where the Commission upheld the government's view (at page 116) that the Swedish amended Code of Parenthood ban on corporal punishment of the child (incorporated into the school curriculum) represented a legitimate attempt 'to strengthen the rights of children and encourage respect for them as individuals ... this humanitarian objective ... to be pursued by way of a general policy of education in its broadest sense'.

17.   In my view, section 43 of the *Code* is incompatible with the State's obligation to ensure the child's right to education at school which requires, in part, as set out at CRC Article 28(2) that: 'States Parties shall take all appropriate measures to ensure that school discipline is administered in a manner consistent with the child's human dignity and in conformity with the present Convention' and at Article 29 (b)(d), respectively, that the State be directed also to: 'the development of respect for human rights and fundamental freedoms and for the principles enshrined in the Charter of the United Nations' and 'The preparation of the child for responsible life in a free society.' The child subjected to corporal punishment under colour of law per section 43 of the *Code*, especially where beyond *de minimis*, learns, contrary to democratic principles, that he or she in the eyes of the State has no inherent right to respect for his or her human dignity and has no reason then to consider that others who are equally or more vulnerable would or should have such a right affirmed and implemented.

18.   That corporal punishment is an affront to the human dignity of the child is evident when one considers the issue from a child-centered perspective as is required in assessing the impact of legislation on the human dignity of the person whose constitutional rights are at issue (*Gosselin v Quebec (Attorney General)*, [2002] SCC 84 at paragraph 25, page 464). Corporal punishment, especially that beyond *de minimis*, as an affront to human dignity, is antithetical to democratic values in that it represents a repudiation of the victim (here the child) as a rights-bearing person. Respect for human dignity is a fundamental principle of justice as part and parcel of the State obligation to afford each individual fair treatment under the law ('The principles of fundamental justice require that each person, considered individually, be treated fairly by the law' (*Rodriquez v the AG (Canada) and the AG (BC)* [1993] 3 SCR 519 at page 523)) and a foundational integrating democratic value underlying the *Charter* as a whole:

> The fundamental importance of human dignity in Canadian society has been recognized in numerous cases ... The Court must be guided by the values and principles essential in a free and democratic society which I believe embody, to name a few, respect for the inherent dignity of the human person ... (*Kindler v Canada* [1991] 2 SCR 779 at page 813)

In a democratic State, the child's right as a person to respect for his/her human dignity is, as noted by the Israeli Supreme Court, 'a super-legislative constitutional right' (*A v Israel supra* paragraph 28) and, I hold, part of being recognised as having natural legal personality.

19.   I concur with the majority (at paragraph 31) that 'Statutes should be construed to comply with Canada's international obligations' but I disagree that this is possible in regard to section 43 of the *Code* and the CRC. In my view, the majority (at paragraph 33) erroneously holds that CRC Article 19 (1) does not prohibit the use of all corporal punishment of the child because there is no explicit reference made to such a complete prohibition. Article 19(1), however, sets out the State obligation 'to protect the child from all forms of physical or mental violence ... while in the care of parent(s), legal guardian(s) or any other

person who has the care of the child'. At the same time, corporal punishment falls, in the particular case, somewhere in the range of severity from *de minimis* to what would qualify at the other extreme as a violation of Article 37(a) of the CRC which incorporates a prohibition on cruel treatment or punishment. In addition corporal punishment of the child, in that it negates the child as a rights-bearing person, infringes the International Covenant on Civil and Political Rights (ICCPR) Article 16: 'Everyone shall have the right to recognition everywhere as a person before the law' and Article 24: the right of all children 'to such measures of protection as are required by his status as a minor, on the part of his family, society and the State.'

20.   Section 43 of the *Code* sends a powerful anti-democratic message in that: 'It is the State that denies protection' (*Vriend v Alberta* [1998] 1 SCR 493 at page 551) to the child. Yet section 43 was upheld by the majority notwithstanding that, as Arbour J (at paragraph 132) points out, parents and teachers are already shielded from untoward criminalisation for applying reasonable corrective force to the child in their charge given: (i) the opportunity for the exercise of prosecutorial discretion and (ii) the availability of the *de minimis* and necessity defences.

21. *Conclusion:* I find that section 43 of the *Code*, in designating categories of 'persons-in-authority' to act under colour of law in furtherance of a governmental child education objective (the misguided attempt to mould children into good citizens by force including corporal punishment), creates a nexus between those section 43 actors and government sufficient to trigger the section 12 *Charter* element of 'treatment by the State'.

B.   Cruel and Unusual Treatment of the Child by the State Under Section 43

22.   The section 12 *Charter* guarantee is not restricted to the judicial context and penal sentences. Rather, section 12 of the *Charter* sets out that '*Everyone* has the right not to be subjected to any cruel and unusual treatment or punishment' (emphasis added) and does not refer to any particular context. The term 'treatment' in section 12, as contrasted with the term 'punishment', has been held to have a much broader scope and to be applicable outside the penal or quasi-penal context (see *Rodriquez* above at pages 610–11). In contrast, the US Constitution refers to a prohibition on cruel and unusual 'punishment' and does not include reference to such 'treatment'. As a consequence, the Eighth Amendment to the US Constitution prohibiting cruelty by an agent of the State has not generally, if at all, been held applicable outside of the penal context (see ie *Ingraham v Wright*, above).

23.   The majority (at page 78), relying on a circular definitional rationale, takes the position that cruel and unusual treatment of the child is completely precluded under the section 43 *Code* defence. Yet, at the same time, the majority (at paragraph 41) concedes that borderline cases may occur but adopts Gonthier J's view in *R v Nova Scotia Pharmaceutical Society*, [1992] 2 SCR 606 (at page 639) that this is not a fatal flaw (here in the section 43 *Code* provision). Yet, this Court has held previously that the constitutionality of a statute under section 12 of the *Charter* requires consideration of all reasonably foreseeable cases (ie, *R v Morrisey* [2000] 2 SCR 90 at pages 92, 93). In the section 43 constitutional case at bar the majority concedes the reasonable foreseeability of borderline cases. These would include cases where the child has in point of fact suffered cruel and unusual treatment by a section 43 person-in-authority but, given the borderline aspect of the surrounding facts and circumstances, (i) the case was successfully defended under section 43, or (ii) the

criminal charge was not laid in the first instance. Such borderline cases are perhaps even more likely when it comes to those where significant psychological harms not immediately evident were inflicted through corporal punishment. This, in that assessment of the seriousness of the attack on the child's human dignity through corporal punishment, cannot be made through objective measures alone but must take into account also, among other factors, the individual child's age, frailties, unique subjective experiences and perceptions and hence is vulnerable to error. Strikingly, in contrast to the majority's acceptance of the potential for and likely probability of some borderline cases under section 43 of the *Code* involving corporal punishment of the child, this Court has rejected as acceptable any cases involving corporal punishment in the penal context: 'at a minimum the infliction of corporal punishment … will not be tolerated' (*Kindler v Canada* (Minister of Justice) [1991] 2 SCR 779 at page 815) as a judicial treatment or punishment.

24.   Since section 12 of the *Charter* encompasses a non-derogable *jus cogens* right, borderline cases, such as the majority concedes can occur under section 43, *are* in my respectful view, fatal to the constitutionality of section 43 of the *Code*. Consequently, section 43 represents an abrogation of Canada's international obligations in regards to the upholding of the peremptory norm prohibiting cruel and unusual punishment or treatment embodied in section 12 of the *Charter* and incorporated into various international treaties to which Canada is a party (ie CRC Article 37(a) above). (See the *Case of Tyrer v the UK*, [1978] (application No 5856/72) concerning judicial corporal punishment of a child wherein the European Court of Human Rights Chamber (at paragraph 38) held that the prohibition against degrading punishment or treatment is absolute and (at paragraph 33) that corporal punishment by agents of the State amounted to being treated as an 'object' without respect for one's dignity as a person; see also *HLR v France* [1997] (Application no 24573/94) where the ECHR Grand Chamber held (at paragraph 40) that 'Owing to the absolute character of the right guaranteed the Court does not rule out the possibility that Article 3 of the Convention … may also apply where the danger emanates from persons or groups of persons who are not public officials'.

25.   Section 12 of the *Charter* is *not* precluded from the section 33 *Charter* notwithstanding clause override. Hence, despite the *jus cogens* principle embodied in section 12 of the *Charter*, the existence of section 43 of the *Criminal Code* leaves children in Canada in increased jeopardy of cruel and unusual treatment should the section 33 override be instituted for any period at some certain point.

26.   This Court has recognised that under various international instruments, including the CRC, children (generally defined under the CRC as persons under age 18) are owed a high level of protection as a vulnerable group (see *Baker v Canada supra* at paragraph 71, page 862). Further, as noted in *B(R) v Children's Aid*, above at 432: 'The rights enumerated in the *Charter* are individual rights to which children are clearly entitled in their relationships with the state and all persons …' Yet, the majority holds the contradictory and, with respect, I contend, the insupportable view that children over two and under 13 can properly be subjected to corporal punishment by a section 43 person-in-authority as so-called 'reasonable correction' (alleged disciplinary education) while children outside that age range are to be exempted. (I concur with Arbour J (at paragraphs 132 and 138) that limitations cannot, in any case, be 'read into' a statutory defence without a constitutional imperative and that this is not the role of the Courts). Further, the majority adopts this

view while, at the same time, conceding that section 43 allows for borderline cases, some of which will, as a factual matter, involve cruel and unusual treatment of the child. However, there can be no justification for exposing any child, regardless of specific age under 18, to the risk, due to section 43, of cruel and unusual treatment (Recall that the UN Human Rights Committee in its General Comment 20 on the Article 7 ICCPR guarantee of protection against cruel or degrading treatment or punishment affirms that the 'prohibition must extend to corporal punishment ... including excessive chastisement ... as an educative or disciplinary measure ...' (UN Doc HRI/GEN/1/rev. 1 at 30 (1994) at point 5). Section 43 of the *Code* thus represents a failure to protect and to adequately respect the human dignity and *Charter* rights of all children. Respectfully, I disagree with Binnie J's suggestion (at paragraph 124), that even absent successful criminal prosecution of the section 43 person-in-authority in the particular case the child protection system offers adequate recourse to ensure the child's welfare in future. Rather child protection agencies may intervene too late (assuming an intervention even occurs) to prevent the child significant harm as the cases cited by Arbour J (at paragraph 150–70) reveal.

27. *Conclusion:* Section 43 does not fully preclude cruel and unusual treatment of the child by the State.

28. *Disposition:* For the reasons given I find that section 43 of the *Code* does not adequately preclude cruel and unusual treatment of the child by the State and therefore infringes section 12 of the *Charter*. I find also that there can be no justification for such derogation of the *jus cogens* prohibition against cruel and unusual treatment through prescribed law which would be reasonable and consistent with the democratic value of respect for human dignity. Thus section 43 of the *Code* is not saved under the section 1 exception set out in *R v Oakes* [1986] 1 SCR 103. As this finding is sufficient to hold section 43 of the *Code* unconstitutional, it is unnecessary for me to address the applicant's section 7 and section 15 *Charter* challenge. I would have allowed the Appeal with costs.

C. Obiter Dictum

29. I take judicial notice of the fact that there are currently few, if any, instances of recognised arguably non-derogable specific 'children's rights' (see *Michael Domingues v United States*, Case 12.285, Report No 62/02, Inter-Am CHR Doc 5 rev 1 at 913 (2002)). The matter of certain 'children's rights' as non-derogable is ripe for legislative and juridical development. Clearly the 'best interest of the child' standard does not always serve children well ie the majority, on my respectful view, erroneously holds section 43 of the *Code* to be in children's 'best interests' notwithstanding the fact that it violates children's right to the *jus cogens* protection guarantee under section 12 of the *Charter*.

Part V

Children's Rights and Criminal Justice

22

Commentary on *Roper v Simmons*

EMILY BUSS

Roper v Simmons is widely perceived as a children's rights judgment and a judgment that has had an important influence on the continuing development of children's rights, particularly in the criminal context. In *Roper*, the United States Supreme Court ruled that sentencing juvenile offenders to death violated the Constitution's prohibition against cruel and unusual punishment, set out in the Eighth Amendment. In her rewritten judgment, Justice Woodhouse replaces the majority opinion, taking issue, not with *Roper*'s outcome, but with the legal basis for the Court's decision. Rather than grounding the right in the criminal-sentencing focused Eighth Amendment, Woodhouse calls for the recognition of children's broad constitutional right to a protected and supported opportunity to grow up.

I. Legal Background

The Eighth Amendment prohibits the administration of punishments that are 'Cruel and Unusual', a prohibition construed to require that criminal sentences are 'proportionate' to the offence and the offender. This requirement of proportionality has imposed few limitations on the state and national governments' ability to impose most criminal sentences, but it has been given some special force in the death penalty context. States have been directed to ensure that sentences of death are only imposed on offenders who commit 'a narrow category of the most serious crimes.'[1] In assessing whether specific applications of the death penalty are unconstitutionally cruel and unusual, the Supreme Court has placed considerable weight on trends in law-making and actual sentencing practices by juries. Where this evidence reveals a trend away from the imposition of death sentences for a certain class of offenders or offences, the Supreme Court has concluded that 'evolving standards of decency'[2] have rendered such sentences cruel and unusual.

This accounting of state laws and the trends in laws and practice served as a primary basis for the Supreme Court's conclusion, in *Thompson v Oklahoma* (1988),[3] that the imposition of the death penalty for murders committed by those 15 years old and younger was cruel

---

[1] *Roper v Simmons*, 543 US 551, 553 (2005) (quoting *Atkins v Virginia*, 536 US 304, 319 (2002)).
[2] *Trop v Dulles*, 356 US 86, 100–01 (1958) (plurality opinion).
[3] *Thompson v Oklahoma*, 487 US 815 (1988).

and unusual punishment but also served as the exclusive basis for the Court's determination in *Stanford v Kentucky*[4] a year later that it was not cruel and unusual punishment to sentence someone to death for a murder committed at the age of 16 or 17. This state-by-state accounting also served, in the same term, as a justification in *Penry v Lynaugh* for the Court's decision that the Eighth Amendment did not categorically prohibit the execution of individuals with significant cognitive impairments.[5]

In 2002, however, the Court reversed its decision in *Penry*. In holding, in *Atkins v Virginia*, that it was cruel and unusual punishment to execute cognitively impaired offenders, the Court relied not only on state legislative and sentencing trends away from the imposition of the death penalty on these offenders, but also on the Court's 'independent evaluation of the issues.'[6] This shift in approach and outcome in *Atkins* set the stage for a reconsideration of the Court's *Stanford* decision as well.

II. The Original Decision

While the Supreme Court's decision in *Roper* engaged in state-by-state accounting of legal trends and concluded (controversially, as Justice Woodhouse notes) that the states were trending away from the imposition of the death penalty on juvenile offenders, the heart of the *Roper* opinion, and the aspect of the opinion with the greatest influence on subsequent legal developments, was the Court's independent consideration of the differences between adults and adolescents that bore on an assessment of their relative culpability. In this section of its opinion, the Supreme Court drew heavily on the findings of developmental psychologists to conclude that juveniles 'cannot with reliability be classified among the worst offenders'.[7] The Court noted three relevant psychosocial differences that lessened juvenile offenders' culpability: adolescent's greater impulsivity and risk taking; their greater vulnerability to social pressure, particularly peer pressure; and their less fully formed characters. The Court concluded that because judges and juries lacked the expertise to distinguish the few juvenile offenders mature enough to be held fully culpable for their offenses from the majority who lacked the requisite maturity, the Eighth Amendment imposed a categorical prohibition on the imposition of capital punishment on juvenile offenders.

The Court also found support in the 'stark reality that the United States is the only country in the world that continues to give official sanction to the juvenile death penalty'.[8] It further noted the express prohibition of capital punishment for juvenile crimes in Article 37 of the United Nations Convention on the Rights of the Child (CRC), acknowledging, with apparent disapproval, the United States' partnership with Somalia as the only two countries that had not ratified the Convention at the time (Somalia subsequently ratified). But the tone of this part of the opinion is defensive and limiting. The Court made

---

[4] *Stanford v Kentucky*, 492 US 361 (1989).
[5] *Penry v Lynaugh*, 492 US 302 (1989).
[6] *Atkins v Virginia* 536 US 304, 321 (2002).
[7] Above n 1 at 553.
[8] ibid at 575.

clear that because 'the task of interpretation remains our responsibility', the clear international consensus had no controlling effect.[9]

The Supreme Court's decision in *Roper* was widely celebrated by children's advocates both for its outcome and for its reliance on development science to justify a distinct and more protective treatment of children under law. *Roper* also inspired a great deal of additional children's rights litigation, particularly in the criminal context, and within less than a decade, the Supreme Court issued three additional decisions which relied on differences between children and adults to recognise special substantive and procedural protections for children under the Constitution.[10] I return to these decisions after considering Justice Woodhouse's rewritten judgment.

III. The Rewritten Judgment

Justice Woodhouse, of course, does not alter the Supreme Court's holding. She agrees with the original Court panel that minors have a constitutional right not to be executed for their juvenile offences. She concludes, however, that this right should not be grounded in our Eighth Amendment, Cruel and Unusual Punishment doctrine, which she sees as problematic for two reasons. Woodhouse's first objection to the Eighth Amendment analysis is its focus on state legislative and sentencing trends. Woodhouse refuses to make the right in any sense contingent on state laws and practices. Woodhouse's second objection is to the Eighth Amendment's focus on culpability, which narrows the Court's consideration of children's developmental differences to those that might reduce their culpability in the eyes of the law. Woodhouse focuses instead on children's unique capacity to grow and change, and concludes that that capacity to change, children's very process of growing up, is entitled to protection as a fundamental right. In stepping outside the Eighth Amendment, she describes a right that could reach all aspects of children's lives from their relationships with their parents, to their access to education, to their opportunities to make important decisions on their own behalves.

While at times Justice Woodhouse's opinion appears to reject the *Roper* Court's reliance on developmental science in reaching her decision, important differences between children and adults and the differences in legal treatment tied to these developmental differences clearly motivate much of her opinion. She offers a long list of laws, including constitutional laws, that take children's special vulnerabilities into account to support her call for children's special right of protection.[11] What Justice Woodhouse resists is the suggestion that culpability as a legal concept can be dictated by developmental findings. Unlike mental

---

[9] ibid at 578.

[10] *Graham v Florida*, 560 US 48 (2010); *JDB v North Carolina*, 564 US 261 (2011); and *Miller v Alabama* 132 S Ct 2455 (2012).

[11] This part of her rewritten judgment adopts significant portions of the Brief of Juvenile Law Center, Children and Family Justice Center, Center on Children and the Families, Child Welfare League of America, Children's Defense Fund, Children's Law Center of Los Angeles, National Association of Counsel for Children, and 45 other organizations, as Amicus Curiae in Support of Respondent Simmons, 2004 WL 1660637, which Barbara Woodhouse coauthored.

disabilities, which impose categorical limits on the behaviour and understandings of individuals, ongoing maturation confers a blend of changing deficits and capacities that vary from one child to the next and over time. What is categorically true of all children is that they are in the process of changing, and it is that process of change and the potential for the future implicated by that process that Justice Woodhouse seeks to protect.

Justice Woodhouse grounds children's fundamental right to grow up with some protection of their developmental potential in the Constitution's due process ('liberty') and equal protection ('equality') principles. As someone who has endorsed an approach to law that focuses on our obligation to children as protectors and supporters of their ongoing development,[12] I am especially intrigued by Woodhouse's suggestion that such an approach could be enshrined as a constitutional right. Her approach has some vulnerability, however, a vulnerability articulated by many critics of the Supreme Court's recent same-sex marriage decision in *Obergefell v Hodges*.[13]

In *Obergefell*, Justice Kennedy grounded the right to marry any person of one's choosing on the due process clause's protection of unenumerated 'liberties'. This form of 'substantive due process' analysis is notoriously vague. Even among many of us who applauded *Obergefell's* outcome, the lack of doctrinal rigor in the Court's opinion has raised serious concerns about the coherence and stability of the precedent it established.[14] It seems to resolve an important and contentious legal issue for all citizens based on the personal views of the majority of the justices, and offers little doctrinal analysis that could guide a court in resolving future right to marriage claims, including a claim of a right to be married to multiple people at the same time.

Similarly, although it is attractive as a policy matter to base the abolition of the juvenile death penalty on a fundamental right to the protection of children's 'capacities for growth to maturity', it is not clear what legal analysis undergirds the recognition of Justice Woodhouse's right. And while, perhaps, a great value of a rewritten judgment could be its potential to remake the law, including the legal foundations on which other law is built, there are special dangers associated with 'rights of protection' defined in only general terms. Most distinctly, rights of protection could be found to be at odds with rights of autonomy, and there is nothing in Justice Woodhouse's analysis that tells us how such potential conflicts should be analysed. Of course, many have suggested that affording children opportunities to make decisions in their own lives is a key aspect of children's healthy development,[15] a view which Justice Woodhouse likely shares. The point is not that a right of protection could not be squared with the preservation of important children's autonomy rights, but rather that it might not be. Broad and amorphous rights leave us vulnerable to decisions by judges who, when the next case is before them, do not share our view of the world.

---

[12] E Buss, 'What the Law Should (and Should Not) Learn from Child Development Research' (2009) 38 *Hofstra Law Review* 13.

[13] *Obergefell v Hodges*, 135 S Ct 2584 (2015).

[14] See eg A Koppelman, 'The Supreme Court Made the Right Call on Marriage Equality, But They Did it the Wrong Way' *Salon* (29 June 2015) www.salon.com/2015/06/29/the_supreme_court_made_the_right_call_on_marriage_equality_%e2%80%94_but_they_did_it_the_wrong_way/.

[15] See eg M Freeman, *The Rights and Wrongs of Children* (London, Frances Pinter, 1983); F Zimring, *The Changing Legal World of Adolescence* (New York, The Free Press, 1982); J Eekelaar, 'The Interests of the Child and the Child's Wishes: The Role of Dynamic Self-Determinism' (1994) 8 *International Journal of Law ad the Family* 42.

This likely objection to Justice Woodhouse's approach—that it constitutes a usurpation of democratic lawmaking by unelected judges—echoes a central objection made by opponents of the actual *Roper* decision.[16] In the original decision, within its Eighth Amendment analysis, the Court reduced the relevance of state legislative and sentencing developments, and increased the importance of the Justices' application of their independent judgment. While the constitutional foundation of the right in the original judgment and Justice Woodhouse's judgment is entirely different, both relied heavily on the justices' own best understanding of childhood to interpret provisions of the Constitution that provided no guidance on how to take account of childhood or child development. For those who favour leaving a heavier share of law- and policy-making to the democratic process, both decisions suffer from the same basic weakness.

In addition to her due process analysis, Justice Woodhouse relies on the Equal Protection Clause, and this aspect of her analysis is particularly interesting. Equal protection analysis focuses on the right to be treated *the same* as others, whereas Justice Woodhouse calls for a constitutional right to be treated differently. In this sense, she is calling for a right of unequal, or special protection, based on minors' membership in a distinct class. Again, the idea is a powerful one, but an idea that is difficult to ground in our constitutional law. Perhaps Woodhouse is suggesting a new way of weaving our constitutional right of liberty and equality together: whereas the two rights have often been understood in combination—a constitutionally protected liberty right creates a special right against discrimination where that liberty right is at issue[17]—perhaps our long-accepted legal tradition of distinguishing children from adults establishes a fundamental right to distinct treatment. In other contexts, our history and traditions have served as an important doctrinal basis for defining and limiting the Court's potentially amorphous expansion of fundamental rights.[18] Perhaps that same analysis supports children's right for unequal, for special, treatment here.

I note with some interest that Justice Woodhouse invokes but does not rely on the international norms or the United Nations Convention on the Rights of the Child. In this sense, her opinion mirrors the original *Roper* judgment, noting that these international norms 'confirm' but do not 'control' the American judgment. This avoidance, even in a rewritten judgment that aims to depart, in ambitious ways, from the original, suggests the depth of the United State's resistance to international legal influence. And where a reliance on the CRC's prohibition against the imposition of the death penalty on juveniles would have had no effect on the law as articulated in the original judgment, a reliance on the Convention as a whole in Justice Woodhouse's opinion could have filled out her account of rights of protection considerably. In this sense, Justice Woodhouse gave up much more than the original Court in towing the line on America's legal independence from the rest of the world. Justice Woodhouse is right, however, to recognise that a reliance on the Convention would be a significantly greater departure from precedent than her shift from a narrow Eighth Amendment right to a broad Fourteenth Amendment right.

---

[16] See eg W Myers, 'Roper v Simmons: The Collision of National Consensus and Proportionality Review' (2006) 96 *Journal of Criminal Law and Criminology* 947.

[17] See, eg, *Zablocki v Redhail*, 434 US 374 (1978); *Loving v Virginia*, 338 US 1 (1967).

[18] *Michael H v Gerald D*, 491 US 110 (1989); *Moore v City of Cleveland*, 431 US 494 (1977).

A. Post-*Roper* Developments and the Implications of the Rewritten Judgment

To a significant degree, Justice Woodhouse's shift in emphasis from minors' difference in current capacities to their difference in capacity to change occurred in the Supreme Court's analysis in *Graham v Florida* and *Miller v Alabama,* which followed *Roper.* In those cases, the Supreme Court increasingly recognised children's special capacity to change as a consideration distinct from their lesser culpability. Addressing the constitutionality of juvenile life without parole sentences, the Supreme Court suggested that minors have a special right to have the opportunity to grow into individuals whose later development demonstrates that their crimes reflected 'unfortunate yet transient immaturity' rather than 'irreparable corruption'.[19] The thrust of *Graham,* which held that all life without parole sentences for non-homicide offences committed by juveniles violated the Eighth Amendment, and *Miller,* which held that even juvenile homicide offenders were entitled to an individualised assessment of their circumstances before they were sentenced to life without parole, was that it was cruel and unusual punishment to deprive a juvenile offender of all hope that he might reap some benefit from his future growth and reform.

Contrary to Justice Woodhouse's approach, however, the Supreme Court continued in these cases to ground its decisions in the Eighth Amendment and therefore the decisions' application in other legal contexts is highly uncertain. Advocates have argued that the Court's new 'developmental approach' should be applied in all contexts in which the law affects children, but it is too early to say to what extent the courts will endorse this approach. *Roper* as rewritten, more comfortably supports this expansion to other areas of the law.

What would such an expanded application look like? The Court would be called upon, in all contexts in which the law affects children, to ask how the law, as written and as applied, shapes children's ongoing development. While the rewritten *Roper* suggests that, at a minimum, the right includes the right 'to continue as a living, breathing human being', the full reach of a right to grow and mature is difficult to define. Justice Woodhouse suggests that the right contemplates protection, including protection from a minor's own mistakes. Does this right take the form of other rights recognised as fundamental under our Constitution, rights generally defined as 'negative' rights; that is, rights of protection against government interference? This would limit the right to instances, such as criminal sentencing, where the government threatens to step in and impose developmentally harmful consequences on a minor. Or does the right create affirmative obligations akin to those recognised in the CRC? In the past our Supreme Court has concluded that there is no constitutionally protected right to education[20] or right of protection against violence at the hands of a private individual.[21] It seems likely that these rulings would be overturned by Justice Woodhouse's approach as well.

---

[19] *Graham v Florida,* 560 US 48 (2010).
[20] *San Antonio Independent School District v Rodriguez,* 411 US 1 (1973).
[21] *DeShaney v Winnebago County,* 489 US 189 (1989).

Supreme Court of the United States

Roper v Simmons

Justice Woodhouse delivered the opinion of the Court.

In *Stanford v Kentucky*, 492 US 361 (1989), this Court considered and rejected the argument that the Eighth Amendment of the Constitution, which prohibits 'cruel and unusual' punishments, bars capital punishment for persons who committed their crimes as minors. The Supreme Court of the State of Missouri, relying on our subsequent decision in *Atkins v Virginia*, 536 US 304 (2002), disagreed and vacated the death penalty at issue in this case. We granted certiorari and now affirm the judgment, but for reasons that differ markedly from the reasoning of the Missouri Supreme Court and from our own prior decisions analysing the constitutionality of capital punishment for crimes committed by minors.

I.

Respondent, Christopher Simmons, was sentenced to death for a murder committed when he was only 17 years old. His early life had been marked by trauma and family dysfunction. His parents had separated before he was born and he grew up in a household dominated by a physically and psychologically abusive, alcoholic stepfather. Despite his troubled home life, his school records showed that he was an average student until he entered adolescence. Christopher's grades plummeted and there was a dramatic change in his behaviour. He began abusing alcohol and marijuana as a young teenager. By age 17 he was skipping school to drink to intoxication several times a week and consuming four to five marijuana cigarettes a day. To escape the brutal stepfather whom he feared, he resorted to running away from home, often for weeks at a time. During the summer of 1993, it was clear that Christopher was in a downward spiral, physically, socially and emotionally. Along with a group of other teenagers, he had been spending more and more time at the home of an older man named Brian Moomey—a 29 year-old who had served time in prison for burglary and assault. Moomey had befriended a group of local adolescents, encouraging them to congregate at his house to get away from their parents who 'picked on them', and supplying them with drugs and alcohol in exchange for their services. The adolescents began calling themselves the Thunder Cats and referred to Moomey as their 'Thunder Dad'.

On 9 September 1993, when he was 17 years old and entering his junior year of high school, Christopher was arrested on suspicion of murder. Fishermen had found the body of a drowned woman, later identified as Mrs Shirley Crook, floating in the Meramec River in St Louis County, Missouri. Her arms and legs had been bound and her face covered with a towel and duct tape. After learning that Christopher and a teenage friend may have been involved in the crime, police went to the high school to arrest Christopher. The police took him to the station house and read him his *Miranda* rights. He waived his right to counsel and initially denied any involvement in the crime. After two hours of intense police interrogation, including being told (falsely) that his accomplice had confessed and that he must cooperate if he wanted to escape the death penalty, he began to cry and asked to speak to the detective alone. He told the detective that at about 2:00 a.m. on September 9th, he had gone with a teenaged friend to Moomey's house. After trying and failing to wake Moomey, they had set out to burglarise a nearby dwelling. Moomey later testified against Christopher at trial, claiming that some days before the crime he had heard the youths talking about committing a burglary and murder but admitting he had not intervened or reported the plot. Christopher told the detective that, when they entered the dwelling they were burglarising, Mrs Crook, the sole occupant, awoke and called out 'Who is there?' On entering her bedroom, Christopher recognised her from a minor traffic accident in which he had been involved immediately after receiving his driver's licence. Christopher 'panicked', believing she also recognised him. The two boys bound her, put her in the back of her van, drove to Castlewood State Park, covered her face with a towel and duct tape and threw her off a railroad trestle into the Meramec River below.

Asked to re-enact the crime on videotape, Christopher agreed and accompanied the police to Castlewood State Park for a reenactment. Based on this confession, and the reenactment, the State of Missouri charged him with burglary, kidnaping, stealing and murder. As Christopher was over 16 at the time of the crime, he was outside the jurisdiction of Missouri's juvenile court system. See Mo Rev Stat 211.021 and 211.031 (Supp 2003). Christopher was tried in an adult criminal court, under the same procedures and with the same penalties as apply to adults.

At Christopher's trial, the State introduced Christopher's confession and the videotaped reenactment of the crime, along with testimony that Christopher had discussed the crime in advance and bragged about it later. The defence called no witnesses in the guilt phase. The jury returned a verdict of murder. The trial then proceeded to the penalty phase. Despite Christopher's youth, and the fact that this was his first offense, the State sought the death penalty. Prior decisions of this Court require that the prosecution prove aggravating factors enumerated in each State's law in order to justify imposition of capital punishment and that the defence be free to submit mitigating evidence. *Godfrey v Georgia*, 446 US 420, 428–29 (1980) (plurality opinion); *Eddings v Oklahoma*, 455 US 104, 110–12 (1982). As aggravating factors, the State pointed to evidence that the murder was committed for the purpose of receiving money; was committed for the purpose of avoiding, interfering with, or preventing lawful arrest of the defendant; involved depravity of mind and was outrageously and wantonly vile, horrible and inhuman. The State called Shirley Crook's husband, daughter and two sisters, who presented moving evidence of the devastation her death had brought to their lives. In mitigation Christopher's attorneys called an officer of the Missouri juvenile justice system, who testified that he was a first offender with no prior convictions and that no previous charges had been filed against him. Christopher's mother, father, two younger half brothers, a neighbour and a friend took the stand to tell the jurors of the close relationships they had formed with Christopher and to plead for mercy on his behalf. His mother, in particular, testified to the responsibility he had demonstrated in taking care of his two younger half brothers and of his grandmother and to his capacity to show love for them.

During closing arguments, both the defence and the prosecution addressed Christopher's age, which the trial judge instructed the jurors they could consider as a mitigating factor. Defence counsel reminded the jurors that persons under age 18 are barred by law from drinking alcohol, serving on juries or even seeing certain movies, because 'the legislatures have wisely decided that individuals of a certain age aren't responsible enough'. Defence counsel urged that Christopher's young age at the time of the crime should make 'a huge difference to [the jurors] in deciding just exactly what sort of punishment to make'. In rebuttal, the prosecutor gave the following response: 'Age, he says. Think about age. Seventeen years old. Isn't that scary? Doesn't that scare you? Mitigating? Quite the contrary I submit. Quite the contrary.' After finding the State had proved each of the three aggravating factors submitted to it, the jury recommended death. Accepting the jury's recommendation, the trial judge imposed the death penalty.

Christopher obtained new counsel, who moved in the trial court to set aside the sentence based on ineffective assistance of counsel at trial. As evidence of ineffective assistance, the new counsel called as witnesses Christopher's trial attorney, Christopher's friends and neighbours, and two expert clinical psychologists who had evaluated him. The trial attorney testified that Christopher neither understood the legal process nor appeared fully to comprehend that he was facing the death penalty. The mental health experts reported that Christopher at age 17 had been 'very immature', 'very impulsive', and 'very susceptible to being manipulated or influenced'. He often seemed 'naïve and child like' and reacted to stress with frustration. 'When he turns that frustration inward, he becomes depressed and there may be periodic suicide attempts … When he turns it outward, he may strike out at others.' The witnesses also testified about Christopher's troubled childhood, his downward spiral on reaching adolescence, and the physical and psychological abuse he suffered at the hands of his stepfather. However, the trial court found that the failure to present these facts to the sentencing jury did not rise to the level of ineffective assistance of counsel and denied his motion for post-conviction relief. The Missouri Supreme Court affirmed and the federal courts denied Christopher's petition for a writ of habeas corpus.

While Christopher was awaiting execution, this Court handed down *Atkins v Virginia*, 536 US 304 (2002), holding that the Eighth Amendment, as incorporated via the Fourteenth Amendment, prohibits the execution of a mentally retarded person. Christopher filed a new petition for state post-conviction relief, arguing that *Atkins* provided a basis for revisiting the constitutionality of the juvenile death penalty. The Missouri Supreme Court agreed, and concluded that, in the period since this Court had last considered the question in *Stanford*, 'a national consensus has developed against the execution of juvenile offenders.' *State ex rel Simmons v Roper*, 112 SW 3d 397, 399 (2003). It pointed to the fact that 18 states now bar executions of minors, that 12 other states bar the death penalty altogether, that no state has lowered its age of execution below 18 since our decision in *Stanford*, that five states have legislatively or by case law raised or established the minimum age at 18, and that the imposition of the juvenile death penalty has become truly unusual over the last decade. The Missouri Supreme Court set aside Christopher's death sentence and resentenced him to life imprisonment without eligibility for parole.

We granted certiorari and we now affirm the decision of the Missouri Supreme Court that the death penalty for crimes committed by minors is unconstitutional. However, our holding rests not on the Eighth Amendment but on the Due Process and Equal Protection Clauses of the Fourteenth Amendment.

II.

The Eighth Amendment, as interpreted by this Court, erects formidable barriers to emerging claims of rights. It reads, 'Excessive bail shall not be required, nor excessive fines imposed, *nor cruel and unusual punishments inflicted.*' US Const, Am VIII (emphasis added). Defendants must show that a particular punishment is both cruel *and* unusual. These words were part of the Bill of Rights, ratified by the original 13 States in 1791. Under our precedents, to qualify as *cruel*, a punishment must be inherently barbaric or excessive in relation to the crime. *Coker v Georgia*, 433 US 584 (1977) (prohibiting execution for rape). The punishment must not be disproportionate to the crime, and must be tailored to the defendant's 'personal responsibility and moral guilt.' *Enmund v Florida*, 458 US 782, 801 (1982) (prohibiting execution for felony murder). In prior cases, we have held that the death penalty may not be applied to individuals whose culpability is diminished because of mental illness or mental retardation. *Ford v Wainwright*, 477 US 399 (1986) (mentally ill); *Atkins*, above.

Although we have held that we 'must draw its meaning from the evolving standards of decency that mark the progress of a maturing society', *Trop v Dulles*, 356 US 86, 100–01 (1958), our precedents require extreme deference to the status quo. In examining the evolution of the Eighth Amendment, we must look to the laws enacted by the legislatures of the States as providing the 'clearest and most reliable objective evidence of contemporary values'. *Penry v Lynaugh*, 492 US 302 331 (1989). Some have argued that only overwhelming opposition to a challenged practice over a long period of time is sufficient. See *Atkins*, above, at 342–45 (Scalia, J., dissenting).

In prior juvenile cases we have followed the path marked out by our Eighth Amendment precedents. *Thompson v Oklahoma*, 487 US 815 (1988) (setting aside the death penalty imposed on a 15 year old offender); *Stanford*, above (upholding death penalty for 16 year old). We have dissected the body of criminal laws, state by state, in search of objective evidence that a sufficiently airtight consensus has developed. We have compared the number of states that have proscribed execution of children of various ages with the numbers of states that permit such punishments. We have debated the significance of how many executions actually occur in those states that *do* permit the death penalty for juveniles. We have argued over whether states that have entirely abolished the death penalty for any crime regardless of the perpetrator's age should be counted in the column of states opposing this sanction, debating whether non-death-penalty states should be disregarded in our computations of how many states regard the death penalty for minors of various ages as cruel and unusual. We have calibrated the relative pace of abolition by state legislatures of the death penalty, comparing youth as a class and at different ages with mentally retarded and mentally ill individuals, and have theorised about the significance of popular trends toward harsher as well as more lenient punishments. The dissenters defend this history and even reject the very concept of a categorical age-based exemption from the death penalty. *Roper v Simmons*, 543 US 609 (Scalia, J., dissenting). They argue that, as long as *some* adolescent murderers of a particular age are sufficiently mature to deserve the death penalty, juries should be left free to determine whether it is merited in the individual case. *Roper v Simmons*, 543 US 551 (O'Connor, J, dissenting). We cannot agree.

This macabre process—of tallying the executions of young persons who committed crimes while still legally children in order to gauge the continuing popularity of the practice—reached its nadir in *Stanford*, above. In *Stanford* a bare majority of the Court concluded that the Constitution did not proscribe the execution of juvenile offenders over the age of 15. The Court based its holding on the continued existence of the juvenile death penalty in 22 of the 36 states that had failed to abolish the death penalty entirely. *Stanford*, 370–71. A plurality of the Court also 'emphatically reject[ed]' the suggestion that this Court should bring its own judgment to bear on the acceptability of the juvenile death penalty. *Stanford*, at 377–78 (Scalia, J, joined by Rehnquist, CJ, White, J, O'Connor, J and Kennedy, J). Perhaps the most telling comment on our decision in *Stanford* came from the Governor of Tennessee, where the crime took place. After we handed down our decision, he commuted Kevin Stanford's death sentence, stating 'we ought not to be executing people who, legally, were children.' *Lexington Herald Leader*, 9 December 2003, p. B3, 2003 WL 65043346.

Our Eighth Amendment analysis has numerous drawbacks when applied to children's rights. First, it fosters a simplistic understanding of complex developmental and neurological science. Children as young as 14 may exhibit well developed cognitive abilities, enabling them to 'understand' many ideas and make certain choices, especially when guided by parents or other responsible adults. However, full maturity, including foresight, resistance to peer pressure, and mature impulse control, does not typically arrive until the mid-20s. Brief for the American Psychological Association et al as *Amici Curiae* 4–12; Brief for American Medical Association et al as *Amici Curiae* 3–20. While developmental science confirms our societal judgment that children are different, it does not and *cannot* tell us when children pass from childhood to adulthood as a matter of law. Our Eighth Amendment cases carving out exemptions for the mentally ill and developmentally disabled have turned on the extent and immutability of the defendant's disability. In dealing with youthful offenders, this disability approach misses the mark. Minors are qualitatively different precisely because of their rapidly evolving moral and cognitive capacities—they are a work in progress. Minors, as a class, have an innate capacity to grow and change that deserves constitutional respect and protection.

Second, our Eighth Amendment analysis vests disproportionate power in the whims of the electorate. As we discuss below, the constitutional issues posed by the juvenile death penalty transcend the Eighth Amendment's narrow prohibition of 'cruel and unusual' forms of punishment and implicate the fundamental rights of the child. Our precedents are clear that 'fundamental rights may not be subjected to a vote; they depend on the outcome of no elections.' *West Virginia Bd of Ed v Barnette*, 319 US 624 (1943) (striking down a penalty against minors refusing to salute the American flag on religious grounds). Original intent is a beginning and not an end of our analysis. Recognition of newly emerging claims of rights has been the hallmark of our constitutional order. As Justice Ginsburg has explained, 'A prime part of the history of our Constitution is the story of the extension of constitutional rights and protections to people once ignored or excluded.' *United States v Virginia Military Academy*, 518 US 515 557 (1996). See also *Lawrence v Texas*, 539 US 558 (2003) (rejecting the Court's erroneously narrow definition of the rights at issue in *Bowers v Hardwicke,* 478 US 186 (1986) as the right to engage in sodomy); *California Fed Sav & Loan Assn v Guerra*, 479 US 272, 284 (2000) (rejecting reasoning of *General Electric Co v Gilbert*, 429 US 125 (1976), that disparate treatment of pregnant women fails to state a claim of gender discrimination). We must acknowledge, as we did in overruling *Bowers v Hardwick*, that our past reliance on a narrow construction of the right at issue has resulted in a tragic miscarriage of justice. While we have quibbled over whether the juvenile death penalty is sufficiently cruel and unusual here at home to satisfy the Eighth Amendment, virtually every other nation has recognised that it is a violation of children's human rights. Brief for Human Rights Committee of the Bar of England and Wales et al as *Amici Curiae* 17–18; Brief for European Union et al as *Amici Curiae* 6–11. Far from being premature, as Missouri has argued, our decision today comes too late for the 19 juvenile offenders executed since our deeply flawed decision in *Stanford*. *See* V Streib, 'The Juvenile Death Penalty Today: Death Sentences and Executions for Juvenile Crimes, January 1, 1973-December 31, 2004'). It is time to go beyond the narrow Eighth Amendment framework and to recognise that children as a class have special rights to protection under our Constitution.

III.

The Fourteenth Amendment's Due Process and Equal Protection Clauses provide the overarching source of protection for fundamental rights and liberties not specifically enumerated in the Bill of Rights. We long ago concluded that 'neither the Bill of Rights nor the Fourteenth Amendment is for adults alone.' *In re Gault*, 387 US 12, at 13 (1967). The identification and protection of fundamental rights is an enduring part of the judicial duty to interpret the Constitution. That responsibility, however, 'has not been reduced to any formula.' *Poe v Ullman*, 367 US 497, 542 (1961) (Harlan, J., dissenting). Rather it requires courts to exercise reasoned judgment in identifying interests of the person so fundamental that the state must accord them its respect. *Poe v Ullman*, above; *Meyer v Nebraska*, 262 US 390 (1923). The process of interpretation is guided by many of the same considerations relevant to analysis of constitutional provisions that set forth broad principles rather than specific requirements. Our Constitution is a living document. As emerging fundamental rights, to privacy, to family, to form intimate relationships, and to protection from invidious discrimination have been recognised, we have struck down as unconstitutional policies that were once widely regarded as a matter for local authorities and state legislatures. See *Loving v Virginia*, 388 US 1 (1967) (striking down laws criminalising interracial marriage); *Turner v Safley*, 482 US 78 (1987) (striking down rules prohibiting incarcerated persons from marrying); *Skinner v Oklahoma ex rel Williamson*, 316 US 535, 541 (1942) (prohibiting laws requiring sterilisation of felons).

Our precedents have also identified classes of persons in need of special protection because of their historically marginalised status. *United States v Carolene Products Co*, 304 US 144, footnote 4 (recognising the danger of discrimination against 'discreet and insular minorities' unable to protect themselves through the political process); *Trimble v Gordon*, 430 US 762 (1977) (applying heightened scrutiny to laws burdening illegitimate children); *United States v Virginia*, above (applying heightened scrutiny to gender classifications). In determining their constitutionality, we asked whether laws burdening a 'suspect class', such as racial minorities, were narrowly tailored and necessary to furthering a compelling state interest. Laws burdening a 'quasi-suspect class', such as classifications based on gender, had to be substantially related to an important state interest. In recent cases, even without finding a suspect class or fundamental right, we have applied 'searching scrutiny' to determine if a law that discriminates based on membership in a class of persons or burdens essential liberties passes muster under the Fourteenth Amendment. See *Lawrence v Texas*, 539 US 558 (2003) (striking down law criminalising homosexual sodomy); *Cleburne v Cleburne Living Center*, 473 US 432 (1985) (striking down zoning ordinance that discriminated against mentally retarded persons); *Plyler v Doe*, 457 US 1131 (1982) (striking down Texas law denying education to undocumented immigrant children).

As we explained in *Moore v City of East Cleveland*, the Constitution protects a societal institution because the institution 'is deeply rooted in this Nation's history and tradition.' 431 US 494, 503 (1977) (striking down zoning ordinance that excluded minor grandchild from definition of family). Childhood, like family, is an institution deeply rooted in this Nation's history and tradition. Children have long enjoyed a special status under our laws. Age-based protections and exemptions from criminal penalties are older than our Constitution. For centuries before the founding of this Nation, the common law had drawn the lower limit of criminal responsibility at age seven. *Stanford,* above, at 368. Children aged seven through 13 were presumed incapable of criminal intent but the presumption could be rebutted. Children 14 and older were presumed to have criminal capacity. These age-based categories were partially rooted in judgments about young people's capacities but also reflected cultural benchmarks dividing adulthood from childhood. These benchmarks have changed as society has changed. See M Grossberg, 'Changing Conceptions of Children Welfare in the United States 1820–1935' in M Rosenheim et al, *A Century of Juvenile Justice* 142, 144–45 (Chicago, University of Chicago Press, 2002). As the American legal tradition has consistently acknowledged, 'there *are* differences which must be accommodated in determining the rights and duties of children as compared to adults.' *Goss v Lopez*, 419 US 565, 590–91 (Powell, J dissenting). Countless federal and state laws reflect these age-based differences. We make assumptions 'about children as a class; we assume that they do not yet act as adults do, and thus we act in their interests by restricting certain choices that we feel they are not yet ready to make with full benefit of the costs and benefits attending such decisions.' *Thompson*, 487 US at 825 n 23.

While developmental research is constantly deepening our *scientific* understanding of brain development, a *legal* bright line, endorsed in the vast majority of our laws, already exists between childhood and adulthood. In the United States today, age 18 marks the legal transition from child to adult. For most civil purposes, no state sets the age of majority below 18. As a nation, we treat persons under 18 years of age differently in virtually all respects—from the exercise of fundamental constitutional rights such as voting and reproductive choice, to participation in mundane activities, such as smoking cigarettes, drinking alcohol, driving a car or even patronising a tanning saloon or tattoo parlour. A person must be at least 18 to serve on a jury, enter military service, make a will, enter into a binding contract, marry without parental permission, gamble, or obtain an unrestricted driver's licence. Eighteen is the benchmark for full access to constitutionally protected activities, including reproductive choice, choice in marriage, access to media deemed, and issuance of a passport without consent of the custodial parent. Four out of five US cities with a population of more than 30,000 had nighttime curfews for youth, most commonly defined as persons below 18 years of age. Far from rejecting or relaxing these restrictions, in recent years, many states have increased restrictions on adolescents or adopted new ones, such as those increasing the age for consumption of alcohol to age 21, and those prohibiting body piercing or tattooing without parental permission. See Brief of Juvenile Law Center, Children and Family Justice Center, Center on Children and Families, Child Welfare League of America, Children's Defense Fund, Children's Law Center of Los Angeles, National Association of Counsel for Children and 45 Other Organizations, as Amicus Curiae in Support of Respondent.

This Court has endorsed constitutional distinctions between minors and adults in a broad range of contexts where minors are seen as needing greater protections from external influences or from their own impulsivity or lack of mature judgment. See eg, *Haley v Ohio*, 332 US 596 (1948) (interrogations); *In re Gault*, 387 US 1 (1967) (juvenile court procedures subject to the Due Process Clause of the Fourteenth Amendment, unless they are found to advance the therapeutic or rehabilitative benefits of the juvenile court); *McKeiver v Pennsylvania*, 403 US 528 (1971) (refusing to grant juvenile defendants the right to a jury trial to avoid making proceedings fully adversary); *Bellotti v Baird*, 443 US 622 (1979) (conditions on access to abortion); *Parham v JR*, 442 US 584 (1979) (allowing involuntary civil commitment by parent or third party); *New Jersey v TLO*, 469 US 325, 341–42 (1985) (allowing school searches); *Hazelwood Sch Dist v Kuhlmeier*, 484 US 260 (1988) (First Amendment not violated by censorship of school newspaper authored by minors); *Ashcroft v American Civil Liberties Union*, 124 S Ct 2783 (2004) (protecting minors from harmful internet images is compelling state interest).

In light of our opinions and the overwhelming consensus of state laws treating minors as categorically different and in need of protection, it is difficult to determine what legitimate purpose can be served by abandoning the age of 18 as the line dividing minority from adulthood, in cases where the state, far from protecting the minor, seeks to end his life. Christopher's case illustrates the danger in treating minority status at the time of a murder as just one among many potentially mitigating factors that a jury may take into account. During the last decade of the twentieth century, in the grip of a moral panic over a supposed epidemic of 'juvenile predators', many legislatures and prosecutors rejected our longstanding focus on rehabilitation of youthful offenders. 'Reformers' carved out exceptions to the jurisdiction of the juvenile courts, 'deeming' adolescents to be adults, based on the severity of their crimes. Laws were radically changed in a climate of fear that was later shown to be unwarranted. Laurie Schaffner, 'An Age of Reason: Paradoxes in the US Legal Construction of Adulthood' (2002) 10 *International Journal of Children's Rights* 201; Sacha M Coupet, 'What to do with the Sheep in Wolf's Clothing: The Role of Rhetoric and Reality About

Youth Offenders in the Constructive Dismantling of the Juvenile Justice System' (2000) 148 *University of Pennsylvania Law Review* 1303. The prosecutor in Christopher's trial played on just such fears when he argued to the jury: 'Think about age. Seventeen years old. Isn't that scary? Doesn't that scare you? Mitigating? Quite the contrary I submit. Quite the contrary.'

We have justified the legal disabilities of minors not only because, as a class, they are more prone to making mistakes, but also in recognition of the special nature of childhood as a period of growth to adulthood. In striking down laws that burden children's development, we have given expression to a societal commitment to fostering the process of growth and maturation of the next generation. See, eg, *Meyer*, above, *Plyler*, above, *Brown*, above. Laws that authorise execution of a person for acts committed while he was still, legally, a child constitute deprivations of the most fundamental liberty of the child—the right to continue developing as a living, breathing human being. Juvenile executions forever deny the individual's capacity for growth and maturation. It is arbitrary and irrational for the law to treat 16 or 17 year olds as children, categorically preventing them from getting a tattoo, entering into a contract or voting, and then declare them to be adults for purposes of trial and execution.

Confirming, but not controlling, our decision is the fact that the United States now stands alone in a world that has turned its face against the juvenile death penalty. Brief for Human Rights Committee, above; Brief for Respondent 49–50. Article 37 of the United Nations Convention on the Rights of the Child contains an express prohibition of execution for crimes committed by juveniles under 18. This bright line, age-specific prohibition is part of a larger scheme of rights of the child that recognises a duty on the part of governments to protect the young and enable their growth to maturity. International norms confirm our own Nation's commitment to minority as a legal and cultural institution conferring special protections on our Nation's youth.

IV.

Today we hold unequivocally that children have a unique set of fundamental rights under the Equal Protection and Due Process Clauses of the Fourteenth Amendment to protection of their capacities for growth to maturity. Concern for the welfare and development of the young and a special duty to foster their survival and growth to adulthood are deeply rooted in our own Nation's history and tradition. Numerous laws in every state impose legal disabilities on minors and assign control of their lives to parents and other adults. We justify these categorical restrictions on youthful freedoms based on a presumption that adults and governments have a duty to act in the best interest of the child. We treat minors as a work in progress, requiring special protections, including protection from their own mistakes. When the state executes an individual for acts committed while he was still, legally, a child, it violates fundamental rights of the child protected by our Constitution.

The judgment of the Missouri Court is hereby affirmed.

It is so ordered.

23

Commentary on *R v JTB*

KATHRYN HOLLINGSWORTH

The 1990s represented a low-point for the rights of children in conflict with the law in England and Wales. The murder of toddler James Bulger by two 10 year old boys in 1993 garnered support for Tony Blair's ambition to be 'tough on crime, tough on the causes of crime';[1] and, following New Labour's 1997 election victory, the youth justice system in England and Wales was radically overhauled in an attempt to 'nip crime in the bud'[2] through early intervention and increased responsibility. It was against this backdrop that Parliament legislated to abolish the centuries' old rebuttable presumption that children over the minimum age of criminal responsibility (10 years) but under the age of discretion (14 years) were *doli incapax*: incapable of committing a criminal offence. However, section 34 of the Crime and Disorder Act 1998 (CDA)—the relevant legislative provision—was ambiguous and a question remained as to whether it abolished only the *presumption* of *doli incapax* (a presumption that had to be rebutted by the prosecution) or whether it also removed the defence of *doli incapax*. It was this question that came before the House of Lords in *R v JTB*.[3]

I. *Doli Incapax* and its Abolition

The doctrine of *doli incapax* had existed in English common law for over 800 years.[4] Prior to 1998 its relevance was two-fold. First (and which remains the case), children under the minimum age of criminal responsibility (MACR) are conclusively presumed to be *doli incapax*; no criminal proceedings can be brought against them. Second, children over the MACR and under 14 years were presumed to be *doli incapax* unless the prosecution could prove that the child knew that what she had done was seriously wrong and not just naughty.

Given the low MACR—one that contravenes the United Nations Convention on the Rights of the Child (CRC) soft law provisions[5]—the presumption of *doli incapax* for 10–13

---

[1] *New Statesman*, 29 January 1993 (available at www.newstatesman.com/2015/12/archive-tony-blair-tough-crime-tough-causes-crime).
[2] Home Office (1997) *No More Excuses: A New Approach to Tackling Youth Crime in England and Wales*.
[3] *R v JTB* [2009] UKHL 20; [2009] All ER 211.
[4] T Crofts, *The Criminal Responsibility of Children and Young Persons* (Aldershot, Ashgate, 2002) chs 2 and 3.
[5] Art 40 CRC requires a minimum age of criminal responsibility but does not specify what it should be. However, the UN Committee on the Rights of the Child has criticized the low MACR in England, and in *General Comment No 10* it stated that an MACR below 12 is internationally unacceptable.

year-olds provided a 'buffer zone' for children who, on account of their age and development, lacked capacity. But the presumption was not without its judicial or academic critics and in 1994 the concerns about *doli incapax* came to a head in *C (a minor) v DPP* when, in the wake of James Bulger's murder, Mr Justice Laws purported to abolish the presumption.[6] He did so because it was outdated (universal education meant younger children knew the difference between right and wrong and they no longer need protecting from the death penalty); it was perverse and divisive (it prosecuted children from 'good homes' who knew right from wrong and absolved those from 'bad homes' who were more likely to offend); and it made prosecution difficult.

The House of Lords subsequently overturned this decision on constitutional grounds (that to abolish a long standing common law doctrine went beyond proper judicial function)[7] and instead called on Parliament to reconsider the continuation of the doctrine; a call to which the legislature responded in 1998. The removal of the presumption by Parliament was significant practically and symbolically.[8] Practically, more young children were brought into the criminal justice system (CJS).[9] Symbolically, it represented a shift towards the responsibilisation of children that was underpinned by two conflicting constructions of child/hood: first, children were 'adulterised' and constructed in the mould of the abstract, liberal, (and crucially) responsible agent who should be held accountable; second, children were imagined as 'becomings' such that holding them accountable would *develop* their responsibility.[10]

Following the CDA 1998, there was some academic and judicial support that section 34 had succeeded *only* in removing the presumption of incapacity and that a child could still invoke *doli incapax* as a defence.[11] The argument was based on (i) evidence that the two concepts (the rebuttable presumption and the defence) could be distinguished in the case law and (ii) a literal interpretation of section 34. It was these issues that went before the House of Lords.

II. Facts and Decision

JTB was 12 when he was convicted of causing or inciting a child under 13 to engage in sexual activity. There was no question he had committed those acts. His appeal therefore was against the trial judge's ruling that the defence of *doli incapax* was unavailable as a

[6]   *C (a minor) v DPP* [1994] 3 WLR 888.
[7]   *C (a minor) v DPP* [1996] AC 1 (HL) at 37.
[8]   L Gelsthorpe, 'Much Ado about Nothing—a Critical Comment on Key Provisions Relating to Children in the Crime and Disorder Act 1998' [1999] *Child and Family Law Quarterly* 209.
[9]   Following the abolition there was a marked increase in the cautions and convictions of 10–14 year olds. See further T Bateman, 'Criminalising Children for No Good Purpose: the Minimum Age of Criminal Responsibility in England and Wales' (London, NAYJ, 2012).
[10]   E Stokes, 'Abolishing the Presumption of Doli Incapax: Reflections on the Death of a Doctrine' in J Pickford (ed), *Youth Justice: Theory and Practice* (London, Cavendish, 2000).
[11]   C Walker, 'The End of an Old Song?' (1999) 149 *New Law Journal* 64; obiter comments of Lady Justice Smith in *DPP v P* [2007] EWHC 946 (Admin); [2008] 1 WLR 1005; and M Telford, 'Youth Justice: New Shoots on a Bleak Landscape—*Director of Public Prosecutions v P*' (2007) 19 *Child and Family Law Quarterly* 505.

result of section 34 CDA. The Court of Appeal dismissed his appeal, holding that both the presumption and the defence had been abolished: a decision with which the House of Lords unanimously agreed.

Lord Phillips' leading opinion focused on two issues: whether a common law defence of *doli incapax* existed independently from the presumption, and the mischief to which the legislation was directed. Extrinsic materials (Hansard and Home Office consultation and white papers) were used to identify the mischief and also, problematically, to establish the meaning of the doctrine in common law.[12] Lord Phillips concluded that the statutory reference to the presumption *was* to be taken to include the whole doctrine. Thus, the separate defence that had existed in common law could not survive section 34.[13]

The reasoning in JTB represents the antithesis of a children's rights approach in at least three ways. First, no reference was made to the CRC even though JTB's counsel had raised it in argument and even though the focus of the case was the ambiguity of section 34 (in which case a court can use relevant, ratified human rights treaties, such as the CRC, as an aid to interpretation). Given that this case concerned the state's use of coercive force against children, their rights were undoubtedly engaged and the failure to refer to the CRC suggests the Court's blindness to children's rights. Nor was there reference to research on children's development, including their capacity for understanding what is, and is not, right and wrong vis-à-vis appropriate sexual behaviour.

Second, the jurisprudence and scholarly material selected by Lord Phillips created a narrative of a benevolent youth justice system, thus making the otherwise unpalatable outcome (the exposure of more young children to the harms of the penal system) more acceptable. Support was given, for example, to Lord Jauncey's statement in *C v DPP* that the absence of the presumption in Scotland is not regarded as an injustice[14] and Glanville Williams' observation that 'at the present day the "knowledge of wrong test" stands in the way not of punishment but of educational treatment'.[15] This narrative is problematic. The Court's attribution of the 'outdatedness' of *doli incapax* to the less punitive criminal justice system reveals a fundamental flaw in its reasoning: if criminal responsibility (and *doli incapax*) is about knowledge of right and wrong then what happens within the penal system is irrelevant. Furthermore, Lord Phillips did not question the notion that children should be criminalised in order to receive 'educational treatment' and he left the quotes to stand without any acknowledgment that Scotland has a welfare-based youth justice system (which mitigates some of the potential injustice) or the vast evidence that children *are* harmed in today's English penal system.[16] A children's rights narrative would have emphasised those harms, and thus the desirability of keeping children *out of*, rather than within, the CJS.

---

[12] F Bennion, 'Mens Rea and Defendants Under the Age of Discretion' [2009] *Crim LR* 757.

[13] Here his reasoning differed from the Court of Appeal who did not accept that there was a separate common law defence.

[14] *R v JTB*, above n 3, [Para [28]].

[15] ibid, para [21].

[16] Bennion, above n 12 at 760. Harms include the increased likelihood of re-offending and escalation through the system (See L McAra and S McVie's, 'Youth Justice?: The Impact of System Contact on Patterns of Desistance from Offending' (2007) 4 *European Journal of Criminology* 315–45), the impact of a criminal record, and the significant harms experienced in custody (for an overview of the literature see K Hollingsworth, 'Assuming Responsibility for *Incarcerated* Children: A Rights Case for Care-Based Homes' (2014) 67 *Current Legal Problems* 99.

Third, the judgment focused heavily on the mischief that the legislation sought to redress: the difficulty of securing a prosecution. The House of Lords, following the Court of Appeal, readily accepted (i) that the presumption was difficult to rebut in practice and (ii) that addressing this mischief required the removal of the doctrine in its entirety. Both of these presumptions should have been subject to greater scrutiny. In relation to (i) no evidence was provided that *doli incapax* hindered prosecutions.[17] A court might legitimately be reluctant to conduct its own investigations into the evidence underpinning governmental or parliamentary statements, but it could require some evidence in support of those statements. With regards to (ii) the Lords did not articulate the difference between the rebuttable presumption and the defence vis-à-vis the mischief: even if the presumption created a barrier to prosecutions, the same cannot be said of the defence where the burden of proof lies on the child. Furthermore, by conflating the defence with the presumption the Lords created a counter-mischief (exposing children who lack capacity to the criminal law) which Bennion argues could not have been Parliament's presumed intent.[18] Unpacking the presumptions underlying the purported mischief would have helped secure a more favourable children's rights outcome (excluding children who do not understand the nature of their action) whilst allowing prosecutions against those who do.

III. The Implications of the Decision

Following *JTB*, children can no longer rely on as a defence a lack of capacity to know right from wrong. Instead, children who would have fallen within the *doli incapax* doctrine must now use other mechanisms to avoid conviction.[19] These include the exercise of prosecutorial discretion; (un)fitness to plead (in the Crown Court);[20] the Mental Health Act 1983 and Powers of the Criminal Courts (Sentencing) Act 2000 (in the youth court);[21] and staying proceedings as an abuse of process where, either under the common law or Article 6 European Convention on Human Rights (ECHR), the child will not receive a fair trial. Although there is a 'large measure of overlap' between *doli incapax*, fitness to plead and a fair trial[22] none of these alternatives is adequate.[23] Prosecutorial discretion is subject only to minimal supervision; section 37(3) of the Mental Health Act 1983 only applies to imprisonable offences and requires defendants to have a 'mental disorder'; accommodations to facilitate children's participation in court are rarely adequate; and staying proceedings as an abuse of process is 'rarely granted and provides no effective remedy'[24] and does not give

---

[17] Crofts, above n 4, notes that the Government was unable to point to evidence during the Parliamentary debates to show that the presumption had resulted in a large number of acquittals.

[18] Above n 12 at 768.

[19] For a full account see N Stone, 'Old Heads upon Young Shoulders: "Compassion to Human Infirmity" following R v T' (2010) 32 *Journal of Social Welfare and Family Law* 287–97.

[20] This allows a trial on the facts without the attribution of criminal responsibility.

[21] See s 37(3) and s 11(1) respectively; this allows a hospital order without conviction.

[22] *CPS v P* [2007] EWHC 946 (admin); [2007] All ER (D) 244.

[23] See Stone, above n 19.

[24] Law Commission (2016) *Unfitness to Plead: Summary* at 6 (full report Law Comm 364).

the defendant the opportunity of an acquittal.[25] Thus existing criminal justice processes 'do not provide suitable outcomes for many, particularly young, defendants'.[26] It is this wider context—the lack of alternative, effective provision to account for children's age-related (in)capacity—combined with a low MACR that compounds the potential harms resulting from the abolition of the presumption *and* the defence of *doli incapax*.

IV. Lord Arthur's Rewritten Judgment

Lord Arthur's rewritten judgment—an imaginary House of Lords dissent—differs from the original in three ways. First, it provides a different narrative. Whereas the original judgment sought only to interpret the abstract principle of *doli incapax*, considering its application to *all* children by drawing on generalised and inaccurate presumptions about childhood, Lord Arthur contextualises the doctrine by setting out the particular circumstances of this applicant—a boy he humanises by giving him the pseudonym 'Tim'. He provides facts that were excluded in the appeal courts,[27] and in so doing reminds us of the nature of childhood offending—that children can engage in immature, sometimes ill-advised games and activities, that may be consensual but that nonetheless can land them in serious trouble—and thus reminds us too of the consequences of removing the defence for an *actual* child. He also excludes from his opinion the unsupported presumptions concerning the nature of the youth justice system included in Lord Phillips' speech.

Second, Lord Arthur's reasoning is markedly different. He starts by rejecting the premise that the legislation is ambiguous and argues that on a purely literal view section 34 abolishes only the presumption. However, he also goes on to consider the proper interpretation should the legislation be deemed ambiguous. Here it becomes clear how judicial choice (and it is a choice) of extrinsic aids to interpretation shapes the reasoning and the outcome. Lord Arthur considers irrelevant the Government's consultation documents published prior to the legislation and instead turns to the CRC, citing previous House of Lords' decisions, to argue that Articles 40 and 3 can be used to interpret section 34 and thus support the retention of the defence. Article 40, read alongside the Beijing rules, places emphasis on the child's maturity and intellectual and emotional maturity and the obligation on state parties to take account of the special position of children in the criminal justice system.[28] This, Lord Arthur holds, requires that 'criminal proceedings should consider whether a child can live up to the moral and psychological components of criminal responsibility'. Article 3 demands that where two statutory interpretations are possible, the one that best protects the child's best interests should be followed. Both of these provisions, he decides, support an interpretation that retains the defence of *doli incapax*.[29] In adopting

---

[25] See Smith LJ, *C v DPP*, above n 6 at para 58.
[26] Law Commission, above n 24.
[27] These were provided to Ray Arthur by counsel for JTB, Peter Blair.
[28] Rewritten judgment, para [18].
[29] There is a lot of discretion involved in determining 'best interests' especially if there are different children involved. Here it would be in the best interests of potentially any child, including Tim, because it would help ensure that a child who lacks capacity is not convicted.

this holistic interpretation of the CRC, he moves beyond the text of Article 40—which is silent on the issue of *doli incapax*—to understand the purpose of the provisions according to the general principles.

However, there is a hurdle facing Lord Arthur and his use of the CRC. General Comment No 10 of the UN Committee on the Rights of the Child, which provides the authoritative interpretation of the Convention regarding juvenile justice, says that the adoption by some states of two MACRs (a lower conclusive one and a higher one that depends on the child's capacity) 'is often not only confusing, but leaves much to the discretion of the court/judge and may result in discriminatory practices'.[30] Prima facie, the lack of certainty and consistency of *doli incapax* would not support an interpretation of section 34 that retains the doctrine. However, the Committee's concerns apply less to *doli incapax* as a defence than as a presumption: the MACR is consistent and individual children can argue a lack of maturity allowing the use of alternative non-criminal proceedings instead in a way that is in-keeping with Article 40(3).[31] Indeed, given the Committee's continued criticism of the UK for its low MACR(s), it would be surprising if it was not supportive of mechanisms that provide some children with an 'escape route'.

Lord Arthur's children's rights approach does not stop at the CRC as an aid to interpretation. He also utilises the Human Rights Act (HRA) *and* the common law, and the concept of the rule of law. He reminds the Appellate Committee that fundamental rights can only be set aside by the clearest of parliamentary language and that the long-standing defence of *doli incapax* constitutes, for children, a fundamental right. This is a crucial element of Lord Arthur's reasoning. The UK Government has stated its intention to repeal the HRA and should it do so the primary vehicle for the CRC in English law will be lost. There is thus a strong imperative to locate children's rights within the common law, even where those rights might also be found in the ECHR, and to interpret those 'fundamental rights' for children using the CRC.

Thus, Lord Arthur's reasoning leads to the third difference with the original decision: the outcome. He finds in favour of retaining the *doli incapax* defence, and that Tim should be re-tried with the defence available to him.

V. Concluding Comments

Arguing for the retention of the *doli incapax* defence is not one that sits easily within a children's rights perspective. Its lack of certainty and consistency is one shortcoming but there are others. *Doli incapax* 'focused narrowly and simplistically on one aspect of cognitive development and functioning' (knowledge of right and wrong)[32] and did not consider reasoning and judgment, volitional control or relational capacities such as empathy

[30] UN Committee on the Rights of the Child, *General Comment No 10 (2007)* CRC/C/GC/10 (25 April 2007) at para 30.
[31] That is, the local authority may have duties to such children under Children Act 1989, s 17 if they are deemed a 'child in need'.
[32] Stone, above n 19.

and compassion, all of which may be less developed in children. This is unsurprising of course, given that it is the narrow liberal idea(l) of autonomy (the only condition of which is rationality) that underpins much of the criminal law. Further, *doli incapax* only applied to children up to the age of 14; if it is/was argued to be a *children's* right then why did it not apply to those aged 14–17 years? Finally, and more fundamentally, *doli incapax* continued to link children's criminal responsibility to their internal capacities (whether presumed for a certain age range or individually assessed) rather than on a consideration of the harm criminalisation causes either to their immediate welfare and rights or to their longer-term capacity for global, and full, autonomy.[33]

In truth then, Lord Arthur's children's rights judgment is a compromise adopted against the backdrop of an extremely low MACR. Judges in England and Wales—even ones who reason and decide using a children's rights approach—can only go as far as the wider legislative framework allows, even when that legislation conflicts with international standards. It was not open to Lord Arthur, therefore, to do what he perhaps would like to do: raise the MACR.

---

[33] K Hollingsworth, 'Theorising Children's Rights in Youth Justice: The Significance of Autonomy and Foundational Rights' (2013) 76 *Modern Law Review* 1046–69.

House of Lords

R v JTB

Lord Arthur:

My Lords,

1.   I have had the advantage of reading in draft the opinion of my noble and learned friend Lords Phillips and the concurring opinions of Lords Rodger, Carswell, Brown and Mance. I find myself unable to agree with them in deciding the outcome of this case.

2.   This Court is required to consider whether the effect of section 34 of the Crime and Disorder Act 1998 has been to abolish the defence of *doli incapax* altogether in the case of a child aged between 10 and 14 years or merely to abolish the presumption that the child has that defence, leaving it open to the child to prove that, at the material time, he was *doli incapax*. The focus of this case to date has been on the interpretation of section 34 of the Crime and Disorder Act 1998, which states that: 'The rebuttable presumption of criminal law that a child aged ten or over is incapable of committing an offence is hereby abolished.' However, this is a case which raises profound questions about the scope of courts' powers to convict children aged under 14 years who do not understand the wrongfulness of the criminal acts with which they have been charged.

The facts

3.   This case concerns a 12 year old boy whom I shall refer to as Tim, rather than simply T. Tim and a group of his friends, all under 13 years of age, were playing a game that they had developed called 'Flinch'. One of the boys would try to make the other boys, who were standing still, 'flinch'. Flinching would result in the loss of a game card. Tim discovered that he could get the other boys to flinch by touching them in a sexualised way and simulating sexual activity. As the game progressed Tim's actions became bolder and he put his hands inside their trousers and simulated sex between their buttocks eventually leading to masturbation, oral sex and anal penetration with his penis. One of the boys complained to his parents about this game. In interview Tim admitted the activity but said that he had not thought that what he was doing was wrong. Subsequently Tim was convicted of offences of causing or inciting a child aged under 13 to engage in sexual activity contrary to section 13(1) of the Sexual Offences Act 2003. The law must protect any victim who does not consent to sexual activity including children as young as the victims in this case who do not have the capacity to consent. Yet this case forces this House to think about childhood, sexuality and how children are held to account for their behaviour.

Tim's counsel submitted to the court a psychologist's report that expressed serious doubt that Tim realised that what he was doing in this game with other children was 'seriously wrong' as he was quite naïve about sexual matters. As such Tim sought to advance the defence of *doli incapax* and advances the same defence in this House.

4.   The trial judge and the Court of Appeal ruled that this defence had been abolished by section 34 of the Crime and Disorder Act 1998. In this House, Lord Phillips of Worth Matravers in his opinion accepts that the defence of *doli incapax* has always had an existence separate from the presumption. However, Lord Phillips finds that once extrinsic aids to interpreting section 34 of the Crime and Disorder Act are taken into account (notably references to Hansard), then section 34 represents Parliament's intention to abolish both the presumption and the defence, even though the section simply says that the presumption is abolished. Lords Rodger, Carswell, Brown and Mance concur with this opinion, with Lords Rodger and Carswell stating that they would have reached this conclusion solely on reading section 34 and without the need to take account of the passages in Hansard.

The presumption of Doli incapax

5.   *Doli incapax*, most commonly translated as 'incapable of committing an offence', has always had a twofold significance in English law. First, it constitutes an exclusion from criminal liability of children below a minimum age on the basis of an irrebuttable presumption of lack of capacity. The minimum age of criminal responsibility in England and Wales was set at 10 years by the Criminal Justice Act 1963, thus excusing all children below 10 years of age from criminal liability as such children are considered morally not responsible and therefore lack blameworthiness.

6.   Second, *doli incapax* operated as a defence to a criminal charge for children within a certain age group coupled with a rebuttable presumption that such children were incapable of committing an offence. According to the rebuttable presumption of *doli incapax*, children did not automatically become fully criminally responsible for their actions once they reached the age of criminal responsibility. They would only be held criminally responsible if, in addition to committing the *actus reus* and *mens rea* of a criminal offence, the prosecution could also prove, beyond reasonable doubt, that when doing the act, the child knew that what he or she was doing was seriously wrong. The common law position was stated in Archbold, and approved by Lord Lowry in *C (A Minor)* [1996] 1 AC 1, 24 as follows:

> at common law a child under 14 years is presumed not to have reached the age of discretion and to be *doli incapax*; but this presumption may be rebutted by strong and pregnant evidence of a mischievous disposition ... (Archbold (1993) volume 1, paragraph 1–96).

The rebuttable presumption of *doli incapax* recognised the possibility that some children aged between the minimum age of criminal responsibility and 14 years of age were incapable of understanding the gravity of their criminal actions because they did not have the prerequisite normal capacities akin to the adult offender. In order to rebut the presumption of *doli incapax* and secure a conviction, the prosecution had to prove that the child was fully capable and aware that what was alleged was seriously wrong. Only then could the child justifiably accept criminal responsibility for his or her actions; otherwise the child would be acquitted.

7.   The presumption recognised that children mature at differing levels and protected the child who was 'merely mischievous' due to immaturity and consequent lack of understanding. As *Blackstone* noted in the eighteenth century, the capacity of 'doing ill, or contracting guilt, is not so much measured in years and days, as by strength of the delinquent's understanding and judgment' (Blackstone, W. (1769) *Blackstone's Commentaries on the Law of England* Book IV, Chicago: University of Chicago Press, 23–24). The modern test upon which the presumption of *doli incapax* was based was: did the child know that the act was wrong, not merely wrong but 'gravely wrong, seriously wrong' (*R v Gorrie* (1918) 83 JP 186). The presumption required courts to consider whether the child defendant had more than simply a child-like knowledge of right and wrong, but instead had the capacity to understand their actions and judge whether these actions were right or wrong in a moral sense and an ability to act on that moral knowledge.

8.   Prior to the Crime and Disorder Act 1998, the validity and fairness of the rebuttable form of the presumption had been increasingly questioned by the courts. In *A v Director of Public Prosecutions* ([1992] Crim LR 34) Bingham LJ discussed the court's concerns regarding *doli incapax* as 'children have the benefit of the presumption which in this case and some others seems to me to lead to results inconsistent with common sense'. However, that comment was directed to the presumption rather than to the defence of *doli incapax*. In *C (A Minor) v Director of Public Prosecutions* ([1994] 3 All ER 190) the Divisional Court, in a judgment delivered by Laws J, purported to abolish the presumption of *doli incapax*. Laws J referred to the presumption as being in principle objectionable and disturbing (197), even nonsensical, as capable of giving rise to the risk of injustice (198) and concluded that 'the presumption relied on by the appellant is no longer part of the law of England' (200). The Appellate Committee considered the case of *C (A Minor) v DPP* ([1996] 1 AC 1). Lord Jauncey stated (at page 20) that:

> The presumption has been subject to weighty criticism over many years, by committees, by academic writers and by the courts … I add my voice to those critics and express the hope that Parliament may once again look at the presumption …

9.   It is clear from Lord Jauncey's speech (with which the other members of the appellate committee agreed) that the perceived problem with the presumption was the difficulty the prosecution faced in rebuttal. Four of the five members of the appellate committee expressed the hope that Parliament would review the operation of this aspect of the law. However, it should be noted that in *C (A Minor) v DPP* Lord Lowry commented that:

> Whatever change is made, it should come only after collating and considering the evidence and after taking account of the effect which a change would have on the whole law relating to children's anti-social behaviour. ([1996] AC 1, at 40)

The judgment in *C v DPP* provided the essential background for the changes enacted in section 34 of the 1998 Act.

Literal interpretation of section 34 of the Crime and Disorder Act 1998

10.   Most statutory enactments are expressed in language which is clear and unambiguous and does not give rise to any serious controversy. Unfortunately, section 34 of the Crime and Disorder Act 1998 is not such a provision. Rather unusually, it uses the latin

doli incapax in the heading but not in the section itself. The text of section 34 refers to the rebuttable presumption that a child aged 10 or over is 'incapable of committing an offence'. Based on a literal interpretation of section 34 of the Crime and Disorder Act 1998, in my view and contrary to the majority opinion of this House it is clear that the 1998 Act abolished the presumption of *doli incapax*. The common law defence of *doli incapax*, which makes some allowance for the fact that using criminal penalties to punish a child who does not appreciate the wrongfulness of their actions lacks moral justification, was not abolished.

11.   The majority in this House agree that the presumption and the defence of *doli incapax* are two different things. Nevertheless, they rule that over time it has generally been understood that when the presumption was referred to, this meant both the concept of *doli incapax* and the way it was to be applied. The Court of Appeal concluded in its judgment that the presumption of *doli incapax* had no existence separate from the concept of *doli incapax* and therefore abolition of the presumption necessarily involved abolishing the whole concept of *doli incapax*. These teleological interpretations, which are unsupported by any evidence, may cast doubts on the literal meaning of section 34. In light of this, and acknowledging that some may consider my literal interpretation to be incorrect, I continue the process of interpretation by attempting to discover the broad purpose of section 34.

Purposive approach

12.   In my view, it seems that the mischief at which the provision was aimed was the difficulty faced by the prosecution in having to rebut the presumption in every case. It also appears from the comments of the Solicitor General, Lord Falconer of Thoroton, that the underlying defence would remain available in 'genuine' cases. In closing the debate on the Crime and Disorder Bill in the House of Lords Lord Falconer acknowledged that:

> The possibility is not ruled out, where there is a child who has genuine learning difficulties and who is genuinely at sea on the question of right and wrong, of seeking to run [*doli incapax*] as a specific defence. All that the provision does is remove the presumption that the child is incapable of committing wrong. (16 December 1997, col 596)

Lord Phillips dismisses Lord Falconer's statement as an exception which is 'at odds with … other Ministerial statements' (paragraph 34). However, in *Pepper v Hart* [1993] AC 593 this House held that 'significance should … be attached' to clear statements by the Minister or other promoter of a Bill which are directed to that very issue of interpretation which the courts are called on to resolve (per Lord Browne-Wilkinson page 637). The House reasoned that it is reasonable to assume that the members of the legislature in enacting the statutory provision will have relied upon such statements made by a Minister or other promoter of the Bill and therefore Parliament passed the Bill on the basis of that statement (ibid pages 633–34). On that view, Lord Falconer's statement should be given greater weight. Lord Falconer's interpretation makes proper allowance for the fact that children such as Tim are still developing their understanding, knowledge and ability to reason. Further support for this interpretation can be found throughout the Parliamentary debates.

13.   When the Crime and Disorder Bill came before Parliament in December 1997, the second reading in the House of Lords was moved by Lord Williams of Mostyn. He stated that the Bill proposed the abolition of the presumption of *doli incapax*. He referred to the recommendation in this House in *C (A Minor)* ([1996] 1 AC 1) that it should be reviewed

'since it could produce inconsistent results' (16 Dec 1997, column 533) and to the parliamentary consensus that 'the ancient presumption of *doli incapax* is wholly out of date' (12 Feb 1998, column 1323). In the course of the parliamentary debate, Lord Ackner, who had been a member of the appellate committee in *C v DPP*, explained to the House the basis of that decision. He stressed the practical difficulties which the prosecution faced in rebutting the presumption:

> The present presumption obliges the prosecution to prove not only that a child under 14 committed a criminal act but also that he knew that the act was seriously wrong as opposed to being merely naughty or mischievous. That is all we are concerned with -nothing else. (12 Feb 1998, column 1318).

The Secretary of State for the Home Department (Mr Jack Straw) in the House of Commons also emphasised the difficulties created by the rebuttable presumption, 'Lawyers acting for offenders between the ages of 10 and 13 use the presumption of *doli incapax* … to run rings around the court system, and to avoid proper sanctions for young offenders' (19 May 1997, column 390). The Parliamentary Under-Secretary of State for the Home Department (Mr Mike O'Brien) when discussing the Crime and Disorder Bill argued that '[the government] thought that it should not be necessary for the prosecution effectively to have to prove that the child knew the difference between right and wrong.'

14.   On the other hand, as Lord Phillips acknowledges in his opinion, in November 1997 the White Paper *No More Excuses: A new approach to tackling youth crime in England and Wales* (Cm 3809, London: The Stationery Office, 1997) expressly stated that the intention of the Crime and Disorder Bill was that the whole concept of *doli incapax* would be abolished. The government stated its view that the defence of *doli incapax*, was 'contrary to common sense' and that retaining the defence of *doli incapax* would perpetuate difficulties prosecuting children under 14 years. The government explicitly rejected the reverse burden scheme, as it wished to send a clear signal that children aged 10 and over should be held accountable for their actions.

15.   What matters when interpreting a statute is not what the government thought it was doing but the meaning of the words which Parliament used. As Lord Reid once put it, 'We are seeking not what Parliament meant but the true meaning of what they said.' (*Black-Clawson International Ltd v Papierwerke Waldhof-Ashaffeburg AG* [1975] AC 591, at 613). Furthermore, Lord Nicholls of Birkenhead in *R v Secretary of State for the Environment, Transport and the Regions and Another, ex parte Spath Holme Limited* ([2001] 2 AC 344, 396) stated that:

> The task of the court is often said to be to ascertain the intention of Parliament expressed in the language under consideration … It is not the subjective intention of the minister or other persons who promoted the legislation … Citizens … should be able to rely upon what they read in an Act of Parliament.

16.   Using the purposive approach does not help in clarifying the meaning of section 34 of the 1998 Act. When the meaning of a statutory provision has been found to be unclear the courts can apply a number of presumptions. One such presumption is that domestic law is not inconsistent with our international obligations. Treaties and international conventions, therefore, may be used as an interpretive aid. Particularly relevant in this context is the 1989 United Nations Convention on the Rights of the Child (UNCRC).

The United Nations Convention on the Rights of the Child (UNCRC)

17.   The UNCRC was ratified by the UK in 1991. Article 40.1 of the UNCRC provides:

> States Parties recognise the right of every child alleged as, accused of, or recognised as having infringed the penal law to be treated in a manner consistent with the promotion of the child's sense of dignity and worth, which reinforces the child's respect for the human rights and fundamental freedoms of others and which takes into account the child's age ...

Article 40 of the UNCRC also requires each state to set a reasonable minimum age of criminal responsibility. The United Nations Standard Minimum Rules for the Administration of Juvenile Justice (the Beijing Rules) 1985 recommend that the minimum age of criminal responsibility shall not be fixed at too low an age level, bearing in mind factors, such as levels of emotional, mental and intellectual maturity. The important consideration, as outlined in Rule 17 of the Beijing Rules, is whether a child, by virtue of his or her individual discernment and understanding, can be held responsible for their behaviour. Neither the Beijing Rules nor the UNCRC set a minimum age of criminal responsibility as it was recognised that different jurisdictions have systems of youth justice and social care which inter-relate in different ways. However, the Commentary to the Beijing Rules stresses that there should be a close relationship between the age of criminal responsibility and the age at which young people acquire other social rights such as marital status and the right to vote. Although the Beijing Rules and the Commentary are purely recommendatory and are non-binding in that they have no direct legal impact upon either international or national legislative bodies, they serve to identify current international thinking on human rights for children and they represent the minimum recommended standards on youth justice issues.

18.   The UNCRC has not been incorporated into domestic law and is therefore not directly justiciable in UK courts. Even if an international treaty has not been incorporated into domestic law, our domestic legislation has to be interpreted so far as possible so as to comply with the international obligations which we have undertaken. *R v G* ([2004] 1 AC 1034) was not referred to in any of the previous opinions of this House or in judgments of the Court of Appeal, but for reasons which I shall now explain, consideration of this judgment is particularly relevant to the present case involving Tim. This case concerned two boys aged 11 and 12 years who went camping overnight without their parents' permission. During the course of this trip they threw lit newspapers under a plastic wheelie bin and caused £1m of damage to a shop. The boys thought there was no risk of the fire spreading in the way it eventually did. In *R v G* ([2004] 1 AC 1034, 1061) Lord Steyn stated that the UNCRC creates a norm which requires the criminal justice system to take account of a defendant's age, level of maturity, and intellectual and emotional capacity. This House ruled that the provisions of the UNCRC impose both procedural and substantive obligations on state parties to protect the special position of children in the criminal justice system. In my view, compliance with Article 40 of the UNCRC requires that criminal proceedings should consider whether a child can live up to the moral and psychological components of criminal responsibility; that is, whether a child, by virtue of her or his individual discernment and understanding, can be held responsible for their behaviour.

19.   Support for my view can be found in the opinion of Baroness Hale in *R v Durham Constabulary* ([2005] 2 All ER 369). This case was also not referred to in any of the previous

judgments in the present case involving Tim. Nonetheless it is particularly salient to Tim's case. This case involved a 15 year old youth who had received a final warning for indecently assaulting girls at his school. The final warning was issued without the consent of the young person or any appropriate adult, nor was any explanation provided as to the implications of accepting the final warning. Baroness Hale cited section 44(1) of the Children and Young Persons Act 1933 and Article 3 of the UNCRC in support of the proposition that the first objective of the youth justice system is the promotion of the well-being of the child. Section 44 of the Children and Young Persons Act 1933 imposes an important welfare principle which requires every court to have regard to the welfare of a child who is brought before it, either as an offender or otherwise. The welfare principle's main virtue is that it requires a decision made with respect to a child to be justified from the point of view of a judgement about the child's interests, objective immaturity, vulnerability and comparative lack of control over their immediate surroundings. Baroness Hale noted that this principle is also reflected in Article 3(1) of the UNCRC which confers on a child a right to have his or her best interests treated as a primary consideration. Article 3 of the UNCRC is an interpretative principle which holds that where a legal provision is open to more than one interpretation, that which more effectively serves the child's best interests should be adopted (per Baroness Hale's speech in *Smith v Secretary of State for Work and Pensions and Another* [2006] 3 All ER 907, 930–931).

20.   The effectiveness and appropriateness of *doli incapax* have been repeatedly questioned, as noted by Lord Phillips. However, the criticisms levelled at *doli incapax* do not convince me of the need for any weakening of the protection it potentially provides. The defence of *doli incapax* is based on a fundamental principle of criminal law, that a person should not be punished unless he freely chose to do something which he knew to be wrong. Children do not have this ability to discern from birth but develop it gradually as they grow up. The *doli incapax* defence allows for account to be taken of the fact that the path of development of the child is not steady and consistent and that children gradually develop an appreciation and understanding of wrongfulness and its consequences. The defence acknowledges that there is no identifiable single age at which it can be said that physical and mental development have reached maturity. Young people may experience differing levels of cognitive maturity.

The Human Rights Act 1998

21.   Section 3(1) of the Human Rights Act 1998 imposes a specific mandatory obligation on the courts to interpret legislation so far as possible in conformity with the rights guaranteed by the European Convention on Human Rights (ECHR). In accordance with the Vienna Convention, the European Court of Human Rights (ECtHR) may have regard to principles of international law, including international conventions, for the purpose of interpreting the terms and notions in the text of the European Convention (*Demir v Turkey* (2008) 48 EHRR 1272, paragraphs 65, 67, 85). The ECtHR has shown a growing willingness to interpret the European Convention dynamically in a way which ensures protection of the rights enshrined in the UNCRC (for example *Sahin v Germany* [2003] ECHR 340, *Sommerfield v Germany* [2003] ECHR 341). Consequently, the European Convention rights protected in our domestic law by the Human Rights Act can also be interpreted in the light of international treaties, such as the UNCRC.

22. Article 6 of the European Convention on Human Rights guarantees the right to a fair trial. The ECtHR in *V and T v UK* ((2000) 3 EHRR 121) ruled that the minimum age of criminal responsibility in England and Wales is low at 10 years of age, but this does not in itself violate Article 6. However, Lord Justice Scott Baker in *R (TP) v West London Youth Court* ([2006] 1 All ER 477) held that the minimum requirements of a fair trial include, amongst other issues, that the court is satisfied that the accused had the means of knowing that their actions were wrong. This ruling reaffirms the requirement under Article 40 of the UNCRC that criminal proceedings should consider whether a child, by virtue of her or his individual discernment and understanding, can be held responsible for his or her behaviour. It is presumed that Parliament must have legislated in conformity with these principles unless very clear language is used to the contrary. In Tim's case this involves interpreting section 34 of the Crime and Disorder Act as ensuring that protection is provided to children who lack the cognitive and experientially based abilities necessary for a fair trial.

Protecting fundamental rights

23. Other presumptions of statutory interpretation are also relevant in the present case. One such presumption is that Parliament has no intention to encroach upon fundamental rights. Lord Scott said in *R (Edison) v Central Valuation Officer* ([2003] 4 All ER 209, 243):

> where rights of citizens regarded of fundamental importance appear to be encroached upon by a particular application of a statute … it is presumed that Parliament, if it intended the statute to encroach upon the important fundamental right, would have expressly said so.

Lord Hoffman in *R v Secretary of State for the Home Department, ex parte Simms* ([2000] 2 AC 115, 131) held that 'Fundamental rights cannot be overridden by general or ambiguous words'.

24. The criminal law, and the UNCRC, have always recognised that a young person such as Tim, whose capacity to appreciate or control his actions have not sufficiently developed, may be blameless. In the present case involving Tim, the lengthy opinions in this Court and the judgments in the Court of Appeal were devoted to interpreting the meaning of section 34 of the Crime and Disorder Act 1998 and there has been no consideration of Tim's particular circumstances. Both Courts should have considered their duty, as a public authority under section 6 of the Human Rights Act 1998, to protect the rights of all involved in the case, including Tim's rights as a child, his right to a fair trial and to consider any evidence regarding Tim's immaturity and the circumstances of the offence. Had Tim been allowed to raise the defence of *doli incapax*, then the Court would have had to consider whether Tim understood the substance of the ingredients of the offences under the Sexual Offences Act 2003 and in particular that he understood that his actions were 'sexual' as required by the 2003 Act.

Changes to common law rules

25. The defence of *doli incapax* is a rule of common law that recognises that not all children under 14 years of age are sufficiently mature to accept criminal responsibility for their behaviour. When considering changes to common law rules, Lord Browne-Wilkinson in *R v Secretary of State for the Home Department, ex p Pierson* ([1998] AC 539 at 573) emphasised that 'Parliament is presumed not to have intended to change the common law

unless it has clearly indicated such intention either expressly or by necessary implication'. In my opinion the wording of section 34 of the Crime and Disorder Act 1998 is insufficiently clearly drawn as to indicate that Parliament intended to abolish the common law defence of *doli incapax*.

The rule of law

26.   Statutes are enacted on the basis that principles of the general law apply unless Parliament has excluded them expressly or by implication. The most important general principle of law is undoubtedly the rule of law itself. In his *Law of the Constitution* 10th edition (1959), Dicey explained the context in which Parliament legislates, at page 414: 'By every path we come round to the same conclusion, that Parliamentary sovereignty has favoured the rule of law'. As Lord Steyn stated in *Pierson* [1998] AC 539, 587, 'Parliament legislates for a European liberal democracy' and the courts may approach legislation on the initial assumption that unless there is the clearest provision to the contrary, Parliament did not legislate contrary to the rule of law (at 591). The ECtHR also has referred to 'the notion of the rule of law from which the whole Convention draws its inspiration' (*Engel v The Netherlands (No 1)* (1976) 1 EHRR 647, 672, paragraph [69]; *Golder v United Kingdom* (1975) 1 EHRR 524, 589, para [34]).

27.   The rule of law has never been comprehensively defined. Lord Bingham of Cornhill set out a number of its features in 'The Rule of Law' ((2007]) 66(1) *CLJ* 67), including:

— the law must be accessible and, so far as possible, intelligible, clear and practicable;
— the law must afford adequate protection of fundamental human rights; and
— the existing principle of the rule of law requires compliance by the state with its obligations in international law.

Professor Lon Fuller in his book, *The Morality of Law* (New Haven, Yale University Press, 1964), identified several elements of law as necessary for a society aspiring to institute the rule of law, including: laws should be written with reasonable clarity to avoid unfair enforcement; laws must avoid contradictions; laws must not command the impossible. Clearly the rule of law enforces minimum standards of fairness, justice and fundamental (substantive and procedural) rights. Accordingly, if a decision is made to prosecute a child for a criminal offence, the prosecutor and the court ought to be alive to the possibility that the child might not, for one reason or another, understand the criminal nature of their behaviour. It is my view that the defence of *doli incapax* is still available, as to hold otherwise is to assume that there are no psychological differences between child and adult offenders that are important to criminal responsibility. Such an assumption is manifestly absurd and could not have been intended by Parliament unless specifically stated, which it has not been. Therefore the law must remain alive to the possibility that the child might be *doli incapax* and the defence should be available for children such as Tim to argue.

28.   Returning to the case of *R v G* (([2004] 1 AC 1034), Lord Steyn held that 'Ignoring the special position of children in the criminal justice system is not acceptable in a modern civil society' (at 1061). In the same case Lord Bingham held that conviction of serious crime should depend on proof not simply that the defendant caused (by act or omission) an injurious result to another but that his state of mind was culpable when so acting (at 1055). As Lord Diplock stated, in the differing context of the partial defence of

provocation to murder, 'to require old heads on young shoulders is inconsistent with the law's compassion of human infirmity' (*Camplin* [1978] AC 705, 717). In *Camplin* Lord Diplock expressly acknowledged that the law must make allowances for youthful immaturity rather than insisting on the impossible, that the young person must at all times demonstrate the same standard of self-control as an adult. It would be misguided to equate the failings of a young person with those of an adult. Only by retaining some recognition of the differences in capacity and capabilities of children aged under 14 years and those aged over 14 years and adults, can courts ensure that the criminal trial is consistent with fundamental principles of fairness, due process and the rule of law.

Conclusion

29.   Tim's case has traversed through the judicial system without any discussion of the need to recognise that children may have not yet fully developed the capacity to be mentally culpable for their behaviour or the relevance of children's rights in this regard. This failure to consider these factors has meant that the judgments have been confined to a narrow discussion of the meaning of the words used in section 34 of the Crime and Disorder Act, with no consideration of the wider assumptions that Parliament must have legislated in conformity with children's rights as enshrined in the UNCRC, common law principles, principles of justice and to protect substantive basic or fundamental rights. In my view, section 34 of the Crime and Disorder Act 1998 abolished the presumption of *doli incapax* but it did not abolish the common law defence of *doli incapax*.

For these reasons I would allow the appeal and recommend the case be re-tried with Tim allowed to raise the defence of *doli incapax* to argue that, owing to his status as a child, he did not understand the 'sexual' nature of his behaviour and therefore did not comprehend that he was engaging in conduct contrary to the provisions of the Sexual Offences Act 2003.

24

Commentary on *The Prosecutor v Thomas Lubanga Dyilo*

CONRAD NYAMUTATA

I. Introduction

On 14 March 2012, the International Criminal Court ('ICC') found the Democratic Republic of the Congo ('DRC') rebel leader Thomas Lubanga Dyilo ('Lubanga') guilty as a co-perpetrator in the conscription and enlistment of children under the age of 15 years and of using them to participate actively in hostilities.[1] The Office of the Prosecutor ('OTP') resolved to charge Lubanga with only the crime of recruitment of children during the war, a decision which drew a lot of criticism. Contrary to the findings of the Pre-Trial Chamber (PTC), the Trial Chamber (TC) ruled that the DRC conflict was non-international in character, thus charging Lubanga under Article 8(2)(e)(vii) of the Rome Statute which criminalises the conduct of '*conscripting* or *enlisting* children under the age of 15 years into armed forces or groups or *using* them to participate actively in hostilities'[2] in non-international armed conflicts. There were several key procedural and material issues which had a bearing on the outcome of the case. These included the use of intermediaries, participation and credibility of victims and witnesses during the trial, the nature of charges, determining age and scope of participation in the conflict. Trevor Buck's rewritten judgment examines the effects of these and seeks to create new, child-centred narratives.

II. Rewritten Judgment

Lubanga, the ICC's first ever case, happened to focus on child soldiering. However, both prosecutorial and judicial approaches seemed to have missed an opportunity for a rigorous child-focused inquiry in a landmark trial focussing exclusively on children. For a crime relating to children's rights, the parsimonious reference[3] to the relevant legal instruments,

---

[1] Trial Chamber I, Case No ICC-01/04-01/06 14 March 2012.
[2] Emphasis added.
[3] Only six references can be found in the Judgment: at paras 604 and 607, and nn 1652, 1801, 1815 (and n 4 in Judge Fulford's separate opinion).

principally the United Nations Convention on the Rights of the Child (CRC), in the verdict, is glaringly counter-intuitive. The CRC is the most useful treaty in the interpretation of procedural and substantive issues related to children. The references to the CRC were only limited to Article 38 on outlawry of recruitment of children under the age of 15. Buck's rewritten judgment (an alternative majority judgment), by contrast, develops more detailed arguments based on the CRC. Under the Rome Statute, the Court is under a duty to apply, where appropriate, applicable treaties and the principles and rules of international law.[4] Overall, Buck draws from the broader international child law framework.

III.   International or Non-international?

The revised judgment immediately departs from the traditional superfluity of classifying conflicts, opting to place charges which cover *both* international and non-international armed conflict, because the 'protection of children would not be served by a prescriptive and rigid test.' In respect of child militarisation in particular, it would seem of little relevance whether children were recruited for an international or non-international armed conflict. More significantly, Buck's judgment analyses prosecutorial flaws and judicial inadequacies in a number of areas.

A.   Intermediaries

First, he notes the detrimental effect of the OTP's decision to delegate investigatory duties to intermediaries which resulted in the assemblage of unreliable witnesses and victims. The direct testimony of all the witnesses who claimed they had served in Lubanga's militia was excluded on the ground of unreliability. Lubanga's UPC/FPLC was described as an 'army of children.'[5] With such prevalent use of children in the armed conflict in the DRC, it is, thus, remarkable that genuine child soldiers could not be identified. To be sure, intermediaries constituted an integral part of the witness protection system and their involvement was considered 'best practice' during investigations.[6] Gathering evidence in conflict zones is challenging. However, the OTP failed to provide adequate supervision over the investigations carried out by the intermediaries.[7]

The main distinguishing feature of Buck's judgment is its attempt to contextualise the prosecutorial inadequacies within the broader children's rights framework. The CRC in particular provides an alternative construction of children premised on the four

---

[4] Art 21(1)(b).

[5] Human Rights Watch, Ituri: 'Covered in Blood' Ethnically Targeted Violence in Northeastern DR Congo 46 (July 2003) [hereinafter Human Rights Watch], at 46–47. available at www.hrw.org/reports/2003/ituri0703/DRC0703full.pdf.

[6] *Lubanga*, ICC-01/04-01/06-2690-Red2, Defence Application Seeking a Permanent Stay of the Proceedings, para 124 (citing *Lubanga*, ICC-01/04-01/06-2678-Conf, Prosecution Confidential Filing, para14).

[7] *Lubanga* judgment, ICC-01/04-01/06-2842, para 482.

foundational principles of non-discrimination, best interests of the child, the right to life, survival and development, and the right to be heard.[8]

IV. Truth-telling and On the Record Experience

Buck's rewritten judgment interprets the impact of the irregularities through the prism of the child's right to be heard (Article 12 of the CRC) and its related General Comment which applies to 'all relevant judicial proceedings affecting the child, without limitation, including, for example … victims of armed conflict and other emergencies.'[9] Buck points out that the rights of child soldiers to be heard within the framework of the CRC require an accurate and reliable record to emerge. The exclusion of witness testimony resulting from the unsupervised use of intermediaries by the OTP resulted in a failure to capture fully the child's voice. The ICC's innovative facility for victim participation ought to have resulted in a clear record of the daily indignities suffered by child soldiers.

With the evidence of unreliable witnesses discounted, Lubanga was convicted, but not on the evidence of those who were alleged to be the victims of the crimes he had committed.[10] The Court relied on visual, documentary and expert evidence. The absence of credible witnesses did sap strength from the prosecution's case, 'for it tended to put distance between the actual experiences of children in the militia and the credited evidence of those experiences.'[11] Buck's arguments on the dearth of children's voices and the need for an accurate record in court proceedings lend themselves to the understudied 'theory' of the expressive function of law.[12] For a seminal trial on a pernicious global problem, the most plausible philosophical justification for prosecuting Lubanga would be the expressive value.[13] Expressivism transcends retribution and deterrence in claiming as a core aim the crafting of historical narratives, their authentication as truths, and their pedagogical dissemination to the public.[14] The 'power to discover and represent facts provides these trials a unique opportunity to shape the historical knowledge of the atrocities that transpired.'[15]

---

[8] Arts 2, 3, 6 and 12 of the Convention on the Rights of the Child.

[9] Committee on the Rights of the Child, *General Comment No 12: The right of the child to be heard*, CRC/C/GC/12 (20 July 2009), para 32.

[10] Lubanga's conviction was based on the evidence of FPLC soldiers over 15 years old and other witnesses, *Lubanga* judgment, paras 645–731; as well as video material, paras 644, 710–18, 774, 779, 792–93, 860–62; and documentary evidence, paras 732–58, which included Lubanga's own speech, paras 1242–46.

[11] D Amann, 'Children and the First Verdict of the International Criminal Court' (2013) 12 *Washington University Global Studies Law Review* 411.

[12] R Sloane, 'The Expressive Capacity of International Punishment: The Limits of the National Law Analogy and the Potential of International Criminal Law' (2007) 43 *Stanford Journal of International Law* 39; M de Guzman, 'Choosing to Prosecute: Expressive Selection at the International Criminal Court' (2012) 33 *Michigan Journal International Law* 265, C Nyamutata, 'Lubanga, Child Soldiering and the Philosophy of International Law' (2015) Unpublished PhD Thesis, De Montfort University.

[13] Nyamutata, ibid.

[14] M Dumbl, *Atrocity, Punishment, and International Law* (Cambridge, Cambridge University Press, 2007) 173.

[15] V Padmanabhan, 'Norm Internalization through Trials for Violations of International Law: Four Conditions for Success and Their Application to Trials of Detainees at Guantanamo Bay' (2009) 3 *Journal of International Law* 427, 438.

However, the historical record in *Lubanga*, as discussed in the rewritten judgment would have been helped by proper selection of witnesses, giving an authentic voice to genuine victims and truth-telling as well as inclusion of sex crimes.

V. Victim Participation

Departing from the orthodoxy of witness-centred inquiry, one of the innovative aspects of the Rome Statute is the provision for victims to participate in proceedings and to claim reparations.[16] From an expressivist standpoint, the inclusion of victims' narratives enriches the historical record. The ICC granted 129 applicants (including 28 under the age of 18) the right to participate in the proceeding. All the applicants claimed to have suffered harm, either as a result of the crime of enlisting and conscripting children under the age of 15 into the FPLC, or their use to participate actively in the hostilities, and others as a result of sexual violence,[17] torture and other forms of inhuman treatment which are not the subject of the charges against Lubanga.[18] Whereas victim participation has always been (in one form or another) at the heart of the modern truth commission, its role in the courtroom is now said to 'mark a great advance in international criminal procedure.'[19] However, the novelty of victim-participation at the ICC was undermined by the use of intermediaries by the OTP which jeopardised children's rights to participate effectively as victims. The status of three participating victims[20] was revoked because of inconsistencies. In rebuking the OTP, Buck enjoins the prosecutor's office to familiarise itself with the *Guidelines on Justice in Matters involving Child Victims and Witnesses of Crime*[21] which set standards and recognises the adversities of children's participation in the judicial process.

VI. Expedition and Social Recovery

The trial of Lubanga focused on events that occurred nine to 10 years before. *Lubanga* underscored the need for fastidious filtering of witnesses and participating victims in the future. As Buck notes, the resultant delays in justice have a negative impact on affected societies, particularly on children who participated in conflict who are known to have incurred long-term physical and psychological damage. If *Lubanga* is to be viewed as a transitional exercise, delays in justice slow down the post-conflict healing processes.

---

[16] Art 68 of the Rome Statute.

[17] 30 victims (18 female and 12 male) referred to acts of sexual violence which they either suffered or witnessed; *Lubanga* Trial Judgment fn 54.

[18] Lubanga was only charged for the crime of enlisting, conscripting and using children under the age of 15. Sexual offences were not prosecuted and neither were torture and other forms of inhuman treatment charged.

[19] A Cassese, 'The Statute of the International Criminal Court: Some Preliminary Reflections' (1999) 10 *European Journal of International Law* 144, 167.

[20] Victims: a/0225/06, a/0229/06, and a/0270/07.

[21] UN Economic and Social Council (ECOSOC), *UN Economic and Social Council 2005/20: Guidelines on Justice in Matters Involving Child Victims and Witnesses of Crime*, 22 July 2005, E/RES/2005/20.

The value of international criminal trials is often affected by the distance between locations for trials and affected communities. The ICC is located in The Hague. It is perhaps worth noting the importance of ICC's Outreach programmes for direct engagement with communities traumatised by conflict. As has been noted, 'Outreach is needed all the more because the ICC may often hold trials far away from the scene of the alleged crimes, and apply law with which most people in the communities affected by the crimes are unfamiliar.'[22] However, such engagements would be unsuccessful if they excluded children, particularly in places where they are prone to recruitment for warfare.

VII. Determining Age

For a crime that centres on the age of victims, determining the ages was a central component of the trial, compounded by the attendant difficulties arising from a lack of systematic birth registrations. Buck correctly observes that the methodology[23] used to determine ages of the victims was barely conclusive because poor nutrition and disease factors could distort results. Medical tests are simply unreliable and a much more nuanced and dignified interdisciplinary approach should be advocated.

Another issue concerning age is that in all other respects, the CRC defines and offers protection to a child as any person under the age of 18. However, it also drops the threshold to 15 for child soldiers. Other international standards reflect a growing international consensus that children under the age of 18 should not participate in armed conflict. The Optional Protocol to the Convention on the Rights of the Child on the involvement of children in armed conflict, for instance, establishes 18 as the minimum age for direct participation in hostilities for compulsory recruitment, and for any recruitment or use in hostilities by irregular armed groups.[24] However, international criminal law has yet to catch up with this age threshold. The ICC still sets below 15 as the age of non-recruitment. Yet it does not prosecute anyone under the age of 18. Buck regrets the discrepancy and passes the buck to international legislators to resolve the incongruence. As international child law stands in this particular regard, it, rather unhelpfully, creates two categories of children.

VIII. Sexual Violence

Perhaps the most controversy of the trial revolved around sex crimes, for two reasons: first because of the OTP's omission of charges on sexual violence, and second on whether such crimes could fall within the scope of 'using' child soldiers to participate 'actively' in hostilities under the already preferred charge. During the trial evidence was adduced that

---

[22] See Lawyers Committee for Human Rights, 'Effective public outreach for the International Criminal Court' January 2004, 1 http://web.undp.org/comtoolkit/why-communicate/docs/Best%20Practices/EffectivePublicOutreachfortheInternationalCriminalCourt.pdf.

[23] *Prosecutor v Thomas Lubanga Dyilo*, Transcript of 12 May 2009, ICC-01/04-01/06-T-172-ENG.

[24] Arts 1 and 4(1).

girl soldiers were held as sex slaves by different commanders who called them their 'wives'.[25] However, the prosecutor had not presented separate charges of sex crimes before the PTC. Therefore, the evidence was considered irrelevant.[26] The TC thus did not make any findings of fact on the issue, particularly as to whether responsibility was to be attributed to Lubanga.[27] The omission was most regrettable because it tended to disregard an increasing and pernicious gender-based crime during armed conflicts. In the real judgment, Justice Odio Benito, dissenting, argued that sexual violence ought to have been included within the legal concept of 'using child soldiers to participate actively in the hostilities' because sexual violence is an intrinsic element of the criminal conduct associated with forcing someone to 'actively participate in hostilities.'[28] The TC concluded that a child would be participating actively if they were a 'potential target' and exposed to 'danger.'

Clearly, the judgment's concept of 'danger' was limited to the military acts of the external enemy and precluded harm that could be experienced by children as 'targets' of the same armed group that recruited them.[29] Buck rightly observes that the TC's 'potential target' test tends to focus on the military significance of children rather than their overall protection. Rather than use 'sexual abuse', Buck opts for the term 'sexual services' so that the acts fit within the other ancillary services such as cooking, guarding, spying duties and so on— considered indirect in traditional international humanitarian law (IHL) but active by the ICC judgment. However, some authors have argued that even 'adopting an extensive interpretation, it appears difficult to encompass sexual violence within the explicit or implicit meaning of the provision in question.'[30]

Had the original judgment retained the standard IHL concepts of 'direct' and 'indirect' participation, a case could be made, as Buck does, for 'sexual services,' or crimes, as part of the latter category. Buck holds that sexual services ought to be treated as active participation where they can be said to provide significant support and maintenance to the military operations at issue. However, a conclusion that, for instance, a rape occurring away from the battlefront would constitute participating 'actively' in hostilities remains contentious. In the context of the Rome Statute, the situation would have been different if the OTP had charged Lubanga separately with sex crimes in accordance with Article 8 (2) (e) (vi) Rome Statute.[31] As Buck observes, a key component of the offence of child soldiering was, as a result, omitted, denying the Court an opportunity for historical inquiry and construction of a plausible record of the crime. Again, this affected the expressivist goal of constructing a fuller picture of child soldiering. This ought to have been a principal prosecutorial objective in a novel case.

[25] *Lubanga* judgment, para 894.
[26] For the purposes of Art 74 of the Rome Statute which states that the '[T]he decision shall not exceed the facts and circumstances described in the charges and any amendments to the charges.'
[27] *Lubanga* judgment, para 896.
[28] Separate and Dissenting Opinion of Judge Odio Benito, attached to the Judgment, 20.
[29] *Lubanga* judgment, paras 18–19.
[30] T Mariniello, 'Prosecutor v Thomas Lubanga Dyilo: The First Judgment of the International Criminal Court's Trial Chamber' (2012)1 *International Human Rights Law Review* 137–47.
[31] The prosecutor did seek consideration of sex crimes as aggravation in sentencing attracting rebuke from judges for not including the crimes or applying for them to be included. *Prosecutor v Lubanga* Decision on Sentence pursuant to Art 76 of the Statute ICC-01/04-01/06-2901 (hereinafter 'Lubanga Sentencing Decision') para 60.

IX. Interpretation of Articles 8(2)(b)(xxvi) and 8(2)(e)(vii) of the Rome Statute

Lubanga was charged under Article 8(2)(e)(vii) of the Rome Statute which criminalises the conduct of '*conscripting* or *enlisting* children under the age of 15 years into armed forces or groups or *using* them to participate actively in hostilities' in non-international armed conflicts.[32] Previous jurisprudence and *Lubanga* concur that conscription connotes some element of coercion while '[e]nlistment is a voluntary act, and the child's consent is therefore not a valid defence.'[33] This is due to the fact that a girl or a boy under 15 years of age is incapable of providing 'genuine and informed consent when enlisting in an armed group or force.' Had the Rome Statute imposed an 18 year threshold, excluding the defence of consent would have been much more difficult.[34] However, Buck cautions against the notion that children lack individual agency. This would tend to conflate conscription and enlistment, rendering the distinction in the statute irrelevant. According to Drumbl the 'faultless passive victim' image of the child soldier[35] is a 'legal fiction.'[36] Some children joined wars voluntarily. Further, refusal to recognise agency of children would contradict children's rights instruments which recognised children's independence of thought.

However, such conclusions are problematic when complexities of childhood and the real context of warfare are considered. It is possible that some children subscribe to ideologies of armed conflicts. But when the socio-economic realities, particularly in war-prone poor countries where child soldiering is rife, are factored in, victimhood ceases to be a fiction. Children, some orphaned, are threatened or enticed to join wars with promises of, among other things, money, food and security or protection of themselves and families. Given these contexts, the defence of consent becomes difficult to advance.

X. Using Children 'to Participate Actively in Hostilities'

For all its good intentions, the original judgment might have accidentally discarded key protections provided by international human rights and IHL. The Additional Protocol I to the Geneva Conventions, distinguishes direct and indirect participation in armed conflict. IHL treats 'active' and 'direct' as synonymous.[37] This is meant to protect civilians,

---

[32] Emphasis added.

[33] *Prosecutor v Brima, Kamara and Kanu*, Case No SCSL-04-16-1 (*AFRC* case) (Judgment) 20 June 2007, para 735; see also, *Child Recruitment Decision*, Dissenting Opinion of Justice Robertson, para 5(b): *Lubanga* judgment, para 613.

[34] M Kurth, 'The Lubanga Case of the International Criminal Court: A Critical Analysis of the Trial Chamber's Findings on Issues of Active Use, Age, and Gravity' (2013) 5 *Goettingen Journal of International Law* 431.

[35] M Drumbl, *Reimagining Child Soldiers in International Law and Policy* (Oxford, Oxford University Press, 2012).

[36] ibid.

[37] C Jenks, 'Law as Shield, Law as Sword: the ICC's Lubanga Decision, Child Soldiers and the Perverse Mutualism of Participation in Hostilities' (2013) 3 *University of Miami National Security and Armed Conflict Law Review* 106.

including children, from being deemed to be participating actively or directly in hostilities. The TC concluded that an 'indirect' role is to be treated as 'active participation' in hostilities if the support provided by the child to the combatants exposed him or her to real danger as a 'potential target'.[38] The TC held that the reference to the expression 'to participate actively' covers a wider range of activities contrary to the expression 'direct participation' used in IHL. The effect of the judgment is the conflation of both direct and indirect participation. As Buck notes, encompassing the types of behaviours that constitute children actively participating in hostilities was well-intended and expanded Lubanga's liability; nonetheless, it could compromise the safety of children not directly involved in combat. When a civilian, including a child soldier, directly participates in armed conflict, they relinquish pivotal protection from being made the legitimate object of attack.[39] As such, the original judgment's conclusion might ultimately not have been in the best interests of children participating in armed conflict.

XI. Concluding Comments

For a trial whose central concern was the welfare of children, it fell short in fulfilling this objective. Buck's rewritten judgment offers alternative narratives by invoking broader international child law instruments, and is, in instances, radical in discarding some international law traditions and contradicting the original verdict. The strength of Buck's recasting of the original judgment should be viewed within its interpretation of the deficiencies of the trial as a novelty. For a seminal trial on a global stage, handling a historically under-judicialised crime, the objective ought to have transcended retribution and deterrence. The most plausible and primary justification for the prosecution of Lubanga is the expressive function of law. Trials are 'expressive acts broadcasting the news that mass atrocities are, in fact, heinous crimes',[40] and in this case, an opportunity existed to present the atrociousness of child soldiering to its fullest extent. However, the prosecutorial flaws which resulted in the absence of credible witnesses, charges on sex crimes and important records diminished the expressive impact of the trial.[41] The original judgment failed to draw from extant child-centred legal frameworks. On the whole, Buck's rewritten judgment is a bold departure from the original judgment and international law traditions, highlighting the importance of international human rights instruments to international criminal law.

[38] *Lubanga* judgment, para 628.
[39] Jenks, above n 37.
[40] D Luban, 'Fairness to Rightness: Jurisdiction, Legality, and the Legitimacy of International Criminal Law' Georgetown Law Faculty Working Papers (2008) 9.
[41] Amann, above n 11, 429.

International Criminal Court

The Prosecutor v Thomas Lubanga Dyilo

Judge Trevor Buck, Revising Judge

I. Factual Context

1.   The Union des Patriotes Congolais ('UPC') was created on 15 September 2000. The accused, Thomas Lubanga Dyilo ('Lubanga') was one of the UPC's founding members and its President. The UPC and its military wing, the Force Patriotique pour la Libération du Congo ('FPLC'), took power in Ituri in September 2002. The UPC/FPLC, as an organised armed group, was involved in an internal armed conflict against the Armée Populaire Congolaise ('APC') and other Lendu militias, including the Force de Résistance Patriotique en Ituri ('FRPI'), between September 2002 and 13 August 2003. At different times during the same period it is alleged that the Democratic Republic of the Congo ('DRC'), Uganda and Rwanda had used these and other militia groups as proxies for their own underlying international conflicts.

2.   The DRC became a State party to the International Criminal Court ('Court' or 'ICC') on 11 April 2002 and, pursuant to Article 14 of the Rome Statute ('Statute'), President Kabila referred the situation in the DRC which involved inter-ethnic armed conflict in the Ituri region of that country to the Office of The Prosecutor (OTP) in March 2004. Pre-Trial Chamber I concluded that the case falls within the Court's jurisdiction pursuant to Article 19 of the Statute.

3.   It is alleged that the accused, jointly with others, was responsible for the widespread conscription and enlistment of children under the age of 15 years into the armed group of the UPC/FPLC and that he used them to participate actively in hostilities between 1 September 2002 and 13 August 2003. Further, these UPC/FPLC child recruits were sent either to the headquarters of the UPC/FPLC in Bunia or its military training camps. Video evidence shows recruits, believed to be under the age of 15, in the Rwampara camp. The military camps ran harsh training regimes and child recruits were subjected to a variety of severe punishments. Some children, mainly girls, were used by UPC/FPLC commanders to carry out domestic work, and it was alleged that girl soldiers were subjected to sexual violence and rape.

4. Children were deployed as soldiers in Bunia and elsewhere, and they took part in fighting. The UPC/FPLC used children under the age of 15 as military guards, and a special 'Kadogo Unit' was formed, which was comprised principally of children under the age of 15. The commanders in the UPC/FPLC frequently used children under the age of 15 as bodyguards or they served within the presidential guard of Mr Lubanga.

II. Legal Context

Sources of Law

5. The Court must apply the law as set out in this Statute. The key allegations in this case are that:

Thomas Lubanga Dyilo is responsible, as co-perpetrator, for the charges of enlisting and conscripting children under the age of 15 years into the FPLC and using them to participate actively in hostilities within the meaning of articles 8(2)(b)(xxvi) and 25(3)(a) of the Statute from early September 2002 to 2 June 2003; and within the meaning of articles 8(2)(e)(vii) and 25(3)(a) of the Statute from 2 June to 13 August 2003.

6. This Court 'may apply principles and rules of law as interpreted in its previous decisions' (Article 21(2) of the Statute). Clearly, reliance on 'previous decisions' is not possible as this is the first case to be brought to a verdict in this Court. Although the decisions of other international courts and tribunals are not part of the directly applicable law under Article 21, it is in principle important that this Court is assisted by the jurisprudence of other relevant courts and tribunals. In particular, the similarity between the relevant provisions of the Statute of the Special Court for Sierra Leone[1] (SCSL), which was based on the wording contained in the Rome Statute, means that the SCSL's case law is likely to assist in the interpretation of the relevant provisions of the Rome Statute. In addition to applying the above Articles, this Court is also under a duty to apply 'where appropriate, applicable treaties and the principles and rules of international law, including the established principles of the international law of armed conflict' (Article 21(1)(b)).

7. The Chamber is conscious of the fact that this is the first ICC case to be delivered to verdict. Consequently, we must look to other relevant sources of law to ensure that its jurisprudence is steered in the right direction and sends out a clear message to the international community to end a culture of impunity in relation to these crimes in accordance with recognised international standards.[2] We believe, that in respect of the war crimes set out above which have children under the age of 15 years as their focus, it would be a damaging omission if this Court did not apply 'where appropriate' the UN Convention on the Rights of the Child of 1989 (CRC). The CRC contains a comprehensive and authoritative code of children's rights and is famously ratified by *all* States Parties (including the DRC, Rwanda and Uganda) other than the United States and Somalia. The CRC has established itself as

---

[1] UN Security Council, *Statute of the Special Court for Sierra Leone*, 16 January 2002.
[2] eg *Principles and Guidelines on Children Associated with Armed Forces or Armed Groups* (The 'Paris Principles'), February 2007, paras 8.1–8.5.

the central international instrument on children's rights and has influenced the operation of international, regional and domestic law and policy. The increased international attention given to children's rights from the 1980s to the present is also reflected by the important references to children in the Statute.[3] The priority given to the protection of children in the Statute[4] is also reflected in its focus on sexual or gender violence and violence against children.

International or Non-international?

8.   The Pre-Trial Chamber in its Confirmation of Charges Decision[5] determined that there was sufficient evidence for Mr Lubanga to be charged with the recruitment and use of children under the age of 15 in hostilities in armed conflict that could be legally characterised *both* as of an international and non-international nature, ie pursuant to respectively Articles 8(2)(b)(xxvi), 8(2)(e)(vii) and 25(3)(a) of the Statute during the relevant periods as noted in paragraph 5 above.

9.   During the trial process the question arose as to whether the conflict was sufficiently internationalised for Article 8(2)(b)(xxvi) to apply. The Chamber considers that the relevant inquiry is whether between September 2002 and 13 August 2003, the UPC/FPLC, the APC and the FRPI were used as agents or 'proxies' for fighting between two or more states (namely Uganda, Rwanda or the DRC). Despite credible evidence detailing the involvement of both Rwanda and Uganda in the conflicts within the Ituri region, it has been argued that neither of these countries nor the DRC had sufficient 'overall control'[6] of their alleged proxy armed groups for the conflict to be sufficiently internationalised to justify the charge under Article 8(2)(b)(xxvi).

10.   The Chamber has concluded that the Pre-Trial Chamber was nevertheless correct in their conclusion that there was sufficient evidence to ground both charges. The Chamber is mindful of the fact that these charges, in addition to their overall aim to hold perpetrators to account for their international crimes, are also directed to *protect children*. Such children, associated with armed conflict, would be better protected if the 'overall control' test were approached more fluidly to widen that protection. A binary division between non-international and international conflicts does not correspond with the more complex scenarios today that involve multi-dimensional domestic, regional and global tensions. The protection of children would not be served by a prescriptive or rigid application of this test.

11.   Accordingly, the Chamber rejects calls by the defence team to apply Regulation 55 of the Regulations of the Court to change the legal characterisation of the facts. The Pre-Trial Chamber's decision[7] to charge both offences of an international and non-international nature is upheld.

---

[3] Preamble §2, Arts 6(e), 7(2)(c), 8(2)(b)(xxvi), 8(2)(e)(vii), 36(8)(b), 42(9), 54(1)(b), 68(1) & (2) and 84(1) of the Statute.
[4] Preamble §2.
[5] 29 January 2007, ICC-01/04-01/06-803tEN, paras 220, 236.
[6] ICTY, *Prosecutor v Tadić*, Case No IT-94-1-A, Appeals Chamber, Appeals Judgment, 15 July1999 ('*Tadić* Appeal Judgment') para 137.
[7] 29 January 2007, ICC-01/04-01/06-803tEN, paras 220, 236.

The Burden and Standard of Proof

12.   Under Article 66 of the Statute, the accused is presumed to be innocent until the Prosecutor has proved his guilt. For a conviction, each element of the crimes charged must be established 'beyond reasonable doubt'.

III. Trial Process Issues

Intermediaries and Witnesses

13.   An issue that occupied the Chamber for a significant part of this trial concerned the use by the prosecution of local intermediaries in the DRC to select, investigate and brief witnesses. The Chamber is of the view that the OTP should not have delegated its investigative responsibilities to the intermediaries, notwithstanding the extensive security difficulties that it faced. A series of witnesses have been called during this trial whose evidence, as a result of the essentially unsupervised actions of three of the principal intermediaries, cannot safely be relied upon.

14.   The Chamber spent a considerable period of time investigating the circumstances of a substantial number of individuals whose evidence was, at least in part, inaccurate or dishonest. The prosecution's negligence in failing to verify and scrutinise this material sufficiently before it was introduced led to significant expenditure and time-wasting on the part of the Court. The lack of proper oversight of the intermediaries also enabled potential coercion of the witnesses they contacted. Irrespective of the Chamber's conclusions regarding the credibility and reliability of the alleged former child soldier witnesses, given their youth and likely exposure to conflict, they were vulnerable to manipulation.

15.   The Chamber has withdrawn the right of six dual status witnesses to participate in the proceedings due to the questionable reliability and accuracy of these witnesses. Likewise, the Chamber has not relied on the testimony of the three victims who testified in Court (a/0225/06, a/0229/06, and a/0270/07), because their accounts are unreliable. Given the material doubts that exist as to the identities of two of these individuals, which inevitably affect the evidence of the third, the Chamber decided to withdraw the permission originally granted to them to participate as victims.

16.   The Chamber has concluded that there is a risk that intermediaries P-0143, P-316 and P-321 persuaded, encouraged, or assisted witnesses to give false evidence. These individuals may have committed a number of offences against the Court's administration of justice (Article 70 of the Statute). Pursuant to Rule 165 of the Rules of Procedure and Evidence[8] ('Rules') the responsibility to initiate and conduct investigations in these circumstances lies with the prosecution. Investigations can be initiated on the basis of information communicated by a Chamber or any reliable source. The Chamber communicates the relevant information to the OTP, and the Prosecutor should ensure that the risk of a conflict of interest is avoided for the purposes of any investigation.

---

[8] Adopted by the Assembly of States Parties First session New York, 3–10 September 2002 Official Records ICC-ASP/1/3.

17.　The progress of this case has clearly exposed problems associated with the prosecution's delegation of duties to intermediaries and the need for the development of more child-sensitive procedures to be deployed in the management of witnesses and victims. That may include an appropriate use of intermediaries fully trained and, in particular, properly supervised by the OTP.

IV. Truth-Telling and 'On the Record' Experience of Children Associated with Armed Conflict

18.　The nature of the offences under consideration in this case perhaps inevitably draws attention, in broad terms, to what adults *do* to children and therefore there is a tendency to regard children as passive recipients of criminal behaviour by the perpetrators of these offences. The framework of international human rights law provided by the CRC provides an alternative construction of children as active, autonomous agents who should be able to access their rights, in particular the four foundational principles of non-discrimination, the best interests principle, the right to life, survival and development, and the right to be heard.[9]

19.　The Statute's innovative approach in the area of victim participation has the potential to capture the authentic voice of children associated with armed conflict. The process of victim participation in the trial should provide an important and clear record of the quotidian indignities suffered by child soldiers and also a reflection of their resilience in such damaging environments. It is therefore regrettable that the procedural and substantive difficulties concerning the role played by intermediaries in selecting (and manipulating) witnesses in this case has weakened the potential for this Chamber to communicate in detail the lived experiences of former child soldiers.

V. Evidence and Child Soldier Witnesses

20.　The Trial Chamber heard 67 witnesses, and there were 204 days of hearings. The prosecution called 36 witnesses, including three experts, and the defence called 24 witnesses. Three victims were called as witnesses following a request from their legal representatives. Additionally, the Chamber called four experts. The prosecution submitted 368 items of evidence, the defence 992, and the legal representatives 13 (1373 in total).

21.　The direct testimony of all the witnesses who claimed they had served in the defendant's militia was excluded on the ground of unreliability, in the context of an inappropriate delegation of investigatory powers to intermediaries by the OTP. The Chamber emphasises that the child witnesses' evidence had to be excluded on this basis alone; the Court applied no presumption that the evidence of children would necessarily be more or less reliable than that of adult witnesses.

[9] Arts 2, 3, 6 and 12 of the CRC.

22.   The videotape evidence provided the turning point in persuading the Court that the defendant was responsible for the recruitment of children and participated in the use of those children in the armed conflict.

23.   The procedural and other irregularities that have emerged in this case urgently prompt this Court to declare strongly its dissatisfaction with the OTP's mishandling of these issues throughout the course of the trial process.

24.   The violation of children's rights consequent upon the crimes of enlistment, conscription and use of children under the age of 15 in hostilities have been exposed in this case in several respects. In this trial, the exclusion of witness testimony consequent upon the mishandling of the investigatory process by the OTP has resulted in a failure to capture fully the child's voice, in contravention of one of the four foundational principles of the CRC, the child's right to express their views freely and be heard (Article 12 of the CRC). Further assistance as to how this right can be implemented is available in the General Comment issued by the Committee on the Rights of the Child ('Committee'), which states, inter alia, that:

> every effort has to be made to ensure that a child victim or/and witness is consulted on the relevant matters with regard to involvement in the case under scrutiny, and enabled to express freely, and in her or his own manner, views and concerns regarding her or his involvement in the judicial process.[10]

There is little evidence in this case that such procedures have been adopted to comply with this guidance. This is particularly regrettable as it has damaged the Court's ability to exercise fully its expressive function and send out the clearest possible truth-telling message about the damage to children caused by these crimes, and that impunity for these war crimes shall not be tolerated.

25.   The rights of child soldiers to be heard within the framework of the CRC require an accurate and reliable record to emerge from this judgment. The failures in capturing the authentic experience of children recruited and used in hostilities in an armed group provide a further reason to call upon the OTP to review urgently their shortcomings in the course of this trial in order to ensure that future cases are not similarly debilitated.

VI. *Victim Participation*

26.   The child's right to express views freely and to be heard in any judicial and administrative proceedings affecting the child (Article 12 of the CRC) also supports children's active participation and agency in decisions, such as this Court's proceedings, which affect their lives. The Statute provides an innovative and robust means for victim participation in the Court's proceedings (Article 68 of the Statute). In accordance with Article 68(3) of the

---

[10] Committee on the Rights of the Child, *General Comment No 12: The right of the child to be heard*, CRC/C/GC/12 (20 July 2009), para 63.

Statute, victims have participated in the case, and in particular they have applied to intro-duce evidence, questioned witnesses and have advanced written and oral submissions with the leave of the Chamber and with the assistance of their legal representatives. The total number of individual victims authorised to participate in the proceedings is 129 (34 female and 95 male victims).

27.   The Committee's General Comment emphasises that Article 12 of the CRC applies to 'all relevant judicial proceedings affecting the child, without limitation, including, for example … victims of armed conflict and other emergencies',[11] and it also references useful guidance produced by the UN's Economic and Social Council.[12]

28.   The Economic and Social Council's *Guidelines on Justice in Matters involving Child Victims and Witnesses of Crime*[13] provides a comprehensive code of good practice for all professionals working in this field at national, regional and international levels. It recog-nises that, in particular, children 'may suffer additional hardship when assisting in the jus-tice process', and that professionals responsible for the well-being of those children must respect a number of cross-cutting principles, including a right to participation in the judi-cial process.[14] In this case there were security issues involved in identifying suitable victims and witnesses. The Guidelines have developed a 'right to safety' which involves, for example, the training of professionals in 'recognizing and preventing intimidation, threats and harm to child victims and witnesses.'[15]

29.   The OTP and the Office of Public Counsel for Victims ('OPCV') need to emphasise further these Guidelines in their training and staff development programmes. The devolu-tion of responsibility for the investigatory process to intermediaries by the OTP has jeop-ardised children's rights to participate effectively as victims in this case. For example, the status of three participating victims[16] was revoked on account of internal inconsistencies which undermined their credibility. There is a real possibility that two of them stole the identities of two other individuals in order to benefit from the perceived advantages of victim status at the ICC.

30.   In future cases, where hopefully there will be less delay than experienced in this case, the participation of victims in general, and child victims in particular,[17] will need to be carefully developed to conform to the Guidelines. It should be recalled that the origins of the provisions relating to victim participation in the Statute were that they could meet 'not only a punitive but also a restorative function', reflecting the 'growing international consensus that participation and reparations play an important role in achieving justice for victims'.[18]

---

[11]   ibid, para 32.
[12]   ibid, para 62.
[13]   UN Economic and Social Council (ECOSOC), *UN Economic and Social Council 2005/20: Guidelines on Jus-tice in Matters Involving Child Victims and Witnesses of Crime*, 22 July 2005, E/RES/2005/20.
[14]   ibid, Annex, paras 7(a), 8(d).
[15]   ibid, Annex, paras 32–34.
[16]   Victims: a/0225/06, a/0229/06, and a/0270/07.
[17]   Approximately 28 victims were under the age of 18 years at the time of the Chamber's decision.
[18]   See ICC, *Report of the Court on the Strategy in Relation to Victims*, ICC-ASP/8/45 (10 November 2009), para 3.

VII. The Need for Expedition and Social Recovery

31.   It is now eight years since the investigations were commenced by the ICC into the war crimes committed in the DRC, and six years since Mr Lubanga was committed into the custody of the ICC. The trial process has focused on events that occurred nine to 10 years ago. The mismanagement of the selection of witnesses and victims has cast a shadow on the reputation of this Court. More importantly, the delays in justice have a particularly powerful impact on children.

32.   The need for expedition in proceedings involving children has been recognised in the superior courts of many States parties and in a range of international instruments.[19] This case has demonstrated clearly the future need for a robust filtering of witnesses and participating victims to ensure their testimony is elicited in a child-sensitive environment and to provide the Court with reliable, consistent evidence that is fit for purpose in these proceedings.

33.   The potential merits of victim participation need to be balanced judiciously with the need for greater expedition than has been seen here. In the context of children associated with armed conflict, where the physical and psychological damage to individuals has been shown to be profound and long-lasting and affects their prospects of social reintegration, there is an even stronger argument for expedition.

VIII. Determining Age

34.   The offences at issue in this case axiomatically concern the recruitment and use of children in hostilities under the age of 15 years. This 15 year threshold was a particularly contentious issue in the drafting of Article 38 of the CRC in 1989, and dissatisfaction with it prompted the arrival of the Optional Protocol to the Convention on the Rights of the Child on the Involvement of Children in Armed Conflict ('OPAC')[20] which has raised this threshold to 18 years.[21] Interestingly, the African Charter on the Rights and Welfare of the Child of 1999 already contained the 18 year threshold.[22]

35.   This Court regrets the discrepancy that has arisen between the 15 year threshold found in international humanitarian law and the 18 year threshold found in the principal international human rights instruments, but recognises that it will be a matter for international legislators to correct this rather than this Court which is bound by the 15 year threshold as set out in the Statute.

---

[19] Art 10(1) of the CRC; Arts 2 and 11 of the Hague Convention on the Civil Aspects of International Child Abduction; Art 11(3) of the Revised Brussels II Regulation; and Art 9(b) of the Hague Convention on Protection of Children and Co-operation in Respect of Intercountry Adoption.

[20] UN General Assembly, Adopted and opened for signature, ratification and accession by General Assembly resolution A/RES/54/263 of 25 May 2000.

[21] Arts 1–3 of OPAC.

[22] Organization of African Unity (OAU), *African Charter on the Rights and Welfare of the Child*, 11 July 1990, CAB/LEG/24.9/49 (1990), Arts 2 and 22.

36.   The determination of age per se, is an evidential issue which poses challenges for this Court, in particular in relation to a crime where age is integral to the *actus reus*. Other international tribunals too have struggled with the difficulties of proving that individuals are below the 15 year threshold.[23] Regrettably, in this trial process there has been very little *conclusive* evidence about children's chronological age. The two medical experts used the 'Greulich and Pyle' method of skeletal examination (involving X-ray of the wrist and hand and teeth),[24] but conceded that poor nutrition and disease factors could distort results. This model of medical examination however, is based on European and American rather than African populations and the methodology has not been updated for 50 years. Were it not for the videotape evidence showing the defendant surrounded by bodyguards who were obviously under 15, it might have been impossible to establish the presence and use of under 15 year olds in the military environment.

37.   Within the framework of the CRC, age is clearly a crucial component and the identification of age thresholds is supported further by Article 7 which mandates birth registration. In a *Day of General Discussion* in 2004, the Committee recommended States parties 'to undertake all necessary measures to ensure that all children are registered at birth, inter alia, by using mobile registration units and make birth registration free of charge'.[25] Unfortunately, in many of the territories where child soldiers have been deployed, the civil administration is weak and the prospect of contacting local informants may pose insuperable security issues for the Court. The Committee noted in its recent 'Concluding Observations' on the DRC's report on OPAC, 'the very low level of birth registration in the State party'.[26]

38.   There are obvious dangers in relying on the subjectivity of witness estimations of children's ages. A more objective and methodologically rigorous approach to medical examination needs to be developed for future cases. Newer interdisciplinary approaches to the determination of age, drawing upon socio-psychological evidence in addition to medical evidence and approaches which emphasise the importance of non-invasive medical procedures, need to be developed in this context.

IX. Role of Sexual Violence

39.   In this case, 30 victims (18 female and 12 male) referred to acts of sexual violence which they either suffered or witnessed. There is an emerging realisation that rape and other forms of sexual violence are increasingly being deployed against vulnerable

---

[23] 'The Chamber is cognisant that these estimations of age were generally made on the basis of a child's appearance or height, rather than on objective proof of age.' *Prosecutor v Sesay, Kallon & Gbao (Judgment)*, SCSL-04-15-T, 2 March 2009, para 1627.

[24] *Prosecutor v Thomas Lubanga Dyilo*, Transcript of 12 May 2009, ICC-01/04-01/06-T-172-ENG.

[25] Committee on the Rights of the Child, *Day of General Discussion on Implementing Child Rights in Early Childhood'*, Report on the thirty-seventh session, CRC/C/143 (12 January 2005) paras 532–63, at 547.

[26] *Concluding observations: Democratic Republic of Congo*, CRC/C/OPAC/COD/CO/1, 7 March 2012, paras 26–27.

populations in conflict areas including children.[27] There are three issues to consider here. First, whether Lubanga ought to have been charged with additional offences under the Statute relating to the alleged sexual violence conducted by UPC/FPLC. Second, the extent to which such behaviour could nevertheless be considered as part of the war crime of 'using' children under the age of 15 'to participate actively in hostilities'. Third, how far could the victim's child status rank as a discrete aggravating factor in sentencing.

40.   On the first issue, the Chamber has concluded that the defendant ought to have faced additional charges of crimes of sexual violence. The Statute provides for these as separate crimes.[28] Despite frequent references to sexual violence during the trial, and the insistent demands by the legal representatives of the victims that new charges be added, the prosecution opposed it.[29] This Court strongly deprecates the position of the Prosecutor who failed to include such crimes in the original charges and actively opposed their inclusion throughout the trial process. However, as the facts relating to sexual violence were not included in the Decision on the Confirmation of Charges, and the Statute provides that the Court's decision 'shall not exceed the facts and circumstances described in the charges' (Article 24(2)), it would be impermissible for the Chamber to base its Decision pursuant to Article 74(2) on the evidence introduced during the trial that is relevant to this issue.

41.   I shall return to the second issue in the course of this Judgment at paragraphs 48–53 below. As this Chamber has already decided that there should be a separate hearing to determine the sentence, the third issue will have to be considered thoroughly in that hearing. Suffice it to say here that the Chamber recognises that, as matter of law in determining the sentence, the Court should not only take into account 'such factors as the gravity of the crime and the individual circumstances of the convicted person' (Article 78(1)), but also under the Rules it must consider, amongst other factors 'the means employed to execute the crime'.[30]

42.   The evidence of sexual violence that has emerged during the long course of this case relates to all children, but particularly to girls. It is relevant here to recall the special protection of the girl child provided by the Optional Protocol to the Convention on the Rights of the Child on the Sale of Children, Child Prostitution and Child Pornography of 2000[31] ('OPSC'). One of the Committee's Days of Discussion was given over to consideration of the girl child.[32] While there are commonalities between the experience of girls and boys in conflicts, girls' experiences can be very different and are at risk of being 'invisible' in release and reintegration programmes.[33] The evidence in this case does indicate that sexual

---

[27] See Sara Meger, 'Rape of the Congo: Understanding Sexual Violence in the Conflict in the Democratic Republic of Congo' (2010) 28 *Journal of Contemporary African Studies* 119. See also: UN Security Council, Working Group on Children and Armed Conflict, Conclusions on children and armed conflict in the Democratic Republic of the Congo, S/AC.51/2011/1, 1 March 2011.

[28] Arts 7(1)(g) and 8(2)(e)(vi) of the Statute.

[29] Trial Chamber I (status conference), 25 November 2008, ICC-01/04-01/06-T-99-ENG ET WT 25-11-2008 1-44 NB T, ICC-01/04-01/06-T-99, p 39.

[30] Rule 145(1)(c).

[31] Adopted and opened for signature, ratification and accession by General Assembly resolution A/RES/54/263 of 25 May 2000 entered into force on 18 January 2002. See, for example, preamble §5.

[32] Committee on the Rights of the Child, *Day of General Discussion on 'The Girl Child'*, Report on the eighth session, CRC/C/38 (27 January 1995) [275–99], at 296.

[33] *Principles and Guidelines on Children Associated with Armed Forces or Armed Groups*, (The 'Paris Principles'), February 2007, paras 4.0–4.3.

violence was used, in particular in relation to girls, as a 'means employed to execute the crime'[34] of child soldier recruitment and use. The sentencing Court should be aware that the Trial Chamber considers such sexual violence one of the 'aggravating circumstances' set out in the Rules,[35] which it will need to balance along with all other relevant factors pursuant to Rule 145(1)(b).

X. Interpretation of Articles 8(2)(b)(XXVI) and 8(2)(e)(VII) of the Rome Statute

43.   The general conclusion of the SCSL on the similarly worded crimes in that Court's Statute[36] confirmed that these offences constituted a crime under customary international law, and that there were three distinct modes of enlisting, conscripting and using children to participate actively in hostilities.[37]

44.   The Chamber agrees that the relevant provisions of the Rome Statute also contain an *actus reus* consisting of three discrete acts of enlistment, conscription and use; and, liability for one does not necessarily preclude liability for another.[38]

Enlistment and Conscription

45.   In the AFRC Trial judgment, the SCSL ruled that '[e]nlistment is a voluntary act, and the child's consent is therefore not a valid defence.'[39] In the case before me I agree that conscription connotes some element of coercion while enlistment suggests a voluntary joining by children, but I disagree with the contention raised by the prosecution that an individual is incapable of consenting to join a militia. If the conflation of these two categories were accepted, then any real distinction between the crimes of enlistment and conscription would disappear. That result would contradict well-recognised canons of interpretation suggesting that wherever possible every word and provision in a legal text should be given effect. Equally, if the provisions in the Statute had followed the earlier singly proscribed 'recruitment' category in the Additional Protocols to the Geneva Convention and in the CRC[40] then the prosecution's refusal to acknowledge the potential consent of child enlistees would be more credible.

---

[34]   Rule 145(1)(c).

[35]   Rule 145(2)(b)(i) to (vi).

[36]   See Art 4(c) of the Statute of the Special Court for Sierra Leone.

[37]   *Prosecutor v Moinina Fofana and Allieu Kondewa (CDF case)* (Appeal Judgment), Special Court for Sierra Leone, Case No SCSL-04-14-A (28 May 2008), para 139.

[38]   *Prosecutor v Thomas Lubanga Dyilo*, ICC-01/04-01/06-803-tEN (Decision on the Confirmation of Charges), 29 January 2007, paras 242–48.

[39]   *Prosecutor v Brima, Kamara and Kanu*, Case No SCSL-04-16-1, *(AFRC case)* (Judgment) 20 June 2007, para 735; see also, Child Recruitment Decision, Dissenting Opinion of Justice Robertson, para 5(b).

[40]   Protocol Additional to the Geneva Conventions of 12 August 1949, and Relating to the Protection of Victims of Non-International Armed Conflicts (Protocol II), adopted 1977. Article 4(3)(c). The compacted 'recruitment' formulation is also contained in Art 38(3) of the CRC, though a distinction between compulsory and voluntary recruitment appears in Arts 2 and 3 respectively of OPAC.

46.   The development of the non-forcible 'enlistment' element of this war crime has been analysed ably in Justice Robertson's Dissenting Opinion in the SCSL. He recognised the difficult issues surrounding the voluntariness of children in the enlistment process, in particular he identified a number of structural factors that may cast doubt on the voluntariness of enlistment.[41]

47.   However, a refusal to entertain that a child could conceivably consent freely—even enthusiastically—to join a militia, seriously undermines the increasing recognition in international law of children's 'agency'. It also undermines, in my view, the broader intention to produce a triple-tier hierarchy of international criminal liability containing 'enlistment' at the bottom, 'conscription' in the middle and 'using' at the top of this structure. It is interesting to observe that some States parties provide increasing sentences for each element of this hierarchy.[42] This Chamber, while recognising the enumeration by Justice Robertson of the types of difficulty associated with identifying the reality of children's voluntariness in the enlistment process, nevertheless rejects the contention that children should be *presumed always* to have been forcibly recruited. The issue of testing the voluntariness or otherwise of child recruitment needs to be examined with care and on a case by case basis.

Using Children to Participate Actively in Hostilities

48.   It was noted in the AFRC case that 'using children to participate actively in hostilities' encompasses putting their lives directly at the risk in combat and that '[a]ny labour or support that gives effect to, or helps maintain, operations in a conflict constitutes active participation.'[43] I consider that the phrase 'using [children] to participate actively in hostilities' allows broadly three approaches to its interpretation. First, it could refer exclusively to the deployment of children as frontline combatants. Second, it could apply where children have been exposed to real danger as a 'potential target' beyond the immediate scene of the hostilities. Third, it could include not only combat-related harms but also a number of supporting roles even if these occur far from the military theatre of activity.

49.   I have concluded that the first possibility is much too narrow a construction, and is certainly much narrower than the formula preferred by the SCSL in the AFRC case. The evidence presented in this case, and in the influential Machel report of 1996 on the impact of armed conflict on children, demonstrates that the use of children in hostilities goes much further than merely deployment in the battlefield. As the author of that report states:

> One of the most alarming trends in armed conflict is the participation of children as soldiers. Children serve armies in supporting roles, as cooks, porters, messengers and spies.[44]

---

[41] *Prosecutor v Sam Hinga Norman (Decision on Preliminary Motion based on lack of Jurisdiction (Child Recruitment)*, SCSL-2004-14-AR72(E), 31 May 2004, Dissenting Opinion of Justice Robertson, 7419, para 8.

[42] Australia provides prescribed maximum penalties of 17 (using), 15 (conscripting) and 10 (enlisting) years imprisonment: International Criminal Court (consequential Amendments) Act 2002 Number 42 (Cth), Section 268.68 of the Criminal Code Act 1995 (Cth).

[43] *AFRC* case para 737.

[44] UN General Assembly, *Impact of armed conflict on children: note / by the Secretary-General*, 26 August 1996, A/51/306, para 34.

50.   Second, although a 'potential target' test has some merit in broadening the definition of active participation in hostilities, it provides a constrained definition that focuses more on the *military significance* of child deployment rather than the overall *protection of children* in an armed conflict as required by the CRC framework.[45] Being brought into a dangerous arena as a potential target is only one harmful outcome for child recruits; there are other forms of active participation which involve harmful results.

51.   The Chamber has concluded that the third approach is the correct one. The phrase 'using [children] to participate actively in hostilities' ought to be interpreted to include, not only combat-related deployment (direct participation) and other activities that expose the child as a potential target, but also to encompass a number of *supporting roles* (indirect participation) even if these occur far from the military theatre of activity. One such role evidenced in this case and prevalent in other armed conflicts around the world is the abusive and endemic provision of sexual services by child recruits. This case has exposed substantial evidence of sexual violence which has been deployed in an organised fashion as an integral element of the operations of armed conflict.

52.   Such sexual and gender violence is an inherent part of the criminal conduct set out in Articles 8(2)(b)(xxvi) and 8(2)(e)(vii) of the Statute. Without its inclusion as an element of the crimes at issue a critical aspect of these crimes would be invisible.

53.   What then should the test be to identify supporting roles, such as sexual services, which could be regarded as indirect participation? I have concluded that such roles are to be treated as active participation where they can be said to provide significant support and maintenance to the military operations at issue. This matter has to be a question of fact and degree in each case. Active participation can include both direct and indirect participation. This is important as those who 'directly' participate in hostilities will lose the protection offered in international humanitarian law from direct attack in contrast to those who may be regarded as 'civilians'.[46] It should be clear that the inclusion of a range of supporting roles constituting 'indirect' participation will not expose such individuals to the same loss of international humanitarian law protection for those participating directly.[47]

XI. Disposition

54.   For the foregoing reasons and on the basis of the evidence submitted and discussed before the Chamber at trial, and the entire proceedings, pursuant to Article 74(2) of the Statute, the Chamber finds Mr Thomas Lubanga Dyilo:

---

[45]   See: Arts 38(4) and 39 of the CRC; and Preamble §5 and §6 and Arts 4 and 7 of OPAC.
[46]   Art 51 of the *Protocol Additional to the Geneva Conventions of 12 August 1949* ('Additional Protocol I'), 1125 UNTS 17512; Geneva Convention Relative to the Protection of Civilian Persons in time of War of August 12 1949, 76 UNTS 287.
[47]   See: Nils Melzer, Int'l Comm of the Red Cross, 'Interpretative Guidance on the Notion of Direct Participation in Hostilities Under International Law' (2009) 90 *International Review of the Red Cross* 991, 1013–14 (adopted by the assembly of the international committee of the Red Cross on 26 February 2009).

55.   *GUILTY* of the crimes of conscripting and enlisting children under the age of fifteen years into the FPLC and using them to participate actively in hostilities within the meaning of Articles 8(2)(e)(vii) and 25(3)(a) of the Statute from early September 2002 to 13 August 2003 and within the meaning of articles 8(2)(b)(xxvi) and 25(3)(a) of the Statute from early September 2002 to 2 June 2003.

56.   At the request of the defence and in accordance with Article 76(2) of the Statute and Rule 143 of the Rules, the Chamber will hold a separate hearing on matters related to sentencing and reparations.

57.   The Chamber communicates to the Prosecutor, pursuant to Article 70 of the Statute and Rule 165 of the Rules, its findings that P-0143, P-0316 and P-0321 may have persuaded, encouraged or assisted witnesses to give false evidence.

25

Commentary on *Farooq Ahmed v Federation of Pakistan*

URFAN KHALIQ

I. Introduction

The decision of the Lahore division of the Punjab High Court in *Farooq Ahmed v Pakistan* is reflective of many of the inherent conflicts, tensions and contradictions endemic not only in the law in Pakistan dealing with children but also more broadly within the legal system and indeed the state itself. Abdullah Khoso's imaginary judgment, presented with an eye to the original case still pending before the Pakistan Supreme Court, seeks to adopt an approach which is friendlier to the notion of children's rights as that term is understood both in international human rights treaties and also, importantly, in the context of Pakistan, Islamic values and norms.

II. Background to the Case

At dispute in *Farooq Ahmed* is the Juvenile Justice System Ordinance, 2000 (JJSO). The JJSO was adopted in 2000 and, in the aftermath of the 1999 coup that brought General Pervez Musharraf to power, was one of the first major pieces of legislation adopted by his military regime. The JJSO sets out in 15 sections a series of measures which are intended to reform the juvenile justice system and in part also help Pakistan comply with some of its obligations under the United Nations Convention on the Rights of the Child (CRC).[1] The fact that all aspects of the criminal justice system in Pakistan needed a complete overhaul was beyond doubt. Endemic corruption at all levels of society, a lack of effective civilian institutions, the absence of essential infrastructure, prisons which are positively dangerous, the widespread use of torture and inhuman treatment to secure confessions, as well as a Penal Code, subject to some amendments, adopted in 1860 are the perfect cocktail

---

[1] Convention on the Rights of the Child, 1989, 1577 UNTS 3. See, for example, the heavy emphasis placed on the JJSO in Committee on the Rights of the Child, Consideration of Reports Submitted by States Parties under Art 44 of the Convention, Pakistan, CRC/C/PAK/3-4, 19 March 2009.

for a system which is positively Dickensian.[2] The added vulnerability of juveniles in such a system, where the age of criminal responsibility had, until early in 2016, been set at seven, simply underlined the need for systematic reform.[3]

The JJSO sets out, inter alia, that: a child be defined as someone under the age of 18;[4] each child accused of the commission of an offence be provided with free legal assistance paid for by the state;[5] juvenile courts with special procedures be established;[6] no adult and child be jointly tried;[7] there is an assumption of privacy where children are being tried;[8] and the arrest, bail and detention conditions of children are to differ from those of adults.[9] The JJSO also makes clear that no child shall: be executed for a crime committed while under the age of 18; be ordered to carry our labour during any time spent in detention; be put in fetters; or administered corporal punishment.[10]

III. The Facts and Original Judgment

Two persons were accused of sodomising and subsequently killing the eight year old son of the petitioner, Farooq Ahmed. Further to the two accused submitting to the trial court that they were juveniles, based upon their school leaving certificates, they were afforded the rights and protection set out in the JJSO, in particular that they could not be executed, a sentence routinely passed in such cases. The petitioner filed a complaint before the Lahore division of the Punjab High Court that the accused were not juveniles but rather adults and thus not entitled to any of the protections afforded by the JJSO. Further, the petitioner argued that the JJSO itself was defective and challenged its validity.

The Lahore division of the Punjab High Court in December 2004 heard the petition and further to giving a very significant number of reasons as to why the JSSO should be 'struck off the statute book' decided accordingly to do so. The Pakistan Supreme Court in early 2005, however, suspended the judgment of the Lahore High Court subject to a final determination by it.[11] At the time of writing (October 2016) the Supreme Court's final decision is still pending and the JJSO is currently in force in Pakistan notwithstanding the decision of the Lahore High Court.

---

[2] On torture in Pakistan and prison conditions see, inter alia, Report of the Special Rapporteur on Torture and Other Cruel, Inhuman or Degrading Treatment or Punishment, Report of his visit to Pakistan in February to March 1996, E/CN.4/1997/7/Add.2 and Report of the Special Rapporteur on Torture and Other Cruel, Inhuman or Degrading Treatment or Punishment, A/HRC/7/3/Add.2, 97 et seq.

[3] See s 82, Pakistan Penal Code, (Act XLV of 1860), 6 October 1860. In March 2016, this was raised to 10. s 82 has been subject to s 83 which grants a judge discretion to ignore the age stated in s 82 and raise it to 14 (prior to March 2016 this was 12) years of age, in the case of a child 'who has not attained sufficient maturity of understanding to judge the nature and consequences of his [or her] conduct on that occasion.'

[4] s 2(b) JJSO.

[5] s 3 JJSO.

[6] ss 4 and 6 JJSO.

[7] s 5 JJSO.

[8] s 8 JJSO.

[9] ss10 and 11 JJSO.

[10] s 12 JJSO.

[11] This was further to an application to the Supreme Court by the Society for the Protection of the Rights of the Child (SPARC) a civil society organisation. All indications suggest that it was granted unilaterally by the then Chief Justice.

Foremost among the reasons cited by the Lahore High Court is one which is tucked away in what are presented as almost throwaway observations but which relate directly to some of the submissions made by the petitioner. At the very end of its reasoning the Court notes:

> If the impugned Ordinance had been preceded by a parliamentary or at least a public debate then the same would not have suffered from the maladies and infirmities noticed therein.

> On the basis of the reasons recorded writ petition is allowed and the Juvenile Justice System Ordinance, 2000 (Federal Ordinance No XXII of 2000) is hereby struck off the statute book on account of its being unreasonable, unconstitutional and impracticable. It, however, goes without saying that the Parliament may, if it so desires, enact a fresh law in this regard after attending to all the infirmities of the impugned Ordinance highlighted.[12]

It was hardly a startling revelation for anyone in Pakistan that Parliament was suspended and that a state of emergency declared at the time the JJSO was adopted.[13] There was thus no chance of a Parliamentary debate or the measure going through the Parliamentary legislative process. Many key parts of legislation in Pakistan have been adopted by Ordinances while there has been a state of emergency; since independence in 1947, Pakistan has been under military rule for almost half of its existence. These Ordinances inter alia criminalise sexual intercourse outside of marriage, the penalty for which is either 100 lashes or stoning to death. Such Ordinances have been systematically abused and are enormously problematic and not only in terms of Pakistan's international human rights treaty obligations.[14] Yet the judiciary has not sought to tackle the validity of these other Ordinances due, in part, to the backlash that would unleash among the religious establishment and due to their own personal sympathies with such laws which purportedly implement Islamic principles and punishments. Indeed, the Lahore bench in their reasoning striking down the JSSO display this sympathy by noting, '[h]ow can one forget in this context that the concept of avoidance of *fasad-fil-arz* is a cornerstone of Islamic system of dispensation of criminal justice.' *Fasad-fil-arz* is, broadly speaking, committing severe mischief or trouble in the (Islamic) territory in question, and thus the bench refer to this concept arguing that the JSSO is contrary to it as it provides protection to juveniles who engaged in such mischief. This is thus an implicit but not express reference to the principle in the Pakistani Constitution that no law shall be contrary to Islamic beliefs.

The Lahore High Court, inter alia, also cited the following reasons for striking down the JJSO: Pakistan's legal and social development was not advanced enough to withstand the demands of the JJSO and nor 'was the rights-based approach appropriate in Pakistan';

---

[12] No paragraph number given.

[13] The Ordinance notes this very clearly in its preamble, 'whereas the National Assembly and the Senate stand suspended …; and whereas the President is satisfied that circumstances exist which render it necessary to take immediate action; … in exercise of all powers enabling him …, the President … is pleased to make and promulgate the following Ordinance.'

[14] See eg, the Offence of Zina (Enforcement of Hudood) Ordinance, 1979; Ordinance No VII of 9 February 1979. s 8 of the Ordinance requires either a confession or four males who witnessed the act of penetration. In the case of rape, a person who cannot produce four male witnesses is deemed to have confessed to sexual intercourse outside of marriage and is thus liable to the penalties stipulated. Numerous such cases are reported each year. There are nationally next to no reported convictions of rape. In the context of children's rights relating to these earlier Ordinances see, for example, the Concluding Observations of the CRC regarding Pakistan, CRC/C/PAK/CO/3-4, 15 October 2009, paras 10, 26 and 68.

the age identified to achieve majority, 18, was arbitrary and unjustifiable; many of the provisions were badly drafted; poverty, a hot climate and the 'consumption of hot and spicy food all lead towards speedy physical growth and an accelerated maturity' which necessitated that there cannot 'be one yardstick' for all juveniles; the JJSO in requiring children be tried separately from adults and also be granted bail on different grounds from adults was impracticable; the rights of the victims of crimes were being sacrificed by granting the rights in the JJSO to children accused of crimes; and the JJSO was widely being abused with criminals either claiming they were under the age of 18 or children were committing crimes on behalf of their families knowing that as they were under 18 years of age they would not be subject to the death penalty.[15] A few aspects of the Court's more general reasoning are noteworthy. First, every, ground the Court cited for striking down the JJSO had been pleaded by the petitioner. The Lahore bench did not filter the arguments and focus on those that were meritorious. Second, the Court verbatim used much of the language of the petitioner in coming to its decision. While the use of such language in judicial reasoning is not uncommon amongst the more senior Pakistani courts, the acceptance of all pleaded grounds, no matter how 'scattergun' the approach, certainly is. This suggests a determination to strike down the JJSO, no matter what, once the opportunity presented itself.

The Lahore High Court's reasoning and also the approach adopted by Abdullah Khoso's imaginary judgment do draw attention to some of the difficulties of defining international standards with regard to children's rights. One point that neither addresses, however, is the necessity to reform institutions and the need to commit resources with a view to implementing certain rights. Both these issues are dealt with below.

IV. The Children's Rights Judgment

A. Cultural Relativism

The Lahore High Court in its reasoning stated inter alia that: a rights-based approach is not appropriate to Pakistan; and that a hot climate and the consumption of hot and spicy food leads to 'speedy physical growth and an accelerated maturity' which necessitates that there cannot 'be one yardstick' for all juveniles.

With regard to the first of these grounds—a rights-based approach is not appropriate—it is difficult to see how a court in Pakistan can logically adopt such an approach. A series of fundamental rights, hence a 'rights-based' approach, are set out in the first substantive chapter of the Constitution of Pakistan.[16] Furthermore, on a global level the era since 1948 when the Universal Declaration of Human Rights was adopted, coinciding almost exactly from the time Pakistan achieved independence is, to use Louis Henkin's famous and apt phrase, the 'age of rights'.[17] Pakistan as a state has played its role in the development of international human rights standards although there are of course significant grounds for

---

[15] No paragraph numbers given.
[16] Pt II—Ch I, The Constitution of the Islamic Republic of Pakistan.
[17] L Henkin, *The Age of Rights* (New York, Columbia University Press, 1990).

disagreement as to what certain of those rights should be and how they should be framed.[18] Read in isolation, the approach of the High Court is a rejection of rights per se. However, if the reasoning given by the Court is considered holistically it is more accurate to consider its approach strongly relativist not rejectionist. Indeed the argument that a hot climate and the consumption of hot and spicy food leads to 'speedy physical growth and an accelerated maturity' which necessitates that there cannot 'be one yardstick' for all juveniles is also notably Orientalist in approach—the irony of which was no doubt lost on the High Court bench.[19]

Abdullah Khoso's proposed judgment categorically rejects the Orientalist and anti-child rights approach of the Lahore High Court. Human rights as defined in treaties extend to all by virtue of their being human and cannot be denied due to some alleged wrongdoing or other. The basic premise is that there is no discrimination between individuals on grounds which cannot be objectively justified. Impoverishment, a spicy diet and a tropical climate, have never as far as is known been considered by any UN human rights treaty body or regional human rights court to be grounds, either individually or collectively, upon which to treat some individuals differently from others. Nor is there any credible medical evidence to suggest that such factors speed up the development and maturity of an individual in any part of the world. A child is a child everywhere, regardless of wealth, climate and diet and is entitled to be protected according to internationally agreed standards entailed in treaties to which a state is party. Abdullah Khoso's judgment upholds these basic principles.

Both the Lahore High Court and Abdullah Khoso's imaginary judgments display their sensitivity to cultural and religious considerations when referring to Islamic principles and edicts. In the context of a Muslim majority state, where religion has always been a volatile ingredient in an increasingly febrile environment, religious legitimacy is a key legal and political consideration the importance of which is easily underestimated outside of Pakistan. The Lahore High Court referred to *fasad-fil-arz* in the context of adopting a more punitive approach to prohibiting and punishing 'mischief' committed by juveniles. Abdullah Khoso equally refers to Islamic principles to support his approach. In arguing that children deserve to be treated differently from adults he refers to the notion that Islamic principles treat 'children and other weak people ... with special care and attention ... compassion and forgiveness are central.'[20] Khoso's judgment also notes that separate trials for adults and children 'does not represent a specifically Western approach' but is part of Islam's tenets of compassion and forgiveness.[21] These are interesting observations as they pay heed to religious sensibilities but also display the malleability of 'Islamic' principles where some can be cited in support of a proposition and others to oppose it. As a sovereign state, Pakistan is party to numerous human rights treaties which it has ratified of its own volition.

---

[18] For an illuminating example, see the differing perspectives of states during the drafting of what became Art 18 (freedom of religion and belief) of the International Covenant on Civil and Political Rights, 1966, 999 UNTS 171. For detailed discussion see U Khaliq, 'Freedom of Religion in International Law: A Comparative Analysis' in A Emon, M Ellis and B Glahn (eds), *Islamic Law and International Human Rights Law: Searching for Common Ground?* (Oxford, Oxford University Press, 2012) 183–225 at 187 et seq.

[19] I use the term in the sense argued by Edward Said in his classic work *Orientalism* (London, Routledge and Kegan Paul, 1978).

[20] para 9.

[21] ibid.

Such obligations have not been imposed upon Pakistan or other Muslim majority states by either Western States or donor agencies—a key criticism of the JJSO cited by the Lahore High Court. Many Muslim majority states were active and vocal participants in the drafting of multi-lateral human rights treaties, in particular, the CRC.[22] It would have been especially welcome in Abdullah Khoso's proposed judgment to see the Supreme Court of Pakistan openly and warmly endorse international human rights treaties, to which the state is party, so to highlight the universal ownership of protected rights and not to seek to ground such rights primarily in Islamic edicts, notwithstanding how important that is for a state such as Pakistan.

B. Resources and Reform

Regardless of Abdullah Khoso's attempt in his proposed judgment to reinstate the JSSO, the crux of the problem from a children's rights perspective is that though the JJSO has been 'on the books' there has been neither the systematic institutional reform nor the commitment to allocate the resources needed to ensure the JJSO's full effect. The provisions relating to the prohibition on the passing of certain sentences, such as the death penalty or the administration of corporal punishment, do not require new procedures or institutions as they are prohibitive in nature. Measures needed to give effect to some of the guarantees in the JJSO such as that relating to differing bail conditions for children are also relatively easy to implement. Others, however, such as those relating to probation—which would require the setting up of something like a probation service—require significant reform and ongoing investment of resources. Neither the International Covenant on Civil and Political Rights, 1966 (ICCPR) nor the CRC[23] permits differential treatment for developing nations when it comes to due process related rights. Nonetheless there is something to the argument that Pakistan's level of economic development does not easily lend itself to, for example, providing legal aid. Indeed the ICCPR does not require free legal assistance, only access to a translator if one is needed, while the CRC is vague as to this matter only stipulating the provision of appropriate assistance.[24] The JJSO therefore goes beyond the treaties' required minimum standards in requiring free legal assistance to children. But legal aid simply does not exist in Pakistan and furthermore, there is no culture of pro bono work among the legal community. Since the JJSO was adopted, the only pro bono legal assistance for children accused of crimes has come from local civil society organisations funded by external donors.[25]

In terms of reforming to the extent needed the court structure and providing legal aid, as the JJSOs' provisions require, those are undeniably enormous undertakings and require a long-term strategy accompanied by massive investment. In the shorter term, however, suitable amendments to the Pakistan Penal Code and Code of Criminal Procedure 1898 to

---

[22] See for example the numerous references in S Detrick, *A Commentary on the United Nations Convention on the Rights of the Child* (Leiden, Martinus Nijhoff, 2012).

[23] See Art 14(4) ICCPR on criminal trials involving juveniles and further General Comment No 32. Art 14: Right to Equality Before Courts and Tribunals and to a Fair Trial, CCPR/C/GC/32, 23 August 2007, paras 42–44.

[24] See Art 14(4) ICCPR, and Art 40 (2)(b)(ii) CRC and further General Comment No 10 (2007): Children's Rights in Juvenile Justice, CRC/C/GC/10, 25 April 2007, paras 49–50 which confirms this.

[25] Examples are organisations such as SPARC and Project Advocate. Free legal assistance has only been provided pro bono to children, not to all, and the JJSO was the catalyst for this.

accompany the JJSO would have made enough changes to both give some effect to certain procedural aspects of the JJSO and to make it much more difficult for the Lahore High Court to dismiss the JJSO out of hand. Such amendments could, for example, stipulate separate hearings for adults and children and would help realise to some extent or other what were and are illusory rights and guarantees.

V. Conclusions

It is undeniably the case that the JJSO has attracted opposition and opprobrium from certain quarters. It shortcomings are clear but they are primarily not substantive. The reality is that the massive level of investment, structural reform and need for ongoing resources that was and still is needed to give practical effect to the JJSO has simply not been forthcoming but the Ordinance was adopted and brought into force nevertheless. The JJSO's close association with what became a deeply unpopular military regime did not assist matters at all, notwithstanding the progressive manner in which it sought to develop juvenile justice in Pakistan. Children's rights as encapsulated in the JSSO represented a low cost, indeed an easy, opportunity for parts of the judiciary to strike back at the Musharraf regime. Lahore is the cultural and intellectual hub of all of Pakistan, the most important city in Punjab and the power base of Nawaz Sharif and his family—Musharraf's greatest adversaries. The Lahore branch of the High Court had been at the forefront of the provincial judicial opposition to the military regime and the measures Musharraf adopted to 'Constitutionalise' his coup.[26] The fact that it was the Punjab High Court based in Lahore which struck down the JJSO is not unrelated to these other considerations. Two matters, however, are especially striking. First, the High Court is not competent to strike down legislation.[27] Second, even if it had such competence, it is a provincial court and its powers do not extend to the entire federation but that is precisely what it sought to do. The JJSO needs to be effectively realised not undermined by those tasked with dispensing justice. The pending case before the Supreme Court represents an ideal and much needed opportunity for the most authoritative court in Pakistan to emphasise not only the legitimacy but also the legality of those children's rights that the JJSO articulates. If the approach in Abdullah Khoso's imaginary judgment were to be adopted by the Supreme Court of Pakistan it may go some way toward achieving this objective.

[26] For example, Provisional Constitution Order No 1 of 1999, 15 October, 1999. The opposition stemmed not from judgments per se but the refusal to swear oaths of allegiance to the military government and Lahore based legal challenges to the coup.

[27] See Arts 192–203 of the Constitution. But this is especially so further to the Provisional Constitution Order of 1999 which deprived all courts of the power to challenge measures adopted by the military regime and provided immunity from challenge.

The Supreme Court of Pakistan

Farooq Ahmed v Federation of Pakistan

Abdullah Khoso J:

1.   This is an appeal against the impugned judgment of the Lahore High Court (LHC), made on 6 December 2004, to revoke throughout the whole of Pakistan the Juvenile Justice System Ordinance (JJSO). The Lahore High Court's order was made following a petition by Farooq Ahmed that the two persons accused of sodomising and murdering his eight year old son should not be able to rely on the protections of the JJSO because they were (i) over 18 years of age and (ii) the JJSO was unconstitutional, discriminatory and conducive to corruption and crime.

2.   The JJSO provides for a range of special protections for juveniles (those under the age of 18 years) accused of crimes, and includes a prohibition on the use of the death penalty. The Lahore High Court's order revoking the JJSO considered each of its sections—from the arrest of the child until the child's rehabilitation—and held that the provisions of the JJSO were against the constitutional rights of others citizens; and that in any event all of the protections are otherwise covered by existing legal provisions. Specifically, the arguments against the JJSO were made in the following manner:

i.   It had been asserted that the JJSO has unconstitutionalities, infirmities, impracticalities, absurdities, obscurities and unreasonableness. It does not fit into the constitutional and legal system of dispensation of criminal justice and, therefore, the law needs to be struck down in the interest of society.

ii.   The matter of treatment of a child accused of committing a crime has already been adequately and satisfactorily taken care of by sections 82, 83 and 299 (a) (adult means a person who had not attained the age of 18 years) and (i) (minor means a person who is not an adult) of the Pakistan Penal Code (PPC), 1860 as well as by section 399 (confinement of youthful offenders in reformatories) of the Code of Criminal Procedure (CrPC), 1898. Thus the JJSO has created unnecessary confusion.

iii. The provisions of Articles 25(3) and 26(2) of the Constitution of Pakistan do not envisage extending protection to children in a manner that leaves others unprotected from these children.

iv.   The matter of sentencing of a young offender always receives a careful and generally sympathetic consideration by the courts. Thus, there was no reason for the JJSO to categorically forbid the death penalty against children below the age of 18 years.

v.   The prohibition of the death sentence to juveniles in the JJSO has encouraged adults to settle their feuds by using children to kill their enemies since these children will be given a lesser sentence. It is argued that such misuse of the provisions of the JJSO has promoted murders and thus denied victims their right to life as guaranteed by Article 9 of the Constitution of Pakistan. It is also argued that the JJSO has encouraged and promoted corruption in society, inasmuch as fake certificates and documents are being prepared to show the age of an offender to be less than 18 at the time of the offence so that a possible sentence of death may be avoided.

vi. The JJSO has been introduced by an unrepresentative government without prior public debate and in the absence of any discussion in Parliament, and under the pressure of the Western governments and foreign donor organisations without appreciating that in view of the peculiar social, economic, climatic and dietary factors, a child in our part of the world attains maturity of understanding at an earlier age than in the West. Thus, it has been asserted, Western standards in this regard should not be applied in Pakistan.

3. The Supreme Court finds little, if any, valid justification for the revocation of the JJSO in the judgment of Lahore High Court. The Supreme Court analyses the matter in following manner:

The application of the JJSO to the accused

4. The two persons are accused of a gruesome and shocking offence: the sodomisation and murder of an 8 year old boy. The School Leaving Certificates (SLCs) show that the accused were minors at the time of the offence, and thus they used these to argue that they should be treated as juveniles under the JJSO. In contrast, the medical certificates—upon which the respondent Farooq Ahmed relies—suggest the accused were, in fact, over 18. However, in order to argue against the JJSO the respondent has also maintained that incorrect medical opinions about age are being procured. This may suggest that the medical certificate upon which he now seeks to rely is also incorrect, and possibly procured by unlawful means. The ambiguity and uncertainty creates doubt about both official documents. In such doubtful circumstances, the Court should give weight to the official document produced first (the SLC). The accused should be presumed to be under 18 years of age.

The constitutionality of the JJSO

5. Internationally and within the Constitution of Pakistan, children are considered to be deserving of special treatment due to their vulnerability and lack of proper understanding of the nature or consequences of their conduct.

6. This special protection applies to all children, including children in conflict with the law. Such children are often victims of their circumstances with little power and few rights, and like many children across the globe and in Pakistan may have been victims of abuse, violence and exploitation. The United Nations Convention on the Rights of the Child (UNCRC) (which has been ratified by almost all of the members of the UN, and by Pakistan in 1990) requires special treatment for children in conflict with the law; not merely for the best interest of children themselves but also for the greater good by rehabilitating the child through positive discipline and the nurturing of constructive values.

7. Thus children accused of crimes should be entitled to all rights that extend to adults, but adapted to take account of their vulnerability and lack of maturity. This broad principle is captured in the Constitution of Pakistan and in the UNCRC:

8.   The Constitution of Pakistan 1973:

i.   Article 4 (1). Right of individuals to be dealt with in accordance with law: To enjoy the protection of law and to be treated in accordance with law is the inalienable right of every citizen, wherever he may be, and of every other person for the time being within Pakistan.

ii.   Article 9. Security of person: No person shall be deprived of life or liberty save in accordance with law.

iii.   Article 25 (3). Equality of citizens: Nothing in this Article shall prevent the State from making any special provision for the protection of women and children.

9.   The UNCRC:

i.   Article 3. In all actions concerning the child … full account [shall be taken] of his or her best interests.

ii.   Article 40(1). Every child alleged as, accused of, or recognised as having infringed the penal law to be treated in a manner consistent with the promotion of the child's sense of dignity and worth … which takes into account the child's age and the desirability of promoting the child's reintegration and the child's assuming a constructive role in society.

Article 40(2) UNCRC goes on to set out a number of procedural guarantees.

10.   The JJSO, in providing special protections for children in conflict with the law, is therefore compliant with Pakistan's international obligations under the UNCRC and is consistent with the Constitution of Pakistan. Furthermore, the JJSO does not represent a specifically Western approach (as argued in the Lahore High Court) but accords also with Islamic principles, where children and other weak people are treated with special care and attention (for example, Islam forbids parents to force their children for prayers), and where compassion and forgiveness are central. The JJSO protects children and helps them to learn forgiveness and to become useful citizens of an Islamic country.

The relationship of the JJSO with existing law

11.   The Supreme Court noted that before the introduction of the JJSO there were laws and practices that provided for sympathetic and concessionary treatment of children in conflict with law. These laws related to the capacity to commit a crime; bail and custody (as is evident from the provisions of sections 82 and 83 of the Pakistan Penal Code and sections 29-B, 497 and 399 of the Code of Criminal Procedure); sentencing (where the courts had regard to the age of the offender before passing sentence) and disposals (including the use of Borstal Institutions and Reformatory Schools for young prisoners).

12.   However, these laws and practices were extremely weak; and they also received less consideration by the courts than the JJSO attained in four years (from 2000 to 2004). There were no procedural guidelines for those working within the criminal justice system on how to protect the rights of children who are accused of an offence.

13.   The JJSO is therefore compatible with other laws but it provides much needed additional protection for children given the harsh legal framework and environment which was created by a colonial mindset that criminalised the poor and was designed to deal with

hardened criminals, not children whom we in Pakistan and the international community now recognise as a vulnerable group.

The definition of a child

14.   Section 2 (b) of the JJSO defines a 'child' as 'a person who, at the time of commission of an offence, has not attained the age of eighteen years'. There is no need to differentiate between boys and girls in the definition of a 'child'—a child is a child below 18 years of age whether it is male or female. This does not, however, mean that boys and girls must be treated the same. The specific needs of female juveniles may require different treatment for girls because Pakistan's criminal justice is designed around the needs of boys/men.

15.   The Court notes that the age of a child in the JJSO—a person under 18 years—has not been fixed arbitrarily and randomly: it is the internationally accepted definition of the child in the UNCRC (Article 1).

16.   Also, the majority of countries are heading towards defining a child as under 18 years, in accordance with the UNCRC. English law now consistently treats a child as a person under the age of 18 (since the Criminal Justice Act 1991) and in India too, a child is defined as a person below 18 years of age. In fixing an internationally approved age, it is easier for local courts to follow one fixed criterion and help to determine matters accordingly. Acceptance and practice of a single universal standard of the age for children and juveniles as recommended by the UN Committee on the Rights of the Child would surely pave the best way to fix problems that children face in Pakistan.

17.   Furthermore, in Pakistan, other laws treat those below 18 years of age as children. Section 3 of the Majority Act of Pakistan, 1875, fixes the age of majority as 18 years and in one particular situation 21 years; those under 18 are not provided with a computerised National Identity Card, they cannot have a Driving Licence; they do not have the right to vote; and have no right to use property if their parents have died. Even for boys, marriage is not possible below 18 years of age. These rules signify that the legislators had used their logic and rationale in drafting JJSO.

18.   It should be noted that although the JJSO fixes the upper age of a 'child' at 18 years, it does not affect the minimum age of criminal responsibility. Section 82 of the PPC has until recently provided that 'Nothing is an offence which is done by a child under seven years of age' and Section 83 of the PPC provides that 'Nothing is an offence which is done by a child above seven years of age and under twelve, who has not attained sufficient maturity of understanding to judge the nature and consequences of his conduct on that occasion.' The UK Parliament had enacted Sections 82 and 83 of the Pakistan Penal Code (at that time known as the Indian Penal Code, 1860), which at that time was the same as the law in England. However, according to section 50 of the Children and Young Persons Act, 1933 (of England) as amended by section 16 of the Children and Young Persons Act, 1963, there is now a conclusive presumption that no child under the age of 10 years can be guilty of any offence. In Pakistan also, the minimum age of criminal responsibility has, as of 2016, been raised to 10 years of age. This is clear evidence of the acceptance of international standards when it concerns the minimum age of criminal responsibility though it remains low at the age of 10. The Parliament should address this and increase the minimum age of criminal responsibility as recommended by the UN Committee on the Rights of the Child.

19.   One reason why children should be treated differently from adults in criminal proceedings is because, regardless of gender, below 18 years of age a child does not attain sufficient discretion and intelligence to fully understand the criminal process, the trial and
some of the implications of his or her actions further to being charged with an offence. This
is further reinforced by evidence that because of poverty many children in Pakistan suffer
from malnutrition which can stymie the development of their mental abilities and capabilities (see Fernando Monckebert, Susana Tisler, Sonia Toro, Vivien Gattás and Lucy Vega
in 'Malnutrition and Mental Development' (1972) 25(8) *The American Journal of Clinical
Nutrition* 766–72 and also Daniel Hackman, Martha Farah and Michael Meaney in 'Socio-
economic Status and the Brain: Mechanistic Insights from Human and Animal Research'
(2010) 11(9) *Nature Reviews Neuroscience* 651–59).

20.   It is mental, not physical, maturity that is relevant to a child's criminal responsibility
and to their special treatment in the criminal justice system. The Lahore High Court was
wrong to suggest that children in Pakistan experience a speedy physical growth and an
accelerated maturity because: they are in close proximity and interact with adults due to
social and economic conditions; do odd jobs and get employed at a relatively young age; live
in a hot climate; and eat exotic and spicy food. Physical maturity is not relevant to criminal
responsibility. If it were, then in England the minimum age of criminal responsibility would
be lowered since there is evidence that improvement in diet is leading to the earlier onset of
puberty (see the British Broadcasting Corporation (BBC) in 2007 which reported research
findings of different universities which suggest that in 'one girl in six reaches puberty before
the age of eight—18 months earlier than their mothers'). Even if special treatment of juveniles were related to physical maturity, this would not support the respondent's argument
since a less healthy diet in Pakistan and other factors mean children mature at a slower, not
quicker, rate than children in England.

Defects in draftsmanship

21.   The Supreme Court notes that because the JJSO was not well-drafted as to its overarching effect on other laws, it has been taken not to apply to other special laws such as the
Anti Terrorism Act. Section 14 JJSO has created confusion in the trials of accused juveniles
and the jurisdiction of the juvenile court. It says 'The provisions of the JJSO, shall be in
addition to and not in derogation of, any other law for the time being in force'. Since it does
not have an overriding effect on other laws such as the Anti Terrorism Act, the Juvenile
Courts remain unable to assert their authority to try children in such cases.

22.   Nonetheless, special protections are needed for juveniles regardless of the offence
committed, as made clear by section 4(3) JJSO which provides that 'The Juvenile Court
shall have the exclusive jurisdiction to try cases in which a child is accused of commission of
an offence'. Parliament may consider redrafting the JJSO to clarify that it applies to all other
laws. In the meantime, having regard to the child's best interest, this Court will presume this
is the case in order to keep children out of the adult courts.

23.   The Supreme Court observes that in other regards the JJSO is not the finest example of
legal draftsmanship (inasmuch as its language as well as its content is weak in many ways).
However, the Courts—including the Lahore High Court—do not have powers to remove
laws from the statute book; they can merely suggest changes to the legislative assembly in

matters which are found to be inconsistent, vague and unconstitutional. In making such recommendations the court can rely on the UNCRC, Beijing Rules, Riyadh Guidelines and recommendations by the UN Committee on the Rights of the Child set out in the Concluding Observations on Pakistan in 2003 and 2009. In this case, a defect in the form or language of a legislative instrument can be overlooked for the sake of greater good; a defective law is still better than no laws at all.

Requirements of the JJSO

24.   Section 5 of the JJSO provides that 'no child shall be charged with or tried for an offence together with an adult'. This is in accordance with the UN Convention on the Rights of the Child and Article 25 (3) of the Constitution of Pakistan, which as noted above provides that 'Nothing in this Article shall prevent the State from making any special provision for the protection of women and children'. In a case involving adult and child co-defendants separate trials are to be conducted, with the child appearing in the Juvenile Court and the adult in the adult court. This practice takes place in other jurisdictions, including India, and protects children from the potentially negative influence of the adult co-defender, and helps to ensure her best interest and the right to fair trial because of the special procedures.

25.   The provincial governments are duty bound to arrange special judges for juvenile courts and for separate trial and other arrangements for juveniles. It implies that children should not suffer for any disadvantage that may result from the joint trial. However, the spirit of Section 5 JJSO is invariably ignored by the trial courts; the same Sessions Judges and Additional Sessions Judges are functioning both as the ordinary courts as well as the Juvenile Courts. More often than not a 'child' is tried by the same judge who tries the adult accused, and the evidence recorded in the adult's trial is usually transferred and adopted by such courts for the purposes of the child's trial. Such a practice is highly objectionable and counterproductive to the interests of the child, particularly as he is not even present before the ordinary court at the time of recording of the evidence in the adult's trial.

26.   If Parliament had formally launched this law it would likely have strengthened the judicial system to protect children in a similar way as children are protected in India through the Juvenile Justice (Child Protection and Care) Act 2000, and in compliance with the UNCRC and related guidelines. As this is not the case, this Court urges the Government to take extra administrative measures for arranging special courts and judicial officers for juveniles.

27.   Section 10 JJSO provides for bail for a child accused and subsection (3) of section 10 contemplates a situation where a child accused of even a bailable offence may not be released on bail if

> it appears that there are reasonable grounds for believing that the release of the child shall bring
> him into association with any criminal or expose the child to any danger, in which case, the child
> shall be placed under the custody of a Probation Officer or a suitable person or institution dealing
> with the welfare of the children if parent or guardian of the child is not present, but shall not under
> any circumstance be kept in a police station or jail in such cases.

Section 10 is designed to protect the child, not merely by releasing a child accused of a bailable offence, but ensuring he is placed in the care of the right person in the right place.

28.   The prohibition of the death sentence for children by the JJSO protects the right to life. However, the petitioner sought to argue in the High Court that this was contrary to the laws of other countries and that

> In England the Children Act 1908 made an immunity from the sentence of death available to an offender who is less than sixteen years of age and in India such an immunity is available under the Juvenile Justice Act 1986 to a boy less than sixteen years of age and a girl less than eighteen years of age.

This is wrong. Neither India nor England allow children to be sentenced to death.

29.   It was also argued that the prohibition of the death sentence on juveniles encourages persons below 18 years of age to commit heinous crimes. However, many judicial officers and lawyers are not aware of the JJSO, so it is unlikely that children know about it (even the educated class do not know about their human rights). Furthermore, if it was the case that children were no longer deterred from committing crime then the number of juveniles in detention centres would have increased alarmingly. However, a research article ('Detention of Juveniles in Pakistan') published in *Chronicle* 2012 (January Edition) reveals that the number of juveniles in the prisons has reduced since the promulgation of the JJSO. At the end of 2002, there were 4979 juveniles in prison of Pakistan; in 2004 this had reduced to 2539.

30.   Arguments were also put before the court that the abolition of the death penalty has led to parents encouraging their children to commit crimes. But if a parent were to force their child to commit an offence, then it is the responsibility of the state to protect such children from those people who misuse or exploit them, not to subject them to harsh punishment. Providing special care and arrangements to juveniles in the criminal justice system is not against society and its values, and it does not leave other citizens more vulnerable; the death penalty is not a deterrent. The JJSO cannot be declared unconstitutional and unreasonable law because adults are exploiting children.

31.   There are indeed problems associated with the implementation of the JJSO. Disputes relating to age are raised for the first time in appeals before the High Court and the Supreme Court without these having been taken care of by the trial court; at appeal level, these matters consume time and resources. And almost every day, cases are coming up before us where fake School Leaving Certificates have been obtained, incorrect medical opinions about age procured, forgeries and interpolations committed in the Registers of Births maintained at Union Councils, and false marriage certificates of parents of accused persons prepared with a view to show the age of an accused person to be less than 18 years so that a possible sentence of death may be avoided against him in cases of terrorism, murder, gang-rape or trafficking in narcotics, etc. There is, therefore, a possibility that undeserving people have exploited the JJSO's provision of age to get a benefit; indeed, any law on the statute book in one or other way is considered a reason of promoting falsehood, lies, forgeries and corruption in the society. But if the Union Council or doctors are giving fake certificates, it is not the fault of the JJSO; it is the fault of the society that is misusing it. The problem is with individuals who misuse the law and with the authorities, not with the law itself.

Conclusion

32.   On the matter of the two accused, who provided documents in order to secure protection under the JJSO, the Supreme Court orders that they be treated as juveniles. The School

Leaving Certificates are official documents and were submitted prior to the medical certificates and the opinions formed from these.

33.   On the matter of the constitutionality of the JJSO, the Supreme Court of Pakistan, after a thorough examination of the JJSO, the United Nations Convention on the Rights of the Child, the Lahore High Court's Judgment, and the arguments provided by the petitioner, the state and others concerned in the case, has reached the conclusion that the JJSO is a reasonable, constitutional and practical law to protect juveniles. The appeal is granted and it is ordered that the purported revocation by the Lahore High Court of the JJSO be set aside. There should be no doubt the JJSO is on the statute book.

34.   Accordingly, the JJSO should guide all agencies and institutions of the criminal justice system in Pakistan and compensate for the lack of an overarching law to protect children in conflict with the law. As a necessary consequence of the declaration made and the order passed, the Juvenile Courts established under the said Ordinance shall continue to work and all the cases pending before all such courts shall ipso facto continue to be tried by the juvenile courts as given in the JJSO.

35.   For the purpose of removal of a possible doubt, a clarification may be necessary. From the date of promulgation of the JJSO to the date of the present judgment accused persons below the age of 18 years have the right to protection from the death sentence.

36.   It goes without saying that Parliament may, if it so desires, enact a fresh law or amend the JJSO to bring improvement in light of the developments on international standards on the juvenile justice system provided by the United Nations. We would urge Parliament to consider amending all the laws which define the male and female child differently and which discriminate against girls, as recommended by the Committee on the Rights of the Child in its Concluding Observations and Recommendations in 2003 and 2009 (see paragraphs 26 and 27 of 2009) and to raise the minimum age of criminal responsibility in line with international standards.

The writ petitions filed by the State and others are permitted.

Judge Approved for reporting.

26

Commentary on *The Case of John Hudson*

SUE FARRAN AND RHONA SMITH

I. Introduction

This contribution is different from others in the collection. Not only is it from an earlier century (from 1783, making it the oldest by far to be revisited) but is also a rewrite of a trial transcript rather than a judicial opinion. This eighteenth century criminal case concerns an eight year old child, John Hudson, found guilty of stealing and sentenced to transportation after a cursory trial in which he was tried alongside adults in a busy Old Bailey court. He was brought there from Newgate gaol where he would have been held in the same conditions as adults. Children, provided they were over seven years old, were regarded as no different from adults in the criminal law of the time. Cross-questioning of witnesses and the use of defence counsel was in its infancy though in the original case the judge demonstrated some concern over John's age and capacity. We have built on this and introduced a defence counsel—William Garrow, who was in the Old Bailey that day, to arrive at a different outcome. We have retained the facts and evidence as presented in the transcript and indicated our changes in italics. In so far as possible we have tried to keep within the style of the reports of the time. However due to challenges of finding a suitable type-face we have not reproduced the original style of writing.

John's trial fate is illustrative of the life and experience of many children of the period. At the time of his conviction, the idea of children as people in their own right was yet to emerge and we were still some way from regarding them as rights-holders in the sense that we understand the concept in theory and practice today. Therefore, in revisiting the case we have had to look beyond modern literature on children's rights to more broadly consider the then-emerging ideas about children, the poor and criminal justice.

This case is interesting not only for its historical context but also because it reminds us of the continuing injustices experienced by children, especially those who are often 'forgotten' in contemporary debates about children's rights:[1] those children who have not had a 'childhood' or who have had to be adult before their time.[2]

---

[1] See R Holden, *Orphans of History, the Forgotten Children of the First Fleet* (Melbourne, Text Publishing Company, 1999). There are of course many forgotten children of the twenty-first century.

[2] Can we really argue that 'children are not yet suitably proficient judges of where their own well-being lies' because of 'their lack of experience of the world and of themselves'—as suggested by AF Hall, 'On Becoming

II. The Emerging Child

In the late eighteenth century the emergence of the child as a person distinct from an adult came to be evidenced through consumerism rather than law. Industrialisation brought more disposable wealth to a growing number of people and there was a market for private education for children, children's books and children's toys.[3] Children were also appearing in paintings,[4] and as central figures in literature.[5] These were indicative of changes in the material world of children and adult attitudes towards them.[6] Foyster, writing of the rise of child abductions at the time, also points to the emerging rhetoric of parent-child relationships.[7] By the eighteenth century Blackstone indicated that the bond of affection between parent and child was recognised,[8] although not all writers agree.[9] Eekelaar for example suggests that the child's interests were only protected in so far as this was beneficial to the father.[10] Moreover, as Mathisen points out '[t]he history of childhood has largely been dominated by examination of the relationships between child, mother and father, often within the rubric of the history of the family'.[11] Despite this there is evidence during the eighteenth century that children outside the family were attracting attention. In particular orphaned and destitute children, such as John, provided philanthropists and reformers with material for social experimentation: for example, the Foundling Hospital in London and various other medical hospitals and dispensaries used children in their care to explore the advancement of medical treatment for children,[12] while the London Philanthropic Society, focused its reform zeal on the children of convicts, and the 'infant poor' engaged in vagrant or criminal activity.[13]

An example of child-focused philanthropy which is particularly relevant to our case was the work of Jonas Hanway.[14] In the 1760s he campaigned for improvement of the situation

An Adult: Autonomy and the Moral Relevance of Life's Stages' (2013) 63 *The Philosophical Quarterly* 223, 225, when they have to fend for themselves from an early age, or are full-time carers?

[3] See JH Plumb, 'The New World of Children in Eighteenth-Century England' (1975) 67 *Past and Present* 64.

[4] See for example the painting by Joshua Reynolds 1788 'The Age of Innocence'.

[5] See A O'Malley, *The Making of the Modern Child: Children's Literature and Childhood in the Late Eighteenth Century* (Abingdon, Routledge, 2003).

[6] Plumb, above n 3.

[7] E Foyster, 'The "New World of Children" Reconsidered: Child Abduction in Late Eighteenth- and Early Nineteenth-Century England' (2013) 52 *Journal of British Studies* 669, 684.

[8] W Blackstone, *Commentaries on the Laws of England* 1.16 7th edn (1975) 450 quoted by J Eekelaar, 'The Emergence of Children's Rights' (1986) 6 *Oxford Journal of Legal Studies* 161, 165.

[9] Eekelaar, ibid 161, see also J Tobin, 'Courts and the Construction of Childhood: A New Way of Thinking' in M Freeman (ed), *Law and Childhood Studies: Current Legal Issues* Volume 14, 2012, Oxford Scholarship Online.

[10] Eekelaar, ibid 167.

[11] A Mathisen, 'Mineral Waters, Electricity, and Hemlock: Devising Therapeutics for Children in Eighteenth-Century Institutions' (2012) 57 *Medical History* 28, 30.

[12] ibid. The campaign to establish a Foundling Hospital (for illegitimate children) was started by Thomas Coram in 1720. Had John Hudson's mother brought him to the Foundling Hospital he could have stayed there until the age of 15 when he might have left to go into service or the army.

[13] See M Whitton, *Nipping Crime in the Bud: How the Philanthropic Quest was put into Law* (Hook, Waterstone Press, 2010).

[14] See 'Jonas Hanway, the Philanthropist' (1795) *The Gentleman's Magazine* 296.

of chimney sweep apprentices (our accused has been 'sometimes a chimney sweep'),[15] publishing in 1785 his *Sentimental History of Chimney-Sweepers*. Although a law in 1788 set a minimum age of eight for child sweeps, it was never enforced and it was not until 1834 that the Chimney Sweeps Act prohibited the apprenticing of children under 10 years old. Despite subsequent Acts raising the age threshold it was only in 1875 that licensing and police enforcement of the regulations was made law. Garrow's argument for the defence in our re-written judgment is based on the 1817 Report of the House of Commons Committee set up to investigate non-compliance with the 1788 Act.[16] Hanaway had also published 'An Earnest Appeal for Mercy to the Children of the Poor' in 1766,[17] drawing attention to the high mortality rates of children placed in parish care and arguing for the education, religious instruction and apprenticeship of children from an early age and he was instrumental in founding the Marine Society in 1756 (see below).[18] Although philanthropic causes dependent on charitable giving had to make their causes attractive to middle class benefactors,[19] it is clear that in the latter part of the eighteenth century not only were children in the emerging middle classes becoming a focus of attention, but also those in less fortunate circumstances, among whom we might include John Hudson.

III. Philosophies of the Time

Despite the developments above, theories about children and children's rights were only just beginning to emerge and we have to search more broadly for the intellectual debates of the day with which our judge might be familiar. In 1767, the English translation of Cesare Beccario *Dei Delitti e delle Pene* had introduced new ideas about crime and punishment based on the enlightenment. These marked a condemnation of barbaric forms of punishment and advocacy of a system of punishment that was rational and certain—crimes should suit the offence, deter potential offenders and prevent the culprit from further offending. Beccario advocated deprivation of liberty and hard labour—preferably in public. His ideas were advocated in Parliament in 1770 by Sir William Meredith MP: criminals should be made 'safely useful'.[20] In 1771, Willian Eden published *Principles of Penal Law*, rejecting capital punishment and transportation and like Meredith and Beccario advocating public display of useful punishment. Unlike the other two however, he did not support imprisonment believing that it made offenders worse. In 1777 the philanthropist John Howard published *The State of the Prisons in England and Wales*, drawing to public attention the shocking state of prisons in the country, especially when compared to similar institutions abroad. In 1778 he gave evidence before the House of Commons on the conditions of the 'hulk' prisons and

---

[15] His work, J Hanway, 'The Status of Chimney Sweepers' Young Apprentices', appeared in 1773.

[16] It is reported in an article entitled 'Chimneys and Chimney-Sweepers' in the *Penny Magazine* 1842, 322–23.

[17] J Hanway, *An Earnest Appeal for Mercy to the Children of the Poor* (Reprint, Cambridge, Cambridge University Press, 2013).

[18] London Lives 1690–1800, www.londonlives.org.

[19] For example by focusing on a regime of religious education, hard work, strict discipline and little leisure. See Whitton, above n 13.

[20] Extracted in C Emsley, *Crime and Society in England 1750–1900* (London, Longman, 1987) 216.

his work and reputation attracted considerable public attention.[21] In 1779, Parliament did pass legislation: the Penitentiary Act 1779, providing for the construction and administration of model penitentiaries but these were never built.[22] Nevertheless a new penal ideology began to emerge in the late eighteenth century and reform and punishment were to become central to public order debate.[23]

There had also been some philosophical writing on children. John Locke writing in 1693 and Rouseau writing in 1762 had both focused on the question of education for children. Locke had suggested that children would learn better and correct themselves when their behaviour was disciplined by a system of rewards and shame.[24] Locke believed that children had the ability to recognise and correct their own mistaken judgements or behaviour. Plumb suggests that 'Locke's book encapsulates what was clearly a new and growing attitude towards child-rearing and education which was to improve the lot of the child in the eighteenth century'.[25] Rousseau advocated education through experience, supporting the romantic notion that children were by nature good and were only corrupted through exposure to society.[26] Locke appears to have supported the idea of children in a natural state, not of innocence but of blankness; 'a tabula rasa' lacking any innate ideas but also vulnerable to the wrong influences. David Hartley writing in 1749 had classed the insane, idiots, drunkards, criminals and children together. He held that children were prone to errors of judgment and lacked the perfection of reasoning attributable to an adult, but suggested that children could eventually be brought to a state of reasoning perfection through discipline of the mind and body.[27]

Thus, by the late eighteenth century there appears to have been a spectrum of views ranging from the child as an innocent to the child as inherently sinful and corrupted by experience. This has to be located alongside views about the poor and the distinctions made between the deserving poor and the undeserving poor—vagrants, criminals, drunkards and so on. Any or all of these views may have informed the approach taken by the Court in John Hudson's case.

IV. The Criminal Law and Punishment

The criminal law of the eighteenth century conferred autonomy on the child in so far as he or she was held to be aware of his or her acts and liable for them. The age of criminal responsibility was seven, although a child under the age of 14 was presumed *doli incapax* unless it could be shown that he or she knew that what he or she had done was wrong.

---

[21] The Howard League for Penal Reform was named after him.

[22] Emsley, above n 20, 217–18.

[23] JM Beattie, *Crime and the Courts in England 1660–1800* (Oxford, Clarendon Press, 1986) 500.

[24] J Locke, *Some Thoughts Concerning Education* 1693 (Available as a Modern History Sourcebook, Fordham University).

[25] Plumb, above n 3, 67.

[26] J-J Rousseau, *Emile* 1762. (Available in translation: B Foxley, (London and Toronto, Dent,1921)). See in this vein the poems of W Blake 'Songs of Innocence and Experience' written 1789–94.

[27] D Hartley, *Observations on Man, his Frame, his Duty and his Expectations* (London, Richardson, 1749).

Langbein has written that

> [o]nly a small fraction of eighteenth-century criminal trials were genuinely contested inquiries into guilt or innocence. In most cases the accused had been caught in the act or otherwise possessed no credible defence. To the extent that trial had a function in such cases beyond formalizing the inevitable conclusion of guilt, it was to decide the sanction. These trials were sentencing proceedings.[28]

In the original trial John is sentenced to transportation.

Transportation, which had been facilitated and accelerated by the 1718 Transportation Act, continued until the mid-nineteenth century.[29] Initially transportation was to the North American colonies but after 1775 a new penal colony had to be found.[30] In the interim, those condemned to transportation lingered in the 'Hulks'—rotting barges moored in the Thames or Newgate prison. The Transportation Act 1784 confirmed the continuation of the practice of transportation; a punishment seen by some as an improvement on the old system of corporal punishment and the frequent use of the death penalty even for children.[31] It offered an alternative punishment for

> those offenders who, for a variety of reasons—their youth, actual nature of their offence, the fact that it was a first-time offence—were not considered to be deserving of the death penalty but to be deserving of something more than a whipping and a discharge.[32]

Rubin suggests that while sparing the lives of those condemned to transportation might be seen as a good thing, in fact transportation had the consequence of widening the net and punishing those who otherwise might have escaped a penal response.[33] Between 1788 and 1868, 160,000 convicts were transported and 50 of the 1,500 first fleeters were children. In fact John was sentenced to transportation at a time when there was uncertainty as to the convict destination. It was clear in 1783 that convicts would not be welcome in the newly independent American colonies but the Cabinet did not approve of Botany Bay in Australia until 1786. This hiatus in transportation, during which time John's trial was heard, gives us space to consider an alternative outcome.

Reference to cases decided the same day as John's trial show that the courts did not only use hanging or transportation. John might have been pilloried or whipped. Fining him would have been pointless. Had he been pilloried the crowd might well have taken pity on him and come to his defence and, similarly, if he had been whipped in public the crowd might have turned on the flogger.[34] The record of punishment for the day of his trial, 10 December 1783, in table 1 below, indicates the variety of sentences received.

---

[28] JH Langbein, 'Shaping the Eighteenth-Century Criminal Trial: A View from the Ryder Sources' (1983) 50 *University of Chicago Law Review* 1, 41.

[29] For early transportation information see A Rubin, 'The Unintended Consequences of Penal Reform: a Case Study of Penal Transportation in Eighteenth-Century London' (2012) 46 *Law and Society Review* 817, 819.

[30] Rubin, ibid 820, points out that between 1718–75 of the 50,000 offenders who were transported to America 18,600 were from London and its environs.

[31] On the death penalty see D Hay, P Linebaugh, J Rule, EP Thompson and C Winslow, *Albion's Fatal Tree: Crime and Society in Eighteenth Century England* (New York, Pantheon, 1976).

[32] Emsley, above n 20, 203.

[33] Rubin, above n 29.

[34] See Emsley, above n 20, 215, for such incidents.

Death sentence	23
Transportation for 14 Years	2
Transportation for 7 Years (including John)	29
Hard labour for two years in the House of Correction	1
Hard labour for one year in the House of Correction	4 (these were all women)
Six months hard labour	22
Three months in Newgate	3
One month in Newgate	8
Publicly whipped	20

Despite the alternatives, capital punishment remained fairly common at least until the early decades of the nineteenth century and public executions continued until 1868, although by the end of the eighteenth century few children were hanged,[35] and a number of those sentenced to capital punishment had their sentences commuted on appeal (see below). This was largely due to the fact that felonies—which included serious and many minor crimes—in common law were punishable by death. Had the goods John Hudson stole amounted to 40 shillings or more in value the crime would have attracted the death penalty.[36] The 'Bloody Code', which contained over 200 capital offences by the nineteenth century,[37] was not revised until the beginning of the nineteenth century.[38] Both capital punishment and transportation gradually gave way to incarceration, but at the time of John's arrest incarceration was only used to a limited extent and usually pending trial or pending transportation or execution.[39] Emsley includes statistics which show that in London and Middlesex in the period 1775–1784 there were 185 convictions for burglary (one of the offences with which John was charged) and of these 108 offenders were executed.[40] Rubin however suggests that death sentences and executions declined in the seventeenth and eighteenth centuries.[41] Nevertheless the risk of, if not execution of, the death penalty remained high and at the time of John's arrest, which coincided with the end of the American war of independence and the return of troops, public concern about law and order in London was rife. Indeed '[i]n March 1786 the Lord Mayor and Aldermen of the city of London petitioned George III about "the rapid and alarming increase in crimes and

---

[35] In 1776 a 15 year old was hanged for arson and in 1792 an 18 year old was hanged for murdering her child www.capitalpunishmentuk.org/child.html.

[36] See a case heard on the same day: Mary Moody, Ann Parker, Elizabeth Parker, Bridget Price: Reference Number t17831210-11 www.oldbaileyonline.org/browse.jsp?div=t17831210-11, in which the judge pointed out to the jury that if the value of the stolen goods was 40s it was a capital offence. He found three of the accused guilty of stealing goods to the value of 39s. One accused was, however, sentenced to death.

[37] Rubin, above n 29, 818.

[38] Emsley, above n 20, 201, refers to the work of Romilly, Mackintosh, Peel and Russell.

[39] Transportation continued until the mid-nineteenth century and the death penalty remained until 1965. B Godfrey and P Lawrence indicate that between 1800–1859 imprisonment became the default option, *Crime and Justice 1750–1950* (Cullompton, Willan, 2005) 90. See also Emsley, above n 20), ch 9, the opening of new prisons (Millbank 1816 and Pentonville 1842) and the centralisation of prison administration 1835 and 1877.

[40] Emsley, above n 20, 212.

[41] See Rubin, above n 29, 817. Compare however Whitton, above n 13, 19, who suggests that between 1783–87 there was an 87 per cent increase in executions over the previous five years.

depredations in this city and its neighbourhood, especially within the last three years".[42] In such a climate the criminal courts were unlikely to want to appear to be too lenient, and it was common for the theft of goods over two shillings to attract transportation,[43] unless the judge—perhaps swayed by the more enlightened thinking of the time indicated above—was prepared to intervene.

What were the alternatives open to the judge in this case that could have reflected a more child-orientated approach? We are confronted by the evidence of a child's footprint, proximity to the scene of the crime and being in possession of stolen goods. Unless challenged, circumstantial evidence would be accepted at face value. Even if the jury found John guilty—as they did in the actual case (guilty of the felony, not the burglary)—there were two possibilities for a more benign outcome.

The first was to consider if John could be placed in an apprenticeship. Besides parish apprenticeships for pauper children aged seven or over,[44] it might have been possible to send John to Bridewell Hospital which was not only a house of correction (see punishment table 1 above) but also an industrial school. Boys could be referred to Bridewell for apprenticeship or imprisonment by Justices of the Peace hearing sessions. Felonies could be heard at sessions, although in London the practice seems to have been to refer these to the Old Bailey,[45] so if session Justices had the power to send offenders to Bridewell then it would seem to follow that judges sitting in the Old Bailey would have a similar power.

The second possibility would be to place John in the hands of the Marine Society. In 1756 John Fielding, a Bow Street Magistrate had raised funds to send 400 'ragged and iniquitous, pilfering boys that … infest the streets of London' to join the British Navy. Combining forces with Jonas Hanway—who had established a charity for clothing poor sailors—the Marine Society was established to apprentice boys to the navy, thereby removing them from a life of crime and serving the nation.[46] Between 1756 and 1940 about 110,000 boys were sent to sea. However, there were obstacles in John's case: boys had to be at least 12 (John was under 12), 4'3" tall, and express a willingness to join the navy. Also, from 1769 recruitment shifted away from the ragged poor and pilfering boys of London to the respectable poor, the sons of artisans and craftsmen.[47] Alternatively the Philanthropic Society might have come to his rescue. The aims of the society were

> the prevention of crimes by removing out of the way of evil counsel, and evil company, those children, who are, in the present state of things, destined to ruin … the children of convicts, or other poor who are engaged in vagrant or criminal courses.[48]

In 1788 the Philanthropic Society had rescued a boy of similar age from transportation to Botany Bay, securing a pardon from the king on condition that the boy was received into the programme of reform of the society.

---

[42] Emsley, above n 20, 218.
[43] Simple grand larceny was the theft of goods valued over 1/-; petty larceny was for goods under 1/-.
[44] K Honeyman, *Child Workers in England 1780–1820: Parish Apprentices and the Making of the Early Industrial Labour Force* (Aldershot, Ashgate, 2007) 266.
[45] The Old Bailey was the assize court for London and Middlesex.
[46] 'Jonas Hanway, the Philanthropist' *The Gentleman's Magazine* 296–303.
[47] D Payne, 'Rhetoric, Reality and the Marine Society' (2005) 30 *The London Journal* 66.
[48] Holden, above n 1, 86, quoting from the 1799 account of the Society.

Finally, could John have received a reprieve? In London and Middlesex sessions the reprieve was not considered immediately after the case had been heard. Rather the convict was held in custody pending any outcome of a reprieve application. Langbein explains that

> Although appellate remedies in the modern sense were virtually non-existent, the executive clemency process served something of the function of a system of appellate review. The pardon power was employed to set aside verdicts thought to be against the evidence or to ameliorate outcomes felt to be too harsh.[49]

The court recorder presented the cases to His Majesty in Council. The convicted person could make a personal application for reprieve, but in John's case this would seem unlikely. Fortunately, Langbein states that '[t]he judge might instigate this review process, reprieving the convict on his own motion and referring the case to the monarch with a recommendation for commutation or pardon.'[50] A reprieve could apply to capital sentences and transportation. McLynn writes that 'Courts made wide use of reprieves and pardons to palliate the excesses of the Bloody Code'.[51]

V. Criminal Process

At this time, most prosecutions were instigated by the victims of crime. In our case this was William Holdsworth, the householder claiming to have been robbed. As a chemist he would have been a man of some means. Emsley suggests it was rare for there to be defence counsel in an ordinary criminal trial even into the early nineteenth century. However Emsley also suggests that

> Judges may have begun to allow counsel to appear for the accused because of the concern about the weakness of the accused's position; this concern also led to a greater querying of hearsay and circumstantial evidence as the eighteenth century wore on, and confessions were often rejected.[52]

Even if there was defence counsel it was not until reform in 1836 that counsel was allowed to sum up the defence argument for the benefit of the jury.[53] Evans points out that '[m]ost trials in the 18th century were still lawyer-free however and, as a result, the accused still had to rely on the discretion of the judge and jury'.[54] We know however that William Garrow was in court the day of John's trial.[55] Having been called to the bar in November 1783, Garrow was to make his name as an advocate of laws of evidence including the non-admissibility of forced confessions and the rule against hearsay.[56] The developing role of counsel in trials was also to lead to the adversarial system in English law which we know

[49] Langbein, above n 28, 19.
[50] Idem.
[51] F McLynn, *Crime and Punishment in Eighteenth-century England* (London, Routledge, 1989) 277.
[52] Emsley, above n 20, 152.
[53] Prisoner's Counsel Act 1836.
[54] H Evans, 'The Bloody Code' (2013) 28 *Manchester Student Law Review* 2, 34.
[55] Mr Garrow appears in the case of Sarah Slade and Mary Wood, 10 December 1783, Old Bailey Proceedings Online www.oldbaileyon-line.org Case Reference t17831210-44.
[56] J Hostettler and R Braby, *Sir William Garrow, His life, Times and Fight for Justice* (Hook, Waterside Press, 2011); J Beattie 'Garrow for the Defence' (1991) *History Today* www.historytoday.com/jonh-beattie/garrow-defence.

today. Taking advantage of Garrow's presence in the Old Bailey on 10 December 1783 we have let him into our courtroom.

There were murmurs about police reform from about 1750 but at the time of John's arrest the system in place was that of the Old Police,[57] consisting of parish constables and night watchmen. A special group of thief-takers, the 'Bow Street Runners', had been established by Bow Street magistrates, John and Henry Fielding, in the mid-eighteenth century and there were private thief-takers who made a living off commissions and court rewards and brought the profession of 'thief-taking' into some disrepute. We attribute this role to one of our witnesses. Garrow was particularly critical of thief-takers who would accept bribes to bring persons before the courts. In our case it appears that John Hudson was apprehended by one of the 'runners' as there is reference to the fact that 'the runners said it was the third time they had had him within ten days'.

VI. The Role of the Judge

John Beattie has described the eighteenth century criminal justice system in England as one which 'was shot through with discretionary powers'.[58] Similarly McLynn writes '[b]y the late 1770s judges had very wide discretionary powers in non-capital cases'.[59] The judge in this case was Edward Willes (1723–87). He was a justice of the court of the King's Bench by the time this case was heard. He was very much a member of the 'Establishment' having been educated at Oxford and Lincoln's Inn, and had served as an MP for Old Sarum in 1747, Aylesbury 1747–54 and Leominster 1767–68. He would therefore be familiar with reformist trends from parliamentary debates.[60]

Langbein suggests that there were four phases in the criminal process that could mitigate the harshness of the law:

1) the victim's decision whether and how to charge;
2) the judge's powers to influence the jury's verdict and to affect sentence;
3) the adjudicative work of the jury, when it convicted an offender of a lesser offense than he had committed or when it acquitted a culprit outright; and finally,
4) the crown's conduct of the clemency process.[61]

To this might be added the possibility of the accused presenting a character defence. John probably could not have supplied a character witness to swear to his good character, but in the case of Mary Moody and others (see above) heard on the same day, Bridget Price was sentenced to be privately whipped and discharged for her part in the theft, having called three witnesses to give her a good character.

---

[57] Godfrey and Lawrence, above n 39, 12. The New Police were not to come into existence until the next century with the establishment of the Metropolitan Police in 1829 and the Municipal Corporations Act 1835.

[58] Evans, above n 54.

[59] McLynn, above n 51, 280.

[60] The History of Parliament www.historyofparliamentonline.org/volume/1715-1754/member/willes-edward-1723-87.

[61] Langbein, above n 28, 47.

In re-writing this judgment we have built on Langbein's second proposal and drawn on the resources indicated above and capitalised on evidence in the original trial transcript that the judge has some sensibilities regarding John's age and vulnerability. Shoemaker suggests that the record of the case published by the Proceedings might very well not have included all the evidence or the judge's summing up,[62] which gives us the possibility of inserting some new material by way of Garrow's questioning of the witnesses and the Judge's instructions to Garrow. This builds on the idea that:

> Judges in the 18th century held extensive discretionary power and they exercised it to mitigate and to nullify the law. In the absence of defence counsel the judge would ensure fair play by questioning the witnesses and commenting on the evidence.[63]

We have tried to present the judge here as an enlightened individual aware of the thinking of his day and prepared to use the discretion afforded to him in his official role to arrive at a more child-orientated outcome which is not out of line with the time.

VII. Postscripts

A. What did Happen to John Hudson?

John was transferred in 1784 from Newgate prison to the *Mercury* for transportation to the Americas. The ship sailed for Georgia on 2 April 1784. Six days later there was a mutiny on board and the convicts commandeered the ship putting into Torbay in Devon a few days later. Here the escaping convicts were arrested and detained in Exeter jail before being removed to the prison hulk, *Dunkirk*.[64] John was on the *Dunkirk* in Plymouth for three years before boarding the *Friendship*, one of the transportation ships on the so-called 'First Fleet', bound for the new convict colony of Botany Bay, New South Wales.[65] He was the youngest convict on board. We know that John arrived in Australia on 21 January 1788 having sailed from Portsmouth on 13 May 1787.[66] Conditions on the first fleet were harsh,[67] but perhaps better than John had experienced in London. Life was also hard for the early convicts in a penal colony without much infrastructure,[68] and a serious shortage of food. Pressure on resources led to about half the settlement of convicts being relocated to Norfolk Islands in 1790.[69] John was among this group and, according to the records, he departed Port Jackson on 4 March 1790 for Norfolk Island aboard HMS *Sirius*, aged 15 and by now

---

[62] RB Shoemaker, 'The Old Bailey Proceedings and the Representation of Crime and Criminal Justice in Eighteenth-Century London' (2008) 47 *Journal of British Studies* 559, 572.

[63] Evans, above n 54, 30.

[64] Facilitated by the Hulks Act 1776. *The Dunkirk* was in fact an unregulated hulk with no regulations governing its use until 1784—Holden, above n 1, 82.

[65] John's age at the time was recorded as 13. There were two other child convicts on the first fleet and 34 children in total, rising to 50 by the time the fleet arrived in Australia. There were about 200 convicts in total. Holden, above n 1, 2.

[66] Convict records www.firstlanding.com.au/.

[67] A Frost, *The First Fleet, the Real Story* (Melbourne, Penguin Random House, 2012).

[68] See also, N Brennan, *Child Convicts* (Newtown, Black Dog, 2013).

[69] Discovered by Captain James Cook in 1774 and named after his patroness the Duchess of Norfolk.

having served over six years of his sentence. One year later, on 15 February 1791, he is recorded as receiving 50 lashes for being out of his hut after nine o'clock.[70] Norfolk Island was to become notorious as a penal settlement but in these early days it appears to have simply been chaotic, with various governors trying to impose order and ensure survival.[71]

There is little corroborated evidence as to what happened to John after Norfolk Island. One source notes he became a freeman at the end of his sentence,[72] though others say his whereabouts cannot be traced. The ticket of leave system was not introduced until after 1800.[73] Nevertheless, it can reasonably be assumed he became a free man, as there is no record of his death during detention, and his period of incarceration was short. Many convicts changed names when granted their freedom so it is possible, perhaps probable, that this happened. Life in the colony was hard, even for free men. Nevertheless, many flourished and their descendants remain in Australia, proud of their convict heritage.

B. Two Hundred Years Later …

Transportation to the colony of New South Wales was abolished in 1850. However, today all those, including children, who try to directly seek asylum in Australia are treated in an eerily similar manner.[74] In April 2016, the last asylum-seeking children detained on the mainland were freed pending determination of their status.[75] However, the Gillard, Abbott then Turnbull governments have sought proactively to limit the number of boats trying to reach Australia[76] by refusing entry onto the mainland without prior permission (visa or authorised asylum),[77] creating centres to process asylum claims offshore. This approach has been widely condemned.[78]

All asylum seekers, including unaccompanied children, are now sent to specific detention facilities on Manus Island off mainland Papua New Guinea or on Nauru. There are other centres on Christmas Island though no children. Conditions in the centres are difficult and have been widely criticised.[79] Philip Moss' 2015 report into the allegations of physical and

[70] Lashing was commonly inflicted: Holden, above n 1, 147.
[71] M Hoare, *Norfolk Island: a Revised and Enlarged History 1774–1998* (Rockhampton, Central Queensland University Press, 1999).
[72] A Boardman and R Harvey, *The First Fleet* (Scoresby, Five Mile Press, 1982).
[73] Introduced by Governor King and mainstreamed by Governor Brisbane.
[74] J Philips, 'Asylum seekers and refugees, what are the facts', Australia Government research papers, 2015, www.aph.gov.au/About_Parliament/Parliamentary_Departments/Parliamentary_Library/pubs/rp/rp1415/AsylumFacts#_ftnref52.
[75] They had been brought to the mainland due to ill health of relatives on Nauru.
[76] Operation Sovereign Borders; see Migration and Maritime Powers Legislation Amendment (Resolving the Asylum Legacy Caseload) Act 2014 issuing temporary visas for refugees.
[77] In 2015, for example, Australia agreed to grant refuge to 12,000 people from Syria and Iraq. They were given visas and flown direct to Australia.
[78] See, for example, many comments made during the working group review of Australia's second universal periodic review, report UN Doc A/HRC/31/14, January 2016, 136.238–136.290. Many states called for the detention centres on Manus and Nauru to be closed; others recommended removing children from detention.
[79] UN Committee Against Torture, Concluding observations on the combined fourth and fifth periodic reports of Australia, UN Doc CAT/C/AUS/CO/4-5 (2014): 'The Committee remains concerned that detention continues to be mandatory for all unauthorized arrivals, including for children, until the person concerned is granted a visa or is removed from the State party' (para 16).

sexual abuse in the Nauru offshore processing centre, and thereafter the senate report, were critical of the facility and the conditions under which so many (children) were detained.[80] The UN sub committee on the prevention of torture visited Nauru in April 2015.[81] Their report has been transmitted to Nauru but the government has not yet chosen to make it public. Nauru incident reports leaked in August 2016 evidence the scale of the problem.[82] In September 2015, however, the UN Special Rapporteur on the situation of migrants cancelled his imminent planned official visit as he considered that Australia could not guarantee compliance with the UN guidelines, especially concerning protection of those speaking and meeting with special procedures.[83] In 2016, the Supreme Court of Justice in Papua New Guinea declared detention in Manus unconstitutional,[84] whilst the High Court of Australia upheld detention in regional processing countries, albeit not indefinitely.[85]

Over 200 years on, Australia has changed direction from a host state for vulnerable children and adults transported to the new colony to an independent state which refuses entry to all undocumented and irregular asylum seekers and keeps children in detention in regional processing centres offshore for months, even years, whilst seeking to resettle them in Cambodia or Nauru. One wonders if the life chances of marginalised children such as John have greatly improved over the intervening centuries.

---

[80] P Moss, 'Review into recent allegations relating to the conditions and circumstances at the regional processing centre in Nauru', February 2015; followed by the senate enquiry, 'Taking responsibility: conditions and circumstances at Australia's Regional Processing Centre in Nauru', 2015 www.aph.gov.au/Parliamentary_Business/Committees/Senate/Regional_processing_Nauru/Regional_processing_Nauru/Final_Report.

[81] Established by the Optional Protocol to the UN Convention on the Prevention of Torture, Cruel, Inhuman or Degrading Treatment or Punishment, Advisory visit to Nauru, May 2015, report transmitted to the state in December 2015 but not yet public (2 April 2016).

[82] Guardian database, the Nauru files, www.theguardian.com/australia-news/ng-interactive/2016/aug/10/the-nauru-files-the-lives-of-asylum-seekers-in-detention-detailed-in-a-unique-database-interactive.

[83] Migrants/Human rights: Official visit to Australia postponed due to protection concerns—www.ohchr.org/en/NewsEvents/Pages/DisplayNews.aspx?NewsID=16503&LangID=E#sthash.vRmzYrEj.dpuf. Francois Crepeau, UN Special Rapporteur on migrants, September 2015.

[84] *Belden Norman Namah v Papua New Guinea & Ors*, SC1497 decision 26 April 2016.

[85] *Plaintiff M68/2015 v Minister for Immigration and Border Protection & Ors* [2016] HCA 1.

The Case of John Hudson:
The Old Bailey, London

Report of Old Bailey Proceedings[1]

19. JOHN HUDSON (A child of nine years old) was indicted for burglariously and feloniously breaking and entering the dwelling house of William Holdsworth at the hour of one in the night, on the 10th of October last, and feloniously stealing therein, one linen shirt, value 10 s five silk stockings, value 5 s one pistol, value 5 s and two aprons, value 2 s the property of the said William.

Court to Prisoner. How old are you?—Going [on] nine.

What business was you bred up in?—None, sometimes a chimney sweeper.

Have you any father or mother?—Dead.

How long ago?—I do not know.

Court. I wanted to see whether he had any understanding or no, we shall hear more of him by and by.

    WILLIAM HOLDSWORTH sworn.

I live in East Smithfield, I am a chymist: On the morning of the 17th of October, about eight o'clock, the maid informed me we were robbed; we have parted with her since; I got up and went to a back dining-room and found the shutters secure, but on opening them I found the sashes had been thrown up to the top, the shutters were fastened within-side, I immediately went down into the parlour and found some glass on the floor, and one of the panes in a narrow sky-light on the top of the sash was broken, part of the glass had been carefully taken out, and laid on some leads; than other part had fallen down parlour, found

---

[1] This report is taken from The Proceedings of the Old Bailey, 1674–1913—Central Criminal court, Old Bailey Online Reference Number t17831210-19 at https://www.oldbaileyonline.org/browse.jsp?id=t17831210-19-defend309&div=t17831210-19&terms=John_hudson#highlight. The online record includes an image of a page from the original Old Bailey Session Papers, the original of which is held by Harvard University. For comment on the reliability of the Proceedings of the Old Bailey—see Shoemaker (n61) who states that by 1778 'the City imposed the requirement that the *Proceedings* provide a "true, fair, and perfect narrative"' 562. The passages in italics are those added by the authors in the re-written judgment. The italicised passages do not appear in the original transcript.

upon the window shutter the marks of toes, as if somebody had slided down the window, in the inside of the shutters.

Court. Were they small toes or large toes?—They were small toes, I observed a table that stood very near the window, there I found the mark of footy [sic] (sooty?) feet, I saw a bar bent that went across the window curtain: I took the impressions of the foot and toes that were on the table upon a piece of paper as minutely as I could.

(The paper produced.)

Court. What reason have you to suspect the prisoner?—None, I did not hear till the next day any thing about him: We found the things were of the (same that?) were mentioned in the indictment which were my property: On the next sent to the pawnbrokers: The boy the robbery till the time that his foot was examined by this piece of paper, acknowledged it.

Court. How do you apprehend the boy got out again?—He said there was another boy with him.

Court. I do not much like the confession of a boy of nine years old, I would rather do without it if I could. How high was your sky-light?—About three yards from the ground, it was impossible for him to get out by himself.

SARAH BAYNES sworn.

I lodge in East Smithfield at a shoe warehouse at Mr. King's, going down on Friday morning the 17th of October about ten into the yard, into a little place that belongs to the lodgers, I staid there about five minutes, and coming out I found the prisoner at the water-tub, which was too high for him to reach without getting to the edge of the tub, I asked him what business he had there, he said, he was going to wash himself; he was all sooty: I told him it was water we made use of for drinking, and I did not chuse he should wash himself there; on putting him away; there is a place that formerly been a kitchen, and there are stairs that go up either into the street or into the lodging place; in this place where dirt is kept, I found a damask table cloth: I called to the boy, for nobody had been down but the boy and me, he said, he knew nothing of it: I found afterwards a parcel of silk stockings in the same place, I believe there were five tied up in a parcel: I then called in two men who found a parcel of things in the same place: Two aprons and a black silk stocking; upon the sink in the same place there was a pistol put in a thread stocking: One of the men going up stairs saw the prisoner coming out of the yard, and they fetched him back, and said he was the same boy: At first he said he knew nothing of them. Then Mr. King said, he would fetch somebody that would make him know, then the boy said, that there was another boy.

Court. That is threatening him, I cannot take a boy's confession after that.

JOHN SMITH sworn.

I am a pawnbroker, on the 17th of October, the boy at the bar brought this shirt to pledge about seven in the morning; he said it belonged to his father, I asked him who sent him with it, he said, his mother, I stopped him.

(The shirt deposed to by prosecutor who saw his daughter making it: It had never been washed.)

JOHN SADDLER sworn.

I apprehended the prisoner.

Court to Prosecutor. What passed before the Justice, were there any promises or threats made use of?—He first denied it, and then he told the Justice that there was another boy with him, and that the other boy broke through the window and got into the room; after the foot was measured by the paper he then confessed he had been in the house.

(The pistol and stockings deposed to.)

Court. Did the boy seem to want understanding before the Justice?—He said very little.

Court to Bayners. Did he appear to you to want understanding?—No: the runners said it was the third time they had had him within ten days.

Court to Garrow. Mr Garrow you appear as Council for the prisoner John Hudson?[2]

Garrow to Court. I do.

Court to Garrow. You may cross examine the witnesses and present a defence but you are not to instruct the jury.

Garrow to Court. I understand.

Garrow to Holdsworth. You are the householder who brings this prosecution?—I am.

You had no reason to suspect the boy when you discovered the broken window—No. I did not know of the boy until the pawnbroker identified him as the person who had brought a shirt to be pawned.

Looking at the boy do you think he could have bent the bar?—It seems doubtful he is but a puny lad.

Could the foot print have been made by another boy with small feet?—It could. He said there was another boy. He could not have got out by himself.

You say the burglary was discovered by your maid—Yes.

Why is she not in court to give evidence?—We dismissed her from service.

Why was that?—She was found to be untrustworthy.

Garrow to Saddler. How do you make a living?—I am a thief-taker.

You say the boy said very little. Could that be because he was frightened?—As to that I couldn't say.

Garrow to Bayners. You say the runners had had this boy three times in ten days—Yes so they said.

What had had they had him for?—They did not say.

Garrow to Baynes. You came across the boy openly in the yard by the water tub—Yes.

Did he appear to be running away from anything?—No he was trying to wash himself. He was all sooty.

The place where the parcel of silk stockings and other things been found has stairs going up to the street and to the lodging place, is that correct?—Yes.

---

[2] As indicated above the italicised portion of this judgment reflects the re-written judgment.

So other people could have gone into the place where the dirt is kept?—Only the prisoner and myself went down at that time.

Who were the men you called?—Mr King and another.

Mr King told the boy that he would fetch someone who would make him know. Is that correct?—Yes.

Garrow to John Smith. You are a pawnbroker?—Yes.

In your experience is it usual for children to bring things to be pawned on the instruction of others?—Yes it happens often that way.

Why did you stop him then?– He were a sweep.

Court to Jury. The boy's confession may be admitted, in evidence, but we must take it with every allowance, and at the utmost it only proves he was in the house; now he might have got in after daybreak, as the prosecutor was not informed of it till eight the next morning. The only thing that fixes this boy with the robbery is the pistol found in the sink; that might not have been put there by the boy: his confession with respect to how he came there, I do not think should be allowed, because it was made under fear; I think it would be too hard to find a boy of his tender age guilty of the burglary; one would wish to snatch such a boy, if one possibly could, from destruction, for he will only return to the same kind of life which he has led before, and will be an instrument in the hands of very bad people, who make use of boys of that sort to rob houses.

Court to Prosecutor. Could the boy go through this hole without scratching himself?—The glass was taken perfectly out.

Prisoner Hudson's defence delivered by Mr Garrow Council for the Prisoner

The prisoner is a sweep who from an early age has been subject to hard labour, spare diet, wretched lodgings and harsh treatment. He has been kept destitute of education, and moral or religious instruction. Because his work is done early in the day he has been turned out onto the streets to pass his time in idleness and depravity. He and others like him are an easy prey to those whose occupation is to delude the ignorant and entrap the unwary. The evidence which has been laid against him is circumstantial. It seems almost certain that at least one other was involved. His confession is unreliable because it was made under threat. He is a child.

Court: This boy appears to be under nine years old and could be less. He is small for his age. I have some doubts that he knew what he did was wrong or understood the charge. The fact that the runners have had him within ten days suggests to me that he is being used as the instrument of very bad people. His confession is unreliable and not conclusive. He appears fearful. He is a boy of tender age who may be easily influenced by bad people. He is an orphan bereft of the guidance of parents. The value of the goods is less than 40s so this is not a capital charge. I could sentence the accused to transportation but at present there is some uncertainty over this and it would mean detaining the accused in the company of those who would almost certainly have a bad influence on him. It is established he handled stolen goods and took them to the pawn broker. Also that he was found in the property where the theft occurred. His presence there may have been circumstantial.

NOT GUILTY of burglariously and feloniously breaking and entering a dwelling house or of feloniously stealing

Tried by the first Middlesex Jury before Mr Justice WILLES.

Part VI

Children's Rights and International Movement

27

Commentary on *RCB as Litigation Guardian of EKV, CEV, CIV and LRV v The Honourable Justice Colin James Forrest*

RHONA SCHUZ

I. Introduction

The issue of separate representation for children in proceedings under The Hague Convention on the Civil Aspects of International Child Abduction (hereinafter the Abduction Convention), which lies at the heart of this case, is important from a children's rights perspective for two main reasons. The first relates to the scope of the child's right to separate representation and its purpose; the second to the children's rights implications of the Abduction Convention. A brief consideration of each of these topics is a necessary background to understanding the context of the judgment and the significance of the rewritten judgment.

A. Separate Representation

The right to be represented in legal proceedings to which one is a party or which have a direct effect on one's life is universally recognised as a basic human right. In the case of children, this right was traditionally realised by parents representing their child, usually by means of a lawyer instructed by them. However, the growing acceptance of the fact that children have rights independent of their parents,[1] together with the acknowledgment of the fact that parents may not be able to represent their children's interests adequately, have led to an increasing recognition that children have a right to be independently represented in certain situations.[2] On the other hand, concerns have been expressed about the harm caused to children by being directly involved in litigation between their parents.[3]

---

[1] J Fortin, 'Children's Representation through the Looking Glass' (2007) 37 *Family Law* 500, 503.
[2] T Eitzen, 'A Child's Right to Independent Legal Representation in a Custody Dispute' (1985) 19 *Family Law Quarterly* 53, 73–77 and 64–66.
[3] Fortin, above n 1.

It is important to clarify that whilst separate representation is one method of enabling the child to participate in legal proceedings, the right to separate representation is wider than the right of the child to participate. Separate representation is not only a method of enabling the child's voice to be heard, but is a method of ensuring that the child's case is presented to the court in a persuasive and professional manner. Hearing the child indirectly or directly does not per se satisfy his right to representation because it does not allow him to engage in the proceedings[4] and does not provide him with an opportunity to have his position put forward in an equal manner to the others involved in the case, who are usually represented by professional lawyers.

The child's separate representative is called by different names in different countries, such as counsel for the child, separate representative, independent children's lawyer and guardian *ad litem*. However, the name does not necessarily reflect the duties expected of the representative and the debate as to the role of the child's representative seems to be virtually universal.[5] Three discrete functions may be involved in representing the child.[6] First, the representative may be expected to evaluate which outcome best serves the welfare of the child and to justify his conclusion to the court. Second, the representative may be seen as an amicus curiae, ensuring that all relevant information is presented to the court. In particular, there may be information to which the parents do not have access or are not interested in disclosing to the court. Last, but certainty not least, the child's representative may be expected to act as an advocate for the child, presenting the child's views and position to the court in the most persuasive way. It now seems to be recognised that a single function approach rarely provides adequate representation for the child and that his representative needs to put forward the child's position, whilst at the same time protecting him.[7]

B. The Abduction Convention

The Abduction Convention mandates the judicial or administrative authorities in the state to which the child has been wrongfully removed or retained to order immediate return of an abducted child to the state of his or her habitual residence prior to the abduction, unless one of the narrow exceptions in the Convention is established.

Whilst it is clear from the Preamble that the main motivation of the drafters was to protect the interests of children, the Abduction Convention has been perceived by some as primarily a procedural vehicle for allocating jurisdiction and enforcing foreign court judgments speedily. According to this approach, children's rights are not engaged in the Convention process itself. Rather, their rights need to be protected in the substantive proceedings relating to parenting arrangements in the country of origin. However, over the years, the fallacy of this approach has been exposed by scholars,[8] who have explained the

---

[4] See per Ryder J in *Re C (Abduction: Separate Representation of Children)* [2008] EWHC 517 [44]; J Fortin, *Children's Rights and the Developing Law* 3rd edn (Cambridge, Cambridge University Press, 2009) 264.

[5] See Eitzen above n 2, 66.

[6] P Parkinson and J Cashmore, *The Voice of the Child in Family Law Disputes* (Oxford, Oxford University Press, 2008) 51–53.

[7] See eg Eitzen, above n 2, 68, 69.

[8] See eg R Schuz, 'The Hague Child Abduction Convention and Children's Rights' (2002) 12 *Transnational Law and Contemporary Problems* 393; MH Weiner, 'Intolerable Situations and Counsel for Children: Following Switzerland's Example in Hague Abduction Cases' (2008) 58 *American University Law Review* 335.

various ways in which children's rights are engaged in Abduction Convention proceedings, inter alia because of the fateful implications such proceedings may have for the lives of children both in the short-term and often also in the long-term.[9]

II. Participation and Separate Representation in Abduction Convention Proceedings

The extent to which and method by which children participate in Abduction Convention proceedings varies from jurisdiction to jurisdiction. In particular, in common law jurisdictions, children are usually heard indirectly by welfare officers or other court agents. Many judges and others take the view that this form of participation is adequate,[10] but a number of scholars have argued that the child's right to participate is not fully realised unless he is given the opportunity to express his views directly to the decision-maker[11] and trends towards more judicial interviews can be identified in some jurisdictions.[12]

Similarly there are divergent views as to what extent courts should exercise their discretion to order separate representation of the abducted child. The arguments given against separate representation include lack of necessity, delay, cost and potential harm to the child.[13] In contrast, a number of scholars have refuted these arguments and explained why various characteristics of Abduction Convention cases mean that the child will often not be properly represented without independent representation.[14]

Whilst, to the best of the author's knowledge, the only countries which mandate the separate representation of children in Hague Abduction cases are Switzerland[15] and South Africa,[16] a greater judicial willingness to order separate representation can be detected in some other jurisdictions, such as England and Wales[17] and New Zealand.[18]

---

[9] The Ontario Supreme Court in *AMRI* v *KER* [2011] OJ No 2449 [128] referred to the 'life-altering effect' of Hague Convention applications.

[10] eg Lady Hale in *Re D (A child)* [2006] UKHL 51; Practice Guide for the Application of the New Brussels II Regulations (drawn up by the European Commission 2005) updated 1 June 2005.

[11] M Freeman and AM Hutchinson, 'Abduction and the Voice of the Child: Re M and After' (2008) *International Family Law* 163; C Piper, 'Barriers to Seeing and Hearing Children in Private Law Proceeding' (1999) 26 *Family Law* 394; R Schuz, *The Hague Child Abduction Convention: A Critical Analysis* (Oxford, Hart Publishing, 2013) 380–83.

[12] Schuz, ibid 376–80.

[13] ibid, 396–99.

[14] ibid, 399–403; Weiner, above n 8; E Pitman, 'Making the Interests of the Child Paramount: Representation For Children in the Hague Convention on the Civil Aspects of International Child Abduction' (2009) 17 *Cardozo Public Law, Policy & Ethics Journal* 515. See also advantages outlined by Bennett J in Australian case of *State Central Authority & Best (No 2)* [2012] FamCA 511.

[15] Art 9(3) of the Swiss Federal Act on International Child Abduction of 2007 (see translation in A Bucher, 'The New Swiss Federal Act on International Child Abduction' (2008) 4 *Journal of Private International Law* 139, 161–65).

[16] s 279 of the South African Children's Act 38 of 2005.

[17] M Freeman and AM Hutchinson, 'Half Price for Children? The Voice of the Child and the Child's Fight for Party Status in Cases on International Child Abduction' (2007) 29 *International Family Law* 177; eg, (Fam); *De L v H*] 2009] EWHC 3074 (Fam); *In The Matter of M (A Child)* [2010] EWCA 178.

[18] See Practice Note of Principal Family Court Judge, www.justice.govt.nz/courts/family-court/practice-and-procedure/practice-notes/practice-note-hague-convention-cases-new-zealand-family-court-guidelines-on-the-appointment-of-lawyer-for-the-child-counsel-to-assist-specialist-reports-and-on-views-of-the-child.

In stark contrast to these trends, Australia enacted legislation in 2000, which expressly restricted appointment of separate representatives for children in Abduction Convention cases to those where there were exceptional circumstances.[19] This legislation forms the backdrop to the case of *RCB*, the focus of this commentary.

III. The Original Judgment in *RCB*

A. The Facts and Decision

The case concerns four sisters aged between nine and 15 who lived in Italy until June 2010 and were in the joint custody of their divorced parents pursuant to a parental separation agreement. In June 2010, the mother brought the children to Australia for a one month holiday, at the end of which she failed to return them to Italy as agreed. At the request of the father, the Director General of the Queensland Department of Communities applied to the court for an order for return of the child under the Family Law (Child Abduction) Regulations 1986 ('the Regulations'), which implement the Abduction Convention in Australia. Forrest J held that since there had been a wrongful retention and no exception had been established, the children were to be returned to Italy.[20] His finding that the child objection exception had not been made out was based on the Family Consultant's opinion that the children's objections did not show a strength of feeling beyond the mere expression of a preference or of ordinary wishes, as required by the Regulations, and that the children had not reached a degree of maturity at which it was appropriate to give weight to their views.[21]

Subsequently, the maternal aunt, acting as a case guardian *ad litem* brought proceedings in the High Court of Australia, claiming that natural justice had not been afforded to the children in this case because they had not been represented by an independent lawyer, who would present their views to the court and pursue the outcome which they desired. That Court dismissed the application.

B. Reasons

A number of reasons for the dismissal of the application can be identified in the judgment of the plurality and the separate opinion of Heydon J. First, the judges took the view that the need for the Court to determine the strength of the children's objection and their maturity in a way which was procedurally fair to all who are affected by the decision, including the children, was satisfied by the appointment of a family consultant.

In addition, under section 68L(2A) of the Family Law Act 1975, separate representation could only be ordered in proceedings under the Regulations where there were exceptional

---

[19] s 68L(3), added by Family Law Amendment Act 2000. KM Bowie, 'International Application and Interpretation of the Convention on the Civil Aspects of International Child Abduction' (March 2001) 23–24 (on file with author), reports on opposition to this reform by family lawyers and judges.

[20] *Department of Communities & Garning (Child Safety Services)* [2011] FamCA 485.

[21] In the family consultant's view, the two younger girls 'lacked cognitive sophistication' and the 'ability for abstract thought and future forecasting' of the older sisters was not yet fully formed, ibid [119]–[120].

circumstances and in this case it had not been suggested that there were circumstances which could properly be characterised as exceptional.[22] Indeed, no application had been made for the appointment of an independent lawyer and, in any event, such an appointment would not answer the claim made by the plaintiff, because such a lawyer is not obliged to act on the instructions of the children,[23] but must rather form his own independent view of the best interests of the child.[24] Moreover, in Heydon J's view, the assumption that children are capable of instructing a lawyer is 'legally incoherent' in respect of most children and even children whose capacity can be equated with that of a capable adult should not usually be accorded party status in litigation between their parents.[25]

C. Analysis of the Original Judgment

This judgment adopts an 'invisible approach' to children's rights;[26] no mention is made of the United Nations Convention on the Rights of the Child (CRC), and the phrase 'children's rights' does not appear. Whilst the Court acknowledges that the decision will affect the children, it takes the view that no legal right is involved in the process of assessing the strength of their objections and maturity.[27]

The judgments indicate a complete lack of awareness of children's right to participate and to have their interests properly represented. Thus, for example, the plurality's view that the question of procedural fairness for the children is essentially a practical question of ensuring that the court has the information on which to base its findings in relation to the child's objections and his maturity ignores the fact that the child's right to be heard is not purely an instrumental right. Rather, participation recognises that a child is a moral and social actor in his own right and empowers him.

Similarly Heydon J's comment that the judge had not been asked to appoint a representative for the children ignores the duty of the state to provide the child with an opportunity to be heard in proceedings concerning him and to ensure that he has proper representation.[28] Moreover his blanket assumption about the incapacity of most children and his view that even capable children should not be given party status is inconsistent with the UNCRC's developing capacities approach, and with the notion of children as right bearers in general, and their right to participate in particular.

D. Impact of the Original Judgment

A search on the website of the Family Court of Australia (in February 2015) revealed only one case in which the case of *RCB* was cited in support of a decision not to appoint an

---

[22] *RCB* [2012] HCA 47, [34]–[36].
[23] ibid [55], citing FLA s 68LA (4).
[24] ibid [38], citing FLA s 68LA(2)(a).
[25] ibid [52].
[26] J Tobin, 'Judging the Judges: Are They Adopting The Rights Approach in Matters Involving Children' (2009) 33 *Melbourne University Law Review* 579, 593.
[27] *RCB*, above n 22, [43].
[28] *cf AJJ v JJ & Others* [2011] EWCA Civ 1448, in which the English Court of Appeal held that the court should have engaged the mature children in the process.

independent lawyer in Hague proceedings[29] and thus there is no evidence that the decision has had any significant practical impact.[30] Indeed, a search did reveal quite a number of cases where there were independent children's lawyers in Hague cases. However, since most of them do not report the actual appointment of the lawyer,[31] it is not clear what approach was taken to the exceptional circumstances barrier.[32]

IV. Rewritten Judgment

The rewritten judgment engages directly with the impact of children's rights in abduction cases, citing the relevant provisions of the CRC and the reference to that Convention in the Australian Family Law Act. The judgment then goes on to deconstruct the reasons given in the original judgment by taking a child-centric approach.

A. The Family Consultant's Report

The rewritten judgment holds that the family consultant's report did not ensure procedural fairness to the children, since they were entitled to have a lawyer cross-examine the family consultant in order to test the reliability of the report. This conclusion reflects justifiable misgivings about parts of the family consultant's report. Indeed, that report provides support for concerns expressed in the literature[33] that experts reporting on children's wishes are liable to be influenced by their own subjective opinions.[34]

The rewritten judgment could have gone further and considered whether the children had been given the right to be heard, as mandated by Article 12 of CRC. In my view, the answer is clearly in the negative, since they had not been afforded the opportunity to express their views directly to the Court and the family consultant was not putting forward their views on their behalf,[35] but was rather fulfilling an evidence-collecting function on behalf of the Court.[36]

---

[29] *Commissioner of Police South Australia (Central Authority) & Wimborne* [2013] FamCA 343.

[30] In the recent case of *Te Mata & Butler* [2016] FamCA 89, Bennett J comments that the independent children's lawyer appointed in that case had played that role in 'very many Hague Convention applications in this registry.' This suggests that that court had continued with Bennett J's pro independent lawyer policy enunciated shortly before *RCB* in *State Central Authority & Best (No 2)* [2012] FamCA 511.

[31] eg *State Central Authority & Castillo*, [2015] FamCA 792, Department of Family and Community Services & Dayan [2015] FamCA 1166.

[32] *cf Commonwealth Central Authority & Cotter* [2015] FamCA 1202.

[33] Schuz, above n 11, 384.

[34] The family consultant's view that it was not in the children's interests to have their objections upheld, because of the potential impact on their future relationship with their father, seems to have coloured her view as to the maturity of the two older children.

[35] General Comment No 12 (July 2009)—The right of the child to be heard, drawn up by the Committee on the Rights of the Child, http://www2.ohchr.org/english/bodies/crc/comments.htm, recommends that children are given the opportunity to be heard directly (para 35) and emphasises that the representative must represent only the child (para 37).

[36] The information which she had obtained from the children was also referred to in relation to other issues which arose in the cases, see *DCS v Garning*, above n 20.

B. Appointment of an Independent Lawyer

The Australian legislative restriction on the appointment of an independent lawyer in Abduction Convention cases to exceptional circumstances (in section 68L(3)) appears to be a statutory impediment to adopting a children's rights approach.[37] The rewritten judgment attempts to overcome the statutory restriction by holding that the skills of an independent lawyer are important in determining the strength of the child's objections, and so cases where objections arc raised are to be considered exceptional. However, this reasoning is hard to reconcile with the intent of the legislature, since the very purpose of the legislative restriction was to overcome the effect of the case of *De L*, which had held that separate representation should be ordered in cases where children's wishes arise.[38] A more convincing and principled line of reasoning might be that the exceptional circumstances requirement has to be interpreted in a way which is consistent with children's rights, in light of the later addition of section 60B(4), which expressly states that one of the objects of Part VII of the FLA is to give effect to the CRC.

Indeed, the rewritten judgment does note that, to the extent that section 68L seeks to limit the appointment of independent lawyers, 'it appears to be inconsistent with universal norms of children's rights and should be revisited by the Parliament.' It might be added that the provision is also inconsistent with the changing approach to the Abduction Convention and developments in other Member States.[39]

C. The Role of the Independent Lawyer

The rewritten judgment deconstructs Heydon J's formalistic argument that the independent lawyer does not in fact represent the child. It points out that whilst it is true that the Family Law Act requires that such a lawyer has to act in what he believes to be the best interests of the child and that he is not obliged to act on the child's instructions, these provisions are designed to free the lawyer from an obligation to act on the child's instructions where the child is not sufficiently mature to instruct him. Thus, they certainly do not prevent the lawyer from acting on the instructions of a mature child. Indeed, it will often be in the best interests of a mature child to have his views presented to the court by a lawyer representing him and in such a case the independent lawyer will surely be obliged to put forward those views. Furthermore, the more mature the child is, the more weight the independent lawyer will have to give to his views.

This interpretation reflects a hybrid approach to separate representation, under which the lawyer will act as an advocate for the child's views, unless this is not in the child's interests.

---

[37] Tobin, above n 26, 621.
[38] *RCB*, above n 22, [34].
[39] See comment of Bennett J in *State Central Authority & Best (No 2)* [2012] FamCA 511, that there exists 'a tension between the "exceptional circumstances" threshold in s 68L(3) and our national responsibilities under UNCRC as well as to conformity with the practice of other contracting states to the 1980 Convention in relation to a requirement to hear children, directly or indirectly, or permit their interests to be represented.'

D. Children's Capacity, Participation and Representation

The rewritten judgment expressly refers to the development of the principle of meaningful participation of children, citing changes in our understanding in relation to children's capacity to participate and the benefits they derive therefrom. Furthermore, it is pointed out that the legislative requirement to ascertain children's views must assume that children are capable of expressing their views.

It might have gone further and clarified that the right of children to have their interests represented properly is wider than the right to participate, as explained above. This means that it may be necessary to order separate representation even where the child has already been given a right to express his views directly to the judge, and sometimes even in cases where the child is not old enough to express his views.

E. Potential Impact

The rewritten judgment could be expected to have a broader impact than simply allowing for a wide interpretation of the 'exceptional circumstances' threshold for appointing independent lawyers in Abduction Convention cases in Australia. Its main significance lies in its express statements about the need to apply that Convention in a way which protects children's rights and complies with the obligations of the state under the CRC. This marks a departure from the approach of the Australian High Court in previous cases which, although taking a liberal approach to the Abduction Convention, focuses on procedural fairness to the adults involved.[40] In addition, the skepticism expressed about the Family Consultant's conclusions in relation to the older children's maturity sounds an important warning against taking a paternalistic approach to assessing children's capacity.[41] Finally, the clarification of the obligation of the independent lawyer to give serious weight to the views of mature children should impact on the role played by such lawyers in all types of family law proceedings and ensure that greater account is taken of children's perspectives by those who represent them.

---

[40] It is particularly striking that in the case of *Re De L* (1996) 187 CLR 640, the High Court's decision that separate representation should be ordered was based on the inaccurate directions given to the family consultant and the difficulties confronting the abducting mother in establishing that the children objected.
[41] See Schuz, above n 11, 324–25.

High Court of Australia

RCB as Litigation Guardian of EKV, CEV, CIV and LRV v The Honourable Justice Colin James Forrest

Simpson CJ (Delivering the judgment of the Court):

1. This case is primarily about the extent to, and the manner in, which we listen to children when making decisions that affect their lives. It is also about how the use of the Convention on the Civil Aspects of International Child Abduction ('the Hague Convention') reconciles the interests of children with the recognition of the orders of overseas courts as its main purpose.

The facts of this case

2. The case before the Court involves four children, aged from nine to 15. The father of the four girls is Italian and the mother is Australian. After the parents separated, they agreed to have joint custody of the children in Italy. In June 2010 their mother took her daughters to Australia telling the father that it was for a holiday. However, she did not return and the father then sought the return of the children to Italy under The Hague Convention. The Director-General of the former Queensland Department of Communities (Child Safety Services) applied to the Family Court for a return of the children under the Family Court (Child Abduction Convention) Regulations 1986 that implement the Convention in Australia.

3. In June 2011 the Family Court of Australia made an order for the return of the children to Italy and in May 2012, a warrant was issued that required the mother to deliver the children to an airport for that purpose. The mother applied for the discharge of that order but this was dismissed. The maternal aunt of the children then applied to this Court as the children's litigation guardian for the discharge of the return order. In late May 2012 a single judge of this Court referred the matter to the Full Court. The central ground for the application to this Court was that the children were denied procedural fairness in that they were denied separate legal representation in the process that determined they be returned to Italy.

The relevant law

4. The Hague Convention states its objects as:

   a) to secure the prompt return of children wrongfully removed to or retained in any Contracting State; and

b)   to ensure that rights of custody and of access under the law of one Contracting State are effectively respected in the other Contracting States." (Hague Convention, article 1).

5.   Article 11 of the Convention also requires that judicial and administrative authorities 'shall act expeditiously in proceedings for the return of children.' The emphasis on the need to return children to their country of habitual residence leads to statements about the need for courts to avoid their usual inclination to conduct a close examination of the child's interests as the aim of the Convention is to have that done by the Courts of the country to which the child is being returned. (*De L v Director-General, NSW Department of Community Services* (1996) 187 CLR 640, at 648–49, citing John Eekelaar, 'International Child Abduction by Parents' (1982) 32 *University of Toronto Law Journal* 281 at 305). This concern with returning the child often leads to it being said that the paramount consideration in Hague Convention cases is not the best interests of the child (See *Director General of Family and Community Services & Davis* (1990) FLC ¶92-182).

6.   However, the Convention does provide that the interests and views of the child being returned may be considered in certain circumstances. This is reflected in the 1986 Regulations that give effect to the terms of the Convention in Australia. These regulations embody the principles of the Convention with respect to the desirability of returning the child to the country of habitual residence in order to resolve any disputes about their care and welfare. But the regulations also set out the qualifications (also present in the Convention) to that obligation. Regulation 16(3), inter alia, provides that a court may refuse to order the return of a child where 'there is a grave risk that the return of the child under the Convention would expose the child to physical or psychological harm or otherwise place the child in an intolerable situation' (Regulation 16(3)(b)), or 'the child objects to being returned' and 'the child's objection shows a strength of feeling beyond the mere expression of a preference or of ordinary wishes' (Regulation 16(3)(c)) or 'the return of the child would not be permitted by the fundamental principles of Australia relating to the protection of human rights and fundamental freedoms.'(Regulation 16(3)d)).

7.   The Convention clearly has aims that are in tension with each other. On the one hand there is the aim of the return of children to the jurisdiction in which they habitually reside for matters about their care to be determined in the courts of that jurisdiction. This is where the Convention can be said to be about respecting the capacity and appropriateness of the home jurisdiction to properly determine the child's best interests as well as not 'rewarding' the abductor by having the courts of the country to which they have been removed decide their interests. On the other hand, the law also contains provisions that prevent a return order where this would be against the welfare interests of the child. As Kirby J acknowledged in *De L*:

It is not strictly correct to say that the Convention is an exception to the usual concern of our law for the welfare or best interests of a child. What the Convention, reflected by the regulations, has done is to recognise that it is in the best interests of children of a class not to be subjected to the turmoil and emotional divisiveness of international child abduction. (*De L v Director-General, NSW Department of Community Services* (1996) 187 CLR 640 at 684).

8.   The exceptions to the requirement to return a child are narrowly drawn so as not to undermine the purpose of the Convention. However, the narrowness of those exceptions is not in issue in this case. What this Court is being asked to do is to decide whether the appli-

cability of those exceptions to the making of a return order can be properly determined without the legal representation of the child.

9.   In this case, the central issue relates to that part of the Convention (and regulations) which justifies non-return of a child to its home jurisdiction where 'the child objects to being returned and has attained an age and degree of maturity at which it is appropriate to take account of its views.'(Article 13 and Regulation 16(3)(c)(iii)). The importance of this provision is that it is a clear recognition of the possibility of the child's views in the process, and that those views are a matter for proper inquiry in the process. In the case before us the ages of the children range from nine to 15. The participation of children in legal processes that directly affect them is an important principle as it ensures that the ultimate decision maker has properly informed themselves of all relevant views. It also relies on a view of the child that accepts that as they develop they become more able to express their views (see *Gillick v West Norfolk and Wisbech Area Health Authority and the Department of Health and Social Security* [1986] AC 112, especially per Lord Scarman). In addition, to exclude the views of the child may also inhibit their development into autonomous and socially engaged adults.

Recent developments that impact on the process in Hague Convention cases

10.   There have been many developments in how the law thinks about children and family life since the drafting of the Hague Convention. While the idea of children's rights is not new, we now have a much more sophisticated understanding than we did in the past of the capacity and resilience of children that supports their inclusion in processes which impact on their lives. With respect to family life, our understanding of the reality of family violence and the difficulties that families face in their everyday lives is now more understood in the law. We are also a more mobile society, which further adds to the complexity of family relationships.

11.   In the UK Supreme Court decision in *E (Children) (FC)* [2011] UKSC 27, Lady Hale and Lord Wilson commented on the changing nature of Hague Convention cases as having moved away from the concern at the time of its creation about 'a dissatisfied parent who did not have the primary care of the child snatching the child away from her primary carer.' ([2011] UKSC 27at paragraph 7).

> Nowadays, however, the most common case is a primary carer whose relationship with the other parent has broken down and who leaves with the children, usually to go back to her own family. There are many more international relationships these days than there were even in the 1970s when the Convention was negotiated, so increasingly returning to her own family means crossing an international boundary. International travel is also much easier and cheaper …

> It is also common for such abducting parents to claim that the parental relationship has broken down because of domestic abuse and ill-treatment by the other parent … Critics of the Convention have claimed that the courts are too ready to ignore these claims, too reluctant to acknowledge the harm done to children by witnessing violence between their parents, and too willing to accept that the victim, if she is a victim, will be adequately protected in the courts of the requesting country: see, for example, M Kaye, 'The Hague Convention and the Flight from Domestic Violence: How Women and Children are being returned by Coach and Four' (1999) 13 Int J Law, Policy and Family 191 … [paragraph 7].

12.   Hague Convention cases are often about the very real needs of children to be protected from harm. Such claims cannot be simply taken at face value and require proper investigation by the court. Yet the aim of returning the child promptly to their place of habitual residence for the courts of that country to determine the child's ongoing care needs may then also involve placing the child back into the care of an abusive parent. In such cases what are the risks of not listening directly to the children involved?

Development of children's rights

13.   The increased awareness of the manner in which the exclusion of children from legal processes that impact their lives can prevent their interests being articulated properly underpins the development of children's rights in international law and in Australian family law. As a community we have become more aware of the capacity of children to participate in the legal process rather than to draw generalisations about their incapacity (See eg Australian Law Reform Commission *Seen and heard: priority for children in the legal process* (ALRC Report 84, 1997), paragraph 4.4–4.9). A children's rights approach aims to place the interests of children more centrally in the relevant process. For example, article 3(1) of the United Nations Convention on the Rights of the Child (UNCRC) provides: 'In all actions concerning children, whether undertaken by public or private social welfare institutions, courts of law, administrative authorities or legislative bodies, the best interests of the child shall be a primary consideration.'

14.   Article 12 of UNCRC provides that 'the child who is capable of forming his or her own views has the right to express those views freely in all matters affecting the child, the views of the child being given due weight in accordance with the age and maturity of the child.' To achieve this 'the child shall in particular be provided the opportunity to be heard in any judicial and administrative proceedings affecting the child, either directly, or through a representative or an appropriate body, in a manner consistent with the procedural rules of national law.' (UNCRC, Article 12(2)).

15.   The Family Law Act now also makes specific reference to giving effect to the UNCRC as an object in children's proceedings (Family Law Act 1975 (Cth), section 60B(4)). Section 60B, for example, emphasises the rights of children with respect to knowing their parents, spending time with their parents, grandparents and other significant persons, and their right to enjoy their culture. Section 60CC(3) which deals with how a court is to determine the best interests of a child, begins with the need to consider 'any views expressed by the child and any factors (such as the child's maturity or level of understanding) that the court thinks are relevant to the weight it should give to the child's views.' Section 60CD(2) states that a child's views can be expressed by a report to the court by a family consultant, through an independent children's lawyer or in any other manner the court thinks appropriate.

16.   These provisions rest on a substantially different view of the child from that which prevailed in past years. Long gone is the notion that a child should be seen but not heard, and it has been replaced with the requirement that a child's views are to be *expressed* and *considered*. Such a legal requirement must be taken seriously and can only rest on the understanding that children are capable of so expressing their views whether to a report writer under section 68CD(2)(a), to an independent children's lawyer under section 68CD(2)(b), or in some cases even directly to the judge. This does not mean of course that the child's

views or wishes are simply given effect to, or that a report writer or a children's lawyer may not put other views of the child's interests to the court. What it does mean is that the child's views play a central part in the process in family law. Of course, there is often a legitimate concern to protect children from the stress and trauma of the legal process. But we must also be careful not to impose a form of paternalism that in effect prevents the voice of children being heard in a way that prevents an informed decision being made. However, legal representation of the child is not the only way to achieve this aim. The various ways in which the child's views and interests can be ascertained, described above, suggest that the particular approach will depend on the child and specifics of each case.

Does procedural fairness require a child to be legally represented in Hague Convention cases?

17.   I come now to the central issue in this case. Section 111B of the Family Law Act 1975 (Cth) and the Family Law (Child Abduction Convention) Regulations which implement the Hague Convention in Australian law provide for judicial proceedings to determine cases brought under that process. This means that they must adhere to the principles of procedural fairness. But do those principles require a child to be legally represented?

18.   Section 68L of the Family Law Act governs the appointment of the independent representation of the child's interests. This section provides for the appointment by the Family Court of a lawyer to independently represent the interests of a child in proceedings if it appears to the court that ought to occur (section 68L(1)). However, under section 68L(3) where the proceedings relate to matters under section 111B, that is Hague Convention cases, the court may only order that the child be independently represented by a lawyer 'if the court considers there are exceptional circumstances that justify doing so' (section 68L(3)(a)) and 'must specify those circumstances in making the order.' (section 68L(3)(b)).

19.   The role of the independent children's lawyer is not to represent the child but to represent the interests of the child. Section 68LA requires the independent children's lawyer to '(a) form an independent view, based on the evidence available to the independent children's lawyer, of what is in the best interests of the child; and (b) act in relation to the proceedings in what the independent children's lawyer believes to be the best interests of the child.' (section 68LA (2)). Sub-section 68LA (4) also makes it clear that the independent children's lawyer 'is not the child's legal representative' and 'is not obliged to act on the child's instructions in relation to the proceedings.' However, to suggest that this is based on the child's incapacity and lack of maturity would be mistaken. Clearly, family law cases deal with children at various stages of development. The case before us is concerned with the lives of four children who range from nine to 15 years of age. To suggest that a child of 15 would be expected to lack any insight into their circumstances because of a lack of maturity seems fanciful at best. On the other hand, a child of nine may well be at a different stage with respect to their level of understanding of what should happen to them. It is important to stress that children of any age, however, must have the right to participate in legal processes that affect them in a way that is meaningful for them.

20.   There is nothing in section 68LA to prevent the independent children's lawyer from forming the view that the child's interests are best served by putting before the court what the child wishes to occur. Section 69L(4) provides that the independent children's lawyer 'is not *obliged* to act on the child's instructions in relation to the proceedings.' To not permit

the independent child lawyer from putting to the court the child's views of what should happen to them would make a mockery of the 'best interests of the child' principle as there must be many cases where the child's views reflect his or her best interests. In addition, the independent lawyer cannot establish the child's best interests without ascertaining his or her views.

21.   The importance of this discussion is that an argument that procedural fairness requires the child to be legally represented may fail if there exists other means to establish the child's best interests. In the decision of this Court in *De L* (1996) 187 CLR 640 this Court acknowledged that reports from court counsellors (now family consultants) can be used to ascertain the views of the child, but that there is also a need to ensure that such evidence is properly focused on the issues before the court in a Hague Convention case, viz, the reasons for refusing an order under regulation 16. As this Court observed, the provision of separate legal representation of a child in such cases does not necessarily hinder the aim of the Convention to have the child returned promptly, but may assist that process. The Court also observed that:

> 'Prompt listing for hearing is one thing; an over-hasty and insufficient hearing is another ... Further, there may be cases where, consistent with those precepts, some, even if restricted, cross-examination upon affidavits is appropriate to assist the court to reach a decision whether to refuse an order for the return of the child.' (*De L* (1996) 187 CLR 640 per Brennan CJ, Dawson, Toohey, Gaudron, McHugh and Gummow JJ, at pages 660–61).

22.   In *De L* this Court decided that a child objecting to being returned, with a degree of maturity to express that view, should ordinarily be separately represented. Section 68L was subsequently amended to restrict the appointment of an independent children's lawyer only where there were 'exceptional circumstances'. It has been argued that this operates to impose a severe restriction on when a child may be legally represented in Hague Convention cases, even though the Act is silent as to what constitutes 'exceptional circumstances'.

23.   A close reading of the decision in *De L* indicates that this Court did not suggest that separate legal representation of a child should be the norm. In that case children with a degree of maturity had expressed an objection to being returned to the United States. Under section 111B(1) of the Act an objection by the child cannot be taken into account 'unless the objection imports a strength of feeling beyond the mere expression of a preference or of ordinary wishes.' The need for a strong feeling against being returned may require careful consideration, including close cross-examination of the evidence of the family consultant. In such cases the skills of an independent children's lawyer to assist the court in determining that issue would be important. Thus, once the child's objections are raised as a real issue in the case, there would appear to be sufficient grounds to justify the conclusion that there are exceptional circumstances such that would support the appointment of an independent children's lawyer under section 68L. Kirby J in *De L* even suggested that the need to appoint a lawyer for the children is by definition exceptional:

> If the judge is uncertain, from anything that appears in the evidence, including the counsellor's report, he or she would be entitled to secure relevant information by such other means as was thought appropriate. In a proper case, the judge might interview the child concerned. In an exceptional case, the judge might require that the child, or children, have separate legal representation. (*De L* (1996) 187 CLR 640, per Kirby J, at page 688).

24.   Importantly, he also noted that ultimately the discretion of the judge must prevail as to how to proceed:

> So long as the judge keeps clearly in mind the limited purpose of the jurisdiction conferred, the ordinary way in which the Regulations and the Convention are expressed to operate and the need for a clear and compelling case to sustain an objection which permits an exception to the ordinary duty to order the return of the child, it can be left to the judges to deal with individual cases as the evidence requires. (*De L* (1996) 187 CLR 640, per Kirby J, at pages 688–89).

25.   Given these observations one may ask what the addition of the need for 'exceptional circumstance' in section 68L before an independent children's lawyer may be appointed actually achieves. In *De L*, it was the exceptional circumstances of a child with some maturity possibly having an objection to being returned that led to the conclusion in that case that separate representation should have been ordered to ascertain that issue. In other words, the court was in effect identifying exceptional circumstances. However, this Court would also observe that given the importance now placed on the participation of children in the legal process and that in certain cases this may be best achieved by the appointment of an independent children's lawyer, then to the extent that section 68L seeks to limit such appointments, it is a provision that appears to be inconsistent with universal norms of children's rights and should be revisited by the Parliament.

What does procedural fairness require in this case?

26.   In this case a psychologist commissioned by the mother prepared a report based on interviews with the four children. The report stated that three of the children wished to stay in Australia and return for holidays and the fourth child was content to return to Italy. Forrest, J also directed a family consultant to prepare a report for the court. This report addressed whether the children objected to being returned to Italy. It stated that all the children wished to remain in Australia with their mother and that their father had been violent towards them and had used inappropriate physical disciplining. They also said they would go back to Italy if their mother came with them.

27.   The report writer described the children's objections as 'age-appropriate' and 'based on their own views.' She then said that the two younger children 'lacked cognitive sophistication for their views to be taken into consideration fully.' She said that the two older children 'had reached a more advanced degree of maturity' but was of the opinion that 'their ability for abstract thought and future forecasting would not have been fully formed.' She concluded that 'they would lack the ability to truly predict what impact their choices or views would have for their future relationship with their father.'

28.   The issue for this Court is whether such a report is a proper and adequate way of ascertaining the views of the child, or whether the appointment of a lawyer to represent the children's interests is necessary to meet this requirement.

29.   While family consultants provide an important and essential service to the operation of the family law courts this does not mean that the use of their reports is unproblematic. We know that judgements contained in psychological and social work reports about the needs and interests of children can be affected by various biases in the report writer, be they cultural, racial, gender or otherwise. (See, for example, Australian Human Rights

Commission *Bringing Them Home: Report of the National Inquiry into the Separation of Aboriginal and Torres Strait Islander Children from Their Families* (1997), page 479).

30.   In this case the report refers to the two older children having 'a more advanced degree of maturity' but 'that their ability for abstract thought and future forecasting would not have been fully formed.' With the greatest respect to the family consultant I find considerable difficulty with the concept of 'future forecasting'. To the extent it implies being able to see into the future, I doubt that this is an attribute that many adults possess (if any). Nor am I convinced that a fully formed ability for abstract thought is something that all mature adults possess let alone children. Family Court judges often refer to the subjectivity and difficulty involved in the task of predicting the impact of their decisions and so, on what basis do we expect of children 'the ability to truly predict what impact their choices or views would have for their future relationship[s]'?

31.   The problem this Court sees in the report of the family consultant is that the law clearly accepts that some children will have the maturity to make the objections they must make to justify no order for return being made. The wording of the family consultant's report suggests that a child may never be able to make that judgement. It is important to note that the eldest child in this case was 15 years old. She was less than one year away from being outside the jurisdiction of The Hague Convention when the law accepts that such a child will be making their own decisions about where they live. While it is true that each case must be decided with reference to the particular children and their individual level of maturity, it would have been a fair question to put to the family consultant in this case at what age and level of maturity the child must be in order to make their own judgements in such matters. Additionally, it might also have been asked whether the family consultant considered that the allegation of family violence made by the children gave rise to a mature response in terms of not wanting to return to Italy. As far as who should put such questions the only conclusion that this Court can reach is that a lawyer appointed to represent the children's interests would be the appropriate person to do so. While we respect the skills of the family consultant we must also respect the skills of independent children's lawyers to cross-examine witnesses on matters that go to the interests of children.

32.   It is not disputed that once a child objects to being returned to their country of habitual residence under The Hague Convention procedural fairness requires that this matter be investigated by the court making the determination under the Convention. But the question of what is procedurally fair to all parties involved—including centrally the children involved—must be assessed against the context of the evolution of children's rights in the last 30 years. This evolution has been one that has recognised the centrality of the child's interests in matters that affect them and the development of the principle that children should meaningfully participate in proceedings that determine what will happen to them.

33.   It has been put to us that the question of procedural fairness in this case is essentially a practical one. The problem in approaching the matter in this way is that matters of practicality often disguise the reality of competing principles. In Hague Convention cases the perceived practicality of a prompt return of the children is in fact the upholding of a set of principles about where the long-term interests of the children should be determined. While this may be a fair principle to uphold, there is clearly the competing principle that the child's immediate situation may require a decision to ensure the child's protection. Beyond that, there is the principle that the inclusion of children in the process ensures their long-

term interests as autonomous individuals. Recognition of a strong objection to return by the child in the Convention itself as a ground to refuse return is clearly an acceptance that children have some autonomous rights.

34.   As Kirby J in *De L* said, the process should not be 'over-hasty and insufficient.' The provision of legal representation for the child is not inconsistent with the need for promptness in Convention cases. The importance of the need to ensure the child's participation in the process is part of the matter that goes to the determination of the strength of their objection to return. This also goes to the matter of what is procedurally fair in the case.

35.   Reliance on the family consultant's report to satisfy this requirement was clearly insufficient in this case. The children objected to being returned to Italy and cited reasons for this view that must be of central concern to any court deciding where a child will live. For the reasons noted above in relation to the discussion of section 68L these were clearly exceptional circumstances such that would justify the making of an order for the appointment of an independent children's lawyer. While we do not question that the family consultant aimed to act in the interests of the children in the preparation of the report, the children were entitled to have that report's veracity and reliability tested in the proceedings by someone skilled in cross-examination in the context of children's proceedings. This means that a lawyer should have been appointed to represent the children's interests and the failure to do so means that the children did not receive procedural fairness.

Conclusion

36.   The application is granted and the matter is returned to the Family Court to be reheard in accordance with the directions above, which means the children must be legally represented.

28

Commentary on *Povse v Austria*

RUTH LAMONT

Povse v Austria[1] provided the opportunity for two European supranational courts, the Court of Justice of the European Union (CJEU) and the European Court of Human Rights (ECtHR), to consider the protection of children's rights by the legal framework governing international child abduction, and its effect on Sofia, a child born in Italy and unlawfully moved to Austria by her mother. The case was heard first in the CJEU as a preliminary reference on a point of interpretation of EU law on child abduction under the Brussels II*a* Regulation.[2] Enforcement of an order to return Sofia from Austria to Italy was then subject to an application to the ECtHR, alleging return would breach both the child's and her mother's Article 8 right to respect for their private and family life under the European Convention on Human Rights and Fundamental Freedoms 1950 (ECHR). This commentary encompasses both the judgment of the CJEU and the ECtHR to provide a critique of the constitutional arrangements between the two supranational courts for the effective protection of children's rights, accepted as a limitation by Lara Walker in her re-written ECtHR judgment.

The ECtHR refers to the ECHR to determine whether signatory States' actions have breached individual rights. The ECHR is not explicitly a children's rights document, but the ECtHR will attach particular importance to the best interests of the child within the scope of Article 8.[3] The EU has its own fundamental rights document, the Charter of Fundamental Rights of the European Union,[4] to which the CJEU refers, along with the ECHR, in interpreting EU law.[5] In contrast to the ECHR, the Charter contains specific provision for the protection of children's rights. Under Article 24, children's views shall be taken into consideration on matters concerning them, in accordance with their age and maturity; in all actions relating to children the child's best interests must be a primary consideration; and every child has the right to maintain a relationship with both parents unless contrary to the child's best interests. When called upon to review the actions of an EU Member State in implementing EU law for compliance with the rights expressed in the ECHR, in *Bosphorus*[6]

---

[1] *Povse v Austria* [2014] 1 FLR 944.
[2] Reg 2201/2003 concerning jurisdiction and the recognition and enforcement of judgments in matrimonial matters and the matters of parental responsibility, [2003] OJ L338/1.
[3] *Johansen v Norway* (1997) 23 EHRR 33.
[4] [2000] OJ C364/1.
[5] Art 52(3), Charter states that where the rights correspond, the meaning and scope of Charter rights are the same as the Convention right.
[6] *Bosphorus v Ireland* (2006) 42 EHRR 1, para 103.

the ECtHR has found the system of rights protection provided by the EU to be equivalent to the Convention system. Member States implementing EU law are deemed compliant with the rights expressed in the ECHR unless there is evidence that the protection provided was manifestly deficient.

I. The Dispute in *Povse*

The child, Sophia, was born in Italy where she lived with her Italian father, MA, and Austrian mother, Doris. Following allegations of violence made against MA, the mother removed Sofia to Austria, in breach of MA's rights of custody. The removal of a child to another state in breach of the rights of custody of another parent constitutes abduction. The Hague Convention on the Civil Aspects of International Child Abduction 1980 provides a remedy of returning the child to the state from which they were removed under Article 12. This is subject to exceptions, including that the child will be placed at grave risk of harm if they are returned. Brussels IIa governs recognition and enforcement of parental responsibility judgments and child abduction, adopting the Convention return remedy but amending its operation. It creates an additional procedural layer when the return of the child is initially refused. Under Articles 11(6)–(8), the court of the state from which the child was unlawfully removed, in this case Italy, may be petitioned to hear substantive custody proceedings and issue a full welfare judgment which may entail the return of the child, despite the initial refusal. If the issuing court certifies that it has heard from the child and the parties, the judgment entailing return is automatically enforceable under Article 42, Brussels IIa. There are no defences to recognition of the judgment; the authorities of the state to which the child was removed must enforce return.

Povse demonstrates the difficulties of these processes in practice. Sofia was removed from Italy to Austria in February 2008. MA had contact with Sofia in Austria on 15 occasions up to 2009. He began proceedings for the return of Sofia to Italy in June 2008. The Austrian court refused Sofia's return to Italy in January 2009 on the ground that she would face a grave risk of psychological harm under Article 13(b), Hague Convention 1980. Following the rejection of his return application, in April 2009, MA made a further application to the Venice Youth Court under Article 11(8), Brussels IIa for a substantive custody hearing in relation to Sofia. The mother had counsel at the hearing and made written submissions. The Venetian courts should have considered Sofia's best interests under Italian national law on the custody of children and the substantive content of the Venetian Youth Court's decision on custody was not directly disputed. The July 2009 judgment ordered Sofia's return to Italy to live with her mother, and having contact with her father. If Doris did not return to Italy, Sofia was to live with her father.

The Venice court certified this judgment for automatic enforcement in Austria under Article 42, Brussels IIa. In September 2009, MA requested enforcement of the return order in Austria. This should have ensured that Sofia was sent back to Italy, even if her mother refused to travel with her. However, the Austrian courts felt that the risks posed to Sofia by return to Italy remained. In April 2010, the Austrian Supreme Court requested a preliminary reference from the CJEU concerning the interpretation of Brussels IIa in these circumstances.

II. CJEU Preliminary Reference

Once the Venetian court certified the custody judgment, under the terms of Brussels II*a*, the Austrian court was obligated to enforce the return of Sofia to Italy. However, given significant changes in Sofia's family circumstances, the Austrian court referred the case to the CJEU to establish whether enforcement of the judgment to return Sofia could be refused.[7] The Austrian court was concerned that, if it could not refuse enforcement of the judgment under Brussels II*a*, Sofia would be returned to Italy, experiencing very serious disruption of her family life in Austria.

The CJEU's judgment clarified that, because the Italian courts retained jurisdiction, the subsequent judgment on custody of the child in Austria could not preclude the enforcement of the Italian judgment entailing the return of the child. Even where the child's circumstances had changed after the Italian judgment was issued and certified for enforcement, the proper remedy was to petition the Italian court to suspend the enforcement. The CJEU stated that Brussels II*a* protected the child's right to maintain a personal relationship and direct contact with both parents under Article 24, Charter. This took 'precedence over any disadvantage which moving might entail.'[8] However, this does not engage with the balance between the right of the child to contact with both parents and the requirement that decisions be taken with the child's best interests as a primary consideration.[9] The judgment reflects the overall approach of the EU in addressing children's rights by encouraging the adaptation of rights to fit with the European legal framework, even if the incorporation of rights is somewhat uncomfortable and poorly articulated.[10]

The Austrian court had identified that the change in circumstances caused by the substantial time delays had affected the child's best interests. This consideration was treated by the CJEU as a purely procedural issue concerning which court to petition regarding the enforceability of the judgment. The CJEU adopts a legitimate, textual approach to interpreting Brussels II*a*, but does not address the question of whether the child's best interests were adversely affected by the actual structure of jurisdiction and enforcement of judgment rules in the Regulation. The decision on custody is a matter for Italian law if that court holds jurisdiction, but procedural issues such as identifying the correct jurisdiction is also a decision to be made with the best interests of the child as a primary consideration.[11] The effect of procedural processes on this particular child, and the practical and financial difficulties of petitioning the Italian court to address the point of change in circumstances, was not considered. The capacity of the Regulation to secure the child's best interests is assumed by the CJEU, and indeed the Regulation is regarded as providing increased protection for the interests of the child.[12]

---

[7] Case C-211/10 PPU *Povse v Alpago* ECLI:EU:C:2010:400.

[8] ibid, para 63.

[9] R Lamont, 'Article 24 of the Charter of Fundamental Rights of the European Union' in S Peers and others (eds), *The EU Charter of Fundamental Rights* (Oxford, Hart Publishing, 2014).

[10] H Stalford, *Children and the European Union: Rights, Welfare and Accountability* (Oxford, Hart Publishing, 2012).

[11] Committee on the Rights of Children 'General Comment No 14 on the right of the child to have his or her best interests taken as a primary consideration' 2013, para 17.

[12] *Povse*, above n 7, para 60.

There is evidence that the abduction provisions of Brussels II*a* are not being correctly used in practice and, in particular, that certificates issued by courts to ensure automatic enforceability of judgments are not properly scrutinised.[13] In the majority of cases the child does not return, even if the state from which they were abducted orders their return following a substantive judgment on custody considering the child's best interests under Article 11(8). The effect of these provisions, as demonstrated by *Povse*, could be traumatic for the individual child if they were enforced.

III. ECtHR Judgment

The CJEU's judgment re-affirmed the enforceability of the Italian judgment in Austria, irrespective of the delay and change in circumstances affecting Sofia. In November 2011 the Venice court awarded sole custody of Sofia to MA and ordered Sofia's return to her father in Italy. Doris did not appeal against this judgment in Italy. Doris and Sofia subsequently petitioned the ECtHR alleging that enforcement by Austria of the custody judgment returning Sofia to Italy would constitute a breach of Article 8 ECHR.[14] The order was not enforced and, when the ECHR petition was decided, Sofia still remained in Austria where she had lived for five years.

The effect of *Bosphorus* and the principle of equivalent protection form the essence of the judgment in *Povse*. Both the Brussels II*a* Regulation and judgment of the CJEU are assumed by the ECtHR to be compliant with the rights expressed in the ECHR. In enforcing the judgment for return, the Austrian court was complying with the strict obligations of EU law, in which it has no discretion, and therefore Austria was not in breach of the Convention.[15]

The decision of *Bosphorus* meant that ECtHR scrutiny of the decision to return the child and the structures of Brussels II*a* were heavily circumscribed. The ECtHR acknowledges that the enforcement of the return order itself is a breach of Article 8[16] in affecting the family life of the abducting parent and child, but justifiable and proportionate under Article 8(2) ECHR to secure the right to family life and rights of custody of the left behind parent. However, in *Povse*, the ECtHR adopts the approach of the CJEU in suggesting that it is for the Italian courts to protect the fundamental rights of the parties and these should be asserted in Italy.[17] The protection of children's rights is restricted to an assessment of where rights may be considered, rather than interrogating whether the procedural legal framework itself is compliant with Article 8. The ECtHR fails to consider either the effect of the enforcement of the return order on Sofia, or the potential limitations on the protection of children's rights provided by Brussels II*a*.

---

[13] P Beaumont, L Walker and J Holliday, 'Conflicts of EU Courts on Child Abduction: The Reality of Article 11(6)–(8) Brussels II*a* Proceedings across the EU' (2016) 12 *Journal of Private International Law* 211, 251.

[14] *Povse v Austria*, above n 1.

[15] ibid, para 77.

[16] *Maumousseau v France* (2010) 52 EHRR 35.

[17] *Povse v Austria*, above n 1, para 86.

IV. Re-writing the ECtHR Judgment

The re-written, alternative ECtHR judgment accepts the constitutional arrangements between the two supranational courts created by the decision in *Bosphorus*. In approaching her judgment, Walker has two options.

The ECtHR in the original judgment ruled that there was no breach of the child's Article 8 right in the enforcement of the return order, and that any petition regarding change of the child's circumstances should be addressed to the Italian court. However, the evolution in Sofia's family life, including the lack of contact with her father since 2009, her inability to speak Italian and her stable family relationships in Austria, meant that the expectation of return was unrealistic. In these circumstances the legal framework was inflexible and unresponsive, but the ECtHR chose not to review the legal framework or the effect return would have on the child.

By contrast, Walker concludes that there was a breach of Article 8 in enforcing a judgment returning the child on the particular facts of the case. The enforcement of the Italian order to return in the circumstances is deemed a disproportionate method of protecting the father's Article 8 rights, infringing the child's best interests to an unacceptable degree. The system of return and enforcement in Brussels IIa is not questioned in this approach, as this is subject to the *Bosphorus* shield and is not manifestly in breach of the Convention, but a personal and contextual analysis of Sofia's circumstances is conducted. Relying on the relatively controversial decision in *Neulinger*,[18] where the ECtHR ruled the return of an abducted child constituted a breach of Article 8 on the basis that the failure to consider the individual child's best interests as a primary consideration rendered return disproportionate, Walker deems the enforcement of the return order disproportionate because of the lapse of time. Practical and operational delays can cause a breach of the Convention[19] without affecting the underlying legal framework. However, this approach places Austria in the position of breaching the obligation under EU law to enforce the order. Whether an ECtHR judgment would act as a defence against such a breach is unclear.

As an alternative, Walker could have utilised the *Bosphorus* formula and asserted that the Brussels IIa provisions governing abduction cases may represent a manifest breach of the child's Article 8 right.[20] Had she adopted this approach, she would have had to suggest that the combined operation of Articles 11 and 42 Brussels IIa mean that the child's best interests were not effectively protected in the enforcement of a custody judgment entailing return. This approach is less feasible since, in effect, the ECtHR would be undermining the entire legal framework surrounding child abduction in the EU by questioning the capacity of the mechanism in Article 11, Brussels IIa to consistently protect the child's Article 8 ECHR rights. The CJEU had considered the protection of children's rights in its judgment on *Povse*, and asserted that the resumption of the relationship between Sofia and MA was in Sofia's best interests and secured by the enforcement of the judgment of return. The ECtHR

---

[18] *Neulinger v Switzerland* (2012) 54 EHRR 31.
[19] *Deak v UK* (2008) 47 EHRR 50.
[20] The ECtHR has subsequently accepted this possibility in the context of mutual recognition of a commercial judgment, see *Avontins v Latvia* (2017) 64 EHRR 2.

would be replacing the CJEU's judgment with a different interpretation of the protection of Sofia's rights. The weaknesses in protecting the child's rights in this case perhaps lie in the CJEU, rather than in the ECtHR.

V. Supranational Courts and Children's Rights Protection

The judgment in *Povse* demonstrates the constraints on supranational courts as protectors of children's rights, restricted both by their constitutional architecture and reasoning, and potentially by the form of proceedings. The modes of representation of children's interests in the supranational courts are difficult as the dispute gains both geographical and legal distance from the child. Elevating a legal decision from the national context affects the representation and active participation of children in the legal process, especially under the EU's preliminary reference procedure, which is solely concerned (in theory) with interpretation of legislation and does not contemplate hearing the child in proceedings.[21] The risk of elevating disputes is that the context and real lives of children are lost in the decision-making process, and particularly in the judgment. *Povse* demonstrated that, where the child has not been promptly returned, the retention of jurisdiction by the court of origin, combined with the automatic enforcement of a custody judgment entailing return under Article 11(8), is likely to create a situation where the child's family and social life will be severely and harmfully disrupted.

The effect of *Bosphorus* is to shield EU law from full review by the ECtHR. Article 6, Treaty on European Union provides competence for EU accession to the ECHR, but the CJEU has disrupted this process.[22] If accession is achieved, it has been suggested a more intensive form of review by the ECtHR would develop.[23] The reasoning and nature of the review conducted by the courts responsible for protecting children's rights is just as important as the scope of the rights themselves. Systems and legal structures also have to facilitate consideration of the child's best interests to ensure that the protection of children's rights through law is a realistic possibility.

---

[21] Consolidated Rules of Procedure of the Court of Justice of the European Union [2012] OJ L173.

[22] Opinion 2/13 *Accession of the European Union to the European Convention for the Protection of Human Rights and Fundamental Freedoms*, ECLI:EU:C:2014:2454.

[23] T Lock, 'The Future of the European Union's Accession to the European Convention on Human Rights after Opinion 2/13: is it Still Possible and is it Still Desirable?' (2015) 11 *European Constitutional Law Review* 239, 260.

European Court of Human Rights

Povse v Austria

The European Court of Human Rights (First Section), sitting as a chamber composed of Lara Walker and Judges U, V, W, X, Y and Z delivers the following judgment.

The Facts

1.   The first applicant, Ms Sofia Povse, born in 2006, is an Austrian and Italian national. The second applicant, Ms Doris Povse, born in 1976, is an Austrian national. The applicants live in Austria.

2.   The Austrian Government ('the Government') were represented by their Agent, Ambassador H Tichy, Head of the International Law Department of the Federal Ministry.

I. The Circumstances of the Case

3.   The facts of the case, as submitted by the parties, may be summarised as follows. The first applicant, Sofia, was born in Italy in December 2006, where she lived with the second applicant, her mother Doris, and her father MA, in MA's apartment. Under Italian law, Doris and MA have joint custody of Sofia. The relationship between MA and Doris deteriorated and there are allegations that MA allegedly inflicted violence on both Doris and Sofia. In February 2008, Doris removed Sofia to Austria, her home country, to live with her parents. In subsequent proceedings for Sofia's return to Italy under the Hague Abduction Convention 1980, the Austrian courts rejected MA's application because of the grave risk of psychological harm to Sofia if she was returned. Having previously had contact with Sofia in Austria, from June 2009, MA refused subsequent contact.

4.   MA issued proceedings in the Italian Venice Youth Court under Article 11(8), EU Regulation 2201/2003 (Brussels IIa) for custody of Sofia and her return to Italy. In July 2009, the Venice Youth Court held custody proceedings in relation to Sofia. Doris was represented at

this hearing but has no legal aid to pursue further proceedings in Italy. The Venice Youth Court ordered the return of Sofia to Italy with Doris with whom she was to live, and issued a certificate of automatic enforceability of the return order under Article 42, Brussels IIa to which there is no defence. In April 2010, the Austrian Supreme Court requested a preliminary reference from the Court of Justice of the European Union (CJEU) regarding the interpretation of Brussels IIa and the enforceability of the Venice Youth Court order to return Sofia to Italy. In July 2010, the CJEU issued a preliminary ruling (Case C-211/10 PPU) which stated that the judgment for the return of Sofia was automatically enforceable in Austria, and that any change in the child's circumstances must be pleaded in the Italian court to suspend operation of the judgment in the child's best interests. In November 2011, the Italian Venice Youth Court issued a new order which withdrew Doris's custody rights, awarded sole custody to MA, and required Sofia to live in Italy with her father. This order has not been enforced to date.

The Applicants' Current Family Situation

5.   Since their arrival in Austria in February 2008, Sofia has been living with Doris. In 2009 Doris entered into a relationship with a new partner. She gave birth to a son in March 2011. Doris, her new partner and the two children are living in a common household. It appears that Sofia does not speak Italian and has not seen her father since mid-2009. MA has refused to travel to Austria to facilitate contact with his child. Doris faces criminal charges in Italy for child abduction.

II. Relevant International Law, European Law and Domestic Law

The Hague Convention on the Civil Aspects of Child Abduction of 25 October 1980

Article 12

Where a child has been wrongfully removed or retained in terms of Article 3 and, at the date of the commencement of the proceedings before the judicial or administrative authority of the Contracting State where the child is, a period of less than one year has elapsed from the date of the wrongful removal or retention, the authority concerned shall order the return of the child forthwith. The judicial or administrative authority, even where the proceedings have been commenced after the expiration of the period of one year referred to in the preceding paragraph, shall also order the return of the child, unless it is demonstrated that the child is now settled in its new environment. Where the judicial or administrative authority in the requested State has reason to believe that the child has been taken to another State, it may stay the proceedings or dismiss the application for the return of the child.

Article 13

Notwithstanding the provisions of the preceding Article, the judicial or administrative authority of the requested State is not bound to order the return of the child if the person, institution or other body which opposes its return establishes that: …

(b) there is a grave risk that his or her return would expose the child to physical or psychological harm or otherwise place the child in an intolerable situation. The judicial or administrative authority may also refuse to order the return of the child if it finds that the child objects to being returned and has attained an age and degree of maturity at which it is appropriate to take account of its views. In considering the circumstances referred to in this Article, the judicial and administrative authorities shall take into account the information relating to the social background of the child provided by the Central Authority or other competent authority of the child's habitual residence.

Council Regulation (EC) No 2201/2003 of 27 November 2003

6.   The most relevant provisions are Articles 11(6)–(8), 42 and 47.

Article 11

6. If a court has issued an order on non-return pursuant to Article 13 of the 1980 Hague Convention, the court must immediately either directly or through its central authority, transmit a copy of the court order on non-return and of the relevant documents, in particular a transcript of the hearings before the court, to the court with jurisdiction or central authority of the Member State where the child was habitually resident immediately before the wrongful removal or retention, as determined by national law. The court shall receive all the mentioned documents within one month of the date of the non-return order.

7. Unless the courts in the Member State where the child was habitually resident immediately before the wrongful removal or retention have already been seized by one of the parties, the court or central authority that receives the information mentioned in paragraph 6 must notify it to the parties and invite them to make submission to the court, in accordance with national law, within three months of the date of notification so that the court can examine the question of custody of the child. Without prejudice to the rules on jurisdiction contained in this Regulation, the court shall close the case if no submissions have been received by the court within the time limit.

8. Notwithstanding a judgment of non-return pursuant to Article 13 of the 1980 Hague Convention, any subsequent judgment which requires the return of the child issued by a court having jurisdiction under this Regulation shall be enforceable in accordance with Section 4 of Chapter III below in order to secure the return of the child.

7.   Pursuant to Article 40(1)(b) of the Regulation, its section 4 applies to 'the return of a child entailed by a judgment given pursuant to Article 11 (8)'. Article 42 in section 4 provides as follows:

Article 42

1. The return of a child referred to in Article 40(1)(b) entailed by an enforceable judgment given in a Member State shall be recognised and enforceable in another Member State without the need for a declaration of enforceability and without any possibility of opposing its recognition if the judgment has been certified in the Member State of origin in accordance with paragraph 2. Even if national law does not provide for enforceability by operation of law, notwithstanding any appeal, of a judgment requiring the return of the child mentioned in Article 11(b)(8) the court of origin may declare the judgment enforceable.

2. The judge of origin who delivered the judgment referred to in Article 40(1)(b) shall issue the certificate referred to in paragraph 1 only if:

(a)   the child was given an opportunity to be heard, unless a hearing was considered inappropriate having regard to his or her age or degree of maturity;
(b)   the parties were given an opportunity to be heard; and

(c)   the court has taken into account in issuing its judgment the reasons for and evidence underlying the order issued pursuant to Article 13 of the 1980 Hague Convention. In the event that the court or any other authority takes measures to ensure the protection of the child after its return to the State of habitual residence, the certificate shall contain details of such measures. The judge of origin shall of his or her own motion issue that certificate using the standard form in Annex IV (certificate concerning the return of child(ren)). The certificate shall be completed in the language of the judgment."

Article 47

1. The enforcement procedure is governed by the law of the Member State of enforcement.

2. Any judgment delivered by a court of another Member State and declared to be enforceable in accordance with Section 2 or certified in accordance with Article 41(1) or Article 42(1) shall be enforced in the Member State of enforcement in the same conditions as if it had been delivered in that Member State. In particular, a judgment which has been certified according to Article 41(1) or Article 42(1) cannot be enforced if it is irreconcilable with a subsequent enforceable judgment.

Austrian Law Relating to the Enforcement of Custody Decisions

8.   The enforcement of custody decisions is based on section 110 of the Non-Contentious Proceedings Act (*Außerstreitgesetz*). This provision applies also to the enforcement of decisions under the Hague Convention and, according to the Supreme Court's case-law, to the enforcement of return orders under Article 11(8) of the Brussels IIa Regulation.

Section 110(1), taken in conjunction with section 79(2), provides for the imposition of fines or imprisonment as coercive measures for contempt of court. As more lenient measures the court may also reprimand a party or threaten to take coercive measures.

Section 110(2) allows for the use of reasonable direct coercion. Direct coercion may only be applied by court organs and is in practice entrusted to specially trained bailiffs.

Section 110(3) provides that the court may refrain from continuing with the enforcement if and as long as it constitutes a risk for the well-being of the minor.

9.   Before this Court, the Government of Austria has argued that in accordance with the CJEU ruling in Case C-211/10 PPU of 1 July 2010, that the Austrian courts were not entitled to rely on section 110(3) of the Non-Contentious Proceedings Act to review a return order on the merits or to examine whether there were reasons for granting a stay of enforcement, even if it was alleged that there had been a change in circumstances. It is exclusively within the competence of the courts of the State of origin to rule on a request for a stay of a return order given under Article 11(8) of the Brussels IIa Regulation.

Complaint

10.   Sofia and Doris have complained under Article 8 of the Convention that the Austrian courts' decisions have violated their right to respect for their family life. In particular, they have argued that the Austrian courts limited themselves to ordering the enforcement of the Italian court's return order and had not examined their argument that Sofia's return to Italy

would constitute a serious danger to her well-being and lead to the permanent separation of mother and child. They have submitted that Sofia has not had any meaningful contact with her father since mid-2009 and does not speak Italian, while her father does not speak German. Moreover, they claim that Doris would be unable to accompany Sofia to Italy or to exercise any access rights as criminal proceedings for child abduction are pending against her in Italy.

The applicants acknowledge that the position taken by the Austrian courts corresponded to the interpretation of Brussels II*a* expressed by the CJEU in its ruling of 1 July 2010 but assert that the Austrian courts' failure to examine their arguments against the enforcement of the return order nevertheless violates Article 8 of the Convention.

The Law

11.   The applicants have complained that the Austrian courts' decisions ordering the enforcement of the Italian courts' return order had violated their right to respect for their family life. They rely on Article 8 of the Convention, which, in so far as relevant, reads as follows:

1. Everyone has the right to respect for his private and family life, …

2. There shall be no interference by a public authority with the exercise of this right except such as is in accordance with the law and is necessary in a democratic society in the interests of national security, public safety or the economic well-being of the country, for the prevention of disorder or crime, for the protection of health or morals, or for the protection of the rights and freedoms of others.

The Court's Assessment

Was there an Interference?

12.   It is not in dispute that the decisions of the Austrian courts, ordering the enforcement of the Venice Youth Court's orders, interfered with the applicants' right to respect for their family life within the meaning of Article 8 of the Convention.

13.   Such interference violates Article 8 unless it is 'in accordance with the law', pursues one or more of the legitimate aims referred to in paragraph 2 of that Article, and is 'necessary in a democratic society' to achieve the aim or aims concerned.

Was the Interference in Accordance with the Law?

14.   In the present case the decisions ordering the enforcement of the Venice Youth Court's orders were based on Article 42 of the Brussels II*a* Regulation. The Regulation is directly applicable in Austrian law. However the mechanisms for enforcement and methods used are still a matter for national law, and Austria is obliged to enforce the decision in accordance with national law under Article 47 of Brussels II*a*. The Austrian law allows for the

reasonable use of coercion, but recognises that enforcement can be stopped where the child seriously resists enforcement and the coercion required would be harmful to the child (§ 8). This Court therefore concludes that the interference was 'in accordance with the law'.

Was the Interference Legitimate and Proportionate?

15.   The interference, which was aimed at reuniting Sofia with her father, pursued one of the legitimate aims set out in the second paragraph of Article 8, namely the protection of the rights of others, in this case the right of MA to have contact and a meaningful relationship with his child under Article 8. Furthermore, this Court has stated that compliance with EU law by a Contracting Party constitutes a legitimate general interest objective (see, *Bosphorus, Hava Yolları Turizm ve Ticaret Anonim Şirketi v Ireland* [GC], (no 45036/98, ECHR 2005-VI) § 150–51, and *Michaud v France*, no 12323/11, 6 December 2012) § 100). This Court has also held that the EU legal system creates an 'equivalent', or at least comparable protection of human rights to the ECHR system (see *Bosphorus*, cited above, § 155). Although this presumption is rebuttable, the *Bosphorus* presumption of 'equivalent' protection can only be departed from where the protection of the applicant's human rights is manifestly deficient (see *Bosphorus*, cited above, § 166). This presumption is even stronger where the case has already been decided by the Court of Justice of the European Union (CJEU), and this Court has particular regard to the role of the CJEU (see *Bosphorus*, cited above, §§ 160–65, and *Michaud*, cited above, §§ 106–11).

16.   Applying the *Bosphorus* principles in the present case, the Court reiterates that it has already found that the protection of fundamental rights afforded by the EU is equivalent to that of the ECHR system as regards both the substantive guarantees offered and the mechanisms controlling their observance. The Court also reiterates that the threshold for rebutting this presumption is exceptionally high. The Court has some concerns about the human rights protection afforded by national courts when applying Articles 11(6)–(8) Brussels IIa, particularly in relation to the protection of the best interests of the child under Article 24 of the European Charter on Fundamental Rights (the Charter) and Article 3 of the United Nations Convention on the Rights of the Child (UNCRC) both of which Member States are bound by (See *Šneersone and Kampanella v Italy*, no 14737/09, 12 July 2011). This application is made against Austria, rather than Italy, so the Court cannot assess the human rights protection afforded by the Italian courts. However, prima facie there is no manifest deficiency in the protection provided for by Brussels IIa because it provides for hearing the child, and the Charter provides a mechanism for protecting fundamental rights under EU law. The Court cannot assess whether the Venice Youth Court actually complied with these requirements in this hearing, but the Austrian courts were complying with Brussels IIa and the CJEU judgment in their decisions. Therefore the Court cannot conclude that the protection afforded to Sofia's or Doris's human rights by the Austrian authorities was manifestly deficient at any time. If the applicants wish to assert that there was a breach of Article 8 by the Italian courts, which would include a failure to hear Sofia, they must bring an application against Italy.

17.   However, the Court must look at the specific characteristics of each case when assessing the protection of the best interests of the child (see *Neulinger and Shuruk v Switzerland* (Application no 41615/07) § 138). This job is primarily for the domestic authorities where

they enjoy a certain margin of appreciation. However, the decisions authorities have taken in the exercise of their discretion remain subject to review by this Court (see, for example, *Hokkanen v Finland*, 23 September 1994, § 55, Series A no 299-A, and *Kutzner v Germany*, no 46544/99, ECHR 2002-I, §§ 65–66; see also *Tiemann v France and Germany* (dec), nos 47457/99 and 47458/99, ECHR 2000-IV; *Bianchi v Switzerland*, no 7548/04, § 77, 22 June 2006 § 92; and *Carlson v Switzerland*, no 49492/06, 6 November 2008 § 69). With regard to Sofia the Court considers that it is necessary to look beyond the initial enforcement of the original order to return in 2009, and the CJEU judgment of July 2010 falling within the *Bosphorus* presumption, to the realisation of the enforcement of the decision of November 2011 at the present time and whether this is proportionate under Article 8(2). The Court has previously, albeit in different circumstances, ruled that the subsequent enforcement of an order would result in a violation of Article 8 without assessing whether or not the order itself violated Article 8 (see *Neulinger and Shuruk v Switzerland*, cited above, § 151). In *Neulinger* there was excessive delay between the issuing of the decision and the decision of the Grand Chamber; the child had not seen his father for five years and the enforcement of the order was not in the child's best interests. When considering the excessively delayed enforcement of an order, it is not necessary to look at whether the judgments were manifestly deficient, but simply whether or not the enforcement of the order is, in the current circumstances, a proportionate response to protect MA's rights.

18.   It is now June 2013, almost four years after the first decision of the Venice Youth Court, which allowed Sofia to reside with her mother (albeit in Italy) and three years after the CJEU's confirmation that the first decision should be enforced. Within this four year period there has been a complete breakdown in the relationship between Sofia and her father. There is also no common language between Sofia and her father so at present they cannot communicate with each other. Any decision now must prioritise Sofia's best interests, which are protected by Article 8 ECHR, Article 3 of the UNCRC and Article 24 of the Charter, as a key factor. The best interests of the child is a primary consideration in all actions concerning children (see, to that effect, *Gnahoré v France*, no 40031/98, § 59, ECHR 2000-IX), and the Court will attach 'particular importance to the best interests of the child' (*Johansen v Norway* (App no 17383/90) 7 August 1996 § 78). In order to effectively prioritise Sofia's best interests the national court delivering further decisions regarding the upbringing of Sofia must determine Sofia's views.

19.   The best interests of the child have to be determined on a case-by-case basis. Where enforcement of a judgment relating to a child is to take place a substantial time after the order was made, actions in accordance with the judgment should only be taken if this is still in the child's best interests. Where a child has settled in a host country it is 'necessary to take into account the child's best interests and well-being, and in particular the seriousness of the difficulties which he or she is likely to encounter in the country of destination and the solidity of social, cultural and family ties both with the host country and with the country of destination.' (*Neulinger and Shuruk v Switzerland*, cited above § 146; *Emre v Switzerland*, no 42034/04, § 68, 22 May 2008). This should include the determination of Sofia's views on her circumstances, which are likely to be strong given that she has brought an application before this court and shown maturity. The child's best interests are a primary consideration of each court at all stages of the legal process.

20.   The Venice Youth Court's decision of November 2011, which required Sofia to live with her father, whom she no longer knows, exacerbated the situation further. The decision was taken to protect the relationship between Sofia and her father but, because of the delay and change in circumstances, the enforcement of the order for Sofia's return is not proportionate to the legitimate aim of protecting MA's right to family life. Enforcement will harm Sofia and therefore will not be in Sofia's best interests, breaching her own right to family life under Article 8. Further Article 11(6)–(8) proceedings are intended to be welfare proceedings, rather than summary proceedings for the return of the child following an unlawful abduction. The text indicates that national courts should 'examine the question of custody of the child' (Article 11(7) Brussels II*a*), and the requirements in Article 42, (giving the parties an opportunity to be heard and ensuring safeguards are in place where appropriate) should be met before an Article 42 certificate is issued. Therefore it is essential that the best interests of the child are examined fully in Article 11(6)–(8) proceedings, and children are heard where appropriate in order for national courts to comply with Article 24 of the Charter and Articles 3 and 12 of the UNCRC. Where this does not occur there will be a breach of Article 8 of the ECHR. The Court notes that there are also allegations that MA was violent towards Doris and Sofia. This Court is not in a position to determine these allegations. However national courts must investigate all relevant allegations and evidence available when examining a question on the custody of the child in order to reach a decision that is in the best interests of the child.

21.   MA does have a right to know Sofia and to have meaningful contact with her under Article 8 ECHR. The parents' interests, especially in having regular contact with their child, are one factor when balancing the various interests at stake (*Sahin v Germany* [GC], no 30943/96, § 66, ECHR 2003-VIII; see also *Haase v Germany*, no 11057/02, § 89, ECHR 2004-III, and *Kutzner v Germany*, cited above, § 58, ECHR 2002-I, and the numerous authorities cited therein). The child's best interests may, depending on their nature and seriousness, override those of the parents (see *Sahin v Germany* [GC], cited above, § 66, ECHR 2003-VIII). Previously the Court has indicated that a parent's right to family life is not absolute (see for example *Nuutinen v Finland* (Application no 32842/96) and *Johansen v Norway* cited above):

> The obligation of the national authorities to take measures to facilitate meetings between a parent and his or her child is not absolute, especially where the two are still strangers to one another … Whilst national authorities must do their utmost to facilitate such cooperation, any obligation to apply coercion in this area must be limited since the interests as well as the rights and freedoms of all concerned must be taken into account, and more particularly the best interests of the child and his or her rights under Article 8 of the Convention. Where contacts with the parent might appear to threaten those interests or interfere with those rights, it is for the national authorities to strike a fair balance between them … the Court must strike a balance between the various interests involved, namely the interests of the applicant's daughter and her *de facto* family, those of the applicant himself and the general interest in ensuring respect for the rule of law. (*Nuutinen v Finland*, cited above § 128–29).

22.   Forcing Sofia to return to Italy and live with her father when she does not know him, and does not share a common language with him, is inconsistent with her best interests. It will also severely affect Sofia's education. This would be very disruptive for Sofia and is against her expressed wishes. The enforcement of the order would also have the effect of

separating Sofia from her current secure family relationships, her mother, brother and step-father. This would be exceptionally harmful for Sofia, a child who is very close to her family, and has not had contact with her father in the interim.

23.   Initially, on her arrival in Austria, Sofia did see her father regularly but unfortunately her father chose to stop travelling to Austria to see her in June 2009.[1] This was the father's choice; the Austrian government submits that the mother cooperated. Therefore, although the initial removal from Italy was disruptive to the family relationship, it was the father's behaviour that resulted in the complete breakdown in the relationship between himself and Sofia. As Sofia no longer knows her father, having had little contact with him over the four year period due to the father's own actions, it will not be in the Sofia's best interests to enforce the judgment. It will be important to try and repair the relationship between the Sofia and her father, via suitable mechanisms in a safe environment, but a parent cannot be entitled under Article 8 to have measures enforced that would harm the child's health and development (see, among many other authorities, *Elsholz v Germany* [GC], no 25735/94, § 50, ECHR 2000-VIII, and *Maršálek v the Czech Republic*, no 8153/04, § 71, 4 April 2006). Therefore forcing Sofia to move to Italy and live with her father is not proportionate to the legitimate aim pursued by the order.

24.   The Court is also concerned that the Austrian enforcement law allows for coercive measures. The Court has previously held, in the context of the 1980 Hague Convention, that 'coercive measures against children are not desirable' (*Maire v Portugal* (Application no 48206/99) § 76), although they cannot be ruled out in the case of manifestly unlawful behaviour by the parent with whom the child lives. In general, the use of coercive measures against children to remove them from their primary carer is not suitable. Children need to be spoken to, informed of decisions and encouraged to comply with them. Where children do not wish to comply with the order then they should not be forced to do so. The Austrian authorities should not use coercive measures against Sofia, as to do so would not be in her best interests, would not be in line with her views and would violate her right to private and family life under Article 8 of this Convention.

25.   The Court reiterates that the Article 8 rights of all family members must be balanced, but the best interests of the child is a primary consideration. If the enforcement of an order will be detrimental to a child because it separates them from their secure family relation-ships in the country in which they are settled and the use of coercion, which can harm a child, is necessary for that enforcement to take place, then these enforcement measures do not fall under the *Bosphorus* presumption of equivalent protection (infra § 26). The effect of the enforcement of the order, given by the Venice Youth Court, will be to separate Sofia from her mother. Doris is unable to return to Italy with Sofia because she is facing criminal proceedings there. Doris also has a young baby and partner in Austria whom she cannot leave for a long period of time. Therefore the only possible outcome of the enforcement of the order would be a breakdown in the relationship between Doris and Sofia and a clear breach of both applicants' right to respect for their family life under Article 8.

26.   Article 47 Brussels II*a* provides that enforcement is a matter of national law, so enforcement action taken by Austria is not protected by the *Bosphorus* presumption. All

---

[1] Sofia initially saw her father at the contact centre 15 times over a 10 month period.

actions taken by Austria to enforce the order, including coercive measures, under national law are subject to the scrutiny of this Court and must be legitimate and proportionate. It is clear that if such enforcement measures were protected under the *Bosphorus* presumption then the rights afforded by this Convention would not be real and effective.

27.   Therefore, in light of all the foregoing considerations, the Court considers that it would not be in Sofia's best interests for her to return to Italy in the current circumstances, particularly if an enforced return resulted in the Austrian authorities using coercive measures against Sofia. Consequently, there would be a violation of Article 8 of the Convention by the Austrian authorities in respect of Sofia if the decision on residence and custody, which requires Sofia to return to Italy without her mother, were to be enforced.

29

Commentary on
Case C-34/09 *Zambrano v Office national de l'emploi*

CHARLOTTE O'BRIEN

Ruiz Zambrano[1] was a game-changing, but notoriously laconic,[2] judgment, setting out the basis for a child's autonomous EU citizenship-based right to reside in their state of nationality, and extending that right to their third country national primary carers. But by doing so in very few words, and in failing to place the children whose rights were at issue at the centre of the judgment, the Court left the way open for Member States to embroider their own conditions and limitations into the right, significantly curbing its effects in ways that impact upon the welfare of *Zambrano* children.

I. Background, Dispute and Preliminary Reference

EU citizenship entails the 'right to move and reside freely within the territory of the Member States'.[3] Prior to *Zambrano* this had been interpreted as conferring a right to reside in *other* Member States, leading to criticism that EU citizenship, far from being a fundamental status, was a contingent status that could only be invoked in the case of cross border mobility,[4] so was meaningless to those without the means to exercise their free movement rights. By implication it was not a status that children could personally rely upon at all, being at best the parasitic family members of free movers, or more likely, being static and economically inactive.

Mr Ruiz Zambrano and his wife, Mrs Marina López, both Columbian nationals, accompanied by their child, also a Columbian national, had made repeated applications for asylum/to regularise their stay in Belgium since 1999. The circumstances of the asylum claim get no attention within the original judgment, but are explained in Advocate General Sharpston's Opinion.[5] Most striking is that the judgment makes only a passing, incidental

---

[1] *Ruiz Zambrano* [2011] ECR I-01177.
[2] N Nic Shuibhne, 'Seven Questions for Seven Paragraphs' (2011) 36 *EL Rev* 162.
[3] Art 20(2)(a) Treaty on the Functioning of the European Union.
[4] S Currie, 'The Transformation of Union Citizenship' in M Dougan and S Currie (eds), *50 Years of the European Treaties: Looking Back and Thinking Forward* (Oxford, Hart Publishing, 2009).
[5] Case C-34/09 *Zambrano* [2011] ECR I-01177, Opinion of AG Sharpston delivered on 20 September 2010.

reference to the eldest child having been abducted by a criminal gang for a week in Columbia. In spite of his applications being refused, Mr Zambrano found work, declared his employment to the social security authorities, and his wages were subject to social security deductions. The couple then had two more children, Diego and Jessica,[6] both of whom acquired Belgian nationality.

Some years after he had started working, a government inspection discovered that Mr Zambrano was in work, and his contract was terminated immediately. He was then refused entitlement to unemployment benefits on the ground that his work had not been lawfully completed, so the family were denied income through either work or welfare. The tribunal hearing the challenge to the unemployment benefit refusal stayed proceedings and made a reference to the Court of Justice of the European Union (CJEU), asking whether EU law conferred a right on a Union citizen to reside in their state of residence, even though they had not exercised free movement rights. It also asked whether EU law required a right to reside for their primary carer, and further, whether that carer should be exempted from work permit requirements.[7]

II. The Original Judgment, its Implications and Consequences

The Court found that Union citizenship could confer a right to reside in the state of nationality even when free movement had not been exercised, in certain circumstances. In sharp contrast to the Advocate General's detailed and thorough analysis, the Court reached its conclusions in a startlingly short judgment. The key statements were:

> Article 20 TFEU precludes national measures which have the effect of depriving citizens of the Union of the genuine enjoyment of the substance of the rights conferred by virtue of their status as citizens of the Union.

> A refusal to grant a right of residence to a third country national with dependent minor children in the Member State where those children are nationals and reside, and also a refusal to grant such a person a work permit, has such an effect.[8]

This appeared to be a watershed moment for Union citizenship, and inspired some excited academic discussion about the interpretation and reach of the new 'substance of rights' doctrine—the finding that EU citizenship could protect own-nationals even when they have not exercised free movement rights, where the substance of their EU citizenship rights were at stake—for instance, where to find otherwise would result in them having to leave not only the country, but the territory of the EU.[9] The Court curbed its findings in

---

[6] Their names were used throughout proceedings, and so we have continued to do so, though note that domestic courts would most likely assume anonymity for minors, especially in such circumstances.

[7] The questions in the rewritten judgment are taken from the original application, so use the pre-Lisbon Treaty numberings (Treaty establishing the European Community–EC); the body of the judgment uses post-Lisbon numbering, referring to the Treaty on the Functioning of the European Union (TFEU) as in the original judgment.

[8] *Zambrano* judgment, paras 42–43.

[9] D Kostakopoulou, 'The Evolution of European Union Citizenship' (2008) 7 *European Political Science* 285; D Kochenov, 'A Real European Citizenship; A New Jurisdiction Test: A Novel Chapter in the Development of the Union in Europe' (2011) 18 *Columbia Journal of European Law* 55; K Hailbronner and D Thym, 'Case C-34/09, *Gerardo Ruiz Zambrano v. Office national de l'emploi (ONEm)*, Judgment of the Court of Justice (Grand Chamber) of 8 March 2011' (2011) 48(4) *Common Market Law Review* 1253.

McCarthy[10] appearing to limit the doctrine to children, so that an adult EU national (who had dual citizenship but had not exercised free movement) could not claim that refusing her third country national spouse a right of residence jeopardised her EU citizenship rights. In *Dereci*,[11] it was further limited, through finding that a *Zambrano* right only comes into effect if the threatened expulsion of the third country national creates a strong presumption of de facto expulsion for the children. In *Iida*,[12] the Court further found that *Zambrano* does not create a right to reside for a parent in a Member State different from that of the child's residence, when a third country national sought to rely on *Zambrano* to enable him to stay within the EU, albeit in a different country to his child. It only applies to own-national children—in *NA*, the Court found it did not cover a non-national Union citizen child who had lived in the host Member State since birth.[13] Some proposed limitations go too far—in *CS* and *Rendón Marín* Member States were not permitted to automatically preclude carers with criminal convictions from having *Zambrano* rights.[14]

However, the focus of this commentary, and the driving force behind the rewritten judgment, is the failure of the Court in *Zambrano* to frame any of its judgment around the best interests of the children at the centre of the case. This has had two significant consequences for how the right has been recognised in the UK. First, the Court's failure to mention the welfare of the children has led UK authorities to interpret the right as excluding any entitlement to equal treatment with regard to welfare. Second, the UK readily switches primary carership to an absent parent in order to find that the actual carer has no right to reside.

The UK government acted swiftly in response to *Zambrano*, enacting legislation that recognised the right to reside,[15] and legislation that made it clear that this did not count for entitlement to benefits.[16] In *Harrison*,[17] the Court of Appeal of England and Wales stressed that the right was 'not a right to any particular quality of life or to any particular standard of living'.[18] The same Court qualified its position in *Sanneh*,[19] finding that total destitution could undermine the benefits of EU citizenship, but that UK provisions for last resort protection under section 17 of the Children Act 1989 was at least in theory sufficient to meet the UK's obligations, so that excluding *Zambrano* families from standard benefit entitlement did not undermine their right to reside in the EU. The Court acknowledged that the adequacy of this support had been questioned, but added that this was not a question before them, so they were to proceed as though section 17 did suffice to meet the needs of the families. However, this misses the key issue. Section 17 support is different—and inferior[20]—to equal treatment with regard to 'normal' welfare benefits: it may amount

[10] Case C-434/09, *McCarthy*, [2011] ECR I-3375.
[11] Case C-256/11, *Dereci* EU:C:2011:734.
[12] Case C-40/11, *Iida* EU:C:2012:691.
[13] Case C-115/15 *Secretary of State for the Home Department v NA* EU:C:2016:487.
[14] Case C-304/14 *Secretary of State for the Home Department v CS* EU:C:2016:674 and Case C-165/14 *Rendón Marín* EU:C:2016:675.
[15] The Immigration (European Economic Area) (Amendment) (No 2) Regulations 2012, SI 2012 No 2560.
[16] The Social Security (Habitual Residence) (Amendment) Regulations 2012; and The Child Benefit and Child Tax Credit (Miscellaneous Amendments) Regulations 2012 SI 2012 No 2612.
[17] *Harrison v Secretary of State for the Home Department* [2012] EWCA Civ 1736, 27.
[18] ibid, para 67.
[19] *Sanneh & Ors v Secretary of State for Work and Pensions* [2015] EWCA Civ 49.
[20] *R (G) v Barnet LBC* [2003] UKHL 57 established that under s 17 social services do not have to meet every assessed need and can take their resources into account when identifying which needs they will meet. In *R(1.PO 2.KO 3. RO) v London Borough of Newham* [2014] EWHC 2561 (Admin) it transpired the local authority in question derived their subsistence rates from child benefit rates—which the High Court deemed inadequate.

to significantly less to live on. It is a measure of last resort. Because families exercising a *Zambrano*-based right to reside are excluded from Housing Benefit, support under section 17 may involve them losing their home and being relocated in emergency accommodation. And the general benefit exclusion applies even though the parents in question may be workers, and even though the children in question are British citizens. *Sanneh* (renamed *HC*)[21] has been given permission to appeal to the Supreme Court.[22] The UK national children of *Zambrano* families are thus treated differently, and less well, than other UK national children, and also than EU national children able to rely upon *Teixeira*.[23]

As well as curbing the effects of *Zambrano* status, the UK authorities have made it difficult to invoke that status in the first place. The Home Office guidance states that decision-makers 'must refuse an application for a derivative residence card if there is another person in the UK *who can care* for the relevant person'.[24] Another parent is deemed someone who 'can' care for the child, if they have had some contact in the last 12 months (which can be an email), and demonstrated some (undefined) financial commitment to them at some point.[25] The child's wishes or best interests are not mentioned. The guidance states that 'a lack of financial resources or a lack of willingness to assume caring responsibilities would not, by itself, be a sufficient basis for a person to claim they are unable to care for the relevant person'.[26] It is hard to see how a child's interests could not be ill-served by switching primary carership to a parent with no financial resources to care for them, or who does not want to care for them. The guidance acknowledges that a parent may be an unsuitable carer if they are on the sex offender's register, but that is rather at the extreme end of unsuitability.

III. The Re-written Judgment

The new judgment reaches the same conclusions as the original, but frames them around the *rights-holders* at the heart of the case—the children. The new judgment pays greater attention to the Court's own equal treatment and EU right to reside case law. And it begins from a subtly different perspective—bringing the children and the family unit to the fore early on, drawing out some of the detail of the backstory of the first child's abduction.

Extra consideration is given to the 'scope and substance' of EU citizenship rights, particularly equal treatment as regards welfare benefits and other entitlements. This goes unmentioned in the original, but its inclusion is hardly a stretch since the reference arises in the

---

[21] *HC—R (on the application of HC) v Secretary of State for Work and Pensions and others UKSC 2015/0215.*
[22] For an analysis of the arguments raised in *Sanneh* see C O'Brien '"Hand-to-mouth" Citizenship: Decision Time for the UK Supreme Court on the Substance of *Zambrano* Rights, EU Citizenship and Equal Treatment' (2016) 38(2) *Journal of Social Welfare and Family Law* 228.
[23] Case C-480/08 *Teixeira* [2010] ECR I-1107.
[24] Home Office 'Derivative rights of residence, version 2.0 Valid from April 2015' (2015) p 69. Accessed at www.gov.uk/government/uploads/system/uploads/attachment_data/file/488448/Derivative_rights_of_residence_v2.0_ext_clean.pdf, emphasis added.
[25] ibid, 70.
[26] ibid, 71.

context of a welfare benefit claim. The judgment makes clear that the right to reside and equal treatment are intertwined rights, referring to 'family-related rights of residence and equal treatment'. It highlights the cases that have established EU law-based rights to reside, and notes that while some are subject to conditions and limitations, the right to reside necessarily entails some equal treatment; and it is the *child's* right to equal treatment at issue, regardless of whether benefits are claimed in the carer's name. The judgment points to *Teixeira* and *Ibrahim*,[27] in which families were entitled to equal access to welfare in order to support the child's right to reside. In those cases it was noted that there was no basis for finding that a *Baumbast*-based right to reside depended on self-sufficiency, and the same principle is applied here.

The Court needs to show that the 'wholly internal' rule does not prevent own-nationals who have never exercised free movement from claiming protection from discrimination, and so notes that equal treatment can be invoked on behalf of own-nationals, as a 'general principle' of EU law. The judgment recalls *Eman and Sevinger*,[28] in which states could not arbitrarily treat their own nationals differently in matters of European Parliament suffrage, and suggests that the *Zambrano* children are entitled to equal treatment with EU national children from other Member States. Reverse discrimination against own nationals is in general permitted, but *Walloon Government v Flemish Government*[29] suggests that that is only the case in situations that fall outside of the scope of EU law. There, Belgian nationals from other regions were excluded from a local Belgian benefit, in contrast with EU nationals who were entitled to it. This was considered lawful, except where Belgian nationals had brought themselves within the scope of EU law by exercising free movement rights. This judgment notes that this situation falls within the scope of EU law, so suggests that *Zambrano* children are entitled to equal treatment with other EU national children.

The judgment acknowledges the Court's duty to interpret EU law in accordance with the United Nations Convention on the Rights of the Child (CRC)[30] and to consider the best interests of the child, in particular through reference to the Charter of Fundamental Rights. It also makes the considerations of the right to respect for family life central,[31] pointing to the Court's own case law on its duty to interpret free movement provisions in light of that right.[32] The re-written judgment's emphasis on the right to family life, and rooting of the *Zambrano* right in the child's best interests preclude the cavalier administrative rearrangement of family units and switching of primary carership in order to deny a *Zambrano* residence right.

---

[27] Case C-310/08 *Ibrahim* [2010] ECR I-01065.

[28] Case C-300/04 *Eman & Sevinger* [2006] ECR I-08055.

[29] Case C-212/06 *Walloon Government v Flemish Government* [2008] ECR I-0683.

[30] See H Stalford, 'The CRC in Litigation under EU Law' in T Liefaard and JE Doek, *Litigating the Rights of the Child: The UN Convention on the Rights of the Child in Domestic and International Jurisprudence* (Dordrecht, Springer, 2015).

[31] H Stalford, 'For Better, for Worse: the Relationship between EU Citizenship and EU Family Law' in N Nic Shuibhne, M Dougan and E Spaventa, (eds), *Empowerment and Disempowerment of the EU Citizen* (Oxford, Hart Publishing, 2012).

[32] Case C-60/00 *Carpenter* [2002] ECRI-6279; Case C-200/02 *Zhu and Chen* [2004] ECR I-9925; Case C-127/08 *Metock* [2008] ECR I-6241.

IV. Conclusions

The Court in *Zambrano* said too little about the right it was creating, opening the way for the UK's highly restrictive interpretations. The revised judgment cleaves more closely to previous case law, to show that equal treatment is an inherent part of an EU law based right to reside. Moreover, such equal treatment is required as a general principle of EU law, and own-national *Zambrano* children are entitled to equal treatment with EU national children. To find otherwise would deprive their EU citizenship of substance, prevent them from benefitting 'from the special relationship of solidarity and ... rights and duties, which form the bedrock of the bond of nationality',[33] and imperil their welfare and best interests contrary to EU law. This revised judgment places the children's citizenship at the heart of the case, considers the implications *for the children* of the rights that stem from their status, and interprets the rights through the prism of the right to family life—in line with CJEU case law. Such a perspective precludes an interpretation that strips out equal treatment rights, or summarily re-allocates primary carership.

The *Zambrano* case reminds us that children are rarely at the forefront of the Court's mind,[34] even when it is their citizenship rights at stake. This problem is echoed in *Commission v UK*,[35] a case about restrictions imposed on EU nationals accessing child benefits and child tax credits; again the interests of the children did not get a look in.[36] But the CJEU is empowered—or even obliged—to take account of their interests. Article 3 Treaty on European Union (TEU) introduced the 'protection of the rights of the child' as a Union objective, while the Charter of Fundamental Rights states that '[i]n all actions relating to children, whether taken by public authorities or private institutions, the child's best interests must be a primary consideration.'[37] Before the *Zambrano* judgment was released, the Commission stated that the 'standards and principles of the CRC must continue to guide EU policies and actions that have an impact on the rights of the child'.[38] If anything, support for this perspective has increased; a 2012 European Parliament report argued that the rights of the child 'now constitute an integral part of fundamental rights which the EU and Member States are bound to respect by virtue of European and international law.'[39] If children's best interests are to be a primary consideration, the CJEU first needs to show that they are a consideration at all; it needs to take children's rights seriously.

---

[33] Case C-135/08 *Rottman* [2010] ECR I-01449.

[34] Stalford and Drywood noted in 2009 the Court's 'unease' and tendency to pay 'lip service' to the CRC: H Stalford and E Drywood, 'Coming of Age? Children's Rights in the European Union' (2009) 46(1) *Common Market Law Review* 143, 162.

[35] Case C-308/14 *Commission v UK* EU:C:2016:436.

[36] C O'Brien 'The ECJ sacrifices EU citizenship in vain: *Commission v UK*' (2016) 54(1) *Common Market Law Review* 209.

[37] Art 24(2).

[38] EU Commission, "Communication from the Commission to European Parliament, the Council, the European Economic and Social Committee and the Committee of the Regions: An EU Agenda for the Rights of the Child", (2011), COM(2011) 0060, final.

[39] European Parliament, DG Internal Policies, 'EU Framework of Law for Children's Rights' April 2012, PE462.445, accessed at www.europarl.europa.eu/RegData/etudes/note/join/2012/462445/IPOL-LIBE_NT(2012)462445_EN.pdf.

Court of Justice of the European Union

Case C-34/09 *Zambrano v Office national de l'emploi*

THE COURT (Grand Chamber),

composed of XX, President, XX (Rapporteur), XX, Presidents of Chamber, XXXXX and H Stalford Judges.

Judgment

1.   The reference for a preliminary ruling concerns the interpretation of Articles 12 EC, 17 EC and 18 EC, and also Articles 7, 21, 24 and 34 of the Charter of Fundamental Rights of the European Union ('the Charter of Fundamental Rights').

That reference was made in the context of proceedings between Mr Ruiz Zambrano, a Columbian national, and the Office national de l'emploi (National Employment Office) ('ONEm') concerning the refusal by the latter to grant him unemployment benefits under Belgian legislation.

[The relevant legislation listed in the original judgment is not repeated for reasons of space. Where necessary, it is integrated into the judgment below].

The Dispute in the Main Proceedings and the Questions Referred for a Preliminary Ruling

2.   The applicant, Mr Ruiz Zambrano, and his wife, Mrs Moreno López, have three children. The eldest was born in Columbia in 1996 and is of Columbian nationality. That child is now 15 years old. His younger brother, Diego, now 8 years old, was born on 1 September 2003 in Belgium and is of Belgian nationality. The youngest child, Jessica, was born in Belgium on 26 August 2005 and also acquired Belgian nationality. She is now 6 years old.

3.   Mr Zambrano applied for asylum in Belgium on 4 April 1999, having travelled there on a visa issued by the Belgian embassy in Bogota. The asylum application was based on significant concerns around the safety of Mr Zambrano, his wife and their son in the light

of the ongoing civil war in Colombia. Mr Zambrano had fled from Colombia after enduring 3 years of serious threats, extortion demands and assaults on his family at the hands of private militias. The final straw came when his son was abducted for a week in 1999 at the age of 3.

Mrs Moreno López applied for asylum in Belgium the following year, in February 2000.

4.   The Belgian authorities refused Mr and Mrs Zambrano's applications for asylum on 11 September 2000 and ordered the family to leave Belgium. However, the order included a non-refoulement clause stating that they should not be sent back to Colombia because of the threat posed to their security and welfare by the deteriorating conditions associated with the civil war.

Since 18 April 2001, the family had been registered in the Belgian municipality of Schaerbeek. On 2 October 2000, Mr Zambrano signed an employment contract with a Belgian company despite not holding a work permit. His work was declared to the National Social Security Office and his pay was subject to statutory social security deductions.

5.   On 20 October 2000, Mr Zambrano applied to have his situation in Belgium regularised on the basis of the family's impossibility of returning to Colombia, their progress in integrating into Belgian society, including learning the French language, and the disruption it would cause to their son's education given that he was now attending pre-school. Mr Zambrano also referred to the fact that any removal was likely to exacerbate his own post-traumatic syndrome from which he had been suffering since the abduction of his son in 1999. While it was not explicit in his arguments, such a removal may also have a detrimental impact on the welfare of their son given the trauma he had already endured.

That application was rejected by the Belgian authorities on 8 August 2001 and by the Conseil d'État on appeal on 22 May 2003.

6.   Nearly four months later, on 1 Sept 2003, Diego was born. He automatically acquired Belgian nationality by virtue of Article 10(1) of the Belgian Nationality Code. Colombian law does not recognise Colombian nationality for children born outside Colombia where the parents have not taken specific steps to have them so recognised. In acquiring Belgian nationality, Diego also acquired the status of EU citizen by virtue of Article 20(1) TFEU.

At the time of Diego's birth, his father continued to work and provide sufficient resources to support the family.

7.   On 9 April 2004, the parents again applied to have their situation regularised, this time supporting their claim by reference to the birth of Diego and to Article 3 of Protocol 4 of the European Convention of Human Rights (ECHR) which prevents a child from being required to leave the territory of the state of which he is a national.

8.   Jessica was subsequently born on 26 August 2005 and also acquired Belgian nationality (and, by implication, EU citizenship) on the same basis as her brother, Diego. Her parents then sought residence on the basis of Article 40 of the relevant Belgian legislation (the Law of 15 December 1980) on the grounds that they are ascendants of Belgian nationals. On 13 September 2005, Mr Zambrano was given provisional authorisation to stay in Belgium pending a final decision on his appeals against the various decisions refusing him a residence permit.

9.   On 10 October 2005 the father's employment contract was temporarily suspended on economic grounds. This led him to make his first application for employment benefits

which was eventually rejected on 20 Feb 2006. He appealed against that decision on 12 April 2006 but later resumed working anyway.

10.   In the meantime, on 8 November 2005, the father submitted a separate application to take up permanent residence. This was rejected on the grounds that he had failed incorrectly to register Jessica (and, presumably Diego) with the diplomatic or consular authorities for the purposes of acquiring Colombian nationality, but had instead opted to adhere to all of the procedures to acquire Belgian nationality mainly with a view to legalising their own residence. The same allegation of 'legal engineering' formed the basis of the decision to reject the mother's application for residence on 26 January 2006.

11.   Moreover, the Office des Étrangers, whilst accepting that they could not deport the parents while an application to regularise their status was ongoing, informed the parents that they could not pursue any employment. The father's employment contract was therefore terminated with immediate effect and without compensation. This left the family without any source of income, either through employment or through unemployment benefits. The latter had also been refused by the National Employment Office (ONEm) on the basis that the father had not completed the requisite number of working days to qualify for such benefits under the law governing foreign workers.

12.   On 23 July 2007, more than three years after the initial application, the parents were notified that their application to regularise their situation had been rejected.

On 19 November 2007, Mr Zambrano sought an annulment of the decision not to grant them residence. He strongly contested the allegation of 'legal engineering' inherent in the authorities' decision, arguing that the acquisition of Belgian nationality by Diego and Jessica was as a result of the legitimate application of the relevant Belgian legislation. Furthermore, he argued that the decision infringed Articles 2 and 7 of Directive 2004/38, as well as Article 8 and Article 3(1) Protocol 4 ECHR.

Similarly, Mr Zambrano challenged the decision not to grant him unemployment benefits on the basis of his right of residence and associated benefits under the EU free movement provisions. Specifically, as the ascendants of minor children who are nationals of an EU Member State and citizens of the EU (Diego and Jessica), the parents enjoy a derived right to reside and access benefits on the same basis as other nationals' family members in the host state and are exempt from the requirement to hold a work permit.

The Questions Referred for a Preliminary Ruling

13.   In the proceedings brought against the two decisions of the National Employment Office refusing Mr Zambrano's claim to unemployment benefits, the Brussels Employment Tribunal referred the following questions to the Court of Justice for a preliminary ruling:

1. Do Articles 12 [EC], 17 [EC] and 18 [EC], or one or more of them when read separately or in conjunction, confer a right of residence upon a citizen of the Union in the territory of the Member State of which that citizen is a national, irrespective of whether he has previously exercised his right to move within the territory of the Member States?

2. Must Articles 12 [EC], 17 [EC] and 18 [EC], in conjunction with the provisions of Articles 21, 24 and 34 of the Charter of Fundamental Rights, be interpreted as meaning that the right which they recognise, without discrimination on the grounds of nationality, in favour of any citizen of the Union to move and reside freely in the territory of the Member States means that, where that

citizen is an infant dependent on a relative in the ascending line who is a national of a non-member State, the infant's enjoyment of the right of residence in the Member State in which he resides and of which he is a national must be safeguarded, irrespective of whether the right to move freely has been previously exercised by the child or through his legal representative, by coupling that right of residence with the useful effect whose necessity is recognised by Community case-law [Zhu and Chen], and granting the relative in the ascending line who is a national of a non-member State, upon whom the child is dependent and who has sufficient resources and sickness insurance, the secondary right of residence which that same national of a non-member State would have if the child who is dependent upon him were a Union citizen who is not a national of the Member State in which he resides?

3. Must Articles 12 [EC], 17 [EC] and 18 [EC], in conjunction with the provisions of Articles 21, 24 and 34 of the Charter of Fundamental Rights, be interpreted as meaning that the right of a minor child who is a national of a Member State to reside in the territory of the State in which he resides must entail the grant of an exemption from the requirement to hold a work permit to the relative in the ascending line who is a national of a non-member State, upon whom the child is dependent and who, were it not for the requirement to hold a work permit under the national law of the Member State in which he resides, fulfils the condition of sufficient resources and the possession of sickness insurance by virtue of paid employment making him subject to the social security system of that State, so that the child's right of residence is coupled with the useful effect recognised by Community case-law [Zhu and Chen] in favour of a minor child who is a European citizen with a nationality other than that of the Member State in which he resides and is dependent upon a relative in the ascending line who is a national of a non-member State?

Consideration of the Questions Referred

14.   While the issues referred to arise from an appeal by the father, Mr Zambrano, it is the status, experiences and rights of his children that are fundamental to determining whether his claims for residence, a work permit and unemployment benefits are well-founded.

15.   The strength of the applicant's claim relies almost entirely on whether or not the children, in this case Diego and Jessica, are recognised as citizens of the European Union under Articles 20 and 21 TFEU and as falling within the scope of the EU free movement provisions, governed by Directive 2004/38. With that in mind, the questions posed by the referring court are considered in the light of, first, whether the status of EU citizenship is conferred upon the children notwithstanding the fact that the children have never exercised free movement between Member States of the European Union; second, whether the children's status as EU citizens under Articles 20 and 21 TFEU confers a derived right of residence and employment on their parents, as relatives in the ascending line on whom they are dependent, without their need to obtain a work permit; and third, the scope and substance of their status as EU citizens under Articles 20 and 21 TFEU, specifically whether the children have a right to equal treatment as regards access to social welfare benefits and other entitlement on the same basis as nationals.

Children's EU Citizenship and the Requirement of Free Movement

16.   Turning to the first issue of whether free movement between the EU Member States is required to trigger individuals' enjoyment of the status and benefits associated with EU citizenship, Article 20 TFEU confers the status of citizen of the Union on every person

who holds the nationality of a Member State (see Case C-224/98 *D'Hoop* [2002] ECR I-6191, paragraph 27, and Case C-148/02 *Garcia Avello* [2003] ECR I-11613, paragraph 21). Article 20 TFEU makes no distinction between adults and children in conferring EU citizenship; indeed, Article 19 TFEU expressly prohibits any discrimination based on age. This status is not contingent on the exercise of free movement but, rather, on being a national of an EU Member State.

17.   It is for national law to determine the conditions under which individuals acquire nationality. Insofar as Diego and Jessica satisfy the conditions for Belgian nationality, it follows that they also enjoy the status of EU citizenship. The rights associated with EU citizenship are closely aligned with the right to move and reside freely within the territory of the Member States (Article 21(1) TFEU, and such rights extend to family members as defined by Article 2 Directive 2004/38, including parents and carers in the ascending line.

18.   The fact that neither Diego nor Jessica have exercised free movement, but rather were born and have always lived in Belgium, raises a fundamental question of whether EU citizenship gives rise to the same family-related rights of residence and equal treatment. The Court has indicated on previous occasions that it does confer some such autonomous rights, asserting that EU citizenship as defined by Articles 20 and 21 TFEU is a 'fundamental status' that gives rise to more than simply rights associated with free movement (Case C-413/99 *Baumbast and R* [2002] ECR I-7091, paragraph 82; *Garcia Avello* [2003] ECR I-11613, paragraph 22; *Zhu and Chen* [2004] ECR I-9925, paragraph 25).

19.   Insofar as the Zambrano children are EU citizens within the scope of EU law, their right to reside freely within the territory of the Member States (Article 20(2)(a)), is protected, even though they have never exercised free movement. This includes a right to reside in their own home state and extends to their third country national primary carers. This right is further supported by international human rights law which protects an individual's right to reside in their country of nationality (Article 8 UN Convention on the Rights of the Child 1989, Article 3 of Protocol 4 ECHR 1950, Article 12(4), International Covenant on Civil and Political Rights).

The Relationship between the Right to Reside and the Right to Equal Treatment

20.   The right to reside under EU law also triggers the right to equal treatment on the same basis as nationals (Case C-85/96 *Martinez Sala* [1998] ECR I-02691 (4), Case C-456/02 *Trojani* [2004] ECR I-7573 (40, 44) and Case C-184/99 *Grzelczyk* [2001] ECR I-6193 (30)), subject to some limitations and conditions such as a requirement of economic activity or habitual residence. In substance, this entails a right to equal access to social welfare benefits, employment and other rights that are available to nationals and other EU citizens lawfully resident in the host state.

21.   The fact that the parents are the claimants of such entitlement is of little relevance where such claims are limited to those who have children and are intended to directly benefit those children. This Court has accepted that enabling non EU-national parents who care for the child access to those benefits is instrumental to supporting the child's right to reside and the child's right to equal treatment (Case C-480/08 *Teixeira* [2010] ECR I-1107 and Case C-310/08 *Ibrahim* [2010] ECR I-01065). To prevent Mr Zambrano from making

a living, either through paid employment or through claiming the full range of benefits normally available to the primary carers of national children, would effectively deprive the children's EU citizenship and their associated right to equal treatment of any useful effect.

22.   The children in the present case are not only protected against discriminatory treatment by virtue of EU law; as Belgian nationals who were born and have always lived in Belgium, they also benefit from the special relationship with and protection by the Belgian authorities (Case C-135/08 *Rottman* [2010] ECR I-01449).

Any difference in treatment between national children and their parents who acquire their residence rights as a direct result of their EU citizenship status (as in the present case), as compared to children from other EU Member States who acquire their rights by virtue of the free movement of persons provisions, may infringe the principle of equal treatment, as one of the 'general principles of Community law' and so must be objectively justified as appropriate and proportionate in the light of the circumstances (Case C-300/04 *Eman and Sevinger* [200] ECR I-08055).

23.   Moreover, as this situation falls within the scope of Union law, it is not a 'wholly internal' situation in which so-called reverse discrimination might be permitted. In circumstances already within the scope of Union law, a Member State's own nationals may invoke the specific protection against discrimination on the ground of nationality under EU law in the same way that EU nationals from other Member States can (Case C-212/06 *Walloon Government v Flemish Government* [2008] ECR I-0683).

24.   Whether the difference in treatment is justified in the present case should be considered by reference to the potential implications for Diego and Jessica of failing to extend residence and employment rights to their parents. It is beyond doubt that if the children's parents are removed from Belgium this will have significant consequences for the children and potentially amount to a serious breach of their fundamental rights. The only way for the children to continue to exercise their fundamental freedom to reside within the EU as EU citizens, would be through being separated from their parents and cared for by someone else in Belgium. This would be an infringement of their right to respect for family life, as laid down in Article 8 ECHR and reinforced by Articles 7 and 24(3) of the Charter of Fundamental Rights of the European Union.

25.   The right to reside and the right to equal treatment, as rights arising out of EU law, must be interpreted in the light of fundamental rights, as expressed in both the EU Charter of Fundamental Rights and in international human rights law by which the Member States are bound. In particular, EU law must be interpreted in the light of the requirement of respect for family life (Case 249/86 *Commission v Germany* [1989] ECR 1263; Case C-60/00, *Carpenter*, [2002] ECRI-6279, paragraph 41; *Zhu and Chen*; *Baumbast*, paragraph 72; Case C-127/08, *Metock* [2008] ECR I-6241, paragraphs 77–79).

26.   Such an interference will infringe the ECHR if it does not meet the requirements of paragraph 2 of Article 8, that is unless it is 'in accordance with the law', motivated by one or more of the legitimate aims under that paragraph and 'necessary in a democratic society', that is to say justified by a pressing social need and, in particular, proportionate to the legitimate aim pursued (see, in particular, *Boultif v Switzerland*, no 54273/00, §§ 39, 41 and 46, ECHR 2001-IX; *Mehemi v France*, 26 September 1997 § 34, ECHR 1997-VI; *Dalia v France*, 19 February 1998 § 52, ECHR 1998-I). Derogation from the right to respect for family life

on public policy grounds entails a proportionality test that takes into account factors such as how settled the family is, the good faith of the claimant, the practicalities of establishing family life elsewhere, and the potential impact of such a move on any children concerned (*Sen v Netherlands*, Application No 31465/96, ECHR 21 Dec 2001, § 40; *Tuquabo-Tekle v the Netherlands*, Application No 60665/00, ECHR 1 March 2006).

The Importance of Interpreting EU Law by Reference to the Child's Best Interests

27.   In conducting this assessment, the European Court of Human Rights routinely interprets Article 8 by reference to the principle of the best interests of the child which, according to Article 3 of the UN Convention on the Rights of the Child (UNCRC), should be a 'primary consideration' ... 'in all actions concerning children'. Similarly, EU law has to be interpreted in a manner that is consistent with the obligations contained in the UNCRC with a view to protecting the rights and interests of the child (*Parliament v Council* [2006] ECR I-5769; Case C-244/06 *Dynamic Medien Vertriebs GmbH v Avides Media AG* [2008] ECR I-505; Article 3(3) TEU).

28.   The Belgian authorities' decision to remove Mr Zambrano from the host state of which Diego and Jessica are nationals cannot be interpreted as affording primary consideration to the children's best interests given the inevitable disruption such a move would pose to their social, educational, and emotional well-being. The children rely on both parents for their day-to-day care and for economic support. This reasoning has been confirmed by the European Court of Human Rights. In *Boultif v Switzerland* (Application No 54273/00 ECHR 2 August 2001) it was confirmed that consideration should be given to the impact parental deportation would have on any children in the family when determining if it is a proportionate response. This involves some consideration of whether there is a de facto caring relationship between the children and the parents and of the best interests and well-being of the children, in particular the seriousness of the difficulties which any children of the applicant are likely to encounter in the country to which the applicant is to be expelled; and the solidity of social, cultural and family ties with the host country and with the country of destination.

29.   Whilst neither Article 8 ECHR nor the UNCRC embody a right to regularise illegal stay (judgment of 37 July 2008, No 265/07, *Omoregie v Norway*, paragraphs 58–68), that does not prevent EU citizenship from offering a higher standard of human rights protection (Article 53 ECHR), particularly if it would better serve the interests of any children concerned.

30.   The fact that Mr Zambrano is not a legal resident does not, therefore, preclude reliance on the right to family life under EU law (*Carpenter*). In the present case, given the extreme nature of the circumstances endured by the family, and particularly the threats posed to the welfare of the children, a return to Colombia is not an option. The Belgian court has acknowledged as much in attaching a non-refoulement clause to the order for removal of Mr Zambrano. But even if a move to another country were possible, this would present significant and disproportionate challenges to the children; all of the children are settled in school and in their local community in Belgium and the two youngest children have never known life anywhere else.

31.   Article 24 of the EU Charter is particularly relevant in assessing the proportionality of removing Mr Zambrano (and, by implication, the rest of the family) from Belgium. This states that:

(1) Children shall have the right to such protection and care as is necessary for their well-being. They may express their views freely. Such views shall be taken into consideration on matters which concern them in accordance with their age and maturity.

(2) In all actions relating to children, whether taken by public authorities or private institutions, the child's best interests must be a primary consideration.

(3) Every child shall have the right to maintain on a regular basis a personal relationship and direct contact with both his or her parents, unless that is contrary to his or her interests.

32.   This provision should be read in conjunction with the UNCRC to which all EU Member States, including Belgium, are signatories and which, as an international human rights treaty, forms part of the general principles of EU law on the same basis as the ECHR (Article 6(3) TFEU; Case C-540/03, *Parliament v Council*, [2006] ECR I-5769, paragraphs 53–59).

33.   EU law cannot be interpreted in such a way that disregards the specific, fundamental rights of children expressed in this provision, nor can it be interpreted in such a way that might deprive the children of a right granted to them by the EU. The effect of Article 24(2) of the Charter, in particular, is that the child's best interests must be a primary consideration in all decisions adopted by the Member States. Previous judgments of this Court have shown a willingness to uphold non-national parents' rights to remain in the host state, even when they themselves do not qualify under the free movement provisions, on the basis of their children's best interests and educational rights (*Baumbast*). This interpretation has even been extended to parents and carers who are neither EU nationals nor economically self-sufficient (*Texeira*, paragraph 20; *Ibrahim*).

34.   If it is accepted that it is in the children's best interests to remain in Belgium, their country of nationality, under the care of their parents, then it must also be accepted that it is in their best interests for their parents to be allowed to provide for their basic needs, either through employment or through claiming unemployment benefits. To do otherwise would not only potentially deprive the children of a right granted to them by EU law, but also present a serious and disproportionate threat to the children's welfare, to their right to life and development (Article 6 UNCRC), to their right to a standard of living adequate for their physical, mental, spiritual, moral and social development (Article 27 UNCRC) and to economic and social protection (Article 17 European Social Charter).

35.   In the light of the above considerations, the answer to the questions referred is that children who are nationals of an EU Member States enjoy an independent status as EU citizens under Article 20 TFEU. Article 20 TFEU precludes any national measures which have the effect of depriving EU citizens of the genuine enjoyment of their rights as EU citizens.

36.   All of the rights arising out of children's status as EU citizens must be interpreted in the light of what is in their best interests (Article 3 UNCRC; Article 24(1) Charter).

37.   A refusal to grant parents a right to reside in the Member State of which their children are nationals for the purposes of caring for them not only undermines their children's best

interests, but deprives their children's citizenship status of any useful effect; it would necessitate the children either moving with their parents to another country with which they have no connection, or to remaining in their country of nationality without essential care from their parents with whom they enjoy a loving and close relationship.

38.   Similarly, any national measures that seek to restrict the parents' entitlement to engage in paid employment or to claim benefits significantly limits their capacity to support their family and, in particular, poses a serious threat to the well-being and stability of their children.

30

Commentary on *Antwi and others v Norway*

ELLEN NISSEN

The *Antwi* ruling presented the European Court of Human Rights (ECtHR) with the opportunity to clarify the scope and meaning of the preceding judgment in *Nunez*, which concerned a similar situation.[1] In *Nunez*, which concerned the deportation of a parent who had been residing irregularly in Norway, the ECtHR examined for the first time whether sufficient weight was attached to the best interests of the children involved, with explicit reference to Article 3 of the UN Convention on the Rights of the Child (CRC).[2] It furthermore referred to the child abduction case, *Neulinger v Shuruk*, another landmark case in which the best interests of the child was at the forefront of proceedings.[3] This commentary aims to discuss both the original and rewritten judgment in light of these preceding cases as they are closely intertwined.

The case law of the ECtHR must also be viewed against the backdrop of two other highly influential cases; the *Zambrano* ruling of the Court of Justice of the European Union (CJEU) (re-written for the purposes of this collection) and the *ZH (Tanzania)* ruling of the United Kingdom Supreme Court.[4] Similarly to the situation in *Antwi*, both cases concerned the deportation of (a) parent(s) of citizen children. This commentary will draw on these cases to provide context to the adopted approach in the rewritten judgment.

I. Facts and Original Judgment

The case concerned a 10 year-old Norwegian girl whose father was threatened with deportation to Ghana. The father's residence permit was revoked and a re-entry ban of five years was imposed after the Norwegian authorities discovered that he had used a forged identity in order to obtain the permit. It was argued before the ECtHR that this measure constituted a disproportionate measure vis-à-vis the child.

---

[1] *Antwi and others v Norway* (2012) 26940/10 ECHR 259.
[2] *Nunez v Norway* (2011) 55597/09 ECHR 1047.
[3] *Neulinger and Shuruk v Switzerland* (2010) 41615/07 ECHR 1053.
[4] *Ruiz Zambrano* [2011] ECR I-1177; *ZH (Tanzania) v Secretary of State for the Home Department* [2011] 2 AC 166.

In examining whether the expulsion of the father would contravene Article 8 European Convention on Human Rights (ECHR), the ECtHR repeated the principles of its settled case law, most notably that when 'the persons involved were aware that the immigration status of one of them was such that the persistence of that family life within the host State would from the outset be precarious' exceptional circumstances are required in order to find a violation of Article 8 ECHR.[5] The Court applied the exceptional circumstances doctrine without examining how the logic underpinning that test relates to the child involved. The ECtHR concluded that the decision did not constitute a violation of the rights of the parents under Article 8 ECHR, and subsequently discussed the circumstances and interests of the child. Even though the Court held that the removal of the father would not be beneficial to the girl, it considered that the family could enjoy family life in Ghana, or at least maintain regular contact, since both parents originated from Ghana. After examining how the case at hand differed from the *Nunez* case, the Court found that no exceptional circumstances were present and held that, for this reason, sufficient weight had been attached to the best interests of the child.[6] It concluded that the state had struck a fair balance between the public interest and the interests of the family members.[7]

There are two main themes that emerge in the original judgment that are especially problematic from a children's rights perspective and which the re-written judgment seeks to address; the treatment of children as extensions of their parents and the lack of recognition of children as independent rights holders.

II. The Treatment of Children as Extensions of their Parents

John Tobin persuasively argues that the conception of the child that underlies courts' reasoning has a significant impact on the way in which decisions are made. Upholding the construction of the child as rights-bearer means recognising children's claim 'to an independent legal status with interests and entitlements that exist by virtue of their humanity.'[8] In the immigration context, the child as rights-bearer is generally not the dominant conception that underlies decisions. According to American scholar, David Thronson, immigration systems are often based on a modern 'children as property' model, which does not mean that children are seen as actual property but that the immigration system 'makes assumptions about children deeply analogous to those it adopts in thinking about property.'[9] These notions of property are reflected in the conceptualisations of parents as active rights-bearers and of children 'as passive objects subject to their control'.[10] Immigration decision-makers view children through this 'property lens' which leaves

---

[5] *Antwi*, above n 1, para 89.

[6] ibid, 103.

[7] ibid, 105.

[8] J Tobin, 'Judging the Judges: Are They Adopting the Rights Approach in Matters Involving Children?' (2009) 33 *Melbourne University Law Review* 579, 586.

[9] DB Thronson, 'Kids Will Be Kids—Reconsidering Conceptions of Children's Rights Underlying Immigration Law' (2002) 63 *Ohio State Law Journal* 979, citing Barbara Bennett Woodhouse, '"Who Owns the Child?": Meyer and Pierce and the Child as Property' (1992) 33 *William & Mary Law Review* 995, 1051.

[10] ibid, 979.

their independent rights ignored, their perspectives unexamined and their voices silenced, according to Thronson. The sovereign right of nation-states to control their borders and the restraint with which immigration courts are to review such cases make it difficult for courts to escape this paradigm.

Despite the introduction of the best interests principle in *Nunez*, and its presence in the *Antwi* case, the Court's settled line of reasoning was not significantly altered. The father's choice to breach immigration rules is still central to the decision, which leads to a large margin of appreciation for signatory states and to the application of the exceptional circumstances doctrine. The parents' conduct, rather than the best interests of the child, thus forms the point of departure. Furthermore, in justifying why the girl can be expected to live in Ghana the Court only refers to the situation of the parents, namely, that they are both from Ghana and that they have travelled there with their daughter on three different occasions.

The Court is somewhat inconsistent when it comes to the relationship between the conduct of parents and the independent rights and interests of the child. In *Nunez* and *Antwi* this relationship is not explicitly addressed. In the previous case of *Osman* concerning a girl who was refused re-entry in Denmark after her father had sent her to Kenya to be 're-educated', the Court held that 'in respecting parental rights, the authorities cannot ignore the child's interests including its own right to respect for private and family life.'[11] By contrast, in *Butt*, concerning the expulsion of young adults after having resided in Norway for many years without a residence permit, the Court held that there

> were generally speaking strong immigration policy considerations in favour of identifying children with the conduct of their parents. If it were to be otherwise, there would be a great risk that parents exploited the situation of their children to secure a residence permit for themselves and for the children.[12]

The Court is consistent to the extent that a child whose parent(s) resided irregularly is defined by that status first, and by his or her status as a child second.

The rewritten judgment, by contrast, provides clarity by clearly stating that the child 'cannot be held responsible for her parents' actions.'[13] Consistent with this statement, the exceptional circumstances doctrine is omitted from the judgment since the doctrine flows from the choice made by the parents to continue their residency in Norway despite being aware of their precarious residency status.

III. The Rights of the Child

The Court considers the best interests of the Norwegian girl but, in doing so, fails to let this assessment be guided by the rights of the child while both ECHR and CRC rights are arguably at stake in the case.[14] Three clusters of rights seem to be of main relevance here; the rights relating to private life, citizenship and development.

---

[11] *Osman v Denmark* (2011) 38058/09, 14 June 2011.
[12] *Butt v Norway*, 47017/09, 4 December 2012. Ruled after the *Antwi* judgment.
[13] Rewritten judgment, para 95.
[14] Tobin, above n 8, 592.

A. The Child's Right to Respect for Private Life under Article 8 ECHR

The child's own right to respect for private life is left unconsidered in the original judgment. Jane Fortin, criticised the United Kingdom Supreme Court for adopting a similar approach. She argues that there is a difference 'between ensuring that a child's best interests are seen as "a primary consideration" and ensuring that a child's position is respected as a Convention rights holder with an equal status to that of the adults involved in the litigation.'[15] In *Nunez*, the parents of the children were divorced and the family judge had awarded custody to the father, as remaining in Norway was considered to be in the best interests of the children. For this reason, the ECtHR did not consider the possibility of the children following their mother abroad. In *Antwi*, however, the possibility of the girl following her parents abroad was an important part of the ECtHR's considerations. If the girl were to follow her parents she would have had to leave behind her country of citizenship, where she was born, raised, went to school and spoke the language. How does this situation respond to her individual right to respect for private life? The Court does not explicitly mention the rights to respect for private life as laid down in Article 8 ECHR nor does it apply any established set of principles connected to that right to the situation of the girl. This can be explained in two ways. First, it is the father, and not the girl, who is being expelled. The girl is a Norwegian citizen, and the place in which she is to reside is constructed as a choice of the parents rather than a choice that is forced upon her by the state. Second, as discussed above, the legal position of the child is first and foremost defined by the immigration status of the child's father. As he is considered to have resided irregularly, the principles that are applicable to the removal of individuals with legal residency are left aside by the Court.

The original judgment draws the general conclusion that the deportation of the father would not be 'beneficial' to the girl but subsequently concluded that there was no insurmountable obstacle in the way of the girl moving to Ghana or of remaining in regular contact since the mother was able to provide care on her own, leaving it to the parents to ensure a satisfactory solution and the well-being of the child.[16] The rewritten judgment, by contrast, rigorously examines the child's rights and interests in relation to both scenarios, thereby acknowledging the state's responsibility in ensuring the well-being of the child and its role in creating the situation.

In answering the question whether the girl can follow her parents abroad, the argument made in the rewritten judgment largely centres on the girl's citizenship status (see next section) rather than on her right to respect for private life. The rewritten judgment therefore does not take the opportunity to develop the approach taken by the ECtHR in the *Neulinger* case.

This case concerned a Swiss boy who had been taken to Switzerland by his mother without the required permission of his Israeli father.[17] In assessing the best interests of the child, and examining whether the child had 'settled in the host country', the Court employed the same principles it used to answer the question whether an adolescent who had committed felonies after spending his entire life in the host country could be expelled without violating

---

[15] J Fortin, 'Are Children's Best Interests Really Best? ZH (Tanzania)(FC) v Secretary of State for the Home Department' (2011) 74 *Modern Law Review* 947, 960.

[16] *Antwi*, above n 1, para 97.

[17] *Neulinger*, above n 3.

his right to respect for private life.[18] In the *Berisha* ruling, which followed the *Antwi* ruling, the dissenting judges made the case for adopting this *Neulinger*-approach to the situation of three children who had travelled into Switzerland without the required residency permits for the purpose of residing with their parents. The judges reasoned—similar to the rewritten judgment—that 'the children cannot be held responsible or suffer for their parents' incorrect or even illegal behaviour.'[19] In line with this view it was argued that the ties of the children ought to be evaluated in accordance with the principles that are applicable to legally residing immigrants who are threatened with deportation, despite the fact that the children's ties to Switzerland were formed during irregular stay.

While the rewritten judgment significantly strengthens the legal position of citizen children, by ensuring that the legal position of these children is defined by their citizenship status rather than the immigration status of a parent, it arguably could have strengthened the legal position of non-citizen children to a greater extent. The opportunity to ensure the immigrant child is seen as a child first and an immigrant second, by acknowledging the child's independent right to respect for private life under Article 8 ECHR, is left unused. The rewritten judgment thus respects the constraints imposed by the ECtHR's settled case law in this context.

B. The Child's Citizenship Status

Another notable aspect is that, besides noting that the girl is a Norwegian citizen, and operating on the assumption that she would return to Norway 'later in life',[20] the ECtHR attaches little importance to her status as a Norwegian citizen in the original judgment. This is consistent with earlier case law in which the Court considered the citizenship status of children—whose parents face deportation—not to be of 'particular significance'.[21] As noted in the introduction of this commentary, the *Antwi* case was handed down against the backdrop of two landmark cases that explicitly address the citizenship status of children and the rights attached to this status; the *Zambrano* ruling by the CJEU and the *ZH (Tanzania)* ruling by the UK Supreme Court. Both cases centre on what has been described in academic literature as de facto—or constructive—deportation.[22] A state cannot deport its own citizens, yet, when the parents (the primary carers) of a citizen child are deported it raises the question to what extent children have the freedom to remain. This lack of choice inhabits a central place in both judgments.

In *Zambrano* the CJEU considered it contrary to EU law to force EU citizens to leave the territory of the Union insofar as it deprives them of the genuine enjoyment of the substance of the rights conferred by their status as EU citizens.[23] In *ZH (Tanzania)* it was also deemed crucial by Lady Hale that the forced removal of the primary carer of children would—in

---

[18] *Maslov v Austria* (2007) 1638/03 ECHR 221.

[19] *Berisha v Switzerland* (2013) 948/12 ECHR 765, joint dissenting opinion of Judges D Jočienė and I Karakaş, para 4.

[20] *Antwi*, above n 1, para 96.

[21] *Sorabjee v United Kingdom*, 23938/94, 23 October 1995.

[22] J Bhabha, 'The "Mere Fortuity" of Birth? Are Children Citizens? (2004) 15 *Differences: A Journal of Feminist Cultural Studies* 91, 94.

[23] *Zambrano*, above n 4, paras 41–44.

her view—inevitably result in a departure of the children and their inability to exercise the rights they have as citizens.[24] Furthermore, the citizenship status of the children was also considered a relevant element for the assessment of the best interests of the child.[25] Lord Kerr eloquently articulated that it 'seems self-evident that to diminish a child's right to assert his or her nationality will not normally be in his or her best interests.'[26] These developments undeniably provide an opening to debate questions concerning a child's interest in growing up in his or her country of citizenship but also concerning the value of citizenship as an intrinsic part of ECHR rights, such as the right to respect for private life and Article 3 of Protocol Number 4 ECHR, which prohibits the deportation of a state's own nationals.[27]

The rewritten judgment constructs the decision to deport the father and impose a re-entry ban of five years as possibly obliging the girl to move to Ghana. This obligation is deemed 'unreasonable' by the Court because of the detrimental impact of this move on the well-being, identity and citizenship status of the girl.[28] Consequently, the Court's focus moves from the question whether or not there are insurmountable obstacles in the way of the family settling together in Ghana, to the question whether a separation of the father and child would violate Article 8 ECHR. Thus, rather than presuming that a child is able to move to his or her parents' home country, the rewritten judgment presumes that the child remains in his or her country of citizenship so as to enable the child to exercise this status.

C. The Child's Right to Development

The word 'development' is not mentioned by the ECtHR in the *Nunez* nor in the *Antwi* case. By contrast, in *Neulinger* the ECtHR considered that it is 'in the child's interest to ensure its development in a sound environment' and subsequently assessed the case from a 'personal development perspective'.[29] The absence of a developmental perspective has at least two consequences. First, it hampers the achievement of substantive equality by failing to recognise the specific characteristics of children and their particular vulnerabilities.[30] Second, by not recognising the centrality of the holistic development of the child to the best interests principle, the principle is at risk of becoming empty rhetoric rather than a guiding human rights principle with substance and meaning.

The contribution made by the rewritten judgment lies, in this respect, most significantly in the introduction of the developmental perspective in the immigration context by relying on the ECtHR's own case law in the context of child abduction.[31] This is an essential

---

[24] *ZH (Tanzania)*, above n 4, paras 32–33.

[25] ibid, para 30. Lady Hale let the right of every child to be registered and acquire a nationality (Art 7) and to preserve her identity, including her nationality (Art 8) guide the best interests assessment.

[26] ibid, para 47.

[27] See E Nissen, *The Rights of Minor EU Member State Nationals Wishing to Enjoy Family Life with a Non-EU Parent in their Country of Nationality* (Oisterwijk, WLP, 2013) 32–36, for a discussion of the ECtHR's case law on Art 3 of Protocol No 4 ECHR and the value of citizenship under Art 8 ECHR.

[28] Rewritten judgment, para 99.

[29] *Neulinger*, above n 3, paras 137–38.

[30] L Ferguson, 'The Jurisprudence of Making Decisions Affecting Children: An Argument to Prefer Duty to Children's Rights and Welfare' in A Diduck, N Peleg and H Reece (eds), *Law in Society: Reflections on Children, Family, Culture and Philosophy—Essays in Honour of Michael Freeman* (Leiden, Brill, 2015).

[31] Rewritten judgment, paras 95–96.

first step toward substantive equality for children and the application of the best interests principle in line with General Comment number 14.[32]

IV. Conclusion

The original *Antwi* judgment failed to consolidate and develop the progress made in the *Nunez* judgment. The rewritten judgment, by contrast, takes important steps in acknowledging and further developing the status of children as independent rights holders. It makes a bold attempt at achieving something that neither the ECtHR nor the CJEU has managed to do, namely, to view fundamental rights in conjunction with the rights attached to citizenship. This paradigm shift, to a certain extent, addresses the unsatisfactory and incoherent jurisprudence as a result of two separate European legal frameworks and jurisdictions.[33] In doing so, the rewritten judgment echoes the ruling in *ZH (Tanzania)* in its focus on the legal position of citizen children as well as in its negligence towards the legal position of immigrant children.[34]

[32] UN Committee on the Rights of the Child (CRC), *General comment No 14 (2013) on the right of the child to have his or her best interests taken as a primary consideration (Art 3, para 1)*, 29 May 2013, CRC /C/GC/14.
[33] G Davies, 'The Family Rights of European Children: Expulsion of Non-European Parents' (2012) 4 *EUI Working Paper RSCAS*, 13.
[34] Fortin, above n 15, 961.

European Court of Human Rights

Antwi and others v Norway

The European Court of Human Rights (First Section), sitting as a chamber composed of Maria Papaioannou and Judges U, V, W, X, Y and Z delivers the following judgment.

Procedure

1.   The case originated in an application (no 26940/10) against the Kingdom of Norway lodged with the Court under Article 34 of the Convention for the Protection of Human Rights and Fundamental Freedoms ('the Convention'), on 11 May 2010, by Mr Henry Antwi ('the first applicant'), a Ghanaian national who was born in 1975; by his wife, Mrs Vivian Awere Osei ('the second applicant'); a Norwegian citizen who was born in Ghana in 1979; and by their daughter, Ms Nadia Ryan Pinto ('the third applicant'), a Norwegian national who was born in September 2001.

2.   The applicants were represented by Mr A Humlen, a lawyer practising in Oslo. The Norwegian Government ('the Government') were represented by Mr M Emberland, Attorney, Attorney-General's Office (Civil Matters), as their Agent, assisted by Ms A Matheson Mestad, Attorney of the same office.

3.   The applicants alleged that the Norwegian immigration authorities' decision to expel the father from Norway and to prohibit his re-entry for five years would, if implemented, give rise to a violation of his, his wife's and his daughter's right to respect for family life under Article 8 of the Convention.

4.   On 19 May 2010 the President of the First Section decided to apply Rule 39 of the Rules of Court, indicating to the Government that it was desirable in the interests of the parties and the proper conduct of the proceedings not to deport the first applicant until further notice. The President further decided to give priority to the application (Rule 41).

5.   On 1 July 2010 the application was communicated to the Government. It was also decided to rule on the admissibility and merits of the application at the same time (Article 29(1)).

The Facts

I. The Circumstances of the Case

A. Factual Background

6.   Mr Antwi arrived in Germany in 1998, where he obtained a forged passport and a birth certificate under a false identity indicating that he was a Portuguese national named Jey Jey Pinto (not the real name).

7.   Mrs Vivian Awere Osei is of Ghanaian origin. In 1997, she reunited with her father and three siblings living in Oslo, and in 2000 she obtained Norwegian citizenship. During his stay, Mr Antwi met Mrs Awere Osei, who was travelling in Germany and, soon after, he moved to Oslo and started cohabiting with her.

8.   On 23 December 1999 Mr Antwi was granted a five year residence- and work permit from 13 April 2000 to 13 April 2005 as an EEA national on the basis of the forged Portuguese passport.

9.   On 23 September 2001 the couple had a daughter Ms Lisa Pinto (the third applicant).

10.   On 11 February 2005 the couple married in Ghana. According to the applicants, it was in that connection that the second applicant had become aware of the first applicant's true identity when he obtained a Ghanaian passport.

11.   On 15 July 2005 the first applicant was arrested in the Netherlands while travelling to Canada, as the Dutch authorities discovered that his passport was forged. Subsequently, the first applicant provided his true identity to the Norwegian authorities. After a few months he returned to Norway.

(…)

2. The Court's Assessment

87.   The Court affirms that the relationship between the applicants constituted 'family life' for the purposes of Article 8 of the Convention, which is applicable to the present case. The Court notes that this was not disputed by the parties.

88.   The Court observes that expulsion measures against an alien when his close relatives reside or have the right to reside in a contracting state may give rise to infringements of Article 8 (*Jerry Olajide Sarumi v the United Kingdom* (dec), no 43279/98, 26 January 1999).

89.   In the present case, in 1998, the first applicant obtained a forged passport and birth certificate stating false identity. Work and residence permits were issued on the basis of false identity information contained in the documents. On these grounds, the first applicant applied for renewal of the permit and for Norwegian citizenship. The Court observes that it is for the Contracting States to maintain public order, in particular by exercising their right, as a matter of well-established international law and subject to their treaty obligations, to control the entry and residence of aliens and notably to order the expulsion of aliens convicted of criminal offences. The Court sees no reason to disagree with the assessment made by the national immigration authorities and Courts as to the repetitive and aggravated character of Mr Antwi's administrative offences under the Immigration Act. By

having intentionally provided a false identity, Mr Antwi had obtained residence and work permits, none of which he had been entitled to. Thus, the Court affirms that Article 8 does not entail a general obligation for a state to respect an immigrant's choice of the country of their residence and to authorize family reunification (see *Nunez v Norway*, no 55597/09, 28 June 2011 §70, *Emre v Switzerland*, no 42034/04, § 65, 22 May 2008).

90.   The Court notes in the first place that the impugned expulsion and five year prohibition on re-entry had been imposed on the *first* applicant with regard to violations of the Immigration Act. It is well-accepted that expulsion would constitute an important means of general deterrence against gross or repeated violations of the Immigration Act (see *Nunez*, cited above, § 71, and *Darren Omoregie and Others v Norway*, no 265/07, § 67, 31 July 2008; see also *Kaya v the Netherlands* (dec) no 44947/98, 6 November 2001) justified by a pressing social need and a legitimate aim pursued in a democratic society and does not, as such, constitute a violation of Article 8 of the Convention.

91.   However, the Court recalls that on various occasions International Human Rights Courts have determined the effect of deportation on family life and whether such interference is proportionate. In an effort to balance a deportee's rights to remain in a host country and a state's interest to protect its immigration policies, various factors have been taken into consideration inter alia: the existence of family ties in the host state; the extent of hardship the non-citizen's deportation poses for the family in the host state; the extent of the non-citizen's links to the country of origin; the nature and severity of the non-citizen's criminal offence(s) (See for instance *Wayne Smith, Hugo Armendariz et al v US Case*, IACHR REPORT no 81/10, paragraph 57), the length of time spent and the cultural and social ties in the receiving state (*Mehemi v France*, no 25017/94, Judgment of 10 April 2003).

92.   The Court observes that the first applicant had grown up in Ghana, where his family lived. At the time he obtained the false travel documents, he was an adult with no links to Norway. He started co-habiting with the second applicant, a Norwegian national, upon his arrival, aware that his residence status was not legitimate. At no point could the first applicant have any reasonable legal base to remain in the country.

93.   The second applicant had also grown up in Ghana. She reunited with her father's family at the age of 17. She became a Norwegian citizen with family ties and social links to Norway. Given her long presence and the strong links with her country of residence and of current citizenship, the Court notes that a temporary resettlement in Ghana would be impossible for her. Furthermore, the second applicant became aware of the precarious legal status of the first applicant in connection with their marriage in Ghana on 11 February 2005, only after her child's birth. Consequently, the Court endorses the High Court's view that expulsion of the first applicant would amount to a disproportionate measure.

94.   As to the third applicant, the Court will examine whether deportation measures would entail infringements under Article 8 in the light of the children's best interests. The Court notes that the best interests of the child as enshrined in Article 3 of the UN Convention on the Rights of the Child (CRC) shall be a primary consideration in all actions taken by public authorities concerning children (see *Neulinger and Shuruk v Switzerland* [GC], no 41615/07, paragraph 135), even in the case of children of non-citizens (ECHR *Maslov v Austria*, Judgment of June 23 2008, no 1638/03, paragraph 82 citing *Üner v Netherlands*, Judgment of October 18, 2006, no 46410/99, paragraph 58). Following the legal reasoning in *Nunez*, the

Court notes that children suffer the negative consequences of fraudulent conduct of their parent, thus the authorities should always examine the effects of an expulsion on children and on the enjoyment of private and/or family life as protected by Article 8 ECHR. With regard to the proportionality test of an expulsion measure concerning a child, it is necessary to take into account the child's best interests and well-being (*Neulinger* and *Shuruk*, cited above, paragraph 146, *Üner v the Netherlands* [GC], cited above paragraph 57, ECHR 2006-XII). 'Such wellbeing is determined by a variety of individual circumstances, such as the age, the level of maturity of the child, the presence or absence of parents, the child's environment and experiences.' (UNHCR Guidelines on Determining the Best Interests of the Child, May 2008). It is also examined by reference to the extent to which family life [would be] effectively ruptured by the expulsion (see *Rodrigues da Silva* and *Hoogkamer*, cited above, § 39).

95.   In this regard, the third applicant is a Norwegian national. She was born in Norway in September 2001 and lived there ever since. She speaks the Norwegian language and she is fully integrated into the Norwegian social, educational and cultural system. In comparison, her only direct link to Ghana is the three visits she made there with her parents. Furthermore, her father had a significant and active role in the child's daily care and up-bringing as he was looking after and actively supporting her on a day-to-day basis (taking her to and from school and, sport activities etc). Given her age, 10 years, the guardianship of Mr Antwi determines the child's sense of security, stability and development. As a child of her age, she is as strongly attached to her father as she is to her mother and she cannot be held responsible for her parents' actions.

96.   The Court draws on the High Court's observations that depriving the child of her relationship with her father would be a serious measure and could have disturbing effects on the child's development as well as on the relations between the child and the parent with whom he or she does not live (*Macready v the Czech Republic*, no 4824/06 and 15512/08, 22 April 2010; *Maumousseau and Washington v France*, no 39388/05, § 83, ECHR 2007-XIII) even if the remaining parent is able to provide satisfactory care or in the absence of insurmountable obstacles in, at the least, maintaining regular contacts with the expelled parent.

97.   The Court recalls that in *Nunez* the Grand Chamber concluded that 'as a result of the decisions taken in the expulsion case a child would in all likelihood be separated from its parent practically for two years, a very long period for children of the ages in question'. (*Nunez* paragraph 81). The Court takes especially into account the age of the third applicant and her close relationship with her father, noting that since birth the first applicant had been very involved in her care. Given the similarities with the facts in *Nunez* (which concerned children of a similar age and a legally residing parent able to take care of the child) and the less aggravated character of the first applicant's violations of domestic law in the present case (the absence of previous criminal offences, or history of entry on false documents as in *Nunez* case) a five-year entry ban would impose a disproportionate burden on the third applicant in the circumstances.

98.   As in *Nunez* (cited above, see the submissions in §62 and 64 of that judgment) an application for family reunification could only be made after expiry of the ban and there was no guarantee that a residence permit would be granted.

99.   With regard to the third applicant's family resettlement in Ghana, the Court considers the third applicant, a Norwegian citizen, is totally integrated into the country's societal and

linguistic context. In this context, an enforced resettlement could have a detrimental impact upon her well-being and identity and significantly undermine her citizenship status.

100.   In light of the above, the Court shares the view of the High Court's minority that the applicant's expulsion with a five year re-entry ban is a disproportionately severe measure which undermines the child's best interests in the context of her right to respect for private and family life under Article 8.

101.   Having regard to all of the above considerations, notably the child's long lasting and close bonds to her father, the Court is not satisfied that sufficient weight was attached to the best interests of the children for the purposes of Article 8 of the Convention interpreted in the light of Article 3 UN CRC (*Harroudj v France*, no 43631/09, 4 October 2012, paragraph 42) and Council of Europe's Guidelines on child friendly justice, 17 November 2010). In particular, the Court emphasises that children are holders of human rights in her own right.

102.   Accordingly, the Court concludes that the first applicant's expulsion from Norway with a five year re-entry ban would entail a violation of Article 8 of the Convention.

31

Commentary on *Defence for Children International (DCI) v Belgium*

GAMZE ERDEM TÜRKELLİ

The European Committee on Social Rights (ECSR) is a quasi-judicial body of the Council of Europe tasked with monitoring compliance with the European Social Charter. The Charter has been called 'the counterpart, in the field of economic and social rights, of the Council of Europe's (CoE) much better known European Convention on Human Rights'.[1] ECSR carries out its monitoring duty through state party reporting and the collective complaints mechanism.[2] The collective complaints mechanism of ECSR allows for institutional complainants and defendant states to present allegations and arguments on broader policy matters. In the absence of an additional individual access to the complaints mechanism, however, this de-personalised complaints approach is problematic with regards to children's right to be heard in judicial and administrative proceedings affecting them, especially because ECSR does not have a mandate to hear testimony or conduct interviews with affected individuals, even when these are children.[3] From a broader human rights standpoint, the collective complaints mechanism of the European Social Charter does not respond wholly to accountability challenges. As Churchill and Khaliq note:

> As an *actio popularis,* the CCP cannot and is not designed to provide individual remedies and thus is of limited utility to provide redress for individual grievances … Any action taken by the defendant state seeking to rectify the situation will almost certainly not be retrospective in effect and will seek only to ensure that the Charter is not breached in future, no matter the degree of detriment already suffered by individuals.[4]

Despite the shortcomings, the collective complaints mechanism of the ECSR has been one of the ways through which pressing policy issues on economic and social rights have been brought to the forefront.

---

[1] RR Churchill and U Khaliq, 'The Collective Complaints System of the European Social Charter: An Effective Mechanism for Ensuring Compliance with Economic and Social Rights?' (2004) 15(3) *EJIL* 417, 418.

[2] ECSR, Rules of the Committee (9 September 2014) para 2.

[3] G Lansdown, 'Every Child's Right to be heard: a Resource Guide on the UN Committee on the Rights of the Child General Comment No.12' (Save the Children, 2011) 24.

[4] Churchill and Khaliq, 'The Collective Complaints System', above n 1, 454.

I. The Decision: *DCI v Belgium*

A complaint under the collective complaints mechanism was submitted to the ECSR on 21 June 2011 by non-governmental organisation, Defence for Children International (DCI), alleging that Belgium was in contravention of its legal obligations under the Revised European Social Charter (the Charter) as regards the rights of unaccompanied and accompanied foreign minors unlawfully present, resident or seeking asylum in its territory for failing to provide adequate 'protection (social, legal and economic), as well as medical assistance'.[5] The complaint alleged that Articles 7 § 10, 11, 13, 16, 17 and 30 of the Charter 'read alone or in conjunction with Article E'[6] of the European Social Charter were violated.

The ECSR's decision made a number of important overtures regarding bringing children within the personal scope of the Charter, even when the children in question are 'not literally included in the Charter's scope' (paragraph 36). The ECSR's assessment, that the personal scope of application (the persons to which the provisions of the Charter apply) may be expanded, is conceptually linked to its assertion that the Charter should be interpreted in line with international law (above all jus cogens (paragraph 29)), including the Convention on the Rights of the Child (CRC) (paragraph 31), employing a teleological approach that it had previously adopted from the European Court of Human Rights to best achieve its object and purpose of 'giv[ing] life and meaning in Europe to the fundamental social rights of all human beings' (paragraph 30).[7]

The ECSR noted that 'the personal scope of the Charter must be determined according to the principle of the child's best interests' with respect to the case, citing the CRC Committee's General Comment 5 (paragraph 32). In addition, the ECSR pointed out a heightened risk of impairment of fundamental rights and thus a heightened duty on the part of states when conditions of 'vulnerability and limited autonomy' are combined (for instance, in the case of 'migrant children unlawfully present in a country'), especially when these children are unaccompanied (paragraph 37). The ECSR concluded thus that accompanied and unaccompanied foreign minors unlawfully resident in the territory of a contracting party should be considered rights holders under the Charter based on the fact that denying them the status of rights-holder would put their fundamental rights in serious jeopardy and 'expos[e] the children and young persons in question to serious threats to their rights to life, health and psychological and physical integrity and to the preservation of their human dignity' which would run contrary to a State's positive obligations under Article 17 of the Charter (paragraph 38). In fact, the ECSR had already noted in a previous decision that Article 17 of the revised charter was 'directly inspired' by the CRC and therefore

---

[5] *Defence for Children International (DCI) v Belgium* (Complaint No 69/2011), Complaint ECSR (27 June 2011) 8.

[6] The rights enumerated in the complaint under relevant articles are: 'The right of children and young persons to protection' (Art 7) entailing the obligation 'to ensure special protection against physical and moral dangers to which children and young persons are exposed, and particularly against those resulting directly or indirectly from their work' (under Art 7 § 10), 'The right to protection of health' (Art 11), 'The right to social and medical assistance' (Article 13), 'The right of the family to social, legal and economic protection' (Art 16), 'The right of children and young persons to social, legal and economic protection' (Art 17), 'The right to protection against poverty and social exclusion' (Art 30).

[7] H Cullen, 'The Collective Complaints System of the European Social Charter: Interpretative Methods of the European Committee of Social Rights' (2009) 9(1) *Human Rights Law Review* 73 and 76.

'protect[ed] in a general manner the right of children and young persons, including unaccompanied minors, to care and assistance', even if this right was a limited one.[8]

This being said, the ECSR underscored that the application of the Charter's provisions to foreign persons unlawfully present in a state party, including accompanied or unaccompanied children, such as in the present case, was 'entirely exceptional' and only justified in cases where the non-application would result in 'seriously detrimental consequences for their fundamental rights' (paragraph 35).[9] In addition, under these exceptional circumstances of application, the unlawfully present foreigners would only be entitled to the protection provided by Charter provisions 'whose fundamental purpose is closely linked to the requirement to secure the most fundamental human rights' (paragraph 36). Thus, the application of the Charter would have to follow a right-by-right approach.[10] The ECSR's decision followed a methodical analysis and interpretation of Charter provisions and international law as they related to the case and showcased an acute aptitude for situating the Charter within the different human rights and international law frameworks.

The complaint alleged that although an adequate legal framework on social assistance to minors was in place, unaccompanied minors had been excluded from such assistance in practice due to a lack of capacity at reception centres (paragraph 40). DCI noted that the Belgian government had not provided accompanied and unaccompanied foreign minors unlawfully residing in Belgium accommodation in reception centres affiliated with the Federal Agency for the Reception of Asylum Seekers (FEDASIL) or through other alternative means since 2009, notwithstanding 43 court orders to provide such accommodation to families and recommendations made by the Federal Ombudsmen.[11] The ECSR's decision dated 23 October 2012 found that Article 17 of the Charter was breached, as Belgium had not guaranteed 'effective rights' (paragraph 69) by failing to resolve the capacity issue (paragraph 82). In addition, the ECSR considered Belgium's 'fail[ure] to find a care solution' for the foreign minors unlawfully present (paragraph 95) and the corresponding exposure of these children and young persons to 'very serious physical and moral hazards' to be breaches of Article 7 § 10 (paragraph 97). Furthermore, noting the total lack of access to healthcare of accompanied foreign minors and the partial lack for those unaccompanied (paragraph 116), the ECSR found that Belgium had violated the right to protection of health by not providing the minimum prerequisites in the form of 'housing and foster homes' (paragraphs 117–18). The ECSR, on the other hand, found no violation of Article 13 on the right to social and medical assistance since the right of medical assistance guaranteed by law was found to be working effectively in practice (paragraph 131). The ECSR found that obligations under Article 30 on the 'right to protection against poverty and social exclusion' would be beyond the level of obligation incumbent on States Parties 'in respect of foreign minors who are in a country unlawfully' (paragraph 146). Likewise,

---

[8] *International Federation of Human Rights Leagues (FIDH) v France* (Complaint No 14/2003), Decision on the Merits ECSR (3 November 2004) para 36.

[9] The fundamental rights to which the ECSR referred included 'the right to life, to the preservation of human dignity, to psychological and physical integrity and to health'.

[10] Accordingly, while violations of certain rights such as the rights to protection and health were ascertained, other rights such as protection from social exclusion and poverty under Art 13 or the application of the non-discrimination principle were deemed non-applicable.

[11] *DCI v Belgium* (Complaint No 69/2011), Complaint (Translation) ECSR (27 June 2011) III. Merits, 1. Complaint, 12.

the ECSR considered that the principle of equal treatment could not be triggered in the specific case as the state had the discretion to treat individuals differently depending on their lawful or unlawful presence, their accompanied or unaccompanied situation or their asylum seeker status and also found Article E on non-discrimination in the enjoyment of rights non-applicable (paragraphs 149–51).

The Belgian government issued a memorandum on the ECSR decision on *DCI v Belgium* to the CoE Committee of Ministers, noting that measures had been taken in response to the decision, including the following:

— FEDASIL had undertaken measures to increase accommodation capacity by enhanced co-operation between different government bodies, including the Guardianship Department and Aliens Office.
— A winter plan for reception of unaccompanied minors for the year 2012–2013 had been put in place, with a number of new unaccompanied minors accommodated.
— A proposal was made to increase the number of guardians to be appointed for unaccompanied minors and set up a system of coaching and support for these guardians.
— FEDASIL had cooperated with emergency welfare system SAMU social to provide winter accommodation to a number of 'illegally resident families'.
— A decision was taken to establish an open centre for returning migrants, for unsuccessful asylum seekers and unlawfully resident families that voluntarily return home.[12]

A 2013 decision by the Committee of Ministers referred to the statement made by Belgium, welcoming the measures that the government had taken and expressing interest in further reporting by Belgium to demonstrate the longer term measures taken to bring the situation in conformity with the Charter.[13]

II. The Concurring Opinion

The ECSR does not have a widespread practice of including concurring opinions in its decisions, although its rules explicitly allow for their inclusion. When concurring opinions have in fact been included, they have not had a clear style and tended to be relatively short. Vandenhole's concurring opinion follows the approach that many judges in the European Court of Human Rights (ECtHR) have chosen to take in drafting their concurring opinions. This is also in line with the ECSR's more general practice of seeking to adopt decisions that are structured similar to ECtHR judgments in their analysis and reasoning.

The ECSR provided strong and progressive reasoning to demonstrate that minors constituting the subject of the complaint came within the scope of the Charter's Article 17 on the 'right of children and young persons to social, legal and economic protection' (paragraphs 28–39). Because of the decision's strengths in the analysis surrounding the essential nature of immediate assistance (paragraphs 80–83) and the active obligation to protect children from physical and moral hazards and to provide access to healthcare even for these

---

[12] Memorandum submitted by the Representative of Belgium at the GR-SOC meeting of 9 April 2013 (translation), *Appendix to Resolution CM/ResChS(2013)11, DCI v Belgium* (Complaint No 69/2011) ECSR (9 April 2013).
[13] CoE Committee of Ministers, Resolution CM/ResChS(2013)11, *DCI v Belgium* (Complaint No 69/2011) ECSR (11 June 2013).

children unlawfully residing in a state's territory (paragraphs 85 and 101–02, respectively), Vandenhole has decided to produce a concurring opinion in lieu of rewriting the existing opinion. The concurring opinion also agrees with the assessment and conclusions of the ECSR with regards to whether violations have in fact taken place.

What the concurring opinion does is to address the points that were not as strongly or convincingly reasoned in the appraisal of alleged violations in the decision on merits. For instance, the ECSR highlighted the particularly difficult situation of unaccompanied foreign minors (paragraphs 78–80). The ECSR also pointed to the need for implementation beyond mere legislation (paragraph 69), which requires resources and may entail progressive realisation as long as this is backed by 'measurable progress' within 'a reasonable time frame' and characterized by the 'optimum use' of resources (paragraphs 70–71). Yet, in arriving at its conclusion that Belgium had breached its corresponding obligations, the ECSR neither explored what the particular situation of unaccompanied minors meant for Belgium's obligations nor provided further direction in its decision about why it considered that the principle of progressive realisation based on measurable progress had not been respected by Belgium. Related to the latter point are the responsibilities that parents are required to undertake and whether a clear distinction between accompanied and unaccompanied minors can easily be drawn in terms of what is incumbent on the state where these minors are residing. The concurring opinion focuses on three aspects of the decision on the merits where the ECSR could have elaborated more strongly on the protection of children's rights: progressive realisation, parental responsibilities and the vulnerability imagery surrounding the migrant child.

A. Progressive Realisation

The ECSR noted, in its consideration of merits related to Article 17, that states are obliged to 'provide for the requisite resources and procedures to facilitate full exercise of the rights guaranteed by the Charter' (paragraph 70). The ECSR's interpretation also allowed for the realisation of rights in 'a reasonable timetable, securing measurable progress' with the 'optimum use' of resources at disposal in cases where implementation is 'highly complex and costly' (paragraph 72), which is squarely in line with the child rights-based approach as outlined in the CRC. On the other hand, in the case of unlawfully present children and young persons, the ECSR considered immediate assistance to be essential (paragraph 81). The concurring opinion of Vandenhole addresses the reasoning gap in the original judgment by bridging the divide between progressive realisation and the necessity of immediate assistance through reference to the concept of 'core obligations'.[14]

The UN Committee on Economic, Social and Cultural Rights (CESCR) concluded in its General Comment 3 on the Nature of States parties' obligations that 'a minimum core obligation to ensure the satisfaction of, at the very least, minimum essential levels of each of the rights is incumbent upon every State party'.[15] While progressive realisation of rights of an economic and social nature had been allowed for in both the International Covenant on Economic, Social and Cultural Rights (ICESCR) and the CRC, a minimum core obligation for each right was an immediate one. The CESCR enumerated rights to 'essential

---

[14] W Vandenhole, Concurring Opinion, para 5.
[15] CESCR, 'General Comment No 3 on the nature of States parties' obligations' (1990) E/1991/23, para 10.

foodstuffs, ... essential primary health care, ... basic shelter and housing, or ... the most basic forms of education' as rights contained within the definition of core obligations.[16] The CRC Committee clarified that the core obligations surrounding the right to health included '[e]nsuring universal coverage of quality primary health services, including prevention, health promotion, care and treatment services, and essential drugs'.[17] The CRC Committee's General Comment 19 on budgeting for the realisation of children's rights further strengthens the immediate and minimum nature of core obligations by noting that they 'shall not be compromised by any retrogressive measures, even in times of economic crisis'.[18] ECSR was confronted with the question of progressive realisation once again in its *Conference of European Churches (CEC) v the Netherlands* decision. CEC brought a complaint before the ECSR alleging that the Netherlands 'failed to fulfil its obligations under the Revised Social Charter ... to respect the rights of undocumented adults to food, clothing and shelter'.[19] In assessing alleged violations, the ECSR referred to 'core obligations' as set out by the CESCR[20] and concluded:

> [A]ccess to food, water, as well as to such basic amenities as a safe place to sleep and clothes fulfilling the minimum requirements for survival in the prevailing weather conditions are necessary for the basic subsistence of any human being.[21]

B. Parental Responsibilities

The ECSR decision was unclear on the relationship of accompanied minors to their parents and the roles of the parents with respect to the rights in question. The accompanied versus unaccompanied minor distinction is drawn upon in the concurring opinion to fill a vacuum left in the ECSR decision about the role of the parents. The concurring opinion acknowledges the parents' role as primary caregivers[22] but also recognises that these primary caregivers—due to their situation as migrants unlawfully resident in Belgium—should be assisted by the state in order to be able to fully carry out their duties. As such, the concurring opinion seeks to highlight that the state has an enhanced obligation not only as regards unaccompanied minors but also accompanied minors. Unaccompanied minors need protection and assistance precisely because these children do not enjoy the support that their families would normally extend them. In addition, the state has an obligation to support children accompanied by their parents and to assist the parents of these children so that they are able to effectively care for their children.[23]

The Belgian Constitutional Court dealt with this question in 2003, in the wake of the Belgian government's decision to cut assistance to undocumented persons, children as well

---

[16] ibid.

[17] CRC Committee, 'General comment No 15 on the right of the child to the enjoyment of the highest attainable standard of health (art 24)' (2013) CRC/C/GC/15, para 73.

[18] CRC Committee, 'General comment No 19 on public budgeting for the realization of children's rights (art 4)' (2016) CRC/C/GC/19, para 31.

[19] *Conference of European Churches (CEC) v The Netherlands* (Complaint No 90/2013) Complaint ECSR, (21 January 2013) '1. Purpose of the Complaint', 1. (The complaint alleged that the Netherlands had breached its obligations under Art 13 § 4 (the right to social and medical assistance) and Art 31 § 2 (the right to shelter) of the Revised Charter (*CEC v the Netherlands*, Complaint ECSR 3)).

[20] *CEC v the Netherlands*, Decision on the Merits ECSR (1 July 2014) para 114.

[21] ibid, para 122.

[22] Vandenhole, Concurring Opinion, para 5.

[23] ibid, para 3.

as adults. The Constitutional Court ruled that accompanied minors unlawfully present in the territory of Belgium alongside their parents were still entitled to a right of material assistance and not merely to urgent healthcare as had been provided by the legislator, because denying such material assistance would force a child to live under conditions detrimental to his/her health and development.[24] The Court clarified that while children were entitled to this assistance, parents themselves did not have any right to social assistance apart from urgent medical care.[25] The Court devised three conditions for granting of social assistance to children unlawfully present:

1. 'Parents do not or are not in a position to carry out their duty of care',
2. 'The request for social assistance comprises expenses vital to the development of the child in whose benefit the assistance is being delivered', and
3. 'The social assistance provided would exclusively be used to cover these expenses'.[26]

In the 2012 *Popov v France* judgment, the ECtHR also tackled the question of what the relationship between state obligations and parental responsibilities is in situations where parents and children are seeking asylum. ECtHR ruled that the presence of parents alongside children could not be considered a sufficient condition for 'exempting the authorities from their duty to protect children and take appropriate measures as part of their positive obligations under Article 3 of the Convention'.[27] The ECtHR further argued that migrant children unlawfully resident in a territory have particular needs arising not solely from 'their age and lack of independence' (and thus perceived vulnerability) but also from their disadvantaged situation as asylum seekers.[28] Furthermore, the ECtHR recalled a previous reference to Article 22 of the CRC, reiterating that states should ensure that a child who is seeking refugee status 'enjoys protection and humanitarian assistance, whether the child is alone or accompanied by his or her parents'.[29] In the Grand Chamber case *Tarakhel v Switzerland*, the ECtHR underscored the crucial nature of the requirement of 'special protection', especially when those concerned were children.[30] The ECtHR's *Tarakhel v Switzerland* judgment built on the *Popov* judgment, holding that this requirement of special protection continues to apply 'even when … the children seeking asylum are accompanied by their parents'.[31] In the case *VM and Others v Belgium*, the ECtHR concluded that its case law required competent authorities to consider that the status as a child trumped the status as an unlawfully present foreigner.[32]

---

[24] *Arrêt n° 106/2003 de la Cour d'Arbitrage statuant sur une question préjudicielle relative à l'article 57, § 2, de la loi du 8 juillet 1976 organique des centres publics d'aide sociale* (M.B. du 04/11/2003, p 53695), 22 July 2003, para B.7.5.

[25] ibid, para B.7.4.

[26] ibid, para B.7.7 (translated from French to English).

[27] *Popov v France*, nos 39472/07 and 39474/07, § 91, 19 January 2012.

[28] ibid.

[29] Originally in *Muskhadzhiyeva and Others v Belgium*, no 41442/07, § 62, 19 January 2010 (original judgment in French) also later referenced in *Popov v France*, nos 39472/07 and 39474/07, § 91, 19 January 2012.

[30] *Tarakhel v Switzerland* [GC], no 29217/12, § 119 ECHR 2014 (extracts).

[31] ibid.

[32] *VM and Others v Belgium*, no 60125/11, § 138, 7 July 2015 (original judgment in French). (The case is currently on appeal, having been sent to the Grand Chamber in December 2015.)

C. Vulnerability

The concurring opinion calls for a nuanced portrayal of migrant children's lives, where vulnerability is not unduly emphasised and treated as inherently antithetical to a migrant child's autonomy.[33] In fact, most migrant children's experiences demonstrate that there are points of vulnerability and resilience in coexistence. Therefore, a balanced approach to vulnerability and resilience discourses serves better to illuminate migrant children's experiences. As Ensor and Gozdziak note:[34]

> Migrant children facing adversity may very well be, owing to the many limitations associated with both young age and displacement, particularly vulnerable to a variety of risk factors. Focusing exclusively on children's weakness, on the one hand, may harm their self-esteem and undermine their efforts to overcome the challenges they might face. An excessive emphasis on resilience and coping, on the other hand, could obscure individual vulnerabilities or even result in blaming those individuals who appear more vulnerable for their failure to cope. Thus, it is important to acknowledge that children's agency, and their ability to overcome the challenges of migration, is framed by their evolving capacities and reflects their own individual and socially generated vulnerabilities and resilience.[35]

In addition, the concurring opinion also highlights that using the vulnerability imagery and limited autonomy arguments as the basis for protection with regard to children (both accompanied and unaccompanied) may also create the false impression that migrant adults, some of whom may be parents that have caregiving duties vis-à-vis their children, themselves do not have protection needs by virtue of their autonomy and perceived capacity of 'choice'.[36] The ECtHR, for instance, considers adult and child asylum seekers alike as 'member[s] of a particularly underprivileged and vulnerable population group in need of special protection'.[37] In *VM and Others*, the ECtHR reiterated its conclusion in *Tarakhel* that vulnerabilities of asylum seekers are heightened in the case of families with children.[38]

---

[33] Vandenhole, Concurring Opinion, para 2. (The following works provide more in-depth insights on the autonomy and vulnerability debate: SR Benporath, 'Autonomy and Vulnerability: On Just Relations between Adults and Children' (2003) 37 *Journal of Philosophy of Education* 127; EH Boyle, T Smith and K Guenther, 'The Rise of the Child as an Individual in Global Society' in SA Venkatesh and R Kassimir (eds), *Youth, Globalization, and the Law* (Stanford, Stanford University Press, 2007); MA Fineman, 'The Vulnerable Subject: Anchoring Equality in the Human Condition' (2008) 20 *Yale Journal of Law and Feminism* 20; J Herring, 'Vulnerability, Children, and the Law' in M Freeman (ed), *Law and Childhood Studies* (Oxford, Oxford University Press, 2012); A Shultheis Moore, 'Spectrally Human: African Child Soldier Narratives at the Limits of Legal Personhood' in A Shultheis Moore, *Vulnerability and Security in Human Rights Literature and Visual Culture* (Abingdon, Routledge, 2016); S Tomanovic, 'Negotiating Children's Participation and Autonomy within Families' (2003) 11 *International Journal of Children's Rights* 51).

[34] MO Ensor and EM Gozdziak, 'Migrant Children at the Crossroads: Introduction' in MO Ensor and EM Gozdziak (eds), *Children and Migration: At the Crossroads of Resiliency and Vulnerability* (Basingstoke, Palgrave Macmillan UK, 2010) 7.

[35] References omitted. The original reference to 'evolving capacities and individual and socially generated vulnerabilities and resilience' comes from MO Ensor, 'Children, Climate Change and Disasters: Challenges and opportunities for Disaster Anthropology' (2008) 49 (4) *Anthropology News* 13.

[36] Vandenhole, Concurring Opinion, para 2.

[37] *MSS v Belgium and Greece* [GC], no 30696/09, § 251, ECHR 2011.

[38] *VM and Others v Belgium*, above n 32.

III. Contextualising the Concurring Opinion

The concurring opinion strengthens the reasoning of the ECSR with regards to conceptual questions on vulnerability, progressive realisation and the accompanied versus unaccompanied minor distinction. In doing so, the concurring opinion illustrates how an inherent vulnerability parlance and imagery may be avoided in recognition of autonomy and agency, reconciles progressive realisation with the obligation to provide immediate assistance by invoking core obligations, and pointing to the need for protection of, in addition to care and assistance to, unaccompanied minors. As the original complaint by the DCI went to challenge Belgium's implementation of its existing legislation in the context of providing minors with reception places and did not contest Belgian legislation on migration and asylum as such, the ECSR did not conduct an assessment of how the Belgian legislative framework was framed and whether it fell short in any respects of the requisite protection in line with its obligations arising from international human rights law, including the Revised European Social Charter or the law of the European Union (EU). It should be noted, however, that at the time of the complaint, Belgium as a Member State of the EU also had obligations to provide access to healthcare, education, legal support, social assistance and accommodation to children covered by the complaint under relevant EU acquis on asylum and international protection, guided by the best interests of the child.[39] For unaccompanied minors, these obligations also included appointing legal guardians or representatives to act as children's advocates, placing these children in most appropriate environments and providing family tracing.[40] While the ECSR has pronounced an unfavourable opinion on the 'presumption of conformity of EU law with the Charter',[41] *DCI v Belgium* presents a clear case where the adequate implementation of the relevant EU acquis would bring Belgium in conformity with its obligations under the Charter. The points that the concurring opinion makes about the core obligations of states in providing access to accommodation, healthcare, food and basic education with regards to both accompanied and unaccompanied minors are critical in light of the mass movement of migrants since 2014 attempting to reach the EU. In 2015, 29 per cent of the 1.3 million asylum seekers in the EU were children and 23 per cent of these children were unaccompanied.[42]

---

[39] See: Directive 2011/95/EU of the European Parliament and of the Council of 13 December 2011 on standards for the qualification of third-country nationals or stateless persons as beneficiaries of international protection, for a uniform status for refugees or for persons eligible for subsidiary protection, and for the content of the protection granted; Council Directive 2003/9/EC of 27 January 2003 laying down minimum standards for the reception of asylum seekers (revised in 2013 by Directive 2013/33/EU of the European Parliament and of the Council of 26 June 2013 laying down standards for the reception of applicants for international protection).

[40] Dir 2011/95/EU (13 December 2011) Art 31.

[41] *Swedish Trade Union Confederation (LO) and Swedish Confederation of Professional Employees (TCO) v Sweden* (Complaint No 85/2012) ECSR (5 February 2014) para 74, *Confédération Générale du Travail (CGT) v France* (Complaint No 55/2009) ECSR (13 September 2010) para 35.

[42] The European Union (EU) Committee, *Children in crisis: unaccompanied migrant children in the EU* (HL 2016-17, 34) 5; European Commission, *Compilation of Data, Situation and Media Reports on Children in Migration* (Update 11 July 2016) http://ec.europa.eu/justice/fundamental-rights/files/rights_child/data_children_in_migration.pdf; M Townsend, '10,000 refugee children are missing, says Europol' *The Observer* (London, 30 January 2016) www.theguardian.com/world/2016/jan/30/fears-for-missing-child-refugees.

A recent House of Lords inquiry noted that more than 10,000 unaccompanied migrant children are estimated to be missing in the EU.[43] In addition to formal asylum seekers, there are also many more children unlawfully resident in EU Member States that do not introduce formal asylum claims or are reportedly dissuaded from doing so,[44] putting the actual numbers of these children in need of immediate assistance at higher figures. Given resource constraints, in order for the rights of accompanied and unaccompanied foreign minors to be effectively protected when they are unlawfully residing in a given country, states should deliver first and foremost on their core obligations all the while working towards the progressive realisation of these rights in the longer term.

[43] The EU Committee, ibid, 6.

[44] The House of Lords EU Sub-Committee on Home Affairs heard testimony regarding Belgium as well as other member states that discouraged children from applying for asylum in the country they were residing, withholding immediate registration while implicitly suggesting that another member state may be a better place to seek asylum. (ibid, 24–25).

European Committee of Social Rights

Defence for Children International (DCI) v Belgium

1. The complaint submitted by Defence for Children International (DCI) was registered on 21 June 2011. DCI alleges that unaccompanied foreign minors unlawfully present or seeking asylum and illegally resident accompanied foreign minors are denied the rights to its full development, social, health, legal and economic protection, social and medical assistance and protection against poverty, in breach of articles 7 § 10, 11, 13, 16, 17 and 30 of the Revised European Social Charter ('the Charter') read alone or in conjunction with Article E. Even though they are legally entitled to receive social assistance in Belgium, they are currently being denied such assistance in practice.

…

The Law

I. Alleged Violation of Article 17 of the Charter

…

Applicability of Article 17 to the Persons Concerned by the Complaint

23. Under paragraph 1 of the Appendix to the Charter:

> 1. Without prejudice to Article 12, paragraph 4, and Article 13, paragraph 4, the persons covered by Articles 1 to 17 and 20 to 31 include foreigners only in so far as they are nationals of other Parties lawfully resident or working regularly within the territory of the Party concerned, subject to the understanding that these articles are to be interpreted in the light of the provisions of Articles 18 and 19.

> This interpretation would not prejudice the extension of similar facilities to other persons by any of the Parties.

...

Assessment of the Committee

28.   The Committee notes that, according to an argument put forward by States Parties in response to other complaints concerning the rights of foreign minors unlawfully present in the country (*Defence for Children International v the Netherlands*, § 8, and *International Federation of Human Rights Leagues v France*, § 18), the implication of paragraph 1 of the Appendix to the Charter is that the persons concerned by this complaint (accompanied and unaccompanied foreign minors unlawfully present in a country) would not come within the personal scope of Article 17, as they are not nationals of other Parties 'lawfully resident or working regularly' within the territory of the Party concerned. The Committee nonetheless points out that the restriction of the personal scope included in the Appendix should not be read in such a way as to deprive foreigners coming within the category of unlawfully present migrants of the protection of the most basic rights enshrined in the Charter or to impair their fundamental rights such as the right to life or to physical integrity or the right to human dignity (*Defence for Children International v the Netherlands*, Complaint No 47/2008, ibid, § 19; *International Federation of Human Rights Leagues v France*, ibid, §§ 30 and 31).

29.   The Committee indeed considers that, beyond the letter of paragraph 1 of the Appendix, the restriction on personal scope contained therein should be interpreted—as is generally the case for any provision of an international treaty—in the light of the object and purpose of the treaty concerned and in harmony with other relevant and applicable rules of international law (Vienna Convention on the Law of Treaties, 23 May 1969, Article 31, paragraphs 1 and 3), including first and foremost the peremptory norms of general international law (jus cogens), which take precedence over all other international norms and from which no derogation is permitted (Vienna Convention on the Law of Treaties, 23 May 1969, Article 53).

30.   Concerning the object and purpose of the Charter, the Committee reiterates that it is a human rights treaty which aims to implement at a European level, as a complement to the European Convention on Human Rights, the rights guaranteed to all human beings by the Universal Declaration of Human Rights of 1948. As the Committee already found (*International Federation of Human Rights Leagues v France*, Complaint No 14/2003, decision on the merits of 8 September 2004, §§ 27 and 29), the purpose of the Charter, as a living instrument dedicated to the values of dignity, equality and solidarity, is to give life and meaning in Europe to the fundamental social rights of all human beings. It is precisely in the light of that finding that the Committee considers—as the Government pointed out in its submissions—that a teleological approach should be adopted when interpreting the Charter, ie it is necessary to seek the interpretation of the treaty that is most appropriate in order to realise the aim and achieve the object of this treaty, not that which would restrict the Parties' obligations to the greatest possible degree (*World Organisation against Torture v Ireland*, Complaint No 18/2003, decision on the merits of 7 December 2004, § 60). It is in point of fact this teleological approach that leads the Committee not to interpret paragraph 1 of the Appendix in such a way as to deny foreign minors unlawfully present in a coun-

try (whether accompanied or unaccompanied) the guarantee of their fundamental rights, including the right to preservation of their human dignity.

31.　In addition, such a strict interpretation of the Appendix, which would deprive foreign minors unlawfully present in a country of the guarantee of their fundamental rights, would not be in harmony with the United Nations Convention on the Rights of the Child, which all member states of the Council of Europe have ratified. It is therefore justified for the Committee to have regard to this convention, adopting the interpretation given to it by the United Nations Committee on the Rights of the Child, when it rules on an alleged violation of any right conferred on children by the Charter (see *World Organisation against Torture v Ireland*, Complaint No 18/2003, decision on the merits of 7 December 2004, § 61).

32.　In this connection, following the guidance of the Committee on the Rights of the Child, the Committee considers that in the present case the personal scope of the Charter must be determined according to the principle of the child's best interests. In this respect it notes that, according to General Comment No 5 (document CRC/GC/2003/5, §§ 45–47) of the Committee on the Rights of the Child

> Every legislative, administrative and judicial body or institution is required to apply the best interests principle by systematically considering how children's rights and interests are or will be affected by their decisions and actions—by, for example, a proposed or existing law or policy or administrative action or court decision, including those which are not directly concerned with children, but indirectly affect children.

33.　Furthermore, this choice in applying the Charter follows from the legal need to comply with the peremptory norms of general international law (jus cogens) such as the rules requiring each state to respect and safeguard each individual's right to life and physical integrity. A strict interpretation of paragraph 1 of the Appendix, which would result in the non-recognition of the States Parties' obligation to guarantee foreign minors unlawfully present in their territory the enjoyment of these fundamental rights, would be incompatible with international jus cogens.

34.　In the light of the latter observations and of the mandatory, universally recognised requirement to protect all children—requirement reinforced by the fact that the United Nations Convention on the Rights of the Child is one of the most ratified treaties at world level, the Committee considers that paragraph 1 of the Appendix should not be interpreted in such a way as to expose foreign minors unlawfully present in a country to serious impairments of their fundamental rights on account of a failure to give guarantee to the social rights enshrined in the revised Charter.

35.　However, although the restriction of personal scope contained in the Appendix does not prevent the application of the Charter's provisions to unlawfully present foreign migrants (including accompanied or unaccompanied minors) in certain cases and under certain circumstances, the Committee wishes to underline that an application of this kind is entirely exceptional. It would in particular be justified solely in the event that excluding unlawfully present foreigners from the protection afforded by the Charter would have seriously detrimental consequences for their fundamental rights (such as the right to life, to the preservation of human dignity, to psychological and physical integrity and to health) and would consequently place the foreigners in question in an unacceptable situation, regarding the enjoyment of these rights, as compared with the situation of nationals and of lawfully resident foreigners.

36.   Since it is exceptional to apply the rights enshrined in the Charter to persons not literally included in the Charter's scope under paragraph 1 of the Appendix, the Committee considers that this category of foreigners (which includes accompanied or unaccompanied minors not lawfully present in a country) is not covered by all the provisions of the Charter, but solely by those provisions whose fundamental purpose is closely linked to the requirement to secure the most fundamental human rights and to safeguard the persons concerned by the provision in question from serious threats to the enjoyment of those rights.

37.   Moreover, the risk of impairing fundamental rights is all the more likely where children—*a fortiori* migrant children unlawfully present in a country—are at stake. This is due to their condition as 'children' and to their specific situation as 'unlawful' migrants, combining vulnerability and limited autonomy. As a result, in particular, of their lack of autonomy children cannot be held genuinely responsible for their place of residence. Children are not able to decide themselves whether to stay or to leave. Furthermore, if they are unaccompanied, their situation becomes even more vulnerable and the state should be managed entirely by the state, which has a duty to care for children living within its territory and not to deprive them of the most basic protection on account of their 'unlawful' migration status.

38.   In the light of the above general observations, the Committee, referring specifically to Article 17 of the Charter and recalling its decisions (*International Federation of Human Rights Leagues v France*, Complaint No 14/2003, decision on the merits of 8 September 2004, §§ 30–32; *Defence for Children International v the Netherlands*, Complaint No 47/2008, decision on the merits of 20 October 2009, §§ 34–38), considers that this provision is applicable to the persons concerned by this complaint. Article 17, in particular paragraph 1 thereof, requires States Parties to fulfil positive obligations relating to the accommodation, basic care and protection of children and young persons. Not considering that States Parties are bound to comply with these obligations in the case of foreign minors who are in a country unlawfully would therefore mean not guaranteeing their fundamental rights and exposing the children and young persons in question to serious threats to their rights to life, health and psychological and physical integrity and to the preservation of their human dignity.

39.   Consequently, the Committee considers that the children and young persons concerned by this complaint come within the scope of Article 17 of the Charter.

Alleged Violation of Article 17

...

B—Assessment of the Committee

68.   The Committee notes that the DCI does not contest the essence of the legislation, but rather the fact that it is not being applied.

69.   The Committee recalls that when considering several complaints, it has specified the nature of States' obligations vis-à-vis implementation of the Charter. The purpose and aim of the Charter is to protect not theoretical but effective rights (*CIJ v Portugal*, Complaint No

1/1998, decision on the merits of 9 September 1999, § 32; *FEANTSA v Slovenia*, Complaint No 53/2008, decision on the merits of 8 September 2009, § 28). It considers that proper application of the Charter cannot be achieved solely through legislation if its application is neither effective nor strictly controlled.

70. In connection with the means of achieving the aims set out in the Charter, the Committee stresses that for the application of the Charter, it is incumbent on States Parties not only to take legal initiatives but also to provide for the requisite resources and procedures to facilitate full exercise of the rights guaranteed by the Charter (*International Movement ATD Fourth World v France*, Complaint No 33/2006, decision on the merits of 5 December 2007, § 61).

71. The Committee underlines that, where the implementation of the rights proves highly complex and costly, the States Parties must endeavour to achieve the aims of the Charter according to a reasonable timetable, securing measurable progress and making optimum use of such resources as can be mustered.

72. The Committee also recalls that the States Parties must pay particular attention to the impact of their choices on the most vulnerable groups and on the other persons concerned (mutatis mutandis, *International Association Autism-Europe v France*, Complaint No 13/2002, decision on the merits of 4 November 2003, § 53).

73. The Committee refers to the content of Article 17, which concerns the aid to be provided by the State where the minor is unaccompanied or if the parents are unable to provide such aid. The Committee also recalls the importance of paragraph 1 (b) of Article 17, because failure to apply it would obviously expose a number of children and young persons to serious risks to their lives or physical integrity.

74. The Committee notes that the only substantive complaint of DCI relates to the lack of reception places, which is allegedly rendering ineffective any access to accommodation and all the other measures provided for legal, economic, medical and social protection.

75. The Committee notes the Government information on the increase in the number of reception places available: 8000 additional reception places have been introduced since 2008 and that measures have been taken to reduce the duration of the procedure for granting asylum, and thus the length of stay of asylum seekers in reception centers.

76. The Committee recalls that the present complaint relates to the fulfilment by Belgium of its obligations under Article 17 vis-à-vis two categories of persons:

— minors illegally resident with their families;
— unaccompanied foreign minors and asylum-seeking unaccompanied foreign minors.

77. In connection with illegally resident accompanied minors, the Committee notes that no further such families, with their children, have been taken in since 2009 because of network saturation. The Committee takes note of the fact that in 2011 FEDASIL received 43 court orders to provide accommodation for families and that the Federal Ombudsmen have addressed a series of recommendations to FEDASIL. According to the DCI, 774 families received a negative response to their applications for accommodation between January 2011 and April 2012. These decisions concerned 3011 persons (the DCI did not know how many children were involved). In 2011, 553 families were refused accommodation; the latter comprised 901 adults and 1242 minors. The Government provides no data, but

acknowledges that they were unable to find an alternative accommodation solution for these families.

78.   Where unaccompanied foreign minors are concerned, the Committee notes that the statistics on the number of such minors seem to be approximate, varying widely according to the source of information used. According to the DCI, Guardianship Department statistics suggest that 461 such minors were turned away in 2011 as compared with 258 in 2010. On the other hand, when taking into consideration the number of arrivals of unaccompanied foreign minors, this figure is much higher. According to the DCI, over 1300 young people were not accommodated in appropriate structures. There are no data on the number of asylum-seekers among non-accommodated unaccompanied foreign minors, but it emerges from the complaint that such minors are prioritised for reception facilities. The Government does not supply statistics on the number of such minors who failed to obtain a reception place.

79.   The DCI estimates the number of unaccompanied foreign minors put up in hotels at 668, while the Government estimates 166 such minors in hotels at 12 March 2012.

80.   The Committee also notes the observations of the UNHCR according to which, unaccompanied foreign minors must be placed as quickly as possible in an appropriate reception structure and their needs must be meticulously assessed in order to keep any changes to a minimum. This period is crucial, because it is when the first links are forged between the minor and the social actors involved. If unaccompanied foreign minors are not properly provided for, they are simultaneously deprived of any chance of exercising the right of asylum.

81.   The Committee considers that immediate assistance is essential and allows assessing material needs of young people, the need for medical or psychological care in order to set up a child support plan. In the same spirit, the guiding principles on extreme poverty and human rights, submitted by the Special Rapporteur on extreme poverty and human rights, Magdalena Sepúlveda Carmona and adopted by the United Nations Human Rights Council on 27 September 2012 state:

> §32. Given that most of those living in poverty are children and that poverty in childhood is a root cause of poverty in adulthood, children's rights must be accorded priority. Even short periods of deprivation and exclusion can dramatically and irreversibly harm a child's right to survival and development. To eradicate poverty, States must take immediate action to combat childhood poverty.
>
> …
>
> §34. Poverty renders children, in particular girls, vulnerable to exploitation, neglect and abuse. States must respect and promote the rights of children living in poverty, including by strengthening and allocating the necessary resources to child protection strategies and programmes, with a particular focus on marginalized children, such as street children, child soldiers, children with disabilities, victims of trafficking, child heads of households and children living in care institutions, all of whom are at a heightened risk of exploitation and abuse.

82.   In the light of the above, the Committee considers that the fact that the Government has, since 2009, no longer guaranteed accompanied foreign minors unlawfully present in the country any form of accommodation in reception centres (through either through the FEDASIL network or other alternative solutions) breaches Article 17§1 of the Charter.

The persistent failure to accommodate these minors shows, in particular, that the Government has not taken the necessary and appropriate measures to guarantee the minors in question the care and assistance they need and to protect them from negligence, violence or exploitation, thereby posing a serious threat to the enjoyment of their most basic rights, such as the rights to life, to psychological and physical integrity and to respect for human dignity. Similarly, the fact that at least 461 unaccompanied foreign minors were not accommodated in 2011 and the problems posed by inappropriate accommodation in hotels, lead the Committee to the conclusion that the Government failed to take sufficient measures to guarantee non-asylum seeking, unaccompanied foreign minors the care and assistance they need, thereby exposing a large number of children and young persons to serious risks for their lives and health.

83.   Consequently, the Committee holds that there is a violation of Article 17§1 of the Charter.

Concurring Opinion Wouter Vandenhole

1.   I agree with the majority that Belgium has violated Article 17 of the Charter by failing to offer sufficient places to migrant minors in its reception centres. I would like to provide a different reasoning however on three points: the differentiation of obligations with regard to accompanied and unaccompanied minors; the framing of obligations; and the relationship between state obligations and parents' responsibilities. Before addressing these points, I will make a preliminary comment on the construction of migrant childhood, which is of relevance to most of the following reasoning.

2.   The majority constructs the condition of migrant children unlawfully present in a country as 'combining vulnerability and limited autonomy' 'due to their condition as "children" and to their specific situation as "unlawful" migrants' (paragraph 37). It continues:

> As a result, in particular, of their lack of autonomy children cannot be held genuinely responsible for their place of residence. Children are not able to decide themselves whether to stay or to leave. Furthermore, if they are unaccompanied, their situation becomes even more vulnerable ....'
> (paragraph 37).

I would like to make two comments. First, the argument runs the risk of being subverted into an *a contrario* reasoning with regard to adults: adults may be said, *a contrario*, to be genuinely responsible for their place of residence. I would regret such a conclusion, since migration often is not so much a matter of choice, but rather of necessity and need, of push as much as pull factors. Presenting the children that illegally resided in Belgium as completely dependent on their parents may have a detrimental impact on the way the human rights of adults migrants in an undocumented situation are understood (ie since they have choice, they have to bear full responsibility for the consequences of their decisions). Such a representation makes it also all the more unlikely that legal developments in the area of children's rights translate into stronger protection of the rights of parents. Children should not be pitted against parents, nor should children's rights be protected at the expense of human rights of adults, as this Committee may be said to have done to some extent in the first case in which it addressed the rights of undocumented migrants (*International Federation of Human Rights Leagues v. France*, Complaint No 14/2003, §§ 34–37). Not surprisingly, subsequent complaints, including the current one, have focused exclusively on violations suffered by *children* that are illegally resident (see also *Defence for Children International v the Netherlands*, Complaint No 47/2008). When dealing with complaints about children's rights violations, this Committee should keep in mind its mandate to protect human rights of all human beings, including adults. I would therefore not have put so much emphasis on migrant's children lack of autonomy.

This is connected to the second and more fundamental point that I would like to make: the children illegally residing on Belgian territory were not inherently vulnerable, nor unequivocally in a vulnerable situation. Vulnerability has to do with a complex web of both internal and external factors, not just with inherent characteristics of children. These migrant children were not exclusively in a vulnerable situation either: they may have employed tactical agency and may have shown a remarkable degree of resilience. This is not to say that they were not at all in a vulnerable situation: many of them undoubtedly were. However, ironically, a one-sided emphasis on vulnerability may have an essentialising effect, and may actually enhance the factual vulnerability of these children. Whereas the Committee is not in a position to know what the effects of its approach are on children, it is widely accepted in the human rights community that stereotyping is harmful and needs to be avoided. Some could argue that less emphasis on children's vulnerable situation may lead to lower levels of protection. Children's rights are not exclusively, and arguably, even not primarily rooted in vulnerability, but as much in human dignity and autonomy. The same level of protection as offered by the majority in this case to the children illegally residing on Belgian territory could have been justified therefore by invoking human dignity, as the majority does accept in its assessment of the applicability of the Charter (see §§ 28 and 35), and as the Committee argued in *Defence for Children International v the Netherlands*, Complaint No 47/2008, § 25:

> The Charter firstly treats children as individual rights' holders since human dignity inherent in each child fully entitles her/him to all fundamental rights granted to adults.

In the latter case, this Committee justified specific rights for children by pointing out 'the specific situation of children, which combines vulnerability, limited autonomy and potential adulthood.' (ibid).

The differentiation that the majority introduces in this case between accompanied and unaccompanied minors builds on a mistaken one-sided vulnerability imagery, and seems to introduce further degrees of vulnerability, this time among categories of children. Admittedly, the majority systematically refrains from hinting at inherent vulnerability, but refers rather to vulnerable situations. Vulnerable *situations* are co-created by the circumstances of migration and the absence of, or inappropriate, reception facilities. With regard to unaccompanied minors, the majority argues that 'their situation becomes even more vulnerable and should be managed entirely by the State …' (paragraph 37). I find that highly problematic and at best an unnecessary, and at worst a dangerous, distinction that creates different levels of protection commensurate to assumed degrees of vulnerability.

3.   In paragraphs 82 and 83, the majority concludes that Article 17 of the Charter has been violated with regard to accompanied and unaccompanied minors residing illegally

on the territory. Unfortunately, the majority does not reason in detail why and how the absence or inappropriate accommodation of unaccompanied foreign minors violates that provision. Part of that missing reasoning can easily be found in the Committee's earlier jurisprudence, in which it has argued that Article 31 § 2 of the Revised Charter is directed at the prevention of homelessness, which requires states to provide shelter to children unlawfully present on their territory as long as the children are in their jurisdiction (*Defence for Children International v the Netherlands*, Complaint No 47/2008, § 61). In that case, the Committee further held that 'the obligations related to the provision of shelter under Article 17 § 1.C are identical in substance with those related to the provision of shelter under Article 31 § 2.' (ibid, § 70). To this reasoning I would like to add that a state has an enhanced obligation towards children and young people deprived of their family's support (See Article 17(1)(c) of the Charter), *a fortiori* when they are unaccompanied *migrants*. That enhanced obligation is twofold: it has a care and assistance dimension as well as a protection dimension. The majority completely overlooks this protection dimension in its reasoning (paragraph 82) with regard to unaccompanied minors, whereas it explicitly mentions it with regard to accompanied minors (see below number 6). This is not only surprising, but even contradictory in light of its earlier differentiation of vulnerability, whereby it counted unaccompanied foreign minors among the most vulnerable. Whereas I question the majority's unidimensional emphasis on their vulnerability, they unmistakably are very often in a vulnerable situation, and their need for protection in most instances cannot be denied therefore.

4.   Article 17(1) Revised European Social Charter (RESC) guarantees the right of children and young people to social, legal and economic protection. It requires states 'to fulfil positive obligations relating to the accommodation, basic care and protection of children and young persons.' (paragraph 38). In the decision's section on the applicability of the Charter, the majority links these obligations directly with 'fundamental rights such as the right to life or to physical integrity or the right to human dignity' (paragraph 28). It equally argues that

> (n)ot considering that States Parties are bound to comply with these obligations in the case of foreign minors who are in a country unlawfully would therefore mean not guaranteeing their fundamental rights and exposing the children and young persons in question to serious threats to their rights to life, health and psychological and physical integrity and to the preservation of their human dignity. (paragraph 38).

In other words, Article 17 of the Charter is construed as touching on 'peremptory norms of general international law (jus cogens) such as the rules requiring each state to respect and safeguard each individual's right to life and physical integrity.' (paragraph 33). Moreover, a teleological approach is advocated, so as to ensure foreign minors in an undocumented situation 'the guarantee of their fundamental rights, including the right to preservation of their human dignity.' (paragraph 30). This reasoning is embedded in earlier case law on the applicability of the Charter to children who are illegally residing on the territory of a State (most recently in *Defence for Children International v the Netherlands*, Complaint No 47/2008, §§ 34–38), and I fully agree with it. However, this emphasis on the jus cogens nature and the close link with human dignity advocated in the *applicability* section of the decision starkly contrasts with the Committee's subsequent *substantive* analysis of the alleged violation. There, the majority suggests that the obligations under Article 17 of the

Charter are relative ones, ie not immediate ones, and subject to the availability of resources (paragraph 71 implicitly), in line with the generally accepted notion of progressive realisation of economic, social and cultural rights (ESC rights). For sure, when the achievement of one of the rights in question is exceptionally complex and particularly expensive to resolve, a state party must take measures that allows it to achieve the objectives of the Charter within a reasonable time, with measurable progress and to an extent consistent with the maximum use of available resources (*Autism-Europe v France*, Complaint no 13/2002, § 53). But how can this notion of progressive realisation be reconciled with a right that is of a jus cogens nature and so closely related to human dignity? In my view, it would have been more coherent for the Committee to argue that the core obligations under Article 17 RESC are intrinsically related to the right to life and human dignity, the inevitable consequence of which would be that these core obligations have to be realised immediately, regardless of the economic situation and the availability of resources. The majority also acknowledges later in the decision that 'immediate assistance is essential' (paragraph 81). Core obligations could be further developed by drawing in particular on the interpretative work undertaken by the Committee on Economic, Social and Cultural Rights and the Committee on the Rights of the Child of the United Nations in their general comments. Typically, core obligations need to be prioritized if not realised immediately, and include 'the satisfaction of, at the very least, minimum essential levels' of a right (Committee on Economic, Social and Cultural Rights, General Comment No 14, document E/C.12/2000/4, § 43).

A similar outcome, ie the immediacy and absolute nature of the obligations at stake, could also be construed on the basis of the obligation to 'pay particular attention to the impact of (the) choices (States make) on the most vulnerable groups' (paragraph 72). However, I am less in favour of such an argument because of the risk of over-emphasising vulnerability (see my comment under 2). Foreign minors who stay irregularly in a country do find themselves undeniably in a very vulnerable situation, no doubt about that. That vulnerable situation can be said to give rise to absolute and immediate obligations. However, in developing this line of reasoning, one has to be careful not to overemphasise in a one-dimensional way that vulnerability, in order to avoid essentialising and reducing these young persons to vulnerability alone.

5.   With regard to *accompanied* migrant children, the majority remains vague about the relationship between the responsibility of parents and the obligations of the state under Article 17 of the Charter. Unaccompanied migrant children are said to be in an 'even more vulnerable' situation, therefore their situation 'should be managed entirely by the State, which has a duty to care for children living within its territory and not to deprive them of the most basic protection on account of their "unlawful" migration status' (paragraph 37). But what does that mean for accompanied migrant children?

Article 17(1)(a) of the Charter explicitly references the 'rights and duties' of parents when spelling out the obligations incumbent on the state to take all appropriate and necessary measures of care, assistance, education and training. This is in line with the deference to the rights and responsibilities of parents in articles 5 and 27 of the UN Convention on the Rights of the Child. The majority, however, remains silent on the subsidiary role of the state with regard to accompanied minors. There is only a vague general reference to 'the content of Article 17, which concerns the aid to be provided … if the parents are unable to provide such aid.' (paragraph 73).

It would have been better to explicitly acknowledge the parents' role as primary caregivers, rather than to make them almost invisible as passive onlookers, and to point out that given their situation as undocumented migrants, they are unable to play their parental role independently in full, so that they need the assistance of the state.[1]

6.   Related to this is the confusing reference to the need of *accompanied* minors to *protection* from negligence, violence or exploitation, whereas with regard to unaccompanied minors, the majority regrettably, as argued earlier, only focuses on care and assistance (paragraph 82). If the reference is to protection against their own parents, this amounts to a rather unfortunate stigmatisation of the parents. If the parents are unable themselves to take care of their children, this may be primarily due to the conditions of (undocumented) migration. If the reference is to protection against third parties, again the responsibilities of parents themselves seem to be ignored or downplayed. The rights of children cannot and should not be disconnected artificially from the rights of their parent(s). I would rather have omitted any reference to protection in this instance, and emphasised the need for aid and assistance, as explained above.

---

[1] Compare the Belgian Constitutional Court judgment of 22 July 2003, no. 106/2003, §§B.7.2-B.7.4.

INDEX